# Remedies in
# Contract and Tort

## Law in Context

Below is a listing of the more recent publications in the Law in Context Series

Editors: William Twining (University College, London) and Christopher McCrudden (Lincoln College, Oxford)

Ashworth: *Sentencing and Criminal Justice*
Bercusson: *European Labour Law*
Birkinshaw: *Freedom of Information: The Law, the Practice and the Ideal*
Cane: *Atiyah's Accidents Compensation and the Law*
Collins: *The Law of Contract*
Scott and Black: *Cranston's Consumers and the Law*
Elworthy and Holder: *Environmental Protection: Text and Materials*
Fortin: *Children's Rights and the Developing Law*
Harlow and Rawlings: *Law and Administration: Text and Materials*
Harris: *An Introduction to Law*
Harvey: *Seeking Asylum in the UK: Problems and Prospects*
Lacey and Wells: *Reconstructing Criminal Law*
Moffat: *Trusts Trusts Law- Text and Materials*
Norrie: *Crime, Reason and History*
Oliver and Drewry: *The Law and Parliament*
Oliver: *Common Values and the Public- Private Divide*
O'Dair: *Legal Ethics Text and Materials*
Palmer and Roberts: *Dispute Processes: ADR and the Primary Forms of Decision Making*
Reed: *Internet Law- Text and Materials*
Turpin: *British Government and the Constitution: Text, Cases and Materials*
Twining: *Globalisation and Legal Theory*
Twining and Miers: *How to Do Things with Rules*
Ward: *Shakespeare and the Legal Imagination*
Zander: *Cases and Materials on the English Legal System*
Zander: *The Law Making Process*

# Remedies in Contract and Tort

Second edition

## Donald Harris
*Emeritus Fellow, Balliol College, University of Oxford*

## David Campbell
*Professor of Law, Cardiff Law School
and ESRC Research Centre for Business Relationships,
Accountability, Sustainability and Society, Cardiff University*

## Roger Halson
*H K Bevan Professor of Law, Hull University*

Butterworths
LexisNexis™

**Members of the LexisNexis Group worldwide**

| | |
|---|---|
| United Kingdom | LexisNexis Butterworths Tolley, a Division of Reed Elsevier (UK) Ltd, Halsbury House, 35 Chancery Lane, LONDON, WC2A 1EL, and 4 Hill Street, EDINBURGH EH2 3JZ |
| Argentina | LexisNexis Argentina, BUENOS AIRES |
| Australia | LexisNexis Butterworths, CHATSWOOD, New South Wales |
| Austria | LexisNexis Verlag ARD Orac GmbH & Co KG, VIENNA |
| Canada | LexisNexis Butterworths, MARKHAM, Ontario |
| Chile | LexisNexis Chile Ltda, SANTIAGO DE CHILE |
| Czech Republic | Nakladatelství Orac sro, PRAGUE |
| France | Editions du Juris-Classeur SA, PARIS |
| Hong Kong | LexisNexis Butterworths, HONG KONG |
| Hungary | HVG-Orac, BUDAPEST |
| India | LexisNexis Butterworths, NEW DELHI |
| Ireland | Butterworths (Ireland) Ltd, DUBLIN |
| Italy | Giuffrè Editore, MILAN |
| Malaysia | Malayan Law Journal Sdn Bhd, KUALA LUMPUR |
| New Zealand | Butterworths of New Zealand, WELLINGTON |
| Poland | Wydawnictwo Prawnicze LexisNexis, WARSAW |
| Singapore | LexisNexis Butterworths, SINGAPORE |
| South Africa | Butterworths SA, DURBAN |
| Switzerland | Stämpfli Verlag AG, BERNE |
| USA | LexisNexis, DAYTON, Ohio |

© Reed Elsevier (UK) Ltd 2002

A CIP Catalogue record for this book is available from the British Library.

ISBN  0 406 90410 3

Printed in Great Britain by Clays Ltd, Bungay, Suffolk

**Visit Butterworths LexisNexis *direct* at www.butterworths.com**

# Preface

Donald Harris welcomes David Campbell and Roger Halson who have joined him in producing this second edition, which goes well beyond the normal revision expected in a new edition of a students' textbook. The two new editors have brought their own teaching and research experience to this edition, and have re-invigorated the book by extensive re-writing and by producing some entirely new chapters based on their own original thinking. For instance, David Campbell has completely re-organised Part 3 on Literal Enforcement and written two new chapters on Restitution (16 and 17); while Roger Halson produced a new, longer, chapter on Personal Injury Damages (22) and has extensively rewritten chapter 23 on Fatal Accidents. In many ways, this book deserves to be reviewed as a new book. Although we have had the opportunity of commenting on each other's drafts, we have each taken sole or major responsibility for revising or re-writing the particular chapters which bear our individual names in the Table of Contents; the new chapters naturally carry the author's name.

This second edition continues an important focus of the first edition on the use of legal rules in situations outside the courtroom, particularly in negotiations to compromise disputes. This edition also continues the emphasis on empirical data (whenever available) which show the way in which some of the rules work out in practice; and on using economic concepts to deepen our understanding of the function of the rules. Other insights derived from the social sciences are also used throughout the book.

We have taken account of the overlaps between contract, tort and restitution; indeed, Part 3 is devoted entirely to Restitution, and Chapter 29 considers concurrent liability in contract and tort. But we remain unconvinced that these traditional categories of the common law should now be merged into a single category of 'Obligations': the borderlines between the categories may be a little blurred, but the paradigm situations in each category deserve still to be separately recognised. We have endeavoured to state the law up to mid-2001, but it has been possible to incorporate into the final few chapters some later material, such as the House of Lords decision in *Farley v Skinner*.

Donald Harris wishes again to thank those who commented on drafts of the first edition of this book (whose names are listed in the Preface to that edition).

David Campbell would like to thank David Miers and, even more, Richard Lewis for their very extensive comments on Chapter 24; James Davey for reference to the insurance literature briefly discussed in Chapter 30; and the staff of the Law Section of the Arts and Social Sciences Library, Cardiff University, for their informed and extremely diligent assistance with all his work on this book.

Roger Halson wishes to thank Hull Law School for granting him a period of study leave in the final stages of this long project.

Donald Harris                           *26 February 2002*
David Campbell
Roger Halson

# Contents

Services rendered by C to D   235
Rescission for common mistake and frustration   241

## 17   The expansion of restitution   [D Campbell]   255

The problem of uncompensated loss   255
D's hypothetical release from literal enforcement   257
Can hypothetical release damages be regarded as compensatory?   258
The restitutionary disgorgement of the gains from breach   262
Would restitution correct the wrong?   268
Is there a 'wrong' in 'wrongful' breach?   272
The proper limits of restitution following non-performance of a
  contractual obligation   282

SECTION 2

TORT: REMEDIES FOR WRONGDOING

PART 5

GENERAL ISSUES IN TORT REMEDIES

## 18   Objectives of the law   [D Harris]   289

Introduction   289
Defining and protecting certain rights and freedoms   289
Regulating behaviour: deterrence   290
  Appraisal of deterrence in personal injury accident cases   292
General or 'market' deterrence   293
Inquests into accidents   294
Compensation   294

## 19   Causation, mitigation and contributory
negligence   [D Harris]   296

Limits on recovery of damages   296
Causation   297
  Medical or scientific evidence   298
  Multiple tortfeasors   300
  Successive causes of disability   300
  Omissions   301

PART 6

COMPENSATION FOR PERSONAL INJURIES AND DEATH

# Table of statutes

# Table of cases

PAGE

Andrews v Grand & Toy Alberta Ltd (1978) ............................ 373
Andros Springs (Owners) v Owners of World Beauty, The World Beauty (1970),
    CA ........................................................................ 534
Anglia Television Ltd v Reed (1972), CA ..................... 127, 131, 173
Appleby v Myers (1867), Ex Ch ........................................ 249
Appleton v Garrett (1996) ............................................. 581
Arab Bank plc v John D Wood (Commercial) Ltd (2000), CA .............. 77
Arafa v Potter. See Potter v Arafa
Archer v Brown (1985) ............................. 557, 581, 588, 591, 596
Arcos Ltd v EA Ronaasen & Son (1933), HL ............................. 55
Argentino, The. See Gracie (Owners) v Argentino (Owners), The Argentino
Ariston SRL v Charly Records Ltd (1990), CA .......................... 135
Armory v Delamirie (1721) ............................................ 543
Arnold v Teno (1978) ................................................. 373
Arpad, The (1934), CA .......................................... 320, 550
Arthur v Anker (1997), CA ............................................ 336
Asamera Oil Corpn Ltd v Sea Oil and General Corpn (1979) ............. 223
Ashington Piggeries Ltd v Christopher Hill Ltd. See Hill (Christopher) Ltd v
    Ashington Piggeries Ltd
Associated British Ports v Transport and General Workers' Union (1989),
    CA; revsd (1989), HL ............................................. 611
Associated Japanese Bank (International) Ltd v Crédit du Nord SA (1989) ... 245
Associated Newspapers Ltd v Dingle (1964), HL ....................... 593
Astley v Austrust Ltd (999) .......................................... 578
Astro Exito Navegacion SA v Southland Enterprise Co Ltd (No 2) (Chase
    Manhattan Bank NA intervening), The Messiniaki Tolmi (1983), HL .. 612
Atlantic Lines & Navigation Co Inc v Hallam Ltd, The Lucy (1983) ........ 559
Atlas Tiles v Briers (1978) .......................................... 345
Attica Sea Carriers Corpn v Ferrostaal Poseidon Bulk Reederei GmbH,
    The Puerto Buitrago (1976), CA ............................ 162, 163
A-G v Birmingham Borough Council (1858) ............................ 479
A-G v Blake (Jonathan Cape Ltd third party) (1997); revsd (1998), CA; affd
    (2001), HL ....................................74, 79, 216, 231, 256,
                                                 257, 261, 262, 263, 264,
                                                 265, 266, 267, 268, 269,
                                                 270, 271, 274, 278, 491,
                                                 570, 606, 608
A-G v Doughty (1792) ............................................... 498
A-G v Guardian Newspapers Ltd (No 2) (1990); on appeal (1990), CA; affd
    (1990), HL ...................................................... 257
A-G (at the relation of Allen) v Colchester Corpn (1955) ................. 189
Australian Hardwoods Pty Ltd v Railways Comr (1961), PC ............... 185
Auty v National Coal Board (1985), CA ............................... 345


### B

BBMB Finance (Hong Kong) Ltd v Eda Holdings Ltd (1991), PC ........... 544
BICC plc v Burndy Corpn (1985), CA ............................... 62, 148
BP Exploration Co (Libya) Ltd v Hunt (No 2) (1982); affd (1982), CA; affd
    (1983), HL ......................... 236, 247, 249, 250, 251, 252, 254
Bacon v Cooper (Metals) Ltd (1982) ............................. 113, 532
Bailey v Bullock (1950) .............................................. 595

# Section 1
# Remedies for unfulfilled contractual undertakings

# 1 Introduction: the function and structure of remedies for failure to perform a contractual obligation

## Introduction

This section of this book considers 'remedies' in the sense of the courses of action open to a claimant, C, who wishes to take some step to cope with the consequences of the defendant, D's, (threatened) failure to perform his contractual obligation. These steps are all legal in the sense of not involving any illegality, but a distinction must be drawn between 'legal' remedies which ultimately rely on the judgment of the court and 'self-help' remedies which do not. Our use of the term 'remedies' will include self-help by C, or action taken by non-judicial agencies, or C's seeking an out-of-court compromise with D. C may have guarded against the risk of D's breach by seeing that the contract included a clause dealing with the consequences of a breach. If C was prudent and capable of doing so, he may have got D to agree to a remedy which did not require any judicial action. C may also have taken out his own insurance protection against the risk of D's failure to perform, but since this is not a remedy directly against D, it is not considered here.

One possible action open to C following D's failure to perform is, of course, forebearing to do anything, or at least forebearing to seek to pursue a remedy as it has just been defined.[1] Though forebearance therefore is, in a sense, tangential to the subject matter of this book, it is a course of action following non-performance that practical experience and empirical studies of contractual action have shown to have great importance. Forebearance will, then, be discussed as such in chapter 2 and will be in the background of all our discussion of contractual remedies.

---

1   WLF Felstiner, 'Avoidance As Dispute Processing: An Elaboration' (1975) 9 Law and Society Review 695.

Since this is a book on remedies, in this section it is almost always assumed that C can prove the existence of an enforceable contract.[2] That according to the rules of the substantive law of liability the contract was initially valid and that D has breached it are almost always never directly at issue in this section. These assumptions do not apply to the discussion of two exceptional remedies for a failure to perform with a lawful excuse, which are therefore not treated as a breach: discharge for common mistake and frustration. In the discussion of even these remedies, however, the relevant facts and rules about the initial validity of the contract or its subsequent discharge are also assumed. Generally, then, this section is concerned not with determining liability for a failure to perform but with the choice between the various remedies potentially available to C after the failure to perform, and with fashioning the remedy to meet the particular situation.

When C is faced with a breach of contract committed by D, he could, as a layperson, expect the law to provide a number of possible remedies. The first thing which, it would seem from the experience of first-year teaching, occurs to a layperson is to ask the court to compel D to do exactly what he promised, if he still is able to do so (although there might well be some delay after the time when D originally promised to do it). But even when C still wants actual performance, he may no longer want performance by D. He may no longer trust an unwilling but coerced D to produce performance of the expected standard, and so would prefer to be able to choose a third person to do exactly what D had promised. C would then wish to ask the court to compel D to pay for any extra cost involved in obtaining this 'third party' or 'substitute' performance. In this section, these two possible remedies will, following the now common (if loose) usage, be referred to as the 'literal enforcement' of the contract, and will be discussed in Part 3. The third possible remedy which C might seek is an order by the court compelling D to pay a sum of money to 'make up' or 'compensate' for the loss of the benefit which C had expected to receive if both parties had fully performed their obligations under the contract. C may also seek money from D to compensate him for consequential losses and expenses arising from D's breach. These 'compensatory' damages will be discussed in Part 2. Damages quantified on an other than compensatory basis, to make D disgorge any benefit he may have gained by not performing or to punish him for breach, will be discussed in Part 4 on 'restitution' and chapter 30 on exemplary damages. In sum, this section of this book will examine how the law has responded to the layperson's desire for these different remedies.

2   This assumption does not apply to the discussion of misrepresentation in pp 553-560 below.

The law leaves the initiative to C. It does not compel him to take any action at all, and certainly does not compel him to seek any remedy from the court. But if he does resort to legal action, the law usually allows him to choose the remedy he wants.[3] The award of compensatory damages is by far the most important remedy,[4] and C's claim to it is not subject to the exercise of any discretion by the court. (There are, of course, rules about how such a claim can properly be framed.) However, the special remedies of enforcement of D's performance are subject to such a discretion, and the award of third party performance damages are subject to limits analogous to that discretion; but they both are granted only if C asks for them. If, however, the court does not grant either form of literal enforcement, C may fall back on the usual remedy of damages for his loss in not getting the benefit of performance.

### The function of the law of contract

Though it is not appropriate in a textbook treatment to spend a great deal of time discussing the economic, legal and social theory of the law of remedies for failure to perform a contractual obligation, some brief statement of the theory which underlies that treatment is needed in the interests of clarity. All such treatments are informed by a theoretical position, whether this is recognised or not, and the lack of self-consciousness which follows from a failure to recognise this can lead only to confusion.

This section of this book deals with capitalist economies in which the principal mechanism for the allocation of economic goods is regular, proportional exchange motivated by the desire of the parties to the exchange to maximise their wealth, wealth being the amount of satisfaction or utility afforded by the economic goods to which the parties have some form of title.[5] The parties exchange goods or services for money, each in the belief that by so doing he will realise a surplus utility.[6] At the time of agreement, each party commits his existing resources, representing a certain utility, to the exchange and expects that, after performance of the exchange, he will obtain a resource which represents an increased utility over that with which he began. The sale of goods which have cost £1m to make for a price of £1.1m is the most clear example of the capitalist exchange, in which proportional exchange and surplus, in the form of a

3   See see p 83 below.
4   Claims in debt and for recovery of monies paid, which are the most common proceedings, are examined in ch 11 and see pp 232-235 below. Both are largely (but not entirely) congruent with a compensatory damages claim.
5   M Weber, *Economy and Society* (1968) ch 2.
6   HH Gossen, *The Laws of Human Relations* (1983) ch 7.

net money profit, are obvious. In what remains the leading contribution to the analysis of contractual remedies, that of Fuller and Perdue,[7] the surplus realised at the completion of performance, or rather the expectation of that surplus which arises at the time of the agreement, is called 'the expectation interest'. The institution of contract is the general form of regulation of economic exchange,[8] but, in a most important sense, the legal contract is not what is essential to the exchange. It is the economic exchange, and particularly the surplus, that is essential. The actual performance of the contract is incidental to the obtaining of the surplus, indeed it is a cost of obtaining that surplus, and an understanding of contract remedies turns on seeing that 'expectation' is what fundamentally matters, not 'performance'.[9]

Fuller and Perdue called the sum of resource which a party commits to the contract in reliance on the other party's promise of performance 'the reliance interest'. In the above example (assuming that D breaches after the goods were put in a deliverable state), the reliance interest is the cost of the production of the goods. It is obvious that in some circumstances a combination of the expectation and the reliance interests may be needed properly to protect the expectation interest. For example, when, as has just been said, goods have been put in a deliverable state, full protection of the expectation interest would require compensation of lost net profit (expectation) and lost production costs (reliance).[10] If the breach took place before any work had been done (and no resale was possible), a bare expectation award would sufficiently compensate. These matters will be dealt with at much greater length in Part 2 below.

One can contemplate economic exchange without contract, and there would appear to be widespread evidence of this in pre-capitalist economies[11] and, less certainly and perhaps not fully understood,[12] exceptional examples of this within overall capitalist economies.[13] However, the law of contract has proven to be a necessary institutional

---

7    LL Fuller and WR Perdue Jr, 'The Reliance Interest in Contract Damages' (1936) 46 Yale Law Journal 52 and 373. This is widely regarded as the most important article on contract law: R Birmingham, 'Notes on the Reliance Interest' (1985) 60 Washington Law Review 217.

8    H Collins, *Regulating Contracts* (1999) ch 6.

9    For an argument quite to the contrary see D Friedman, 'The Performance Interest in Contract Damages' (1995) 111 Law Quarterly Review 628, which is discussed in ch 17 below.

10   It is possible to quantify lost expectation using a 'costs avoided' figure in a way which allows one to work with a gross, rather than a net, profits figure, but this is, it is submitted, less theoretically clear and this method will not be used here.

11   B Malinowski, *Crime and Custom in Savage Society* (1962) chs 2-5, 8-9.

12   As it is argued at pp 33-38 below, these cases are examples not of 'non-contractual' relations but of bargaining in the shadow of the law.

13   Eg F Pyke et al (eds), *Industrial Districts and Inter-firm Co-operation in Italy* (1990).

support for the capitalist economies based on generalised exchange, by providing the security to C of being able ultimately to obtain a legally enforceable remedy against D when D breaches by failing to perform without a lawful excuse. The law of contract provides a framework within which parties can, if they wish, turn their voluntary agreement into a binding arrangement subject to external sanction. Although market forces would often induce performance, a third-party enforcement mechanism (such as a court) would be needed to deal with the recalcitrant promisor even in the case of an otherwise perfectly well functioning contract. Even if the parties had made an 'ideal' contract, there would be problems in deciding disputed questions of fact, in settling a disputed question of interpretation, and in compelling an unwilling party to pay the penalties for breach laid down in the contract. The law thus enables the parties to make arrangements which are ultimately much more reliable than those which depend exclusively on sanctions within their own control. (However, the latter sanctions are still important: this book places weight on 'self-help' remedies for breach of contract.)

The relationship of the exchange and the contract is realised in the distinction, central to the law of contractual relationships, between 'primary' and 'secondary' obligations.[14] The primary obligations are the parties' obligations under the exchange. In the above example, the seller's obligation is to deliver the goods[15] and the buyer's is to pay £1.1m. Each party's secondary obligation under the contract is to provide a remedy for a failure to perform (part or all of) his primary obligation. This secondary obligation is created at the time of agreement of the contract, but it is latent until breach, when C gains the right to seek it. The remedy may completely take the place of D's original performance, or may be combined with some residual part of it after breach. In the exceptional case where the remedy sought is compulsion of D's original performance, the primary and secondary obligations apparently merge, though we shall see that there is a very significant practical difference between a performance which D renders voluntarily in the expectation of profit and one which he renders under the compulsion of the court.[16]

**The reason(s) for breach**

The obvious question raised by this analysis of contract in terms of primary and secondary obligations is why D breaches? If we know that contract

---

14  The *Hong Kong Fir Shipping Case* [1962] 2 QB 26 at 64 and *Photo Productions Ltd v Securicor Transport Ltd* [1980] AC 827 at 848.
15  There probably also will be obligations that the goods are of the right quantity and of satisfactory quality, etc.
16  See pp 187-193 below.

works by providing the threat of remedy, we have to ask why that is needed if we are to assess how well contract works. One obvious and indisputably correct answer to the question why D breaches which has already been implied is that D may act in bad faith. By virtue of having entered into a contract with C, D may be placed in a position where he may make a gain by not performing. If, in the example above, the buyer pays for the goods in advance of delivery, the seller will obviously have an incentive not to deliver the goods, for by avoiding the costs of delivery, he will be able to treat all of the payment as a profit, instead of being confined to the net profit that he would realise after delivery. (The prudential as well as moral reasons why the seller should not do this are obvious.) One may, indeed, dispense with 'exchange' at all and just steal. It is obvious that the very same individualistic orientation towards the maximisation of wealth that can lead to productive exchange can also lead to actions that undermine an exchange economy, such as violent expropriation, duress, fraud, etc.[17] The law of contract, and even more other bodies of law including the criminal law, would appear to have a vital role in providing a framework of 'peacefulness'[18] which keeps the maximisation impulse within parameters which mean that it broadly works towards productive exchange.[19] As Macneil has put it in the most thorough treatment of the issue by a contract scholar:

> [C]ontract between totally isolated, utility-maximising individuals is not contract, but war ... contractual solidarity – the social solidarity making exchange work ... at a minimum holds the parties together so that they will not kill and steal in preference to exchanging. [This is a matter of the] external god providing social stability, enforcement of promises, and other basic requirements. Within these rigid confines, the parties are free to maximise their individual utilities to their hearts' content.[20]

This role of the 'external god' may be traced back to Hobbes[1] and it is a vital part of the social contract as the political foundation on which the capitalist economies have been built.[2] The consequences of attempting

---

17  VI Pareto, *Manual of Political Economy* (1970) p 341: 'the efforts of men are utilised in two different ways: they are directed to the production ... of economic goods, or else to the appropriation of goods produced by others'.
18  L von Mises, *Socialism* (1981) p 36.
19  EA Cannan, 'Review of NG Pierson, *Principles of Economics*' (1913) 23 Economic Review 331, p 333: 'the working of self-interest is generally beneficent ... because human institutions are arranged so as to compel self-interest to work in directions in which it will be beneficent'.
20  IR Macneil, *The New Social Contract* (1980) pp 1, 14.
1   T Hobbes, *Leviathan* (1968) p 196.
2   CB Macpherson, *The Political Theory of Possessive Individualism* (1963).

to encourage 'economic' action in the absence of the moral and political constraints which are the indispensable but often, highly mistakenly, taken for granted institutional framework of capitalism, have very sadly been visited on the former COMECON economies, the 'liberalisation' of which has led to widespread or even general gangsterism.[3] However, it is the argument of this section of this book that, *in the 'high trust'*[4] *established capitalist economies*, it is possible to treat as relatively marginal those cases in which D is motivated by bad faith, and in the majority of cases, those cases which it is most important to understand in order to grasp the function and structure of the law of remedies, breach of contract should be seen as a rational economic choice. In the established capitalist economies, the remedies for breach of contract, it will be argued, both essentially are and should be designed to regulate, and thereby facilitate, that choice.

The way in which this facilitation takes place is that there is a general preference for the award of compensatory damages rather than literal enforcement.[5] Either form of literal enforcement, whether D or a third party performs, is likely to cost (a great deal) more than the cost of D's original performance. For reasons which will be set out fully in Part 2, compensatory damages, however, can cost less than literal performance and perhaps even less than original performance. The crucial point which arises from this which it is necessary to grasp to understand remedies is that these cost differentials mean that D may choose voluntarily to breach for an economically rational reason. Put bluntly, D will breach when he believes that breach will, by a significant margin, more greatly maximise his resultant wealth than performance. This is the only reason there can be for breach on the basis of rational self-interest. As the law of contract is a legal institution for the facilitation of economic exchange, and as such exchange is at its heart motivated precisely by parties' wishes to maximise their wealth, much overtly moralistic criticism of breach as a dishonourable failure to keep one's promises is contradictory, or rather beside the point.[6] (Of course, this does not apply to gratuitous promises which are, precisely, non-contractual.)[7] This is even more the case when,

---

3   D Campbell, 'Breach and Penalty as Contractual Norm and Contractual Anomie' [2001] Wisconsin Law Review 68. The situation in Russia is described in S Hedlund, *Russia's Market Economy: A Bad Case of Predatory Capitalism* (1999) and S Menshikov, *Catastrophe or Catharsis?* (1990).

4   F Fukuyama, *Trust* (1995) Pt 3.

5   C is given a very strong incentive indeed – instructively, this incentive is commonly called a duty – to follow this general preference by the causation and mitigation rules which govern the quantification of compensatory damages: see chs 6-7 below.

6   PS Atiyah, *Promises, Morals and the Law* (1981) ch 6.

7   MA Eisenberg, 'The World of Contract and the World of Gift' (1997) 85 California Law Review 821.

as we will see, breach performs a central, legitimate function in the market economies and, indeed, significantly contributes to such efficiency as those economies possess. If one's understanding of contract takes it that obligations should always be performed and that the courts play the principal role in this enforcement, then the actual picture of contract revealed by empirical studies – of ubiquity of breach and absolute rarity of court enforcement of primary obligations (indeed, of court action at all)[8] – is simply hopelessly bewildering. However, it is the shortcomings of that understanding of contract that produces the bewilderment, rather than it being the case that the actions of the contracting parties lack rationality. When properly understood, non-performance is perfectly rational.[9] The position taken in this book is that the function of the law of remedies for breach of contract is not to 'enforce' (primary obligations under) contracts but to regulate the occasions of breach; that is to say, to provide a framework which will allow breach in wealth maximising circumstances.

Of course, were there no rules regulating the terms and occasions of breach, then the law of contract would have no function. One must bear in mind that breach analytically is not just walking away from a contract (though this does in practice occur when C's damages are nominal). It is, as it were, walking away, but on terms, those terms essentially being the compensation of C based on protection of his expectation interest. In order that the underlying trust in the market economy be preserved, C should have his lost expectation compensated by D's payment of damages, and the law of contract has this compensation as its principal function.[10] This is the first rule of contractual remedies, the famous rule in *Robinson v Harman*, that a remedy should aim to put C in the position he would have been in had the contract been performed.[11] In any consideration of contractual remedies, then, the necessity of compensating C is never an issue, though how and how far this goal is realised is. With this in mind, let us examine what, analytically, are the only two reasons which there can be for breach according to rational self-interest. These are the maximisation of gain and the minimisation of loss through breach. In what immediately follows it will be argued that the function of the law of contract is best understood not as the general prevention of breach but as the regulation of the terms on which breach may legitimately be made.

8    See ch 2 below.
9    Collins, *Regulating Contracts*, above p 6, n 8, ch 6.
10   GH Treitel, *Law of Contract* (10th edn, 1999) p 7. Though it is too complex an argument to pursue here, by attempting to give certainty to compensation liability through the rules of causation, remoteness and mitigation, the damages rules allow D to fix the price of its goods accurately, for the cost of (inevitable occasional) failure should be part of the price of the good: see ch 6 below.
11   (1848) 1 Exch 850 at 855. See further ch 5 below.

**Breach in order to maximise gain: the concept of efficient breach**

A powerful incentive to breach a contract arises where D expects to make a net profit from the opportunities created by his proposed breach. Although the courts are often concerned to see that C, the non-breaching party, is not better off as a result of the breach – the remedy for the breach should not be more valuable to him than performance would have been – they do not usually accept the converse. There is, in fact, a good economic case for so-called 'efficient' breach of contract based on the view that society should allow D not to perform whenever the breach will leave him better off after fully compensating C. An important reason for C's choosing, after breach, to seek money rather than compulsion of D's promised performance is that he may want to be completely free in deciding how to use that money. C may not even want to use the money to buy a substitute performance from a third person because, in the light of some new circumstances, he may have found a better opportunity, a new use for the money. Similarly, if D had not yet completed performance on his side, he would often wish to be released from that obligation so that he could redeploy to other uses the resources he would have devoted to the contract, eg his own time and labour. This freedom might be especially valuable to D because, since the contract was made, a more profitable opportunity might have opened up. It is claimed that society as a whole will benefit if D can deploy his resources to a more profitable use which will leave him with a net profit or surplus after he has paid damages to compensate C.[12]

The efficiency of allowing breach in this sort of case can best be appreciated by taking a contractual-type problem and transforming it into a similar problem within a single firm which is subject to an overall decision-making body (the central management). Instead of a contract between two strangers, suppose a similar arrangement between two branches of the same firm. How would the central management deal with a change in circumstances which affected the profitability of the arrangement? They would ask themselves the question whether, in the light of all the information *then* available, the firm as a whole would be better off by continuing the arrangement or by stopping it (viz which alternative would maximise profits overall or minimise losses overall?). Since the relevant circumstances may change over time, an arrangement

---

12  RA Posner, *Economic Analysis of Law* (5th edn 1998) p 133. The case most often cited in support of efficient breach of this profit maximising sort is not, on its facts, clear authority for this principle: *Teacher v Calder* 1897 SC 661. However, in that case it was firmly stated that C cannot recover from D the profits D made from his breach of contract but can recover only for his own (C's) losses: ibid at 672-673; affirmed on this point [1899] AC 451 at 467-468 (HL(Sc)).

between the branches which was initially the best which could be made, may cease to be so. New information may become available which shows, for instance, escalating costs in the branch supplying an item to the other branch so that it would be cheaper for the latter to obtain it from an outside supplier. Or, a new opportunity may arise for the supplying branch to make a greater profit by switching its production to meet the needs of an outside customer who is willing to pay an attractive price. The central management, not being bound by any contract, can make adjustments from time to time so as to achieve the most efficient use of the firm's resources. When the arrangement takes the form of a contract between two separate legal persons, there is no higher decision-making body to make the adjustments which may be in their joint interest and may lead to a more efficient use of society's resources overall. If circumstances change there are only two methods of adjustment open to the parties to a contract: either they will negotiate a modification by subsequent agreement, or one party will unilaterally take advantage of the rules by breaching the contract and leaving the other to claim damages (or, more likely, by settling a prospective damages claim).

This illustration should be borne in mind when breach is analysed. Efficiency requires that resources be allocated and risks assigned so that all possible gains from beneficial exchanges are exhausted. The economist assumes that, at the moment of making the original contract, each party (as a rational person) valued the promise of the other more than (or at least as much as) any alternative which he could then find in exchange for his own promise. At that time, the contract was 'efficient', but circumstances may change thereafter, and it is this which leads to the concept of 'efficient' breach. It is argued that D will break his contract if, at the time of the breach, he can find a better opportunity for his labour and resources, under which he will make (after fully compensating C for the loss caused by the breach) a greater profit than he would have done if he had performed his promise. It is claimed that this result is 'efficient' and should be encouraged by the law because, by maximising the total value or utility of the two parties, it benefits society. Remedies under contract law should aim to discourage 'inefficient' breaches, by which is meant breaches which impose total costs on the parties in excess of the total benefits accruing to them. As the decision to breach lies with the defendant, it is necessary that he should be required to make good the loss suffered by C if we are to have a proper test of the economic efficiency of the breach. The defendant will have to decide whether to breach in light of the costs of the breach to both parties. If, in anticipation of paying full compensation (damages) under this rule, D still decides to break his promise, the implication is that the resources released by the breach are being allocated to more efficient uses, and that society as a whole therefore benefits. The law is, in effect, permitting D to break his contract, provided he pays C the monetary equivalent of the lost benefit which performance would have given him.

It is essential to bear in mind, however, that D's calculation of 'resultant wealth' may very well extend beyond the horizon of the specific contract which D may consider breaching. There is a strong extra-legal incentive on D to maintain his business reputation so that others (the other party to the contract and third parties aware of his conduct) will do business with him in the future, either by continuing in a long-term relationship or by reaching new agreements with him. When D has made a promise, he will be deterred from breach by the fear of getting a reputation for unreliability.[13] The limited empirical evidence we have leads to the conclusion that solicitude for reputation, or the extra-legal remedy of loss of reputation, is of more significance in determining whether or not D will breach than any of the legal remedies.[14]

### Breach in order to minimise loss

The very considerable attention which efficient breach has received is in marked contrast to the (from the perspective which is being advanced here) other form of breach,[15] though this form is far more important; indeed determining the correct policy towards it is the most important issue in the law of contractual remedies. The purpose, as we have seen, of efficient breach is to allow D to maximise a gain. Far more important is breach which has the purpose of minimising loss. This is, indeed, the typical case of breach, though not generally recognised as such.

When D undertakes a primary contractual obligation, he does so in the belief that performance of that obligation will cost a certain amount. That this belief inevitably will be based both on imperfect information about the state of the world at the time of the agreement and a limited ability to compute what is involved in performance means that risk always attends a contractual undertaking.[16] In some cases, this risk is manifested over the course of performance by a rise in the cost of performance. Any rise in the cost of complete performance above D's original estimate will reduce D's expected profit margin, and thus D's own expectation interest, and beyond a certain point the rise will extinguish that margin completely

---

13 D Charny, 'Non-legal Sanctions in Commercial Relationships' (1990) 104 Harvard Law Review 373. See further pp 44-45 below.

14 B Klein and B Leffler, 'The Role of Market Forces in Assuring Contractual Performance', in DB Klein (ed), *Reputation* (1997) 289.

15 Cf the distinction between the 'fortunate' and the 'unfortunate' contingency in R Cooter and T Ulen, *Law and Economics* (3rd edn 2000) p 238.

16 R Dye, 'Costly Contract Contingencies' (1985) 26 International Economic Review 233.

(leaving D in a 'break-even' contract, where receipts equal costs) or make the margin negative (leaving D in a 'losing contract', where receipts are lower than costs). The enormous variation in the empirical circumstances which give rise to these outcomes – unanticipated shortage of raw materials, destruction of premises by fire, etc – should not obscure the fact that, in all cases other than bad faith, it is a rise in the cost of his performance that gives D a motive for breach.

In terms of dealing with breach,[17] the principal function of the law of remedies is to allocate risks of non-performance.[18] Parties expect to improve their welfare by making agreements which reduce uncertainty about the future and enable reliance to be placed on each other's promise. The law is needed to support the agreement in this regard because, leaving aside bad faith, on their own the parties cannot adequately guard against the risk that a promise might not be fulfilled. The economist sometimes postulates a hypothetical, ideal world to clarify our thinking. In such a world, in which each party was fully informed about all the circumstances and could accurately predict the future, and the costs of negotiating were negligible, the parties would draw up a 'completely contingent contract', that is, one which exhaustively specified all the parties' rights and obligations in every possible situation, and which provided a set of procedures and penalties to deal with every conceivable aspect of non-performance. But, of course, finding all the relevant information and fully negotiating terms to incorporate it into the contract would involve costs now generally referred to as transaction costs.[19] Given the existence of these costs, contracts cannot be the completely contingent products of perfect rationality but are the imperfect products of 'bounded rationality'.[20] The state of the world will not be as assumed by the parties at the time of the contract, for their knowledge of that state and its potential for change, and their ability to calculate the consequences of what they do know, will be bounded, and this will impose risk. The practical point

---

17  As, one imagines, most contractual obligations are relatively unproblematically performed, it is probably right to say that the principal function of the law of contract in established capitalist economies is the crystallisation or 'presentation' of the parties' intention to exchange by setting standards of communication with which those parties must comply to make an enforceable agreement: Macneil *The Relational Theory of Contract* (2001) ch 6.

18  AM Polinsky, 'Risk Sharing Through Breach of Contract Remedies' (1983) 12 Journal of Legal Studies 427.

19  RH Coase, 'The Problem of Social Cost', in RH Coase *The Firm, the Market and the Law* (1986) 95, p 114. See further KJ Arrow 'The Organisation of Economic Activity: Issues Pertinent to the Choice of Market Versus Non-market Allocation', in KJ Arrow, *Collected Works*, vol 2 (1983) ch 7 and CJ Dahlman, 'The Problem of Externality' (1979) 22 Journal of Law and Economics 141, p 148.

20  HA Simon, *Administrative Behaviour* (4th edn 1997) p 20.

is not that a completely contingent contract would be infinitely costly to draw up. It is that, long before a party needs to consider the infinite cost of a completely contingent contract, he would reach a point where the transaction costs of continuing to specify an ever more precise contract did not yield any marginal return in terms of materially assisting the planning of performance.[1] In a complex building contract, for example, the only way exactly to price the works is to carry them out (and thus those contracts must be based on variable estimates).[2]

In all contracts, then, there is a reciprocal allocation of risks to each party. Much of the future is uncertain, but one way of partially reducing that uncertainty is to obtain binding promises from others that they will perform (or refrain from performing) certain acts. If one party is risk-averse in relation to a specified future uncertainty, whereas the other is not (being either a risk-taker or risk-neutral), there is a mutually beneficial opportunity for the risk to be undertaken by the latter. The promisor can therefore often be considered as a kind of insurer: he is the party better able to bear a specified risk, either by spreading its cost among all his customers or by controlling its occurrence. He is rewarded for this risk-taking by the price or counter-promise from the other party. This approach justifies holding the promisor liable for the loss caused to the other through his involuntary failure to fulfil the promise: this failure is the 'insured event' which activates the promisor's liability to meet the promisee's loss. Contract law should therefore facilitate the allocation of risk between the parties by upholding the agreed exchange of risk-taking.

The allocation of risk takes place within certain limits to the extent to which D can be required to absorb risk. There is a fundamental limit to the extent to which D could be obliged to perform even when his costs were rising. This upper limit is set by the possibility of D becoming bankrupt or going into liquidation. There is a lower limit set by the possibility of the contract being discharged for common mistake or frustration, to which we will return in chapter 16. In the great majority of cases, however, a more relevant limit is set, and the general possibility of breach *created*, by the compensatory principle on which damages are calculated.[3]

Let us consider an example in which D is to deliver widgets to C six months after agreement, but D's premises are flooded one week after agreement. If D can repair the flood damage within a time which will still allow him to deliver to C, his expectation will be lowered because his

1   P Diamond and E Maskin, 'An Equilibrium Analysis of Search and Breach of Contract' (1979) 10 Bell Journal of Economics 282.

2   D Campbell, 'Fixing Prices to Shift Risk' (June 1992) The New Gazette (Law Society of Hong Kong) 28.

3   R Birmingham, 'Breach of Contract, Damages Measures and Economic Efficiency' (1970) 24 Rutgers Law Review 273.

costs of performance will be increased by the cost of the repairs, but, nevertheless, D may still deliver at a profit, and may choose to do so. Should the repair be more costly, D will still have an incentive to repair and deliver up to the point where the costs of performance exceed the costs of breach. If, for example, widgets are generally available at only a small extra cost, giving C an incentive to buy them from a third party, by breaching and compensating him only for that cost will be cheaper than D's performing.[4] The costs of breach to D if a compensatory solution is pursued are the damages which will have to be paid to C and D's own wasted expenditure and lost profits. One easily can see that beyond a certain level of cost of repair, D will have a rational incentive to breach.[5]

If the damages system works in the sense that damages actually do compensate, or are an 'adequate' remedy as it is put, C should be indifferent whether D pays damages or performs. The only issue should be whether D be made to perform or to pay compensatory damages, and, if damages are adequate, D obviously should be allowed to breach. If D decides that breach is less costly than performance and the damages that are part of the cost of breach do compensate C, then D should be allowed to breach. To compel D to perform will protect C's expectation, but *ex hypothesi*, damages will do this more cheaply than literal enforcement.[6] As no benefit will be conferred by making D protect C's expectation by the more expensive method of literal enforcement, D should be allowed to elect the cheaper method. (This idea of mitigation of loss also applies to the quantification as well as the election of damages, indeed it is more clearly understood in regard of quantification.[7] If two methods of quantification both protect C's expectation but one is cheaper for D than the other, the cheaper should be chosen.) To do otherwise than adopt this 'principle of joint-cost minimisation'[8] would be to incur pointless 'social waste'.[9] In sum:

> remedies for breach of contract ... attempt to accommodate two
> competing goals ... (1) securing to the injured party the benefit of

---

4    This is the principal application of the mitigation principle. See ch 7 below.

5    For ease of exposition, we consider here only this single sale. Whatever the analysis of D's position in respect of this single sale, D may well have an incentive to repair and perform in order to maintain his reputation for reliable delivery.

6    W Bishop, 'The Choice of Remedy for Breach of Contract' (1985) 14 Journal of Legal Studies 299, p 316.

7    See ch 7 below.

8    CJ Goetz and RE Scott, 'The Mitigation Principle' (1983) 69 Virginia Law Review 967, pp 972-973.

9    Concern about such social waste, whether this is explicitly recognised or not, lies behind most of the difficult decisions whether to grant literal enforcement discussed in Pt 3 below, nb 154-157 and 222-226.

the bargain, (2) without imposing unnecessary costs on the breaching party.[10]

When one wishes to evaluate the efficiency of a contractual remedies rule, it is absolutely vital to appreciate that it does not necessarily matter whether 'the contract' is enforced. What is essential is that the legal rule realises, so far as possible, the purpose of the underlying exchange, that of realising a surplus, by protecting the expectation interest. After a breach, this cannot be done as cheaply as it could under the terms originally envisaged by the parties, for, by virtue of D's having breached, something has happened to disrupt those terms. But it should, in order to avoid this waste, be done as cheaply as possible. The law of contract's general recourse to compensatory damages rather than literal enforcement can be explained on this basis. In sum, we might modify *Robinson v Harman* to say that the fundamental goal of the law of contract is to put C in the position he would have been in had the contract been performed; that is, to protect C's expectation, but *at least cost to D*.

It is obvious that in the capitalist economies which are composed of countless trillions of exchanges of varying degrees of complexity, dealing with contracts in which D finds his costs of performance growing in an unanticipated way is a major problem. Finding a mechanism for handling this problem is central to the efficiency of the economy. The fundamental mechanism is an agreed adjustment of obligations by the parties, but this takes place within the limits to which the original performance can be insisted upon. Much more importantly even than insolvency, which nevertheless itself has a crucial role,[11] and certainly more importantly than discharge for common mistake and frustration, which is somewhat otiose because it is so rarely granted,[12] breach sets this limit. Breach allows flexibility into the system of exchanges, allowing parties relief from unanticipatedly expensive obligations when further performance would merely be wasteful because C can be adequately compensated in damages. In this sense, the function of the law of contract is to allow breach, but on the right occasions and on the right terms.[13]

10  EG Andersen, 'Good Faith in the Enforcement of Contracts' (1988) 73 Iowa Law Review 299, p 306. One might say that the first, compensation, principle of damages is supplemented by a second, efficiency, principle, in an instance of the common law's combination of compensation and efficiency discussed in R Cooter's seminal 'Unity in Tort, Contract and Property: The Model of Precaution' (1985) 73 California Law Review 1, p 1.
11  RM Goode, *Commercial Law in the Next Millennium* (1998) pp 45-6: 'business failure should be seen as a necessary consequence of a market-oriented society'.
12  RA Hillman, 'Contract Excuse and Bankruptcy Discharge' (1990) 43 Stanford Law Review 132.
13  A comparison with the extreme rigidities characteristic of the centrally planned command economies is useful. In such economies an analogue to specific

It must be stressed that this understanding of breach is quite opposed both to the understanding of breach as a 'wrong' which is the import of that common language in which a breaching party is a 'wrongdoer' and a non-breaching party 'innocent'.[14] Some breaches may be made deceitfully or in bad faith, and arguably these should be regarded as wrongs and treated as such, with punishment or deterrence in view.[15] But other breaches are legitimately made by parties acting in good faith and should be treated as such, when punishment or deterrence is not appropriate. (It is a shortcoming of the understanding of all breaches as wrongs that it cannot easily accommodate a doctrine of good faith.)[16]

This understanding of breach also calls into question the more subtle distinction which has been drawn between voluntary and involuntary breach. Faced with what has been called here the rising costs of performance, D who contemplates what has here been called a breach to minimise loss may well not look at the matter in these explicitly economic terms. He will see his breach as involuntary in the sense that he wishes to perform but feels that he cannot because changed circumstances have prevented him. This is the common sense view that performance has become 'impossible' that gives superficial plausibility to the idea of widespread excuse for frustration. Recognising this, Macneil has put forward the following criticism of efficient breach:

---

performance played the major role as a remedy for failure to comply with obligations under the plan because satisfaction of the plan was the goal of economic action: Wang Liming, 'Specific Performance in Chinese Contract Law: An East-West Comparison' (1992) 1 Asia-Pacific Law Review 18. Of course, as much as in any system, obligations were entered into under imperfect information and with limited computational power, and so their performance was subject to unexpected rises in costs. Though a whole legion of semi-illicit devices for modifying the plan would seem to have arisen (bribes to those who held scarce goods, lying about plan fulfilment, etc), the absence of a general possibility of an analogue to breach to deal with these rises would appear to have caused an inflexibility which was a major weakness of these economies: J Kornai, *The Socialist System* (1992) chs 6-8.

14   P Birks, 'Restitutionary Damages for Breach of Contract' [1987] Lloyd's Maritime and Commercial Law Quarterly 421 and G Jones, 'The Recovery of Benefits Gained from a Breach of Contract' (1983) 99 Law Quarterly Review 443.

15   See ch 30, below.

16   D Campbell, 'The Relational Constitution of the Discrete Contract,' in D Campbell and P Vincent-Jones (eds), *Contract and Economic Organisation: Socio-legal Initiatives* (1996) 40, pp 62-63. On good faith in consumer contracts see sec 3.10 below; on good faith in commercial contracts see sec 32.3 below; and, as the isssue emerges from the current extension of restitution remedies following breach of contract, see ch 17 below.

In the real world of commerce, opportunities for gain through "efficient breach" of transactions in goods other than true futures deals are so rare as to be almost non-existent. There simply are not many chances for deliberate breaches of this kind, and general propositions about remedies based on them tell singularly little about efficiency in the real world. What does happen in the world of contracts – often in clear violation of legal rules of contract remedies – is that people get themselves into trouble in an incredible variety of ways, both ingenious and disingenuous, and are unable or at the very least think themselves unable to perform. Their position *at that time* comes much closer to impossibility and serious impracticability than it does to deliberate breach, even when they led themselves into the morass.[17]

But though this no doubt is an accurate description of how the matter is often now understood by all but the most rational business parties, if it is allowed that breach be efficient if it minimises loss as well as when it maximises gain, then this ultimately is a misleading understanding of the matter. Except in the almost empty set of cases classed as common mistake or frustration, D does not escape liability because of his subjective feeling that performance has become impossible. The only commercially sensible response to the situation initially felt to be 'impossible' is to do the calculation of the optimal time to breach which we have set out, though even then it may well not be understood in this way. In the hypothetical example above, until D exhausts all his resources it is quite wrong to say that he *could not* perform by, say, engaging in the incredibly rapid and expensive repair of his factory. His decision not to do this and breach can only be really understood in economic terms and not by reference to impossibility of performance and the involuntariness of breach.[18] Ultimately, the nature of contractual obligation and breach must be understood economically, for the two cases Macneil opposes are not opposed, and the latter case, which he sets against efficient breach, is in fact the most important example of efficient breach. 'Even if ... breach is deliberate, it is not necessarily blameworthy',[19] for the deliberateness may just follow from clarity of thought.

Grasping the function of the two forms of efficient breach and therefore of breach as such allows us to come to terms with a paradox in the law of remedies for breach which arises if that law is thought to have the purpose

---

17   IR Macneil, 'Contract Remedies: A Need for a Better Efficiency Analysis' (1988) 144 Journal of Institutional and Theoretical Economics 6, p 15.

18   The same applies to the decision to enter administration or voluntary liquidation, when non-rational aspects of the decision may be even more to the fore of the business party's thinking.

19   *Patton v Mid-continent Systems Inc* 841 F 2d 742 at 750 (1988).

of enforcing primary obligations by generally deterring D from breaching them or of punishing D for their breach. As has been mentioned, the law reports contain many statements to the effect that the court should not give C any remedy for D's breach of contract which would put C into a better position than he would have been in if D had fully performed his obligations. There is no corresponding principle that D should not be better off as a result of his breach, and in most cases where D deliberately breaks the contract, despite his ability to perform, he expects to profit from the breach, or at least to avoid a greater loss. The law of remedies for breach which, as Farnsworth famously put it: 'shows a marked solicitude for men who do not keep their promises',[20] will be incomprehensible unless it is appreciated that breach is a *legitimate* legal institution, governing a rational economic response to the limitations of bounded rationality, which it is one important function of compensatory damages *to allow*.

Greater self-consciousness of the nature and limits of a contractual undertaking might, it is submitted, be of assistance to business parties in understanding the function of contract.[1] What is needed is to recognise that *the rules stipulate co-operation in the normal case of breach*. Let us return to our hypothetical example. When the costs of performance exceed the costs of breach, D has a rational incentive to breach. As the costs of breach are D's *and* C's lost expectation and wasted reliance, the costs of breach can be lower than the costs of performance only if damages are normally quantified on the basis of compensation of C's net loss and C has a 'duty' to mitigate; or, to put it the other way around, when literal enforcement and punitive damages are only exceptionally available. This has the result that the most important sensible course of action for C after breach is to find a substitute and be compensated for his net loss, if any. Exceptions to the basic position must be considered when cover is inadequate to protect C's expectation.

The point of relevance to us is that breach is both efficient and co-operative in a way that undercuts the typical opposition of these qualities. In circumstances when C can be compensated in damages, breach obviously is efficient, for insisting upon anything else would be to satisfy C's expectation at a higher cost to D than the costs of breach, and what would be the point of that? The breach is efficient in this case because it minimises *D's* loss. But this efficiency emerges only where C co-operates by accepting breach and mitigating. Allowing D to breach and placing the burden of mitigation on C enlists C's co-operation in dealing with

20  EA Farnsworth 'Legal Remedies for Breach of Contract' (1970) 70 Columbia Law Review 1145, p 1216.
1   See ch 17 below.

D's problems, one aspect of this co-operation being that it makes legal action unnecessary in cases where compensation is adequate. In this way, the efficient breach is, we suggest, the fundamental provision giving an incentive to co-operation in contract.[2]

Policy towards efficient breach should, however, bear in mind the possible external effects of widespread recourse to such breach. We have acknowledged that welfare enhancing capitalist economies enjoy and depend on a high level of reliance on the fulfilment of contracts. Business and the ordinary life of individual citizens could not be carried on if it was not possible to rely on most contractual promises being performed. Though a certain level of breach must be encouraged, each breach tends to weaken public confidence in the reliability of contractual promises, especially since most breaches will come to the knowledge of third parties. It is obvious that bad faith breach is inimical to the contract system. But more than this, it must be acknowledged that extending our conscious tolerance of breach will allow a larger margin for bad faith breach, and this will tend to undermine general reliance on contracts and thereby cause an external cost (which is not taken into account in the assessment of damages for the loss caused to C). We suspect that a more condemnatory attitude toward specifically bad faith breach, which will require acceptance of a general duty of good faith, will be able to deal with this problem far more adequately than the current, futile treatment of all breach as wrong.[3] Nevertheless, support for the concept of efficient breach of contract must be kept within boundaries which preserve this basic framework of reliance on the sanctity of contract.

### Exceptions to the general preference for compensatory damages

There are three sets of remedies in which the law has developed or is being asked to develop exceptions to the general preference for compensatory damages. They are: restitution, exemplary damages and literal enforcement.

---

2  This argument is made in the course of a criticism of relational contract theory's typical aversion to efficient breach in Campbell, 'Breach and Penalty as Contractual Norm and Contractual Anomie', above p 9, n 3.
3  J Shearmur and DB Klein, 'Good Conduct in the Great Society: Adam Smith and the Role of Reputation', in Klein (ed), *Reputation*, above p 13, n 14, 29.

## Restitution of benefits received by D[4]

In the terms of the contractual interests analysis formalised by Fuller and Perdue, the third ground for C's claim against D is restitution of such valuable benefit as C has conveyed to D (eg repayment of the price paid in advance by C). A claim in restitution is *not* a claim for compensatory damages and the principles of its quantification are distinct from those in contract (or tort).

There are three principal circumstances in which a restitutionary claim can emerge following a failure to perform a contract:

(1) *C conveys a valuable benefit which unjustly enriches D.* If D has failed to perform his side of the contract and C has terminated so that C has not and will not receive any benefit from D's performance, C may seek to get back from D what D had received from C. This may be an issue of recovering money paid or property transferred under a contract (recovery) or receiving a payment for goods delivered or services rendered (*quantum meruit*). C does not allege that he has suffered loss, nor directly that he has incurred expenses in reliance on the contract which have been wasted. The claim rather is that, as C has (part-)performed in expectation of a reciprocal performance but D has not given that performance, D would be unjustifiably enriched if, after his breach, he could retain the benefit he had received from C. A reliance expenditure is necessary (for it is restitution of the benefit conveyed by this that C seeks) but the ground on which recovery, and the quantification of the sum awarded, is sought is not contractual but restitutionary. Such a hybrid claim is 'quasi-contractual', though this description has fallen from usage. Because of the different ways in which a claim in contract (and tort) and a claim in restitution are quantified, C may find a claim in the latter more advantageous than in the former. The law of quasi-contract is, therefore, both distinct from, and complementary to, the law of contract (and tort), and some reference to it is necessary to give a comprehensive view of remedies in contract (and tort).

(2) *Common mistake and frustration.* Following a successful plea of common mistake or frustration, D's failure to perform is not regarded as a breach but as a failure to perform with a lawful excuse. That excuse in substance essentially is that performance had become commercially impracticable, either for reasons which were present but unknown at the time of agreement (common mistake) or for reasons which arose unforeseen during performance (frustration). In such a case of lawful failure to perform, there is no reason why D, who, to repeat, has not breached, should be compelled to compensate C for his lost

expectation. Rather, the appropriate remedy, often called 'rescission,' would be to wipe the slate clean by restoring both parties to the position they would have been in if they had never entered into the contractual relationship. In any contract sufficiently involved for litigation to be envisaged in respect of it, this is a much more difficult matter than it may at first appear. Restitution has been used to try to effect rescission in these circumstances.

(3) *The profit made by D after breach.* The traditional statement of the purpose of awarding damages does not refer to the position of D after the breach. It simply says that the purpose is to put C into the position he would have been in if both parties had performed their respective obligations under the contract. In a typical statement, the Court of Appeal has said that 'we are concerned with the buyer's loss and not with the seller's profit, the latter being wholly irrelevant'.[5] If D makes a windfall profit through diverting his resources elsewhere after efficient breach, it has until recently been said that it is not the objective of the courts to deprive D of this profit, but simply to compensate C for his loss. D may be better off after the breach, but all the courts are concerned with is C's position. C should be no worse off but also no better off: 'It is not the function of the courts where there is a breach of contract knowingly to put the plaintiff in a better financial position than if the contract had been properly performed.'[6] This philosophy permeates the law on damages, but there are signs that the courts are moving away from this approach. Obviously, an award of exemplary damages could deprive D of the windfall profit of a successful efficient breach. However, it is principally through a restitutionary argument for the redistribution of at least some of this profit on the grounds of restitution to C rather than punishment of D that disgorgement of the profits of breach has been mounted, and this has recently been pushed so far as to challenge the quantification of damages by reference to the expectation interest.

## Exemplary damages for breach of contract

Quantification of damages with the goal of compensation analytically precludes attempting to quantify them according to the blameworthiness of D's conduct. The measure of the damages is C's expectation. This is less of a problem than it initially appears once one appreciates that breach typically is legitimate. There are, of course, breaches in bad faith, and the general refusal of the courts to award exemplary damages in contract

5   *The Solholt* [1983] 1 Lloyd's Rep 605 at 608.
6   *C & P Haulage v Middleton* [1983] 1 WLR 1461 at 1468.

meant that D faces no penalty for the most outrageous, deliberate breach. Treating D's bad faith, and even his malice against C as irrelevant both to the issue of his liability in contract and to that of the amount of damages cuts out the possibility of using damages to punish D for bad faith breach. There have, consequently, been attempts to give punitive or 'exemplary' damages, and their more general use presently is being considered.[7]

## Literal enforcement

There are circumstances in which it has been thought best not to allow breach at all but, in effect, to compel performance of the primary obligation. This may be called the literal enforcement of the contract. The rational reason C sometimes elects to pursue literal enforcement, and the reason the court sometimes awards a remedy that effects it, is that, as we will see, damages sometimes do not actually compensate or, as it is put, 'are inadequate'.[8]

7    See ch 30 below.
8    See Pt 3 below.

# Part I
# First-step remedies

# 2 Forebearance, alternative dispute resolution and settlement

## Forebearance

As was mentioned in the previous chapter, one course of action open to C following D's failure to perform is, of course, forebearing to do anything, or at least forebearing to seek to pursue a remedy. Though forebearance therefore is, as was said, in a sense tangential to the subject matter of this book, it is a course of action following non-performance that practical experience and empirical studies of contractual action have shown to have great importance, for the principal fact about the formal remedies for non-performance is what has been called their 'non-use'.

### The non-use of contract remedies

Many writers have implicitly assumed that a breach of contract immediately and automatically brings a legal sanction into operation, and, behind this, that every breach is a wrong which must call forth a remedy effecting corrective justice, or restitution, or whatever.[1] The abiding principle of this view of the law remains *pacta sunt servanda* (contractual obligations should be performed). This view is formalist in the sense that it is based on abstract jurisprudential principles produced by philosophic ratiocination rather than on empirical study or practical experience of the law.[2] For practising lawyers know that, although there are many

1   EJ Weinrib, *The Idea of Private Law* (1995); P Birks, *An Introduction to the Law of Restitution* (rev edn 1989) and P Birks, 'Definition and Division: A Meditation on Institutes 3.13', in P Birks (ed), *The Classification of Obligations* (1997) 1, pp 20-21.
2   EJ Weinrib, 'The Jurisprudence of Legal Formalism' (1993) 16 Harvard Journal of Law and Public Policy 583.

occasions in which disputes arise between parties to contracts, very few indeed of these disputes are settled in the formal setting of the court-room. Though empirical research on the practical use of contract remedies in the UK remains extremely inadequate,[3] its basic thrust repeatedly confirms the early work of Stewart Macaulay in America, that if one assumes *pacta sunt servanda*, then the absolutely defining feature of the law of contract is that it is not used by the parties to the contract to resolve their disputes.[4] A book on contractual remedies which seeks not to construct a formally coherent but (indeed because) practically irrelevant doctrine but rather to give an accurate account of those remedies' practical importance must have their non-use at its heart.

'Non-use' is, however, in some respects a misleading term and it has, to some extent therefore, been difficult to explain. There are two important senses of non-use which should be distinguished. First, there is the non-use which arises when those who wish to use the law are unable to do so because of problems restricting their access to the civil justice system. The Office of Fair Trading (OFT) estimates that some 85.8 million consumer complaints were made in 1999, and in 1.4 million of these cases legal advice was taken (with 'quasi-legal' advice from Citizens' Advice Bureaux, Trading Standards Departments, etc being taken in 2 million cases).[5] But though the Lord Chancellor's Department does not collect the statistics in such a way as to make an accurate estimate of the number of consumer actions possible, in 1998 only 7,148 small claims[6] and 2,900 county court actions above the small claims limit[7] may possibly have arisen from a consumer complaint.[8] (The High Court effectively is barred

---

3    For a review of the British research up to 1995 see D Campbell, 'The Socio-legal Analysis of Contract', in PA Thomas (ed), Socio-legal Studies (1997) 239, pp 252-3. Subsequent empirical research is represented by B Lyons and J Mehta, 'Private Sector Business Contracts: The Text Between the Lines', in S Deakin and J Michie (eds), *Contracts, Co-operation and Competition* (1997) 43 and S Deakin et al, 'Contract Law, Trust Relations, and Incentives for Co-operation: A Comparative Study', in Deakin and Michie (eds), *Contracts, Co-operation and Competition*, loc cit, 105.

4    S Macaulay, 'The Use and Non-use of Contracts in the Manufacturing Industry' (1963) 9 Practical Lawyer 13.

5    Office of Fair Trading, *Consumer Detriment* (OFT 296) (2000) paras 5.1, 5.17.

6    Lord Chancellor's Department, *Judicial Statistics* (1998) table 4.8. These were disputes brought by 'individuals' on 'other matters'. Though the small claims (up to £5,000) procedure now has a statistically dominant position in the civil courts, in 1998 representing over 80% of all defended claims in the civil court system (ibid, table 4.7), the vast majority of these were for debt.

7    Ibid, table 4.12. This certainly is an over-estimate of the number of county court cases brought by consumers.

8    This is not to say that this may not be the right number of small claims in the sense of being the number which it is sensible to use the court system to deal with (J Baldwin, *Monitoring the Rise of the Small Claims Limit* (LCD Research Series 1/97) (1997)), it is merely to stress that consumer disputes obviously are predominantly resolved elsewhere.

to consumers.)[9] Despite the shortcomings of the evidence, innumerable post-war studies confirm that consumers feature but rarely as claimants even in 'the bargain basement of civil justice'.[10] The most recent survey of which we are aware estimated that the court was used to resolve only 1% of the 71% of complaints about unsatisfactory goods which were resolved.[11]

Policy over reform of the civil justice system has not been informed by any systematic attempt to assess what might be the optimal level of use of courts to resolve consumer complaints. That C is the first to bear the risk of the uncertainties and costs of litigation means that delay in procedure, scarcity of judicial time, as well as fear of legal expenses, may all operate to deter C from attempting to hold D to the contract at all, not to speak of pursuing his claim to judgment. No doubt where genuine claims are abandoned for these reasons it is arguable that there is an 'inefficient' level of contract-enforcement, and this may be an inducement to D not to perform adequately. If it is (in proportion to the value of the contract) difficult and expensive to monitor D's performance,[12] D has an incentive to 'cheat' in the hope that C will not discover the breach, or, if he does, will not be able to prove it by evidence satisfying the legal rules of admissibility.

But once one fully acknowledges that legal adjudication has a cost, and courtroom adjudication a great cost, then it is obvious that a policy of seeking to resolve by legal proceedings any significant fraction of the estimated total number of complaints made by consumers is logically[13] and practically[14] absurd. In the absence of an assessment of what it might be possible for the courts actually to do, the call also made innumerable times in the post-war period for more and better access to the civil courts which has now led to the Woolf Report[15] rather founders on the question

9   In 1998 only 70 breach of contract actions brought by individuals as complainants (ie possibly consumer actions) were set down for trial in the Queen's Bench (Lord Chancellor's Department, *Judicial Statistics*, above n 6, table 3.4). To understand this, it is perhaps sufficient to mention that the survey of High Court costs conducted by Professor Hazel Genn for the Woolf Inquiry showed that median taxed costs (ie the winning party's costs only) awarded in High Court claims up to £12,500 (including contract) were £8,318, and that in 40% of such claims those costs equalled or exceeded the amount of the claim: Lord Woolf, *Access to Justice (Final Report)* (1996) annex 3, paras 14, 16.

10  J Baldwin, *Small Claims in the County Courts in England and Wales: The Bargain Basement of Civil Justice* (1997).

11  National Consumer Council, *Seeking Civil Justice* (1995) tables 15, 11.

12  Sophisticated analysis of 'the costly state verification' problem underpins the most plausible accounts of the existence of financial intermediaries to monitor investments: K Dowd, *Competition and Finance* (1996).

13  P Lewis, 'Unmet Legal Needs', in P Morris *et al*, *Social Needs and Legal Action* (1973)  73.

14  Lord Devlin, 'Foreword', in Justice, *Going to Court* (1974) p v.

15  Lord Woolf, *Access to Justice (Interim Report)* (1995) ch 3.

of how much more?[16] The answer commonly assumed to be true – a lot more – is wholly unsatisfactory.[17] Nevertheless, it would appear that at least 43% of consumers presently are left dissatisfied by the handling of their complaints,[18] and it seems undeniable that this problem of what used to be called 'unmet legal need'[19] contributes to a serious loss of welfare for consumers stemming from imperfections in consumer markets, a loss the OFT values at £8.3 billion per annum.[20] The remedies put forward to deal with this problem will be reviewed in chapter 4.

This problem shades into another in which relatively less wealthy parties, including smaller businesses as well as individual consumers, may gain access to the civil justice system but are routinely unfairly defeated or stymied not because of the (lack of) intrinsic merit of their complaint but because of the systematically superior legal resources brought to bear on the matter by the other, typically more wealthy, party,[1] a superiority which, in essence, commercial litigators find it advantageous ruthlessly to exploit.[2] D obviously will have a further incentive not to perform adequately if he has access to legal resources which allow him confidently to hope that C will not be sufficiently determined to hold out until he obtains a judgment in his favour. The want of justice and fairness in such proceedings as do take place was another concern leading to the Woolf inquiry.[3] The substantive law of contractual remedies has been developed with very little or no regard to the facts that legal resources are limited and unequally distributed, despite the obvious truth that the formal provision of justice may be undermined or rendered quite useless by that limit and that inequality. The current elaboration of restitutionary remedies[4] which are so doctrinally complex that, for the foreseeable future and perhaps forever, they will be available only to those able to command extremely competent and expensive counsel in High Court or appeal hearings, is a strikingly complacent example of how those committed to

---

16  M Zander, 'Why Lord Woolf's Proposed Reforms of Civil Litigation Should be Rejected', in AAS Zuckerman and R Cranston (eds), *Reform of Civil Procedure* (1995) 79.

17  H Collins, *Regulating Contracts* (1999) p 354: 'The vogue for policy initiatives designed to improve access to justice has been a distraction'.

18  Office of Fair Trading, *Consumer Detriment*, above p 28, n 5, para 7.1.

19  B Abel-Smith et al, *Legal Problems and the Citizen* (1973) p 226.

20  Office of Fair Trading, *Consumer Detriment*, above p 28, n 5, para 6.14. Cf paras 6.18, 6.25.

1   M Galanter, 'Why the "Haves" Come Out Ahead: Speculations on the Limits of Legal Change' (1974) 9 Law and Society Review 95 and S Macaulay, 'Lawyers and Consumer Complaints' (1979) 14 Law and Society Review 153. This problem is superbly illustrated with reference to *Romalpa* clauses in S Wheeler, *Reservation of Title Clauses* (1991).

2   R Williams, *Saving Litigation* (1999).

3   Lord Woolf, *Access to Justice (Final Report)*, above p 29, n 9, section 1, para 2.

4   See Pt 3 below.

formalism ignore this.[5] Though it may now be widely recognised that justice is itself a scarce economic good,[6] and though criticism of inequality of access to justice is as old as the existence of modern legality itself,[7] it remains the case that a book setting out the positive rather than a normative substantive law of remedies regrettably must proceed largely in ignorance of these vital considerations, for those remedies do not take this vital issue to heart.[8]

## The relational contract

A second type of 'non-use' can, however, play a larger role in a book on the substantive law of remedies. This type of non-use is the one which Macaulay himself developed in his paper on 'Non-contractual Relations in Business: A Preliminary Study'[9] and which has been the cornerstone of all subsequent attempts to deal with non-use. For the assumption that the formal law governs contracting must be dropped even when the parties are broadly equal and legally competent businesses dealing with expensive matters. In 1998, only 210 breach of contract actions brought by firms were settled in the course of proceedings in the Queen's Bench (and only 70 were determined after trial).[10] The issue obviously therefore arises as to what does govern business contracting, and the answer often given which follows the thrust of at least the title of Macaulay's paper has been 'non-contractual' relations. In Beale and Dugdale's British replication of Macaulay's work by a study of engineering firms, for example, it was found that:

> There is not much scope for using contractual remedies. Lawyers and legal remedies ... tend to be  avoided as being inflexible; lawyers are thought not to understand the needs of commerce ... A similar reluctance to use the law was also evident on the planning side.[11]

5   D Campbell, 'Classification and the Crisis of the Common Law' (1999) 26 Journal of Law and Society 369, p 375.
6   WM Landes, 'An Economic Analysis of the Courts' (1971) 14 Journal of Law and Economics 61.
7   G Winstanley, *The Law of Freedom in a Platform* (1973) p 138: 'when money must buy and sell justice, and bear all the sway, there is nothing but oppression to be expected'.
8   D Harris and CJ Veljanovski, 'Designing Rules to Facilitate Out of Court Settlements' (1983) 5 Law and Policy Quarterly 97.
9   (1963) 28 American Sociological Review 55. Cf S Macaulay, 'An Empirical View of Contract' [1985] Wisconsin Law Review 465, pp 466-477.
10   Lord Chancellor's Department, *Judicial Statistics*, above p 28, n 6, table 3.5.
11   H Beale and T Dugdale, 'Contracts Between Businessmen: Planning and the Use of Contractual Remedies' (1975) 2 British Journal of Law and Society 45, p 59.

There obviously are aspects of commerce which turn on the use of formal remedies. The uncontested and, indeed, routinised collection of debt, for example, is by far and away the most widely used court action, but it may well be an exception which proves the rule. It appears largely to arise (though the evidence does not allow one to say this with complete confidence) when a contractual relationship (typically between a business and an impecunious consumer) is already threatened with termination. Much more relaxed attitudes towards recovery of debt, including acceptance of part payment in full accord and satisfaction, are common in business relationships. In all, the overwhelming conclusion of empirical studies is that formal remedies are not used in continuing contractual relationships.[12]

In contractual scholarship, the implications of this finding have been most thoroughly explored by Ian Macneil, who has shown that contracts are agreed and formal remedies exercised within webs of social relations. Macneil has done this by distinguishing discrete and relational contracts, the former – exemplified by a spot sale of a generic commodity – being one in which a sharp definition of the obligations and liabilities it imposes is possible; and the latter – exemplified by a complex design and build engineering contract – being one where such a sharp definition is impossible.[13] The traditional law of contract is ill-suited to a relational contract,[14] where not all future contingencies can be anticipated, and even if they can be, the modification of the relationship appropriate to deal with the contingency will not be clear until it occurs. Incomplete information and limits on computational competence create bounded rationality at the time of agreement, and it is both ultimately impossible, and, beyond a certain point, not cost-effective to try to go beyond these bounds in pursuit of a fully contingent, or as Macneil puts it fully 'presentiated',[15] contract. In a relational contract, the parties need to preserve flexibility to enable them to respond to new circumstances in ways which maximise their joint welfare.[16] Such a contract is more like a partnership in which 'sequential decision-making' is needed, rather than

12  D Campbell and S Clay, *Long-term Contracting: A Bibliography and Review of the Literature* (1995) pp 54-55.
13  IR Macneil, 'The Many Futures of Contract' 47 Southern California Law Review 691 and IR Macneil, *The New Social Contract* (1980).
14  IR Macneil, 'Contracts: Adjustment of Long-term Economic Relations Under Classical, Neo-classical and Relational Contract Law' (1978) 72 Northwestern University Law Review 854.
15  IR Macneil, 'Restatement (Second) of Contracts and Presentiation' (1974) 60 Virginia Law Review 589.
16  D Campbell and D Harris, 'Flexibility in Long-term Contractual Relationships: The Role of Co-operation' (1993) 20 Journal of Law and Society 166. Cf D Baird, 'Self-interest and Co-operation in Long-term Contracts' (1990) 19 Journal of Legal Studies 583.

the pursuit of meticulous planning to anticipate all possible contingencies prior to entering into the agreement. The parties therefore deliberately leave open-ended their planning[17] of such 'incomplete contracts'.[18] Williamson identifies the crucial feature of many relational contracts as the 'asset specific' investment made under them, which refers to the existence of specialised resources invested in the relationship.[19] One party may develop specialised equipment or sources of supply to meet the other's special requirements; or he may develop special knowledge and skills which are unique to the particular relationship ('human capital investment' which results from the 'know-how' developed from 'learning-by-doing'). The unique feature is that the investment cannot (readily) be switched to alternative uses, since it has been developed to meet the specific needs of the other party. Similarly, the party with those needs would find it difficult to get them met elsewhere, and would incur considerable 'search' and 'set-up' costs in any attempt to do so, as well as delay while another party invested resources to develop the specialised equipment and skills. The result is that both parties realise that they are 'locked into' the relationship, and would lose heavily if it was terminated. These losses are likely to be 'idiosyncratic' in the sense that they are so complex and uncertain that C is unlikely to be able to prove them in a contested court action.[1] Each party has the strongest incentive to protect his idiosyncratic investment by continuing to co-operate. Each realises that the joint gains from long-term co-operation greatly exceed any short-term gain which might result from his breaking a particular obligation. Problems which arise should be solved in a forward-looking way against the background of the overwhelming desire of both sides to preserve the relationship. Hence, the pressure is to compromise any dispute which might arise by treating it merely as a hiccup in the smooth running of the relationship. Informal procedures are evolved to deal with problems in much the same way as they would be dealt with within an integrated firm.[2]

### The nature of forebearance

The importance of what Macneil identified as relational contracts, and the limits of the ability of formal contract remedies to deal with such

17   Collins, *Regulating Contracts*, above p 30, n 17, ch 7.
18   A Schwartz, 'Relational Contracts in the Courts: An Analysis of Incomplete Agreements and Judicial Strategies' (1992) 21 Journal of Legal Studies 271.
19   OE Williamson, 'Transaction Cost Economics: The Governance of Contractual Relations' (1979) 22 Journal of Law and Economics 233, pp 238-245.
1    D Cloughton, *Riley on Business Interruption Insurance* (8th edn 1999) ch 1 and PA Gaughan, *Measuring Commercial Damages* (2000).
2    H Beale, *Remedies for Breach of Contract* (1980) ch 10.

contracts, to which Macneil has drawn our attention has perhaps been the most interesting finding made by advanced contract scholarship for 40 years.[3] But the relational concept, especially when considered as an explanation of the non-use of formal remedies, has displayed a shortcoming which is particularly evident when one wishes to draw on it in a book on remedies. The implication of the contrast between discrete and relational contracts is that in the latter the formal remedies effectively are ousted, thereby creating the region of non-use. When, for example, Macaulay sought to give formal remedies any place in this region, his principal example was their use only as a fallback when relations collapse in unusual circumstances such as 'major shocks to the world economic system'.[4] This sort of exceptional use is not, however, an entirely accurate account of the role of remedies, for whether relational contracts really represent 'non-contractual' relations is, it is submitted, highly questionable.[5] Even in functioning relational contracts, the formal remedies remain as possible threats, and the parties' relations are conducted with these threats in the background, but a background that influences events in the foreground. The formal remedies may never be invoked, but they have a most important influence on the actions of the parties, for their existence, and the possibility that they may be invoked, radiates an influence[6] on the nature of any settlement and on any continuing relations.[7]

A striking example of the former was provided by the deregulation of the US gas industry under the Natural Gas Policy Act 1978, following which many natural gas companies tied into very long-term 'take-or-pay' gas supply contracts faced insolvency, for the creation of an unregulated spot market in gas in conditions of over-supply made these long-term commitments extremely onerous to buyers (pipelines).[8] Many of the companies sought to have their liabilities discharged under Uniform Commercial Code 2-615, which excuses non-performance on the ground of commercial impracticability.[9] (As of 1992) all such pleas had been

3   MA Eisenberg, 'Relational Contracts', in J Beatson and D Friedmann (eds), *Good Faith and Fault in Contract Law* (1995) 291, p 303.
4   Macaulay, 'An Empirical View of Contract', above p 31, n 9, p 472.
5   EM Schur, *Law and Society: A Sociological View* (1967) p 131. This is quoted in Beale and Dugdale, 'Contracts Between Businessmen: Planning and the Use of Contractual Remedies', above p 31, n 11, n 4, and that paper strives to emphasise the ways in which it does not amount to evidence of 'non-contractual' relations.
6   M Galanter, 'The Radiating Effects of Courts', in K Boylum and L Mather (eds), *Empirical Theories About Courts* (1983) 117, pp 121-124.
7   C Menkel-Meadow, 'Toward Another View of Legal Negotiation: The Structure of Problem Solving' (1984) 31 UCLA Law Review 754, pp 764-794.
8   JB McArthur, 'The Take-or-Pay Crisis' (1992) 22 New Mexico Law Review 353, pp 355-356.
9   FD Tannenbaum, 'Commercial Impracticability Under the Uniform Commercial Code: Natural Gas Distributors' Vehicle for Excusing Long-term Requirements

rejected, but typically formal remedies were not directly applied, and (on 1989 figures) US$44 billion of liability on those contracts was settled at an average of 18.67c on the dollar.[10] These settlements were, however, reached through an enormous and enormously expensive wave of (threatened) litigation[11] conducted in a climate the nature of which is sufficiently indicated by this episode being generally known as 'the take-or-pay wars'.[12]

In this situation, in which the formal law treats (inevitable) disputes as pathological cases and pushes parties to treat them in this way as well, one suspects that the way remedies presently function even within continuing relations may be markedly sub-optimal, contributing to a 'poor quality' of contracting in the sense that, whilst goods and services may ultimately be produced under a contract, the contract process itself imposes significant avoidable costs on their production.[13] In an empirical project in which one of the authors is presently involved,[14] it would appear to have been found that serious problems with the design and build of aerospace products are *caused* by the contracts under which the work is agreed. These products are at the leading edge of technology and their specification (and hence prices and delivery dates) cannot be precisely agreed before the project is underway but must be modified as the project progresses. The projects are, however, commissioned under contracts which essentially seek to fix those prices and dates. The results have been that when disputes inevitably arise, the contracts are either ignored (and the dispute resolved in other ways) or, even worse, are invoked as threats,

---

Contracts?' (1983) 20 Houston Law Journal 771. Perhaps the best known case of a failed impracticability defence, which Macaulay uses as his principal illustration of a major shock, arose out of Westinghouse's difficulties over uranium supply contracts in the seventies: Macaulay, 'An Empirical View of Contract', above p 31, n 9, p 472. Cf S Macaulay, 'Elegant Models, Empirical Pictures and the Law of Contract' (1977) 11 Law and Society Review 507, p 515. See further Campbell and Harris, 'Flexibility in Long-term Contractual Relationships: The Role of Co-operation', above p 32, n 17, pp 171-172.

10  *Regulation of Natural Gas Pipelines After Partial Wellhead Decontrol* 54 Fed Reg 52,344, 52,356 Table 5.

11  WJ Legg, 'Natural Gas Contract Litigation in Oklahoma' (1986) 11 Oklahoma City University Law Review 63, p 65.

12  JM Medina, 'The Take-or-Pay Wars: A Cautionary Analysis for the Future' (1991) 27 Tulsa Law Journal 283.

13  P Vincent-Jones, 'Responsive Law and Governance in Public Services Provision: A Future for the Local Contracting State' (1998) 61 Modern Law Review 362. In a number of papers, Vincent-Jones and A Harries, though broadly supportive of the reform of incentives in public sector contracting, have shown how the naive importation of what are mistakenly thought to be models of private sector contracting into the public sector provision of services can have very seriously deleterious effects on that provision.

14  T Broughton et al, *Effective Contractual and Other Legal Obligations in the Aerospace Industry*, EPSRC grant GR/M60484.

and that it is barely conceivable that the threat will be carried out in most cases does not prevent their being made, leading to the degradation of the working relationships between the parties. This is an industry which remains absolutely characterised by enormous delays and cost-overruns.[15] The undesirability of obtaining, at very great expense, a contract which, apart from signalling that work of some sort will be done, is useless or pernicious is not lost on those in the aerospace industry, but their response to this mirrors the current shortcomings of our understanding of contract. The Society of British Aerospace Companies, the trade body, has set up a process re-engineering programme, 'Supply Chain Re-engineering in Aerospace', which has produced a Code of Practice[16] which effectively completely contradicts the competitively negotiated contracts on which they continue to do business, thereby reproducing the problem by requiring that contracts, once signed, are utterly ignored.

This sort of distanced influence of formal rules which will apply only, as it were, informally has been analysed as 'bargaining in the shadow of the law', though the analysis has been far more thoroughly applied in areas other than contract.[17] Understanding the nature of this distanced influence of remedies on the contractual relationship is the most important issue for the law of remedies, but this issue is barely recognised in formal scholarship and poorly understood even in scholarship more sensitive to the contextual role of remedies.[18] From the point of view of a book on contractual remedies, the point is not that the relational aspects of contract exclude formal remedies, but that the exercise of remedies is embedded within social relations which influence that exercise.[19] Recently, Hugh Collins has very helpfully described 'three frameworks of contractual behaviour': the 'business relation', the 'economic deal' and 'contract', of which only the last is directly 'constituted by the standards provided by the self-regulation contained in the contract'.[20] Contracts are 'embedded'

15   Public Accounts Committee, 33rd Report, HC 247 (2000).
16   Available from Supply Chain Re-engineering in Aerospace, Duxbury House, 60 Petty France, Victoria, London, SW1H 9EU.
17   R Mnookin and L Kornhauser, 'Bargaining in the Shadow of the Law: The Case of Divorce' (1979) 88 Yale Law Journal 950. The best application to contract is Wheeler, *Reservation of Title Clauses*, above p 30, n 1.
18   Vincent-Jones, 'Responsive Law and Governance in Public Services Provision', above p 35, n 13, n 95: 'Despite the volume of "relational" doctrinal and empirical research on contract, the role of legal norms in orienting practical transacting behaviour and the very meanings of "contract" remain opaque'.
19   This point also applies to what appear to be discrete contracts. It is to be regretted that Macneil's work has been interpreted as implying a radical break between discrete and relational contracts, an interpretation Macneil himself strenuously rejects: D Campbell, 'The Relational Constitution of the Discrete Contract,' in D Campbell and P Vincent-Jones (eds), *Contract and Economic Organisation: Socio-legal Initiatives* (1996) 40.
20   Collins, *Regulating Contracts*, above p 30, n 17, pp 128-136.

in the 'social practices and norms from which they arise'. The general 'social and business relation between the parties both precedes the transaction and is expected to persist after performance', and the specific 'deal or agreement' is the actual object of the economic action. When the 'contract' works well, it should 'assist in the construction of the deal' by giving 'help to plan a transaction and in dispute settlement'. However, these three frameworks generate three sets of, in an important sense, 'competing norms of contractual behaviour', and contract law often handles this very badly. The relation and deal frameworks can generate norms of permanence and flexibility in the parties' economic relationship of a different character from the 'precision planning' of the contract. The formal law tends to undercut this because of its 'taste for litigation', which places far too great an emphasis on the generation of rights at the time of agreement and the prosecution of disputes based on vindication of those rights.[1]

To improve the contribution of the law to business,[2] it would appear to be necessary in future, from the point of view of the substantive law, to design remedies which facilitate more and hinder less the making of the necessary (and therefore legitimate) modifications of obligations in relational contracts. But the formal law of contract, and specifically the doctrine of the insufficiency of consideration arising from existing obligations, has until recently obstructed outright the recognition of essential and reasonable modifications, though they are perfectly common practice.[3] Even though this ridiculous position has been to some degree corrected after *Williams v Roffey Bros and Nicholls (Contractors) Ltd*,[4] as we still but poorly understand the way remedies presently work, this redesign of remedies cannot properly be undertaken.[5] The result of this arguably drastic weakness in the present understanding of the law for a book on contractual remedies written now, is that what it can say about what seems to be the most important aspect of those remedies, the role they play in modifying obligations after (threat of) non-performance, is extremely limited. However, what can be said is as follows.

The vast majority of disputes are settled by direct negotiations between the parties in which compromises are reached in the light of all the factors which they consider relevant. The efficiency and therefore legitimacy of

---

1    Ibid, pp 323-337.
2    RJ Gilson, 'Value Creation By Business Lawyers: Legal Skills and Asset Pricing' (1984) 94 Yale Law Journal 239. See further 'Symposium on Business Lawyering and Value Creation for Clients' (1995) 74 Oregon Law Review 1.
3    RD Halson, 'Opportunism, Economic Duress and Contractual Modifications' (1991) 107 Law Quarterly Review 649.
4    [1991] 1 QB 1.
5    S Macaulay, 'Elegant Models, Empirical Pictures and the Complexities of Contract' (1977) 11 Law and Society Review 507 and Macaulay, 'An Empirical View of Contract', above p 31, n 9.

breach, the value of a continuing relationship or of possible future business, or, more widely, of a commercial reputation, as opposed to the one-shot value of pursuing litigation most ruthlessly, must all be weighed.[6] When C takes a course of action after breach other than seeking a formal remedy, then, if the contract is not ignored, one imagines that this tends to take the form not of self-conscious co-operation but of forebearance from seeking such a remedy. Though the overwhelming weight of evidence is that disputes will be settled out of court by compromise, the present understanding of remedies encourages a 'vindication of rights' mentality.[7] The most aggravated form this takes, now deplored and intended to be corrected by Lord Woolf's reforms, is the tendency of commercial litigation to:

> degenerate into an environment in which the ... process is too often seen as a battlefield where no rules apply. In this environment, questions of expense, delay, compromise and fairness may have only a low priority. The consequence is that expense is often excessive, disproportionate and unpredictable; and delay is frequently unreasonable.[8]

Businesses can, and perforce do, avoid this by eschewing litigation conducted in this way, but it casts its pall over post-breach negotiations in which reference to the contract takes the form of exchanges of surrenders of adversarially asserted claims. The only general present corrective to this seems to be the advice one imagines is given very commonly indeed, that the law in practice falls short of the law in books (in which the client would get his full deserts), which is a very unsatisfactory position indeed.[9] Self-consciousness of the co-operative element of contract set out in the previous chapter is a necessary condition for improving the basic quality of advice in this regard.

## Alternative dispute resolution (ADR)

The principal way in which the vindication mentality in pursuit of remedy seems to be being dealt with as a practical matter is in the use of forms of

---

6    J Shanteau and P Harrison, 'The Perceived Strength of an Implied Contract: Can It Resist Financial Temptation?' (1991) 49 Organisational Behaviour and Human Decision Processes 1.
7    Collins, *Regulating Contracts*, above p 30, n 17, pp 350-355.
8    Lord Woolf, *Access to Justice (Interim Report)*, above p 29, n 15, p 7.
9    I Kant, 'On the Common Saying: That May Be Correct in Theory But It Is Of No Use In Practice', in I Kant, *Practical Philosophy* (1996) 273.

ADR as an alternative to litigation. Following the Woolf Report,[10] the Lord Chancellor's Department actively is promoting the use of ADR.[11] The parties may agree that a form of ADR be followed either preliminary to or as a complete[12] alternative to litigation, either in the contract or after the (threatened) failure to perform takes place.[13] An account of the nature, forms and law of alternative dispute resolution must be sought elsewhere.[14] Here, two points should be made. First, although there is clear evidence that the costs of certain forms of arbitration can rival those of litigation, it remains the case that ADR *can* be markedly cheaper and quicker than litigation and thus potentially may function as an aid to resolving disputes which can *preserve* the parties' relationship rather than, with the huge expense and delay of litigation, which encourages (and then cements) its breakdown. Second, though the private nature of the proceedings makes it difficult to determine what is done in ADR, the nature of ADR adjudication would appear to assist settlement.[15] It is the purpose of assisted negotiation, conciliation and mediation directly to seek compromise,[16] but properly conducted arbitration can also do so.[17] It can be specified that the arbitrator act as '*amiable compositeur*' and give his

10  Lord Woolf, *Access to Justice (Final Report)*, above p 29, n 9, section 1, para 9.
11  Lord Chancellor's Department, *Alternative Dispute Resolution: A Discussion Paper* (2000).
12  England and Wales remain unusual in that there is arguably some possibility of appeal on a point of law from an arbitration, which is not the case under the UN Committee on International Trade Law Model Law on International Arbitration, which is the basis of most other domestic laws of arbitration, including that of Scotland. That this possibility was restricted but not completely excluded in the consolidating Arbitration Act 1996 is widely thought to be a mistake (and may, in the form in which it arises in the Act, be incompatible with EU law) which, if a prediction may be hazarded, eventually will be rectified.
13  IR Macneil, 'A Primer of Contract Planning' (1975) 48 Southern California Law Review 627.
14  D St John Sutton et al, *Russell on Arbitration* (21st edn 1997) and A Redfern and M Hunter, *Law and Practice of International Commercial Arbitration* (3rd edn 1999).
15  Galanter has, however, described a process of the invasion of adversarial litigation based attitudes into ADR, which takes on a form which he therefore calls 'litigotiation': M Galanter, 'Worlds of Deals' (1984) 34 Journal of Legal Education 268.
16  LL Fuller, 'Mediation: Its Forms and Functions' (1971) 44 Southern California Law Review 305.
17  To the extent that commercial arbitration (as opposed to mediation) has begun to involve the huge costs of commercial litigation (J Flood and A Caiger, 'Lawyers and Arbitration: The Juridification of Construction Disputes' (1993) 56 Modern Law Review 412), this obviously is not true: RL Bonn, 'The Predictability of Non-legalistic Adjudication' (1972) 6 Law and Society Review 563, p 573. It is symptomatic and regrettable that a usage distinguishing ADR from litigation *and arbitration* seems to be gaining wide currency: A Glaister, 'A Fair Wind Blows for Adjudication – Where to Arbitration? (2001) 67 Arbitration 263.

award *ex aequi et bono*, that is to say, with latitude to depart from the (technical) legal rules. More than this, however, even when the formal legal rules are not expressly excluded, it would appear that arbitrators tend to apportion losses in a way which is extremely difficult in English litigation.[18] This feature of arbitration adjudication may be encouraged by the use of a non-legal expert versed in the informal custom and usage of trade as arbitrator.

## Some observations on settlement

When we compare the use of legal rules in and outside the court-room, several important differences emerge[19] which should be borne in mind in attempts to reform the law of remedies.[20] The first is the impartial application of the rules by an independent third party in court, whereas in direct negotiations between the parties themselves there is no third person to protect the weaker party.[1] In court the judge treats the parties as equals, and ignores any extra-legal circumstances which might make them unequal, such as their relative wealth, their reputations, business or political support. The judge is avowedly independent in order to neutralise the inequalities of the market-place outside. But in two-party negotiations aimed at an out-of-court settlement, the relative bargaining strengths of the parties may be crucial. Although the weaker party knows that he can escape from his weaker position by going to court to gain an impartial decision, empirical studies all report the many pressures on him to negotiate a settlement. In practice, both the parties to a dispute and their lawyers act on the assumption that it is very likely to be settled out of court. The law-maker should therefore aim primarily at the potential use of his rules in the two-party 'direct negotiations' situation, rather than at their use by an arbitrator or judge. In particular, he should consider the effect of a proposed rule on the relative negotiating strength of the parties:

18   A most commendably self-critical and worthwhile exercise recently carried out by the Chartered Institute of Arbitrators allows one to base this observation on something more than professional gossip. The Institute asked five distinguished arbitrators to give an award in a hypothetical case and published those awards. Though the awards were (a little embarrassingly) rather different, all were characterised by loss-splitting: '*Meadowsweet v Bindweed*' (2000) 66 Arbitration 83.

19   O Fiss, 'Against Settlement' (1984) 93 Yale Law Journal 1073.

20   Harris and Veljanovski, 'Designing Rules to Facilitate Out of Court Settlements', above p 31, n 8.

1    This may be a serious problem with the imposition of arbitration schemes which act to the disadvantage of a weaker party in a way analogous to the way exclusion clauses were inserted into standard form consumer contracts prior to 1977: DS Schwartz, 'Enforcing Small Claims to Protect Big Business' [1997] Wisconsin Law Review 33. See Arbitration Act 1996, ss 89-91.

how will the rule affect the distribution of the 'bargaining chips' between the parties?

The second difference arises from the first: it is the importance of extra-legal factors in negotiations. Unlike the judge, the parties are not restricted to purely 'legal' considerations, and may use against each other many points which would be irrelevant in court, such as the desire to maintain a long-standing relationship, to preserve a reputation, or to avoid an immediate financial crisis. The procedure leading up to a full hearing involves delay, which the contract-breaker can often exploit to his advantage. If the claimant is under some financial pressure, he may accept a smaller sum now rather than face further pressure and uncertainty in the hope that the court will award a larger sum at some uncertain future date. Fear of legal expenses and the risk-averse attitude of many ordinary people also act as powerful incentives to compromise. Similarly, pressure to settle comes from the strain of being involved in a dispute or the fear of giving evidence in a public hearing. Although the court hearing should protect parties from extra-legal pressures, the costs of prolonging the dispute often outweigh this advantage. So, in the real world, the impact of the formal legal rules may be undermined by the impact of extra-legal factors; the law may merely cast a distant shadow across the parties' negotiating positions. Hence, even where lawyers are involved in negotiating the settlement, the legal rules are often applied by them without any precision, because if other factors are likely to prevail, it is a waste of time and expense to investigate the precise legal position.

A third difference between litigation and an out-of-court settlement is that in a settlement the parties can reach a compromise which would not be possible in court. On most issues, a judge must, according to the relevant legal rules, find in favour of one party, who thus wins that issue completely (in economic language, it is a zero-sum game). Judges can seldom resolve doubts in their minds by saying that they find, say, 60% in favour of the claimant, and therefore award only 60% of the damages that they would have awarded had they found with 100% certainty in his favour. Negotiations out of court, however, enable the parties themselves to compromise claims. Uncertainties and weaknesses in a case can be discounted, so that the degree of uncertainty is reflected in a lower sum of damages. Any doubt can be translated into a discount, instead of it risking the failure of the whole claim. In court, the judge must either ignore a doubt or give it decisive weight, but outside the court the doubt becomes merely a negotiating weapon. Legal rules and procedures should therefore be designed with this result in mind. And since most disputes are compromised, it should be recognised that many claimants will accept something less than their full claim.

Throughout this book reference will be made to the way in which the parties can use the rules on remedies to influence a negotiated settlement of their dispute. A general point should, however, be made here. It can be argued that the commercial legal system will always have to make both ADR and litigation available to parties because that system will always throw up different types of disputes requiring different resolution mechanisms. But whilst litigation continues to be characterised by excess of formalism and the vindication mentality (and to some extent resultant procedural shortcomings), the boundary between ADR and litigation will not be rationally determined. The shortcomings of litigation will mean that, of those disputes which it is right to think require relatively formal resolution, too many will be resolved through use of ADR. A particular loss occurs because ADR cannot, of its nature, throw up precedents, and the benefit of litigation to those external to it, of having a precedent set which may be of use in guiding their conduct, is reduced.[2]

2    JL Coleman and C Silver, 'Justice in Settlements', in JL Coleman, *Markets, Morals and the Law* (1988) 202, pp 211-215.

# 3 Self-help

## Introduction

Remedies which lie entirely within the control of C are those to which he
will first resort. They are viewed as 'self-help' because C needs no
assistance from the court or from any third party to effect them. Such a
remedy is typically speedy and inexpensive, and often it is, from C's point
of view, very effective, either in producing the desired performance from
D, or in putting C into a better position than he would be in as the result
of obtaining a judicial remedy. If D objects to the exercise of a self-help
remedy, the burden of initiating any litigation to challenge it is placed
on him.

From an economic perspective, the main advantages of self-help
remedies are the reduction in transaction costs in comparison with judicial
remedies, and the incentive imposed on D to perform. Though there may
be some increase in the transaction costs of negotiating the clause of the
contract which creates the self-help remedy, transaction costs after breach
typically are reduced because there is usually no uncertainty about C's
entitlement to the remedy and he can exercise it without needing anyone
else's consent. There is no need to persuade a court to recognise his right,
as with the quantification of damages,[1] or to exercise its discretion in his
favour, as with specific performance.[2] There is also no need for delay,
and no need for C to give D any opportunity to remedy the breach within
a given time, even where D's breach was inadvertent. No negotiations
between the parties are needed, unless the facts are disputed, or D wishes
to offer C an inducement not to exercise the remedy. C need not incur the

---

1    See chs 5-6 below.
2    See ch 12 below.

cost of proving his loss, unless he wishes to claim damages in addition to exercising his self-help remedy. Nor is C faced with the question whether he acted reasonably to mitigate his loss. C can also avoid the risk of D's insolvency (unlike a claim for damages, where C has to give 'credit' to D until the latter actually pays the damages). The cost of subsequent litigation will seldom be incurred, because D will risk the cost of challenging C's entitlement to the remedy only if he has a strong case against C.

Even where C is entitled to the remedy, however, post-breach negotiations may occur if one or both parties would prefer an outcome other than C's exercising the particular remedy (and the costs of negotiation are not too high). If D wishes to negotiate a compromise, C's entitlement to the remedy puts him into a powerful bargaining position, in the same way as an order for specific relief would do.[3] For instance, if C is entitled to reject goods tendered by D under a contract of sale, he may be able to extract from D a greater reduction in price for accepting them than the amount at which his damages for loss would be assessed under the ordinary rules of damages.

The risk that D's breach or failure to perform could entitle C to exercise a self-help remedy will often give D a powerful incentive to perform. It is an incentive which is not subject to judicial controls, such as the law as to penalties (restricting D's liability to pay a pre-estimated amount as damages for breach),[4] or the rules on mitigation (requiring C to act reasonably after the breach if he wishes to claim damages, eg to seek a substitute performance at the lowest cost).[5] A self-help remedy created by the parties often provides a more powerful incentive to perform than any of the remedies provided by the law, which raises social and political issues about the parties' freedom to create these incentives.[6]

## Complaints and threats to reputation

Upon learning of D's breach, C's first action will usually be to complain directly to D and ask for the breach to be remedied, or some redress given. Should this fail, complaints to third parties may also be made, such as to a business association of which D is a member; to the Trading Standards Department of the local authority; to the local newspaper; or to television or radio programmes on consumer affairs.[7] The well-managed company should welcome complaints as a source of essential information about its

3    See chs 15, 17 below.
4    See ch 9 below.
5    See ch 7 below.
6    See ch 9 below.
7    A Best, *When Consumers Complain* (1981).

performance.[8] Publicity for C's justifiable complaint is a weapon the use of which D will often fear,[9] since his future business or social relations may depend on preserving his reputation for reliability.[10] If D is in or wishes to develop a long-term relationship with C, he will usually value the continuance of that relationship much more highly than any short-term advantage he might derive from breaking one of his contractual obligations to C.[11]

## Withholding performance

In many contracts, C's duty to perform an obligation is made dependent on D's having completed performance of one of his obligations (or on D's ability to perform contemporaneously with C). For example, under 'staged payment' clauses in standard construction contracts, the client comes under an obligation to pay an instalment of the price only when the contractor has completed a specified stage of the building and this has been certified by a third party (usually an architect).[12] Until the contractor's completion of that stage is certified, the client's obligation to pay that instalment does not arise. He can withhold payment, which will act as a strong incentive to the contractor to complete that stage, and so amounts to a temporary 'remedy' for the contractor's breach (if that stage was to be completed by a certain date). Performance by the builder is not coerced by a court order, but by a type of extra-judicial, self-help remedy. The contractor knows that until he actually completes that stage he will receive no payment for any work done since the previous stage was completed. But by withholding performance, C is not terminating the contract. He merely is suspending his own performance.[13]

8   C Adamson, 'Complaint Handling: Its Rationale and Function in Well-managed Companies', in R John (ed), *The Consumer Revolution* (1994) ch 11.
9   Adverse publicity has been given a theoretically sophisticated statement as the base of a 'pyramid' of strategies for enforcing good corporate conduct in B Fisse and J Braithwaite, *Corporations, Crime and Accountability* (1993) ch 5. See further B Fisse and J Braithwaite, *The Impact of Publicity on Corporate Offenders* (1983).
10  DB Klein, 'Trust for Hire: Voluntary Remedies for Quality and Safety', in DB Klein, ed, *Reputation* (1997) 97.
11  See the discussion of the relational contract at pp 31-38 above. A refusal to enter into future contracts may sometimes act as a powerful sanction; hence, a series of short-term contracts, renewable at regular intervals, could give the parties a form of self-help remedy: VP Crawford, 'Long-term Relationships Governed by Short-term Contracts' (1988) 78 American Economic Review 485.
12  Joint Contracts Tribunal, *Standard Form of Building Contract* (1998) (JCT98) sections 30.1-30.2.
13  Another illustration from the sale of goods is the unpaid seller's lien or right of stoppage in transit. See pp 49-50 below. The suppliers of essential services or utilities have had a power to cut off supply if bills are unpaid. However, the possible denial of essential services to chronically impecunious consumers raises

C's right to withhold his performance in this way is sometimes called the 'entire contracts' rule; but it should rather be called the 'entire obligation' rule,[14] since the parties intend that C should be obliged to pay (or perform an obligation on his side) only after D has completely performed one or more of his obligations. Subject to recent amendment of the law of rejection of sales of goods,[15] C may refuse to pay or perform even where he suffers no (or only trivial) loss from the fact that D's performance is incomplete. D has no claim for the benefit which C has already received from D's incomplete performance, even where D's failure is not a breach, eg because of his illness or death.[16] In *Sumpter v Hedges*,[17] D agreed to build two houses for C for a lump sum. Before he completed the work, D ran out of money and could not complete it. C took advantage of D's work by completing it himself, but the court held that D could recover neither the lump sum nor a reasonable remuneration for the partial benefit which C had received from D's work. C had no choice but to use what had been attached to his land; but he was required to pay a reasonable sum for D's loose materials left on the land which he had also used.

The draconian effect of the entire obligation rule is avoided where the courts can interpret the contract as containing a 'severable' obligation or obligations, for D may 'substantially perform' part of such an obligation and recover part of the price for the completed parts of his performance.[18]

---

issues of public concern which have been thought to require the close regulation of this power. National Consumer Council, *In the Absence of Competition* (1989) appendix 1. There has been particular concern over the disconnection of water supplies. A Herbet and E Kempson, *Water Debt and Disconnection* (1995). This recently has led to the withdrawal of the power to disconnect to households, hospitals, etc: Water Industry Act 1999, s 1 (amending the Water Industry Act 1991, s 62).

14  GH Treitel, *The Law of Contract* (10th edn 1999) p 728.

15  Sale of Goods Act 1979, s 15A (inserted by the Sale and Supply of Goods Act 1994, s 4). See further PS Atiyah et al *The Sale of Goods* (10th edn, 2001), pp 501-502.

16  *Cutter v Powell* (1795) 6 Term Rep 320. The (especially to contemporary opinion) vexed aspects of this case now cloud its authority for what is, in itself, a perfectly sensible rule: SJ Stoljar, 'The Great Case of *Cutter v Powell*' (1956) 34 Canadian Bar Review 288. It is arguable that the Apportionment Act 1870, ss 2, 5 and the Law Reform (Frustrated Contracts) Act 1945, s 1(3) might now mitigate the operation of the entire obligations rule on the facts of this case.

17  [1898] 1 QB 673. See also *Bolton v Mahadeva* [1972] 2 All ER 1322.

18  The claim that there can be substantial performance of an entire obligation is quite contradictory: A Beck, 'The Doctrine of Substantial Performance: Conditions and Conditions Precedent' (1975) 38 Modern Law Review 413. It has been dismissed as mere 'semantics' in the leading work on construction law (where it has its principal application): IN Duncan Wallace, *Hudson's Building and Engineering Contracts* (11th edn 1995) para 4.022. We follow Treitel, *The Law of Contract*, above p 46, n 14, pp 730-1 in merging the concepts of the severable obligation and of substantial performance, so that there can be substantial performance only of an obligation interpreted as severable.

Unlike in the case of an entire obligation, C cannot refuse to pay at all on the ground of some relatively minor omission or defect in D's performance. C must pay the price subject to a cross-claim or set-off[19] for damages in respect of the partial breach.[20] Of course, a very serious breach of even a severable obligation creates a right to terminate, and the distinction between levels of seriousness of breach of a severable obligation is considered below.[1] In terms of the threat of withholding performance, the point is that this threat is credible for *every* breach of an entire obligation.

Since the 'entire obligation' rule puts C into a powerful position where he may be enriched without paying for it, the courts are understandably reluctant to interpret the contract so as to produce an entire obligation, unless the wording chosen by the parties compels it.[2] The drafting of the contract is the crucial factor in putting C into this powerful position. If C or his legal adviser can negotiate D's consent to a clause which makes performance of C's obligation dependent on prior or contemporaneous[3] performance by D, C has a built-in security that he need not perform until D has completely performed. Under this arrangement, until his own performance of the particular obligation is completed, D is giving credit to C in respect of any benefit received by C from D's work towards that performance. Unless D obtains some 'security' from C, he is putting his trust entirely on C's contractual promise, and should realise that if he completes his side but C then fails to perform, it is he who must bring legal proceedings against C. So by this arrangement C can also put himself into the favourable position of being the defendant if any dispute arises over whether D has completed his performance.

The 'entire obligation' rule may appear unduly to favour the party who is placed in a powerful negotiating position because he has not yet paid the other, and the Law Commission has recommended that a *quantum meruit*[4] claim should normally, unless the contract stipulates otherwise, be available for part-performance of what would have been regarded as an entire obligation.[5] One can understand the abstract restitutionary logic behind this suggestion, for were it the case that the burdens and benefits arising under a contract would usually be adjudicated to this level of

---

19  See p 61 below.
20  *Hoenig v Isaacs* [1952] 2 All ER 176.
1   See pp 51-56 below.
2   SM Waddams, 'Restitution for the Part Performer', in BJ Reiter and J Swan (eds), *Studies in Contract Law* (1980) Study 6.
3   For an illustration see Sale of Goods Act 1979, s 28, under which delivery of the goods and payment of the price are concurrent obligations (unless the contract stipulates otherwise).
4   See pp 235-241 below.
5   Law Commission, *Law of Contract: Pecuniary Restitution on Breach of Contract*, Report No 121 (1983) Pt 2.

exactness, this would realise a perfect justice.[6] But, with respect, fear that this is not what will happen is just what lies behind the legitimate use of entire obligations. Recognising an obligation to be entire can provide a strong incentive to secure D's complete performance under circumstances where C both fears incomplete performance and would find the threat of legal proceedings to enforce that performance ineffective. In a note of dissent to the Law Commission's recommendation, Brian Davenport QC held that the assumption that the builder's obligation was entire has a useful application in small, informal contracts such as that between a householder and a jobbing builder. The rule, he said, was 'the only effective sanction [which the householder] has against the builder not completing the job'. Under the rule, the householder is legally entitled to say: '[u]nless you come back and finish the job, I shan't pay you a penny.'[7] Thus, the rule has an important influence on ordinary practice since it puts the householder who often cannot credibly threaten proceedings into a strong position to induce a small builder to complete.

## Liens

An important type of withholding performance arises from certain transactions under which C holds chattels belonging to D. A 'lien' is the right of C to retain D's chattel in his possession until D performs a particular obligation owed to C. It is not a right to sell the chattel (which may, however, be conferred separately on C)[8] but merely a right to retain it pending D's performance. A general lien (arising from trade usage or by contract) covers all of D's goods or documents under C's control. It may be exercised inter alia by bankers, solicitors, factors, stockbrokers and insurance brokers.[9] An innkeeper has a general lien (for the unpaid amount of his bill) over all the chattels which his guest takes into the inn.[10] A special or particular lien relates to particular chattels.[11] So if C has repaired or improved D's chattel at D's request, he may retain it until he is paid for his work.[12] At common law, a 'common carrier' has only a particular lien upon the goods carried for payment of his freight. Under the standard form

---

6    A Burrows, *The Law of Restitution* (1993) pp 276-281.
7    Law Commission, *Law of Contract: Pecuniary Restitution on Breach of Contract*, above p 47, n 5, pp 36-37.
8    The Torts (Interference with Goods) Act 1977, ss 12-13 confers a general power of sale on bailees who are in possession of uncollected goods, widening the narrower power under the Disposal of Uncollected Goods Act 1952.
9    *Halsbury's Laws of England* (4th edn 1979) vol 28, paras 525-533; cf para 516.
10    *Chitty on Contracts* (28th edn 1999), paras 33-109-33-113.
11    *Halsbury's Laws of England*, vol 28, paras 534-41.
12    *Chitty on Contracts*, 28th edn, para 33-087.

contracts for the carriage of goods, however, the carrier has a general lien against the owner of the goods.[13]

## Security

Where D gives C additional security for performance of an obligation, C's rights usually go beyond merely withholding performance on his side. (Such security is additional to the necessary transfer of possession that makes a particular lien possible, and may be considered an extension of the technique of the lien when coupled to a power of sale.) A pledge or pawn arises where D delivers chattels to C to hold as security for payment of a debt. As pledgee, C has a special property in the chattels which entitles him to sell them upon D's default.[14] A mortgage to C of D's land is a similar security for repayment of a loan made by C.[15] As mortgagee, C is entitled to various remedies which can be exercised by him without the authority of a court order, such as a power of sale, or a power to appoint a receiver to receive rent accruing from the land.

## Self-help in the sale of goods

The Sale of Goods Act 1979, ss 38-48 gives the unpaid seller of goods some 'real' remedies in respect of the goods themselves, analogous to a form of security over the goods until the price is paid. They often give the seller more protection than a claim for the price, and can put him into a position where he gains preference over the unsecured creditors of the buyer if the latter becomes bankrupt. Until the goods reach the actual possession of the buyer or his agent (and despite the fact that the ownership ('property') of the goods may have passed to the buyer), the unpaid seller may prevent the buyer from obtaining possession. If the seller himself still controls the goods, he may exercise a lien over them, which means that he is entitled to retain possession of them until the price is paid. The lien arises if the buyer becomes insolvent; if the price is to be paid before or on delivery; or where a period of credit has expired without the price being paid. If the buyer becomes insolvent while the goods are still in the control of a carrier, the right of stoppage in transit arises. The seller may,

13  Ibid, para 36-058. For the carrier's right to sell see ibid, para 36-059.
14  Ibid, paras 33-115-33-130. The Consumer Credit Act 1974, ss 114-122 controls many aspects of pledges arising from regulated consumer credit agreements: *Chitty on Contracts*, paras 33-131-33-138.
15  R Megarry and HWR Wade, *Law of Real Property* (6th edn 2000) ch 19. Equitable charges over D's property are another, less formal, type of security: ibid, para 19-040.

by giving notice to the carrier, prevent delivery to the buyer and direct the carrier to redeliver the goods to himself or his agent. The seller regains possession of the goods and is entitled to retain them until the price is paid; he can, in effect, resume his lien. The exercise of this lien is an instance of C withholding performance of his obligation until D has performed an obligation on his part.

The seller's retaining possession will not automatically produce payment of the price, but he is put into a position where he can resell the goods and deliver them to a second buyer. The unpaid seller in possession may pass a valid title to the second buyer because the resale divests the defaulting buyer of any title he had. The unpaid seller's right to resell may arise under an express term in the contract; or following his justifiable termination of the contract; or (under a statutory power) when the goods are perishable or when the buyer fails to pay the price within a reasonable time after he receives notice of the seller's intention to resell.

Sellers nowadays often insert a '*Romalpa*' clause into contracts for the sale of goods.[16] These clauses provide that the seller will retain the ownership of the goods until the price has been fully paid. The formal security given by such clauses is more extensive than the statutory rights of lien or stoppage in transit. The introduction of this security device, which is intended to avoid the normal rules for the perfection and prioritisation of security interests upon insolvency, has further muddied the 'seriously defective' English law on the recognition of claims upon insolvency.[17] Furthermore, a rare but excellent empirical study of the use of these clauses has shown that there are major practical difficulties in enforcing them, as the control of the liquidation process generally resides with an insolvency practitioner who will be trying to keep the assets of the company (and hence the pool from which creditors will be paid through insolvency proceedings) as large as possible. The techniques used include intentional delay in dealing with correspondence and accelerated disposal of goods which may be subject to retention of title.[18] These difficulties call the practical value of the *Romalpa* clause into question, though their inclusion in a contract of sale proceeds as a standard drafting practice despite the difficulties.[19]

---

16   *Benjamin's Sale of Goods* (5th edn 1997) paras 5-135-5-164.

17   RM Goode, *Commercial Law* (2nd edn 1995) p 728.

18   S Wheeler, *Reservation of Title Clauses* (1991).

19   J Spencer, 'The Commercial Reality of Reservation of Title Clauses' [1989] Journal of Business Law 220, pp 231-232. See further I Davies (ed), *Retention of Title Clauses in Sale of Goods Contracts in Europe* (1999).

## Termination for failure to perform

C's withholding of his performance may not produce the desired result that D completes his performance. The ultimate step is for C to terminate the contract, which, as we shall see, cuts off C's obligations to D and makes D liable for C's lost expectation, and therefore is perhaps the most powerful form of self-help available to C. For this reason, C's threat to terminate, or the perceived risk that he might terminate, is a most effective incentive upon D to perform. Although C's power to terminate normally arises on D's breach, it need not be dependent on breach, but on a serious failure of performance. However, since such a failure is normally the result of a breach by D, this section will deal only with that situation.

'Termination' (especially when used synonymously with 'rescission') has been a vexed term.[20] 'Rescission for breach', 'justifiable repudiation' or 'electing to treat the contract as at an end' have also been used to denote the remedy we call termination. By this remedy we mean that C brings to an end *both* his and D's obligation to complete their primary performance and activates D's latent obligation to perform his secondary obligation to provide a remedy.[1] The important point to understand at the outset is that the contract, in the sense of the agreement generating secondary liabilities, continues after termination. It is obvious, then, that termination must be regarded as quite distinct from 'rescission' for eg misrepresentation or fraud, which is rescission *ab initio*, a return (so far as possible) to the situation as if there had been no contract.[2]

C's election to terminate affects both parties, though the impact on each is very different. By 'terminating' in the sense of cutting off any further performance of the remaining contractual obligations, C is unilaterally releasing himself from the duty to perform any obligations still remaining on his side. He need not actually perform them and no claim for specific relief will lie against him; nor will he be liable to compensate D for not performing them. (Of course, C still continues to be liable to pay damages for any breach which he himself may have committed prior to the termination.)

The position of D is radically different. (In the following discussion it is assumed that D is in breach of the contract, as he usually is.) By terminating the contract, C is 'releasing' D from his obligation to perform in a very different sense. C is notifying D: (1) that he (C) will not accept

---

20  W Alberry, 'Mr Cyprian Williams' Great Heresy' (1975) 91 Law Quarterly Review 337; M Hetherington, 'Keeping the Plaintiff Out of His Contractual Remedies: Heresies that Survive *Johnson* v *Agnew*' (1980) 96 Law Quarterly Review 403 and AJ Oakley, 'Chimerical Heresies' [1980] Cambridge Law Journal 58.

1   *Moschi v Lep Air Services* [1973] AC 331 at 350.

2   *Heyman v Darwins* [1942] AC 356 at 399; *Horsler v Zorro* [1975] Ch 302 and *Johnson v Agnew* [1980] AC 367 at 383.

any further performance from D (which means that C is giving up any claim to specific relief against D); (2) that he (C) will no longer be liable to pay for any further performance by D, nor will he be liable to fulfil any of his own duties which, according to the contract, were to be concurrent with, or dependent upon, D's fulfilling his obligations; but (3) that he (C) will hold D liable in damages, not only for the breach which led to the termination (and for any previous breach committed by D), but also for any loss which C suffers from the fact that C will not receive the benefit of D's further performance, viz C's loss arising from the fact that the contractual performance will not now be completed on both sides.³ C is subject to the rules on mitigation, so that his damages will be assessed on the basis that he (C) took reasonable steps to minimise his loss, and that the resources which he would have devoted to performing his own remaining duties have been released for other use. Rejection of the goods by the buyer under a contract for sale of goods is a classic case of termination for breach. For instance, tender by the seller of the wrong quantity of goods may entitle the buyer to reject.⁴

Although termination by C releases both parties from their obligations to continue with actual performance of the contract, it remains alive for

3   It is possible (see pp 45-48 above and ch 9 below) to draft a clause so that *any* breach of it gives C a right to terminate and claim full expectation damages. However, there have been many cases, mainly of the hire purchase of consumer goods, where C has terminated following D's relatively trivial breach of a clause which expressly granted him the right to terminate for *any* breach, but C has then been denied full expectation damages. Compensation for losses caused up to the time of the termination has been awarded, but not for lost future profits. The reasoning given for this is that it is C who causes the loss of future profits by choosing to terminate in circumstances in which, *ex hypothesi*, it was not necessary to do so: *Financings Ltd v Baldock* [1963] 2 QB 104 at 115. See further J W Carter, 'The Effect of Discharge of a Contract on the Assessment of Damages for Breach or Repudiation' (1988) 1 Journal of Contract Law 113 and B R Opeskin, 'Damages for Breach of Contract Terminated Under Express Terms' (1990) 106 Law Quarterly Review 293.
    This reasoning is, with respect, wholly unconvincing: *Lombard North Central plc v Butterworth* [1987] QB 527, discussed in p 145 below. What really is at issue in these situations is the avoidance of the heavy losses imposed by termination on a consumer who cannot, in any real sense, be thought to have agreed that the power to terminate should arise for this type of breach, though the contract expressly provides it. (The resulting losses are exacerbated because, in practice, a consumer receives little benefit from mitigation: *Lombard* involved the lease of a computer, and computers have little resale value.) This reasoning rightly has not been followed in commercial cases where the parties may legitimately be held responsible for the drafting of wider powers of termination: *The Solholt* [1983] 1 Lloyd's Rep 605 at 607. See further JS Ziegel, 'Measuring Damages for Breach of a Chattel Lease: The Supreme Court of Canada Liberalises the Rules' [1988] Lloyd's Maritime and Commercial Law Quarterly 276, 281.
4   Sale of Goods Act 1979, s 30. See also the unpaid seller's power to resell just discussed.

other purposes. Some clauses of the contract are intended to survive termination for breach. Thus, clauses dealing with C's remedy still apply, eg agreed damages and time limit clauses, or arbitration clauses,[5] and in assessing the loss suffered by C from the overall non-performance of the contract, the clauses of the contract which fix the parties' primary obligations will obviously be needed to show the benefit which D's performance was intended to confer on C.

Since C's entitlement to terminate is more a matter of substantive than of remedial law, it is not examined in detail in this book. The following is therefore only an outline.[6] In respect of the remedy of termination, terms of the contract may be divided into three categories.[7] First, the parties may intend (expressly or by implication) that any breach by D of a particular term, irrespective of the actual consequences of the breach, should entitle C, if he so chooses, to terminate the contract. This is, in the traditional language adopted by the Sale of Goods Act 1979, ss 12-15, a breach of a 'condition'.[8] In this situation, the parties regard any breach as so serious in its significance that C's power to terminate is not dependent on his proving that he has suffered (or will suffer) any loss,[9] although one imagines that in most situations such a breach will usually cause serious loss.[10] Secondly, the parties may have the opposite intention, that no breach of the particular term, irrespective of the actual consequences of any breach, should entitle C to terminate, although he will have a remedy in damages for any loss suffered. This type of clause traditionally was termed a warranty. Thirdly, there is an category of 'innominate' or 'intermediate' terms where the parties have not made clear what their intentions were about the power to terminate as a consequence of a breach.[11] Some breaches could have serious consequences, but others less serious ones. Here the courts have inferred that the right to terminate was

---

5   *Heyman v Darwins*, above p 51, n 2.
6   For a full treatment see Treitel, *The Law of Contract*, above p 46, n 14, pp 731-746.
7   *The Hansa Nord* [1976] QB 44 at 61.
8   By reserving 'condition' for a term classified as such by the parties rather than a term the breach of which necessarily is serious (though a breach of a condition as we define it may be serious), we follow Treitel, *The Law of Contract*, above p 46, n 14, p 734.
9   *Bunge Corpn v Tradax Export SA* [1981] 1 WLR 711.
10  For the rules on the time for performance, and on whether D's failure to perform on time entitles C to terminate, see H Beale, *Remedies for Breach of Contract* (1980) pp 80-95 and Treitel, *The Law of Contract*, above p 46, n 14, pp 766-767.
11  Though the terms of the contract obviously influence the classification of a clause as one of these three types, those terms and especially the use of the word 'condition' is not necessarily determinative. Use of the the word 'condition' does not preclude the possibility that the court will interpret the clause so referred to as falling into the third category: *Schuler AG v Wickman Machine Tool Sales Ltd* [1974] AC 235.

intended to be dependent on the actual consequences of the breach in question. If D's breach was 'a serious and substantial breach' or went 'to the root of the contract' or 'deprived [C] of substantially the whole benefit which he bargained for', C is entitled to terminate.[12]

A breach of an intermediate term requires an *ex post* enquiry into the facts, and depends on an assessment of the relative seriousness of the consequences. Although the post-breach transaction costs therefore could be high, C will be entitled to terminate only where the breach in fact causes serious adverse consequences. The fact that D's breach of a term in this category was intentional may be relevant to the issue where the consequences are less drastic, because its deliberate nature might show D's intention not to be bound by the contract. Such a 'repudiatory' breach undercuts the confidence C might have in D's future performance.[13] But D's deliberate refusal to perform in accordance with C's interpretation of a term of the contract will not amount to a repudiation where D *bona fide* believes that the clause provides a contractual right to withdraw from the contract.[14]

The justification for recognising the first two categories of terms is commercial certainty. The parties often need to know exactly where they stand after the breach, so that either the contract continues in force (the second category, warranty) or C has a choice whether or not to terminate it (the first category, condition). Certainty will reduce post-breach transaction costs, and so in *Bunge Corpn v Tradax Export SA*[14a] termination was allowed where D had failed to comply with a precise timetable laid down in the contract, even though the actual consequences were, in the circumstances, minor, because the precision of the timetable, which was intended to let each party know exactly when his respective obligations were activated, was of substantial commercial value.

But allowing termination for breach of condition will enable C to take opportunistic advantage of his power and terminate even where that will lead to social waste (and so be 'inefficient' in economic terms.)[15] The question whether damages would be an 'adequate' remedy for a breach of such a term is not considered to be relevant. By termination C may often place himself in a better position than if he could only sue for damages.

---

12   *Hong Kong Fir Shipping Co Ltd v Kawasaki Kisen Kaisha Ltd* [1962] 2 QB 26 at 70.

13   *Withers v Reynolds* (1831) 2 B & Ad 882. If, before his performance is due, D states (without legal justification) that he will not perform (or his conduct clearly evidences such an intention), C may accept this anticipatory repudiation, terminate the contract and sue for damages without waiting for the time of performance to arrive. See pp 106-107 below.

14   *Woodar Investment Development Ltd v Wimpey Construction UK Ltd* [1980] 1 WLR 277.

14a  See p 53, n 9 above.

15   GL Priest, 'Breach and Remedy for the Tender of Nonconforming Goods Under the Uniform Commercial Code: An Economic Approach' (1978) 91 Harvard Law Review 960.

In *Reardon Smith Line Ltd v Hansen-Tangen*,[16] D attempted to terminate
a contract in which it was to take delivery of a tanker on the basis of an
'excessively technical'[17] interpretation of what it was thought was a
condition that goods sold by description must conform to that description.
In most shipbuilding contracts, before the vessel's launch it is referred to
by the yard in which it is built and a number assigned to it by that yard,[18]
and this tanker was so referred to in the contract. It was, however, built
under sub-contract at another yard, and so was delivered under a different
yard name and number. Though it otherwise was in conformity, D sought
to reject the tanker, being motivated by a serious fall in the tanker market
which it sought to transfer to C. Though sale by description is a condition
under the Sale of Goods Act 1979, s 13(1), this breach was not allowed to
justify termination.[19]

Such cases raise the question whether the courts should exercise some
control over the power to terminate[20] when C simply intends to escape
from what has turned out to be a bad bargain, eg by denying the buyer's
right to reject the goods when he simply plans to take advantage of a fall
in the market price.[1] However, in contractual disputes, the courts have
usually avoided investigation of motives, since that would not only
undermine the degree of certainty attached to commercial transactions,
but also lengthen trials. After weighing these conflicting factors, the Law
Commission recommended revision of the non-consumer's right to reject
goods. The Sale and Supply of Goods Act 1994, s 4 inserted s 15A into
the Sale of Goods Act 1979. The Sale of Goods Act 1979, ss 13-15, implies
conditions for the delivery of goods (of which conformity with description
was one). Section 15A prohibits a non-consumer from rejecting goods for
'a breach so slight that it would be unreasonable … to reject' for that
breach, which must be treated as a breach of warranty. A consumer's right
to reject is left formally more or less absolute because it was feared that
any uncertainty about that right would lead to disputes over rejection
between the consumer and the business person which the consumer would
tend to lose.[2]

16 [1976] 1 WLR 989. Cf *Sanko Steamship Co Ltd v Kano Trading Co Ltd* [1978]
   1 Lloyd's Rep 156.
17 *Reardon Smith Line Ltd v Hansen-Tangen* [1976] 1 WLR 989 at 998.
18 S Curtis, *The Law of Shipbuilding Contracts* (1991) p 18.
19 A number of cases of which this one is but an egregious example have had perhaps
   terminal consequences for the coherence of the concept of sale by description:
   PS Atiyah, *Sale of Goods* (10th edn 2001) pp 81, 141-148.
20 The Consumer Credit Act 1974, ss 88-89, confers power on the courts to exercise
   such control over regulated consumer credit (or hire) agreements. The lessor's
   power to forfeit a lease is also subject to court approval.
1  *Cunliffe v Harrison* (1851) Exch 903 at 907 and *Arcos Ltd v Ronaasen & Son*
   [1933] AC 470.
2  Law Commission, *Sale and Supply of Goods*, Law Com 160, Cm 137 (1987)
   para 4.17. Cf the argument that the entire obligation rule be retained for consumers
   in small building works at pp 47-48 above.

## Termination as a form of self-help

Termination has the advantage that C can act unilaterally and without judicial approval, thus forcing D to bring proceedings if he disputes C's entitlement to terminate, and in this way, C gets the favoured position of defendant in any litigation. C may, however, be compelled to sue as claimant[3] if he seeks restitution[4] from D of any benefit which he had previously conferred on D, eg the benefit of partial performance by C, or money paid in advance to D, or property transferred to D.[5] Termination is a potent form of self-help by which C avoids all the costs and uncertainties of litigation. He can also act quickly, and may be able to avoid the risk of D's insolvency. In the case of breach of condition, recourse to termination does not depend on any proof of C's loss, and he is therefore not faced with the problems of causation, remoteness or mitigation. Unless he intends to claim damages, C need not take any steps to minimise his loss, nor need he act 'reasonably' in deciding whether or not to terminate the contract. If he is entitled to terminate, there is no judicial power to control his choice, whether under the heading of the court's discretion or otherwise; nor, in the case of conditions, are his motives in exercising the choice open to challenge in court. In cases of termination, the sole issue is whether C was legally entitled to terminate.

C must terminate the whole contract. He cannot choose to terminate only in part. Hence, he must return to D any benefits which he has received

3   C will also need to make an application to the court where an order for specific performance has been made in his favour which he now wishes to abandon in order to terminate and claim damages: *Johnson v Agnew* above p 51, n 2.
4   See ch 16 below.
5   Repossession by C, the owner, of land held by a lessee, or of a chattel held by D under a contract of hire-purchase, is subject to some statutory restrictions making, in some circumstances, a court order necessary: Consumer Credit Act 1974, ss 90, 92. For the current law and practice of repossession see J Kruse, *Distress and Execution* (1998) (a commendably objective work commissioned by the bailiffs' trade association, The Association of Civil Enforcement Agencies). That law is deplorably archaic and would appear to allow the systemic oppression, shading into illegality, of poor debtors: A Green, *Undue Distress* (2000). See further DI Greenberg, 'Easy Terms, Hard Times: Complaint Handling in the Ghetto', in L Nader (ed), *No Access to Law* (1980) 379, pp 385-6. On the policy questions raised by court support for repossession see further the Law Commission, *Landlord and Tenant: Distress for Rent*, Law Com No 194 (1991) and also the Law Commission, *Distress for Rent*, Working Paper No 97 (1986) and National Consumer Council, *Response to the Report of the Law Commission on Distress for Rent* (1986). The Lord Chancellor's Department is in the process of what appears to be a very wide ranging reform of the entire enforcement process: Lord Chancellor's Department *Towards Effective Enforcement: A Single Piece of Bailiff Law and a Regulatory Structure for Enforcement* (Green Paper, Cmd 5096, 2001); J Beatson *Independent Review of Bailiff Law* (2000) and Lord Chancellor's Department *Distress for Rent* (Enforcement Review Consultation Paper No 5, 2001). See further W Kennett 'The Enforcement Review: A Progress Report' (2001) 20 Civil Justice Quarterly 36.

under the contract and which are capable of being returned. So if C, the buyer, rejects defective goods, he must make them available for D to collect.[6] But if the benefit to C consists of services rendered by D, or building work on C's premises,[7] it obviously cannot be returned *in specie*. Usually C need not notify D that he is terminating the contract. He need do so only if he has already received performance which he now wishes to reject because it is defective, or where he seeks the return of property or money transferred to D in pursuance of the contract, or where he is treating D's anticipatory breach as a repudiation.[8] Again, C is under no obligation to give D any reasons for his decision to terminate. The court will uphold his decision if he can later show that at the time there were legal grounds for his action. Even if, at the time of terminating, he did not know of these grounds, or gave D another reason which would not entitle him to terminate, he can later justify his action on adequate grounds.[9]

The law does not at present provide adequate alternatives to termination for breach (except for C's withholding performance under a contractual provision for this).[10] It would meet some situations if C had to give D an opportunity to cure the defect in performance, and thus became entitled to terminate only for D's failure to take the opportunity to cure.[11] There is provision for this opportunity in some specific areas of commercial law,[12] and its general use has recently received recognition in the House of Lords.[13] Again, there is no legal machinery to produce a variation in the terms of the contract so as to give C some security against the risk of further, similar breaches: eg when the buyer who was given credit under an instalment contract fails to pay for a delivery at the fixed time after it was made, it would be reasonable for the contract to be varied so that all future deliveries should be made 'cash against delivery'.[14]

6   C has no lien over the goods as security for any claim in damages which he might have against D.
7   Another form of self-help available to C is the power given by the tort of trespass to land to withdraw from a contractor permission to remain on the land.
8   See pp 106-107, 160-165 below.
9   C cannot, however, rely on this rule if D could have cured the defect in the proper time had he been given the proper reason by C.
10  JW Carter, 'Suspending Contract Performance for Breach', in J Beatson and D Friedmann (eds), *Good Faith and Fault in Contract Law* (1995) 485.
11  A Apps, 'The Right to Cure Defective Performance' [1994] Lloyd's Maritime and Commercial Law Quarterly 525.
12  Eg the 'anti-technicality' clauses in charterparties: SC Boyd et al, *Scrutton on Charterparties* (20th edn 1996) p 357 and H Williams, *Chartering Documents* (3rd edn 1996) pp 77-80. See also relief against forfeiture discussed at pp 58-61 below.
13  *The Kanchenjunga* [1990] 1 Lloyd's Rep 391 at 399.
14  GH Treitel, 'Some Problems of Breach of Contract' (1967) 30 Modern Law Review 139, pp 154-5. However, in analogous circumstances, the duty to mitigate can require C to deal on cash terms: *Payzu v Saunders* [1919] 2 KB 581. See further p 111 below.

## Forfeiture of advance payments or of rights over property or arising out of the contract

There are many contracts where sums of money are payable in advance of the performance due from the payee D, or are payable at regular intervals (such as a purchase where the price is payable by instalments). The purpose of these payments may be to provide the payee with working capital to help finance his performance, or as a security against the risk of the payer's insolvency or breach. Subject to any set-off,[15] when C terminates he must normally return to D money paid in advance by D which C has not earned by partial performance. (This obligation to return money may be based on a claim for reliance damages or restitution of monies paid.)[16] However, these contracts may contain a clause which provides that, upon breach by the payer, the payee C may forfeit all the sums paid to him, in addition to terminating the contract (and pursuing expectation damages if they are larger than the forfeit). In contrast to the situation with liquidated damages, the payee does not need to ask the court to award him the agreed sum, since he already has it. He simply claims to be entitled to 'forfeit' the amount he has received, by retaining it for his own beneficial use, leaving the payer to challenge this if he can.

Perhaps the most common forfeiture clause is the 'deposit', which is a sum paid by D to C as a financial security for D's full performance of his obligations under the contract. The courts have traditionally held that the use of the word 'deposit' implies, unless the parties have expressly provided otherwise, that the intention of the parties is that the amount is to be forfeited to C if D defaults.[17] If D fully performs his obligations, the amount is to be credited towards the price or other performance which D has promised. However, if D breaches, C is entitled to forfeit the deposit (that is, he is free to use it for any purpose he chooses) whether or not he has suffered any loss as the result of D's breach, or of the termination of the contract following the breach. If C's losses exceed the amount of the deposit, he may sue to recover damages for the excess. In a contract of sale of goods, the seller who sues the buyer for the price or for damages must give the buyer credit for the deposit paid to him.[18] But if the seller resells the goods and does not sue the buyer for damages, he can retain both the price he receives under the resale and the deposit paid by the

---

15  See p 61 below.

16  See ch 8 and see ch 16 below.

17  *Howe v Smith* (1884) 27 Ch D 89 at 97-8. If it is the party who receives the deposit which breaches, he must return the deposit to the other party if the latter terminates the contract: *Country and Metropolitan Homes Surrey Ltd v Topclaim Ltd* [1997] 1 All ER 254.

18  *Commission Car Sales (Hastings) Ltd v Saul* [1957] NZLR 144 at 146 .

first (defaulting) buyer.[19] A deposit is thus a rare case of a type of payment which the courts have expressly recognised as having the purpose of compelling D to perform, which he will have a strong incentive to do since he knows that he will lose the whole benefit of the deposit if he commits a breach which enables C to terminate the contract. A deposit is: 'an earnest to bind the bargain ... and creates by the fear of its forfeiture a motive in the payer to perform the rest of the contract'.[20]

Furthermore, if D failed to pay C the deposit which he promised, C may recover the amount as damages after he has terminated the contract.[1] In this situation, the amount is awarded just so that it may be forfeited by C, since it can no longer be used by D to render performance. This is an outright case of damages arising out of a contract being awarded as a 'penalty' for breach, irrespective of the loss suffered by C.

The law on penalties strikes down clauses fixing sums payable as damages by D upon his breach, except where the amount is a genuine attempt to pre-estimate loss, and has developed some (admittedly not always very helpful) rules to distinguish genuine pre-estimates (liquidated damages) from outright penalties. But it has traditionally been held that a deposit or other form of forfeiture is not in general subject to the penalty rules, even though the deposit or forfeit may often greatly exceed C's actual loss. There are a number of exceptions to this general position, and perhaps it is more correct to say that it is unsettled whether the amount of a forfeit other than a deposit must be 'usual' or 'reasonable' for it to be treated as an amount which C can choose to forfeit.[2] Certainly concern has arisen both about the disparity between the size of some forfeitures and C's actual loss and about the obvious inconsistency between the rules on penalties, which are regulated, and forfeitures if they are not, when, if anything, as a sum actually deposited rather than owed, the latter will tend to have more impact on D. This concern has led the Law Commission to suggest that the penalty rules should apply to deposits and other forfeitures.[3] In the case of the widely used deposit, this concern

19  Ibid and *Howe v Smith*, above p 58, n 17 at 104-5. The seller resells as a beneficial owner, as in the analogous situation of a *Romalpa* clause: *Clough Mill v Martin* [1985] 1 WLR 111 at 117-118, 122.

20  *Howe v Smith*, above p 58, n 17 at 101. Cf *John Barker and Co Ltd v Littman* [1941] Ch 405 at 412.

1   *Damon Cia Naviera SA v Hapag-Lloyd International SA* [1985] 1 WLR 435. In this case the amount of the deposit exceeded the damages which C could have recovered apart from the deposit.

2   *Linggi Plantations Ltd v Jagatheesan* [1971] 1 MLJ 89 at 94 per Lord Hailsham (PC). Lord Hailsham appeared to maintain both that the law of penalties does not apply to forfeits, including deposits, but also that forfeits must be 'reasonable'.

3   Law Commission, *Penalty Clauses and Forfeitures of Money Paid*, Working Paper No 61 (1975). This recommendation would not apply to deposits below a fixed percentage in sales of land.

is exacerbated as there is little empirical evidence to support the courts' usual construction of the term, in the sense that an ordinary person realises, in contracts not concerning land, that a deposit will be forfeited on his breach.[4]

Nevertheless, recent developments seem to have had the effect of distinguishing the deposit, which it has been in effect affirmed is isolated from the penalty rules, from other forms of forfeiture, which increasingly are being subject to scrutiny. In 1993, in *Workers Trust and Merchant Bank Ltd v Dojap Investments Ltd*,[5] the Privy Council applied the penalty rules when refusing to enforce the forfeit of a 25% deposit on a sale of land when that deposit was higher than was customary and was by no means a genuine pre-estimate of the loss caused by the vendor's default.[6] The Privy Council rejected the argument that a larger deposit was justified by particular features of the Jamaican fiscal system[7] and that 'the test of reasonableness [should] depend upon the practice of one class of vendor, which exercises considerable financial muscle' so as to 'allow them to evade the law against penalties by adopting practices of their own.'[8] Had this case been followed, it would have involved reforming the traditional understandings[9] of deposit in particular and forfeiture in general.[10]

But whereas it would appear to have had some impact on the latter,[11] in respect of the former it has not been followed in any English case and the Privy Council has resiled from its 1993 position. In 1995 in *Bidaisee v Sampath*[12] the Privy Council, without discussion, cited *Workers' Trust* as authority for the proposition that equity has never considered deposits

---

4    For an exemplary empirical study which does state a sound case for the legitimacy of loss of deposits (if regulated) given for package holidays see A Milner, 'Liquidated Damages: An Empirical Study in the Travel Agency' (1979) 42 Modern Law Review 508, p 531.

5    [1993] AC 573.

6    The bank would be entitled to unliquidated damages for any legally recoverable loss.

7    Which required the payment by the transferor of a 7.5% tax. This gave rise to the practice of taking a 17.5% deposit.

8    *Workers Trust and Merchant Bank Ltd v Dojap Investments Ltd*, above n 5 at 580.

9    The previous support for the view that the law as to penalties applies to a deposit was very sparse indeed, and it is clear that the Privy Council exploited the ambiguity in *Linggi Plantations v Jagatheessan* (discussed on p 59, n 2 above) and relied heavily on the isolated *Public Works Comrs v Hills* [1906] AC 368: *Workers' Trust and Merchant Bank Ltd v Dojap Investments Ltd*, above n 5 at 579, 582.

10   H Beale, 'Unreasonable Deposits' (1993) 109 Law Quarterly Review 524.

11   *Cargill International SA v Bangladesh Sugar and Food Industries Corpn* [1998] 2 All ER 406. See further L Smith, 'Relief Against Forfeiture: A Restatement' [2001] Cambridge Law Journal 178, p 182 n 15.

12   Transcript available through LEXIS. The very brief 'report' at [1995] NPC 59 does not carry the relevant discussion.

'as a penalty against which it granted relief'. However questionable this interpretation of *Workers' Trust* may be, the Privy Council has continued to take this line. In *Vaswani v Italian Motors (Sales and Services) Ltd*, *Workers' Trust* was cited in argument but not reported in the judgment in which a deposit was enforced without consideration of its merit (and may have been reasonable).[13] In *Union Eagle Ltd v Golden Achievement Ltd*, an attempt to use *Workers' Trust* to challenge a deposit as a penalty was explicitly rejected. *Workers' Trust* and *Howe v Smith* were cited as authority for the proposition that 'in the normal case of a reasonable deposit, no inquiry is made as to whether [a deposit] is a pre-estimate of damage or not'.[14] The result would appear to be that the traditional view of deposits has been restored.[15]

The courts have a statutory power to grant relief against forfeiture of a deposit under a contract for the sale of land: 'Where the court refuses to grant specific performance of a contract, or in any action for the return of a deposit, the court may if it thinks fit, order the repayment of any deposit.'[16] Although this section gives an unqualified discretion,[17] the courts still exhibit some hesitancy in departing from the common law rule on forfeiture of a deposit.

The cases in which regulation of forfeit is possible and the Law Commission's proposals are considered in the context of the entire range of pre-estimated damages in chapter 9 below.

## Set-off[18]

Outside of the operation of financial markets,[19] the main use of a set-off is as a defence to C's claim against D for a sum of money. The defence arises from the fact that C owes D another sum of money, which D may

13  [1996] 1 WLR 270, PC.
14  [1997] AC 514 at 518, PC. This evasion did not prevent the court from treating a deposit as 'an earnest of performance' in what amounts to a return to the result of *Linggi Plantations Ltd v Jagatheesan*, above p 59, n 2, without reference either to that case or to its consideration in *Workers' Trust*, above p 60, n 5 at 579.
15  See also *SCI (Sales Curve Interactive) v Titus Sarl* [2001] EWCA Civ 591 [2001] 2 All ER (Comm) 416.
16  Law of Property Act 1925, s 49(2).
17  *Universal Corpn v Five Ways Properties Ltd* [1979] 1 All ER 552 at 555. See also *Safehaven Investments Inc v Springbok Ltd* (1995) 71 P & CR 328.
18  R Derham, *Set-off* (2nd edn 1996). See further PR Wood, *English and International Set-off* (1989).
19  The settlement of margin calls by multilateral netting by which financial futures dealing is conducted is a sophisticated development of set-off: J Williams, *The Economic Function of Futures Markets* (1986) pp 1-16. 'Set-off' of this sort has characteristic legal features *sui generis*.

use to reduce or extinguish C's claim against him. In his claim against D, C should give D credit for this if D pays the balance after setting off his cross-claim. It is up to C to challenge it by bringing legal proceedings.[20] The defence began as a set-off of one debt against another debt,[1] such as the deduction of liquidated damages from the price payable by C, but it was later extended to enable the buyer to set off his claim for damages for defective quality of the goods against the seller's claim for the price of the goods.[2] It is now clear that any claim for a debt may be met by a cross-claim for unliquidated damages arising under the same contract.[3] Any claim recognised by equity can also be met by another claim recognised in equity. Thus, a claim to forfeit a lease for non-payment of rent may be met by an equitable set-off against the rent, eg unliquidated damages for breaches of the obligation to repair.[4] Finally, it has been held that against C's claim for the equitable remedy of specific performance on the ground that D has failed to pay a sum due to C, D may set off a legal claim for other sums due from C to D. The court may therefore refuse to grant specific performance.[5]

## Appraisal of self-help remedies

The practical advantage of self-help remedies based on the minimisation of post-breach transaction costs is manifest and this can lead parties capable of doing so to negotiate contracts which afford them such remedies. It is equally manifest, however, that in many individual situations, C's exercise of such a self-help remedy will not be 'efficient' because the current rules governing self-help can be opportunistically exploited.[6] When this is so, a different outcome could be expected to produce a higher level of social welfare. C can act arbitrarily, without considering the interests of D or of third persons (there could be 'external' costs). Nor is C required to prove or to minimise his own loss. Indeed, he sometimes has an incentive to hope that D will commit a breach, because the self-help remedy would

20   On the use of set-off as a counterclaim in litigation see CPR Pt 20, r 2 and Pt 16, r 6.
1    In this context, the significant feature of a debt is that it is an ascertained or 'liquidated' sum, rather than, as with a claim for damages, a sum the quantification of which may be a matter of dispute. See below ch 9.
2    *Mondel v Steel* (1841) 8 M & W 858, which is the basis of Sale of Goods Act 1979, s 53(1)(a).
3    *Gilbert-Ash (Northern) Ltd v Modern Engineering (Bristol) Ltd* [1974] AC 689.
4    *British Anzani (Felixstowe) Ltd v International Marine Management (UK) Ltd* [1980] QB 137.
5    *BICC plc v Burndy Corpn* [1985] Ch 232.
6    See D Friedmann, 'Good Faith and Remedies for Breach of Contract', in Beatson and Friedmann (eds), *Good Faith and Fault in Contract Law*, above p 57, n 10, 399, pp 415-421.

make C better off than full performance would. (It could even be argued that in such a situation C has an incentive to 'lead' D into a position where he is likely to commit a breach. At the very least, C has no incentive to warn D when he is risking committing a breach which would enable C to take advantage of a draconian remedy.) But the assessment of efficiency is an overall social cost-benefit analysis. The fact that self-help remedies often provide powerful incentives to promisors to perform may be counted a social benefit if society wishes to maintain the present level of voluntary performance of contracts in general (or, at least, to avoid a higher level of breaching). The reduction in transaction costs in those contracts with built-in self-help remedies would be another social benefit to be weighed against inefficient outcomes in particular cases. Against these benefits would need to be set the social losses arising from avoidance of the ordinary rules on mitigation and the minimisation of losses.

Attempts by the courts or Parliament to control the exercise of self-help remedies will impose costs both on the parties and on society. For instance, the control of consumer credit by legislation creates costs which initially fall on the businesses providing credit, but ultimately fall on the consumers seeking credit (through higher charges or deposits, or more restrictions on the availability of credit).[7] There is probably little need to control the use of self-help remedies in contracts between businesses, which should be able to look after their own interests. The party entitled to the remedy would have 'bought' it as part of the price paid to secure the contract. Criticism of the use of the remedies arises mainly in standard-form contracts between businesses and consumers, where the former are in the stronger bargaining position, and have ready access to the legal knowledge which can produce the contractual clauses creating the remedies. It is therefore not surprising that most of the controls considered in chapter 4, on 'consumer protection', apply to contracts affecting consumers. The legislature is in a better position than the courts to make the necessary assessment of whether the social benefits of imposing a given control over a self-help remedy would exceed the social costs arising from the control. There is a glaring contrast between the restrictions placed on the availability of the remedies provided by the law, and the absence of restrictions on the use of the self-help remedies. This contrast calls for a comprehensive review of the position rather than the piecemeal approach adopted up to the present time, which has been according to categories of contract (eg hire-purchase). It is not clear that the restrictions on specific relief (particularly the discretion of the court and the test of the inadequacy of damages) and those on damages (causation, remoteness, mitigation, penalties) should be so easily evaded by parties with the expertise to protect themselves by ensuring the creation of self-help remedies in their contracts.

7    C Fried, *Contract as Promise* (1981) pp 103-109.

In the absence of detailed consideration of all the aspects of self-help, the most likely possible control on opportunistic exercise of the self-help remedies may lie in the development of a general[8] doctrine of good faith in performance in English law.[9] It is still correct to say, however, that the English law has no general doctrine of good faith in the performance of a contract.[10] To the extent that this is so, C's motive in exercising a self-help remedy is irrelevant. Not only is he not subject to any test of reasonableness in deciding whether and how to exercise the remedy, his actual malice against D is also irrelevant.[11] The oppressive exercise of self-help remedies which are the products of unequal bargaining power is one of the reasons why the development of a doctrine of good faith in performance has been urged on English law.[12] The experience of other jurisdictions[13] would seem to be that such a doctrine may have a useful role in this respect.[14] In a more limited fashion, we have seen that in cases which are held to turn on the use of intermediate terms, the common law has attempted to assess the seriousness of the consequences of D's breach as a way of regulating C's power to terminate,[15] and it may be worthwhile to extend control of this type to some other forms of self-help, even at the cost of introducing more uncertainty about C's entitlement. Generally to require C to give a short period of notice to D to remedy the breach before C is entitled to take action would be a limited but valuable reform.[16]

8    Explicit consideration of good faith in the regulation of exclusion clauses in consumer contracts has been brought into English law by the Unfair Terms in Consumer Contracts Regulations 1999, SI 1999/2083 (replacing SI 1994/3159), implementing the Directive on Unfair Terms in Consumer Contracts 93/13/EC.

9    Law Commission, *Sale and Supply of Goods*, para 4.18 and *Interfoto Picture Library Ltd v Stiletto Visual Programmes Ltd* [1989] QB 433 at 439. See further R Brownsword et al (eds), *Good Faith in Contract* (1999).

10   *Walford v Miles* [1992] 2 AC 128 at 138. See further M Bridge, 'Does Anglo-Canadian Contract Law Need a Doctrine of Good Faith?' (1984) 9 Journal of Canadian Business Law 385. See generally pp 604-606 below.

11   One might, however, expect a court to try to interpret the relevant clause in the contract so as to prevent an outrageous use of a self-help remedy by C: *The Hansa Nord*, above p 53, n 7 at 70-71.

12   R Brownsword, '"Good Faith in Contracts" Revisited' [1996] 49 Current Legal Problems 111. Cf R Powell, 'Good Faith in Contracts' [1956] Current Legal Problems 16.

13   O Lando and H Beale (eds), *Principles of European Contract Law* (2000) art 1:201.

14   RS Summers, 'The General Duty of Good Faith: Its Recognition and Conceptualisation' (1982) 67 Cornell Law Review 810. See contra SJ Burton, 'More on Good Faith Performance of a Contract: A Reply to Professor Summers' (1984) 69 Iowa Law Review 1.

15   See pp 53-54 above.

16   This is the case in specific contracts governed eg by the Consumer Credit Act 1974, ss 87-88 and the Insolvency Act 1985, s 120(3)(a). There is a general requirement of reasonable notice in sales of goods under the Uniform Commercial Code, s 2-508(a).

# 4 Consumer protection

## Introduction

We have seen that the law of contract as developed by the judges often makes the assumption that contracts are made between parties of equal bargaining strength.[1] But this is not the case where an individual makes a contract with a business: it is often a standard-form contract from which no variation is tolerated by the business. The standard form contract so dramatically economises on transaction costs that its use in consumer dealing is more or less universal,[2] but, of course, such is the typical inequality of bargaining power between the parties crystallised in the standard form that the potential for abuse of such contracts may well arise.[3] In the belief that private negotiations cannot adequately address this problem,[4] the principal regulatory response has been to use public law to protect the private consumer by many statutes, regulations, officials, and consumer organisations.[5] The present chapter can offer only a brief outline of the protection which is now available beyond the law of contract; the

1   Duress and undue influence are examples of situations where the courts have not made this assumption.
2   D Dewees and MJ Trebilcock, 'Judicial Control of Standard Form Contracts' in P Burrows and CJ Veljanovski (eds), *The Economic Approach to Law* (1981) ch 4.
3   IR Macneil, 'Bureaucracy and Contracts of Adhesion' (1984) 22 Osgoode Hall Law Journal 5.
4   F Kessler, 'Contracts of Adhesion: Some Thoughts About Freedom of Contract' (1943) 43 Columbia Law Review 629.
5   GJ Borrie, *Consumer, Society and the Law* (4th edn 1981); GJ Borrie, *The Development of Consumer Law and Policy: Bold Spirits and Timorous Souls* (1984) and C Scott and J Black, *Cranston's Consumers and the Law* (3rd edn 2000).

purpose of this chapter is to indicate the wider background to judicial remedies for breach of contract.

## The consumer's private law remedies

Although the formal rules of contract law appear to give the private individual many rights, in practice he faces serious obstacles in enforcing them.[6] The major one is the basic legal principle that it is up to the person who complains to take the initiative in bringing proceedings. The consumer is seen by the law as a private person with an individual problem which he can solve by taking action on his own. To the consumer, however, the procedure for bringing a claim before the ordinary courts often appears forbidding, slow and expensive. In regard to ordinary small claims the disincentives to suing clearly outweigh the incentives. One response abroad has been to allow a 'class action' under which a representative group of claimants (or a consumer or public agency) sues on behalf of a whole class with similar claims against the same defendant. But this procedure has not been successfully employed in England to enable a single action to be brought by a group of individuals who have all made similar but separate contracts with the same business. Another response has been to set up a special procedure for small claims. Claims with a value not exceeding £5,000 are normally allocated to the 'small claims track' in the County Court, where some of the ordinary rules on evidence and procedure are relaxed.[7] However, the move to informality is limited: parties may be legally represented, and businesses may be claimants. The power to award costs is limited so as to discourage the use of lawyers; courts try to make it possible for litigants to conduct their own cases.

Efforts have been made outside the official court system to improve the consumer's choice of methods to solve his disputes. In order to foster good relations with consumers, some trade associations (such as car repairers) have voluntarily created their own informal and cheap procedures for responding to complaints about their members. These codes of practice may provide for conciliation or arbitration.[8] If the consumer agrees to arbitrate (he may do so in the original agreement itself, or after the dispute has arisen), the arbitration may be conducted simply on written evidence from both sides, and so may not involve the consumer in any further expenditure. Voluntary, privately organised arbitration schemes for any type of small claims made by individuals were also successfully

---

6    R Cranston, *Regulating Business* (1979) and J O'Grady, 'Consumer Remedies' (1982) 60 Canadian Bar Review 549.
7    Civil Procedure Rules 1998, Pt 27; Practice Direction 27.
8    The courts exercise some control under the Arbitration Act 1996.

tried in England on an experimental basis, but they were discontinued when their funding came to an end.

## Advice for consumers

Citizens' Advice Bureaux, Consumer Advice Centres and the Trading Standards Departments of local government authorities all offer advice and assistance to private individuals with consumer complaints.[9] These agencies may help with drafting letters, telephoning and interviewing the business against whom a complaint is made, and may succeed in persuading it to offer some redress for the consumer, eg replacement or repair of defective items, or some allowance against the price. At present the law does not entitle the consumer to require defects to be cured, or the goods to be replaced. The rules on rejection of the goods often make this remedy difficult for the consumer. However, by the EU Directive on the Sale of Goods[10] (which is to be implemented in the UK by January 2002), if goods bought within the EU are faulty or do not match up to the contract, consumers will be able to have them repaired or replaced, or if this is unreasonable or not possible, to obtain a full or part refund.

Special Councils exist to investigate complaints about the operation of utilities, such as electricity, gas and water.

## Private law rights given by statute

Intervention by legislation may directly regulate a contractual relationship without creating offences under the criminal law. For instance, exemption clauses affecting consumers are subject to statutory control;[11] and if a seller tries to foist on to a private person goods which the latter did not order ('inertia selling') a statutory procedure enables the recipient to treat them as a gift after six months.[12] Another, more recent technique is the imposition by statute of a 'cooling-off' period. A sale may be cancelled by a consumer-debtor in some circumstances if it falls within the definition of a regulated consumer credit agreement and was signed by the debtor away from trade premises.[13]

---

9  In 1998, Citizens Advice Bureaux dealt with 1,000,000 consumer complaints, Trading Standards Departments with 900,000: Office of Fair Trading, *Consumer Detriment* (OFT 296) (2000) paras 5.1, 5.17.
10  99/44/EC.
11  Unfair Contract Terms Act 1977 and the Unfair Terms in Consumer Contracts Regulations 1999.
12  Unsolicited Goods and Services Acts 1971 and 1975.
13  Consumer Credit Act 1974, ss 67–73.

## Consumer credit transactions

The Consumer Credit Act 1974, although a very complicated enactment, does give a wide measure of protection to individuals ('debtors' who are given credit up to £25,000). Businesses providing such consumer credit must be licensed. The Act, and the many regulations made under it, control the advertising of consumer credit; the form and content of regulated agreements, including guarantees and indemnities; and the supply to the debtor of copies of the agreement and statements of account. In addition to the 'cooling-off' period already noted, the debtor has a right to settle the credit early (and to receive a rebate of interest and charges). The creditor's power to enforce or terminate the agreement is restricted, and the county court may make 'time orders' giving the debtor more time to pay instalments; and may reopen extortionate credit bargains. Beside the general rules, some special ones apply to hire-purchase and conditional sale agreements and to those for running-account credit; to credit cards and tokens; and to linked transactions. The true annual percentage rate of interest (the APR) must be disclosed to the debtor.

## Intervention by public law

The weaknesses of the private law remedies have led to increasing pressure over the years for intervention by public law. The major response has been through criminal law: many statutes have created offences in order to protect the public as consumers. A few are mentioned here to give an impression of the range of the criminal responsibility which can arise from contractual relationships.

A long history of public control over units and standards of measurement has led to the current legislation, the Weights and Measures Act 1985. Offences under this Act include the use of inaccurate equipment, and the delivery to a buyer of a smaller quantity than that purportedly sold to him. The Trade Descriptions Acts 1968 and 1972 prohibit the use of a false trade description for goods in the course of a trade or business, and regulate many details of the tradesman's offer to supply goods. The Food Safety Act 1990 regulates hygiene in the composition, preparation and handling of food, and its labelling and sale to the public. In 1999, a Food Standards Agency was set up to protect public health in relation to food and to monitor the performance of enforcement authorities. Medicines and drugs are controlled under the Medicines Act 1968: for instance, it is provided that 'No person shall, to the prejudice of the purchaser, sell any medicinal product which is not of the nature or quality demanded by the purchaser'.[14] In addition to

14  S 64(1).

imposing criminal sanctions some statutes expressly give a civil action to someone adversely affected by a breach. The Consumer Protection Act 1987 by section 11 enables regulations to be made to secure that goods are safe and that appropriate information is provided to buyers; to fix standards for classes of goods and to require testing by prescribed methods. Regulations now cover items such as electric blankets, oil heaters and lamps, toys and cosmetic products; the General Product Safety Regulations 1994 lay down a general safety requirement where no specific rules exist. The 1987 Act provides not only that it is an offence to contravene safety regulations but that an obligation imposed on a person by a regulation is a duty owed by him to any other person who may be affected by a failure to perform the obligation. So the buyer or a member of his family who is injured by a breach of the regulations may sue for damages under the Act. Many statutes imposing criminal penalties are silent on this issue, which usually leads to the inference that no civil liability was intended by Parliament. Sometimes, however, a statute provides expressly that breach shall not invalidate a contract of sale.[15]

Various statutes or regulations fix advertising standards,[16] while others deal with such diverse matters as 'pyramid selling', inertia selling, mail orders, mock auctions, trading stamps, labelling and packaging and claims that an item was made by disabled persons.

### Administrative action

A government department, the Office of Fair Trading, is responsible for reviewing commercial activities involving the supply of goods and services to consumers.[17] On the recommendation of the Consumer Protection Advisory Committee, regulations may be made to control a consumer trade practice which adversely affects consumers. The Director-General of Fair Trading is also empowered to recommend delegated legislation on similar matters; to seek a written assurance from a business that it will not persist in conduct detrimental or unfair to the interests of consumers; and, failing such assurance, to apply for a court order to that effect. The Director-General (as well as other representative bodies) may also seek an injunction against someone using a contract term for general use which is unfair to consumers.[18] The Office of Fair

15  Eg Trade Descriptions Act 1968, s 35 and Road Traffic Act 1972, s 60.
16  Eg Cancer Act 1939; Medicines Act 1968; Control of Misleading Advertisements Regulations 1988 and Broadcasting Act 1990. A voluntary code of practice is administered by the Advertising Standards Authority (a non-statutory body).
17  Fair Trading Act 1973. See further Department of Trade and Industry, *Modern Markets: Confident Consumers* (1999).
18  The Unfair Terms in Consumer Contracts Regulations 1999, regs 4, 8 and Schs 2 and 3.

Trading also encourages the preparation of Codes of Practice to guide members of trade or business associations in safeguarding consumers' interests, and publishes information and advice to consumers.

# Part 2
# Compensation

# 5 The protected contractual interests

## Introduction

The main judicial remedies available for breach of contract are the award of money either by a judgment for damages against D or an action in debt against D in respect of money due. Though similar in that they both involve an award of money, damages and debt serve essentially different, and indeed sometimes rival, functions as remedies. The former is a compensatory substitute for D's primary performance; the latter is a means of literally enforcing D's primary obligation when that obligation is to pay money due under the contract, just as an order for specific performance literally enforces D's primary obligation when that obligation is other than to pay money. Debt therefore will be considered in chapter 11, in the course of the discussion of literal enforcement in Part 3. In this Part we will consider the action for damages as it serves as a compensatory substitute for performance.[1]

It follows that the rules on damages are relevant only when three conditions are satisfied. First, C can prove that D has committed a breach of an obligation imposed on him by the contract. Second, C is seeking compensation by means of a payment of money to be assessed by the court, instead of seeking the benefit of actual performance of D's obligation by means of an order for specific performance. Third, C needs the assistance of the court to obtain compensation because no self-help remedy, such as forfeiture of a deposit or other advance payment, is available to him.

---

1  Cost to complete damages straddle this distinction between compensation and literal enforcement, containing an element of both, for they secure a substitute, third party to carry out D's original performance. These damages are discussed in ch 14 below.

Since one of the main grounds for awarding specific performance is that damages are 'inadequate' as a remedy for C, it is more convenient to examine the law on damages before that on specific performance. A claim to damages is a claim that the court should enforce C's legal right, since (unlike a claim to specific relief) the entitlement to damages is not subject to the exercise of any discretion by the court: if C is entitled to damages, the court has no discretion to refuse to award them because it disapproves of his conduct.

## The purpose of awarding damages: compensation for loss

That the aim of an award of damages for breach of contract was to compensate C for his loss was said to be 'beyond dispute' in the Court of Appeal and 'axiomatic' in the House of Lords in its recent decision in *AG v Blake*.[2] Exemplary damages are damages which seek to punish the wrongdoer rather than compensate his victim. Exemplary damages are not available in this country[3] in a purely contractual action and the Law Commission has recently recommended that there should be no change to this rule.[4] The traditional statement of the aim of awarding damages for breach of contract is that compensation should be assessed so as to give C the equivalent in money of the value he would have enjoyed if D had performed the promise according to its terms.[5] Since the function of exchange is to realise a surplus, the central concept of 'loss' following a breach of contract is C's failure to obtain the future expected surplus. The purpose is not to *restore* C to the position he was in before the contract was made, but to give him the monetary equivalent of the future *improvement* in his position which D had undertaken to produce, in return for some price paid or promised by C. Loss of a promised (and therefore expected) benefit, such as the loss of anticipated profits, is the core of the contractual concept: it is typically an attempt to achieve the *post*-performance situation, which is to be contrasted with the attempt in the law of tort typically to restore the *pre*-accident situation.[6] For this

2   *AG v Blake* [1998] 1 All ER 833 at 844, CA and [2001] 1 AC 268 at 282, HL. See also *McAlpine Construction v Panatown* [2000] 3 WLR 946, 987 ('That damages for breach of contract are compensatory has long been established in English law') and 1004 ('The general rule is that damages for breach of contract are compensatory').
3   Cf *Vorvis v Insurance Corpn of British Columbia* (1989) 58 DLR (4th) 193 (Canada).
4   Report No 247 (1997) p 107.
5   The classic statement is in *Robinson v Harman* (1848) 1 Ex 850 at 855.
6   See ch 19 below. Loss of future earnings in a personal injury case is intended to compensate C for the loss of the expectations which he enjoyed through his previous healthy and fit condition.

reason the making good of C's expectations, so far as an award of money can, is sometimes called *the* contractual measure of damages.[7]

The concept of loss recognised by the law of contract can be gleaned only from the many reported cases on the subject of damages. Apart from the test of remoteness considered in chapter 6, there is no test by which the courts decide as a matter of judicial policy which categories of loss should be compensated by damages in contract. But a reading of this chapter will show that 'loss' includes any damage to, or destruction of, C's land, buildings or chattels; any injury to his body, or illness; his physical inconvenience; any injury to his present economic rights (such as a patent or copyright); any diminution in his previous financial position (as by wasted expenditure); his failure to obtain the use of a physical object or an economic or other non-physical advantage, or the benefit of C's services, which he reasonably expected to receive under the contract; and, sometimes, the disappointment of his expectation that he would derive pleasure, enjoyment or peace of mind from D's performance under the contract.

## Expectation losses

### The minimum legal obligation rule

The paradigmatic type of loss in contract is the loss of C's expectations which were created by the contract itself.[8] But in assessing C's loss, the court must ignore any expectation of C's which does not depend on D's minimum legal obligations.[9] If D has not assumed a strict obligation to do something (eg to give the annual bonus which an employee may nonetheless reasonably expect), the court cannot take it into account. If D could have terminated the contract under a power granted to him, it will be assumed that he would have done so.[10] If C has a choice between methods of performance and has not yet chosen one, the assessment will be on the basis of the method which would be the least onerous to him.[11] In making an assessment of C's loss the court will take account of D's overall situation. Damages will not be assessed on the basis that D would tender a minimal performance when the benefit of so doing is outweighed by the damage to his business reputation which such a course of action

---

7  *Nyekredit Mortgage Bank plc v Edward Erdman Group Ltd (No 2)* [1997] 1 WLR 1627 at 1634.
8  LL Fuller and WR Perdue Jr, 'The Reliance Interest in Contract Damages' (1936) 46 Yale Law Journal 52 and 373.
9  *Lavarack v Woods of Colchester Ltd* [1967] 1 QB 278 at 294.
10  *The Mihalis Angelos* [1971] 1 QB 164.
11  *Bunge Corpn v Tradax Export SA* [1981] 1 WLR 711, HL.

would cause. In the words of Lord Diplock 'One must not assume that [D] will cut off his nose to spite his face'.[12]

Nonetheless, the minimum performance rule operates harshly against claimants who prior to breach enjoyed a reasonable expectation of receiving discretionary bonuses eg a sales' 'rep' who in breach of contract is dismissed by his employer and whose 'salary' largely consisted of commission paid at the discretion of the employer. An analogy could be made with the position of commercial agents who, upon termination of their agency, may be entitled to compensation based upon the normal rather than the minimal performance of their principal's obligations.[13]

## The net loss approach

In the typical contract, C hopes to receive both the immediate benefit of D's promised performance (eg the delivery of an item sold to him by D) and the consequential benefit to be derived from subsequently using or enjoying that benefit (eg the expected profits if it was a profit-earning machine). Expectation damages are designed to give C the monetary equivalent of the lost benefit. But a crucial feature of the concept of loss in this context is that it refers to the *net* loss actually suffered by C, that is, the loss of the net benefit which he expected to receive from full performance by D.[14] If, as the result of D's breach, C is relieved of the obligation to complete performance of his side of the contract, the cost which he has avoided must be deducted from the gross benefit which he would have received from D's performance, so as to leave only the net loss to be compensated by the award of damages.[15] Similarly, if C has received some benefit from partial performance by D, that must be taken into account so that the damages compensate him only for the missing part of D's performance. The courts often assert that damages should be no more than C needs to put him in the position he would have been in had there been no breach of contract. They adopt the approach of drawing up a profit and loss account for C's position following the breach.[16] On the 'profit' side will be items such as any benefit received from D's partial performance (eg the salvage value of anything left in C's hands); any expense saved by C because he need not complete his own performance;

12  *Lavarack v Woods of Colchester*, above p 75, n 9 at 295.
13  Commercial Agents (Council Directive) Regulations 1993 and *Page v Combined Shipping & Trading Co Ltd* [1997] 3 All ER 656.
14  *McAlpine v Property and Land Contractors* (1995) 76 BLR 59.
15  This saving of the future cost of C's performance is considered pp 110-111 below.
16  See the language used in the *British Westinghouse* case [1912] AC 673 at 691: 'it is right for the ... arbitrator to look at what actually happened, and to balance loss and gain'. The 'net loss' approach was approved by the House of Lords in the situation where a wrongfully dismissed employee finds another job: *Westwood v Secretary of State for Employment* [1985] AC 20 at 44.

the benefit of substitute performance received by C from a third party; any savings in taxation (which will shortly be discussed) and sometimes[17] any right of recoupment from third parties.[18]
On the 'loss' side will be items such as the failure to receive the benefit of complete performance by D; any of C's expenditure incurred in reliance on the contract and which is wasted as the result of D's breach; any of C's expenditure arising after, and as a result of, D's breach (such as the cost of C's attempts to minimise his loss);[19] and sometimes the cost of a third party completing the performance promised by D.[20] Damages are intended to compensate C only for the debit balance of this profit and loss calculation – in other words, for his net loss. This approach leads to the result that damages seldom give C the monetary equivalent of the benefit of full performance. The 'net loss' approach also means that once D encounters problems which raise the costs of his original performance, a point will usually come when it is much cheaper for D to break his contract than to perform it. If D is tempted not to perform, the rules on damages often provide him with an additional incentive to yield to the temptation. These rules are not designed to encourage D to perform: rather, the message to C is that he should be satisfied if he gets damages calculated to meet his net loss.

## Taxation

This question is of greater importance in personal injury cases (which are usually, but not necessarily, claims in tort),[1] but it can also apply to some

17 Rights of recoupment may be ignored for policy reasons eg to encourage parties to obtain proper insurance: *Arab Bank plc v John D Wood Ltd* [2000] 1 WLR 857 (mortgage indemnity policy which compensated lender if mortgaged property sold for less than debt owed to be ignored when calculating damages recoverable from negligent surveyor) or to avoid stifling the charity of third parties: *Deeny v Gooda Walker (in liquidation)* [1995] 4 All ER 289 at 293-4 (applied by analogy to payments made by Lloyd's out of a central fund to meet the liabilities of 'Names' in an action against their agents). These policy reasons are usually applied in relation to actions for personal injury: see Pt 6 below.
18 *St Albans City and District Council v International Computers Ltd* [1996] 4 All ER 481. In this case, a defective computer system overstated the number of council chargepayers with the result that the council set too low a charge. The council nevertheless was unable to recover the shortfall as damages because it could be recouped by setting a higher charge in the future.
19 For instance, 'a wrongfully dismissed employee will be able to set off against any earnings in a new job to be deducted from his damages the reasonable expenses of travelling and advertising incurred in obtaining that new job': *Westwood v Secretary of State for Employment*, above p 76, n 16 at 44C.
20 See the discussion of *Ruxley Electronics and Construction Ltd v Forsyth* [1996] AC 344 in ch 14.
1 See chs 22-24 below.

other claims in contract, such as damages for wrongful dismissal of an employee.[2] The incidence of taxation will reduce C's damages whenever two conditions[3] are met: (1) the damages themselves would not be taxable in C's hands;[4] and (2) the amount which C has lost would have been taxable as income or as a capital gain if he had received it from D in fulfilment of the contract,[5] eg if C has lost earnings on which he would have paid income tax, his damages should reflect only his net loss. Legislation now imposes tax on damages for wrongful dismissal when they exceed £30,000.[6] So C's saving of tax on the first £30,000 of his damages will be deducted from his award,[7] but tax will be ignored on any amount beyond £30,000.[8]

If C's tax liability is actually reduced as a result of D's breach of contract, the saving will be deducted from C's damages since it is relevant in calculating his net loss.[9]

### The profit made by D after breach

The traditional statement of the purpose of awarding damages does not refer to the position of the contract-breaker D after the breach. It simply says that the purpose is to put C into the position he would have been in if both parties had performed their respective obligations under the contract. If D makes a profit through diverting his resources elsewhere after the breach, it is said that it is not the objective of the courts to deprive D of this profit, but simply to compensate C for his loss. D may be better off after the breach, but all the courts are concerned with is C's position: he should be no worse off, but also no better off. This philosophy permeates the law on damages, though there have long been isolated exceptions to

2    *Beach v Reed Corrugated Cases Ltd* [1956] 1 WLR 807.
3    *British Transport Commission v Gourley* [1956] AC 185 and *Hall v Pearlberg* [1956] 1 WLR 244 at 247. The *Gourley* principle has been rejected in Canada, limited in New Zealand but followed in Australia. See MP Furmston (ed), *The Law of Contract* (1999) para 8.26 for further detail.
4    So if C's damages will be subject to tax, his damages should be assessed at his gross loss without any reduction: *Diamond v Campbell-Jones* [1961] Ch 22 (C dealt in real estate). It does not matter that the tax levied on the damages may be different from that which would have been levied on the lost amount.
5    *Phipps v Orthodox Unit Trusts Ltd* [1958] 1 QB 314 and *Deeny v Gooda Walker (No 2)* [1996] 1 WLR 426.
6    Income and Corporation Taxes Act 1970, ss 148, 188 ( as amended by s 74 of the Finance Act 1988).
7    *Parsons v BNM Laboratories Ltd* [1964] 1 QB 95. C's effective rate of tax is used in the calculation.
8    *Shoe v Downs Surgical Plc* [1984] 1 All ER 7; *Bold v Brough, Nicholson & Hall Ltd* [1964] 1 WLR 201 and *Stewart v Glentaggart* 1963 SLT 119.
9    *Levison v Farin* [1978] 2 All ER 1149.

it. But recently, in *AG v Blake*, the Court of Appeal and the House of Lords
have considered moving away from this approach in general, to the point
where Lord Nicholls was able to say that: 'In a suitable case damages for
breach of contract may be measured by the benefit gained by the
wrongdoer from the breach.'[10] At the moment, such a remedy will only be
available 'exceptionally',[11] but it is the clear thrust of the (formerly minor)
line of cases now culminating in *Blake* that the number of these exceptions
should grow. The entire issue is examined in detail in chapter 17.

### Damages in respect of a third party's interest

When C maintains an action in respect of lost or damaged goods C will
not be able to prove a loss unless he had a property interest in the goods
at the time of the loss or damage. An exception to this rule in the case of
the carriage of goods by sea was described by Lord Diplock in the
*Albazero*[12] whereby the consignor of goods was able to recover substantial
damages from the carrier despite the fact that the consignor had already
sold the goods at the time of the damage or loss. This exception was
necessary to avoid the separation of the cause of action and the loss. The
consignor had a cause of action against the carrier with whom he had a
contract but suffered no loss because the goods were sold for full value.
The consignee who gave full value undoubtedly thereby suffered a loss
but had no cause of action (contract) against (with) the carrier.

This exception became otiose after the Bills of Lading Act 1855[13] but
was given new life in 1994 by the decision of the House of Lords in the
*Linden Gardens* case.[14] A contractor entered a contract with a building
owner for the removal of asbestos. At the time when the contractor breached
this contract the building owner had already sold the property. The
original building owner sued the contractor for breach of contract. The
majority of the House of Lords applied and extended the carriage of goods
by sea exception to the sale or leasing of real property where the ultimate
purchaser or lessee (who suffered the loss) did not have a right of action
against the party in breach of contract.[15] Lord Griffiths took a different

10  *A-G v Blake*, above p 74, n 2 at 283-284 per Lord Nicholls, Lords Goff and
     Browne-Wilkinson concurring.
11  Ibid at 286.
12  [1977] AC 774 at 847. The exception is thought to derive from *Dunlop v Lambert*
     (1839) 6 Cl & Fin 600.
13  S 1 effected a statutory assignment to the consignee of the consignor's right of
     action against the carrier. See now Carriage of Goods by Sea Act 1992.
14  *Linden Gardens Trust Ltd v Lenesta Sludge Disposals Ltd* [1994] 1 AC 85.
15  See the judgment of Lord Browne-Wilkinson with which Lords Ackner, Bridge
     and Keith agreed, especially ibid at 115.

approach and would have allowed the original building owner to maintain an action to recover the cost of remedial work on the basis that *he* had suffered a loss because he had not received the promised contractual performance.[16] It is important to understand the different approaches taken. The majority would exceptionally allow the original owner to recover damages in respect of a third party's loss. By adopting a more expansive definition of loss Lord Griffiths would have allowed him to recover damages on the basis that he was being compensated for his own loss.

The question came before the House of Lords again in *McAlpine Construction v Panatown*[17] where D contracted with C to build an office block and car park on land owned by X, another company in the same group as C. Under a deed D also undertook a direct obligation to X to exercise reasonable care in the contracted construction. Defects were later discovered and C sued D. The majority of the House of Lords[18] held that C's action failed because X's direct right of action against D under the Duty of Care Deed took the case outside the exception formulated by the majority in the *Linden Gardens* case.[19] Only the minority[20] supported the broader formulation of Lord Griffiths in the earlier case which would have allowed C to succeed irrespective of X's direct right of action.

The problem addressed by the courts in the above cases was described as being caused by the fact that the party who has a cause of action for breach of contract is not the same as the person who has most immediately suffered the loss caused by that breach. The courts have shown great ingenuity in their attempt to permit recovery by the party who has the benefit of a direct cause of action. A different approach has been taken by the legislature,[1] which has introduced a general right of action for third parties. In other words the party who has undoubtedly suffered the loss is given a new cause of action. The Contracts (Rights of Third Parties) Act 1999,[2] s 1 provides that a third party to a contract may 'in his own right' enforce a term of a contract if 'the contract expressly provides that he may' or 'purports to confer [such] a benefit on him'. This section creates two distinct categories of third party claimant who can enforce a contract. An illustration of the first would be where X contracts to sell his boat to D in exchange for D's promise to pay C £20k 'who shall enjoy the direct

16   Ibid at 97.
17   [2001] 1 AC 518.
18   Lords Clyde, Jauncy and Browne-Wilkinson.
19   Which, in any case, may have been premised upon a misunderstanding of *Dunlop v Lambert*. See especially the judgment of Lord Clyde.
20   Lords Goff and Millett agreeing with observations in *Darlington Borough Council v Wiltshier Northern Ltd* [1995] 1 WLR 68 by Steyn LJ.
1    Following Law Commission, *Privity of Contract: Contracts for the Benefit of Third Parties*, Law Com No 242 (1996).
2    The Act applies to any contracts concluded after 10 May 2000.

right to enforce D's promise'. Such express provision is likely to be rare particularly in regard to contracts where it is not usual for X to seek legal advice. Therefore the second category of third party claimant is of greater practical importance. The effect of the provision is to create a rebuttable presumption in favour of there being a third party right whenever a contract seeks to confer a benefit on an expressly specified third party. A simple example might be where X contracts to sell his boat as above absent the express conferral on C of a right to sue. The intentions of the original contracting parties, D and X must be ascertained by other means. However, the burden of proof will effectively be borne by D who will have to show that the parties' intention was not to confer an enforceable right on C.

It is unclear whether, if the Act were in force at the time, it would have been of assistance to the third parties in the cases considered above. In *Linden Gardens*, the third party (the new building owner) was not identified in the original contract and so would fall outside s 1.[3] In the *McAlpine* case, it could be convincingly argued that the direct right of action enjoyed by X under the deed would indicate a clear intention that that document should exhaustively define X's rights. However what would be the position where the rights conferred on the third party were more limited?[4] Where third parties do acquire a right under the Act they are entitled to whatever remedy they would be able to exercise if they were a party to the contract.[5] This implies that the limitations (remoteness, mitigation etc) appropriate to an action for damages by a party to the contract will also be applicable to any action by the third party.

## No loss, or speculative loss

Even if C has suffered no loss, or cannot prove any, he will be awarded nominal damages, eg £2 (but he may not get his costs, which are in the discretion of the court). Sometimes, C seeks nominal damages in order to determine his legal rights, but an action for a declaration is now a more appropriate remedy for this purpose.[6]

The fact that (apart from specific relief) compensation must be assessed in money raises many problems in assessing what is the money equivalent of the missing performance: often there is no recognised method of

3   By s 1(3) identification by name, class or description is sufficient.
4   Eg the *Darlington* case where the third party had a direct right of action to recover liquidated damages for delay in constructing leisure facilities on land they owned. The third party, a local authority, was not a direct party to the building contract in order to circumvent central government restrictions on local authority borrowing.
5   S 1(5).
6   See pp 86-87 and chs 6 and 7 below.

translating the loss into money, but the court will attempt an estimate, eg in the 'loss of a chance' cases, as where C was denied the chance of winning a prize in a beauty contest.[7] The difficulty in making an assessment never deters the court from attempting it, even where the loss depends on a contingency.[8]

## Evaluation of loss in terms of the market

As many of the cases on damages concern disputes between businessmen, it is not surprising that they frequently refer to market value as the yardstick of loss. This applies particularly to sales of goods but it covers many other types of contract. For instance, where D, a surveyor, failed to report to his client C that the roof timbers in the house C wished to buy needed replacement, C's damages were the difference between the market value of the house in its actual state with the rotten timbers, and the price C paid for it. C could not recover the cost of putting in new timbers, since that would improve the value of the house. His 'loss' was the difference between the price and the actual value of what he got.[9] The position is similar in respect of other breaches of contract which do not adversely affect the market value. Where solicitors failed to advise C that a covenant prohibited him from building on the land he was buying (on which they knew he intended to build) his damages were nominal, because even with the covenant restricting its use, the land was worth what he paid for it.[10] It would have been worth more without the covenant, but this loss to C was ignored because the market value was taken as the measure of the value of the land to him.

There are relatively rare circumstances in which the market measure of damages will be abandoned in cases of broadly this nature, and they will be examined in chapter 14 below.

## Reliance losses

So far we have considered expectation losses. A second ground for awarding damages for D's breach of contract is to reimburse C for expenditure which he incurred in reliance on the contract, but which is

---

7   *Chaplin v Hicks* [1911] 2 KB 786. See further H Reece, 'Loss of Chances in the Law' (1996) 59 Modern Law Review 188.
8   *Joseph v National Magazine Co Ltd* [1959] Ch 14 at 21, in which C lost the opportunity to enhance his reputation as an expert.
9   *Philips v Ward* [1956] 1 WLR 471.
10  *Ford v White* [1964] 1 WLR 885.

now rendered futile by D's breach; or expenditure which C incurred after, and as a result of, D's breach. This category of loss is loosely described as reliance expenditure, but it should be divided into the sub-categories analysed in chapter 8 below because different factors are relevant to each. The relationship between damages assessed on the expectation measure and those assessed on the reliance measure is also considered in chapter 8 below.

### Restitution of benefits received by D

A third ground for C's claim against D is restitution of what C has transferred to D (or a benefit which D has received from C) in pursuance of the contract (eg repayment of the price paid in advance by C). If D has failed to perform his side of the contract so that C has not received any benefit from D's performance, C may seek to get back from D what he had received from C, so as to restore both parties to the position they would have been in if they had never entered into the contractual relationship. However, it is not a claim for damages and it is available only after C has terminated the contract. C does not allege that he has suffered loss, nor that he has incurred expenses in reliance on the contract. The claim is rather that D would be unjustifiably benefited if, after his breach, he could retain the benefit he had received from C. Being distinct from a claim in contract (or in tort), its principles will be examined separately in Part 4.

### Can C choose the ground for his claim?

There is no simple answer to the question whether C has a free choice between the different grounds on which to make his claim: loss of expectation; reliance; or restitution. The main approach of the courts is to allow C to choose between them, but subject to some limitations which are discussed in the appropriate places below. Sometimes C may be able to claim on more than one ground, provided he can show that there is no overlapping or inconsistency between the different heads of his recovery. C should not be able to recover more than once for any particular head of loss.[11] But incidental and consequential losses may often be recovered in addition to C's net loss of profits.[12]

---

11  See pp 130-132 below.
12  See ibid.

## Restrictions on the recovery of damages

The law on damages can be viewed as a set of rules placing a number of limitations on the extent of D's liability for the consequences of his failure to perform. Firstly, C must shoulder the burden of *proving* that D broke his contractual promise. Secondly, C must prove his *net loss* and that the loss was caused by that breach. Thirdly, there may be special clauses[13] in the contract limiting D's liability for the breach or restricting the remedies available to C, eg a clause fixing the amount of the compensation payable. Fourthly, even where the rules on causation are satisfied, some categories of loss may be held to be 'too remote' a consequence of the breach, so that there was no intention that damages should be awarded in respect of them (see ch 6). Fifthly, the rules on *mitigation* narrow the concept of net loss by taking account of the post-breach opportunities which C had to reduce his loss (see ch 7).[14]

### Causation

C must show that the loss in question was *caused* by D's breach of contract. The courts have avoided laying down any formal tests for causation, relying rather on their common sense to decide whether D's breach was a sufficiently substantial cause of C's loss.[15] It need not be the sole cause:[16] D is liable if his 'breach of contract is one of two causes, both co-operating and both of equal efficacy'.[17]

The chain of causation is normally broken by the voluntary act of a third person which intervenes between D's breach and C's loss. But the court clearly exercises some discretion in deciding the issue. In one case, D, in breach of contract, negligently left a libellous letter from C in a place where it was read by a third party, who was likely to, and did, communicate its contents to the persons libelled; the latter recovered damages for libel

13 There may be some judicial control over the validity or application of these clauses, eg the law on penalties (ch 9 below) or the Unfair Contract Terms Act 1977 and the Unfair Terms in Consumer Contracts Regulations 1999.
14 We shall shortly consider the unsettled question whether contributory negligence applies to breach of contract, so that the damages could be reduced proportionately if the loss was held to be caused partly by the fault of C and partly by the fault of D.
15 *Galoo v Bright Grahaeme Murray* [1994] 1 WLR 1360 at 1375. See further HLA Hart and T Honoré, *Causation in the Law* (2nd edn 1985) ch 11.
16 See the *Monarch Steamship* case below. If D's breach is a substantial cause, he will be liable for all the loss (subject to the rules of remoteness and mitigation); but D may seek contribution from a third party who contributed to the causation and would also have been liable to C: Civil Liability (Contribution) Act 1978, s 1(1).
17 *Heskell v Continental Express Ltd* [1950] 1 All ER 1033 at 1048.

from C, who sued D to recover the damages and costs he had paid. The majority of the House of Lords held that C could recover only nominal damages for D's breach, since the act of the third party was a 'new and independent' cause.[18] But D may owe a contractual duty to C to take care to ensure that a third party is not permitted to intervene. A customer of a bank owes a duty to the bank to draw his cheques carefully so as not to facilitate fraud; where a customer drew a cheque in such a way that the amount could be readily altered, he was held liable to the bank for the increase forged by a third party, who obtained payment of the increased amount.[19] The fact that a crime was necessary to bring about the loss does not prevent its being 'the natural consequence of the carelessness.'[20] So where a decorator leaves a house unlocked he will be liable for the loss of items stolen while he is absent.[1]

Where C has acted voluntarily *after* D committed the breach, several different rules may apply to decide whether C's act prevents D from being liable for the consequences of the action. C may have failed to take reasonable steps to minimise his loss, and so be denied damages under the 'avoidable loss' rule of mitigation considered below. If the principle of contributory negligence applies to the contract in question, the same result might be achieved. But the court may also use the concept of causation to hold that C's loss was not caused by D's breach, but by some other factor for which D was not responsible. So in one case, D could have anticipated that if he failed to supply C with adequate equipment (such as a stepladder) for his work, there might be an accident if C attempted to use makeshift equipment. C was injured in doing this, but the court held that it was C's own act which caused the accident. D's breach of contract merely gave C the opportunity to injure himself if, despite his appreciation of the risk involved, he chose to use equipment which he knew was unsuitable for the task.[2] If, however, D's breach put C on the horns of a dilemma, C is not disentitled from recovering damages where he acted reasonably.[3] So where D chartered a ship and could nominate the port of

18  *Weld-Blundell v Stephens* [1920] AC 956 at 986. (The intervening act of the third party was apparently foreseeable: ibid at 974, 987, 991. But see GH Treitel, *Law of Contract* (10th edn 1999) p 754.)
19  *London Joint Stock Bank v Macmillan* [1918] AC 777.
20  Ibid at 794.
1   *Stansbie v Troman* [1948] 2 KB 48. See also *De la Bere v Pearson Ltd* [1908] 1 KB 280.
2   *Quinn v Burch Bros (Builders) Ltd* [1966] 2 QB 370 (affirmed 381). Cf the similar situation in *O'Connor v BDB Kirby Co* [1972] 1 QB 90. See also *Beoco Ltd v Alfa Laval Co Ltd* [1995] QB 137 (cost of first repair and consequential loss recovered but not losses following explosion caused by poor repair which proper inspection would have revealed to be defective).
3   *Compania Naviera Maropan SA v Bowaters Lloyd Pulp and Paper Mills Ltd* [1955] 2 QB 68 at 88.

loading, the master of the ship, provided he acted reasonably, was entitled to assume that D would fulfil his contractual duty by nominating a safe port.[4] D could escape liability for damage to the ship only where the port was obviously unsafe.[5]

Sometimes D claims that it was an event which intervened between his breach and C's loss. In the *Monarch Steamship* case,[6] D's ship was carrying a cargo from the East to Sweden, where she was due in July 1939. Through D's breach, she was delayed until war broke out in September, when she was diverted by the Admiralty to Glasgow. The House of Lords held that D was liable for the expenses incurred in sending the cargo to Sweden in neutral ships, since his breach had caused the transhipment. Reasonable businessmen, knowing of the possibility of war, would have foreseen that a delay might lead to the risk that the Admiralty would divert the vessel.[7]

## Contributory negligence

The Law Reform (Contributory Negligence) Act 1945 permits apportionment of loss by the reduction of C's damages where he 'suffers damage as the result partly of his own fault and partly of the fault of any other person'; the definition in the Act of 'fault' as (inter alia) 'negligence' raises the question whether D when sued for breach of contract can take advantage of this provision if C has himself contributed to causing his loss by some 'fault' on his part. The question may be academic in many situations, because D may defend by proving that C failed to mitigate his loss,[8] or arguing that C's loss was not caused by the breach.[9] In other words there is an overlap between the doctrines of mitigation, causation and contributory negligence. Nonetheless the question is an unsettled one despite receiving considerable attention from the courts and even the Law Commission.

In this context it is necessary to distinguish three situations:
(1)  Where D's liability arises from some contractual provision which does not depend on negligence on his part ie strict liability in contract.[10]
(2)  Where D's liability arises from a contractual obligation which is expressed in terms of taking care (or its equivalent) but does not

4   *Reardon Smith Line Ltd v Australian Wheat Board* [1956] AC 266 at 282–3.
5   Cf *Lambert v Lewis* [1982] AC 225.
6   Cf *Monarch Steamship Co Ltd v A/B Karlshamns Oljefabriker* [1949] AC 196.
7   But if the ship ran into a typhoon and suffered damage during the delayed voyage, it could not be said that the delay caused the damage: ibid at 215.
8   See ch 7 below.
9   See pp 84-86 above.
10  Eg a seller's obligation under Sale of Goods Act 1979, s 14(2) to provide goods of satisfactory quality.

correspond to a common law duty to take care which would exist in the given case independently of contract ie liability for breach of a contractual duty of care.[11]

(3) Where D's liability in the law of contract is the same as his liability in the tort of negligence independently of the existence of any contract ie concurrent duties of care in contract and tort.[12]

The law is at least clear in relation to category 3 cases where it has been held that C's contributory negligence can operate to reduce the damages for breach of contract which would otherwise be recoverable.[13] This is the most obvious application of the 1945 Act to a contractual action. As the 1945 Act was intended to apply to actions in the tort of negligence it would be absurd if such a reduction could be avoided by C simply asserting the breach of a contractual duty of care. The Court of Appeal has recently held[14] that the 1945 Act is not applicable to category 1 cases. D was employed to clean an asbestos roof under a contract that imposed on him a strict contractual duty. The work was sub-standard but D claimed that C was partly to blame because C had assumed supervisory responsibility for the work. The 1945 Act probably does not apply to category 2 cases.[15] This is contrary to the Law Commission's recommendation that the 1945 Act should be amended so as to apply to category 2 situations.[16]

---

11 Eg a service provider's liability under Supply of Goods and Services Act 1982, s 13 to perform the service with reasonable care and skill.

12 Eg that owed by a solicitor (*Midland Bank Trust Co Ltd v Hett, Stubbs and Kemp* [1979] Ch 384) or other professionals (eg underwriting agents: *Henderson v Merrett Syndicates* [1995] 2 AC 145) to their clients.

13 *Forsikringsaktieselskapet Vesta v Butcher* [1988] 2 All ER 43; affirmed without reference to contributory negligence at [1989] AC 852; *Barclays Bank v Fairclough Building (No 2)* [1995] IRLR 605 (arising out of the litigation discussed in the text below) and *Platform Home Loans v Oyston Shipways* [1998] 4 All ER 252 (reversed with regard to the exact calculation of the reduction in damages at [1999] 1 All ER 833).

14 *Barclays Bank v Fairclough Building Ltd* [1995] 1 All ER 289. In fact D sub-contracted the work to E who in turn employed T. This case involved an action by BB against F; the case of the same name referred to in the note above involved the contract between E and T.

15 *James Pty Ltd v Duncan* [1970] VR 705 (Canada) and *Raflatac v Eade* [1999] 1 Lloyd's Rep 506.

16 Law Commission, *Contributory Negligence as a Defence in Contract*, Report No 219 (1993). In Working Paper No 114 (1990) the Commission had recommended that the 1945 Act should be amended to apply to Category 1 situations as well. The Law Commission were originally influenced by the injustice the present law can cause (eg see *Schering Agrochemicals Ltd v Resibel NV SA*; unreported but discussed in A Burrows, 'Contributory Negligence in Contract: Ammunition for the Law Commission' (1993) 109 Law Quarterly Review 175), but were eventually persuaded that such a reform would create undesirable commercial uncertainty.

# 6 Remoteness

## Introduction[1]

Remoteness rules are a type of 'standard-form' or 'default'[2] provision for the remedy of damages which are to be read into any contract which contains no tailor-made clause on the matter.[3] If the parties have not fixed a 'liquidated damages' or similar clause to specify the remedy for the breach which occurred, the law fills in the gap by providing an all-purpose, standard clause to govern the assessment of compensation. In theory, parties are free to specify the consequences that should follow each potential breach of each of their various promises.[4] In a hypothetical

---

1    For an edited collection of articles discussing the economic and theoretical justification for the remoteness rules see R Craswell and A Schwartz, *Foundations of Contract Law* (1994) pp 22-30, 67-81.

2    The economic justification for so-called default rules in contract has been widely discussed in recent literature. See I Ayres and R Gertner, 'Filling Gaps in Incomplete Contracts: An Economic Theory of Default Rules' (1989) 94 Yale Law Journal 97; I Ayres and R Gertner, 'Strategic Contractual Inefficiency and the Optimal Choice of Legal Rules' (1992) 101 Yale LJ 729; JS Johnston, 'Strategic Bargaining and the Economic Theory of Contract Default Rules' (1990) 100 Yale LJ 615 and RE Scott, 'A Relational Theory of Default Rules for Commercial Contracts' (1990) 19 Journal of Legal Studies 597.

3    The remoteness doctrine is a 'background rule' ie 'it specifies the sanctions that will be applied to any unexcused non-performance'. See R Craswell, 'Contract Law, Default Rules, and the Philosophy of Promising' (1989) 88 Michigan Law Review 489, p 503.

4    In fact the law exhibits what Epstein terms 'an uneasy dualism'. It permits C and D considerable latitude when specifying the primary obligations to be assumed under a contract but considerably restricts their freedom to specify the consequences of breach. See R Epstein, 'Beyond Foreseeability: Consequential Damages in the Law of Contract' (1989) 18 Journal of Legal Studies 105.

'ideal' world where there was full information, complete foresight, and no costs attached to negotiating, there would be no need for the law to provide any rules on remoteness, because each contract would contain a special remedy clause for each contingency. But the transaction costs of negotiating a multitude of such clauses would be infinite and this means that negotiations take place within horizons of bounded rationality.[5] It is much cheaper for most people to leave the remedies to the law, in the expectation that they will seldom be needed because most contracts are fully performed. In this way, the transaction costs over remedies will usually be incurred only after a contract has actually been broken. If, however, the parties do wish to anticipate breach, they enjoy a limited freedom to fix their own remedy.

If the transaction costs could be avoided, it is clear that a special clause would be far superior to any general rule of law, which can be aimed only at the majority of situations and cannot take account of the many variables affecting individual transactions. A negotiated clause on remedies could provide just the optimal mix of variables: the appropriate incentive to perform, the precise allocation of risks according to the different attitudes of the parties to particular risks, plus the level of compensation desired by C for meeting the consequences of the breach. (C may not want a full indemnity against all losses caused by the breach, because D would increase his price in proportion to the risk he was bearing.) The single formulation provided by the law cannot produce optimal results in all situations because there are too many variables.[6]

Most contractual exchanges can be viewed as an agreed allocation of reciprocal risk-taking or a simple form of insurance.[7] D undertakes in respect of each promise the risk that he may not be able to perform his promise – the risk of non-performance – and thus accepts liability for compensating C for his failure to perform. The parties have different abilities to bear a given risk. In normal circumstances, D offers a promise about the future to C when he is better able than C to produce the result which is promised – either he has more skill or experience in producing that result, or he is willing (like an insurance company) to accept the risk of the specified event occurring (which will activate his obligation to pay or to do something). D is in effect saying to C: 'You may rely on me to produce the result which you desire – either I will bring it about, or, if

5   See ch 1 above.
6   And so has been described as an 'untailored default' rule to distinguish it from a 'tailored default' rule which 'attempts to provide a contract's parties with precisely "what they would have contracted for"'. See Ayres and Gertner, 'Strategic Contractual Inefficiency and the Optimal Choice of Legal Rules', above p 88, n 2.
7   See generally PS Atiyah *The Rise and Fall of Freedom of Contract* (rev edn 1985) pp 1-7.

I fail to do so, I will accept responsibility to compensate you for not receiving the benefit of that result.'

But 'accepting the risk of non-performance' needs greater specification when the obligation to compensate actually arises. Which losses are to be taken into account and how is compensation to be assessed? If compensation extended to all consequential losses (and the seller was unable to distinguish high and low loss customers) all purchasers would pay the same price. The low loss customers would effectively be cross-subsidising the high loss ones.[8] In the hypothetical, ideal world the parties would spell out in their contract what losses D is to be liable for, either by fixing an agreed sum to be paid on breach, or by listing the categories of loss for which D is to be liable and fixing a method to quantify those losses in money. But the transaction costs of negotiating such a clause usually preclude this, and most contracts are silent on the point, thus leaving it to the law to fill in the gap with a standard term. This standard term is known as the rule of remoteness of damage. It may be summarised as follows: 'A type or kind of loss is not too remote a consequence of a breach of contract if, at the time of contracting (and on the assumption that the parties actually foresaw a breach of the undertaking in question), it was within their reasonable contemplation as a not unlikely result of that breach.'[9]

The remoteness rule is not usually treated as an implied term in the contract but as a rule of law.[10] Yet the rule is clearly subject to the express intentions of the parties as shown by the terms of their contract. The law is merely providing a formula to make explicit what is implicit in their contract. Putting it in lay terms, we can say that D, merely by making the contractual promise, is implicitly accepting responsibility to compensate C only for the usual or normal consequences of a breach: it is implicit in his promise that he is not accepting responsibility for unusual or abnormal consequences unless the circumstances show that this extra responsibility was intended by the parties. Thus, when there is no indication that D's responsibility extends beyond the usual situation, there is an implicit allocation of risk-taking in any contractual promise: D accepts the risk of liability for the usual losses caused by breach, while C accepts the risk of any unusual losses (in other words, he implicitly agrees not to hold D liable to compensate him for unusual losses). This should be put in terms of the intention of the parties rather than in terms of reasonable contemplation or foreseeability. Although the categories of loss which are reasonably anticipated will often be those for which the parties intend

---

8   GD Quillen, 'Contract Damages and Cross-subsidisation' (1988) 61 Southern California Law Review 1125.

9   *The Heron II* [1969] 1 AC 350.

10   *GKN Centrax Gears Ltd v Matbro Ltd* [1976] 2 Lloyd's Rep 555 and *The Pegase* [1981] 1 Lloyd's Rep 175.

D to be liable, their intention (express or implicit) should be the paramount test: it may sometimes be inferred from the express terms that there was an intention that D should not be liable for a particular loss even though it could have been reasonably anticipated. An exemption clause is a regular method of expressly allocating to C certain risks which, in the absence of such a clause, the law would infer were those implicitly accepted by D.

The test for remoteness has often been explained in terms of encouraging the efficient exchange of information by the parties. The exchange of risk-taking will obviously depend on adequate information being available to the parties. Transaction costs are minimised by assuming that there is no need for the parties to incur the costs of exchanging information about the *usual* risks attaching to each promise. The rule assumes that D is as well placed as C to appreciate the usual risks of losses likely to be caused by breach, and if nothing is said on the point, D is taken to have accepted liability for them. If he is not willing to bear these usual risks, he should contract out of liability by means of an exemption clause which transfers the risks to C. But in regard to unusual risks, D should be safe in assuming that he will not be held liable, unless C informs him about them and he accepts liability for them. This is the justification for the so-called 'second' rule in *Hadley v Baxendale* which places the responsibility on C to disclose information to D about an unusual risk if he intends D to bear that risk. This *incentive*[11] to disclose information which D would otherwise not have is *efficient* in leading to the optimal balance between the need for the exchange of information, and the desire to minimise transaction costs, ie it is an incentive to disclose information *only* when the exchange is necessary.[12] The rules give an incentive to C to disclose relevant information only when he has better access to the information, eg when he knows that breach will cause him

---

11   It has been questioned whether this incentive is always effective (see generally LA Bebchuk and S Shavell, 'Information and the Scope of Liability for Breach of Contract: The Rule of *Hadley v Baxendale*' (1991) 7 Journal Law, Economics and Organisation 284) or necessary (see R Danzig, '*Hadley v Baxendale*: A Study in the Industrialisation of the Law' (1975) 4 Journal of Legal Studies 249, p 281 discussing the situation where D engages in many transactions and so may prefer to 'self-insure' by subsidising occasional larger liability from the profits derived from many other low risk transactions.

12   It may not be efficient to encourage disclosure of the risk of abnormal losses on the part of buyers where the seller is a monopolist supplier. Such disclosure may simply encourage the supplier to increase the price of the goods beyond that justified by the 'insurance' such disclosure effectively purchases. See Ayres and Gertner, 'Strategic Contractual Inefficiency and the Optimal Choice of Legal Rules', above p 88, n 2; Johnson, 'Strategic Bargaining and the Economic Theory of Contract Default Rules', above p 88, n 2 and LE Wolcher, 'Price Discrimination and Inefficient Risk Allocation Under the Rule in *Hadley v Baxendale*' (1989) 12 Research in Law and Economics 9.

some loss which the average person in D's position would not expect to follow breach.[13]

The extent of the risks undertaken by D will clearly affect the price that he charges in the contract, whether the price is in money or by way of counter-promises. The greater the number and the extent of the potential losses for which he assumes responsibility, the higher the price he will charge. A higher than usual price for a particular promise may be a pointer to acceptance of a greater than usual risk-taking by D.[14] The rules on remoteness may operate like exemption clauses in limiting liability, and thus will directly affect the price. (This is one justification for applying the rules at the time of contracting when the 'price' was fixed, and not allowing later information to widen the extent of liability.) One way of applying the remoteness rules would be to ask whether it is reasonable to infer from the contract that C had bought insurance-type protection against the risk of the type of loss in question if it were caused by a breach of contract. It will often be cheaper for C himself to bear the risk of uncertain losses than for him to pay a higher price to D to do so: if the type of loss is unusual and its extent is unpredictable, D might charge too high an 'insurance' premium for bearing it. C is in a better position to assess and control the extent of some losses, and it may therefore be cheaper for him to take responsibility for 'insuring' against them: either he can 'self-insure' by bearing the risk himself, or he can take out insurance with an insurance company. If D does accept responsibility for unusual losses caused by breach, he has the same alternatives of either self-insurance or seeking liability insurance.[15] Acceptance of this extra responsibility would also give D an incentive to take extra care to avoid committing a breach: the more he can control the likelihood of breach, the more likely he is to be better placed to insure the losses.

Let us consider how these factors apply to the classic case of *Hadley v Baxendale*.[16] C's mill was brought to a standstill by the breakage of his

---

13   In technical language the rules are designed to avoid problems of 'adverse selection' referring to the situation where insurance is sought in the main by high-risk parties. The so-called first rule provides sufficient insurance for low risk insureds while the second rule encourages high-risk assureds to reveal themselves as such. See W Bishop, 'The Contract-Tort Boundary and the Economics of Insurance' (1983) 14 Journal of Legal Studies 299.

14   A high contract price may, for similar reasons, justify the conclusion that an exemption clause is unreasonable. See Unfair Contract Terms Act 1977, Sch 2(b).

15   There would be a 'moral hazard' problem if D sought insurance protection against the consequences of a voluntary breach of contract.

16   (1854) 9 Exch 341. See further AWB Simpson, 'Innovation in Nineteenth Century Contract Law' (1975) 91 Law Quarterly Review 247, p 273; D Pugsley, 'The Facts of *Hadley v Baxendale*' (1976) 126 New Law Journal 420 and Danzig, '*Hadley v Baxendale*: A Study in the Industrialisation of the Law', above p 91, n 11.

only crankshaft. D, a carrier, failed to deliver the broken shaft to the manufacturer at the time he had promised to do so (it was needed as the pattern for a new one), and C sued to recover the profits he would have made had the mill been started again without the extra delay. The court rejected the claim on the ground that the facts known to D were insufficient to 'show reasonably that the profits of the mill must be stopped by an unreasonable delay in the delivery of the broken shaft by the carrier to the third person'.[17] (C might have had a spare shaft; D was not told that delay would keep the mill idle.)

The court had to decide whether the risk of loss of profits caused by delay in transporting the shaft should be borne by the mill-owner or the carrier. It has already been argued that, in the absence of an express clause, the answer should depend on the implicit intention of the parties, as revealed by the terms of the contract interpreted in the light of the parties' knowledge at the time of contracting. The court should look at the consequences of either interpretation. If, without being alerted to the risk, the carrier were held to have assumed liability for this type of loss, the cost would ultimately have to be borne by all his customers in the form of some increase in freight costs. Would it be fair on ordinary customers to produce this result, or should the cost fall on the individual customer, the mill-owner? If the carrier were held liable, it would give carriers in general an incentive to obtain more detailed information about the purpose of transporting the goods, so that they could take extra care when there was a risk of loss of profits or refuse to carry the goods at the normal freight charge. Would it be efficient to put the onus on carriers to seek this information in *all* cases? If, on the other hand, the carrier were held not to have accepted this type of risk, the mill-owner would bear the loss himself unless he took steps to cover himself: he could do this either by notifying the carrier of the risk and getting him to accept responsibility for it, or by obtaining from an insurer some insurance protection against the risk. The court, if it were using economic perspectives, might well conclude that transaction costs in society as a whole would be minimised if the initiative to deal with this type of unusual loss were left to the customer, who, after all, is in the best position to know of the risk and to choose the cheapest method of guarding against it.

The remoteness rules are not the only legal rules putting boundaries to the risks undertaken by D. Other risks are (in theory at least) removed from him by the doctrines of common mistake and frustration,[18] by the court's discretion to refuse specific relief (or to refuse to assess damages at the cost of getting a third party to complete performance), and, ultimately, by the law on bankruptcy, which operates to release D (at least

17  *Hadley v Baxendale*, loc cit at 355.
18  See pp 241-254 below.

partially) in the event of his insolvency. All these rules place limitations on the enforcement of a contractual undertaking, and so restrict the risks undertaken by D.

## The detailed legal rules on remoteness

The main proposition in *Hadley v Baxendale* was laid down by Alderson B:

> Where two parties have made a contract which one of them has broken, the damages which the other party ought to receive in respect of such breach of contract should be such as may fairly and reasonably be considered either as arising naturally, ie according to the usual course of things, from such breach of contract itself, or such as may reasonably be supposed to have been in the contemplation of both parties, at the time they made the contract, as the probable result of the breach of it.[19]

This proposition has been re-examined several times by the Court of Appeal[20] but a major reinterpretation came in the House of Lords in 1967 in *The Heron II*.[1] Although their Lordships did not agree upon a common formula, their slightly differing formulations of the principle for remoteness of damage are still based on *Hadley v Baxendale*. Lord Reid said that Alderson B: 'clearly meant that a result which will happen in the great majority of cases should fairly and reasonably be regarded as having been in the contemplation of the parties, but that a result which, though foreseeable as a substantial possibility, would only happen in a small minority of cases should not be regarded as having been in their contemplation'.[2] Lord Reid continued: 'The crucial question is whether, on the information available to the defendant when the contract was made, he should, or the reasonable man in his position would, have realised that such loss was sufficiently likely to result from the breach of contract to make it proper to hold that the loss flowed naturally from the breach or that loss of that kind should have been within his contemplation.'[3] Lord Upjohn stated 'the broad rule as follows: What was in the assumed contemplation of both parties acting as reasonable men in the light of the

---

19   *Hadley v Baxendale*, above p 92, n 16 at 354.
20   *Victoria Laundry (Windsor) Ltd v Newman Industries Ltd* [1949] 2 KB 528 and *Parsons (H) (Livestock) Ltd v Uttley, Ingham & Co Ltd* [1978] QB 791.
1     *Koufos v C Czarnikow Ltd* [1969] 1 AC 350, noted by M Pickering, 'The Remoteness of Damages in Contract' (1968) 31 Modern Law Review 203.
2     *The Heron II*, above p 90, n 9 at 384.
3     Ibid at 385.

general or special facts (as the case may be) known to both parties in regard to damages as the result of a breach of contract.'[4]

Several features of the *Heron II* formulation should be noted. Firstly, in the *Heron II* the test for remoteness in contract is formulated in terms of the 'reasonable contemplation' as opposed to the reasonable foresight (the term used in the test of remoteness in tort) of the parties, even though 'contemplation' and 'foresight' appear to be synonyms. Secondly, the reasonable contemplation test does not apply to the breach itself. It is irrelevant that D could not contemplate, at the time the contract was made, the occurrence of the particular breach he would later commit; the test of remoteness *assumes* contemplation of a breach of the undertaking in question and looks at the consequences of the breach.[5] Thirdly, the test applies only to the *type* or *kind* of loss.[6] The test does not require the parties to contemplate 'the precise detail of the damage or the precise manner of its happening'.[7] If reasonable parties would have contemplated a particular type of loss, they need not have in mind the extent of that loss[8] (except in the case of loss of profits where the normally expected amount of loss places a ceiling on recovery). Thus where D could reasonably contemplate that a breach of contract might cause C's pigs to fall ill, he was liable for their loss through death even though the reasonable man could not contemplate the rare disease they suffered from.[9] The power to categorise losses into general types gives judges considerable discretion in applying the remoteness test. As the cases discussed below will illustrate, broad categories have been used, such as loss of profits; physical damage to a chattel (or building); illness or death of a person; illness or death of an animal; expenses incurred by C in reliance on the contract; or damages and costs paid by C to a third party as a result of D's breach of contract leading to C being held liable to the third party.

Fourthly, in *The Heron II* their Lordships discussed the degree of likelihood that the test requires to be satisfied before the type of loss in question can fall within the reasonable contemplation of the parties. Lord Reid used 'the words "not unlikely" as denoting a degree of probability considerably less than an even chance but nevertheless not very unusual and easily foreseeable'.[10] The phrases supported by at least two of their Lordships were 'not unlikely to occur'; 'liable to result'; 'a real danger';

---

4   Ibid at 424.
5   *Victoria Laundry (Windsor) Ltd v Newman Industries*, above p 94, n 20 at 540.
6   *Wroth v Tyler* [1974] Ch 30.
7   *Christopher Hill Ltd v Ashington Piggeries Ltd* [1969] 3 All ER 1496 at 1524. For the HL decision, which was on other grounds, see [1972] AC 441.
8   *Parsons (H) (Livestock) Ltd v Uttley, Ingham & Co Ltd*, above p 94, n 20.
9   Ibid.
10  [1969] 1 AC 350 at 383. Lord Morris at 406 also used 'not unlikely to occur'.

and 'a serious possibility'.[11] (These phrases require a higher degree of probability than does the corresponding test for remoteness in tort.)[12]

It is crucial to know which facts the court is entitled to use in applying the test. The usual application is based on the *imputed* knowledge of D. What would the reasonable man in D's position have known about the circumstances surrounding the contract and its contemplated performance in ordinary conditions? D's knowledge of the type of business conducted by C is often used to impute to D knowledge of the consequences of a breach. 'As reasonable businessmen, each must be taken to understand the ordinary practices and exigencies of the other's trade or business.'[13] For instance, the parties will be taken to know of the risk that the supply and demand for a given commodity may after the date of the contract, and that this may lead to changes in the market price. In *The Heron II* itself[14] D's ship carried a cargo of sugar for C to a foreign port. Although D did not actually know of C's intention, C intended to sell the cargo as soon as it reached the port. But D did know that there was a market for sugar at the port, and the reasonable shipowner with this knowledge could have contemplated that it was not unlikely that on arrival the cargo would be sold in the market at the then current market price. D broke his contract by making a deviation en route, and the ship reached the port nine days later. During the delay the market price of sugar fell. The House of Lords held that C's damages should be calculated by reference to the low market price prevailing on the actual date of arrival. The type of loss was within the contemplation of reasonable parties to this contract, and the risk that it would be caused by late arrival of the ship satisfied the relevant degree of probability ('not unlikely' and the other phrases referred to above). In contrast it was not possible to impute to a supplier of electricity knowledge that disruption of the supply to a concrete production works would render necessary the demolition of existing work on a major structure because of the need for a 'continuous pour' of cement.[15]

Imputed knowledge will normally be at least as great as D's actual knowledge. C will assume the burden of proving D's actual knowledge only where imputed knowledge would be an insufficient basis for contemplating a particular category of loss.

If the loss is exceptional in its type (or, in the case of loss of profits, its extent), the question of D's liability for it can arise only when he had, at the time of contracting, actual knowledge of the special circumstances which made that loss a not unlikely consequence of the breach in question.

11   Four rejected the colloquialism 'on the cards'.
12   See ch 20 below.
13   *Monarch Steamship Co Ltd v A/B Karlshamns Oljefabriker* [1949] AC 196 at 224.
14   [1969] 1 AC 350.
15   *Balfour Beatty Construction (Scotland) Ltd v Scottish Power* (1994) 71 BLR 20.

(The formulation in *Hadley v Baxendale* was that 'if the special circumstances under which the contract was actually made were communicated by the plaintiffs to the defendants, and thus known to both parties, the damages resulting from the breach of such a contract, which they would reasonably contemplate, would be the amount of injury which would ordinarily follow from a breach of contract under these special circumstances so known and communicated'.)[16] When D is shown to have actual knowledge of special facts, it is sufficient if the reasonable man in D's position with this knowledge would have realised that the type of loss in question was a 'not unlikely' consequence of breach. But liability depends on more than realisation of this risk. The test is whether the reasonable man in D's position would have realised that, by making the promise in these special circumstances, he was *assuming responsibility* for the risk of causing this unusual type of loss. It would make the test too stringent to say that there must be an implied *term* in the contract that D will be responsible for that loss.[17] But, on the other hand, mere knowledge or 'communication'[18] of the special circumstances is not sufficient, because in some situations the reasonable man in D's shoes would not have understood that, simply by making the promise in those special circumstances, he would be taken to assume the risk that his breach might cause that unusual loss.[19] (*A fortiori* if D made it clear to C that he was not willing to accept the risk of that loss.) Indications of the implicit assumption of responsibility[20] would come from D's adjustment of the proposed price, or from his adding some provision to the contract to deal with the risk, such as a clause restricting C's remedy or one which in specified circumstances excused D's non-performance.

D's silence alone may not indicate his willingness to accept the risk: if I tell my taxi driver that I will miss the opportunity of making a profit of £1 million if I fail to reach an appointment on time, his acceptance of me as a passenger should not lead to the inference that he accepts the risk. As we have seen, the economic justification for the rule is that C is likely to have better information about the risk of unusual losses arising from D's breach and that it will reduce transaction costs if D can assume that, unless C actually informs him to the contrary, there are no special circumstances affecting the loss which is likely to result from his breach.

16  *Hadley v Baxendale*, above p 92, n 16 at 355. The poorly reported facts suggested that there was actual communication: Pugsley, 'The Facts of *Hadley v Baxendale*', above p 92, n 16.
17  As was said in *British Columbia Saw Mill Co Ltd v Nettleship* (1868) LR 3 CP 499 at 509.
18  *Hadley v Baxendale*, above p 92, n 16 at 354.
19  *The Heron II*, above p 90, n 9 at 421–2 and *Satef-Huttenes Albertus SpA v Paloma Tercera Shipping Co SA* [1981] 1 Lloyd's Rep 175 at 183–184.
20  'An "implied" undertaking ... to bear it': *Robophone Facilities Ltd v Blank* [1966] 1 WLR 1428 at 1448.

## Illustrations of the remoteness test

Since many of the reported cases deal with contracts between businessmen, it is not surprising that often the disputed issue on remoteness concerns the loss of profits. The cases can conveniently be divided into categories.

### Delayed delivery of a profit-earning chattel

The contrast between actual and imputed knowledge is illustrated by the leading case of *Victoria Laundry*,[1] which concerned the late delivery of a profit-earning machine. The buyer claimed the loss of profits that he would have made in the period between the due date for delivery and the actual date. C was a launderer and dyer who wished to expand his business by installing a larger boiler. D was the engineer who agreed to provide the boiler. As the result of a mishap the machine was damaged while it was being dismantled for delivery, and it was actually delivered to C five months late. C claimed as damages for the delay his loss of profits in respect of (1) the large number of new customers he could have taken on had the boiler been installed on the due date; and (2) the amount which he could have earned under special 'highly lucrative' dyeing contracts with the Ministry of Supply. D knew that C was a launderer and that he wanted the boiler for immediate use.[2] The Court of Appeal held that with such knowledge the reasonable man in D's position could have foreseen that delay in delivery would lead to some loss of business (and therefore loss of profits). But he would not have foreseen the loss of profits under the special contracts, since these were special circumstances not within D's actual knowledge. Hence C could not recover the full loss he had incurred under these contracts, but only the normal loss of profits he would have made under the normal type of dyeing and laundering contracts. C had actually lost profits, and loss of profits was a category of loss that satisfied the reasonable contemplation test. Other examples of knowledge being imputed to sellers on the basis of the obvious profit earning nature of the chattel being sold have involved ships[3] or their essential parts.[4]

C's intention to put equipment supplied by D to some exceptional use must be known to D before he can be held liable for loss of profits arising

---

1   *Victoria Laundry (Windsor) Ltd v Newman Industries Ltd* above p 94, n 20.
2   A carrier (as in *Hadley v Baxendale*) usually knows less about the purpose for which the consignee needs the goods than a seller knows about the buyer's purpose.
3   *Fletcher v Tayleur* (1855) 17 CB 21.
4   *Wilson v General Iron Screw Colliery Co* (1877) 47 LJQB 239 (propeller) and *Saint Line v Richardsons, Westgarth & Co* [1940] 2 KB 99 (engine).

from that intended use. In one case[5] C, a coal merchant, bought the hull of a floating boom derrick from D, who finally delivered it six months later. The normal use of the hull would have been as a coal store, but C (unknown to D) intended to use it for a new method of transferring coal from colliers to barges. C did not claim as damages his loss of the profits which he would have made from his intended use, but only the smaller loss of profits which he would have suffered had he intended to use the hull as a coal store. D claimed that C's damages should be nominal because he had not actually suffered any loss from the expected normal use. But the court rejected this defence and awarded the amount claimed by C. Loss of profits was the contemplated *type* of loss, and C had in fact lost profits; the amount expected from normal use simply placed a *ceiling* on his recovery. Had D been told of C's intended use, and realised, as a reasonable man, that he was undertaking responsibility for the risk of the loss of higher-than-usual profits, he would have been able to demand a higher price from C, or to cover himself with an exemption.

### The seller's loss of profits in contracts for the sale of goods

Recovery of lost profits when buyer D refuses to accept the goods sold to him by dealer C will depend on the state of the market. If the supply of the goods in question exceeds the demand, so that C can satisfy every customer he can find, C can recover his loss of profits on the sale to D: any other customer whom C finds is an *additional* one, to whom C could have sold a further item, on which he would have made a further profit, even if D had performed the first contract (it is a 'lost volume' case).[6] But if the goods are scarce (demand exceeds the supply), and C finds a second buyer following D's default under the first contract, C makes the same profit through the second contract as he would have made through the first one: C may therefore recover only nominal damages from D.[7] If D had performed the first contract, C could not have made a second profit, since he had only one item to sell. When C is not a dealer, the situation is more obvious. If I have a second-hand car that you agree to buy for £1,000 but later refuse to accept and pay for, I may be able to find a substitute buyer who will also pay £1,000 for it. The damages that I could recover from you will be restricted to any extra expenses I may have incurred in making the substitute sale.

---

5  *Cory v Thames Ironworks Co* (1868) LR 3 QB 181.
6  *Thompson (WL) Ltd v Robinson (Gunmakers) Ltd* [1955] Ch 177.
7  *Charter v Sullivan* [1957] 2 QB 117.

## The buyer's loss of profits under a contract of sale

Where C buys goods from D, who fails to deliver them, C's damages depend on whether there is an 'available market' for the goods.[8] The basic concept is the immediate availability of buyers and sellers and their ready capacity to supply or absorb the goods in question: since C is a disappointed buyer, the relevant question is the availability of substitute sellers. (If C were a disappointed seller, the relevant question would be the availability of substitute buyers.) So the normal measure of damages when D fails to deliver the goods is the difference between (a) the market price of the relevant goods at the time and place fixed for delivery and (b) the contract price.[9] One of the justifications for this measure of damages derives from the doctrine of mitigation, since the rule assumes that the reasonable buyer should have gone into the market, immediately following the seller's breach of contract, and bought substitute goods. With the amount of money designated by the difference between the two prices, C should be in the same financial position as he would have been in if D had performed his contractual obligation to deliver.[10] C is not entitled to claim for any loss of profits, since he could have avoided any loss by buying substitute goods in the market immediately following D's breach.

The situation is very different where there is no available market for the goods that D failed to deliver (as in the case where D was to manufacture them especially for C). Here C may well suffer a loss of profits. His damages will be assessed under the general remoteness rules.[11] The assessment must be made on the basis of the value of the contract goods at the time and place of the breach which may be ascertained by any relevant evidence, such as the cost of the nearest equivalent, or a resale price, or the profits which the buyer would have made had he acquired the goods and manufactured them into other articles, as the seller knew that he intended to do.[12]

---

8   The same concept is used in assessing a seller's damages: Sale of Goods Act 1979, s 50(3).
9   Sale of Goods Act 1979, s 51(3). The subsection assumes that the buyer has not previously paid the price to the seller: if he has, the damages must also cover the price.
10   The purpose for which the buyer wanted the goods is normally irrelevant: hence, where the buyer is a non-profit-making organization the ordinary rule still applies: *Diamond Cutting Works Federation Ltd v Triefus & Co Ltd* [1956] 1 Lloyd's Rep 216 at 227.
11   S 51(2) of the Act follows *Hadley v Baxendale*: 'The measure of damages is the estimated loss directly and naturally resulting, in the ordinary course of events, from the seller's breach of contract.'
12   *Leavey (J) & Co Ltd v George H Hirst & Co Ltd* [1944] KB 24 at 29.

Where there is an available market for the goods in question, C's damages for D's failure to deliver are not affected by the fact that C had resold the goods – he could have bought substitutes to fulfil the sub-sale. But where C has resold to a sub-buyer the very same goods that he bought from D, D's failure to deliver will obviously cause C to be in breach under the sub-sale. C can recover damages for his loss of profits under the sub-sale only where D should have contemplated, at the time the first contract was made, both that C was (or was probably) buying for resale, and that C could perform his obligations under a contract of resale only by delivering the same goods.[13] (C may also recover from D damages for his loss incurred by being held liable in damages and costs to his sub-buyer.)[14]

Where D sells land to C, but fails to convey it to him, C may claim the loss of profit which he intended to make from a particular use of the land (eg by converting a building into flats and offices) only if D had actual or imputed knowledge of special circumstances showing that C intended to use the land in that way.[15]

*Profits lost through the defective quality of the goods*

D's breach of the contract of sale may arise from the defective quality of the goods. Where D sold defective seed to farmer C, he was liable for the loss of profits that C expected to make on the crop.[16] Where D knew that C intended to resell the goods, and ought reasonably to have contemplated that a breach of his undertaking as to the description or condition of the goods would be not unlikely to cause C to lose the profit he hoped to make under the sub-sale, C may recover damages in respect of such a loss of profits caused by a breach of D's undertaking.[17] It makes no difference that the goods sold were to be altered by C before onward sale so long as the conversion was in a manner contemplated by both parties.[18] Similarly, D's breach may cause C to suffer a loss of general custom. If, at the time of contracting, it was within the reasonable contemplation of the parties that defects in the goods supplied by D might lead to sub-buyers (C's

13  *Re R & H Hall Ltd & W H Pim Jnr & Co's Arbitration* [1928] All ER Rep 763, HL. The terms of the resale must be reasonable and usual: ibid.
14  Ibid at 767, 769.
15  *Diamond v Campbell-Jones* [1961] Ch 22 and *Cottrill v Steyning and Littlehampton Building Society* [1966] 1 WLR 753.
16  *George Mitchell (Chesterhall) Ltd v Finney Lock Seeds Ltd* [1983] 2 AC 803.
17  *Molling & Co v Dean & Son Ltd* (1901) 18 TLR 217 at 218.
18  *Bence Graphics International Ltd v Fasson UK Ltd* [1997] 1 All ER 979.

customers) withdrawing their custom from C, damages may be awarded for loss of profits on 'repeat orders' from the sub-buyers.[19]

When D sells a profit-earning machine to C he may undertake that it will perform in a specified manner or at a specified rate. If the machine fails to perform in accordance with the undertaking, C may claim damages for the resulting loss of profits. In the *Cullinane* case,[20] D sold a clay-pulverising machine to C and warranted that it had a certain productive capacity, but the machine failed to achieve this. The Court of Appeal held that C was entitled to recover his net loss (ie after deducting from his expected gross profits or gross receipts the necessary expenditure in earning it) of profits during the normal commercial life of the machine. 'The plant having been supplied in contemplation by both parties that it should be used by the plaintiff in the commercial production of pulverised clay, the case is one in which the plaintiff can claim as damages for the breach of warranty the loss of the profit he can show that he would have made if the plant had been as warranted.'[7] But the mitigation rules may apply. For a period after delivery it may be reasonable for C to use the machine to see if it meets the warranty, but as soon as a reasonable buyer would have replaced the defective machine with one which functioned properly or efficiently, or simply stopped using it, C should not be entitled to claim for any further loss of profits.[1]

### Types of physical damage

If it was in the reasonable contemplation of the parties, at the time of making a contract of sale, that the seller's breach of his contractual undertaking as to the quality or description of the goods was not unlikely to cause physical injury to the buyer's person or his property, the buyer may recover damages for the injury so caused. Thus, where defective food was sold for human consumption, the buyer recovered damages for his illness caused by its unsuitable condition.[2] Where the buyer of woollen underwear contracted dermatitis through its defective condition he recovered damages for personal injuries from the retailers.[3] Damages for

19    *GKN Centrax Gears Ltd v Matbro Ltd* [1976] 2 Lloyd's Rep 555 at 573–4, 577, 579–580.
20    *Cullinane v British Rema Manufacturing Co Ltd* [1954] 1 QB 292.
1    The *British Westinghouse* case [1912] AC 673 and *Cullinane v British Rema Manufacturing Co Ltd* above, n 20, 314, 316.
2    *Wren v Holt* [1903] 1 KB 610. If the remoteness test is satisfied, C may be able to recover his expenses incurred when a member of his family suffered injury from eating the defective food: *Priest v Last* [1903] 2 KB 148 and *Jackson v Watson & Sons* [1909] 2 KB 193.
3    *Grant v Australian Knitting Mills Ltd* [1936] AC 85.

personal injury or death caused by breach of contract may include compensation for pain, suffering and loss of amenity, as well as loss of earnings, which are normal heads of damages in the assessment of damages in tort for such injuries.[4] Where D's breach of contract causes physical inconvenience to C damages may be recovered.[5] However despite their description as physical such damages compensate C for the non-pecuniary consequences of the disturbance and so are analogous to damages for distress, disappointment and loss of enjoyment considered below in ch 30.

The remoteness test may also permit the buyer C to recover damages in respect of other property of his which was damaged as the result of the seller D's breach of contract.[6] So where D installed a defective heating system in C's factory, which caught fire through the defect, the replacement cost of a new factory was held to be the measure of C's damages.[7] Similarly, where a game farmer bought compounded meal for feeding to his pheasants and many chicks died and others grew up stunted because the meal contained a toxic substance, he recovered damages for the loss of the birds and the reduced value of the survivors.[8] It is not necessary that the reasonable man in D's position should anticipate the details of the actual consequences of the breach: it is sufficient that the general type of consequence was within reasonable contemplation. In *Parsons (H) (Livestock) Ltd v Uttley, Ingham & Co Ltd*,[9] D supplied C with a hopper for storing pig food. Through a defect in the installation, the pig nuts in the hopper went mouldy because of inadequate ventilation and C's pigs died from a rare disease. It was, however, within reasonable contemplation that defective installation of the hopper might cause its contents to deteriorate, which in turn might cause C's pigs to become ill, and this degree of foresight satisfied the test.

---

4   There may often be concurrent liability in tort, but the advantage in suing in contract is that C may not have to prove D's negligence. See ch 29 below.
5   *Watts v Morrow* [1991] 1 WLR 1421 (£4000 damages for C's inconvenience suffered while repairs effected to holiday home bought in reliance upon D's negligent survey) and *Patel v Hooper & Jackson* [1999] 1 WLR 1792 (£2000 damages awarded for discomfort of living in rented accommodation following purchase of uninhabitable property in reliance on negligent survey).
6   C must show that his use of the goods fell within *one* of the categories of use which meet the reasonable contemplation test: *Henry Kendall & Sons v William Lillico & Sons Ltd* [1969] 2 AC 31.
7   *Harbutt's 'Plasticine' Ltd v Wayne Tank and Pump Co Ltd* [1970] 1 QB 447. (The decision has been overruled on another point: *Photo Productions Ltd v Securicor Transport Ltd* [1980] AC 827.)
8   *Henry Kendall & Sons v William Lillico & Sons Ltd*, above, n 6.
9   [1978] QB 791.

## Distress, disappointment and loss of enjoyment

It is obvious that in many cases a breach of contract will cause distress and disappointment to C, and in some cases when a good which was to be enjoyed by a consumer is lost or spoilt by the breach, that enjoyment will be lost or impaired. Though the position is currently a matter of some uncertainty, these losses have normally been considered too remote in contract, and damages which compensate for any of them are exceptional. The award of such damages will be considered in the context of the discussion of exemplary damages in chapter 30 below.

## Special case: failure to pay money

There are some special situations where the normal remoteness rules are ousted. D's failure to pay C an agreed sum of money on the due date may cause C foreseeable loss when he is not sufficiently creditworthy to be able to borrow elsewhere. But the courts maintain their refusal to award C any general damages for that loss. The agreed sum is recoverable as a debt; interest may be awarded for the period of delay in C's receiving it; and *special* damages may be awarded if C has suffered a particular loss which is not too remote a consequence of D's failure. But it is only in certain exceptional situations that C may recover general damages: eg if D, a bank, fails to pay its customer C's cheque, C may recover general damages for the injury to his credit.[10] Again, if D's failure to pay on time justifies C in terminating the contract, C may recover general damages for loss he suffers.[11]

## The time for assessing damages

Since prices are not constant, it is often important to know the point of time at which C's loss or his costs should be assessed.[12] The general rule is that C's damages should be assessed as at the date of D's breach, which is the date when the cause of action arose.[13] This rule applies where there is a market in which C can readily obtain substitute performance from a third party: if C suffers further loss after this date it is due to his own failure to mitigate. But the House of Lords has denied that breach-date assessment is an absolute rule: 'if to follow it would give rise to injustice, the court

---

10  *Kpohraror v Woolwich Building Society* [1996] 4 All ER 119, abandoning the previous restriction to 'traders'.
11  *Yeoman Credit Ltd v Waragowski* [1961] 1 WLR 1124.
12  SM Waddams, 'The Date for the Assessment of Damages' (1981) 97 Law Quarterly Review 445.
13  *Miliangos v George Frank (Textiles) Ltd* [1976] AC 443 at 468.

has power to fix such other date as may be appropriate in the circumstances'.[14] In the case in which this was said, C had reasonably continued to treat a contract for the sale of land to him as still in force after D had failed to convey the land to him. At first C tried to get specific performance, and it was only at a later date, when D failed to comply with the order, that C terminated the contract on the ground of D's breach and sought damages as his remedy: this was the time when the contract was 'lost', and when C's damages should be assessed. C therefore benefited from the inflation in the value of the land up to that time: any further delay in his receiving compensation should be met by the award of interest. The time for assessment could also be fixed at the time when D's performance became impossible; or at the time when it was reasonable for C to have discovered that D's work was defective[15] and for C to have incurred the cost of repairs or reinstatement.[16] In some cases, it may be reasonable for C to delay getting remedial work done so long as there is a reasonable chance that D will cure the defect.[17]

If C did not learn of D's breach at the time it occurred, his damages will usually be assessed as at the time when he should reasonably have discovered the breach, and was reasonably able[18] to act on that knowledge (as by mitigating). When D delivered sealed packages to C, knowing that they would not be examined until they reached the sub-buyer to whom C intended to send them, the date for taking the market price (in C's claim for damages on the ground that the goods were defective) was the date when the sub-buyer examined them.[19] Even after C learns of the breach, he may have 'a reasonable time to consider his position'[20] if the circumstances justify it.

The courts will not take any account of a fall in the domestic purchasing power of the pound sterling between the date when C's loss is assessed

14  *Johnson v Agnew* [1980] AC 367 at 401.
15  *East Ham Corpn v Bernard Sunley & Sons Ltd* [1966] AC 406.
16  *Dodd Properties (Kent) Ltd v Canterbury City Council* [1980] 1 WLR 433 and *Alcoa Minerals of Jamaica Inc v Broderick* [2000] 3 WLR 23, PC (tort case). See IN Duncan Wallace, 'Cost of Repair and Inflation' (1980) 96 Law Quarterly Review 101; IN Duncan Wallace, 'Cost of Repairs: Date of Assessment' (1980) 96 *Law* Quarterly Review 341; IN Duncan Wallace, 'Inflation and Assessment of Construction Cost Damages' (1982) 98 Law Quarterly Review 406; Waddams, 'The Date for the Assessment of Damages' and SM Waddams, 'Inflation and Mitigation of Damages' (1980) 1 Oxford Journal Legal Studies 134.
17  *Radford v de Froberville* [1977] 1 WLR 1262, discussed at pp 210-211 below.
18  If there is a rising market, D may know that C lacks the financial ability to buy a substitute, which may justify him in not attempting to do so: *Wroth v Tyler* [1974] Ch 30.
19  *Van den Hurck v Martens (R) & Co Ltd* [1920] 1 KB 850.
20  *Sharpe (C) & Co v Nosawa* [1917] 2 KB 814 at 821.

and the date of judgment.[1] For domestic[2] purposes, sterling is treated as constant in value, but the award of interest on any debt or damages will largely compensate C for the loss of domestic purchasing power because the market rate of interest will reflect current expectations of this loss in future. When the date for assessing C's damages is postponed for some time after the date of D's breach, C is protected against inflation until the date of the assessment. He should therefore not be awarded interest at the full market rate for any earlier period.[3]

## Anticipatory breach

Where D repudiates his liability under the contract before his performance is due, C has (subject to certain limitations) a choice: he may either accept the repudiation as a breach and immediately sue for damages, or he may refuse to accept the repudiation, affirm the contract, and continue to treat D as bound by his contractual obligations.[4] If C elects the second alternative, the contract continues to bind both parties and D will commit a breach only if he fails to perform at the due date;[5] the rules on mitigation will apply to C only from that date, and his damages will be assessed by reference to the normal rules about the time of the assessment. The law on the sale of goods illustrates the first alternative. When C treats the repudiation as an immediate breach of contract, the relevant date for taking the market price is, prima facie, and subject to the rules on mitigation, the due date for delivery.[6] If C's claim is heard before the date for delivery arrives, the court must attempt to estimate what the market price is likely to be at that date. But the rules on mitigation apply as soon as C accepts the repudiation: D may prove that C should then have taken reasonable steps to buy or sell in the market.[7] The market price is then taken at the

1   *Philips v Ward* [1956] 1 WLR 471. For this reason, the courts have upheld clauses indexing debts to the value of gold, to a foreign currency, or to a price index.
2   In relation to a foreign currency, sterling has a fluctuating exchange value: *Miliangos v George Frank (Textiles) Ltd*, above p 104, n 13.
3   *Dodd Properties (Kent) Ltd v Canterbury City Council*, above p 105, n 16, (a tort case), discussed in Waddams, 'The Date for the Assessment of Damages', pp 454–455 and J Swan, 'Damages, Specific Performance, Inflation and Interest' (1980) 10 Real Property Reports 267.
4   The issues raised by C's choice are considered at length in ch 11 below.
5   *Tai Hing Cotton Mill Ltd v Kamsing Knitting Factory* [1979] AC 91 at 104.
6   *Garnac Grain Co Inc v HMF Faure and Fairclough Ltd and Bunge Corpn* [1968] AC 1130 at 1140; *Frost v Knight* (1872) LR 7 Exch 111 at 113 and *Roper v Johnson* (1873) LR 8 CC 167.
7   *Roth & Co v Taysen Townsend & Co* (1895) 73 LT 628 at 629–30 (affirmed (1896) 12 TLR 211 at 212).

time when C ought reasonably to have gone into the market for a substitute.[8]

If C accepts D's anticipatory breach and terminates the contract, his damages will be assessed on the basis of D's minimum obligation. Hence, if D himself had an option to terminate the contract, it will be assumed that he would have exercised that option so as to reduce the extent of his liability towards C.[9]

## Interest and special damages for late payment

At common law, interest was payable on a debt only if the contract provided for it; interest could not be awarded by way of *general* damages simply because payment of the debt had been delayed.[10] Now by statute,[11] the court may include simple interest in its judgment[12] for any debt or damages.[13] The court has a discretion to fix the rate of interest, to decide whether the interest should run on all or part of the sum, and for all or any part of the time between the cause of action arising and the date of judgment.[14] The court may also award interest if the debt is paid before judgment but after proceedings for its recovery were instituted, and the same applies to payment of damages for breach of contract prior to the hearing.[15] A recent extension[16] introduced a statutory right to interest[17] for the late payment of commercial debts. It applies to contracts for the supply of goods or services where the purchaser and supplier are each acting in the course of a business. Where D's breach of contract deprived C of the opportunity to put the money to work, the court will regularly use its statutory power to award interest at the current commercial rate at which C would have had to borrow the amount. The common law rules on remoteness of damage may also permit the award of *special* damages

8   *Melachrino v Nickoll and Knight* [1920] 1 KB 693 at 697, 699. If, however, the buyer accepts the anticipatory repudiation, but does not mitigate by then repurchasing in the market, his damages will be assessed at the price prevailing at the due date, if that happens to be lower than the price at the time he ought to have repurchased: ibid at 698.

9   *The Mihalis Angelos* [1971] 1 QB 164.

10  *President of India v La Pintada Compania Navigacion SA* [1985] AC 104.

11  S 35 of the Supreme Court At 1981. (The county court and arbitrators have similar powers.) The claim for interest must be specifically pleaded.

12  A judgment debt in the High Court carries interest at a rate fixed from time to time by delegated legislation.

13  Any terms of the contract providing for the payment of interest will prevail over the statutory rules.

14  Or (in the case of any sum paid before judgment) the date of payment.

15  *Edmunds v Lloyd Italico* [1986] 2 All ER 249.

16  Late Payment of Commercial Debts (Interest) Act 1998.

17  Set generously (ie for creditors) at 8% over base rate.

for interest actually incurred by C where it was within the reasonable contemplation of the parties that, as a result of D's failure to pay money when it was due, C would incur interest charges in obtaining finance from another source.[18]

Special rules apply to interest on damages for personal injuries.[19]

---

18  *Wadsworth v Lydall* [1981] 1 WLR 598, approved by HL in *The President of India* case, above p 107, n 10.
19  See chs 22-23 below.

# 7 Mitigation

## Incentives on D not to perform

The doctrine of mitigation should be seen as one of the incentives to breach (or disincentives to perform) provided by the law, which D will weigh against the incentives to perform when he is deciding whether or not to perform. The doctrine is inextricably linked with the basic measures of recovery.[1] It is also closely associated with the idea of efficient breach of contract which we have used in this book to organise our explanation of our remedies rules.[2] It must be recalled that a breach is efficient when it minimises loss as well as when it maximises gain. Mitigation is central to the efficiency gain in both cases. If C did not, in effect, co-operate with D in dealing with the consequences of breach by mitigating those consequences, efficient breach would not be possible (in most circumstances). Though mitigation therefore is of the first importance at doctrinal, theoretical and practical levels, the relative lack of case law on the topic might be thought to suggest the contrary. The paucity of case law is mainly attributable to the deference of appellate tribunals to the findings of trial judges.[3] In several cases mitigation has been said to involve a question of fact[4] and appeal courts will rarely interfere with the judge's primary findings of fact.

---

1 See the explanation of the doctrine in *Radford v de Froberville* [1978] 1 All ER 33, 44 per Oliver J.
2 See ch 1 above.
3 It may also be attributable to the late development of the doctrine: see CM Schmitthof, 'The Duty to Mitigate' [1961] Journal of Business Law 361.
4 *Payzu v Saunders* [1919] 2 KB 581 at 589 and *The Solholt* [1983] 1 Lloyd's Rep 605 at 618. Cf *Payzu v Saunders*, loc cit at 585.

## The legal rules on mitigation

### Avoidable loss

There are three principal legal rules on mitigation. The first concerns *avoidable loss*: C cannot recover damages in respect of any part of his loss caused by D's breach which he could have avoided by taking reasonable steps. This is sometimes expressed as a 'duty to mitigate', which strictly it is not.[5] Rather it is a restriction on the damages recoverable for the breach, which will be calculated *as if* C had acted reasonably to minimise his loss. (The rule operates in the same way as does contributory negligence.) C has a reasonable time after the breach to decide how to act; the length of time will depend on all the circumstances. C is also protected by the onus of proof being placed on D, who must show that C could have mitigated,[6] and by the judicial view that, since it is D who has breached, C need not meet a high standard of reasonableness. It has been said that the propriety of C's actions to mitigate his losses in an 'emergency' should not be minutely examined at the behest of D who caused the emergency in the first place.[7] For instance, C need not take risks with his money or property, nor embark on difficult[8] litigation against a third party;[9] and C is not expected to take any step which would risk his own commercial reputation such as suggesting to the driver of a Rolls Royce that he should substitute a less prestigious vehicle.[10]

The lenient standard applied to C is illustrated by the case where D's breach of contract led to the circulation of unauthorised currency of C, a national bank. It was held that C could recover the cost of exchanging valid notes for the invalid ones, which action C reasonably considered to be necessary in order to maintain public confidence in the currency. C had acted reasonably despite the fact that D was able to suggest a cheaper way of remedying the situation: C's actions 'ought not to be weighed in

5  Breach of a legal duty by D usually entitles C to compensation. The 'duty' to mitigate is cast on C not D and its breach has the effect of reducing C's recovery. See *The Solholt*, above n 4 at 608.
6  *Garnac Grain Co v HMF Faure and Fairclough Ltd and Bunge Corpn* [1968] AC 1130.
7  *Banco de Portugal v Waterlow* [1932] AC 452.
8  C may be required to undertake simple litigation: *Watt v Medicott & Son* [1999] 1 All ER 685 (a tort case).
9  *London and South of England Building Society v Stone* [1983] 1 WLR 1242. In this case a building society was not required to enforce mortgagor's personal covenant to pay when the defendant surveyor's negligence caused the property to be inadequate security for sum advanced.
10  *HL Motorworks v Alwahbi* [1977] RTR 276 (a tort case). See also *Finlay and Co v NV Kwik Hoo Tong Handel Maatschappij* [1929] 1 KB 400 (C not required to demand sub-buyers accept goods under falsely dated bills of lading).

nice scales at the instance of the party whose breach of contract has occasioned the difficulty'.[11]

The time when C should have mitigated may depend on when he discovered or ought to have discovered that D had broken his contractual obligation. So, as soon as C discovers that an item supplied to him by D is unsafe because it is defective (in breach of D's contract), he cannot continue to use it at D's risk: he must either make it safe or replace it, since he cannot recover damages from D for any loss which arose after he discovered the defect but which he could reasonably have avoided by taking remedial steps.[12] Sometimes C's opportunity to mitigate may arise from an offer from D, which it would be unreasonable for C to reject.[13] Where D refused to deliver goods to C on the agreed credit terms, but offered to do so on terms of 'cash on delivery', it was held to be reasonable to require C to accept this offer because substitute goods could be obtained only at a higher price.[14] C will, of course, have a claim for damages for any loss remaining after this. But if C rejects the goods as defective, he need not accept them when D offers them in mitigation, even at a lower price, since this would undermine C's right to reject.[15] Where D sold a ship to C, but could not deliver on the agreed date, it was held to be reasonable for C to mitigate by accepting its late delivery at the original price:[16] C could still claim damages for any residual loss.

### Protection of steps taken in mitigation

The second rule of mitigation protects C when he attempts to mitigate: he may recover damages for the expenses of a reasonable effort to reduce the loss caused by D's breach, even if that effort was not successful[17] (and indeed, even if greater loss resulted from his attempt to mitigate).[18] It is in the interests of contract-breakers (as well as of society) that C, the person in the best position to minimise the loss, should be encouraged to try to

11   *Banco de Portugal v Waterlow* [1932] AC 452 at 506.
12   *Lambert v Lewis* [1982] AC 225 (defective trailer coupling).
13   But it is not reasonable for the offer to be on terms that C should relinquish his claim against D for damages: *Shindler v Northern Raincoat Co Ltd* [1960] 1 WLR 1038.
14   *Payzu v Saunders*, above p 109, n 4.
15   *Heaven and Kesterton Ltd v Etablissements François Albiac & Cie* [1956] 2 Lloyd's Rep 316.
16   *The Solholt* [1983] 1 Lloyd's Rep 605.
17   Eg costs incurred by the buyer in defending a sub-buyer's claim which results from the seller's breach: see p 130 below.
18   This can occur when the buyer accepts the seller's anticipatory repudiation: the market price at the time of this acceptance may be higher than that at the (later) time fixed for delivery (see pp 106-107 above).

do so. C should be indemnified against the expenses of any reasonable attempt to mitigate, since such attempts are usually successful.

In this connection it might be mentioned that in the course of a mitigation attempt, even a successful one, C may incur extra transaction costs: viz the time and trouble taken in searching for a substitute supplier, checking his reputation for quality etc, and negotiating a new contract. Although in theory C should be entitled to damages for these 'incidental expenses'[19] which are incurred in attempts to mitigate, it would be difficult to quantify these extra transaction costs, and those in C's position appear not to attempt to prove these costs.

### Loss actually avoided

The third rule concerns loss which C actually avoided: if C has *in fact* avoided the potential loss likely to result from D's breach of contract (viz where he took mitigating steps beyond those which he could reasonably be expected to take under the 'avoidable loss' rule), he cannot recover damages in respect of the potential but avoided loss. This is part of the 'net loss' approach:[20] C's actual loss is assessed only after taking into account all the items in his notional profit-and-loss statement for the transaction, which enables his net deficit to be calculated. This rule on avoided loss requires judges to decide whether C's actions after D's breach arose *out of* his attempts to mitigate his loss.[1] Formulating 'a single guiding rule to distinguish receipts by [C] which are to be taken into account ... from those which are not' has been described as a task which has 'baffled many eminent common law judges'.[2] The most popular approach asks whether the benefit which C received was 'independent'[3] of any mitigating action.[4]

---

19   *The Borag* [1981] 1 WLR 274.
20   For a recent restatement of the principle see *McAlpine v Property and Land Contractors* (1995) 76 BLR 59.
1    Further illustrations of the problem are found in *Lavarack v Woods of Colchester Ltd* [1967] 1 QB 278 (see p 118 below) and in the *British Westinghouse* case [1912] AC 673 (see p 119 below).
2    *Hussain v New Taplow Paper Mills* [1988] AC 514 at 527-8.
3    This is sometimes expressed as the distinction between 'direct'(ie non independent) and 'collateral' (ie independent) benefits.
4    A different way of expressing the distinction is to say that C's loss is not reduced by his own subsequent action unless it forms part of a continuous transaction commencing with the original contract. Applying this approach, damages awarded against a surveyor were not reduced when the purchaser of leasehold property was able to persuade the landlord to remedy defects which a competent survey would have revealed: *Gardner v Marsh and Parsons* [1997] 1 WLR 489.

To understand how this judgment of degree is drawn in practice we must examine some circumstances where it has been applied. As with all questions of causation the court's approach is a robust pragmatic one preferring 'common sense' to philosophical niceties.[5] So where C, a seller, decided not to resell the goods immediately after the buyer D's breach but to keep them, and later resold them when the market price rose, his damages were still assessed at the market price at the time of D's breach.[6] In keeping the goods, C was acting at his own risk: he could not have held D liable for any additional loss if the market price had fallen after the breach,[7] so he was entitled to any gain when it rose. The decision to keep the goods was an independent speculation by C. But contrast the case where the buyer C rejected the goods on the ground that they were defective. After continuous negotiations, C finally accepted the *same* goods at a reduced price: this transaction was taken into account since it was not 'independent or disconnected' from the original transaction.[8] As C obtained the goods at a price which was lower than the market price for similar goods at the date of D's breach, his damages were nominal. Nor can C's loss be reduced by the 'benefit' arising from a new replacement for something partly used. So where D's breach caused the destruction of C's building, C's damages for the cost of rebuilding were not reduced on account of any 'betterment' enjoyed by C through having a new building in place of the old one; but a reduction should be made for any improvement, such as extra accommodation, which goes beyond replacement.[9] Another case illustrates the point: as a result of D's breach, a working part of C's machine had to be replaced with a new part which would last longer; C's damages were nevertheless for the full cost of the replacement.[10]

Finally, it should be noted that C will not suffer through his prudence in protecting himself against loss through D's *future* breach. If, by entering a wholly independent transaction, C had guarded against potential loss arising from D's breach (as by C taking out insurance cover,[11] or making

5   *Galoo v Bright Grahme Murray* [1994] 1 WLR 1360 at 1375.
6   *Campbell Mostyn v Barnett Trading Co* [1954] 1 Lloyd's Rep 65.
7   *Jamal v Moolla Dawood, Sons Co* [1916] 1 AC 175 (D failed to accept shares sold to him by C, who kept them after the breach; C could not recover from D the extra loss he suffered because the market price later fell.)
8   *Pagnan (R) and Fratelli v Corbisa Industrial Agropacuaria* [1970] 1 WLR 1306. (C might have been able to claim, in appropriate circumstances, for any consequential loss arising from the delay in obtaining the goods.)
9   *Harbutt's 'Plasticine' Ltd v Wayne Tank and Pump Co Ltd* [1970] 1 QB 447. (This case has been overruled by the House of Lords on another point: *Photo Production Ltd v Securicor Transport Ltd* [1980] AC 827.)
10  *Bacon v Cooper (Metals) Ltd* [1982] 1 All ER 397.
11  Ibid.

a contract with a third party *before* D's breach),[12] D cannot use that extraneous circumstance to reduce the damages payable to C. (After all, C has paid the third party for the extra protection gained through that independent contract.)

## The importance of competitive supply

General recourse to mitigation may be had only in an economy characterised by the ready availability of goods in competitive supply, including a margin of excess capacity, so that, following D's breach, alternative goods and services of the same quality are readily available to C. The capitalist economies are, however, characterised by the availability of goods in this fashion,[13] and its role in allowing 'switching' production when original plans and obligations prove to have been mistaken has been analysed.[14] Mitigation is, then, essential for breach to be efficient, but mitigation requires the ready availability of substitute goods on a market. From the concept of mitigation, then, the 'market price' rule in the sale of goods naturally evolved. Where there is an available market for the goods under a contract to buy and sell, the damages for breach by either party are prima facie to be fixed by reference to the market price prevailing on the day of the breach. Prima facie the damages are the difference between the contract price and the market price at that date, because, with this amount of money, C is enabled either to buy from a substitute seller or to sell to a substitute buyer.

This market price rule reflects C's likely reaction to the breach. Although the breach puts him into a position where he is free to redeploy, in any way he chooses, the resources released by the breach (the price or the goods), he will usually try to find substitute performance from a third party which is as close as possible to the performance which he hoped to obtain from D. This occurs because his preferences have not changed in this respect – a benefit which is as close as possible to the expected benefit of the performance due under the original contract continues to be his first choice among the multitude of ways in which he could deploy the resources needed to buy that benefit. If D defaults in delivering a ton of coal, C will usually buy another ton of coal from a substitute seller because his requirements for coal still need to be met.

In all cases of breach of a contract concerning an item freely available in the market, the market price rule is applied, whether or not C actually bought or sold in the market on that date: his damages are crystallised by

---

12  *Haviland v Long* [1952] 2 QB 80 at 84.
13  D Ricardo, *On the Principles of Political Economy and Taxation* (1951) p 12.
14  JB Clark, *Competition as a Dynamic Process* (1961) p 59.

reference to the market price on that date no matter what he then (or subsequently) chose to do – whether he went into the market to find substitute performance or chose to redeploy his resources in a completely different way. In the market situation, the 'avoidable loss' rule means that C's damages are assessed on the basis that the *only* reasonable step which he could take was to buy or sell in the market on the date of the breach. Many who write from an economic standpoint insist that the rules on mitigation produce an efficient result. As has been argued in chapter 1, this is usually correct in the situation where satisfactory substitute performance is readily available to C in the market. Real and sometimes severe problems arise when no substitute is available. This may lead to a claim for unavoidable consequential loss or to a claim for specific performance (or another form of literal enforcement as appropriate). Literal enforcement will be considered in Part 3.

### Loss actually avoided: alternative uses of C's resources released by D's breach

The third rule of mitigation deserves closer study. This is the rule that C cannot recover damages in respect of potential loss which in fact he succeeded in avoiding. Even where C went beyond the reasonable steps which the 'avoidable loss' rule required him to take, and managed to avoid loss only by taking exceptional measures, D gets the benefit by way of a reduction in his damages. The first rule covers *reasonably* avoidable loss and looks at steps to prevent losses from continuing to mount, or steps to find substitute performance from a third party. It is obvious that C should accept an *exact* substitute (one ton of coal of a specified grade being treated as identical with any other ton of the same grade); but authority is lacking as to whether C should accept a 'near equivalent' of D's performance.[15] It is submitted that it would be good policy obviously consistent with normal commercial principles that the exactness of the substitute should be understood as a matter of commercial convenience rather than of the precision found in natural sciences. If C in fact takes a 'near equivalent' he may recover damages on that basis. For instance, if, following the seller's failure to deliver the contractual goods, there is no available market in which the buyer C can buy substitute goods, C may (provided the court holds that he has acted reasonably) recover as damages the cost of obtaining goods which are the nearest available equivalent in

---

15  Such authority as exists deals with imperfect substitutes offered by the party in breach eg *Payzu v Saunders*, above p 109, n 4.

quality and price[16] to goods of the contractual description.[17] C may also recover any extra cost arising from his adapting the nearest substitute to suit his requirements, to the extent that goods of the contractual description would suit these requirements.[18]

If not even a near equivalent is available to C, the 'avoidable loss' rule is irrelevant. But this does not prevent the third rule (no recovery for avoided loss) from applying. When C terminates the contract on the ground of D's breach, the termination releases for other uses the resources which C would have used to perform his side of the contract. If C was to pay D a price, that sum is now available for another use; if C was to transfer some property to D, C can now devote it to another purpose (including retaining it for his own use); if C was to provide D with labour, whether his own or that of his employees, he can now redeploy that labour to any other use he chooses. Being a rational man, C will choose the next best use of the released resource, judged in the light of the circumstances and opportunities confronting him at the time of the breach of contract. Since C regains his total freedom over the possible uses of the released resources, he can switch them to some use totally unconnected with the purposes of the original contract. The question which arises is whether the assessment of damages for breach of contract should take into account the benefit which C actually receives under *any* alternative use of his released resources. It will be submitted that, in principle, the profit or benefit to C should be deducted to the extent that the opportunity to derive it arose *only* as a result of the breach, ie to the extent that C could not have obtained it if there had been no breach (and therefore no termination) of the original contract.

Nearly all of the reported cases on mitigation are concerned with alternative uses of C's resources which fall within the same general category as the original use under the broken contract. But C will always find *some* use for the resources released by D's breach; he will not keep them idle, but will find what he judges to be his next best use of the resources.[19] It is submitted, however, that the rule on avoided loss should

---

16    The nearest equivalent may be of superior quality and so higher in price: *Diamond Cutting Works Federation Ltd v Treifus* [1956] 1 Lloyd's Rep 216.

17    *Hinde v Liddell* (1875) LR 10 QB 265 and *Erie County National Gas and Fuel Co Ltd v Carroll* [1911] AC 105 at 117.

18    *Blackburn Bobbin Co Ltd v T W Allen & Sons Ltd* [1918] 1 KB 540 at 554 (appeal decided on another ground [1918] 2 KB 467). In the reverse situation, where the buyer fails to accept the goods, and there is no market for the goods in their present condition (eg they were manufactured to the buyer's specifications) the seller may recover as part of his damages the expense incurred in adapting the goods to suit another buyer: *Re Vic Mill Ltd* [1913] 1 Ch 465 at 473, 474.

19    This is connected with the economic concept of opportunity cost: the cost of a resource (capital, labour, etc) used for a particular purpose is its value in its next best alternative use – the foregone opportunity of using the resource elsewhere.

mean that the courts should take into account, when assessing C's damages, the net benefit received by C from any switch of the released resources, even if it is a switch into an entirely different use. If C switches from one profit-making activity (the original contract) into another profit-making activity, the profits made in the new activity should reduce his damages if it was as a result of D's breach (and *only* through that breach) that C was able to undertake the new activity.[20] If C was a builder who abandoned the building trade after D's breach in order to open a fish-and-chips shop, his damages against D should not be the whole of his net loss of profits on the building contract with D: his damages should be reduced to the extent of the profits from his new business which he made during the expected period of D's contract and by using the resources released from performing that contract. A practical limitation will curtail the application of this proposition, however, since D bears the onus of proof that C has mitigated his loss. (Later it will be argued that the deduction should not be of the whole of C's net profits from the new activity, since the law should give some incentive to those in his position to switch their resources to other uses.) Suppose that, after D's breach, because no other building work was available C decided to stay at home reading novels, despite the fact that some other remunerative activity was open to him. Could C avoid any reduction in the damages payable by D, or should the court assume that the value to C of reading novels at home amounted at least to the value of the foregone opportunity to earn in that other activity?

The line of authority in the reported cases which is nearest to this issue concerns damages for wrongful dismissal. An employee C dismissed by D in breach of contract will find that his damages for wrongful dismissal will be reduced as follows[1] (in each case the relevant period will be the minimum period of notice to which he was entitled under the broken contract):

(1) *Hypothetical earnings.* By the amount C could have earned under another contract of employment which was reasonably available to

---

With the scarcity of resources which faces the individual he must choose between competing uses of any resource available to him; the value to him of the use which he chooses for that resource is measured by his willingness to give up alternative uses open to him.

20  The causal test should be (1) that C used substantially the same resources as he would have used in the contractual activity, and (2) that the opportunity for C to use them in the new activity would not have arisen *but for* D's breach of contract, that is, it was the breach alone which released them for the alternative use. For instance, in *Hill v Showell* (1918) 87 LJKB 1106 at 1108, the breach enabled C to execute other profitable orders: it led to 'the situation in which his machinery was rendered *free by reason of the breach*' (italics supplied).

1  *Jackson v Hayes Candy & Co Ltd* [1938] 4 All ER 587 and *Collier v Sunday Referee Publishing Co* [1940] 2 KB 647 at 653.

him. Initially, he may reasonably refuse employment of a different type or at a different level of responsibility. But after a reasonable time within which to seek a comparable job, he may have to lower his sights and take a lower-status job; or

(2) *Actual earnings.* By the amount C actually earned under another contract of employment which he was able to undertake only as the result of the breach of the original contract.[2] Under the avoided loss rule, it does not matter whether C's damages would, under the avoidable loss rule, be reduced if he had refused to take the other employment. Nor does it matter whether the type of work in the new job is similar to or different from that in the first job. The principle seems to be that C's alternative opportunity arose only because of D's breach and that he has redeployed substantially the same personal skills as he would have employed in working for D. If, however, C is required to employ different skills in the new employment, or to put in a greater effort, the courts should, we submit, make allowance for this greater input from C by deducting only a proportion of his substitute earnings.

One of the few illustrations of redeployment of released resources into a dissimilar activity is *Lavarack v Woods of Colchester Ltd.*[3] An employee, C, was wrongfully dismissed by D. C then took employment in another company at a low salary because, following the dismissal, he had purchased half of the shares in the company for £1,500 and stood to make a profit through capital appreciation of his shares if the company prospered. The Court of Appeal took the view that the profit on the shares was 'a concealed remuneration' for his work for the company, and that *part* of it should be taken into account in reducing his damages for wrongful dismissal: 'the expenditure of the time released to him by the wrongful dismissal has enabled him by his work and management during that time to enhance the value of [his shareholding].'[4] For the period of his contractual entitlement to employment with D, the shares increased in value by £3,566, but a reduction was made of 100% of C's original investment of £1,500, leaving £2,066 to be deducted from his damages.[5] This could be seen as taking account of the risk involved in making the original investment (if it was lost, C could not have used the loss to increase his damages from D). We would also refer to two other factors justifying the reduction: first, some return on the capital invested and, secondly, an

2   Exceptionally C may be able to frame his action as one in debt to which the mitigation rules do not apply. See *Gregory v Wallace* [1998] IRLR 387 (contract construed as entitling C to salary in lieu of notice as well as retaining new earnings).
3   [1967] 1 QB 278.
4   Ibid at 300.
5   Ibid at 301.

incentive to those in similar situations to take employment of a different type or employment remunerated in a more speculative way.

It is submitted that the approach taken in the employment cases should be extended to all types of contract. C's termination of the contract releases resources for re-allocation: the fact of their release is the advantage which should be set off against C's claim for damages. The alternative use actually chosen by C is merely the exercise of his freedom to choose. The courts may, however, find it difficult to assess the value of the release of the resources to C without considering the alternative use to which he actually puts them. Courts should be willing to do this, provided the assessment does not deprive those in C's position of all incentive to switch their resources.[6] For this reason, the courts should not deduct the whole of the net benefit accruing from the alternative use. C should be encouraged to show enterprise in choosing the alternative, without the fear that all of the benefit will go to D. The proportion to be deducted should be fixed at a level designed to reward C for finding and adopting the alternative, and to give a sufficient incentive to others like C to take similar initiatives in future 'breach' situations.

The general policy of avoiding social waste which underlies the mitigation rules will be furthered by encouraging C to go beyond the requirements of the 'avoidable loss' rule. The *British Westinghouse* case[7] considered the circumstances in which a buyer C was entitled to claim, as damages for the defective quality of machines bought from D, the cost of buying substitute machines to perform the function intended to be performed by those meeting the contractual quality. The House of Lords accepted that the cost of the substitute machines could be awarded as damages but held that C's damages should take account of any extra profit to C which he gained from replacing the defective machines. D had agreed to erect steam turbines of a specified kilowatt capacity. They were delivered but C complained that they failed to comply with the contractual provisions with respect to economy and steam consumption. Several years later, after experience of the defective supply of power from the turbines, C decided that he would replace the turbines with new turbines from a different manufacturer, which were of an improved type and of a greater kilowatt capacity than those supplied by D. The arbitrator found that the new machines were so superior in efficiency, and in economy of working expenses, that it would have been to C's pecuniary advantage to have replaced the original machines even if the latter had complied with all the contractual specifications. The House of Lords held that though C may not have been under a 'duty' to mitigate his loss in

---

6   Some incentive will come from the fact that C faces the risks of proof, delay and costs in any litigation against D.

7   [1912] AC 673.

this way, when his action in replacing the turbines *in fact* diminished his loss, his claim for damages for the cost of installing the newer turbines must take account of the *extra* profit (including the saving of expenses) resulting from this action. Since this profit exceeded the cost of the substitute, C could not recover the cost as damages from D.[8] In this case C was not bound to buy the more efficient machines, but it was 'reasonable and prudent'[9] to do so.

But in our view, to deduct the whole of the extra advantage would give buyers in a similar situation insufficient incentive to buy more efficient replacements for defective machines: they would have a clear incentive only if the extra advantage was expected to exceed the loss caused by D's breach. But it is in the interests of society (as well as of contract-breakers) that there should be an incentive to replace even where this action will only reduce (but not wipe out) C's loss caused by the breach. Such an incentive would be given if the courts adopted the policy of deducting only part of the benefit accruing to C from the substitute.[10] (This argument, it should be reiterated, does not apply to the situation where C can find an exact or near-equivalent substitute to D's performance.)

## Scope of the rules of mitigation

Parts 3 and 4 of this book discuss mitigation in relation to claims for a debt, for specific performance and injunction, for cost to complete damages, and for restitution. We will see that the extent to which the policy of mitigation influences the court's attitude to these claims is the principal factor in hard cases, even when the formal law on mitigation does not apply.

---

8   It should be noted that the normal measure of damages for defective goods, according to the Sale of Goods Act 1979, s 53(3) is the difference between the value of the goods at the time of delivery and the value they would have had if they had answered to the contractual undertaking as to their quality. If the buyers in the *British Westinghouse* case had claimed this measure of damages, their claim could not have been reduced by the seller's proving that at a later date it would have become more economical to discard their machines and to use the improved type.

9   Ibid at 688.

10  *Lavarack v Woods of Colchester Ltd* [1967] 1 QB 278 gives some support to this submission for only part of the enhanced value of C's shares was deducted: see p 118, above.

# 8 Reliance expenditure

## Damages for C's expenditure rendered futile by D's breach, or incurred as a result of D's breach

Instead of claiming damages on the basis of his loss of expectations, C may claim damages for his expenditure which has been wasted as a result of D's breach of contract. The claim is that C incurred the expenditure in reliance on D's contractual undertaking, and would have benefited from it had D performed his side of the contract: it is a type of reliance loss. Recent cases have raised the question whether C by claiming on this reliance measure is entitled to recover more than he could if he had claimed on the expectation measure. But we must first examine the different categories into which C's expenditure may fall, because different rules might apply to the different categories.

Table 1 (see p 122) gives an outline of all C's claims for money which can arise from D's breach of contract. The two main categories are, first, those claims which are based on C's unfulfilled expectation that D would perform his contractual obligations (heading A). The obvious instance is loss of the benefit which C expected to receive from D's performance (A(1)): this is the central case of expectation damages already considered in chapter 5. The second category is C's claims in respect of losses which are not based on his unfulfilled expectations: these are losses which arise after D's breach, and were caused by the breach (heading B). Under this heading, the losses may arise directly without any intervening act by C (as in B(1)), or they may arise from conscious action taken by C after the breach (as in B(2) and (3)).

The first two categories of C's claims to damages to recover his expenditure fall under A(2) in Table 1, and arise after C has terminated the contract. C's claims under this sub-heading are based on two grounds:

## Table 1

| Different types of claim made by the claimant arising from the defendant's breach of contract | Principles restricting recovery of damages |
|---|---|
| A Claims based on the claimant's *expectation* of the performance promised (but not fulfilled) by the defendant | |
| (1) (*Expectation interest*) *Loss of expected benefits* The claimant's failure to receive the benefits/profits/gains/advantages expected by him from the defendant's performance. | A(1)  Causation; remoteness; mitigation (viz seeking a substitute benefit/profit/consumer surplus); (sometimes) contributory negligence |
| (2) (*Reliance interest*) Expenditure incurred by the claimant (before the breach) in reliance on receiving the defendant's performance (but which expenditure has been rendered futile by the breach) | |
| (a) Expenditure in or towards performing the claimant's obligations under the contract; | A(2)  (a) Causation; remoteness; mitigation (viz seeking performance; seeking the salvage value of result of partial performance) |
| (b) Other (consequential) expenditure incurred in reliance on the defendant's promised performance | A(2)  (b) Causation; remoteness; contributory negligence; mitigation |
| (3) (*Restitution interest*) Recovery (or payment in lieu) of benefits conferred on the defendant by the claimant in pursuance of the contract. | A(3)  Total failure of consideration. (*Not* causation) (*Not* remoteness) (*Not* mitigation) |
| B *Losses caused by (and arising after) the breach (Indemnity interest)* Actual losses suffered by the claimant which arose after, and as a result of the breach: | |
| (1) Losses suffered directly: eg physical loss or damage, death or personal injury | B(1)  Causation; remoteness; mitigation (sometimes) contributory negligence. |
| (2) Expenditure incurred by the claimant in attempting to mitigate: eg the cost of substitute performance; the cost of cure | B(2)  As for B(1); also reasonableness applied to the decision to incur the cost and to the amount of the cost. |
| (3) Compensation paid to third parties: eg damages and costs paid to a sub-buyer or stranger. | B(3)  As for B(2). |

(1) he incurred the expenditure *before* D's breach on the basis that he was relying on D's performance to give him the benefit of that expenditure; and (2) the expenditure has been rendered futile as a result of D's breach. This reliance expenditure would not have been wasted had D fulfilled the contract: two separate sub-categories are distinguished in the following paragraphs.

## Performance expenditure: expenses incurred by C in preparing to perform (heading A(2)(a))

After making the contract with D, C will usually incur some expenses as he prepares to or actually begins to fulfil his own obligations under the contract. This expenditure is part of the cost of C's performance, and if D had fulfilled his side C would have received the benefit of the expenditure when he received the benefit of D's performance (eg the price). When C terminates the contract on the ground of D's breach, he may claim damages to cover his expenditure towards his own performance, but only to the extent that it has been wasted as a result of the breach. If C can salvage any items of value from his preparations for performance, the rules of mitigation require him to deduct from his claim the amount he obtained from selling the salvageable items to a third party (or the amount he ought reasonably to have obtained from doing so). It should be noted that no test of reasonableness is applied to C's incurring his performance expenditure, whereas it is an important restriction on damages for post-breach expenditure (B(2) and (3), considered below). Provided C's expenditure under A(2)(a) was genuinely intended by him to prepare for his performance and falls within the remoteness test,[1] it is apparently recoverable as damages for D's breach without satisfying any further criteria.

When C has completed his side of the contract, he will not normally wish to claim damages for his expenditure as such, because the return of his expenditure is contained within the price payable by D (or the other benefit which D has promised to C: for convenience, the word 'price' when it is used in this section covers any such benefit). Usually, C expects to make a profit on the contract, and recovery of the price will give C both the cost of his own performance and his net profit. If C has completed his performance, the only situation in which he might be tempted to claim his actual *performance* expenditure rather than the price would be where it was a losing contract from his point of view and his expenditure exceeded the price. But the law could not allow C to escape in this way

---

1   See ch 6 above. If C's expenditure was quite unreasonable, it might not satisfy the reasonable contemplation test.

from the ceiling fixed as the agreed price, and the damages for C's performance expenditure should not be more than the amount of the price. If, however, C has not completed his own performance, he cannot sue for the price and is relegated to a claim to damages.[2] In this situation he may find it difficult to prove his loss of profits (the expectation measure: A(1)) and so may fall back on claiming simply his reliance expenditure. But C will often claim both his *net* loss of profits under A(1) *and* his wasted expenditure incurred up to the date of termination. There will be no overlapping in the latter claim if C's net loss of profits is calculated by deducting from the price both his actual performance expenditure to the date of termination and the further performance expenditure which he would have incurred after that date if he had completed his performance. The rules on mitigation preclude C from incurring any further, avoidable expenditure, which leads to a saving which reduces the damages payable by D. If C recovers his performance expenditure wasted by the breach, and the net loss of profits which he would have made on the contract overall, he should be put into the same position as he would have been in if D had paid the price (or fully performed his side).[3]

The problems of the relationship between damages under A(1) and under A(2)(a) are not difficult when C claims both, since it is then obvious that the court must ensure that C calculates his loss of expectation damages after deducting his claim for performance expenditure. If, however, C claims only for his wasted expenditure, the relationship between the two headings is still a problem. In this situation, there must be some reason for C not to claim his net loss of profits. Since the onus of proof of loss rests on him, he may find that he cannot prove what his profits would have been; or he may find in the course of performance that it is turning out to be an unprofitable contract, so that the termination saves him from a loss instead of depriving him of a profit. The question to be decided is whether C's expected gross return from performance (one of the expectation measures under A(1)) should place a ceiling on recovery of damages for C's performance expenditure under A(2)(a).

The courts have tended to see this as a simple matter. 'It is not the function of the courts where there is a breach of contract knowingly ... to put a [claimant] in a better financial position than if the contract had been properly performed.'[4] From this principle the courts have deduced that C can recover damages for expenditure incurred in reliance on the contract

---

2   Unless D's breach was an anticipatory one ie before the time for performance D indicated that at that time he would not be tendering the contract performance and C has both an legitimate interest in continuing with their contract and may tender his performance without any help from D. See ch 11 below.

3   This statement relates only to claims under A(1) and A(2)(a). C may have additional claims under other headings.

4   *C & P Haulage v Middleton* [1983] 1 WLR 1461 at 1467–1468.

## Table 2

|  | Case A | Case B | Case C | Case D | Case E |
|---|---|---|---|---|---|
| 1. Expected gross return from the contract (eg the price, or the *gross* benefit expected by C) | 1,000 | 1,000 | 1,000 | 1,000 | 1,000 |
| 2. *Performance costs incurred by C*<br><br>C's actual costs (or reliance expenditure towards his performance ) up to the date of termination | 1,100 | Nil | Nil | 500 | 1,000 |
| 3. *Performance costs saved by C*<br><br>The expected costs which C would incur in performing during the remaining period of the contract (*expected performance expenditure*) | Nil | 800 | 1,100 | 600 | 100 |
| 4. Amount of damages if based on the loss of expectation measure | 1,000 | 200 | Nominal | 400 | 900 |
| 5. Amount of damages if based on the reliance measure (performance expenditure) | 1,000 | Nominal | Nominal | 500 (possibly 454) | 1,000 (possibly 909) |

only to the extent that it would have been covered by the gross return which C would have received if the contract had been fully performed.[5] It is submitted that this proposition should apply only to C's *performance* expenditure, not to other reliance expenditure (A(2)(b)) nor to C's expenditure incurred after D's breach (B(2) and (3)). It is only his performance expenditure under A(2)(a) which C expects to cover from the price payable by D.

Let us consider the example in Table 2, which illustrates the different stages of performance by C of a contract under which he is to make something for D for an agreed price of £1,000.

*Case A.* Here C has completed performance, but it is a losing contract. His costs of £1,100 exceed the price of £1,000 but no matter how he frames his claim C should not recover more than £1,000. If D refuses to pay the price (thus committing a breach), and C sues for his performance expenditure (line 2) instead of suing in debt for £1,000,[6] he should not

5   *CCC Films (London) Ltd v Impact Quadrant Films Ltd* [1985] QB 16.
6   See ch 11 below.

be awarded more than £1,000: the parties placed this limit on recovery of any of D's costs of performance, all of which they expected to be met out of the price.

All the cases except A assume that D has committed a breach of contract which entitles C to terminate further performance and that C has done so. He thereby saves all his future costs of performance (line 3), but has already incurred the costs in line 2 towards or as part of his own performance. (For the sake of simplicity, it is assumed that there is no salvage value arising from the latter.)

*Case B.* Here C has not begun to perform when D repudiates the contract: no costs have been incurred (line 2) so no claim lies for reliance expenditure (line 5). The loss of expectation measure (line 4) will give C his net profit (line 1 minus line 3). It is assumed that, by redeploying the resources released by D's breach (line 3), C could not make a *substitute* profit which should be set off against the loss of £200 net profit expected under D's contract.[7]

*Case C.* At the time of making the contract C expected his costs to be £800, so that he expected to make a net profit, but by the time of D's repudiation C's expected costs had escalated to £1,100, and thus he faced a potential loss. Since C had incurred no costs (line 2), D's breach has enabled him to terminate the contract, and thereby save all future costs (line 3). D's breach has put C into a better position than he would have been in had there been full performance on both sides, but as C needs no judicial remedy to give him this benefit he can retain it all.

*Cases D and E.* In both these cases, full performance by C would cause him a loss. On the expectation measure, in Case D (line 4) C might recover only £400 (line 1 less line 3), in which case D would benefit from the difference of £100 between the price and the expected total costs (lines 2 and 3). Can C avoid this result by claiming £500 damages as his performance expenditure to the date of termination (line 2)? Three responses are possible. First, it could be held that line 4 should always place a ceiling on recovery under line 5, so that C can recover no more than £400. If the court followed its own rhetoric (that C should be no better off as the result of D's breach) this should be the result. However, the onus of proof could assist C. It has been held that this onus is on D, who must show that C would not have recouped his expenditure if the contract had been fully performed.[8] In the absence of such proof, the court will assume in C's favour that he would have recouped it. But if D can

7    It would be a substitute profit for this purpose if C could fulfil the second contract *only* because D had broken the first contract. If C could have performed both contracts, the profit under the second one is not a substitute profit: see p 99 above.
8    *CCC Films (London) Ltd v Impact Quadrant Films Ltd*, above p 125, n 5.

prove that C would not have recouped it all, the first solution would leave C aggrieved because D's breach would leave him out of pocket. Hence, another solution is more likely to be sought.

The second solution would entitle C to claim his performance expenditure (line 2) up to the limit imposed by the price (line 1). Although C would not be better off in absolute terms than he would be after full performance (recovering £500 instead of £1,000), he would be better off in relative terms. The third solution would be to scale down C's recovery of his performance expenditure to date to the proportionate recovery he would have made on full performance, viz by (line 1)/(lines 2 and 3). In case D, this would produce 1000/(500 + 600) x £500 = £454. Under this solution, C is not put into a relatively better position than he would have been on full performance, but the result is arguably too generous to D. By his breach, D can not only escape paying for the avoided expenditure (line 3) but he can also use the amount saved to make a proportionate reduction in C's recovery of costs actually incurred. In their desire to ensure that C is not better off, the courts should not be so concerned to protect D. It was his breach which entitled C to terminate and thereby to avoid his potential loss becoming an actual loss. If C recovers his actual expenditure, subject to the ceiling imposed by the price, he is still not making a profit, merely avoiding a loss. It is submitted that the second solution is to be preferred, even though in Case E it would give C the same amount as would be payable on his performance.

## Expenditure incurred by C before making the contract with D

C may sometimes incur expenses before making the contract with D, but in the expectation that the expenditure will be needed to enable him to perform the contract he expects to make with D, and that he will be able to recoup the expenditure from the price to be paid by D (or from the benefit of D's performance). If, at the time of contracting, it is within the reasonable contemplation of the parties that C will be able to recoup this expenditure from the price payable by D, C may recover it from D as damages[9] (subject, of course, to C's duty to mitigate, if he can, by selling the benefit of the expenditure for its salvage value, or using it for some other purpose).

An argument against the recovery of damages as described in the paragraph above (and *a fortiori* the one below) emphasises the role of

---

9   *Anglia Television Ltd v Reed* [1972] 1 QB 60 and *Lloyd v Stanbury* [1971] 1 WLR 535 at 546.

contract as a device for the allocation of risk. Can responsibility for the possible waste of money expended by C before a contract is entered be regarded as a risk reallocated upon the making of a contract with D? If C entered no subsequent contract, C would have no redress when the expenditure was wasted. Should the intervention of a contract with D be regarded as effectively insuring C against the risk of wasted expenditure? The answer suggested above and below is that there is no objection to such reallocation when it falls within the remoteness principles.

Instead of anticipating a contract with D, a particular individual, C may incur expenditure in anticipation of making contracts with future customers in general. Suppose that C manufactures engineering equipment to the specification of his customers. Before he makes any individual contract he will have committed himself to many overhead and other costs such as the cost of his premises, equipment, workforce and raw materials. C has incurred these costs in anticipation of future contracts with customers who are not yet specified. But from each contract he does make, C naturally expects to recoup a proportion of his overhead and similar costs. When C makes a specific contract with D, who fails to pay the price, C may not be able to make a substitute contract under which he can recoup the contribution to overheads which he would have received from D. To the extent that he cannot recoup this contribution from a substitute contract, C should be entitled to recover damages from D for his wasted expenditure. If it falls within the remoteness test, it is expenditure which D impliedly promised to meet when he promised to pay the price. If it is *performance* expenditure (A(2)(a)) it should be subject to the restriction discussed in the previous section.

## Expenditure incurred by C in reliance on the contract but not towards performance of his side

Before D's breach of contract, C may incur expenditure in reliance on D's contractual undertaking which, however, is not part of the performance promised by C. It may be within the parties' reasonable contemplation that this expenditure is not unlikely to be incurred by C and also that it is not unlikely that it will be wasted if D commits a breach (A(2)(b) in Table 1). Since the expenditure is not towards C's performance, he does not intend to meet it from the gross return which he expects to receive from the contract with D. Although it is incurred in reliance on D's promise, it is for C's own benefit.

For instance, in one case D sold goods to C, who had some repairs made to them before he found that a third party was entitled to retake them (D having no title to them). It was held that C could recover damages for the

10  *Mason v Burningham* [1949] 2 KB 545.

cost of the repairs, which were wasted from his point of view. It was within reasonable contemplation that C might incur this expenditure in reliance on the title which D purported to transfer to him.[10] In another case, after D promised C to deliver a ship by a certain date, C incurred expenses in taking on a crew and preparing for a voyage. When D delayed delivery, C could recover the cost of the wages paid to the crew while they were idle during the period of the delay.[11] Similarly, where a buyer C sues the seller D for damages for defective quality, C may recover his expenses which the parties could reasonably contemplate that C would incur in reliance on D performing his contractual obligations, eg incidental expenditure such as the cost of painting a machine before it was found to be defective;[12] the cost of transporting goods before they were examined and rejected;[13] or the cost of the extra coal used by defective steam turbines.[14] A final illustration comes from the case where a brewer C bought sugar from D for making beer, but the beer had to be destroyed because the sugar had been contaminated with arsenic. C recovered the market value of the wasted beer, which gave him all the costs of producing the beer – other materials used and labour – as well as his profit. These costs were not incurred by C in order to fulfil his side of the contract to buy the sugar; rather, they were expenses which D ought reasonably to have contemplated as not unlikely to be incurred by C in reliance (inter alia) on his contract with D.[15]

One important reason for distinguishing between expenditure under A(2)(a) and that under A(2)(b) is that the latter should not be subject to any ceiling fixed by C's expected gross return (the price). The parties do not contemplate that the expenditure under A(2)(b) will be met by C from the benefit to be received from D, yet the reasonable contemplation test is satisfied: the expenditure is likely both to be incurred, and to be wasted if D breaks his contract.

### Expenses incurred by C as a result of D's breach

The final categories of expenses fall under heading B in Table 1. As the result of D's breach of contract, C may incur expenses in minimising his

11  *Steam Herring Fleet Ltd v S Richards & Co Ltd* (1901) 17 TLR 731 (C would, of course, have to mitigate if it was reasonable for him to do so).
12  *Cullinane v British Rema Manufacturing Co Ltd* [1954] 1 QB 292.
13  *Molling & Co v Dean & Son Ltd* (1901) 18 TLR 217.
14  *British Westinghouse Electric and Manufacturing Co Ltd v Underground Electric Railways Co of London, Ltd* [1912] AC 673 at 683.
15  *Richard Holden Ltd v Bostock & Co Ltd* (1902) 18 TLR 317. There is probably no need to impose a reasonableness test on C, since if the expenditure is unreasonable either in type or extent, it would not satisfy the reasonable contemplation test.

loss or in dealing with the consequences of breach.[16] The price or gross return expected by C has never been used to place a ceiling on the recovery of his expenses incurred after, and as a result of, D's breach. Provided that his actions satisfy the test of reasonableness, C may recover these expenses as part of his damages (B(2)). So, in the case already mentioned about the arsenic in the sugar, the brewer recovered the cost of printing notices sent to his customers to minimise any loss of business.[17] In another case, D delayed delivery of a crane sold to C, whom he knew to be an importer of timber; C recovered the extra cost of manhandling timber at his wharf.[18]

C may even recover damages paid to a third party (B(3) in Table 1). This situation can arise where D sold goods to C, who sold them on to T. It must have been within the reasonable contemplation of the parties that C would probably resell, and that D's breach in supplying defective goods to C was not unlikely to result in C being liable to pay damages and costs to a sub-buyer for breach of the sub-contract. In these circumstances C may recover from D the amount he has paid T, provided that he (C) acted reasonably in meeting T's claim: eg if C paid T in an out-of-court compromise, it must have been reasonable for him to settle rather than defend the claim in court, and the amount paid must have been reasonable;[19] if C incurred the expense of defending T's claim up to judgment, he can recover the full cost from D only if that was a reasonable course for C to take.[20]

### Claims for both wasted expenditure and loss of profits

The courts have run into difficulties when C has split his claim into two, one part based on his wasted expenditure, the other based on his loss of profits caused by the breach. In the *Cullinane* case,[1] C purchased a

---

16  The cost incurred by C in getting a third party to remedy D's defective performance (see ch 14 below) could be placed under this heading. Eg in *Smith v Johnson* (1899) 15 TLR 179 mortar supplied by a builder was below standard; it was used for a building which the local authority later condemned as unsafe, and the owner recovered from the builder the cost of pulling it down and of rebuilding.

17  *Richard Holden Ltd v Bostock & Co Ltd*, above n 15.

18  *John M Henderson & Co Ltd v Montague L Meyer Ltd* (1941) 46 Com Cas 209 at 219–20.

19  *Biggin & Co Ltd v Permanite Ltd* [1951] 2 KB 314 (C can also recover his own reasonable costs in defending T's claim).

20  In appropriate cases, C may even recover a fine imposed on him as the result of D's breach of contract, eg in supplying C with food which is unfit for human consumption.

1   *Cullinane v British Rema Manufacturing Co Ltd*, above p 129, n 12 (criticised by JK Macleod, 'Damages: Reliance or Expectancy Interest' [1970] Journal of Business Law 19). See also M Owen, 'Some Aspects of the Recovery of Reliance Damages in the Law of Contract' (1984) 4 Oxford Journal of Legal Studies 393.

clay-pulverising machine from D, who warranted that it would function at a certain rate. When it failed to do so, C claimed damages: first, for his net capital loss or expenditure incurred (viz the price paid for the machine, the cost of its housing and ancillary plant, plus interest thereon, *less* the residual value of the machine and plant in their actual condition at the time of the claim); and, secondly, for his loss of profits[2] for the three years up to the hearing of the case (viz the estimated net profit for those years, after deducting interest on capital, depreciation, maintenance and other expenses). The useful commercial life of the machine was expected to be ten years, but in his pleading C limited his claim for loss of profits to three years. The majority of the Court of Appeal held that C could not claim both his capital loss (expenditure incurred) and his loss of gross profits: they were concerned that C should not make a double recovery. In their opinion, C must elect between these two claims, and either seek to be put back into the position he would have been in if the contract had not been made (viz recover his net outlay, his reliance expenditure) or, alternatively, claim what he would have received if the contract had been fully performed (viz the gross profit he would have received if the machine had functioned in accordance with the contractual warranty).

It is submitted that the position taken by the majority in this case is confused: their concern to avoid double recovery led them to overlook the fact that a *net* loss of profit can be calculated in such a way as to avoid overlapping with the wasted capital expenditure. They were correct in holding that the *gross* profit expected to be earned by the machine during its useful life would include the expected return of the capital expenditure incurred by C.[3] But, as Morris LJ pointed out in his dissent,[4] C was not claiming his expected gross profits, but his net profit calculated after a deduction of depreciation, which represented the return to him of the capital element; therefore, his claim for his net capital outlay did not overlap with his claim for loss of net profits. It is submitted that the view of Morris LJ is to be preferred, and that a split claim should be permitted so long as the calculations show that no overlapping occurs in the different heads of claim. In a later case Lord Denning repeated the view that a claimant 'has an election: he can either claim for loss of profits or his wasted expenditure... He cannot claim both'.[5] It is suggested that this statement must be interpreted to refer only to gross not net profits.

---

2   It was clear that the buyer's loss of profits was within the reasonable contemplation of the parties.
3   In *Commonwealth of Australia v Amann Aviation Pty Ltd* (1991) 66 ALJR 123 Mason CJ, Dawson, Brennan and Deane JJ presented the recovery of reliance losses as part of an expectation claim, so creating an 'assumption' of profitability.
4   Above p 129, n 12 at 315, 317–18.
5   *Anglia Television v Reed* [1972] 1 QB 60 at 63-64.

The approach to combining expectation and reliance claims proposed in this book (ie that claims can be combined where there is no overlap) is supported by a later case involving the sale of a racehorse which turned out not to have the parentage warranted by the seller.[6] The buyer's damages included the difference in value between the horse with the warranted pedigree (the contract price so long as the sale was at full value) and its value when its true history was discovered[7] (the expectation claim) in addition to the cost of training and stabling fees (the reliance claim). In an appropriate case it might be possible to combine claims for expectation, reliance and restitution damages without any risk of double recovery. In one case concerning the sale of machinery[8] C recovered his net loss of profit (expectation) as well as installation expenses (reliance) and the price paid (restitution).

6    *Naughton v O'Callaghan* [1990] 3 All ER 191. See also *Millburn Services Ltd v United Trading Group* (1997) 52 Con LR 130.
7    Which was two seasons later. The case therefore represents a departure from the presumption that damages are assessed at the date of breach of contract – as to which see sec 6.4.
8    *Millar's Machinery Co Ltd v David Way & Son* (1935) 40 Com Cas 204.

# 9 Pre-estimated damages

## Clauses fixing the amount of damages

Contracts often provide that, in the event of a breach[1] by D, he shall pay
C a specified sum of money.[2] D's willingness to contract on this basis is
an advantage to C for which D will expect to be paid by an increase in the
price. Such stipulated damages clauses have traditionally been controlled
by the common law and equity.[3] However these mechanisms have recently
been supplemented by the Unfair Terms in Consumer Contract Regulations
1999.[4] The Privy Council recently endorsed[5] the common law test for a
valid, enforceable clause of this type fixing damages in advance which
was 'authoritatively set out in the speech of Lord Dunedin in *Dunlop
Pneumatic Tyre Co Ltd v New Garage and Motor Co*'.[6] The test is whether

---

1   See below for a discussion of payments conditional on events other than a breach
    by D.
2   On obligations other than that to pay a sum of money, see p 143 below.
3   One method of indirect control is by the principles of incorporation. Such clauses
    are often contained in unsigned documents or notices which the courts might
    hold not to be validly incorporated into the parties' contract if, prior to entering
    the contract, C did not take reasonable steps to bring the document or notice to
    the attention of C and the document was of a type likely to contain contractual
    terms: see *Interfoto Picture Library Ltd v Stiletto Visual Programmes Ltd* [1989]
    QB 433. Any clause which 'binds the consumer to terms he had no real opportunity
    of becoming acquainted with before the conclusion of the contract' is
    presumptively unfair under the Unfair Terms in Consumer Contracts Regulations
    1999, Sch 2, para 1(I). For the general conditions of applicability see below p 137
    below.
4   No 2083, replacing earlier regulations of 1994.
5   *Phillips Hong Kong Ltd v A-G of Hong Kong* (1993) 61 BLR 41 at 56.
6   [1915] AC 79 at 86.

the clause represents (in the light of the circumstances known to the parties at the time of contracting)[7] a '*genuine*' attempt to estimate in advance the loss which C was likely to suffer from the breach in question. Such a provision is called 'liquidated damages' and is enforceable upon the breach occurring, irrespective of the actual loss caused by the breach[8] – or, indeed, whether any loss at all was actually caused.[9] If the court finds that the clause did not constitute a genuine attempt to pre-estimate loss, it is labelled a 'penalty' and is unenforceable; the result is that C can claim only unliquidated damages[10] for the loss which he can prove was actually caused by the breach, and that his claim is subject to all the rules on damages, such as those on remoteness and mitigation. Ostensibly, the courts have not simply defined a penalty negatively as a stipulated damages clause which is unenforceable because it is not a genuine pre-estimate of loss. Rather the courts have stated a positive test (was it a deterrent against D's breach, 'a payment of money stipulated as *in terrorem*' of D?).[11] However it is unclear what this positive statement adds to the negative definition and its value has been questioned in more recent cases.[12]

The precise words used by the parties are not conclusive. If the contract describes the sum payable as 'liquidated damages' it may still be held to be an unenforceable penalty, and using the word 'penalty' does not prevent the clause being upheld as valid liquidated damages.[13] Indeed, it is probably more accurate to say that 'the names... are immaterial'.[14] The fact that damages would be difficult to assess strengthens the inference that a genuine attempt has been made to pre-estimate loss and so avoid the difficulties of proof.[15] Another pointer to a genuine attempt is a

---

7   *Public Works Comr v Hills* [1906] AC 368 at 376. However subsequent events 'can provide valuable evidence as to what could reasonably be expected to be the loss at the time the contract was made': *Phillips Hong Kong Ltd v A-G of Hong Kong*, above n 5 at 59.

8   *Diestal v Stevenson* [1906] 2 KB 345. (£90 stipulated in a clause was recovered when the actual loss was more than three times this sum.)

9   *Clydebank Engineering and Shipbuilding Co Ltd v Don Jose Ramos Yzquierdo Y Castenada* [1905] AC 6 at 10 (rejecting the argument that a party who contracted to supply naval vessels was not liable to pay liquidated damages for the failure to deliver on time because, if they had been delivered, they would have been lost in a disastrous naval engagement shortly thereafter!)

10   It is doubtful whether C is entitled to recover *more* than the amount stipulated in the unenforceable penalty: see *Elsey v JG Collins Insurance Agencies Ltd* (1978) 83 DLR (3d) 1 at 15.

11   *The Dunlop case*, above p 133, n 6 at 86.

12   *Bridge v Campbell Discount Co Ltd* [1962] AC 600 at 622.

13   The *Dunlop* case, above p 133, n 6 86.

14   *Sparrow v Paris* (1862) 7 H & N 594 at 599.

15   *Clydebank Engineering and Shipbuilding Co Ltd v Don Jose Ramos Yzquierdo y Casteneda*, above, n 9 at 11. The difficulties in making a pre-estimate of loss are

graduated series of sums payable according to the relative seriousness of the breach, eg so much according to the number of items involved in the breach, or so much for each period of delay in performance.[16] Thus, where the retail price of an article was about one shilling (5p), the sum of £15 was upheld as liquidated damages due to the manufacturer in respect of each sale of the article at a price lower than that fixed in a resale price maintenance agreement.[17]

Sometimes a clause makes the same sum payable for breaches of varying importance. This does not necessarily make the sum a penalty where it is a genuine attempt to average different types of loss which may be difficult to compute in advance. In the *Dunlop* case, D were tyre dealers who agreed (inter alia) not to resell any tyres bought from the manufacturer C to any private customers at less than C's current list prices, and not to supply anyone suspended by C; D agreed to pay £5 by way of liquidated damages for every tyre sold or offered in breach of their undertaking. The House of Lords upheld this sum as liquidated damages: 'the damage caused by each and every one of those events, however varying in importance, may be of such an uncertain nature that it cannot be accurately ascertained'.[18] In another case in the same year,[19] another retailer agreed to pay £250 as 'the agreed damage which the manufacturer will sustain' by a clause similar to that in the *Dunlop* case. The Court of Appeal held that this was a penalty since it was an arbitrary and substantial sum, made payable for various breaches differing in kind, some of which might cause only trifling damage.[20] To similar effect is a more recent case where the same court held that where a sum is stipulated which is a genuine estimate of the loss that could and on the facts did occur, the provision may nonetheless be penal if in respect of other contemplated breaches it would be excessive.[1] However, when applying this test the Privy Council has emphasised that the court should not be over-zealous in striking down clauses in commercial contracts on the basis of 'unlikely illustrations'.[2]

---

illustrated by an empirical study of liquidated damages in the holiday travel industry: A Milner, 'Liquidated Damages: An Empirical Study in the Travel Agency' (1979) 42 Modern Law Review 508.

16 Businessmen, however, seem reluctant to enforce agreed damages clauses for delay: H Beale and T Dugdale, 'Contracts Between Businessmen: Planning and the Use of Contractual Remedies' (1975) 2 British Journal of Law and Society 45, p 55.

17 *Imperial Tobacco Co Ltd v Parslay* [1936] 2 All ER 515.

18 The *Dunlop* case, above p 133, n 6 at 96. *Imperial Tobacco Co Ltd v Parslay*, above, n 17, is an illustration.

19 *Ford Motor Co v Armstrong* (1915) 31 TLR 267.

20 Similarly, a sum liable to fluctuate with *extraneous* circumstances will be a penalty: *Public Works Comr v Hills* [1906] AC 368.

1 *Ariston SRL v Charly Records* (1990) Financial Times, 21 March.

2 *Phillips Hong Kong Ltd v A-G of Hong Kong* above p 133, n 5 at 58-59.

The parties may fix a sum as liquidated damages in the event of one specific breach, and leave C to sue for unliquidated damages if other types of breach occur.

A 'minimum payment' clause is often found in a hire-purchase agreement. Under it the hirer D agrees that in certain events including his breach he will pay 'compensation for depreciation' to bring the total of his payments up to a certain proportion (such as three-quarters) of the total hire-purchase price. Apart from statutory controls,[3] the law on penalties will apply only if the event on which C relies was *in fact* a breach by D.[4] In that case, the minimum payment should be graduated according to the way in which the hired chattel will normally depreciate over time. In one case, the sum payable actually decreased over time as D paid more of his instalments: it was 'a sliding scale of compensation ... that slides in the wrong direction' and was therefore penal.[5]

The 'genuine pre-estimate' test raises a number of unsettled questions. Does the word 'genuine' mean 'honest', 'serious', or 'reasonable'? Could an 'unreasonable' attempt to pre-estimate loss still be a genuine attempt? In the *Dunlop* case the requirement of genuineness suggests that an honest estimate is required. Somewhat confusingly, in *Phillips Hong Kong Ltd v A-G of Hong Kong*[6] Lord Woolf said that Dunlop 'authoritatively set out' the law on penalties but also referred to the test as 'objective' thereby suggesting that the belief should also be a reasonable one.[7] Again, could a clause be a genuine pre-estimate if it ignores the probability that C could mitigate his loss? It could be argued that the doctrine of mitigation should have only as limited an application to the action for liquidated damages as it has to the action for debt, which is also an action to recover a liquidated sum.[8] However such an approach might be criticised for its tendency to encourage waste, as it has been criticised in the case of debt.[9] It is also likely that the parties are permitted to take account of C's losses which would be irrecoverable under the normal rules,[10] eg loss of business reputation. Another question is whether the courts would treat as analogous to liquidated damages a clause which specified a particular measure of damages. For instance, would the courts uphold a clause

---

3    Consumer Credit Act 1974.
4    *Cooden Engineering Co Ltd v Stanford* [1953] 1 QB 86. Cf the situation where the event is not a breach: see pp 143-144 below.
5    *Bridge v Campbell Discount Co Ltd* [1962] AC 600 at 623.
6    Above p 133, n 5.
7    Ibid at 59-60. See also *Darlington Borough Council v Wiltshier Northern Ltd* [1995] 3 All ER 895 at 899 where Dillon LJ spoke of 'a fair pre-estimate of loss'.
8    See p 158 below.
9    See p 162 below.
10    *Robophone Facilities Ltd v Blank* [1966] 1 WLR 1428 at 1448. The opposite approach was suggested by the Law Commission in Working Paper No 61 para 44.

specifying that damages for D's failure to perform will be assessed at the cost incurred by C in obtaining substitute performance through a third party?[11] This would not be a pre-estimate of 'loss' in the market sense of loss and thereby would avoid the test (discussed above and below) which the courts would normally apply to C's claim for damages assessed on this basis. Such a clause would also avoid the court's discretion in granting or refusing an order for specific performance directly against D. The answers to these questions should depend on an examination of the policies behind the law, and the question whether these policies justify any restrictions on the parties' freedom to fashion their own arrangements. Before examining these policies we will consider the statutory control of stipulated damages clauses.

## Unfair Terms in Consumer Contracts Regulations 1999

As their title suggests, these regulations police unfair terms in consumer contracts. Thus the control they exercise over stipulated damages clauses is only a part of a more general regulatory regime. Any unfair term[12] in a contract[13] between a commercial seller of goods or supplier of services[14] and a consumer[15] will not be binding on the consumer.[16] An unfair term is one that has not been individually negotiated which 'contrary to the requirement of good faith ... causes a significant imbalance in the parties' rights and obligations ... to the detriment of the consumer'.[17] Schedule 2 contains what has become known as the 'grey list' of terms which will be presumptively regarded as unfair. These include 'terms which have the object or effect of ... requiring any consumer who fails to fulfil his obligation to pay a disproportionately high sum in compensation'.[18] The common law jurisdiction over stipulated damages clauses is in a number of ways broader than the statutory one. Formally it applies to all such clauses irrespective of the status of the parties and whether the clause was individually negotiated or not. However, there is one respect in which the statutory control may be more extensive. The common law control only applies to sums payable upon breach of contract whereas the

11  See ch 14 below.
12  Not including terms which define the main subject matter of the contract or the adequacy of the price or remuneration. See reg 6(2).
13  Probably including a contract for the sale of land: see below.
14  Ie someone ... acting for the purposes of his trade, business or profession, whether publicly owned or privately owned. See reg 3.
15  Ie someone acting for purposes outside his trade, business or profession. See reg 3.
16  Reg 8(1).
17  Reg 5(1).
18  Para 1(e).

Regulations refer to a consumer who merely fails to fulfil his obligation. Such a failure may not amount to a breach of contract where the consumer can claim that his failure was excused perhaps because the contract was frustrated. Whether when both jurisdictions are applicable the test of 'genuine pre-estimate' and 'disproportionately high sum' will produce different answers remains to be seen.

## Incentives to perform

The test for a valid agreed damages clause is firmly based on the loss concept: if the sum exceeds the expected loss, it cannot, according to present authority, be justified by reference to any other factor. If C desires to give D an incentive to perform rather than to pay damages in lieu of performance, he cannot use a financial disincentive by means of a post-breach payment by D, except to the extent that the risk of paying the cost of C's expected loss acts as a disincentive. (This is exactly what the ordinary law on damages purports to do.) Any added incentive above the level of expected loss is ruled out by the current test. But why should the courts not uphold an agreed damages clause on the ground that it amounts to a reasonable incentive to D to perform? The law's stance towards upholding the various incentives to perform, including some which do not take account of any actual loss suffered by C, is not consistent. The grant of the various forms of literal enforcement or a general restitutionary remedy, all of which encourage performance more than do compensatory damages, yield no coherent overall principle. These remedies can obviously amount to powerful (sometimes 'unreasonable') incentives to D, and if the incentives to perform produced by these rules of law are sometimes acceptable, *a fortiori* the law should enforce an incentive which is tailor-made by the parties.[19] In fact, as shall shortly be discussed, the strength of disapproval of penalties is not displayed towards provisions of a different legal form but which have a similar practical effect of increasing the performance incentive.

Concern about the inequality of bargaining power between the parties is probably the historical explanation[20] – the judges feared that a more

---

19  The conditions of granting literal enforcement are discussed in Pt 3 below and their inconsistency is evaluated in ch 15. The general restitutionary remedy and the attitude that should be taken towards the parties' tailoring of incentives to perform are discussed in ch 17 below.

20  It was the Courts of Equity which held that if the sum fixed was really a penalty to ensure that the promise was not broken, the promisee should receive by way of damages only that sum which would compensate him for his actual loss: J Story, *Commentaries on Equity Jurisprudence* (3rd English edn 1920) para 1316. T Downes, 'Rethinking Penalty Clauses', in P Birks (ed), *Wrongs and Remedies*

powerful party would exact from the weaker party an undertaking to pay a sum which was wholly disproportionate to any expected loss, so that the incentive would be too powerful.[1] But instead of limiting the justification for an agreed damages clause to the concept of expected 'loss', it would have been possible to restrict the parties' freedom by qualifying their power to fix an incentive by reference to a standard of reasonableness,[2] as has been used in so many other contractual situations.[3]

A stronger incentive for D to perform (or at least for D to negotiate his release by paying C a price for his release) is most arguably legitimate in the case of deliberate breach by D to maximise his gain – the paradigmatic case of efficient breach. Would the courts uphold an agreed damages clause which was designed to make D pay a proportion of the profits he makes from a deliberate but in this sense efficient breach? If the 'loss' concept is always used as a ceiling on the agreed sum which can be awarded even in this situation, the courts would be encouraging breach whenever D hopes to make a better profit from a new opportunity. It is submitted that the courts should allow the parties a wide latitude in designing clauses dealing with deliberate breaches. Courts should not inflexibly apply the penalty jurisdiction so as to rule out clauses which legitimately express the intentions of the parties.

### The advantages of pre-estimated damages clauses[4]

As the law stands, the incentive argument just considered is not acceptable. But other justifications are recognised for the validity of agreed damages clauses. In comparison with unliquidated damages assessed under the ordinary rules (causation, remoteness, mitigation, etc), an agreed provision has the following advantages:

---

    *in the Twenty First Century* (1996) 249, p 269 argues that inequality of bargaining power now provides 'an obvious starting point' for identifying stipulated damages clauses which should not be enforced.

1    It has been argued that if C could enforce a penalty clause (viz one giving him more than his estimated loss) he would face a 'moral hazard' if he could in any way influence the likelihood of breach occurring: KW Clarkson et al, 'Liquidated Damages vs Penalties: Sense or Nonsense?' [1978] Wisconsin Law Review 35.

2    M Chen-Wishart, 'Controlling the Power to Agree Damages', in Birks (ed), *Wrongs and Remedies in the Twenty First Century*, ch 12 argues for a 'realignment' of the penalty jurisdiction in a way that explicitly incorporates ideas of substantive fairness.

3    Eg in the doctrine of mitigation; the test for a valid covenant in restraint of trade; and the statutory tests under the Unfair Contract Terms Act 1977.

4    PR Kaplan, 'A Critique of the Penalty Limitation on Liquidated Damages' (1977) 50 Southern California Law Review 1055 and J Sweet, 'Liquidated Damages in California' (1972) 60 California Law Review 84.

(1) *Reduction in post-breach transaction costs.* This is the orthodox argument: C can avoid the cost and difficulty of proving the actual loss which he suffers; he 'derives an advantage from having the figure fixed and so being assured of payment without the expense and difficulty of proof'.[5] The more difficult the proof, the more likely it is that an agreed sum will be enforced; and the higher the probability of enforcement, the greater the incentive on D to settle C's claim out of court. Although there will be a saving in post-breach transaction costs in these relatively rare situations of breach, this saving may be outweighed by certain pre-breach costs. Most obviously these include the extra costs of negotiating the agreed damages clause. However there may be other costs arising from D's protective response to such a clause. It is likely that a party confronted with such a clause would in turn insist on a 'force majeure' clause to protect him from the consequences of a failure to perform which was caused by matters beyond his control[6] which would increase the transaction costs in monitoring performance.[7]

(2) *Avoiding the risk of under-compensation.* At the time of contracting, the promisee C may fear that a damages award assessed under the ordinary principles would be inadequate compensation. Consequential or indirect losses may not be covered, nor may loss of reputation or idiosyncratic losses. An agreed damages clause may be the best way of dealing with these unusual risks[8] – better even than C's informing D of the risks in the hope that damages would be awarded under the second rule in *Hadley v Baxendale*.[9] The agreed sum should also be justifiable by reference to the cost of actually detecting D's breach in the course of monitoring his performance; the general 'hassle' involved for C in coping with a breach and the costs of delay in recovering the agreed sum; legal costs not recoverable from D under the usual rules on costs; and, if the agreed sum assumes that C will be able to mitigate his loss, the hassle involved in seeking

5    *Suisse Atlantique Societe d'Armement Maritime SA v NV Rotterdamsche Kolen Centrale* [1967] 1 AC 361. In *Diestal v Stevenson* [1906] 2 KB 345 at 350 a liquidated damages clause was included in a contract for the sale of coal 'in order to avoid the difficulty, as between shipper at Newcastle and buyer at Lubeck, of proving the value of the goods in a market which is constantly fluctuating'.
6    Beale and Dugdale, 'Contracts Between Businessmen: Planning and the Use of Contractual Remedies', above p 135, n 16.
7    Eg *Suisse Atlantique Societe d'Armement Maritime SA v NV Rotterdamsche Kolen Centrale*, above n 5 (charterer of ship undertook to pay 'demurrage' (a fixed sum per day) if loading took longer than an allowed time, so long as the delay was not caused by strikes or other causes beyond the charterer's control).
8    An agreed damages clause may take into account loss which would be too remote under the normal rules: *Robophone Facilities Ltd v Blank* [1966] 1 WLR 1428 at 1447–1448.
9    See pp 96-97 above.

substitute performance. Since judicial awards of damages often do not cover C against transaction costs which are difficult to establish in court or to quantify, he should be able to use them to support an agreed damages clause.

(3) *An assurance of reliability.* If D the promisor is able to accept an obvious disincentive to breach he can give C an assurance that his promise to perform can be relied upon. D may be unknown to C, a newcomer to the market who as yet has no reputation for reliability. Instead of offering a lower price than his competitors, he may wish to gain the contract by putting himself at greater risk should he commit a breach. If it is C who presses D for the clause, it can function as notice to D that actual performance is what C is paying for, not the right to compensation in lieu of performance.

(4) *Limitation of liability.* An agreed damages clause may perform the same function as an exemption clause: an agreed sum may place a *ceiling* on the financial risk which D is willing to accept. If the parties could anticipate that breach might cause greater loss than would be compensated by the fixed sum, the clause will be enforced as an agreed limitation on the extent of D's liability.[10] (As such, it may be subject to judicial or statutory control over exemption clauses.) Instead of the risk of loss being divided between the categories of unusual and usual losses (as with the remoteness rules), the loss is divided in monetary terms: D accepts liability for loss up to a given value, while C accepts the risk of any excess loss over this figure. These clauses may often be designed as the basis for insurance arrangements to be made by the parties.[11] C may obtain insurance against the risk of loss beyond the agreed ceiling, but D may not be able to obtain insurance against a potentially unlimited risk, or against the consequences of his own failure to perform,[12] and he may be unwilling to accept an uninsurable responsibility for unpredictable loss. An agreed damages clause of this type would seem to be the only efficient way to meet the problem of the component manufacturer who supplies a defective part to the manufacturer of the whole, eg the supplier of a defective nut which could conceivably cause the loss of a valuable machine like an airplane. If the component manufacturer, instead of exempting himself from all liability for consequential loss, were to accept liability

10  *Cellulose Acetate Silk Co Ltd v Widnes Foundry (1925) Ltd* [1933] AC 20.
11  Eg the *Hague Rules* on the carriage of goods by sea provide that the carrier is liable up to a specified limit per package. Cf, on the relevance of the availability of insurance, s 11(4)(b) of the Unfair Contract Terms Act 1977.
12  An insured behaving differently as a result of obtaining insurance is the paradigmatic case of a 'moral hazard'. As KJ Arrow, *Collected Papers*, vol 4 (1984) p 85 puts it: 'the policy might itself change incentives and therefore the probabilities upon which the insurance company has relied'.

up to an agreed ceiling, this might give him the necessary incentive to take care in manufacturing the part he supplies. The price he charges will, of course, reflect the extent of his potential liability.

(5) *Flexibility.* The final advantage is the ability to combine the relevant factors. An agreed damages clause permits the parties to take account of all the factors in any combination. The agreed sum will be a 'trade-off' of the various factors in the foregoing list of advantages, plus any other factors, so as to produce the correct 'mix' of factors to suit the particular case. Among the other factors will be:

(a) The different attitudes of the parties to the risk of the particular breach occurring – one party, usually the promisor D, may be risk-neutral, whereas the other (usually the promisee C) may be risk-averse, and so desire some insurance protection against non-performance. The second factor follows the first:

(b) The extent of insurance protection desired by C. If C obtains the consent of D to an enforceable agreed damages clause, he has purchased a form of lump-sum insurance against the consequences of non-performance. Because of the 'moral hazard' problem (D may be encouraged to breach if he knows that there is an insurance cover for the consequences) neither party may be able to get insurance cover (at least at acceptable rates) against this risk from an insurance company. D, the party in the better position to control the risk, can often provide C with insurance protection at cheapest cost.[13]

(c) C may wish (to the extent permitted by the 'genuine pre-estimate' test) to give D the desired level of incentive actually to perform. If the courts ever allowed a reasonable incentive, there would be great scope for the parties to choose the appropriate degree of incentive.

In view of the advantages of agreed damages clauses, it is not surprising that generally economic analysis[14] supports their enforcement (except in cases of initial 'unfairness or other bargaining abnormalities').

## The scope of the law on penalties

In the major cases on the penalty jurisdiction the discussion is not limited to the judicial control of clauses requiring payments of money by the

---

13  CJ Goetz and RE Scott, 'Liquidated Damages, Penalties and the Just Compensation Principle' (1977) 77 Columbia Law Review 554.

14  Ibid; SA Rea Jr, 'Efficiency Implications of Penalties and Liquidated Damages' (1984) 13 Journal of Legal Studies 147 and A Ham, 'The Rule Against Penalties in Contract: An Economic Perspective' (1989-90) 17 Melbourne University Law Review 649.

party in breach. A term which entitles D to withhold a payment which was otherwise owed to C will also be subject to the jurisdiction.[15] Contractual provisions which require a party to transfer something other than money upon the transferor's breach of contract are also subject to review. On this basis it has been held that a clause obliging the buyer of shares to re-transfer them if he defaulted on the payment of any instalment was a penalty.[16]

However, the applicability of the law on penalties to the range of sums of money which may become payable under a contract is very uneven. It does not apply to the forfeiture of deposits, though a standard of reasonableness has occasionally been considered for these.[17] It does not apply to a sum due on the occurrence of some event other than a breach by D[18] or to a debt, a sum of money due from D in return for C's performance.[19] Therefore it is inapplicable where D, the promisor, has the option to pay a sum of money as the alternative to another form of performance by him. The remedy of termination for breach can operate as harshly as any penalty clause, but it has not been treated as subject to the law on penalties.[20]

In the *Export Credits Guarantee* case,[1] the House of Lords ruled that the law on penalties has no application to a clause providing for D to pay a sum to C upon the happening of a specified event which was *not* the breach of a contractual duty owed by D to C. So it could not be a penalty where D had agreed to reimburse C the amount paid by C to third parties under a guarantee (even where C's obligation to meet the guarantee arose on the occasion of D's breach of his contractual duties owed to other parties). Although it was a guarantee in a complex commercial arrangement, their Lordships' limitation on the scope of the law on penalties was expressed in such wide terms that it would prevent many other clauses from being subject to that law.[2] In one case a hire-purchase agreement permitted the hirer at his option to terminate the hiring during

15  *Gilbert-Ash (Northern) Ltd v Modern Engineering (Bristol) Ltd* [1974] AC 689.
16  *Jobson v Johnson* [1989] 1 All ER 621. See further D Harris, 'Penalties and Forfeiture: Contractual Remedies Specified by the Parties' [1990] Lloyd's Maritime and Commercial Law Quarterly 158. A separate line of authority analogous to the law on penalties has developed to deal with the forfeiture of advance payments made by D. Like the penalty doctrine, this jurisdiction has been extended to clauses not involving the payment of money. See pp 147-150 below.
17  See sec pp 58-61 above.
18  The Unfair Terms in Consumer Contracts Regulations 1999 might apply: see p 137 above.
19  See ch 11 below.
20  See p 145 below.
1   *Export Credits Guarantee Department v Universal Oil Products Co* [1983] 1 WLR 399.
2   The death or bankruptcy of a party might be another event, not constituting a breach, upon which money is to be paid.

the period of the agreement, and provided that the hirer should thereupon pay a sum by way of agreed compensation for depreciation of the chattel. The Court of Appeal held[3] that this sum, being payable upon an event not constituting a breach of the agreement, fell outside the scope of the law as to penalties: the *Export Credits Guarantee* case clearly supports this position. Statutory protection is now available for many hirers,[4] but the common law position is unsatisfactory, because an honest hirer who terminates his agreement when he finds that he cannot keep up the instalments is in a worse position than the hirer who simply breaks his agreement by failing to pay the instalments. Lord Denning described this as 'an absurd paradox' and said '[i]f this be the state of the equity today, then it is in sore need of an overhaul so as to restore its first principles'.[5] The Law Commission agreed with Lord Denning and provisionally recommended 'that the court should have the power to deal with such clauses in the same way whether or not they come into operation by breach'.[6] The difficulty then arises as to how to confine this power of review in a way that does not cause all contractual clauses to be subject to challenge.

Where a contract empowers a party to perform his obligations in more than one way it will not attract the penalty jurisdiction. The key to its avoidance is that the failure to perform in a particular way must not amount to a breach of contract. On this basis a university might grant licenses to occupy rooms in a hall of residence for £500 payable before the beginning of term or £750 payable thereafter. So long as the failure to pay before the commencement of term is not a breach of contract the 'requirement' to thereafter pay an 'extra' £250 falls outside the penalty jurisdiction. Similarly the law on penalties does not apply to an *increase* in the price if certain targets in the contract are bettered or if costs are reduced; eg the price for a specially manufactured machine may be graduated according to its efficiency in operation. A government report has recommended that in building contracts incentive payments should be preferred to agreed damages clauses. [7]

A clause which 'merely provides for the acceleration of payment of the stipulated price'[8] has been said not to amount to a penalty. On this

3   *Campbell Discount Co Ltd v Bridge* [1961] 1 QB 445. On appeal a different view was taken of the facts: [1962] AC 600; but four of their Lordships obiter considered the issue. It is unfortunate that the short speech in the *Export Credits Guarantee* case, above, made no attempt to discuss these opinions.
4   Consumer Credit Act 1974, ss 99, 100.
5   *Bridge v Campbell Discount Co Ltd* [1962] AC 600 at 629.
6   Law Com No 61 para 22.
7   Banwell Report (Report of the Committee on Placing and Management of Contracts for Building and Civil Engineering Work) (1964) para 9.22.
8   *White and Carter (Councils) Ltd v McGregor* [1961] 3 All ER 1178 at 1180-1181.

basis a clause which provided that if one instalment of the price for a service remained unpaid all future instalments were to become payable was said by the House of Lords not to amount to a penalty. This rule appears to be based upon the false premise that the party subject to the clause is only being required to pay what was already due. This is clearly not so. Being required to pay at an earlier date amounts to being asked to pay a larger sum[9] and in any case imposes a real extra burden.

Parties to a contract may expressly provide that a particular clause is to be a condition of the contract ie the breach of that provision will justify C in terminating the contract. The parties' description of the clause or its remedial effect is not conclusive as to its legal classification but is nonetheless highly persuasive. Where this intention is made clear C may terminate the contract and claim damages for loss of bargain. This will sometimes enable a party to recover as unliquidated damages a sum which could not be recovered under a stipulated damages clause. This will be possible where the contract is one for the sale or hire of goods which have little or no resale value. In *Lombard North Central plc v Butterworth*,[10] a finance company leased a computer to D for five years. Clause 2 of the agreement made punctual payment of hire 'of the essence' of the agreement; clause 6 required D to pay all outstanding and future rentals if the finance company terminated the agreement for failure to make punctual payments as it was empowered to do under clause 5. D failed to pay a number of the £500 quarterly payments. The finance company recovered the computer and sold it for only £172. The Court of Appeal held that the effect of Clause 2 was to make prompt payment a condition of the contract the breach of which entitled it to terminate the agreement and claim damages for loss of bargain. These damages extended to all outstanding and future rentals due under the contract.[11] The finance company therefore recovered as unliquidated damages a sum which could not have been recovered under Clause 6 because it was held to be an unenforceable penalty.[12]

---

9   Ie assuming positive inflation.

10   [1987] QB 527.

11   If the finance company had relied upon an express power of termination such as that contained in clause 5 damages would have been limited to instalments which were unpaid at the time of termination. See *Financings Ltd v Baldock* [1963] 2 QB 104. The distinction between an express power of termination (as in *Financings*) and a clause which states a particular breach to be a condition and so triggers the common law right to terminate is a technical one without merit.

12   It was not a genuine pre-estimate of loss because it obliged D to pay all future instalments 'regardless of the seriousness or triviality of the breach'.

## Appraisal

What is the purpose today of the law on penalties?[13] It seems that its only justification is to protect a weaker party against the unconscionable use of a superior bargaining strength: it is 'designed for the sole purpose of providing relief against oppression of the party having to pay the stipulated sum'.[14] If this is its purpose, it is hard to justify limiting judicial scrutiny to this one type of clause. Any type of clause can be drafted unfairly, but the law has never attempted overall control. For instance, no attempt is made by common law or equity to control the price (a debt) or the power to cancel the contract (terminate for breach) or many other types of remedy specified in the contract. The most wide-ranging measure is probably the Unfair Terms in Consumer Contract Regulations 1999.[15] However these Regulations only apply to contracts between a seller or supplier 'acting for purposes relating to his trade, business or profession' and a consumer who is not so acting[16] and do not subject to review any term which defines the main subject matter of the contract or the price to be paid for it.[17] The existing law on penalties can easily be evaded by the clever draftsman producing clauses which fall outside its scope. We have already examined a number of these techniques: offering a 'discount' for early payment, accelerating an existing debt, making prompt payment 'of the essence'. If abuse of a stronger bargaining position is the real evil, it should be attacked directly by a principle which aims at any manifestation of the abuse instead of one which aims selectively at penalty clauses and ignores all other types of clause. Nowadays the need for protection is mainly confined to consumer contracts, and here the courts unfortunately tend to take the view that it should be left to Parliament to provide the necessary protection to consumers. There is almost no prospect of a general doctrine of unconscionability being developed by English judges.

If the present law on penalties is to continue in force for an indefinite period, there is scope for several changes. First, if public policy prevents the parties from effectively choosing specific relief as the automatic remedy for a given breach,[18] a strong argument can be made for permitting them to choose indirect specific performance, by agreeing that the cost of getting a third party to perform should be the measure of damages.

13  See the Law Commission's Working Paper No 61 (1975).
14  *Elsley v JG Collins Insurance Agencies Ltd* (1978) 83 DLR (3d) 1 at 15. This was recognised in the leading case, the *Dunlop* case, above p 133, n 6 at 87.
15  SI 1999 No 2083 which replaced the Unfair Terms in Consumer Contracts Regulations 1994. See p 137 above.
16  Regs 4(1) and 3(1).
17  So far as both appear 'in plain intelligible language': reg 6(2).
18  See p 137 above.

Secondly, the courts should recognise that the law reopens the allocation of risks made by the parties at the time of contracting.[19] If D avoids paying the agreed damages, the price paid by C should be adjusted. C has paid a 'premium' for the clause,[20] which should not be ignored when the clause is held to be unenforceable. When C has paid the price to D, C's unliquidated damages should include an element to return this premium to him.

## Forfeiture of deposits, other advance payments and of rights over property or arising under the contract[1]

It has been shown in chapter 3 that advance payments identified as deposits are not subject to the penalty rules, though the advisability of this has been questioned and is questionable. It is an unsettled question whether the law on penalties applies to a clause in the contract entitling a payee to forfeit advance payments which are not labelled 'deposits', or any other rights. There are many contracts where sums of money (not being deposits) are payable in advance of the performance due from the payee, or are payable at regular intervals (such as a purchase where the price is payable by instalments). The purpose of these payments may be to provide the payee with working capital to help finance his performance, or as a security against the risk of the payers' insolvency or breach. Often these contracts contain a clause which provides that, upon breach by the payer, the payee may forfeit all the sums paid to him, in addition to his remedy of terminating the contract (which relieves him of the obligation to complete his own performance). As with a deposit and in contrast to the situation with liquidated damages, the payee does not need to ask the court to award him the agreed sum, since he already has it: he simply claims to be entitled to 'forfeit' the amount he has received, by retaining it for his own beneficial use, leaving the payer to challenge this if he can. Although the Consumer Credit Act 1974 may give statutory protection to the payer in many situations, the courts also assert a limited degree of extra-statutory control over these clauses.

---

19  In the USA some courts have decided on the enforceability of a liquidated damages clause by conducting a *post hoc* evaluation of the relation between the actual loss suffered by C and the pre-estimate made at the time of contracting. This approach seems to be even more open than the English test to the objection that the original allocation of risks is being reopened.

20  If at the time of contracting the parties actually knew the law on penalties, it might be argued that the price will have discounted the risk that the clause would not be enforceable.

1   The Law Commission, *Penalty Clauses and Forfeiture of Moneys Paid*, Working Paper No 61 (1975) paras 50, 65, 66.

For many years the courts ignored the possible analogy to penalty clauses, despite the existence of a supporting analogy in landlord and tenant cases, where there was a long history of equitable relief against forfeiture of leasehold interests. More recently, however, the courts have begun to grant a limited type of relief against forfeiture in a wider range of situations. A condition said to be necessary before equitable relief may be granted is that the forfeiture clause was inserted in order 'to secure a stated result which can effectively be attained when the matter comes before the court, and where the forfeiture provision is added by way of security for the production of that result'.[2] The wider development began in 1954 with *Stockloser v Johnson*,[3] in which there was a provision, in a contract to purchase plant and machinery by instalment payments, that upon default by the buyer the seller might terminate the contract and forfeit the instalments already paid. The majority of the Court of Appeal held that the court has an equitable jurisdiction to relieve against forfeiture of such instalments, even after termination of the contract, if in the actual circumstances of the case the clause was penal and it would be oppressive and unconscionable for the seller to retain all the instalments. In 1983, the House of Lords upheld the jurisdiction to relieve against forfeiture, but limited it to contracts concerning the transfer or creation of proprietary or possessory rights.[4] Thus it did not apply to the facts of the case before the House, where a shipowner withdrew his ship (chartered under a time charter)[5] on the ground of the charterer's failure to make punctual payment of an instalment of hire. Similarly, the House of Lords has refused relief against the forfeiture of 'mere contractual licences' to use certain names and trade marks.[6] But the Court of Appeal has granted relief (in the form of an extension of time in which a payment could be made by D) in a commercial contract which provided that D's failure to pay a sum on time would entitle C to claim an assignment of patent rights held by D.[7] This decision holds that interests in personal property may be given this limited protection against forfeiture, but it is not clear whether courts will ever do more than give the payer more time in which to pay the sum he failed to pay on time.

2    *Shiloh Spinners Ltd v Harding* [1973] AC 691 at 723. (The case concerned the right to forfeit (re-enter upon) leasehold property for failure to repair fences and to maintain works for the protection of adjoining property.) So relief cannot be granted where the lessee under a finance lease could no longer be put back in possession: *On Demand Information plc v Michael Gerson (Finance) plc* [2001] 1 WLR 155.
3    [1954] 1 QB 476.
4    *Scandinavian Trading Tanker Co AB v Flota Petrolera Ecuatoriana, The Scaptrade* [1983] 2 AC 694.
5    A charter by demise would have given the charterer a possessory interest in the ship.
6    *Sport Internationaal Bussum BV v Inter-Footwear Ltd* [1984] 1 WLR 776.
7    *BICC plc v Burndy Corpn* [1985] Ch 232 at 251–2.

Relief may also be given against the forfeiture of *money* paid in advance in contracts of the appropriate type (involving the transfer of proprietary or possessory rights) and not simply against the forfeiture of the rights themselves.[8] The Court of Appeal has accepted that if, under a contract to purchase premises by instalment payments, the buyer defaulted in payment of an instalment of the price, the court has jurisdiction in a proper case to relieve the buyer against forfeiture of the instalments already paid, by granting an extension of time to him within which he could pay.[9] But the court will not be easily satisfied that the seller's conduct is unconscionable, especially where the buyer has had the use or benefit of the subject-matter of the contract over a period. On the facts of *Stockloser v Johnson*, above, although the majority of the court treated the clause as penal, they did not think that the seller's conduct in retaining £4,750 out of the £11,000 price in one contract, and £3,500 out of the £11,000 price in another, was unconscionable, because the buyer had already received substantial benefits in the form of royalties.[10] It is obvious that the courts are more reluctant to allow recovery of money already paid by the contract-breaker (ie affirmative relief) than to deny recovery of a sum (a penalty) agreed to be payable upon breach by the contract-breaker (ie negative relief) or to give more time to him to make a payment.

Express forfeiture provisions may also be subject to control under the Unfair Terms in Consumer Contracts Regulations 1999.[11] Any contract subject to the Regulations[12] which contains a clause which permits the seller or supplier to retain sums paid by the consumer where the latter decides not to conclude or perform the contract without providing for the consumer to receive equivalent compensation in the event of the seller's cancellation is presumptively unfair and so not binding on the consumer.[13] This provision probably does not apply to deposits which are forfeit by operation of law rather than by virtue of any contractual term.[14] After some doubt it now appears to be thought that the Regulations do apply to contracts for the sale of land.[15]

---

8   This has been established for many years in regard to contracts for the sale of land where the price was payable by instalments: *Re Dagenham (Thames) Dock Co, ex p Hulse* (1873) 8 Ch App 1022; *Steedman v Drinkle* [1916] 1 AC 275 and *Mussen v Van Diemen's Land Co* [1938] Ch 253.

9   *Starside Properties Ltd v Mustapha* [1974] 1 WLR 816.

10  [1954] 1 QB 476 at 484, 492.

11  SI 1999 No 2083.

12  For the general conditions of applicability see p 137 above.

13  Sch 2, para 1(d). For the civil law origins of this provision see GH Treitel, *Remedies for Breach of Contract* (1988) para 182.

14  GH Treitel, *The Law of Contract* (10th edn 1999) pp 942-3.

15  See M Attew, 'Teleological Interpretation and Land Law' (1995) 58 Modern Law Review 696 and S Bright and C Bright, 'Unfair Terms in Land Contracts: Copy Out or Cop Out?' (1995) 111 Law Quarterly Review 655.

The contracts in the cases discussed in the preceding paragraphs all contained an *express* forfeiture clause. If there is no such clause, but the seller terminates the contract upon the buyer's default, the buyer may recover any prepayment or instalments in part payment of the price, subject to a counter-claim by the seller for damages for the breach of contract.[16] Thus, in one case, despite the buyer's repudiation of his contract to buy goods, he was held to be entitled to recover a substantial prepayment (not in the nature of a deposit) made by him, subject to a deduction in respect of the actual loss suffered by the seller through the breach of contract: the court held that if it permitted the whole prepayment to be retained by the seller, it would be permitting the retention of a penalty, not liquidated damages.[17] This decision has been distinguished by two of their Lordships in the House of Lords[18] on the ground that it concerned a sale where no expenditure was intended to be incurred by the seller in reliance on the advance payment. It has been persuasively argued[19] that the payee's rights should depend on the construction of the clause in the contract requiring the advance payment: was the right to retain the payment intended to be conditional upon performance by the payee of his obligations, or was it intended to be a security for performance of the payer's obligations?

16  *Dies v British and International Mining and Finance Corpn Ltd* [1939] 1 KB 724
    (sale of goods); *Stockloser v Johnson*, above p 148, n 3 at 483, 489–90 and
    *Mayson v Clouet* [1924] AC 980 (sale of land).
17  *Dies v British and International Mining and Finance Corpn Ltd*, above n 16.
18  *Hyundai Heavy Industries Co Ltd v Papadopoulos* [1980] 1 WLR 1129 at 1142–
    1143, 1147–1148. (The contract in this case was for work and materials supplied
    in the course of building a ship, and so it was treated as analogous to a building
    contract.) See also the similar case of *Stoczia Gdanska SA v Latvian Shipping Co*
    [1998] 1 All ER 883.
19  J Beatson, 'Discharge for Breach: The Position of Instalments, Deposits and Other
    Payments Due Before Completion' (1981) 97 Law Quarterly Review 389, pp
    391–401 and J Beatson, *The Use and Abuse of Unjust Enrichment* (1991) pp 56–
    61.

# Part 3
# Literal enforcement

# 10 Introduction

## The forms of literal enforcement

In Part 2 it has been shown that the usual remedy for breach of contract is the award of compensatory damages. As Holmes famously put it: 'the only universal consequence of a legally binding promise is that the law makes the promisor pay damages if the promised event does not come to pass. [The law of contract] leaves [the promisor] free to break his contract if he chooses'.[1] In Part 3 we now turn to the circumstances in which the remedy C seeks is not compensatory damages but, in effect, the performance of D's primary obligation, by D or a third party. This may be termed the literal enforcement of the contract.

The remedies which may be sought from the court which literally enforce the contract are:
- claims in debt[2]
- specific performance[3]
- injunctions[4]
- performance by a substitute.[5]

A brief discussion of another legal remedy, that of obtaining a declaration, and of the possibilities of bringing about literal enforcement through self-help are needed to complete this survey of literal enforcement. That

---

1    OW Holmes, *The Common Law* (1881) p 301.
2    See ch 11 below.
3    See ch 12 below.
4    See ch 13 below.
5    See ch 14 below.

discussion will be undertaken as part of a general appraisal of such enforcement.[6]

Before turning to the forms of literal enforcement, however, it is as well to outline what is at issue when the court must choose between compensatory damages and literal enforcement. If compensatory damages did actually fully compensate C,[7] C should be indifferent whether damages were awarded or the primary obligation performed. Indeed, C might often have an incentive to welcome breach. Not only would C be freed from what might be the onerous duty of exacting a performance from D which D did not want to render, but, on present rules, C might actually have the opportunity of realising a windfall profit after the breach. From our earlier discussion of mitigation,[8] we have seen that, in general, where C sues for damages and no reasonable substitute performance is available to him, courts have typically ignored the fact that C's resources have been released. C therefore is in general left better off if D pays expectation damages without any deduction for the advantage which C has in being able to switch his resources to another contract quite different from the contract with D.

In the light of these considerations, C's recourse to literal enforcement shows that breach may occur or C believes it is about to occur in circumstances where this assumption of full compensation does not apply.

## The reasons for seeking and granting literal enforcement

Leaving aside the procedural advantages of claiming in debt which we will examine,[9] the rational reason C sometimes elects to pursue literal enforcement, and the reason the court sometimes awards a remedy that effects it, is that, as we will see, damages sometimes do not actually compensate or, as it is put, 'are inadequate'. There are two general reasons why damages might be inadequate: for consumers, the existence of a consumer surplus, and for commercial parties, the existence of an idiosyncratic loss. These will be discussed, with examples drawn from

6   See ch 15 below. The relationship of literal enforcement to the use of restitutionary damages and/or exemplary damages to deprive D of the gain from his breach, which would have an effect approximating to literal enforcement, is taken up at the end of this chapter and in depth in ch 17 below.

7   'Full' compensation in this sense might be thought to include compensation for the cost of obtaining the compensation, and, after litigation, costs typically follow the cause. However, the award of costs to a successful C never compensates him for the anxiety and trouble of pursuing the claim.

8   See ch 7 above.

9   See ch 11 below.

specific performance, in the survey of specific performance below, and the reader is advised to turn to that discussion now.[10]

As clear a line as possible should be drawn between a breach which, though motivated by self-interest, takes place in reasonable circumstances, in the ideal case of which C is completely compensated for lost expectation, and a breach which leaves C with a substantially or totally uncompensated loss, which, of course, prima facie is unreasonable. That the breach lowers D's costs is not itself unreasonable. The whole point of compensatory damages based on the quantification of C's loss after mitigation is that C's net loss can be smaller than the cost of performance.[11] Damages in this circumstance are adequate. But this reasoning works smoothly only if C *is* fully compensated. If, because of the existence of a consumer surplus or idiosyncratic loss, C is faced with an under- or uncompensated loss,[12] C obviously will have a legitimate reason to seek literal enforcement. We have argued in chapter 1 that the principal function of breach by D (followed by mitigation by C) is to allow D, when committed to an primary obligation which has proved more costly to perform than he anticipated, to satisfy C's expectation in a way which minimises D's costs by turning to a secondary obligation to compensate. That it miminises D's costs is the main reason why breach may be said to be efficient. But D will, of course, have an incentive to breach irrespective of whether C will receive full compensation,[13] and if breach leaves C uncompensated because damages are inadequate, breach is not efficient. It is in those circumstances in which D (obliged to acknowledge liability) seeks to pay only damages which C believes are inadequate that literal enforcement may be granted by the court to protect C's expectation.

But it must be noted that though granting C literal enforcement in these situations will protect C's expectation, it will do so in a way which will impose a heavy cost on D because, by enforcing performance of D's primary obligation, C obviously will not have mitigated his loss. In

10 See pp 167-175 below. Two, as it were, particular reasons for granting specific performance, that a sale of land or a third party beneficiary is involved, are also discussed in this section. These particular grounds also turn on the inadequacy of damages but raise issues specific to themselves.
11 See ch 1 above. A less common but sometimes commercially important other circumstance when damages are smaller than the cost of performance is when, during a period of high inflation, damages are assessed at a date earlier than the time when D would incur the cost of performance.
12 In the interests of economy of expression, henceforward 'uncompensated' will be used to include the argument that C is left partially as well as totally uncompensated by damages.
13 D's interest in preserving existing relationships and/or his reputation will severely curtail the number of occasions in which this incentive will be sufficient to motivate D to breach in these circumstances.

practice, if D can perform, he will dispute C's claim to literal enforcement only when he expects the cost of performance (substantially) to exceed his estimate of C's compensatory damages. If D expects the cost of complying with the order to be no higher than the likely award of compensatory damages, he will (in the absence of some exceptional reason) perform rather than dispute C's claim. In this situation, C may value performance more highly than the award of damages (eg no substitute performance may be available, and the damages may not reflect C's subjective valuation of his consumer surplus). D, being indifferent between performing and paying compensation, will minimise transaction costs by accepting C's choice. (Even if D did dispute the claim for literal enforcement, the court should not agonise over the selection of the remedy where it believes that the cost of compliance would not exceed the damages which would be awarded.)

D, however, may reasonably ask the court to use its powers to refuse literal enforcement by exercising its discretion to refuse specific relief even though damages are inadequate, because he expects a money award to be markedly less costly for him. In such a situation, the denial of literal enforcement has an important impact on the parties. Paying damages is the cheaper alternative for D, but, as damages are inadequate, this will be the less valuable alternative from C's point of view, and so literal enforcement should be considered. It is, as has been said, prima facie unreasonable for D to breach when this will leave C under-compensated. But this does not settle the matter. If the cost to D of literal enforcement is markedly in excess of the benefit such enforcement renders to C, it still may be reasonable for D to breach (and pay damages). This is the situation in which the exercise of the court's judgement over the award of literal enforcement is crucial. The law governing this is most fully developed in respect of the discretion to award specific performance, but similar issues arise in respect of debt, injunction and cost to complete damages, and the factors relevant to the decision should be weighed with this consequence in mind. Do these factors, when weighed against each other to determine the balance of convenience or relative disadvantage of the parties, point to it being fair to relieve D of the full cost, or to it being fair to impose that cost on him in order to be just to C?

We will see that this tension between C's wish to be fully compensated and D's wish to minimise the cost of performance of his secondary obligation runs through the law on all the forms of specific enforcement, to which we now turn. The argument of this Part of this book is that, when balancing the convenience or relative disadvantage of the parties in 'hard cases' of literal enforcement, D's interest in minimising the cost of the remedy should be allowed proper weight against C's interest in the protection of his expectation, in order to minimise the transaction costs of exchange and thereby avoid social waste.[14] A fuller discussion of the concept of social waste is reserved for the conclusion of this part, but the reader may care to turn to it now.[15] However, at this initial stage of our discussion of literal enforcement, in order to appreciate this tension, and to understand literal enforcement at all, it is essential to see that the point of the law of literal enforcement is not to prevent breach as such but to distinguish between reasonable and unreasonable breaches in those hard cases where C and D legitimately claim they face loss.

The restitutionary argument for (partial) disgorgement of the windfall from efficient breach has sometimes been couched in terms of D paying C for a hypothetical release from specific performance (and by extension other forms of literal enforcement). Leaving aside whether such negotiation may be a good idea or not, conducting the argument for it in this way imposes two costs on our understanding of the law. First, it must be insisted that such negotiation is hypothetical and not only does not represent the law of literal enforcement but cannot be generated from that law, which is itself guided by the goal of compensation, but only from restitutionary principles added to that law. To claim otherwise is a mistake, and this in a particularly important way. For, second, the argument that, in the absence of negotiation for release, C has 'lost' the chance to exact a payment for that release conflates the situations of 'actual' loss and loss of windfall. (Indeed, it is the purpose of the argument to conflate these situations.) But the implicit balance of convenience or relative disadvantage reasoning that has guided hard cases in the law of literal enforcement strongly distinguishes these situations for it is (though often insufficiently) conscious of the hardship imposed on D by literal enforcement. The restitutionary argument for (partial) disgorgement of windfalls will be discussed elsewhere.[16] In this Part, we will be concerned only with the situation where D hopes to avoid literal enforcement in order to minimise the cost of his performance.

---

14  *Ruxley Electronics and Construction Ltd v Forsyth* [1996] AC 344 is one of the principal authorities giving weight to the approach advocated in this Part. Though *Bellgrove v Eldridge* (1954) 90 CLR 613 at 618-619, in which the High Court of Australia specifically disapproved of the use of the term 'economic waste', was approvingly cited by Lord Jauncey in *Ruxley* at 359, it is clear that something like this term does describe what is at issue here, and in this Part the term 'social waste' will continue to be used.

15  See pp 222-226 below.

16  See below ch 17. Wider use of exemplary damages in contract would also have an effect approximating to literal enforcement. See below ch 30.

# 11 Claims in debt

## Introduction

A claim in debt is quite distinct from a claim to damages. A debt is a definite sum of money which, under the terms of the contract, D is due to pay C, either: (a) in return for C's completing his performance of a specified obligation under the contract; or (b) upon the occurrence of a specified event or condition (other than a breach of contract committed by D). The first category is illustrated by the price payable upon delivery of the goods under a contract of sale, or by an instalment payable under a building contract when the builder has completed a specified stage of the building. It is a sum which C has earned by completing part or all of his own performance. The second category is illustrated by a sum payable under an insurance policy upon the happening of one of the events specified in the policy, eg theft of an item of jewellery listed in the policy, or the payment of a sum due under the terms of a guarantee. A further illustration is a case where D received an insurance payment from C on the basis of his permanent disablement and C was able to enforce D's undertaking to repay the amount if he later took part in a particular sport.[1]

When C claims a debt, the question before the court is whether the sum is *due* according to the terms of the contract, not whether D has committed a breach of the contract (apart from his failure to pay that sum).[2] This will tend to make a claim in debt much simpler than a claim for damages,[3] and, *ceteris paribus*, more attractive to a claimant. There is no

---

1   *Alder v Moore* [1961] 2 QB 57.
2   A sum payable by D *upon* his breach, as a secondary obligation activated by breach of his primary obligation, is not a debt for these purposes, and is subject to the separate body of rules on liquidated damages and penalties. See ch 9 above.
3   In terms of its legal complexity, debt in this sense 'hardly merits comment': FH Lawson, *Remedies of English Law* (2nd edn 1980) p 50.

question of C proving any 'loss' caused by D's breach, but of his proving that the conditions set out in the contract for the payment have arisen and that he has not received the payment. So none of the rules on the law of damages are relevant. There is no need for C to satisfy the rules on causation of loss, assessment of loss, or the remoteness of damage. C is not required to meet any test of reasonableness under the doctrine of mitigation, since the orthodox view is that this doctrine does not apply to a claim for a debt. (This question is examined throughout this chapter.) Nor is C required to satisfy the rules on liquidated damages, which relate only to sums payable by D in consequence of his having committed a breach of his contract.[4] Unless D enters a defence such as tender before claim,[5] the simplicity of the debt action makes it particularly easy for C to apply for summary judgment against D,[6] and rapidly put him in a position where he can enforce the judgment.[7]

Decisions on contracts of hire highlight the distinction between debt and damages. Where chattels are hired to D by C, the owner, in return for regular payments of hiring charges, if C terminates the contract upon D's breach, the claim for instalments already due lies in debt, but a claim for the *prospective* loss of instalments due in the future can only be a claim for damages.[8]

4    Although failure to pay a debt when it is due can be termed a breach of contract, a claim to *that* debt itself is not treated as subject to the rules on liquidated damages. But these rules would apply if the contract provided that upon D's failure to pay a specified sum, a larger sum became payable by him.

5    A defence that, before C started proceedings, D unconditionally offered to C the amount due.

6    CPR Part 14. See further the Court Service, *Small Businesses: A Guide to Debt Recovery Through a County Court for Small Businesses* (nd).

7    JK Gatenby, *Recovery of Money* (1993). The law of actual enforcement of debt is deplorably archaic and obscure and has long been acknowledged to allow the systemic oppression, shading into illegality, of poor debtors, especially those in rent arrears: The Law Commission, *Distress for Rent*, Working Paper No 97 (1986); National Consumer Council, *Response to the Report of the Law Commission on Distress for Rent* (1986); *Report of the Review Body on Civil Justice*, Cm 394 (1988); The Law Commission, *Landlord and Tenant: Distress for Rent*, Law Com No 194 (1991); JK Gatenby, *Recovery of Money*, *loc cit*, chs 11-12; J Kruse, *Distress and Execution* (1998) (a commendably objective work commissioned by one of the bailiffs' trade associations, The Association of Civil Enforcement Agencies); A Green (National Association of Citizen Advice Bureaux), *Undue Distress* (2000) and J Kruse, *The Law of Seizure of Goods* (2000). See further DI Greenberg, 'Easy Terms, Hard Times: Complaint Handling in the Ghetto', in L Nader, ed, *No Access to Law* (1980) 379, pp 385-6. The Lord Chancellor's Department is in the process of what appears to be a very wide ranging reform of the entire enforcement process: Lord Chancellor's Department, *Towards Effective Enforcement: A Single Piece of Bailiff Law and a Regulatory Structure for Enforcement*, Green Paper, Cmd 5096 (2001); J Beatson, *Independent Review of Bailiff Law* (2000) and Lord Chancellor's Department, *Distress for Rent*, Enforcement Review Consultation Paper No 5 (2001). See further W Kennett, 'The Enforcement Review: A Progress Report' (2001) 20 *Civil Justice Quarterly* 36.

8    *Interoffice Telephones Ltd v Robert Freeman Co Ltd* [1958] 1 QB 190.

A claim for the price of goods sold to D brought by the unpaid seller C is the main instance of a claim in debt. According to the Sale of Goods Act, the buyer must have made default in paying the price, and either the property (ownership) in the goods must have passed to the buyer, or the price must have been due 'on a day certain irrespective of delivery'.[9] (If the goods have not been delivered, the seller who claims the price must continue to be able and willing to deliver them.) But the terms of the contract may entitle the seller to sue for the price in other circumstances, eg 'net cash before delivery', coupled with a provision that property is to pass only on delivery.[10] In addition to the price, the seller may claim interest for delay in receiving it[11] and damages for any consequential loss, such as storage charges for the goods. The rules on claiming the price may provide certainty (and thus encourage out-of-court settlements), but they imply that the seller can compel the buyer to take and pay for the goods even where the seller is better able than the buyer to find a substitute buyer. The parties will normally negotiate the 'efficient' outcome, but an unreasonable seller can sit tight on his claim to the price and refuse to negotiate. The US Uniform Commercial Code, s 2-709 may indicate a preferable position when it permits the seller to recover the price only if he cannot be reasonably expected to resell the goods at a reasonable price.

## Debt and mitigation

In some cases, conceivably the great majority, a claim for debt and a claim for damages amount to the same thing, with C's choice of a debt action being a matter of the procedural ease of that claim.[12] If C has, say, completely performed his obligation to deliver the goods and D has failed to pay, then an action for damages would be equivalent to an action for

9    Sale of Goods Act 1979, s 49.
10   *Benjamin's Sale of Goods* (5th edn 1997) para 16-025.
11   See p 108 above.
12   By far the largest category of 'disputes' which enter the civil legal system are claims for debt. In 1998, 87% of county court summonses were default actions of which debt will have formed a large proportion: Lord Chancellor's Department, *Judicial Statistics (County Court)* (1998). The majority of the work of the civil court system, of bureaucratised, indeed now largely automated, debt collection, therefore lies outside the scope of this book. This is a surprising state of affairs for remedies scholars, one not without significance for a sociologically accurate account of the function of the civil law which, one suspects, would place us in a position analogous to that of Galanter, of being unable to 'escape the conclusion that in gross the courts in the United States are forums which are used by organisations to extract from and discipline individuals': M Galanter, 'Afterword: Explaining Litigation' (1974-5) 9 Law and Society Review 347, 360. See further RA Kagan, 'The Routinisation of Debt Collection: An Essay on Social Change and Conflict in the Courts' (1984) 18 Law and Society Review 323 and H Collins, *Regulating Contracts* (1999) pp 324-5.

debt. The contract price, which would be the subject of a claim for debt, is congruent with the cost of producing and delivering the goods (reliance) plus the lost net profit on the sale (expectation) which would be the subject of a claim for damages.

However, in certain cases, the avoidance of the rules on mitigation in a claim for debt can produce a crucially important difference between debt and damages for C and, as we shall see, even more for D. For instance, if on selling goods to D, C is entitled to claim the price, he need not mitigate by reselling them at the market price prevailing at the date of D's failure to pay the price. In other types of contract, if C can complete his performance, he may also be able to sue in debt and thus avoid any duty to mitigate. In *White and Carter (Councils) Ltd v McGregor*,[13] C was an advertising contractor who agreed to display advertisements for D's garage on litterbins for a period of three years. D repudiated the agreement on the day it was made, but C refused to terminate it and proceeded to prepare and display the advertising plates for the whole three years. The House of Lords held that C could recover the full contract price. C had not accepted D's anticipatory repudiation, with the result that the contract continued in force and C had been able to complete its performance.

We have seen above that C's power to terminate following D's breach can be a powerful remedy, one regulated by the distinction between conditions, warranties and intermediate terms.[14] The purpose of distinguishing between these types of terms is to limit (unless the parties have provided otherwise) C's power to terminate *only* to those cases where the breach is sufficiently serious to justify C terminating, as termination will impose a heavy loss on D. Unreasonable termination is to be avoided. The issue raised by *White and Carter (Councils)* is, as it were, just the opposite, of trying to ensure that C *does* terminate when this will limit D's loss. Starting from a position in which it was thought C had an unfettered power to elect to terminate or affirm (or to waive the right to terminate),[15] the majority of their Lordships allowed C to continue to perform to the point where the debt arose under the contract. By

---

13  [1962] AC 413. See the criticism made at the time by numerous commentators: AL Goodhart, 'Measure of Damages when a Contract is Repudiated' (1962) 78 Law Quarterly Review 263; MP Furmston, 'The Case of the Insistent Performer' (1962) 25 Modern Law Review 364; K Scott, 'Contract – Repudiation – Performance by Innocent Party' [1962] Cambridge Law Journal 12 and PM Nienaber, 'The Effect of Anticipatory Repudiation: Principle and Policy' [1962] Cambridge Law Journal 213.

14  See pp 51-56 above.

15  *Tredegar Iron and Coal Co (Ltd) v Hawthorn Bros and Co* (1902) 18 TLR 716 at 716–717 and *Howard v Pickford Tool Co Ltd* [1951] 1 KB 417 at 421. On the exercise of the power of election or waiver see H Beale, *Damages for Breach of Contract* (1980) 118-124.

implication, that majority[16] decided that the mitigation rules did not apply to C when it could sue for a debt in return for its own performance. According to Lord Reid, even where C's attempt to enforce his strict contractual rights is unreasonable, the court should refuse to control him, since to do so would create too much uncertainty.[17]

The decision in *White and Carter (Councils)* seems to contravene the policy of the mitigation rules[18] and therefore to permit social waste.[19] Such utility as reliance expenditure ultimately has is its utility to D, and in this case D made it plain that it did not want the reliance expenditure made. If C knows that the originally contemplated expense of his performance is now useless to D, why should he be able to insist on completing performance instead of accepting damages to compensate him for both his wasted expense to the date of the repudiation (more or less zero in *White and Carter (Councils) Ltd v McGregor*) and also his loss of profits on the contract as a whole? If expectation damages alone or expectation plus reliance in respect of only expense wasted up to the date of repudiation provide full compensation to C, why should C be able to recover a greater sum? If damages are an 'adequate remedy', why should C be able to get indirect specific performance[20] by *continuing* after D's repudiation to incur expense in performing after D has definitely indicated that performance is no longer useful to her or him?[1] By insisting upon mitigation in these circumstances, the court would merely be restricting the range of remedies available to C, not denying her or him a remedy. American courts have not hesitated to hold that, whether D's repudiation is accepted or not, C is always obliged to mitigate.[2]

Pronounced uneasiness about the result of *White and Carter (Councils) Ltd v McGregor* led Lord Reid, one of the majority in the Lords, to recognise two qualifications of that result, one obvious but the other novel, in his speech. In many contracts, C will need D's co-operation in order to

---

16  The two in the minority thought that C should have mitigated his loss by discontinuing performance after D had repudiated: *White and Carter (Councils) Ltd v McGregor*, above, n 13 at 433, 439-440 per Lords Morton and Keith dissenting.

17  Ibid at 430.

18  See ch 7 above.

19  JW Carter et al, 'Performance Following Repudiation: Legal and Economic Interests' (1999) 15 Journal of Contract Law 97, pp 121-131 and JS Zeigel, 'What Can the Economic Analysis of Law Teach Commercial and Consumer Law Scholars', in R Cranston and RM Goode (eds), *Commercial and Consumer Law* (1993) 249, pp 261-262.

20  *White and Carter (Councils) Ltd v McGregor*, above p 161, n 13 at 433 per Lord Morton dissenting. And, indeed, if it were a claim for specific performance, the court would have a discretion whether or not to grant it. See pp 178-193 below.

1   *Attica Sea Carriers Corpn v Ferrostaal Poseidon Bulk Reederei GmbH, The Puerto Buitrago* [1976] 1 Lloyd's Rep 250.

2   Goodhart, 'Measure of Damages when a Contract is Repudiated', above p 161, n 13, p 267.

complete his own performance, and it is obvious that in the circumstances where D wants C to terminate the contract, this co-operation will not readily be forthcoming. *White and Carter (Councils) Ltd v McGregor* was itself unusual in that no co-operation at all was required for C to continue to be able to perform for three years![3] But in other circumstances, D's reluctance to co-operate when his co-operation is necessary can mean that C will be forced to sue for damages, and so be subject to all the rules on damages, including mitigation. When, for example, the installation of a complex, bespoke telephone system in business premises obviously required active co-operation over the installation, this barred C's affirmation of the contract after D's repudiation.[4]

Of course, the court could issue orders which sought to, as it were, compel co-operation similar to orders for specific performance. But, not only is the court generally entirely correct to be reluctant to embark on what might be prolonged and ultimately fruitless and/or oppressive supervisory duties,[5] it would appear that a perception that the position left by *White and Carter (Councils)* is unsatisfactory has reinforced that reluctance. In the New Zealand case of *Mayfield Holdings Ltd v Moana Reef Ltd*,[6] C was engaged on work on D's land and was restricted to its remedy in damages when D obtained an injunction that it vacate the site, C's own application for an injunction restraining D from removing it from the site having been refused.[7] It is difficult to justify drawing a line with such serious consequences as between debt and damages according to the fortuitous circumstance whether C can perform his remaining obligations with or without D's assent or co-operation, and in the Canadian case of *Finelli v Dee*,[8] the Ontario Court of Appeal simply ignored it. C needed to obtain access to D's property to carry out building works and, knowing that D no longer wished to have the work done, waited until D was away from home to carry out the works. As a matter of fact if hardly of right, C thereby had rendered the question of co-operation otiose. However, flatly refusing to follow *White and Carter (Councils) Ltd v McGregor*, Laskin JA did not award C the contract price.

Lord Reid's second qualification was novel and, it would seem, played no part in the decision in *White and Carter* itself.[9] It was that C should

---

3   *White and Carter (Councils) Ltd v McGregor*, above p 161, n 13 at 429 per Lord Reid.
4   *Telephone Rentals v Burgess Salmon* [1987] CCLR 419.
5   See pp 187-193 below.
6   [1973] 1 NZLR 309.
7   *Hounslow London Borough Council v Twickenham Garden Developments Ltd* [1971] Ch 233 was not followed. In this case, a similar injunction to evict D from C's land was not granted to C because, without a full trial of the matter, Megarry J was uncertain where the rights of the breach claimed by C but denied by D lay: ibid at 268-70.
8   (1968) 76 DLR (2d) 393.
9   *Hounslow London Borough Council v Twickenham Garden Developments Ltd*, above, n 7 at 253.

not be entitled to claim the price if he has 'no legitimate interest, financial or otherwise, in performing the contract rather than claiming damages'.[10] This qualification has been accepted by the Court of Appeal[11] and has since clearly been applied to deny C the contract price in a number of cases. In *The Alaskan Trader*,[12] C owned a ship which was chartered to D for two years. A serious engine breakdown led to repairs taking several months. Although D treated the charterparty as ended, C completed the repairs and told D that the ship was at its disposal. C then kept her at anchor with a full crew ready to sail until the charter expired some seven months later. The commercial court upheld the arbitrator who found that D had breached the contract, but held that C had no legitimate interest in claiming hire for these seven months, instead of claiming damages. This was a 'commercial absurdity'. The essence of the dispute was whether C should have attempted to mitigate its loss by reducing its outgoings or seeking a substitute charterer as soon as the ship was repaired. The judge found the facts 'startling', no doubt because C's keeping the ship idle for seven months was such an obvious waste of resources. Even if no alternative use for the ship could have been found, it would have been much cheaper to lay the vessel up, rather than to keep a full crew on board. The qualification introduced by Lord Reid was applied. C's seeking to sue D in debt for the full hire was 'wholly unreasonable'.

C's conduct in *White and Carter (Councils) Ltd v McGregor* is prima facie puzzling. Standing on the simple right to claim a debt when the sum became outstanding which C understandably thought the law to be prior to Lord Reid's invention of the legitimate interest,[13] C pleaded no such interest and its reasons for pursuing the course it did do not emerge from the case. Nevertheless, this course obviously was a risky one to take, for common sense if not the law on debt would lead C to believe not only that payment might be withheld but that a court might be reluctant to enforce this particular debt. Winning three to two in the House of Lords (after previously losing twice) hardly shows that one has pursued unambiguously the right course. Furthermore, in choosing to perform this contract, C denied itself a potential windfall profit. Following termination of the contract, C may have been able to redeploy the resources thereby released into another contract in the expectation of another profit on that contract. In *White and Carter (Councils) Ltd v McGregor*, C declined to pursue this possibility of increasing its overall profits over the three years in which it was obliged to perform after affirming the original contract by performing another contract as well within those three years. One can only

10   *White and Carter (Councils) Ltd v McGregor*, above p 161, n 13 at 431.
11   *Attica Sea Carriers Corpn v Ferrostaal Poseidon Bulk Reederei GmbH, The Puerto Buitrago*, above p 162, n 1 at 254-5 per Lord Denning MR.
12   *Clea Shipping Corpn v Bulk Oil International Ltd, The Alaskan Trader* [1984] 1 All ER 129.
13   Furmston, 'The Case of the Insistent Performer', above p 161, n 13, p 367 n 20.

assume that C feared that it would sustain some uncompensated loss by terminating. As one imagines its business relationship with D was ended, such loss could not be a property of that relationship, such as mutually devised and understood working practices.[14] But if, for example, C could have found no other work and have had to lay off experienced and loyal employees, this would result in an idiosyncratic loss which would not be fully compensated by an award of damages.

Nevertheless, if the policy underlying the mitigation rules is sound, it should not be avoided by C being able to incur further expense in performing after D's clear repudiation (whether anticipatory or not). The technical rules about C's election whether to 'accept' a repudiation should not become an instrument for flagrant waste.[15] If the courts will inquire into the legitimacy of literal enforcement when C seeks specific performance or a mandatory injunction, surely the same approach should apply in these cases of indirect specific performance. Lord Reid's qualification is sufficiently wide to give the courts the opportunity to bring the legal position close to that achieved by the 'reasonableness' standard of the mitigation rules. Either the Reid qualification or the mitigation rules would protect C whenever his failure to perform would harm his reputation or impose on him loss not covered by the rules on damages (eg because it would be too remote).

Neither a sum due from D on C's performance nor one which is payable upon an event other than a breach by D of his contract with C is subject to the law on penalties.[16]

## Appraisal

Since it is obviously much easier for C to recover a debt than damages, it will always be the endeavour of the astute draftsman to put into the contract clauses permitting his client to claim in debt instead of in damages. Because the extent to which the policy of mitigating loss applies to debt is not certain, there is a possibility that a claim for debt may lie which unreasonably diverges from the consequences of a claim for damages, and a potential reward is therefore available for the party who has access to the services of an expert draftsman. The only real control over this would be a general power of the courts to so expand the category of unfair contract terms secured by abuse of unequal bargaining power to include terms of this sort. A restriction simply on the availability of the remedy would not strike at the heart of the problem.

14  Such a property of the parties' relationship would be an "asset specific" resource. See pp 31-33 above, 171-175 below.
15  EG Andersen, 'Good Faith in the Enforcement of Contracts' (1988) 73 *Iowa Law Review* 299.
16  See ch 9 above.

# 12 Specific performance[1]

## Introduction

An order of specific performance purports to compel the promisor to perform his contractual obligations according to its terms. In English law, such an order has always been treated as an exceptional remedy. The traditional position is that it is available only where, for some special reason, the normal remedy of damages would be 'inadequate'. Historically, the remedy was granted not by the ordinary common law courts but by the Courts of Chancery, under a discretionary, equitable jurisdiction within which the judge was concerned not only with the conduct of the promisor D but could also investigate the conduct of the promisee C to see whether the latter deserved the court's assistance. The discretionary nature of the remedy was not considered to be unfair to C, since he could always fall back on his common law claim to damages if he failed to obtain specific relief.[2] The common law courts had not developed a remedy to

1 G Jones and W Goodhart, *Specific Performance* (2nd edn 1986); ICF Spry, *The Principles of Equitable Remedies* (5th edn 1997) ch 3; RJ Sharpe, *Injunctions and Specific Performance* (2nd edn 1992) Pt 2 and E Yorio, *Contract Enforcement: Specific Performance and Injunctions* (1989).

2 The Supreme Court Act 1981, s 49. With one principal exception, the court's power to withhold specific performance and award damages in lieu under Lord Cairn's Act (The Chancery Amendment Act 1858, s 2; now The Supreme Court Act 1981, s 50) now raises no special issues as it has been settled that any such award should be quantified on the normal principles of common law damages: *Johnson v Agnew* [1980] AC 367 at 400. That exception is the award of damages for hypothetical release from an obligation discussed in ch 17 below. The other circumstances where the residue of Lord Cairn's Act might now apply, if they exist at all as other than theoretical speculations (eg *Ryan v Mutual Tontine Westminster Chambers Association* [1893] 1 Ch 116) are too arcane for a work of this scope and must be sought elsewhere: MP Furmston, ed, *The Law of Contract* (1999) para 8.152.

compel performance (except a claim in debt), since they accepted the view that money was always an equivalent of anything that had been promised.

Since equity supplemented rather than supplanted the common law, the granting of specific performance was cautious and limited. It was granted only when the court could 'do more perfect and complete justice'[3] by awarding it rather than by damages. As imprisonment for contempt of court was the ultimate sanction against D, a promisor who refused to comply with an order, the Chancery judges played safe by granting specific performance only where the threat of imprisonment was likely to lead to the required performance. They were concerned with the problem of supervising D's purported compliance, and their assessment of the parties' behaviour could lead to the exercise of their discretion not to grant an order. The basic condition for granting an order of specific performance is that damages are inadequate. But even if the court finds that damages are inadequate, it still retains the discretion to withhold an order because, overall, to grant the order would not do more perfect and complete justice.

## Inadequacy of damages

The orthodox statement of the law is that specific performance will not be ordered if damages would be an adequate remedy for the disappointed promisee C.[4] Such a statement implies a knowledge of the rules on damages and of the situations in which those rules may fail to give C an acceptable equivalent of what he expected from performance. To understand these situations, we must understand something of the properties of a good in the economic sense.

In the capitalist economy, goods (and services) possess both a use-value and an exchange-value. The former is the use of the good to its consumer, related to the good's physical characteristics. The latter is the value which the good commands in exchange, measured in money.[5] Subject to an assumption to which we shall shortly turn, it follows from this distinction that a party whose interest is in the exchange-value of a good prima facie will be able to be awarded an adequate remedy in damages. The central case where damages normally will be considered adequate is where C is a businessperson seeking profits who can readily buy a substitute good from others in the market. With the money which measures the difference between the contract price and the market price at the time of the breach, the businessperson can have his expectation

---

3   *Wilson v Northampton and Banbury Junction Railway Co* (1874) 9 Ch App 279 at 284.

4   The question of enforcing negative covenants (undertakings not to do something) is considered in ch 13 below.

5   A Smith, *Wealth of Nations* (Glasgow edn 1976) p 44.

protected by being put into as good a position as if D had performed his original obligation. Assuming good faith, D will usually have breached because performance had become unanticipatedly costly. By terminating after D's breach and obtaining a substitute, C protects his expectation in the way least costly to D. This is to say, C mitigates. The principle that specific performance should not be granted in situations where mitigation is possible has not been openly stated in the cases, but it is implicit in the practice of the courts.[6] C generally should not be allowed to avoid mitigation by seeking specific relief.

When no opportunity to mitigate through substitute performance is available, the award of damages may not be effective to produce an 'equivalent' benefit to C. As, in principle, an order of specific performance should give C whatever benefit he expected to derive from performance, then the more difficult it is to assess the value of that benefit in money, the more willing the court should be to make such an order. It can be seen that a remedy based on C obtaining a substitute and/or being compensated in damages if necessary can be the general remedy for breach only if it is assumed that substitute goods and services are available in competitive supply. That most goods and services are so available in the capitalist economies is a distinguishing feature of those economies,[7] and on this assumption the structure of legal remedies in contract is based.[8] There are two strong reasons, common to all forms of literal enforcement including specific performance, why this assumption might not hold: the loss of a consumer surplus and idiosyncratic loss leading to 'commercial uniqueness'. There are, in addition, two peculiar and, as they now stand, ultimately indefensible reasons which have been the basis of grants of specific performance, the fact that the contract is for the sale of land or that the contract has purported to confer a benefit on a third party.

### Consumer surplus

The concept of a 'consumer surplus' traceable to the economist Alfred Marshall[9] is one which, though at first strange to lawyers, has been adapted to, and has proven useful in, the understanding of some legal problems

---

6   Except in sales of land, which will be discussed shortly.
7   K Marx and F Engels, 'Manifesto of the Communist Party', in K Marx and F Engels, *Collected Works*, vol 6 (1976) 477, p 489.
8   Capitalist economies with civil legal systems appear to give far greater precedence to literal enforcement than those with common law systems, but this precedence is so hedged with exceptions that, it would appear, the practical difference is small: GH Treitel, *Remedies for Breach of Contract* (1988) para 41.
9   A Marshall, *Principles of Economics* (8th edn 1920) pp 103-110.

about remedies.[10] It is based on the idea that the subjective value of something to an individual may sometimes diverge from its value as represented by the market price. The simplest example is the situation where a person decides in advance the maximum amount he would be prepared to pay for an item at an auction. If he then buys it for less, the difference is his consumer surplus at the moment of purchase. If he can buy *x* for £100 when he was prepared to pay up to £150 for it, the saving of £50 represents his consumer surplus. His willingness to pay, rather than the market price, is the measure of its value to him.

Unlike the businessperson who seeks a profit, and therefore is concerned with exchange-value, the private party buys things for use, and therefore is concerned with use-value. The consumer seeks the pleasure or utility to be obtained from use or possession. The same holds for services under a contract. A package holiday is worth more to a tourist than its price, since the tourist hopes to gain recreation, pleasure and other non-pecuniary advantages from it. Wedding photographs are worth more to the couple and their relatives than their cost. The purpose of a contract in this circumstance is to give one party a benefit which, from his point of view, is not measured by the price he paid for it. The economist would describe the consumer surplus in terms of the excess 'utility' obtained from a good which is above the utility associated with spending its market price on another purchase.

In many situations, the law on remedies can safely ignore the problem of valuing the consumer surplus expected by C, viz whenever he can obtain a substitute in the market which will give him virtually the same surplus. It is only where it is impossible to mitigate in this way that a problem arises because no substitutes are available at the time in question. The legal significance of the existence of consumer surplus therefore emerges when a good is available only in limited supply. It is axiomatic in neo-classical economics that virtually all goods are scarce in the sense of not being available in infinite, costless supply.[11] Nevertheless, the supply of such goods can be increased, which invites competition in supply, and therefore their market price is a product of the two functions of demand and supply. That price will partly reflect the cost of producing the good, and not simply the demand for it, and the more competitive the market, the closer the market price will be to the cost of supply. Some goods, however, are 'scarce' in the stronger sense that their supply cannot be increased.[12] The supply of timber for door-making can be increased to

---

10  D Harris et al, 'Contract Remedies and the Consumer Surplus' (1979) 95 Law Quarterly Review 581.

11  HH Gossen, *The Laws of Human Relations* (1983) ch 2.

12  D Ricardo, *On the Principles of Political Economy and Taxation* (1951) p 12. This sense of scarcity applies to goods of limited as well as completely fixed supply, so it would include eg the only copy of the Mona Lisa and all the copies of a limited edition print of a Hockney.

the extent that our efforts be committed to that increase, but the supply of a particular ornamental door by the late architect Adam cannot.[13] An attempt to do so would be a forgery. The price of a good scarce in this second sense cannot be influenced by supply, which is fixed. It is a direct function of demand, that is to say, of willingness to pay.

The door by Adam will always be scarce, but circumstances might render otherwise common goods scarce. A clock may be a mass-produced good of a common pattern, but if it is C's grandmother's clock, it may have a sentimental value unrelated to its price which can constitute a consumer surplus. If C agreed to pay £100 for this clock when others of the pattern are available for £150, the difference in market value of £50 will not adequately compensate him. (This is even less the case if, as can readily be conceived, C had, in the circumstances, paid £150 for a clock generally available for £100. In this case C's damages would be nominal.)

If the court makes an order of specific performance compelling sale of a specific good or rendering of a specific service, C may enjoy his expected consumer surplus (perhaps after a delay, which if it is substantial is a consequential loss for which damages should be paid).[14] One can, of course, conceive of a money payment that obviates C's need to claim specific performance. C may, in the example of the clock discussed above, be dissatisfied with £50 but happy to accept £500. D is, of course, at liberty to offer £500 for his own reasons (he may have his own consumer surplus), but this is not the figure which could be fixed as damages, which are quantified so as to compensate C. Compensation for the loss of a consumer surplus could be measured only by the willingness of the court to attempt to put a value on it. But there are serious or intractable problems of proof in attempting to value it. The court could not simply accept C's own evidence as to the value he put on it, since he has an obvious incentive to inflate that value. If the court attempts to assess the value itself, it would be impossible (or at least extremely difficult and costly) to obtain the relevant information about the subjective value that a reasonable person in C's position would have put on it. Consequently, there is a high risk of over- or under-compensation. Against the general reluctance of the courts to run the risk of over-compensating C and giving him a 'windfall' must be weighed the consideration that if they fail to take account of the loss of the consumer surplus which C genuinely expected (and which satisfies the test of remoteness), he will be left uncompensated. An order of specific performance avoids the difficulty or impossibility of trying to put a monetary value on the surplus, which would be very speculative.

13  *Phillips v Lamdin* [1949] 2 KB 33 at 41-42.
14  The special problems raised by the court awarding C damages assessed at the cost of employing a third party to perform exactly what D promised are discussed in ch 14 below.

With an instinctive feeling for this consideration, the courts have for centuries held that specific performance should be granted for cases where performance would confer some peculiar, special, or, as it is often put, 'unique' value on C, eg in contracts about heirlooms and works of art.[15] The point, of course, is not that the good actually is unique. All objects are unique in one sense, their being so is simply a condition or an implication of their being distinguishable objects, and this can hardly be the basis of specific performance. On the other hand, uniqueness for the purposes of an order of specific performance of the sale of the door by Adam can be shared by the clock of common pattern which has a sentimental value.[16] The point is that uniqueness in this sense, like all utility generally,[17] is not a property of the good. It is a property of the relationship of the good to the use to which it is to be put, and in this case that purpose can helpfully be analysed as realisation of consumer surplus.

### Idiosyncratic loss and commercial uniqueness

If C is a commercial party, he cannot have a consumer surplus interest. As a commercial party is interested only in the exchangeable value of a good, prima facie that party should find damages adequate. Even were the good which is the subject of the contract scarce in the stronger sense we have used, if C's interest is only in, say, its value on resale, then he may be compensated in damages. The very same door by Adam which could ground a claim for specific performance by C if it is C's intention, being very concerned with the quality of his decor, to hang it in his home, cannot ground such a claim in the same way if it is his intention, as an art dealer, to sell it.[18] In the latter case, C's interest is only in the exchange value of the good, specifically the profit on (re)sale, and prima facie this can *always* be compensated by an award of money damages, even if the good which is the subject of the contract is allowed to be unique in any or all of the sense we have discussed. In *Societé des Industries Metallurgiques SA v Bronx Engineering Co Ltd*, specific performance was refused of the sale of a machine made to C's specification weighing 220 tons, costing £270,400,[19] and which would take between nine months and a year to

15  AT Kronman, 'Specific Performance' (1978) 45 University of Chicago Law Review 351.
16  Queen Victoria wrote of Crimean War soldiers to whom she had presented medals that 'they won't hear of giving up their medals to have their names engraved on them for fear they should not receive the *identical one* put into *their hands by me*, which is quite touching': *The Letters of Queen Victoria*, vol 3 (1908) p 127.
17  WS Jevons, *The Theory of Political Economy* (1970) pp 105-106.
18  The leading case of *Falcke v Gray* (1859) 4 Drew 651 is notably confused on this point.
19  *Ex works*, in 1973 prices.

replace, because there was 'no suggestion of financial inability in the defendants to meet such a money judgment (whatever its dimensions) as might be awarded against them to cover all such items of damages as the plaintiffs could legitimately rely upon.'[20] The traditional preoccupation with the subject good's uniqueness means that this uniqueness is, however, often discussed at unnecessary length, especially in somewhat older authorities. So when, in *Cohen v Roche*,[1] specific performance was denied to a buyer of furniture who intended to resell it at a profit, great and arguably unnecessary pains were taken to point out that it was 'ordinary Hepplewhite furniture' which 'possessed no special characteristics' at all.

However, even in commercial contracts, the court may take into account types of loss which are so uncertain that there would be 'great difficulty in estimating' them and/or would be too remote for the assessment of damages, eg loss of goodwill and trade reputation in a contract.[2] This may even apply to a commercial good which, in the circumstances, has unusual qualities. In *Behnke v Bede Shipping Co Ltd*,[3] specific performance was ordered of the sale of a ship which, though relatively inexpensive, satisfied exacting German shipping regulations when there was no alternative vessel reasonably available, the only comparable vessel not being for sale. Similarly, in *Dougan v Ley*,[4] specific performance was ordered of the sale of a taxicab which had a valuable operating license, one of a limited number, attached to it.

Because of the domination of ideas drawn from cases of consumer surplus, it is often pleaded that goods in these circumstances are 'unique'.[5] Such a concept of 'commercial uniqueness'[6] is, of course, an oxymoron. What really is at issue when an order for specific performance is made in such circumstances is that C is trying to avoid the risk of being left (partially) uncompensated as a result of the normal operation of the rules for the quantification of compensatory damages. In *Behnke v Bede Shipping Co Ltd*, C obviously faced a consequential loss of profits related to work it would have to forego because it had no ship. Such a loss certainly

---

20  [1975] 1 Lloyd's Rep 465 at 468.
1   [1927] 1 KB 169 at 179-181.
2   *Evans Marshall & Co Ltd v Bertola SA* [1973] 1 WLR 349 at 380.
3   [1927] 1 KB 649; distinguished in *Societé des Industries Metallurgiques SA v Bronx Engineering Co Ltd* [1975] 1 Lloyd's Rep 465 at 468.
4   (1946) 71 CLR 142.
5   *Behnke v Bede Shipping Co Ltd*, above n 3 at 661. The Sale of Goods Act 1979, s 52 requires that, for a court to consider exercising its discretion to grant specific performance to a buyer, the goods must be 'specific or ascertained' (as opposed to 'generic'). Whilst the detailed meaning of these terms must be sought elsewhere (*Benjamin's Sale of Goods* (5th edn 1997) para 17-090), it is basically determined by the unavailability of a reasonable substitute: *The Oro Chief* [1983] 2 Lloyd's Rep 509 at 521.
6   GH Treitel, *Law of Contract* (10th edn 1999) p 952.

would occur, but might be irrecoverable because, in the absence of the evidence of a full order book or something similar, that loss was uncertain or remote. Such a loss, which cannot be quantified and therefore compensated in damages, may be called idiosyncratic,[7] as opposed to the type of loss exemplified by market damages when a substitute good is bought at a higher price, which are readily quantifiable.[8]

The rules for quantifying compensatory damages work well for market damages but not for idiosyncratic loss. The principal reasons why C may face an uncompensated loss are:

(1) *Onus of proof.*[9] The basic rule that the onus of proof is on C means that it is C who must monitor D's performance to discover any breach, and then must be able to find legally admissible evidence to prove the breach and the extent of the loss which it caused. If he cannot find sufficient evidence to prove these, he loses. Any uncertainties over the evidence therefore are at C's risk, as are the risks of delay and the recovery of legal costs. D as defendant can sit tight and wait until C proves his claim. The position of D as defendant, who merely responds to C's claim, is therefore a powerful one. D is also protected by procedural rules designed to give him notice of a claim and a fair opportunity to rebut it. The inability of C to clear all these hurdles will often give D a protection against liability to some extent distanced from the actual extent of that liability,[10] and D may take advantage of this when deciding whether or not to perform.

(2) *Limited use of specific relief.* Except in sales of land, the use of specific performance is rare, which fact must induce the majority of promisors to believe that it is most unlikely that the court will ever compel them actually to perform. They will therefore calculate that the maximum risk is the payment of damages, which, being usually assessed as C's net loss, will seldom cost D as much as actual performance. Restitutionary awards which would have the effect of promoting performance, that is to say, would be an indirect form of specific relief, previously have not been widely available and the current argument that they should be is, it will be argued in chapter 17, very weak.

(3) *Causation and remoteness.* The need for C to prove causation and proximity can provide the major incentive to D to breach in a case of loss not provided for in the contract by, eg a liquidated damages clause,

7   Cases such as *Anglia Television Ltd v Reed* [1972] 1 QB 60, in which no claim was made for lost profits, exemplify this type of idiosyncratic loss. The 'asset specific' investments characteristic of relational contracts are very likely to be idiosyncratic in this sense. See pp 31-33, above.
8   See pp 168-171 above.
9   MG Bridge, 'Expectation Damages and Uncertain Future Losses'in J Beatson and D Friedmann (eds), *Good Faith and Fault in Contract Law* (1995) ch 17.
10  See ch 2 above.

for, in the absence of such a clause, the problems of proof may lead to C remaining under-compensated by an award of damages.

(4) *Limited exemplary damages in contract.* The very limited circumstances in which the courts will award exemplary damages in contract means that D may face no penalty for the most outrageous, deliberate breach. D's bad faith, and even his malice against C, are treated as irrelevant to the issue of liability in contract and of limited relevance to the quantification of damages.[11]

(5) *The law on penalties.* Since there is always the chance that the law on penalties may release D from an agreed damages clause, the incentive to perform provided by the clause is diminished and C, who will have to fall back on the common law rules of quantification if D is released from the agreed damages clause, may be left under-compensated. (C originally thought the agreed damages clause was necessary.) If the penalty test were abolished, an agreed damages clause would obviously become a more powerful incentive to perform, thereby protecting C's expectation.

(6) *Special clauses protecting D.* Exemption clauses, 'conclusive evidence' clauses and other devices to similar effect may operate to protect D from liability for breaches, and thus encourage him to breach without regard to the consequences for C.

When one or a combination of these factors have produced a situation in which C faces an uncompensated loss as a result of D's breach, C's expectation interest arguably can be protected only by literal enforcement. In the absence of this protection, D may breach unreasonably, or 'opportunistically' as economists would put it,[12] because the breach does not, as it should, involve paying (full) compensation to C (which D may do reasonably self-interestedly).

These issues were considered in *Sky Petroleum v VIP Petroleum*,[13] in which specific performance was in effect granted of the sale of fuel to C's petrol stations. Cartelisation of international oil prices by the Organisation of Petroleum Exporting Countries had created a shortage of petrol such that C could not have bought a substitute supply and would, in all likelihood, have had to go out of business following D's refusal to supply. Though D in fact disputed any liability, even had he been liable, C would have had great difficulty in the extremely disrupted business conditions in proving all the loss he would have sustained as a result of D's failure to

11  See pp 594-603 above.
12  OE Williamson, *The Economic Institutions of Capitalism* (1985) pp 47-49.
13  [1974] 1 WLR 576. This was actually a case in which an injunction was sought, but the grant of an injunction constituted, the court clearly recognised, indirect specific performance: ibid at 578. On indirect specific performance generally see pp 200-208 below.

perform, and obviously feared that D's breach would leave him with a very substantial uncompensated consequential loss.

Granting specific relief in circumstances such as these is inconsistent with the normal rules for the quantification of compensatory damages and so one suspects has inefficient consequences. *Sky Petroleum v VIP Petroleum* must itself be suspect in this sense. The injunction granted to D ensured that supplies to him would continue. As supplies were absolutely scarce, however, this could only mean that supplies elsewhere were cut off. The court did not inquire into the global consequences of its ruling, nor, had it done so, would it have been as competent as D to determine where, in these circumstances, it was optimal that supplies be discontinued. One suspects, of course, that it was optimal that it was D's supply that was discontinued.[14] The possibility of gaining such relief is the result of the separate historical development of the compensatory and specific relief remedies. The fact that the normal restrictions on the quantification of damages do not apply to specific relief may perhaps be justified by the exceptional nature of the remedy, which means that the restrictions are avoided only in a minority of cases.

## Sale and purchase of land

Specific performance is the regular remedy for breach of contracts to buy and sell land.[15] Courts regularly assume that, from the purchaser's point of view, each piece of land is unique, and therefore no substitute would be the same.[16] Damages therefore must be inadequate and courts grant specific performance as a matter of course, without enquiring whether damages would be adequate in the individual case.[17] Often this will be correct on the facts, since the market price of a house may not reflect the unique consumer surplus of the purchaser who is a consumer. The particular 'mix' of factors which led to his choosing this house (its location, size, design, price, access to shops, schools, recreational facilities, etc) would seldom be found anywhere else.

---

14  Cf the questionability, which is much more widely perceived, of implying terms which have a similar effect in eg *Liverpool City Council v Irwin* [1977] AC 239.

15  It is also available to enforce a contractual license to occupy land, even where no proprietary interest has been created: *Verrall v Great Yarmouth Borough Council* [1981] QB 202.

16  To the purchaser, 'the land may have a peculiar and special value': *Adderley v Dixon* (1824) 1 Sim & St 607 at 610.

17  For an historical explanation see D Cohen, 'The Relationship of Contractual Remedies to Political and Social Status: A Preliminary Inquiry' (1982) 32 University of Toronto Law Review 31.

But if the purchaser was buying the land as an investment (either to earn income, or to make a profit on resale) and not for personal occupation, it might be thought (as some Canadian cases have held)[18] that damages would be adequate.[19] It is submitted that courts should allow D to argue that another property could be found with similar potential for income or for profitable resale. Even in the case of residential property, the element of uniqueness may be absent, eg one flat in a high-rise building may be almost identical to another, and could be treated as a substitute.

The existence of this possibility has not led the courts to change their general practice. It is possible to argue that this practice brings orderliness to the transfer of ownership and possession of property, and that this is a special case of 'performance' needed to provide certainty in transactions about land. It is submitted that this is, however, too sweeping a generalisation and that the question at least deserves empirical investigation.

On the basis of reciprocity, the vendor of land has also been given the remedy of specific performance.[20] Although, once he has sold, his interest is primarily only in money, he may have found it difficult to sell, or, as ownership of land carries some potentially onerous duties, he may have his own reasons for wanting to get rid of the responsibilities of ownership of this particular piece of land. Again, the particular sale might be one vital link in a chain of house purchases, and the vendor's entitlement to specific performance may prevent the whole chain from collapsing. The strong likelihood that specific performance will be granted to the vendor does mean, however, that he need not, upon the purchaser's breach, take steps to mitigate by finding another purchaser. The practice of granting specific performance puts on the defaulting purchaser the burden of trying to resell the land.[1] If he can find another purchaser, D can usually arrange simultaneous completion so that the price from the resale is available to meet the price under the original sale.

### Enforcement in favour of a third-party beneficiary

The remarkable case of *Beswick v Beswick*[2] established that a contract in favour of a third-party beneficiary may in some circumstances be enforced

18  Sharpe, *Injunctions and Specific Performance*, above p 166, n 1, para 8.30.
19  PJ Brenner, 'Specific Performance of Contracts for the Sale of Land Purchased for Resale or Investment' (1978) 24 McGill Law Journal 513.
20  *Eastern Counties Rly Co v Hawkes* (1855) 5 HL Cas 331 at 376-377. The availability of the remedy in this situation has been criticised in Sharpe, *Injunctions and Specific Performance*, above p 166, n 1, paras 7.820-7.880.
1   For an argument based on the passing of the equitable title to the land immediately upon the making of the contract, see ibid, paras 8.170-8.200.
2   [1968] AC 58.

by specific performance so as to ensure that the benefit is actually received by the third party. In that case, D agreed to pay an annuity to C and W, C's wife, in return for C's transferring his business to D. Reduced payments to W were to continue after C's death. But after C's death, D made only one payment to W. According to the orthodox theory of privity, W, in her own capacity, had no cause of action against D. But W was administratrix of C's estate. The House of Lords ordered specific performance when C's estate sought to enforce D's promise to make payments to W. Either damages allowing purchase of another fund or an order to enforce the annuity payments would have been available had C himself been the beneficiary. Damages were, however, held to be inadequate because C could recover only nominal damages since no loss to the estate could be proven. Specific performance therefore was granted.

One can attempt to defend this decision as law. D had already received the benefit of C's promise to him of the transfer of the business, and, in any case, if C had failed to transfer the business, he could have been specifically ordered to transfer it to D as mutuality was satisfied. Both of these are factors in favour of specific relief.[3] But, it is submitted, it is best to see this case as a strained attempt by their Lordships to avoid the 'most unsatisfactory'[4] 'black hole'[5] of manifest injustice which can follow from the rule that a third party cannot enforce a contractual promise obviously intended to benefit him.[6] The parties in this case were relatives, which may explain why the legal formalities which would have made the annuity enforceable regardless of the contractual position were not observed. D was C and W's nephew and obviously a blackguard. But, nevertheless, damages were not, it is submitted, inadequate. They actually were nominal, for C (as the estate) actually suffered no loss. Of course, one of C's essential purposes in entering into the contract, of providing for W, would have been defeated if specific performance had not been granted (or some other way of avoiding the privity rule not been adopted).

Though there can no doubt that equity was served by the outcome of *Beswick v Beswick*, it is, of course, in obvious respects an unfortunate precedent. The reason which was given why damages were inadequate makes inadequacy an even more difficult concept and in particular suggests that their Lordships would have been willing to make an order of specific performance even if only a single payment to W had been promised or if substantial damages could have been recovered by C.

3   See pp 183-185 below.
4   *Woodar Investment Development Ltd v Wimpey Construction UK Ltd* [1980] 1 WLR 277 at 291.
5   *J Dykes Ltd v Littlewoods Mail Order Stores Ltd* 1982 SC (HL) 157 at 177.
6   *Beswick v Beswick*, above p 176, n 2 at 89.

Hopefully, in future the necessity to use arguments derived from *Beswick v Beswick* to protect the interests of third party beneficiaries will be much reduced. The Contracts (Rights of Third Parties) Act 1999, s 1[7] gives third party beneficiaries, when expressly or implicitly identified in the contract as having the right to enforce that contract, direct rights to enforce contractual provisions in their favour. This is intended to turn the issue for a party in W's position from one of somewhat tortuous remedy to an easier one of liability,[8] and from this liability, remedies should, it is hoped, follow in the usual way, though limitations to the scope of the Act have raised apprehensions that this will not always be so.[9] However, even in cases which might escape the 1999 Act, it is clear that there now is much less tolerance of attempts to use privity to escape justified liability, and any of a range of ways of preventing this will be looked upon favourably.[10]

If it should happen that *Beswick v Beswick* has in future to be called upon because C is obliged to ask for specific performance in favour of a third party inadequately identified in the contract[11] or expressly excluded from a right of enforcement under the 1999 Act,[12] then the conditions normally required in addition to inadequacy for specific relief to be granted should be satisfied, such as the possibility of supervision or mutuality of remedy. D should be able to defend on any ground which applies to the usual two-party situation.

## Equitable factors relevant to the exercise of the court's discretion

The decision to grant specific relief is never automatic. The court always has an overriding discretion to refuse to grant it even if damages are shown

7   See further Law Commission, *Privity of Contract: Contracts for the Benefits of Third Parties*, Consulation Paper No 121 (1991) and Law Commission, *Privity of Contract: Contracts for the Benefit of Third Parties*, Law Com No 242 (1996).
8   Ibid, para 7.2.
9   See pp 79-81 above.
10  *Alfred McAlpine Construction Ltd v Panatown Ltd* [2000] 3 WLR 946 at 961C-G. That liability was ultimately denied in this case turned on an evaluation of the merits of the case, in which C had agreed to a set of contracts which had the effect of isolating D from liability in order to avoid VAT, not on a formal argument about privity: GH Treitel, 'Damages in Respect of a Third Party's Loss' (1998) 114 Law Quarterly Review 527, 534. This evaluation, which treats an attempt to avoid a tax liability as a way of allocating risk, is, however, questionable: IN Duncan Wallace, 'Third Party Damage: No Black Hole?' (1999) 115 Law Quarterly Review 394, 409.
11  Contracts (Rights of Third Parties) Act 1999, s 1(2).
12  Ibid, s 6. See further Law Commission, *Privity of Contract: Contracts for the Benefit of Third Parties* (1996), above n 7, para 5.16.

to be inadequate, and in pursuing its equitable goal of doing 'more complete and perfect justice', the court may take into account many factors which would not be relevant to the questions whether damages should be awarded, and, if so, in what amount. The main reason for this discrepancy is the different historical origins of the remedies, damages being awarded at common law, and specific relief at equity. Equitable relief has always depended on the court's appraisal of all the circumstances, including the behaviour of the parties, as well as on whether damages would be an adequate remedy. In particular, Courts of Equity proclaimed that, as courts of conscience, they would not give a remedy to a party who had acted unconscionably.[13]

Not only may the court take into account factors which a court will ignore in a claim for damages, but the relevant time for considering those factors can be different. The rules on the remoteness of damage are applied on the basis of the facts known (or which ought to have been known) to the parties at the time of entering the contract. (The same time is relevant to the question whether an agreed damages clause is invalid as a penalty.) But when specific relief is sought, the court is free to consider various factors in the light of the information available at the time of the hearing. Clearly the factual situation may change substantially after the time of contracting, and a major problem about the consistency of the law on remedies for breach of contract is this contrast. If, in assessing damages, the court is precluded from considering post-contracting developments which led to categories of loss which were not within the reasonable contemplation of the parties at the time of contracting, why should the court be willing to consider them when C seeks specific relief? We shall return to this question after examining the cases on the discretionary nature of specific relief. Since the question of the relevant time is so important, the cases will be divided by reference to time.

### Factors arising from the factual situation at, or before, the time of contracting

(1) *Mistake and misrepresentation.* Various factors relevant to the exercise of the court's discretion relate to the behaviour of the parties up to the moment of contracting. Mistake and misrepresentation have always been relevant to the validity of a contract (it could be held invalid from the outset or be 'liable to be set aside in equity'). But

---

13 It should be noted that although most of the factors relating to discretion deal with those which justify a denial of the order, some may aid C in obtaining an order, eg the court may wish to encourage the freedoms of speech and assembly by enabling a political conference to be held: *Verrall v Great Yarmouth Borough Council*, above p 175, n 15.

even where the evidence relating to the mistake or the misrepresentation does not lead to this drastic result, it may still be considered by the court when choosing between specific relief or damages. The equitable view was that 'it is against conscience for a man to take advantage of the plain mistake of another, or, at least, that a Court of Equity will not assist him in doing so'.[14]

The most relevant cases are those decided after the fusion of the administration of law and equity, since the same court could then give either remedy.[15] Since this date, however, the courts have not given a wide interpretation to mistake in this context. In *Tamplin v James*,[16] D, the purchaser of a property at an auction, relied on his lifelong knowledge of the property and failed to consult an available plan which showed that it did not include a garden which he believed was part of the property. The Court of Appeal upheld an order for specific performance, since D's mistake, although honestly made, was 'without any reasonable excuse' and, in particular, had not been contributed to by C.[17]

Specific performance was thought not to impose on D 'a hardship amounting to injustice' in *Tamplin v James*.[18] Such hardship was found, however, in *Hope v Walter*, in which the court refused to order the purchase of a property bought at auction by the purchaser which neither party then knew was run as a brothel by the tenant. Similarly, the fact that C has misrepresented a relevant fact may be a ground for denying specific relief. A less serious misrepresentation than would justify rescission of the whole contract, eg a lack of candour on the part of C[19] or a misrepresentation of a collateral aspect of a contract,[20] may nevertheless be a ground for refusing specific performance.[1]

(2) *Unfairness.* In denying specific relief, the courts have also used a general concept of unfairness which arises from unconscionable conduct on the part of C in obtaining the agreement of D, eg sharp practice by C or his unfairly taking advantage of the weaker position of D. The courts have investigated the particular circumstances of each case with reference to a wide range of factors. This is to say,

---

14   *Manser v Beck* (1848) 6 Hare 443 at 448.
15   In the time of separate courts, the Court of Equity could refuse specific performance in the expectation that C, having incurred the costs of that suit, might not be willing to incur the costs of a second suit to claim damages at common law: Sharpe, *Injunctions and Specific Performance*, above p 166, n 1, para 10.60.
16   (1880) 15 Ch D 215.
17   Ibid at 221.
18   Ibid.
19   *Summers v Cocks* (1927) 40 CLR 321.
20   *Holliday v Lockwood* [1917] 2 Ch 47.
1    *Re Terry and White's Contract* (1886) 32 Ch D 14 at 29 and *Lamare v Dixon* (1873) LR 6 HL 414 at 428.

they have not restricted themselves to specific categories of unconscionability. The circumstances may be based on factors such as D's poverty, his urgent need, sickness, disability, old age, mental incapacity, lack of education, or absence of independent advice.[2] C must have exploited D's weak position so as to obtain an unfair advantage to such an extent that would be 'highly unreasonable' to order specific performance.[3] In *Walters v Morgan*,[4] for example, specific performance was refused after D had been pressurised into signing a contract before he could find out the value of the property he had just bought.

Unfairness is often associated with a mistake on the part of D, and with the inadequacy of the consideration provided by C.[5] This inadequacy is also often treated as an element of another discretionary bar, namely hardship to D, to which we shall shortly turn. However, a nominal payment in the contract may be deliberately designed by the parties to make a promise enforceable, as with the grant of an option for £1, and the exercise of such an option has been enforced by specific performance.[6] It has generally been held that specific performance will not be ordered in the absence of consideration, and Fry therefore has argued that a contract under seal should not be specifically enforced.[7] However, the granting of specific performance of a contract supported by nominal consideration should, by analogy, mean that the fact that a contract is under seal, and therefore need not be supported by consideration, should not of itself prevent specific performance if C can show that he in fact provided consideration to D.

## Factors arising after the date of contracting[8]

(1) *Impossibility*. If the facts at the time of hearing make it impossible for D to perform his obligation, the court will obviously not order him to perform. Contempt proceedings would be absurd in these circumstances.[9] Thus, if D promised to transfer an item to C, but later resold and transferred it to a bona fide third party who took it without

---

2  *Blomley v Ryan* (1956) 99 CLR 362 at 405.
3  *Wedgwood v Adams* (1843) 6 Beav 600 at 605.
4  (1861) 3 De GF & J 718.
5  *Wiltshire v Marshall* (1866) 14 LT 396 at 397.
6  *Mountford v Scott* [1975] Ch 258.
7  *Fry on Specific Performance* (6th edn 1921) p 53.
8  Unreasonable delay by C in seeking specific performance is a ground for refusing the order, as is the case with all forms of equitable remedy. See ch 32 below.
9  *Seawell v Webster* (1859) 29 LJ Ch 71 at 73.

notice of C's prior interest, no order for specific performance will be made against D.[10] There must be no legal impediment to D's compliance with the proposed order.[11] Thus, where D, the lessee, had no power under his lease to grant a sub-lease (and would risk the forfeiture of his lease if he did so), he could not be compelled by an order of specific performance to carry out an agreement to sublet.[12] In *Watts v Spence*,[13] specific performance was not ordered where a husband and wife jointly owned a house but the husband alone, without any authority from the wife, agreed to sell it. Similarly, where, in breach of an agreement, D failed to pull down an old wall and build a new one, he could not be ordered to pull down the old wall after arbitrators, acting under statutory powers, decided that it should remain.[14]

(2) *Hardship*. The fact that the contract turns out to be to D's disadvantage is not a sufficient hardship to him to justify refusal of specific relief, eg where D has sold a house only to find it difficult to buy another.[15] A contract is a mechanism for the mutual exchange of risk-taking, and an adverse outcome to one party is an obvious part of this. Although the court is not limited to assessing hardship in the light of the situation when the contract was made, any new circumstances on which a claim of hardship is based should not simply be the occurrence of the normal risks which D undertook by entering into the contract. Thus, specific performance of a mining lease has been granted despite the fact that the mine turned out to be unprofitable.[16] But it was not granted against a purchaser of farming land to which he would have no access, since all the land around it was owned by others and he would have no right of way across any of it.[17] Nor was it granted against D where the effect would be to compel him to take legal proceedings against his wife.[18]

But sometimes the performance of a contractual obligation can become unexpectedly onerous. If there is such a change of circumstances as to make D's obligation 'radically different' from that which he undertook, the doctrine of frustration may operate to

---

10  *Ferguson v Wilson* (1866) 2 Ch App 77. The substantive rules of the sale of goods or, in the case of land, property law produce the same result.
11  *Harnett v Yielding* (1805) 2 Sch & Lef 549 at 554.
12  *Warmington v Miller* [1973] QB 877.
13  [1976] Ch 165.
14  *Seawell v Webster*, above p 181, n 9.
15  *Mountford v Scott* [1975] Ch 258 at 264.
16  *Haywood v Cope* (1858) 25 Beav 140 at 149.
17  *Denne v Light* (1857) 8 De GM & G 774. Cf *Norton v Angus* (1926) 38 CLR 523.
18  *Wroth v Tyler* [1974] Ch 30.

terminate further performance by both parties.[19] But even short of this drastic consequence, the hardship which a 'non-frustrating' change in circumstances would impose on D may be a ground for denying specific performance and leaving C to his claim to damages. Hardship is often based on other factors relevant to granting a discretionary remedy, such as mistake, misrepresentation, unfairness, etc, but it need not be,[20] so that D may plead a hardship for which C was not directly responsible.[1]

On close analysis, the plea of hardship in all cases in which specific performance is contested may be seen actually to be a matter of comparing relative hardship. C may claim that the denial of specific relief may cause hardship to him which would be greater than that suffered by D if he is compelled to perform. It will be argued here that the position taken by the courts when weighing this balance of convenience or relative disadvantage turns on an appreciation of social waste. This consideration is not, however, of relevance only to pleas of hardship in specific performance but to certain attempts to resist all forms of literal enforcement. Discussion of this therefore will be reserved for the summary of literal enforcement as a whole in chapter 15 below.

(3) *A prior breach of contract committed by C.* Several discretionary bars to specific relief depend on the conduct of C after the contract was made. ('He who seeks equity must do equity' or 'he who comes to equity must come with clean hands'.) The first instance occurs when C himself has failed to perform his own obligations under the contract. It is a question of substantive law whether the breach is sufficiently serious to entitle D to terminate the contract.[2] But quite apart from this consequence, if C seeks specific relief, the court has a discretion to refuse it on the ground of his prior breach, provided it is a serious[3] breach. Breaches of provisions relating to the time of performance were not normally regarded by Courts of Equity as being of the essence of C's obligation.[4] Hence, in general and subject to certain exceptions,[5] even where C failed to comply with a stipulation as to time, he might nevertheless be granted specific performance.[6]

---

19  See pp 241-244 above.
20  *Webb v Direct London and Portsmouth Rly Co* (1852) 1 De GM & G 521.
1   *Patel v Ali* [1984] Ch 283.
2   See pp 51-56 above.
3   Specific performance may be granted despite C's trivial prior breach: *Dyster v Randall & Sons* [1926] Ch 932 at 942.
4   *United Scientific Holdings Ltd v Burnley Borough Council* [1978] AC 904.
5   Treitel, *Law of Contract*, above p 172, n 6, pp 768-769.
6   C is, of course, still liable to pay damages for any loss to D caused by his delay.

(4) *Mutuality: securing future performance by C.* Another traditional bar to specific relief has been 'want of mutuality'. If, at the time of the suit, C has not yet performed his side of the contract and could not be compelled to perform specifically, the Court of Equity felt that it would be unfair to compel D to perform. As Ames put it: 'Equity will not compel specific performance by a defendant if, after performance, the common law remedy of damages would be his sole security for the performance of the plaintiff's side of the bargain.'[7] This situation can arise where C is entitled to claim specific performance before he performs his own obligations, ie if the contract requires D to perform before C is due to perform. It might be a hardship on D if he complied with the order only to find that, should C not perform, his sole remedy against C would be damages.

Though one can perceive that doctrinal purity is served by this conclusion, mutuality would appear to have been largely a theoretical speculation[8] on the consequences of the historically different jurisdictions of the common law and Equity Courts.[9] Such cases as raised the question would appear to have had unusual features, such as an infant seeking specific performance of a contract which the rules on capacity meant that he could not be compelled to perform on his side.[10] Mutuality certainly now has limited relevance. In the case where it has most extensively been examined in modern times, mutuality was impossible but specific performance nevertheless was granted because D would be able to be adequately compensated in damages.[11] We recall that the risk that C might not perform, and D be thrown back on damages, is inherent in any contract which D agrees to perform without any overwhelmingly compelling security that C would subsequently perform his part. In addition, the time for assessing mutuality is the time of the hearing,[12] so that if by that time C has in fact performed his side (even though he could not have been compelled to do so), the original lack of mutuality will not prevent an order being made against D.[13] These two considerations will, it is submitted, cover most practically arising matters.[14]

7    JB Ames, *Lectures on Legal History* (1913) p 371.
8    JB Ames, 'Mutuality in Specific Performance' (1903) 3 Columbia Law Review 1.
9    Sharpe, *Injunctions and Specific Performance*, above p 166, n 1, paras 10.530-10.570.
10   *Flight v Bolland* (1828) 4 Russ 298 at 301 and *Lumley v Ravenscroft* [1895] 1 QB 683.
11   *Price v Strange* [1978] Ch 337.
12   Ibid.
13   *Wilkinson v Clements* (1872) 8 Ch App 96.
14   If C's obligation is severable, specific performance may be ordered in respect of the severable parts of the contract which he or she has not performed: see p 194 below.

In those situations in which one might conceive that the court may have no adequate method of ensuring that C will perform after D has complied with the order of specific performance, and this is of importance, the mutality problem can be overcome if the court can find a way of protecting D. The court might give a conditional order which depends on future performance by C[15] or some security being given by C.[16] Thus, where D agreed to transfer shares for a price which depended on the future earnings of the company, the court granted specific performance on condition that the shares should be held by C's solicitors until the price had been ascertained and paid.[17] If C is acting in good faith in asking for the order, it will cost him little extra to give security to guarantee the performance which he already intends to complete. The grant of an order of specific performance improves C's position, since he now has at his disposal the sanction of proceedings for contempt. Giving security for his own performance arguably is a small price to pay for this improvement.

The question of mutuality concerns performance by C after D has complied with an order. An analogous situation is where C's obligations are to be performed at the same time as D performs his. If C seeks specific performance, he must prove that he is ready and willing to perform. Specific performance will therefore be refused if C's conduct casts doubt on his willingness to perform, or on his ability to do so.[18]

(5) *Insolvency.* In the exercise of its discretion, the court may take into consideration any factors which it considers relevant. There is uncertainty whether D's insolvency (potential or actual) may justify an order on the ground that damages could not be collected from him. It is right, of course, that C will be very concerned, should he obtain judgment, with 'the further question – are the defendants good for the money?'[19] But when considering this, the courts should take into account the impact of an order on the rights of third parties. In sales of goods cases, if the seller becomes insolvent after he has been paid the price but before he has delivered the goods, an order for specific performance, by taking the goods out of the seller's estate,

---

15 *Price v Strange*, above p 184, n 11.
16 See also the technique of expressly empowering D to apply for an injunction to be lifted if C fails to perform: *Metropolitan Electric Supply Co Ltd v Ginder* [1901] 2 Ch 799 at 812. An application to lift a continuing injunction could, of course, always be made after sufficient evidence that C had not performed had accrued. This was a large part of the traditional reasoning that lack of mutuality was not relevant to the grant of an injunction: see WW Cook, 'The Present Status of "The Lack of Mutuality" Rule' (1927) 36 Yale Law Journal 897.
17 *Langen and Wind v Bell* [1972] Ch 685.
18 *Australian Hardwoods Pty Ltd v Railway Comrs* [1961] 1 WLR 425 at 432-433.
19 *Evans Marshall & Co Ltd v Bertola SA*, above p 172, n 2 at 380.

will give the buyer priority over the other, unsecured creditors of the seller.[20] If C were given an order, it would amount to giving him preference over D's other unsecured creditors. For this reason, the court should normally not make an order in these circumstances. Of course, other creditors might pursue an order to gain a similar advantage, but obviously not all of them could be given this preference. When D is insolvent, then, specific performance should be given only if it would have been given apart from the insolvency, such as where C has a proprietary interest in a chattel; or where, on the facts of the case, C would not be preferred to D's other creditors, eg because enforcement of the contract would involve a mutually beneficial exchange, such as the price being paid in return for the transfer of a chattel.

(6) *Election to claim damages.* If C, following D's breach of contract, has chosen to terminate the contract and to claim damages, he cannot later change his mind and seek specific performance. The principles governing termination for breach have already been examined.[1] The point here is that once C has definitely chosen this course, both parties are released from further performance of their remaining primary obligations under the contract (although, of course, C keeps alive his claim for damages against D, the contract-breaker). It would be unfair for C to revert to holding D liable to perform the contract. Since specific relief is discretionary, we might expect the principle underlying election to be that C should be held to his decision not to seek specific performance only where it would be unfair to D if C were allowed to change his mind. Such unfairness to D would obviously be caused if he had acted to his detriment in reliance on C's apparent decision not to claim specific performance. (Estoppel is an independent but analogous principle. A buyer may be estopped from seeking an order for specific performance after he has elected to accept damages in lieu of performance.)[2]

If D, the contract-breaker, indicates that he is no longer willing (or able) to perform, he is in effect anticipatorily repudiating his obligations. C may then choose either to ignore the repudiation and continue to hold D liable to perform ('affirming' the contract or 'keeping it alive'), or to 'accept the repudiation' and treat both parties as discharged from actual performance.[3] Acceptance of D's

---

20  Granting a prohibitory injunction will not, however, normally diminish D's assets: Sharpe, *Injunctions and Specific Performance*, above p 166, n 1, para 1.230.
1   See pp 51-56 above.
2   *Meng Leong Development Pte Ltd v Jip Hong Trading Co Pte Ltd* [1985] AC 511.
3   See pp 51-56 and 160-165 above.

repudiation is incompatible with seeking specific performance,[4] but not, of course, with seeking damages.[5] By extension, a restitutionary claim for the recovery of the deposit C paid[6] can be justified only if C has terminated the contract in the sense of abandoning all attempts to obtain actual performance of D's obligations.

## Practical factors relevant to the exercise of the court's discretion

In the exercise of its discretion, the court takes into account not only factors which influence the overall equity of its granting or refusing to grant an order but also factors which affect the practicality of such an order. An order to do something which has become impossible obviously would be impractical, as would an order which is likely to prove ineffective and of which contempt proceedings therefore are a likely consequence. This distinction between 'equitable' and 'practical' factors allows us to understand some cases in which equity apparently would be satisfied by an order but the order is not given, but it is clear that that distinction cannot be maintained rigidly. It may be possible to issue orders to do something which has become very difficult and by threat of imminent imprisonment compel performance, but if the likelihood is that D would be placed in contempt, the order will be refused as securing performance by such a threat is unacceptably oppressive. Practicality, in sum, is assessed from the point of view of obtaining D's performance by reliance on normal incentives once the order has been made.

The most important practical consideration is the possibility of supervision of the order, and, in an instructive sense, other considerations may be regarded merely as variants of this.

### Supervision of compliance with the order

The court will grant an order only where it could, if required, monitor compliance with the order in the expectation of securing performance. No order will be made if D undertook to perform a complicated activity which could not be adequately supervised within the court's procedures for enforcement through a contempt application. This is especially true when the promised activity involves the exercise of care and skill to meet an imprecise standard. Thus, contracts of employment have traditionally

---

4   *Johnson v Agnew* [1980] AC 367 at 392.
5   Ibid at 393.
6   See pp 58-61 above.

been outside the scope of the remedy (with the common law position being consolidated in statute),[7] and the courts have been hesitant to enforce building contracts (where, in most cases, another builder can be engaged).[8]

So reluctant have the courts been to avoid monitoring commitments that it had seemed that the law was that an order would not be granted when that was likely to lead to the court being drawn into 'continued supervision',[9] even though that supervision might not, in fact, be fruitless. But denying an otherwise appropriate remedy on this ground obviously is unsatisfactory to C, and the courts, which after all do not refuse to award damages on the ground that the defendant may fail to meet the judgment,[10] should retain some flexibility. They should be willing to take such steps as can be taken to overcome problems of supervision whenever justice requires this remedy: 'the court should not lightly be deterred by such a consideration from making an order which justice requires'.[11] Dicta to the effect that the problem of supervising an order should no longer be viewed as seriously as it used to be emerged in a number of cases in the 1970s.[12] Ultimately, in a 1985 case the covenant of the landlord of a block of flats to employ a resident porter was specifically enforced, though supervision difficulties arguably would have, and in a previous case had,[13] prevented specific enforcement of the landlord's obligations to eg 'keep clean the common [areas]' which were to be performed by the porter.[14]

Lord Hoffmann recently has helpfully clarified what is problematic about 'continued supervision' in *Co-operative Insurance Society Ltd v Argyll Stores Ltd*. The court should avoid 'the possibility of ... having to give an indefinite series of ... rulings in order to ensure execution of the order,'[15] not because these rulings could not in theory be enforced,[16] but because doing so would be unacceptably oppressive and costly. This possibility of a series of rulings is, of course, more likely if the performance is of its nature indefinite and complicated, and so the old objections are recognised to have force, but also applies when the performance is (though of a relatively simple nature) continued over a substantial period of time,

---

7   The Trade Union and Labour Relations (Consolidation) Act 1992, s 236.
8   See ch 14 below.
9   *JC Williamson Ltd v Lukey* (1931) 45 CLR 282 at 297-298.
10  It is, of course, much easier to decide whether an amount has been paid than whether some promised action has been done properly.
11  *Beswick v Beswick*, above p 176, n 2 at 91.
12  *Giles (CH) & Co Ltd v Morris* [1972] 1 WLR 307 at 318; *Shiloh Spinners Ltd v Harding* [1973] AC 691 at 724 and *Tito v Waddell (No 2)* [1977] Ch 106 at 321-322.
13  *Ryan v Mutual Tontine Westminster Chambers Association*, above p 166, n 2.
14  *Posner v Scott-Lewis* [1987] Ch 25.
15  *Co-operative Insurance Society Ltd v Argyll Stores Ltd* [1998] AC 1 at 14G, HL.
16  *Shiloh Spinners Ltd v Harding* [1973] AC 691 at 724.

rather than being aimed at the production of a specific result. Traditional authority which, on the facts of the decided cases, arguably itself was correct,[17] had been taken to constitute a rule that specific performance would not be granted of a covenant to operate a business.[18] In *Co-operative Insurance Society Ltd v Argyll Stores Ltd*, this 'rule' was rightly regarded merely as an application of arguments about supervision, and the Court of Appeal was prepared to consider these arguments on their merits.[19] However, on the facts of that case the House of Lords agreed, it is submitted correctly, with the trial judge's refusal to order specific performance of a covenant to operate a supermarket for the remaining 19 years of a 35-year lease. In the Court of Appeal, Leggatt and Roch LJJ had been of the opinion that, after the order was granted, D would run the supermarket in the way it had done previously when expecting the supermarket to yield a profit.[20] But as this was bound to entail mounting, large losses this was, with respect, an overly optimistic conclusion which their Lordships were right to reject when reversing the Court of Appeal.[1]

The main question, it is submitted, is whether, when the order is made, D can know with sufficient clarity what he must and reasonably can do to avoid being found guilty of contempt.[2] It is C who must first decide whether D has failed to comply with the order, since it is only on his initiative that the court will be asked to treat the failure as contempt of court. If there is a dispute over compliance, it is most important to predict whether the court will be required to conduct another detailed and costly examination of the factual situation.[3] The question which the court should weigh is whether a dispute over compliance would involve a substantial investment of judicial effort (largely at the taxpayer's expense, since the full cost of litigation is not borne by the parties). Justice to C through specific relief must be balanced against its cost to society, especially when

---

17   *Dowty Bolton Paul Ltd v Wolverhampton Corpn* [1971] 1 WLR 204 at 211 and *A-G v Colchester Corpn* [1955] 2 QB 207 at 217.

18   *Halsbury's Laws of England* (4th edn reissue) vol 27(1), para 444.

19   *Co-operative Insurance Society Ltd v Argyll Stores (Holdings) Ltd* [1996] Ch 286 at 302D-306, CA.

20   Ibid at 298E.

1   *Co-operative Insurance Society Ltd v Argyll Stores (Holdings) Ltd*, above n 15 at 16E-19A, HL.

2   *Dowty Bolton Paul Ltd v Wolverhampton Corpn*, above n 17 (for later proceedings see [1973] Ch 94) and *Joseph v National Magazine Co Ltd* [1959] Ch 14. D must, of course, be put in a position to instruct his employees etc accordingly: *Morris v Redland Bricks Ltd* [1970] AC 652 at 666. So, in the absence of a detailed specification, a covenant to erect a house of a certain value would not be specifically enforced: *Brace v Wehnert* (1858) 25 Beav 348 at 351.

3   *Jeune v Queens Cross Properties Ltd* [1974] Ch 97.

damages can always be awarded in lieu. Contempt proceedings, and imprisonment itself, are costly.[4]

Where D already enjoys the benefit of C's performance, the court is less willing to allow problems of supervision to exclude the remedy. The leading illustration is where C has transferred the ownership or possession of land to D in return for D's promise to build on it for C's benefit, eg to build a wharf on the land,[5] or a road over which C was to have a right of way to other land he kept in his ownership.[6] For the order to be made, however, other problems of constant supervision must be excluded, and so the building work needs to be sufficiently specified in the contract:[7] the 'real question is whether there is a sufficient definition of what has to be done in order to comply with the order of the court'.[8]

### Contracts involving personal service

Traditionally, the courts have been hesitant to use specific orders to force an unwilling party to maintain a long-term personal relationship with the other,[9] since it would infringe personal liberty and thus be against public policy.[10] This has led to a traditional refusal, now recognised in statute,[11] to grant specific performance of contracts which involve personal service, especially those where the quality or standard of the work is crucial but ultimately depends on a subjective appraisal without definite criteria.[12] So artistic performances, or highly skilled work, will not be specifically ordered. It is clear that not only is an issue of public policy raised here but also one of the practicability of granting an order.

The court traditionally was unwilling to order either party to perform. An issue of mutuality is raised, but, more substantially, since an employer needs to have trust and confidence in his employee, the court will not force him to accept an employee in whom he has lost confidence: 'if one party has no faith in the honesty or integrity or the loyalty of the other, to

---

4   *Co-operative Insurance Society Ltd v Argyll Stores (Holdings) Ltd*, above p 188, n 15 at 13C.
5   *Wilson v Furness Rly Co* (1899) LR 9 Eq 28.
6   *Tannenbaum v WJ Bell Paper Co Ltd* (1956) 4 DLR (2d) 177.
7   *Wolverhampton Corpn v Emmons* [1901] 1 KB 515 at 525.
8   *Tito v Waddell (No 2)* above n 12 at 321-322.
9   Though injunctions have been granted in analogous situations involving other personal relationships, eg against expulsion from membership of a social club: *Young v Ladies Imperial Club Ltd* [1920] 2 KB 523. Cf the possibility of a declaration in the case of exclusion from a professional association: *Nagle v Feilden* [1966] 2 QB 633.
10  *De Francasco v Barnum* (1890) 45 Ch D 430 at 438.
11  Trade Union and Labour Relations (Consolidation) Act 1992, s 236.
12  *Southern Foundries (1926) Ltd v Shirlaw* [1940] AC 701 at 722.

force him to serve or to employ that other is a plain recipe for disaster'.[13] The traditional remedy for breach was always damages.

That the climate of opinion has to some extent now changed is evidenced by the passage of legislation making reinstatement or re-engagement an optional remedy in cases of unfair dismissal.[14] This recognises both that common law damages for wrongful dismissal and statutory compensation for unfair dismissal leave an employee who faces future unemployment uncompensated, and that there are in any case advantages of employment from the employee's point of view which cannot be measured in money terms. However, an employer who refuses to comply with an order for reinstatement or re-engagement ultimately will face only an additional liability in damages rather than contempt proceedings, and so an employer who can afford to do so can in the end choose to pay to unfairly dismiss an employee.[15] On the other hand, an important exception exists in that reinstatement has been enjoined by declaration in cases with some public interest element, such as where an employee holds a position created by a statute, eg a public office, and the employer has failed to comply with the procedures laid down for dismissal.[16]

The general question still is unresolved of how far the courts, in deciding whether to order specific performance of personal service contracts, should follow the lead given by Parliament? The answer should depend on how direct and how personal the relationship would be. Most people would accept the principle that personal service should not be turned into slavery by the threat of imprisonment for contempt. But this objection should prevail only where friction might be caused in a direct and personal manner by 'the daily impact of person upon person',[17] or where there is a risk that the threat of enforcing the order could be used oppressively, eg where D, in order to avoid a difficult, personal confrontation, might be forced to pay a high price to buy out C's entitlement to specific performance. But where the work is well defined

---

13  *Chappell v Times Newspapers Ltd* [1975] 1 WLR 482 at 506.
14  Employment Rights Act 1996, ss 113-117.
15  Ibid, ss 129(9), 130.
16  *Vine v National Dock Labour Board* [1957] AC 488; *Ridge v Baldwin* [1964] AC 40 and *Thomas v University of Bradford* [1987] AC 795; [1992] 1 All ER 964. Cf *Francis v Municipal Councillors of Kuala Lumpur* [1962] 1 WLR 1411, in which a declaration was not granted to the employee. An extraordinary attempt to identify all employment as having a public interest element in *R v BBC, ex p Lavelle* [1983] 1 WLR 23 has been so intermittently followed as to have unclear status. On the background policy issues raising the question whether public service employment calls for special regulation, see GS Morris, 'Employment in Public Services: The Case for Special Treatment' (2000) 20 Oxford Journal of Legal Studies 167.
17  *Giles (CH) and Co Ltd v Morris*, above p 188, n 12 at 318.

and does not put an unwilling party into close personal contact with others, the courts should be willing to consider making an order. Modern forms of employment often do not involve the immediate personal relationship which was the norm in the nineteenth century. Perhaps the most influential consideration now is that the courts have come close to circumventing the principle of not specifically enforcing personal service contracts by their willingness to grant an injunction restraining D from breaking a negative promise, eg the promise of an opera singer not to sing for anyone else.[18] Refusal to grant specific performance is rather pointless if this alternative is available. Reinstatement can also sometimes also be achieved by indirect means. In *Hill v CA Parsons*, both parties to the employment contract wished it to continue but a third party (a trade union) brought pressure on the employer to dismiss the employee. The court granted the employee an interim injunction to prevent his dismissal in breach of contract.[19] This has been followed in other cases, where the courts are showing some willingness to grant interlocutory injunctions to protect employees from dismissal,[20] eg in breach of the agreed procedure.[1] Unless the ratio of *Hill* is restricted to cases where the problem is caused by a third party,[2] and it has not been in subsequent cases, it is difficult to see that there is now anything left of a general rule against enjoining dismissal, and by extension specifically enforcing obligations to employ, other than a general reluctance to specifically enforce in circumstances which will lead to difficulties of supervision.

### Avoiding multiplicity of suits

*Beswick v Beswick*[3] stands as authority for the principle that if the promisee is due to receive a regular performance from the promisor, such as, in that case, the payment of an annuity, the court may grant specific performance in order to avoid the trouble and expense of regular claims for debt or damages. However, the vexed qualities of *Beswick v Beswick* mean that this principle is unclear. Not only are damages obviously in principle adequate for the loss of a sum of money, but these are precisely the type of circumstances of continuing performance in which supervision problems might be expected to arise following an order of specific

---

18  See pp 204-208 below.
19  *Hill v CA Parsons Ltd* [1972] Ch 305.
20  *Powell v London Borough of Brent* [1987] IRLR 466 and *Dietmann v London Borough of Brent* [1987] IRLR 259.
1   *Jones v Lee* [1980] ICR 310 and *Irani v Southampton and South West Hampshire Health Authority* [1985] ICR 590.
2   Ibid.
3   See pp 176-178 above.

performance. If it were possible to go into the market to buy another annuity, the court should be content to award the cost as damages for breach of the original contract. But, of course, recourse to damages was exactly what was not possible in this case. The changes to the privity rules in the Contracts (Rights of Third Parties) Act 1999 should make such recourse possible.

## Specific performance on terms

The courts may grant an order subject to conditions, including the award of supplementary damages, which are imposed to implement the parties' intentions, as with the problem of mutuality already discussed.[4] For instance, in *Baskcomb v Beckwith*,[5] D, the purchaser of a parcel of land, did not realise that C, the vendor, retained an adjoining piece of land which was not covered by the restrictive covenant protecting the land sold. C had, by his acts, unintentionally contributed to D's mistaken impression. The court gave C the choice of taking specific performance with the covenant applying to the adjoining land, or not having the order. Similarly, where C has purchased land from D, he may seek specific performance with compensation in the form of an abatement of the price[6] for some deficiency in D's performance, as where D cannot transfer all the land he promised[7] or there is some defect in his title. D cannot force such a transfer on C, but if that is what C wants, and it is not excluded by the terms of the contract,[8] the court should be willing to modify its remedy.[9]

Granting specific performance on terms can have an apparently dramatic effect. In *Grant v Dawkins*[10] the whole price was extinguished by way of abatement to take account of the amounts due under mortgages taken over by C (and, in addition, damages were awarded). But even this outcome is in pursuit of the purpose of the contract, and the grant of remedy should not distort the agreement between the parties, as where there is a serious discrepancy between D's undertaking and what he can in fact

4   See p 184 above.
5   (1869) LR 8 Eq 100.
6   There is traditional authority to the effect that the calculation of these compensatory or abating payments should be conducted somewhat differently from ordinary quantification: *Knatchbull v Greuber* (1815) 1 Madd 153 at 66-7. No general principle seems to inform the minor modern residues of this authority, and it is submitted that none should actually obstruct the quantification of damages according to normal principles: Furmston (ed), *The Law of Contract*, above p 166, n 2, para 8.153.
7   *Rutherford v Acton-Adams* [1915] AC 866.
8   *Jacobs v Revell* [1900] 2 Ch 858.
9   *Topfell Ltd v Galley Properties Ltd* [1979] 1 WLR 446 at 451.
10  [1973] 1 WLR 1406.

transfer.[11] Where it is the vendor who sues for specific performance with compensation to the purchaser because he cannot transfer exactly what he promised, the order may be made only where the mis-description is not of 'a material or substantial point'.[12]

## Specific enforcement of severable obligations

There is traditional authority to the effect that if specific performance of all of D's primary obligation cannot be ordered, then specific performance of any part may not be ordered.[13] There would appear to be no overall justification for this principle, though, of course, in certain circumstances it may in fact prove to be the case that D's obligation is not severable. If that obligation is severable and specific performance of a severable part would not be contrary to the parties' intention, then there would appear to be no reason why it should not be ordered. In *Ogden v Fossick*,[14] an agreement to grant a lease was enforced although that to provide personal services could not be. In *Lytton v Great Northern Rly Co*,[15] D was ordered to build a railway siding, but not to keep it in repair, for the latter part of the obligation would involve supervision problems and damages would be an adequate remedy for failure to repair.

## Contractual clauses affecting specific relief

An important question is whether the parties are free to specify in their contract that specific relief is to be the remedy in the case of breach.[16] The general principle underlying the law of contract is that the parties are free to fashion their own relationship, specifying all its details and the consequences of all eventualities, including breach. The presumption therefore should be that the parties can validly agree that breach of a given clause shall be followed by an order for specific performance (or an injunction, in the case of a negative undertaking). However, we have seen that literal enforcement of all kinds including specific performance can

---

11  *Rutherford v Acton-Adams*, above n 7 at 870. Cf *Durham (Earl of) v Legard* (1865) 34 Beav 611.
12  *Flight v Booth* (1834) 1 Bing (NC) 370 at 377. Cf *Shepherd v Croft* [1911] 1 Ch 521.
13  *Ryan v Mutual Tontine Westminster Chambers Association*, above p 166, n 2 at 123.
14  (1862) 4 De GF & J 426.
15  (1856) 2 K & J 394.
16  Sharpe, *Injunctions and Specific Performance*, above p 166, n 1, paras 7.640-7.810.

in certain circumstances impose a burden on D which would not be imposed by compensatory damages. This consideration alone should lead us to consider the value of some judicial control over these clauses, whether by insisting on the overriding discretion of the court to decide whether to grant relief (as would apply in the absence of such a clause), or in subjecting the clauses to a special test. Whilst this test should ultimately be directed towards determining the genuineness of the agreement, the nature of the ultimate sanction for non-compliance with the court's order, that is, proceedings for contempt of court and the threat of imprisonment, is a further, additional obstacle to conceding the freedom to the parties to stipulate specific performance.[17] If no court would uphold a clause which directly specified that imprisonment was to be the sanction for breach, the same result should not be achieved indirectly through a clause stipulating specific relief as the remedy.[18]

In the analogous situation of an agreed damages clause, the courts have developed a test to control the parties' own stipulation.[19] In order to be valid, the clause must constitute a genuine attempt to pre-estimate the loss expected to result from the breach in question. It would be inconsistent not to impose some such test for clauses purporting to stipulate specific enforcement. If the courts used a special test, such as reasonableness, they would probably treat as relevant all or most of the factors which already govern the exercise of their discretion to deny specific relief, such as the question of social waste or the availability of substitute performance.[20] If the tests for reasonableness would be close to those for the overriding discretion which the court already enjoys, it would be simpler to leave control to the established tests rather than to introduce a special new test. The regular discretion could also serve to prevent unconscionable use of specific remedies in circumstances not envisaged by the parties at the time of contracting, as well as to protect the weaker party from unconscionable use of a stronger bargaining position.[1]

17 *Co-operative Insurance Society Ltd v Argyll Stores Ltd* (HL(E)), above p 188, n 15 at 12G-13B.
18 Sharpe, *Injunctions and Specific Performance*, above p 166, n 1, para 7.790 would allow party stipulation for specific relief except 'where its grant could violate the policy against involuntary servitude or impose an unreasonable burden on the courts'.
19 See ch 9 above.
20 If, at the time of contracting, mitigation was expected to be possible, would the court nevertheless enforce a clause for specific relief?
1 If the common law developed a general doctrine of unconscionability, there would, of course, be no need to treat these clauses as a separate problem.

A number of other considerations also point to the need for some judicial control. It should be remembered that D's liability normally is minimised by mitigation and the law of insolvency provides D with an ultimate protection against money awards which he cannot meet, whether they are based on debt or on liquidated or unliquidated damages. The granting of specific relief has the effect of denying him either type of protection. Again, as little of the full cost of enforcement through contempt proceedings and imprisonment is borne by the parties, there seems no reason for them to be able to obtain this subsidy merely by expressing their own choice of this remedy in their contract.

The factors examined in this section should cast further doubt on two situations in which the practice of the courts is to grant specific relief as a matter of course. The first concerns contracts for the sale of land, where the grant of specific performance is often made without enquiry into the particular circumstances.[2] Although the parties do not expressly stipulate for specific performance, it can be taken for granted in these contracts. It has already been argued that this is suspect as a general practice, though it may be appropriate in a number of empirical situations.

The second situation concerns the practice of granting injunctions as a matter of course to enforce negative stipulations. This practice means that the parties, by casting an obligation in this negative form, can in effect stipulate for, as it were, indirect specific performance. It is submitted that the arguments put forward in this section should preclude the automatic granting of prohibitory injunctions, and this issue is discussed further below.[3]

The objection based on fear of non-compliance leading to imprisonment would not apply, however, to a damages clause which specified the cost of performance by a third party as the measure of damages (as opposed to measuring damages by loss of market value).[4] Although such substitute performance is indirect specific relief, it avoids the threat of imprisonment for contempt and the problems of supervision which arise in the case of specific performance. If it is thought desirable to give more scope to the parties to select a remedy analogous to specific relief, it would be less objectionable to allow them, in situations where it is reasonable, to specify the cost of substitute performance as the basis for the assessment of damages than to stipulate for direct specific relief.

If we leave the level of principle to seek authority in the law reports for party stipulation, we are disappointed. In one case, a contract for the personal services of a film actress expressly provided that the producer would be entitled to an injunction enforcing an undertaking not to act

---

2   See p 175 above.
3   Sec pp 200-208 below
4   See ch 14 below.

for another studio.[5] The court said that 'parties cannot contract themselves out of the law'[6] but that the court could give some weight to the formal recognition by the parties that an injunction would be appropriate.[7] The contract could provide evidence of the factors which the parties deem to be relevant, but the court should also be free to consider any other relevant factor.

A final question is whether the existence of an agreed damages clause should exclude specific relief. The answer in older cases is no,[8] provided that the other conditions for granting such relief are present. Of course, the contract may be interpreted as giving D the choice between the alternatives of performing or paying the fixed sum, and in this situation no specific relief should be given.

---

5    *Warner Bros v Nelson* [1937] 1 KB 209 at 220-1.
6    Ibid at 221.
7    There is American authority to the same effect: *Stokes v Moore* (1955) 77 So 2d 231 at 335.
8    *Howard v Hopkyns* (1742) 2 Atk 371; *Long v Bowring* (1864) 33 Beav 585 at 588-9 and *Magrane v Archbold* (1813) 1 Dow 107.

# 13 Injunctions

## Negative covenants[1]

Where D's contractual promise is negative – a promise not to do something or a promise to abstain from acting in a certain way – the judicial remedy to enforce it is a prohibitory injunction.[2] This will be granted much more readily than when the promise is positive and can be enforced only by an order of specific performance, for the courts do not take a similar stance toward these obligations. When deciding whether to enforce a negative covenant, the courts say that it is not a matter of their assessing the balance of convenience[3] or the risk of damage from breach of the covenant. It is simply literal enforcement of the negative undertaking for which the parties have themselves contracted. The courts do not expect C to prove that he will suffer loss or damage from breach of the undertaking,[4] but rather assume that its inclusion in the contract demonstrates its importance to C. They do not ask, as in the case of liquidated damages, whether the remedy is reasonably proportionate to the expected harm. As will be argued, this difference in approach is questionable. However, it might be suspected that the cost which would be imposed on D in complying with the injunction would not usually be

---

1    This section does not consider the rules on injunctions to enforce covenants in restraint of trade in detail. See JD Heydon, *The Restraint of Trade Doctrine* (1971) ch 9; MJ Trebilcock, *The Common Law of Restraint of Trade* (1986) and, for recent authorities, K Brearley and S Bloch, *Employment Covenants and Confidential Information* (2nd edn 1999) chs 9-10.

2    For mandatory injunctions, which order D to undo an act or reverse a situation, see p 208 below.

3    *Doherty v Allman* (1878) 3 App Cas 709 at 720.

4    *Marco Productions Ltd v Pagola* [1945] KB 111.

out of proportion to the value of the benefit of compliance to C. For although D is forbidden to do one particular act, or to engage in one particular activity, he is free to do anything else.

A prohibitory injunction may be granted to support an order for specific performance. Thus, in *Behnke v Bede Shipping Co Ltd*, in which D was ordered to sell a ship to C, an injunction restrained D from parting with the ship to anyone but C.[5] Similarly, an injunction may prevent D from taking a specific chattel like a ship out of the jurisdiction until the court has adjudicated on C's claim to it.[6] Yet another illustration is provided by *James Jones and Sons Ltd v Tankerville*.[7] Timber sold by D to C was on D's land and the contract gave C the right to enter the land to remove it. An injunction was granted to restrain D from preventing the due execution of the contract. In cases not concerned with personal services, the courts have been willing to *imply* negative stipulations.[8] So, if D charters a ship to C, D will be enjoined from permitting a third person to use the ship in a way which is inconsistent with the charter.[9]

Despite the general principle that negative covenants will regularly be enforced by injunction, the courts still retain some discretion not to grant one.[10] However, the problems of enforcement of negative covenants typically are less serious than with specific performance, because it will often be easy to prove breach of the injunction. The question is simply whether D has acted in the prohibited way. Nevertheless, if, for instance, the breach is of trivial importance, or if C has delayed unduly, no injunction will be granted. If C himself does not act equitably, he may be denied relief.[11] The court may also weigh the effect of factual changes since the contract was made: 'Even where there have been negative words, circumstances may change, so that though the covenant still remains it would not be reasonable that it should be enforced.'[12]

5  *Behnke v Bede Shipping Co Ltd* [1927] 1 KB 649.
6  *Hart v Herwig* (1873) 8 Ch App 860. Cf *Societé des Industries Metallurgiques SA v Bronx Engineering Co Ltd* [1975] 1 Lloyd's Rep 465.
7  [1909] 2 Ch 440.
8  Provided, of course, that the positive obligation is sufficiently precise for the negative obligation to be properly defined: *Bower v Bantam Investments Ltd* [1972] 1 WLR 1120.
9  *Lord Strathcona Steamship Co v Dominion Coal Co* [1926] AC 108.
10 In the case of mandatory rather than prohibitory injunctions, the courts clearly retain their discretion: see pp 208-209 below.
11 *Chappell v Times Newspapers Ltd* [1975] 1 WLR 482.
12 *Doherty v Allman*, above p 198, n 3 at 730.

## Distinguishing between negative and positive undertakings

It is obvious that distinguishing between negative and positive undertakings may be very difficult, and this has given rise to two particular problems: the enforcement of long-term supply contracts and indirect specific performance.

When drawing the line between these undertakings, the courts have looked to the substance of the undertaking, not to its mere form.[13] They recognise that many positive promises could be rephrased in negative terms: 'If I agree with a man to be at a certain place at a certain time, I impliedly agree that I will not be anywhere else at the same time'.[14] Some promises are in substance negative, despite the fact that they have been expressed in positive terms. So, in *Metropolitan Electricity Supply Co Ltd v Ginder*, where D had agreed to take from C (at a fixed price per unit) *all* the electricity required for D's premises for not less than five years, an injunction was granted to restrain D from taking electricity from any other supplier. D had agreed that *if* it used electricity at all, it would take that electricity from C, and so 'by necessary implication' it had agreed not to take electricity from others.[15] The court has used the implication of negative covenants in this way to govern the enforcement of long-term supply contracts.

On the other hand, the courts also recognise that a negative undertaking may amount to a positive one. An undertaking not to dismiss an employee is in substance a positive undertaking to continue to employ him, and, as this would not be specifically enforced,[16] it is questionable whether an injunction should be granted which amounts in effect to specific performance indirectly.

### Long-term supply contracts[17]

Many long-term business contracts involve the supply of a quantity of a particular commodity, some of which have now been studied closely.[18]

---

13  *Wolverhampton and Walsall Rly Co v London and North Western Rly Co* (1873) LR 16 Eq 433 at 430.
14  *Whitwood Chemical Co v Hardman* [1891] 2 Ch 416 at 426.
15  [1901] 2 Ch 799 at 806. Cf *Erskine McDonald Ltd v Eyles* [1921] 1 Ch 631, in which an authoress agreed to give her publisher her 'next three books'.
16  *Davis v Foreman* [1894] 3 Ch 654; *Kirchner & Co v Gruban* [1909] 1 Ch 413 and *Chappell v Times Newspapers Ltd*, above n 11. See, however, the exceptional cases represented by *Hill v CA Parsons & Co Ltd* [1972] Ch 305.
17  RM Sharpe, *Injunctions and Specific Performance* (2nd edn 1992) paras 8.390-8.510,  9.130-9.200.
18  T Daintith, 'The Design and Performance of Long-term Contracts', in T Daintith and G Teubner (eds), *Contract and Organisation* (1986) 164; PL Joskow,

There are economic advantages of such contracts to both parties. The supplier can plan on the basis of a known outlet for its product, while the purchaser can plan on the basis of an assured source of supply. Both parties may also want over a long period the security of a fixed price, or of a price which can fluctuate only in accordance with an agreed index.[19] The exclusive supply arrangements may be part of a franchising system, eg solus agreements between oil companies and franchisee garage proprietors,[20] or a dealership-distribution network, by which a manufacturer arranges for its product to be distributed in an orderly way by dealers in different areas so as to ensure the required levels of pre-sales advice to customers and post-sales service. This is the case with car sales.[1] Such contracts obviously work by reducing the contestability of markets by effectively excluding purchases in spot markets,[2] and they have been the subject of 'deregulatory' measures in a number of industrial sectors, such as the natural gas industry.[3] To be enforceable within the restraint of trade doctrine, the restrictions in such a long-term contract must be reasonable and in the interests of both the parties and the public.[4] In a number of industries, including natural gas, very considerable disruption[5] has followed deregulation because the positive role of long-term contracts[6] had not been fully appreciated, and no replacement mechanism

---

'Contract Duration and Relationship Specific Investments: Empirical Evidence from Coal Markets' (1987) 77 American Economic Review 168 and PL Joskow, 'The Performance of Long-term Contracts: Further Evidence from Coal Markets' (1990) 21 Rand Journal of Economics 251.

19   WE Stockhausen, 'The Commercial and Anti-trust Aspects of Term Requirements Contracts' (1948) 23 New York University Law Review 412, pp 413-4.

20   Monopoly and Mergers Commission, *The Supply of Petrol*, Cm 972 (1990) 6.246-6.291, 6.415-6.423, 8.94-8.100 and GH Treitel, *Law of Contract* (10th edn 1999) 431-434.

1   H Beale et al, 'The Distribution of Cars: A Complex Contractual Technique', in D Harris and D Tallon (eds), *Contract Law Today: Anglo-French Comparisons* (1989) ch 7.

2   Thereby not only giving legal expression to limits on the choice available to the end consumer but also creating the possibility of opportunist exploitation of inequality of bargaining power between the parties to the distribution contract. In relationship to cars see S Macaulay, *Law and the Balance of Power* (1966).

3   The report of the Monopoly and Mergers Commission, *Gas and British Gas plc*, Cm 2314-2317 (1993) gave rise to amendments to the Gas Act 1986 by the Gas Act 1995, and see now the Utilities Act 2000.

4   Heydon, *The Restraint of Trade Doctrine*, above p 198, n 1, ch 9 and Trebilcock, *The Common Law of Restraint of Trade*, above n 1, ch 7.

5   JM Medina, 'The Take-or-pay Wars: A Cautionary Analysis for the Future' (1991) 27 Tulsa Law Journal 283.

6   SE Masten and KJ Crocker, 'Efficient Adaptation in Long-term Contracts: Take-or-pay Provisions for Natural Gas' (1985) 75 American Economic Review 1083.

provided.[7] And, in general, the courts have accepted that a supplier can justify 'maintaining a stable system of distribution throughout the country so as to enable [his] business to be run efficiently and economically'.[8]

In the simplest case, the agreement could be for the supply of a fixed quantity of an item to be delivered at stated intervals over an agreed period of time. But the quantity need not be agreed in advance. The supplier may agree to sell *all* his output (impliedly agreeing not to sell to anyone else); or the purchaser may agree to buy *all* his requirements from the supplier (impliedly agreeing not to buy from anyone else). This has been called a 'requirements contract'.[9]

The parties to such an agreement will usually consider damages to be an inadequate remedy for breach. It is of the nature of such agreements that they generate asset-specific benefits for the parties which are idiosyncratic, eg a mutual understanding of each party's method of working which it would be costly to reproduce with another party but the loss of which is too uncertain to be captured in damages.[10] But specific performance would normally be excluded on the grounds that the goods are not unique and that it would be difficult for the court to monitor compliance with complex obligations over a long period. However, the courts have been willing to grant injunctions to enforce undertakings not to buy from another supplier. They claim to enforce only the negative undertakings in long-term supply contracts, but are not unhappy with the expectation that the injunction will be an incentive to D to fulfil his positive undertakings. If a garage proprietor agrees to take all his petrol and other specified items from a petroleum company, he may be restrained by injunction from purchasing petrol or such items from any other supplier.[11] Similarly, a publican who has made a 'tied house' agreement to take all his beer from one brewer will be prevented by injunction from obtaining his beer from another brewer.[12]

---

7   DB Rice and MA Schleuter, 'Deregulation and Natural Gas Purchase Contracts: Examination Through Neoclassical and Relational Contract Theories' (1985) 25 Washburn Law Journal 43.

8   *Esso Petroleum Co Ltd v Harper's Garage (Stourport) Ltd* [1968] AC 269 at 302.

9   As there is a possibility that the buyer's requirements may in fact be zero, and therefore nothing bought, it has proven tricky to find consideration for these contracts: JN Adams, 'Consideration for Requirements Contracts' (1978) 94 Law Quarterly Review 73.

10  See pp 31-33 above.

11  *Foley v Classique Coaches* [1934] 2 KB 1.

12  *Clegg v Hands* (1890) 44 Ch D 503; *Courage & Co v Carpenter* [1910] 1 Ch 262 and *Catt v Tourle* (1869) 4 Ch App 654. (This actual decision is no longer law: R Megarry and HWR Wade, *The Law of Real Property* (6th edn 2000) para 16-034 n 49.) The basic nature of the restrictive covenant is unaffected by recent regulation aimed at diversifying brewers' supplies of beers to outlets, which obliges

As we have seen in the discussion of negative covenants proper,[13] if, on the facts of *Metropolitan Electricity Supply Co Ltd v Ginder*, D undertook to buy from C all the electricity he needed, the court will imply the negative undertaking not to buy electricity from any other supplier. When granting an injunction to enforce the latter obligation, the court was of the opinion that it was not forcing D to take any electricity at all. If D used gas or oil, he was free to buy his energy from anyone. Only if he used electricity would he be affected by the injunction. Of course, as the costs of switching the form of power supply are hardly negligible, this type of specific relief should, it is submitted, be given only where C has a long-term interest in securing a regular distribution network, since it is often tantamount to an order for specific performance.

And the courts have, indeed, not been so ready to use negative injunctions against the supplier who agrees to sell all his output to C. It has been assumed that the buyer C does not need protection beyond the award of damages, but this reason only holds when the item in question is freely available in the market (as has been the case in the reported cases, eg coal).[14] If, however, C could not find a substitute supplier who could guarantee a regular supply on a long-term basis, the courts should be willing to use an injunction to protect his interest in maintaining a secure supply.

The question remains whether courts should in future be more willing to grant specific performance of these contracts. If alternative outlets or sources of supply could be found, damages could be assessed at the difference in prices between the substitute long-term contract and the original one, and any loss of transaction-specific investment might be offset if not fully compensated by C's being able to rely on the co-operation of a willing, instead of a coerced, contractual partner. But in the absence of such an alternative, the assessment of damages would be highly speculative. The risk of fluctuations in market prices over a long, future period could not be accurately assessed in damages, and it would be difficult to put a figure on the loss of an assured outlet or source of supply. These difficulties would be compounded if the quantity to be supplied was uncertain, as in a requirements contract. The planning of C's whole business may depend on having the security of a long-term contract, and his inability to find a substitute contract may make damages a very inadequate remedy. The commercial uniqueness of the long-term

the brewer/landlord to allow its tenants to purchase a minority of their beer from a source other than the brewer/landlord itself: Monopoly and Mergers Commisssion, *The Supply of Beer*, Cm 651 (1989) 1.28 and the Supply of Beer (Tied Estate) Order 1989, SI 1989 No 2390.

13  See p 198 above.

14  *Fothergill v Rowland* (1873) LR 17 Eq 132.

arrangements could be used to justify specific performance, even though the items in question may be available for purchase on the spot market.[15]

This factor was recognised in *Evans Marshall and Co Ltd v Bertola SA*, in which the Court of Appeal granted an interlocutory injunction to prevent a foreign exporter of sherry from distributing in England otherwise than through the sole distributorship granted to C (and so restrained breach of the distributorship). D wished to bring to an end the long relationship under which (under previous ownership) it had sold sherry to C. Other sherry could, of course, have been obtained. But the 'abrupt termination of an agreement with 14 years to run' would have caused 'loss of goodwill ... disruption in trade, and ... litigation with sub-agents' of a sort which 'cannot be taken into monetary account in a common-law action for breach of contract.'[16] Thus, indirectly through injunctions, courts enforce positive undertakings in long-term supply agreements.

But the courts should be careful not to put C into too powerful a bargaining position. C should not be able to exact a price for a subsequent release from the injunction which substantially exceeds its own loss because the cost to D of complying with the order is substantially greater than that loss, a manifestly inefficient outcome.[17] If the court suspects that C is seeking an injunction merely in order to take advantage of this type of windfall, it should leave him to his remedy in damages. The courts have many factors to weigh in choosing the most appropriate remedy in these contracts, and they should carefully weigh the advantages of specific relief with the disadvantages.

### Indirect specific performance

The courts also recognise that a negative undertaking may amount to a positive one, and this may give rise to a difficulty. Given that a prohibitory injunction may be more easily granted than an order of specific performance, it is obvious that C may seek a prohibitory injunction not

---

15  Subject to C satisfying the definition of 'commercial agents' under reg 2(1), termination of such a relationship may be governed by the Commercial Agents (Council Directive) Regulations 1993, SI 1993 No 3053 (as amended by the Commercial Agents (Council Directive) (Amendment) Regulations 1998, SI 1998 No 2868). C may find damages under these Regulations more adequate, and thus have less need for injunctive relief, because the right to compensation under reg 17 would appear to be more extensive than that recognised by the common law, though the issue is by no means settled: *Page v Combined Shipping & Trading Co* [1997] 3 All ER 656; *Moore v Piretta Ltd* [1999] 1 All ER 174 and *Duffen v Frabo SpA* [2000] 1 Lloyd's Rep 180.

16  [1973] 1 WLR 349 at 379-80. Cf *Decro-Wall International SA v Practitioners in Marketing Ltd* [1971] 1 WLR 361.

17  Cf pp 268-272 below.

to enforce a negative covenant proper but as a way of obtaining indirect specific performance by restraint of breach.[18] The question arises whether a court, if it is not willing to order specific performance of a positive obligation, should refuse to grant an injunction to enforce a corresponding negative obligation? If the negative obligation stood alone, the injunction might be appropriate. But if enforcement of the negative obligation would have the practical effect of forcing performance of the positive obligation, it should be denied on the ground that it would amount to indirect specific performance if specific performance itself would be denied. Thus, no injunction will be granted to enforce an employee's undertaking that, for the agreed period of employment, he will not work in any business other than that of his employer.[19] Similarly, as we have seen above, no injunction will be granted against an employer restraining him from dismissing his employee in breach of contract.

The leading authority on indirect specific performance is *Lumley v Wagner*[20] where D, a famous opera singer, promised to sing at C's theatre for three months, and also not to sing for anyone else during the same period without C's consent. The court accepted that no order could be made compelling D to sing for C, but nevertheless granted C an injunction prohibiting D from singing for anyone else. The problem is whether in practice this type of injunction amounted to compulsion of D to fulfil her positive obligation.[1] If she were faced with the alternatives of starvation or being compelled, against her will, to sing for C, the answer should be clear. Since this would then indirectly constitute an order for specific performance, which the court would not make directly, the negative injunction should be refused. But on the facts of *Lumley v Wagner*, the choice was found not to be so stark, since D presumably could have employed her talents in some way which did not infringe the injunction. If she could earn a livelihood elsewhere, why not enforce the negative undertaking?

18  H McGregor, *Contract Code* (1993) section 421.
19  *Ehrman v Batholomew* [1898] 1 Ch 671. In *Evening Standard Co Ltd v Henderson* [1987] IRLR 64, the Court of Appeal granted an interlocutory injunction restraining an employee D from working for a rival newspaper during the currency of his contract with C, in breach of a clause in the contract prohibiting D from working for anyone else during the period of the contract. But the court was heavily influenced by C's willingness to continue paying D's salary during the period of the injunction.
20  (1852) 21 LJ Ch 898. See also *Lumley v Gye* (1853) 118 ER 749.
1  CD Ashley, 'Specific Performance by Injunction' (1906) 6 Columbia Law Review 82; GL Clark, 'Implications of *Lumley v Wagner*' (1917) 17 Columbia Law Review 687; HJ Glasbeek, '*Lumley v Gye*, The Aftermath: An Inducement to Judicial Reform?' (1975) 1 Monash University Law Review 187; JD Heydon, *Economic Torts*, (2nd edn 1978) 28-47; Heydon, *The Restraint of Trade Doctrine*, above p 198, n 1, pp 64-71 and RS Stevens, 'Involuntary Servitude by Injunction: The Doctrine of *Lumley v Wagner* Considered' (1921) Cornell Law Quarterly 235.

This rather unconvincing reasoning, which seems to hold that obliging D to become, say, a seamstress is much the same thing as allowing her to continue as an opera singer, rather misses the point at issue. There can be no doubt that granting this injunction would have imposed a considerable cost on D. There is no real point denying this. The question really is whether this cost is outweighed by the cost which not granting the injunction imposes on C. The answer should depend on whether C had a legitimate interest in specifically enforcing the covenant, which would not be satisfied by an award of damages. And, indeed, one can speculate that C would have faced a very substantial uncompensated loss. One factor in favour of, in effect, specific relief in *Lumley v Wagner* was that it would not be easy to assess the loss which C would suffer as a result of some of his potential customers being induced to go to a rival's theatre in order to hear D's singing. Another factor is the question of competition. C had a negative interest in D not singing at a theatre in direct competition with him, quite apart from his interest in getting her to sing at his own theatre.[2]

This latter factor in particular could distinguish *Lumley v Wagner* from a later decision criticising it. In *Whitwood Chemical Co v Hardman*,[2a] D had agreed to manage a company and to 'give the whole of his time to the company's business'. The Court of Appeal rejected the argument that this constituted a negative undertaking not to work for anyone else, and refused an injunction. C had no interest in restricting competition. Its only interest in enforcing the alleged negative undertaking would have been to force performance of the contract by way of indirect specific performance.

Subsequent courts, however, have issued *Lumley v Wagner* type injunctions without asking whether C had any interest in the injunction beyond the pressure to fulfil the positive obligation. In *Warner Bros Pictures Inc v Nelson*,[3] D, the film actress Bette Davis, undertook to work only for C's studio and not to work for any other studio without C's consent. An injunction was granted to prohibit her from working for any other studio during the period of the contract. The court said that she was not faced with the alternatives of starvation or working for C, since she could earn a livelihood in some other type of activity. But the court recognised that, since she could earn much more as an actress than in any other activity, the injunction might induce her to perform the positive side of her contract.[4] This reasoning is, with respect, no improvement on *Lumley v Wagner*, but again, however, on the facts, C could have shown a legitimate interest in enforcing the negative undertaking. Since C was obviously in competition with other studios and Ms Davis was the most

2    SM Waddams, 'Johanna Wagner and the Rival Opera Houses' (2001) 117 Law Quarterly Review 431.
2a    [1891] Ch 416.
3    [1937] 1 KB 209.
4    Ibid at 219.

commercially important film star then working, her working for a competitor certainly would cause C a loss of revenue, but that loss would be so extremely difficult to quantify as perhaps to be irrecoverable.[5] The restraint of trade doctrine is the main judicial control over such 'exclusive' undertakings. Although this doctrine was not discussed in *Lumley v Wagner*, it should be applied to restrictions during the period of the contract, as well as to those coming into operation after the termination of the contract.[6] The restriction is valid only if it is reasonable in the interests of the public as well as in the interests of the parties. An 'exclusive' restriction imposed on an ordinary employee without special skills should not pass this test, and so the question of enforcing it by injunction should not arise.[7] The question the court should ask is whether D was left with any other reasonable means of earning his living. Where a negative covenant is expressed too widely, C may restrict his request for an injunction to a severable part of it. So in *Warner Brothers Pictures Inc v Nelson*, though C was granted an injunction to enforce that part of the covenant which prevented D from working as an actress for third parties, no injunction would have been granted to enforce the whole of the covenant, which included a wide undertaking not to engage in any other occupation without C's written consent.

Injunctions have also been used to prevent the breach of exclusive agencies, as in *Evans Marshall and Co Ltd v Bertola SA* discussed above. However, though this case turned on idiosyncratic loss arising from assets specific to the parties' relationship, that relationship was based on 'a commercial agreement between trading companies [and] the fact that some degree of mutual co-operation or confidence is needed does not preclude the court from granting negative injunctions designed to encourage the party in breach to perform his part'.[8] But sole or exclusive agents employed to manage a pop group,[9] and in another case a boxer,[10] have not been successful in obtaining relief by injunction when their employers wished to appoint new managers. The relationship between the manager and his employers was so close and confidential that the courts would not compel

5   It is less easy to detect any legitimate interest C may have had in other cases such as *Marco Productions Ltd v Pagola* [1945] KB 111 or *Grimston v Cunningham* [1894] 1 QB 125. The point, however, is that in *Warner Bros Pictures Inc v Nelson*, loc cit, as in *White and Carter (Councils) Ltd v McGregor* [1962] AC 413 (see pp 160-165), this crucial consideration, though it might have been present, was not explicitly identified.
6   Heydon, *The Restraint of Trade Doctrine*, above p 198, n 1, pp 60-1.
7   See, however, *Lanner v Palace Theatre (Ltd)* (1893) 9 TLR 162 and *William Robinson & Co Ltd v Heuer* [1898] 2 Ch 451.
8   *Evans Marshall & Co Ltd v Bertola SA*, above p 204, n 16 at 379 (for later proceedings see [1976] 2 Lloyd's Rep 17).
9   *Page One Records v Britton* [1968] 1 WLR 157.
10  *Mortimer v Beckett* [1920] 1 Ch 571.

an unwilling party to continue with it. It was accepted that an injunction would in practice compel D to continue with C as manager.

## Appraisal

It is submitted that the courts should no longer place much weight on the attempt to identify a difference in the nature of positive and negative obligations as such. Rather, they should ask whether, by requiring D to refrain from doing something, they are, in the circumstances facing him, really bringing substantial pressure on him to do something positive. If this is so, a prohibitory injunction should be granted only if the court would be willing on ordinary principles, weighing C's and D's interests, to order specific performance of the positive action. For instance, in long-term supply contracts, the effect of an injunction prohibiting D from purchasing his requirements from anyone else will in most practical situations force him to buy from C, and this should be recognised. But if C has such an interest as makes this outcome on balance desirable, the court should grant the necessary relief.

On the other hand, if a positive obligation would not be directly enforced, it should not be enforced indirectly by injunction merely because a negative obligation is implied. In *Fothergill v Rowland*, D, a colliery, agreed to sell to C all the coal it produced for five years. The court refused an injunction to prevent D from selling the colliery during that period. It was not so much that, as Sir George Jessel MR said in that case, the injunction would have amounted to 'specific performance by a roundabout method',[11] but that specific performance of this sort *by any method* was on balance undesirable.

## Mandatory injunctions

A mandatory injunction orders D to undo an act or to reverse a situation. If D's negative undertaking has already been broken by a positive act (such as erecting a building in violation of that undertaking), more than a prohibitory injunction will be needed to undo the act. A mandatory injunction will be required to order D to take positive steps to reverse the situation, eg dismantling the erection.[12] This type of injunction has a much more drastic effect than a prohibitory injunction, which is designed merely to prevent certain conduct for the future. A mandatory injunction usually

---

11  (1873) LR 17 Eq 132 at 140.
12  *Shepherd Homes Ltd v Sandham* [1971] Ch 340 at 348. (For later proceedings see [1971] 1 WLR 1062.)

requires D to spend time, money and materials in complying with it, and it therefore has some similarity to specific performance. 'The basic concept is that of producing a "fair result", and this involves the exercise of judicial discretion.'[13] Hence, the court will use the balance of convenience or relative disadvantage test and will engage in the type of cost-benefit analysis used in cases of specific performance, asking whether the cost of compliance to D will be substantially out of proportion to the value of compliance to C? This test has already been examined at length in relation to specific performance, and will be examined again in relation to cost to complete damages.[14]

In one case, D who had covenanted not to alter the exterior of his house, later put in a window. The court refused an injunction mandating the removal of the window because the market value of C's property was not affected.[15] Similarly, no injunction could be made to prevent a hotel from closing.[16] But where D acted deliberately, in full knowledge and defiance of C's rights, the court may grant a mandatory injunction despite the cost of complying with it, eg where D put up a building to block C's view of the sea, in defiance of a restrictive covenant prohibiting it.[17] Similarly, any 'attempt to steal a march on the court' may be reversed by a mandatory injunction.[18]

---

13  *Shepherd Homes Ltd v Sandham*, loc cit at 351; *Sharp v Harrison* [1922] 1 Ch 502 at 515 and *Charrington v Simons & Co Ltd* [1970] 1 WLR 725 at 730.
14  See pp 182-183 above and 211-214, 221-226 below.
15  *Sharp v Harrison*, above, n 13.
16  *London, Chatham and Dover Rly Co and South Eastern and Chatham Rly Co's Managing Committee v Spiers and Pond Ltd* (1916) 32 TLR 493.
17  *Wakeham v Wood* (1982) 43 P & CR 40.
18  *Shepherd Homes Ltd v Sandham*, above p 208, n 12 at 352.

# 14 Performance by a substitute

## Damages assessed as the cost to complete by a third party

One way of securing C's expected consumer surplus or preventing an uncompensated loss of his commercial expectation is by the indirect route of awarding damages based on what it would cost to obtain performance (or completion of performance) of D's primary contractual obligation by a third party.[1] Such damages are sometimes called 'reinstatement', 'cost of cure' or 'cost to complete damages', and should be regarded as a form of substitute specific performance.

From C's point of view, cost to complete damages may be superior to an order for specific performance.[2] C can choose as the substitute performer a third party in whose work C has confidence, rather than rely on the quality of D's performance when he is acting under compulsion.[3] In this way, cost to complete damages avoid any problems of supervision of D's compliance with an order for specific performance.[3]

In *Radford v de Froberville*,[4] C sold part of his land to D, who promised to separate the two plots by building a wall on his land. D failed to build the wall, but claimed that C's damages should be limited to the reduction in the market value of C's land as the result of not having the wall, which

1  D Harris et al, 'Contract Remedies and the Consumer Surplus' (1979) 95 Law Quarterly Review 581, 589–94.
2  The question whether the parties may in their contract stipulate cost to complete as the measure of damages is considered in pp 136-137 above.
3  If D could choose a substitute performer, he would lack C's incentive to choose carefully. Hence, instead of cost to complete operating as a form of vicarious performance (which would permit D to choose a substitute), it operates as a form of mitigation, under which C chooses the substitute performer under rules limiting the amount which may be spent on the alternative performance.
4  [1977] 1 WLR 1262.

was nominal.[5] C, however, claimed and was awarded the cost of up to £3,400 of getting someone else to build the wall. C's claim for cost to complete arose from his belief that he had a consumer surplus interest in having the wall built which would not be reflected in market values. The wall was worth more to C than the difference (if any) between the market values of his land with and without it, and had he been confined to the diminution measure, that loss of consumer surplus interest would have been left uncompensated.

Cost to complete damages should be viewed as a method of allowing C to protect his expectation when there is no market in which he can immediately obtain from a third party what D promised. They are mainly applicable to cases where D promised to produce a good (in the economic sense) which required complex, lengthy works (eg to build a machine or construct a building to individually agreed plans). As the good is not available in competitive supply, C cannot reasonably mitigate his loss in any way other than by having the work completed.[6] The substitute performer must enter into a similar contract under which he undertakes to produce the same result, eg to complete the construction of the building according to the same plans. Cost to complete damages are so generally apposite to complex construction cases that their award, which we will see can involve a substantial modification of normal mitigation principles, is often called 'the building contracts rule'.[7]

## Limitations on the availability of cost to complete damages

Having been developed as a form of damages, the principles governing the award of cost to complete damages are not consistent with those which govern the granting of a direct order for specific performance. In particular, there is no *explicit* judicial discretion whether to grant the award as there is in respect of specific performance. As these damages can raise serious problems closely analogous to those encountered when deciding whether to grant specific performance, this is rather unfortunate.

5   An expert witness for D expressed the opinion that the value of C's property was indeed *enhanced* by the absence of the wall: ibid at 1268. If this were so, then this would be an example of the 'ugly monument' paradox drawn to general attention by Corbin in the US *Restatement (Contracts)*. If C builds an ugly ornamental monument, it may actually diminish the market value of the land, and if C were always confined to the diminution measure, the contract to build the fountain would always be unenforceable: *Restatement (Contracts)* 2d, sec 344, illustration 4.

6   *Harbutt's Plasticine Ltd v Wayne Tank and Pump Co Ltd* [1970] 1 QB 447 at 473.

7   *East Ham Corpn v Bernard Sunley and Sons Ltd* [1966] AC 406 at 434.

In these cases the court faces a choice between two measures of damages: that based on the cost to complete, and that based on the difference between the market value of D's performance in its defective or incomplete state and the market value of the performance if it had been properly completed.[8] We will call the latter the diminution measure. Where only a small amount of work is unfinished, and relatively little is therefore at issue, the courts invariably award the cost of the remedial work. So where a builder or decorator has completed the work except for minor omissions or defects, the cost of getting a third party to make them good is the usual measure of damages.[9]

Where, however, considerable work remains to be done after breach, the difference between the diminution measure and cost to complete damages can diverge sharply, for the latter may be very considerably higher than the former. In the admittedly absolutely extraordinary *Ocean Island* case, C owned land on an island from which D was permitted to remove phosphate in return for a promise to make certain payments and to restore the worked-out land. The cost of restoration was claimed to be $73,140 per acre and the diminution in market value caused by leaving the land unrestored was $75 per acre. The disproportion between the cost of restoration and the gain it would provide was taken to justify refusing cost to complete damages.[10] Even in more ordinary cases, the burden of cost to complete can be extreme.

Of course, the mitigation rules might normally be expected to confine C to the diminution measure. Instead of asserting judicial discretion over the remedy, as in the case of specific performance or injunctions, the courts have said that C is entitled to the reasonable cost of having the remedial work done if it is reasonable for him to insist on having the work done and either: (a) C has actually had the work done,[11] or (b) C undertakes to have it done,[12] or (c) C has shown a 'sufficient intention' to have the work

---

8    AFH Loke, 'Cost of Cure or Difference in Market Value: Towards a Sound Choice in the Basis for Quantifying Expectation Damages' (1996) 10 Journal of Contract Law 189.

9    *Hoenig v Isaacs* [1952] 2 All ER 176 at 181. This is tantamount to saying that, for all practical purposes in these cases, the two measures coincide or are interchangeable: eg *Dean v Ainley* [1987] 1 WLR 1729. The cost of cure has also been awarded as damages for the defective quality of goods delivered under a contract of sale. See pp 101-102 above.

10   *Tito v Waddell (No 2)* [1977] Ch 106. Though, it is submitted, decided on correct contractual principle, this case is so overlain with issues of the most pressing public and international concern that its use as a precedent in contract is highly suspect. Indeed, its being treated as a contract case is what is suspect about it: Y Ghai et al (eds), *The Political Economy of Law* (1987) 3-4.

11   *Jones v Hexheimer* [1950] 2 KB 106.

12   *Tito v Waddell (No 2)* above n 10, at 333 and *Dean v Ainley* above n 9, at 1737-1738.

done if he receives damages on this basis.[13] In general, the courts are unconcerned with the purpose to which C actually puts an award of damages.[14] However, it is analytically the case that protection of a consumer surplus implies that C has undertaken (a) above or will undertake (b) and (c) above to secure substitute performance. The extra cost of cost to complete can be justified only where C really wants performance. Cost to complete therefore will be denied where the court thinks that C does not intend to have the work done.[15] C, of course, may mount an action for cost to complete simply to attempt to capitalise on the possibility of obtaining the larger award.[16] The requirements in (a), (b) or (c) above are justified and indeed necessary if the award is treated as a substitute for specific performance.

American and Canadian courts have found the cost to complete measure reasonable where the difference in market values was nominal, either because it actually was nil[17] or because it was too speculative to be awarded;[18] or where D's breach was 'either intentional or due to gross neglect'.[19] English courts have tended to choose this measure when they have instinctively recognised a substantial loss of consumer surplus.[20]

In all these jurisdictions, however, the diminution in value measure has been preferred where it is considered that the cost of the remedial work would be grossly and unfairly out of all proportion to the benefit to be obtained,[1] and the award therefore would amount to 'economic waste'.[2] The argument here is in substance the same as that of undue hardship in the similar situation when C seeks specific performance.[3] It is not that C's interest in performance is not recognised,[4] but that its full protection is taken to be unjustifiable in the light of the cost of this to D. In *Ruxley*

13 *Tito v Waddell (No 2)* above p 212, n 10, at 333; *Radford v de Froberville*, above p 210, n 4 at 1284 and *Dean v Ainley*, above p 212, n 9.
14 *Ruxley Electronics and Construction Ltd v Forsyth* [1996] AC 344 at 359, HL.
15 *Wigsell v School for Indigent Blind* (1882) 8 QBD 357 and *Tito v Waddell (No 2)*, above p 212, n 10 at 332.
16 At first instance in *Ruxley*, it was found that C had no intention of rebuilding the pool and therefore to award cost to complete would be to convey to him a windfall profit of £21,560: *Ruxley Electronics and Construction Ltd v Forsyth*, HL, above n 14 at 360.
17 *Chamberlin v Parker* 45 NY 569 (1871).
18 *Sunshine Exploration Ltd v Dolly Varden Mines Ltd* (1969) 8 DLR (3d) 441.
19 *Jacobs and Youngs Inc v Kent* 129 NE 889 at 892 (1921) per McLaughlin J dissenting.
20 Harris et al, 'Contract Remedies and the Consumer Surplus', above p 210, n 1, p 590.
1 *Jacobs and Youngs Inc v Kent*, above n 19.
2 *Tito v Waddell (No 2)*, above p 212, n 10 at 328.
3 See pp 182-183 above.
4 *Pace* B Coote, 'Contract Damages, *Ruxley* and the Performance Interest' [1997] Cambridge Law Journal 537.

*Electronics and Construction Ltd v Forsyth*, Lord Mustill made explicit reference to the consumer surplus analysis developed by Harris, Ogus and Phillips and in the first edition of this book when recognising that 'the law must cater for those occasions where the value of the promise to the promisee exceeds the financial enhancement of his position which full performance will secure'.[5] It was nevertheless decided in that case that C had to be confined to the diminution measure. D had built a swimming pool for C with a diving area only between 6 feet and 6 feet 9 inches in depth rather than the 7 foot 6 inches specified. As the pool remained perfectly suitable for the type of diving contemplated, this breach had no effect on the market value of the property. The Court of Appeal nevertheless awarded £21,560 as the cost to complete (by completely rebuilding the pool, the original price of which was £17,797).[6] This was reversed by the House of Lords because of the obvious disproportion between the high cost to D of conferring a minor or non-existent benefit on C. This manifestly is justifiable and is, in our opinion, the best (or least worse) possible outcome, but it must be stressed that it can leave C with an uncompensated loss.[7] We shall now turn to attempts to address this.

### Another alternative to diminution in value or cost to complete?

If the courts' decision not to award cost to complete damages in cases such as *Ruxley* on the grounds that this would occasion social waste is justifiable, then it has been argued that the diminution measure is not the only alternative. At least two other solutions are possible, though neither, in our opinion, is on balance preferable to the existing law as the default rule which should apply.

First, if C has a substantial consumer surplus but not one sufficient in the circumstances to justify imposing cost to complete damages on D, an

5    HL, above p 213, n 14 at 360E-F.
6    Ibid at 361G. The entire works, which also included an elaborate enclosure for the pool, would have cost over £70,000.
7    This loss is particularly hard to identify in *Ruxley*, which would appear to be either a case of C wishing to stand on his rights or, more likely, in bad faith to attempt to avoid paying the contract price: ibid at 362. In an excellent note on this aspect of *Ruxley*, O'Sullivan has warned against letting the unworthiness of the claimant in *Ruxley* (which she argues the court exaggerates), and similar cases, weigh too heavily against the merits of 'compensating the unfulfilled personal preference', especially where C is a consumer who may well not be able to guard effectively against incomplete performance: J O'Sulllivan, 'Loss and Gain at Greater Depth: The Implications of the *Ruxley* Decision', in FD Rose (ed), *Failure of Contracts* (1997) 1, 7.

attempt might be made to evaluate this surplus and compensate for its loss. Analogies from the law of tort are available for putting an arbitrary figure on an intangible loss like pain and suffering or loss of amenity, and in tort the fact that a genuine loss cannot be accurately measured is not held to be a reason for ignoring it. At first instance in *Ruxley*, C was awarded £2,500 for loss of amenity[8] and whilst it is, with respect, impossible to place any firm logical ground under this further departure from *Addis v Gramophone Ltd,*[9] this award was restored by the House of Lords. In the Court of Appeal in *Ruxley*, Staughton LJ clearly had been influenced to award cost to complete because he shied away from what he saw as the only alternative, of awarding nothing,[10] and this possibility of awarding loss of amenity at least has the advantage of easing the dilemma of awarding nothing or clearly too much posed by the choice between the two measures in this case.[11]

The fact remains, however, that such figures are arbitrary and, as the necessity for arriving at them follows from the diminution measure yielding the figure, in its own terms correctly quantified, of zero, they must be arbitrary. No justification of the figure of £2,500 was given by any of their Lordships,[12] who merely pointed to the fact that D had not challenged it, with Lord Lloyd saying plainly that the size of the figure was a piece of luck for C.[13] Although one might have expected some such compromise payment to be the outcome of ADR or an out of court settlement, it must be questioned whether the introduction of arbitrary tort quanta into appeal cases on contract is an unambiguous good. If parties are to be able to calculate their exposure to risk when entering into a contract, their potential liability must be certain, and recognising 'luck' will hardly increase that certainty. Furthermore, it cannot be a legitimate purpose of appeal courts to state as law what might indeed be the compromise outcome of ADR or pending litigation, for this merely shifts the boundaries of any settlement later reached in the shadow of the law. We believe that attempts to quantify consumer surplus should be rejected because of the uncertainty of the quantification involved.

Alternatively, the 'windfall' comprising the difference between the two measures of damages need not be awarded wholly to one party. In the *Ocean Island* case, the huge windfall was a saving of expense 'awarded'

---

8   *Ruxley Electronics and Construction Ltd v Forsyth*, HL, above p 213, n 14 at 363G, HL.
9   [1909] AC 488.
10  *Ruxley Electronics and Construction Ltd v Forsyth* [1994] 3 All ER 801 at 810H, CA.
11  *Ruxley Electronics and Construction Ltd v Forsyth*, HL, above p 213, n 14 at 359-361.
12  Ibid at 354C, 359E, 361E.
13  Ibid at 373-377.

entirely to D. If D had to negotiate his release from the obligation to replant, C would certainly have demanded a price for the release. Damages for C's loss of the opportunity to negotiate could have been fixed as a price above the market value measure. This possibility was suggested in the *Ocean Island* case, but rejected on the ground that, as D was not liable for anything, it would have paid nothing for release.[14] As it has been observed, this is so, but it rather begs the question,[15] and payment for hypothetical release had been made in the earlier case of *Wrotham Park Estate Co Ltd v Parkside Homes Ltd*.[16] The decisions both to leave C in *Ruxley* under-compensated because of the 'unreasonable', 'disproportionate' cost of fully compensating him but also to make some sort of award have recently been approved by Lord Hobhouse in the course of his powerful dissent in *A-G v Blake*.[17] The most plausible justification of payments in the *Ocean Island* or *Ruxley* situations has been furnished on restitutionary grounds, and this justification will be discussed in connection with restitution in chapter 17 below. The reader is advised to turn to this chapter for the completion of our account particularly of these cases.

---

14  *Tito v Waddell (No 2)*, above p 212, n 10 at 335-336.
15  H Beale, *Damages for Breach of Contract* (1980) p 177.
16  [1974] 1 WLR 798.
17  [2001] 1 AC 268 at 298.

# 15 Appraisal of literal enforcement

## Incentives to perform

This chapter considers the extent to which the currently available legal and self-help remedies do and should provide incentives to the promisor D to perform his contractual obligation. Having acknowledged the general preference for compensatory damages, when reviewing the law relating to literal enforcement we find that Holmes' famous statement,[1] while capturing the basic position, is something of an over-statement, for in a haphazard way the law does provide a number of incentives to perform.

The legal remedies which give D an incentive to perform his primary obligation are:

(1) *Declarations*.[2] A non-coercive remedy available to C is a declaration (declaratory judgment) by the court which sets out C's rights against D, but does not order him to do (or refrain from doing) anything. For instance, C may ask the court to decide whether he is still bound by the contract; whether he is entitled to terminate it; or whether his interpretation of a clause in the contract is correct. The declaration is an authoritative statement of the relevant legal position on which the parties can base their future actions. The court may thus guide the parties in performing a long-term contract, and help them to avoid a conflict, since the remedy is available before any breach of contract has occurred. The court has a discretion whether to grant a declaration. It will pronounce on the parties' legal position only if there is a real, as opposed to a theoretical, question to be solved. Even where D is liable to pay damages, C may claim only a declaration that D is in

---

1  See p 153 above.
2  Lord Woolf et al *The Declaratory Judgment* (3rd edn 2001).

breach, and that the damages amounted to a particular sum.[3] In one case of an overseas sale by instalments, the seller obtained a declaration that the buyer was bound to pay the price upon the seller's fulfilling its obligations, eg upon tender of the shipping documents (the buyer had wrongly claimed that it was entitled to examine the goods before paying).[4]

If D acts in a way which contravenes his legal position as stated in the declaration, he will usually become liable to an ordinary coercive judgment against him.

(2) *Unliquidated damages.* The traditional view of the law of contract is that D's fear of paying damages to C will usually provide a sufficient incentive to D to perform. The expectation measure of damages is designed to give C the full value of the performance promised by D, and the reliance measure may often increase the cost of D's breach by giving C the amount of his wasted expenditure. The risk of paying interest on the damages, as well as the costs on both sides, may add to the incentive on D to avoid being forced to pay damages. But the burden placed on C to prove and value his loss, and by the net loss approach (the rules of mitigation), seriously undermines the incentive effect of the risk of D having to pay unliquidated damages. The fact that promisees often insist on deposits, advance payments, guarantees and other forms of security for performance, indicates their lack of confidence in damages as an adequate incentive upon D.

(3) *Debt.*[5] Where C has a claim in debt, D will often be induced to pay before he is sued because he knows that C can easily obtain summary judgment, costs and interest.

(4) *Specific relief.*[6] The obvious incentive is the risk that the court will make an order for specific performance or grant an injunction. But except in sales of land, this risk is usually remote for most contractual undertakings, and in any case, the court has an overriding discretion to refuse to make an order.

(5) *Substitute performance damages.*[7] Where the court is likely to award C damages assessed at the cost of obtaining substitute performance from a third party (the cost of cure or of reinstatement), D will have an incentive to perform if he can himself complete performance more cheaply. But the effect is diluted because the court has, in effect, a wide discretion in deciding whether to assess damages on this basis.

---

3    *Louis Dreyfuss and Co v Parnaso Cia Naviera SA* [1959] 1 QB 498 (appeal allowed on a different point [1960] 2 QB 49).
4    *Polengi Brothers v Dried Milk Co Ltd* (1904) 10 Com Cas 42.
5    See above ch 11.
6    See above chs 12-13.
7    See above ch 14.

Particularly in the light of recent developments in the law of restitution[8] and exemplary damages,[9] to this list we now must add:
(6) *Depriving D of the gain resulting from his breach.* D obviously would have a strong incentive to perform if the damages rules worked to deprive him of the gain (reduction of loss or windfall profit) which he makes as the result of breach. An effective incentive to perform would be imposed by making D liable to damages assessed at a reasonable 'price' for his acting as if C had agreed to release him from his primary obligation.

This really can be done only if we abandon the basic method of quantifying damages with the aim of compensating C's loss. This would be the case were exemplary damages to be generally awarded in contract or were the restitutionary redistribution of efficient breach windfalls to be widely undertaken. Though both are being strongly advocated, both, it will be argued at length in chapters 17 and 30, are being proposed in such ignorance of the function of breach that they will be incapable of taking a general foothold in the law.

Whatever the outcome of these two proposed developments in the law, it should be pointed out in this context that their strength as incentives to perform will be roughly correlated to the proportion of D's profit they remove. A small proportion may leave a strong incentive to breach; a large proportion may create a strong incentive to perform. The logic of exemplary damages allows them to embrace large proportions, indeed to exceed 100% of the profit, for the quantification of those damages is supposed to be in proportion to what is taken to be the injustice of the breach, and this is not directly or at all related to D's profit. On the other hand, even though the fixing of restitutionary figures has so far been very imprecise, it is difficult to conceive of a restitutionary sum being so high a proportion of the profit. As has been said above, no rational D would have agreed to pay as the price of his release from his obligation a sum which is so high as to deprive him of all of the profit of his breach (and C would therefore lose his extra profit as well). Even were they to become more common, restitutionary awards on this basis are, then, less likely than exemplary damages to work as a form of literal enforcement.

## Contractual provision for literal enforcement

Being aware of the limitations on the literal enforcement remedies, when negotiating a contract which gives rise to the possibility of idiosyncratic and therefore uncompensated loss, C might attempt to insert contractual

8  See ch 17 below.
9  See ch 30 below.

provisions which allow him to take advantage of the following self-help techniques which give D an incentive to perform:

(1) *Withholding performance by use of conditional or entire obligations.* C may be entitled to withhold performance of his obligation until D has performed (or is able and willing to perform) an obligation upon him. The desire to obtain the benefit of C's performance will often induce D to perform. The most significant instance is the 'entire obligation' rule, where D must fully complete his performance before C's obligation is activated. If D fails to perform, he risks losing the benefit of his partial performance and wasting the cost of that effort.

(2) *Withholding performance by termination.* C's power to terminate the contract for a serious breach or failure to perform by D will often be an incentive on D to avoid breach. In partially performing, or in preparing to perform, D will have invested resources the benefit of which he will lose if he allows C the opportunity to terminate. The risk of such an uncompensated loss will often induce D to perform. Nor is C's power to terminate always restricted by the need to prove that he has suffered loss from the breach. (The concept of 'efficient breach' has never applied to this situation.) C may also be entitled to restitution of benefits conferred by him on D, despite D's partial performance of his side. Sometimes, a restitutionary remedy may provide a clear deterrent against breach of D's obligation, as where a principal may recover from a corrupt agent the amount of the bribe received by him from a third party, irrespective of any loss suffered by the principal.

(3) *Forfeiture of a deposit or other advance payments.* The fear that breach might entitle C to forfeit a deposit paid by D will often induce D to perform. He risks losing the benefit of that payment, which C could forfeit following breach whether or not he actually suffered any loss. Similarly, a clause in the contract may create the risk that D's breach might entitle C to forfeit other advance payments made by D or rights enjoyed by him.

(4) *Guarantees and other forms of security.* D may have given C other forms of security for his performance, such as a guarantee from a third party, security over his assets, or retention of title over goods. Breach by D in this situation will cost him as much as, or more than, performance, and he will therefore strive to perform.

(5) *Liquidated damages.* A valid agreed damages clause may also induce D to perform. First, C need not prove his loss after the breach, so that he can more easily obtain judgment for damages, costs and interest against D. Secondly, provided the amount fixed by the clause was a genuine pre-estimate of loss, it may turn out that at the time when D is tempted to breach, the amount is likely to exceed the loss then expected, and will therefore be a greater incentive to perform than unliquidated damages.

(6)   *Clauses invoking literal enforcement.* Clauses which have been discussed throughout this Part which seek to invoke a form of literal enforcement when the default rules would not do so obviously lead to literal enforcement. Indeed, C's automatic entitlement under a clause in the contract to obtain an order is the most powerful incentive which the law could conceivably offer, but the courts are justified in not generally permitting this.

As has been mentioned throughout this Part, these self-help remedies pose a regulatory problem different from that posed by the legal remedies.[10] Self-help remedies are the products of the parties' negotiations, and the regulatory problem is determining how far those negotiations are fair.[11] This is not a matter of evaluating the substance of the remedy but of evaluating the procedure by which that substance was agreed, in essence, of evaluating the (in)equality of bargaining power in the negotiations. When evaluating the legal remedies, which usually function as default rules in the absence of the parties' own agreement of a remedy, it is the substance that is important, for the purpose of these rules is to furnish a fair and efficient outcome. We now turn to an appraisal of these legal remedies.

## Appraisal of the legal remedies providing for specific enforcement

### Issues common to the forms of literal enforcement

Developed as quite separate claims or even, in the case of specific performance and injunction, based in a quite different form of legal reasoning, the forms of literal enforcement have many features peculiar to themselves which have obscured the fact that all these forms raise very similar issues. Nevertheless, one principal problem, or perhaps two principal problems, have emerged from our discussion of literal enforcement. These are the existence of uncompensated loss which follows from the general preference for compensatory damages over literal enforcement (given that these damages sometimes lead to a failure to compensate), and the tension between the unacceptability of such loss and the impossibility of abandoning the general preference whilst pursuing the avoidance of social waste through mitigation. The way this problem emerges and is treated in each of the existing forms of literal enforcement is, from our current perspective, a haphazard product of their

---

10   Lawson calls these remedies 'in the fullest sense consensual', which rather misses the point: FH Lawson, *Remedies of English Law* (2nd edn 1980) p 41.

11   I Ayres and J Braithwaite, *Responsive Regulation* (1992) and G Teubner, 'Substantive and Reflexive Elements in Modern Law' (1983) 17 Law and Society Review 239.

different histories, and this is obviously unwelcome. It should not be the case that basically the same problem of balancing convenience or relative disadvantage should be resolved differently according to the empirical circumstances in which it arises and, given the present state of the law, how therefore it is pleaded. Determining how far this haphazard quality may be reduced requires further discussion of the reasons why the general preference for compensatory damages cannot be abandoned. Any such determination requires us to make explicit a consideration which has so far been allowed to remain largely implicit in our discussion of the forms of literal enforcement, namely social waste.

### The concept of social waste

The placing of a requirement on C to show a legitimate interest in affirming a contract after D has repudiated it, the refusal to grant specific performance or injunction because of undue hardship to D, and restricting C to the diminution rather than the cost to complete measure because the latter would involve 'expenditure ... out of all proportion to the benefit to be obtained'[12] all turn on a recognition that literal enforcement can be wasteful of the limited resources in society. The possibility of D finding itself in a losing contract is endemic to the capitalist economy and an efficient legal system will facilitate release from these contracts which prove to have been mistaken, in an economic if not a legal sense, at least transaction cost. To fail to minimise this cost when such minimisation is reasonably possible is to incur social waste. This issue of social waste is the most important general issue which the courts must weigh, and with varying degrees of self-consciousness have weighed, in deciding whether to grant literal enforcement.

The comparison is between the estimated cost to D in complying with the order and the expected value to C of getting the benefit of performance. If C's expectation is equally protected both by the payment of compensatory damages and literal enforcement, then there is no good reason to impose literal enforcement on D at all. This is generally taken to be case, which is why compensatory damages[13] are typically preferred and why *White and Carter (Councils) Ltd v McGregor*,[14] on the facts as pleaded (in which C's reasons for affirmation do not appear), appears so absurd.

This policy is consistent with the doctrine of mitigation. If C can reasonably obtain a satisfactory substitute, he should accept that in lieu

---

12  *Ruxley Electronics and Construction Ltd v Forsyth* [1996] AC 344 at 367.
13  Or debt in the circumstances where debt produces the same result.
14  [1962] AC 413, discussed at pp 160-165 above.

of performance. When specific performance is ordered, C avoids the responsibility of finding suitable alternatives. Hence, whenever it is reasonable for him, after D's breach, to seek substitute performance through another person, or to switch his resources to the next best use, the court should not grant literal enforcement. If C expects, say, an order of specific performance, he will not take any steps to minimise the effect of D's breach. Although the courts, when considering C's claim for literal enforcement, previously have not discussed his responsibility to minimise his loss, it is implicit in the way they exercise their discretion over granting the remedy that they would not grant it where C should have mitigated.[15] This is the core meaning of the traditional statement that specific relief is given only where damages would be an 'inadequate' remedy.

(However, C may often be faced with uncertainty as to the way the court will exercise its discretion, and it would be unfair on him if, following a finely balanced weighing of the factors relevant to this exercise, the court came down against specific relief and this led to the result that C was then told that immediately after breach he should have mitigated his loss. So long as there are proper grounds on which to base a claim for specific relief, C should not be held to have failed to take reasonable steps to minimise his loss, even though the court ultimately holds that his only remedy is damages.)[16]

What in addition has emerged from our discussion of literal enforcement is that even when, generally because of the existence of consumer surplus or uncompensated commercial loss, C has a good case for literal enforcement, C is not always able to obtain literal enforcement because, when D objects to that enforcement, a balance between C's and D's interests has to be struck. The court cannot look exclusively at C's position, because it is also concerned to avoid putting a burden on D which is disproportionate to the advantage to be gained by C. It is this which, it is submitted, constitutes a policy of avoiding social waste. If the cost imposed on D would substantially exceed the gain to C, society as a whole would be better off if D paid C the full monetary equivalent of the gain but avoided the extra cost beyond this figure, since it would be 'wasted' from society's point of view.

This can be seen if we consider a case where C is seeking an order of specific performance against D. The example set out in Figure 1 assumes that no substitute performance is available, and that C is not seeking to get a third party to perform:

15  The (it is submitted problematic) exception of the sale of land being noted.
16  *Asamera Oil Corpn Ltd v Sea Oil and General Corpn* (1979) 89 DLR (3d) 1 at 26.

*Figure I*

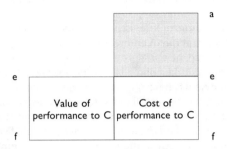

Suppose that the cost of performance which D would incur under an order for specific performance would amount to level *a* in Figure 1, but the value of that performance to C would amount only to *e*. If D were compelled to perform, the social waste would be measured by the shaded area *a* to *e*; if D does not perform, but compensates C by an amount of money *e* to *f*, C receives a value equivalent to performance, but D saves the expenditure *a* to *e*. Now, in the eyes of the economist, a saving of expenditure is as much a benefit as the receipt of money. If the court denies specific performance in this situation, and awards damages measured by *e* to *f*, the effect of its decision is to award the whole of the benefit *a* to *e* to D, the contract-breaker.

Judges have been too prone to look at the situation only from C's point of view. They are concerned that he should be 'fully' compensated (though not 'over-'compensated by receiving more than his 'loss'), but they often ignore the effect of their judgment on D. When D is relieved of the obligation to incur the expenditure *a* to *e*, that is an *award* of the benefit of that saving to him. The denial of C's claim has a negative effect from his point of view as he fails to get the remedy he sought. But it also has a positive effect from D's point of view, in that he is allowed to keep the resources *a* to *e*, freed from the obligation to use them to perform his contractual promise. It is submitted that courts can do justice only by considering the effect of their rulings on both sides, rather than by concentrating merely on C's side. In this regard, the recent dicta of Millett LJ in his dissent in the Court of Appeal's hearing of *Co-operative Insurance Society Ltd v Argyll Stores (Holdings) Ltd* are an exemplary statement of the correct approach: 'It is always necessary to consider the consequence to the defendant of granting such relief as well as the consequence to the plaintiff of leaving him to his remedy in damages. Equitable remedies are instruments of justice: they should be refused where they would be potential instruments of oppression.'[17] (To this we would venture to add

17   [1996] Ch 286 at 304G, CA.

only that the same reasoning should be applied to the analogous arguments which have arisen in regard of the other forms of literal enforcement.)[18]

In *Co-operative Insurance Society Ltd v Argyll Stores (Holdings) Ltd*, C's case for specific performance was particularly strong. D had taken a 35-year lease on part of C's shopping centre development in order to operate a supermarket. The viability of other businesses in the shopping centre and of the shopping centre itself was, as the parties knew at the outset, heavily dependent on the operation of D's supermarket. When D decided to breach its lease because its business was making a loss, C (and the third party owners of other businesses) faced extensive losses,[19] some of which would, because of proof problems, have remained uncompensated.[20] D also would appear to have acted unreasonably in the manner in which it breached.[1] Nevertheless, specific enforcement of a covenant to keep open a supermarket for a further 19 years when D had breached because that supermarket had already made substantial losses would impose excessive, disproportionate loss on D.[2] Leaving aside any difficulties with supervision which purporting to specifically enforce the covenant in these circumstances was likely to lead,[3] the over-riding objection to a grant of specific performance was stated by Millett LJ. In certain circumstances it is a reasonable response to the unfortunate circumstance of a losing contract for D to breach.[4] One only has to postulate the alternative, that, having entered into a 35-year covenant, D could be held to that covenant regardless of whether it might cause a 'potential loss [which is] enormous, unquantifiable and unlimited'[5] to see that this is a commercial absurdity which must have unwelcome consequences:

> Over the years countless tenants with the benefit of legal advice
> have entered into commercial leases ... similar to ... the present ...
> If they had asked their legal advisers whether this meant that they

18   Eg *White and Carter (Councils) Ltd v McGregor*, above p 222, n 14 at 433 and
     439-440 per Lords Morton and Keith dissenting.
19   *Co-operative Insurance Society Ltd v Argyll Stores (Holdings) Ltd*, above n 17 at
     301C, CA.
20   Ibid at 295A.
1    Ibid at 295B-296E, 299E. Cf *Co-operative Insurance Society Ltd v Argyll Stores
     (Holdings) Ltd* [1998] AC 1 at 18C-G, HL.
2    Counsel for C allowed that specific performance could have driven D into
     bankruptcy: ibid at 19A. It must be recalled that D was *not* pleading common
     mistake or frustration, and so seeking to refuse to perform without liability. D
     acknowledged liability in damages.
3    See pp 187-190 above.
4    *Co-operative Insurance Society Ltd v Argyll Stores (Holdings) Ltd*, above p 224,
     n 17 at 304C-D, CA.
5    Ibid at 305D.

could be compelled to keep the premises open for business regardless of the financial consequences, I have no doubt that they would have been told that it did not; they would have been advised that such a covenant sounds in damages only. If the courts were willing to compel performance, I do not see how any tenant properly advised could safely enter into such an obligation. Yet the covenant is of great commercial value to developers, even if it does sound only in damages. If [such a covenant was specifically enforceable in these circumstances] developers may find it difficult to find anchor tenants willing to submit to such a covenant ... The equitable jurisdiction should not be exercised in a manner which would defeat the commercial expectations of the parties at the time they entered into their contractual obligations.[6]

## Conclusion

The position taken generally in this Part of this book is that the positive law is that compensatory damages are typically preferred to literal enforcement and that this is correct. It is correct because it is economically efficient, and evidence that it is so is that it conforms to what we know of legitimate commercial expectations. The position which it has been sought to establish in this Part of this book is that even when C has a case for literal enforcement, its grant both has been and should be considered with reference both to C's and D's interests and the general interest in avoiding social waste. The corollary of these positions is that literal enforcement is and should remain a relatively unusual remedy.

The crucial consequence of any wider availability of literal enforcement would be a corresponding restriction of the scope of the rules on mitigation.[7] We should not literally enforce in those situations where we want promisees to take reasonable steps to mitigate. Is the doctrine of mitigation too wide? The answer lies in understanding the public policy of encouraging a more efficient use of resources if the promisor finds that he has made a bad bargain.[8]

A final way of testing the present rules on specific relief is to ask whether they reflect the kind of terms governing remedies which the average parties would themselves have negotiated in the absence of transaction costs. If the law supplies 'default' rules on remedies which suit most negotiating parties, transaction costs are minimised because they

6    Ibid at 305E-G.
7    See ch 7 above.
8    Or is offered a better opportunity to make a profit, which raises the issue of efficient breach discussed in relation to restitution in ch 17 below.

need not negotiate over them.[9] In general, the rules seem to pass this test. The rule arguably is efficient in the sense that it represents the one that the parties would themselves have negotiated as a general rule if they bear in mind, over time, that they will stand in the position of D as well as C.[10] If C could find a substitute, he would prefer a term permitting him to find one, and then entitling him to claim the difference in cost from D. If he could not find a substitute, he would want actual performance from D.[11] Kronman argues that most promisors (D) would want a term which kept open the option of breaking the contract (should his costs of performance rise or a better offer come along), subject to paying the cost of compensating C for his loss of the bargain.[12] C's entitlement to enforce actual performance would thus be agreed by D only if the price were increased in a bespoke contract actually negotiated between the parties. C would not agree to this increase if substitutes were readily available, but if D's performance were unique, C would be willing to pay extra to ensure actual performance, especially when there is the risk that he may be left uncompensated by a damages award. Entitlement to performance would also mean that C would have the assurance that D would have to pay a price for his release if he did not wish to perform. D would lose the unilateral power to commit a breach so as to force C to mitigate his loss by seeking substitutes. All this is, of course, acceptable if the default rule is ousted after proper negotiation between the parties.[13]

---

9   See pp 88-92 above.
10  Cf J Rawls, *A Theory of Justice* (rev edn 1999) ch 3.
11  C would particularly prefer damages if he wished, upon D's breach, to have the option of redeploying his resources to some different use.
12  AT Kronman, 'Specific Performance' (1978) 45 University of Chicago Law Review 351.
13  The difficulty with this argument arising from the threat of imprisonment standing behind specific performance is considered at pp 189-190 above.

# Part 4
# Restitution

# 16 Existing forms of restitution

## Introduction

C is sometimes entitled to claim from D restitution of the valuable benefit he has conveyed to D by (part) performance of his primary obligation under the contract. This may take the form of recovery of money paid to D or obtaining a reasonable sum for a valuable benefit (other than the payment of money) which C has conveyed to D, the latter now generally being called a *quantum meruit*. Instead of claiming damages for his loss caused by D's breach, C asks for restitution of the valuable benefit he has conveyed by performance on the ground that, as he has not received the performance which D had promised in return, D has been unjustly enriched. The whole jurisprudential basis of a restitutionary claim, based on abhorrence of D's unjust enrichment,[1] is different from that of a claim in damages based on C's expectation interest. Restitution does *not* compensate C for loss caused by D's non-performance.[2] It compels D to make a payment to divest him of the valuable benefit he has received in order to prevent his unjust enrichment.

The possibility of framing a claim in restitution following a breach of contract led Fuller and Perdue in their seminal article to identify the restitutionary interest as the third of the contractual interests.[3] As such a

---

1   *Moses v Mcferlan* (1760) 97 ER 676 at 680; *Fibrosa Spolka Akayjna v Fairburn Lawson Combe Barbour Ltd* [1943] AC 32 at 61; *Lipkin Gorman v Karpnale Ltd* [1991] 2 AC 548 and *A-G v Blake* [1997] Ch 84; revsd [1998] Ch 439; affd [2001] 1 AC 268.
2   The circumstances covered in this chapter are, however, those which Birks calls 'unjust enrichment by subtraction', and the significance of this will be discussed in the next chapter.
3   LL Fuller and WR Perdue Jr, 'The Reliance Interest in Contract Damages' (1936) 46 Yale Law Journal 52, pp 53-54.

claim arose from C's performance and D's non-performance of obligations under a contract, but the assessment of the remedy was not made on a contractual basis, it continued in modern times to be classified as 'quasi-contractual'.[4] However, it is apparent from what has just been said that restitution has no necessary connection with contract, for not only is the remedy following non-performance quantified differently in restitution as opposed to contract, but unjust enrichment may very well arise out of non-contractual situations. At the moment, a determined effort is being made by some writers to reclassify the whole of the law of civil obligations in restitutionary terms. In this general classification, quasi-contract must disappear, for the implicit claim that contract is in some way the foundation of these claims is precisely what is denied in this classification.[5] In this book, 'restitution' will be preferred to 'quasi-contract' but, without wishing to enter into the general doctrinal debate until the next chapter (and then to a very limited extent), we will, when necessary, argue that the complete substitution of 'restitutionary' for 'contractual' rules for the quantification of damages will lead to undesirable outcomes.

A restitutionary remedy is available to C after he has terminated the contract on the ground of D's breach, in cases of common mistake, or (further) performance of the contract has been discharged for frustration. It is consistent with the general reluctance to over-compensate C when claiming contractual damages and would seem to be the position for which there is most authority that C cannot recover both in restitution and in damages. This is to say that he cannot avoid the 'net loss' assessment in the restitutionary part of his claim if he is also trying to hold D liable for loss (such as consequential losses) in another part of his claim.[6] Following breach, then, C must chose whether to claim in restitution or contract and, of course, he will choose the course which will lead to the higher recovery.[7]

By claiming in restitution, C avoids all the rules on contractual damages. Since he is not claiming compensation for his loss, he may have a restitutionary claim even when he has not suffered an expectation loss at all. He need not satisfy the rules on causation, remoteness, mitigation or penalties, and so may be able to claim in restitution when an expectation claim would not fully compensate him. C therefore may sometimes be

---

4   SJ Stoljar, *The Law of Quasi-Contract* (2nd edn 1989).
5   R Goff and G Jones, *The Law of Restitution* (5th edn 1999) pp 5-11. Paradoxically, it was in order to do away with the implied contract fiction that Jackson had earlier attempted to give currency to the use of 'quasi-contract': RM Jackson, *The History of Quasi-Contract in English Law* (1936) section 32.
6   H Beale, *Remedies for Breach of Contract* (1980) p 210.
7   P Birks, 'Inconsistency Between Compensation and Restitution' (1996) 112 Law Quarterly Review 375. On possible limitations on this right in relationship to a *quantum meruit* claim see pp 238-241 below.

able to put himself into a better position through a restitutionary remedy than he could through a claim for specific relief or for damages, eg if he had made a bad bargain and therefore had no expectation, or his losses were so uncertain that he could not prove loss of an expected benefit. But the opposite may (one suspects far more commonly) be true. In many situations, if C can satisfy the usual tests such as causation and remoteness, he may recover more by way of damages than by way of restitution because the former will compensate his lost expectation. Though the present rapid development of restitution in the appeal courts places a question mark against almost any definite statement, it is logically implicit in the notion of restitution that if C has suffered a bare expectation loss or has incurred wasted reliance expenditure which has not conveyed a valuable benefit to D,[8] these losses will not be met by restitution.[9]

There are three principal circumstances in which C may pursue a restitutionary claim following D's failure to perform a contract: after (part) performance by which C has conveyed a valuable benefit which unjustly enriches D; after discharge for frustration (which must be considered together with common mistake); and after efficient breach has presented D with a windfall gain. The first two circumstances will be dealt with in this chapter; the last in chapter 17. The first circumstance embraces C having paid money to D or C having rendered a service to D, and the law treats these separately.

## Recovery of money paid by C to D

The restitutionary claim for the recovery of money paid by C to D is not restricted to situations arising out of non-performance of a contract,[10] but this is the only situation which is directly relevant to this section of this book.[11] C can sue to recover money paid to D under a contract where C has not obtained the benefit of the performance promised by D in return. C's claim that D has been unjustly enriched logically implies that D has failed to provide his promised performance, but how serious such a failure must be to allow C to set aside the normal contractual rules and bring the restitutionary rules into play is an extremely vexed question. That there must have been a 'total failure of consideration' is the phrase which has

---

8   It is not in fact possible to derive a sharp division between reliance and restitution from the leading case of *Planche v Colburn*. See pp 236-238 below.

9   *Mason v Burningham* [1949] 2 KB 545.

10   Eg *Barclays Bank v WJ Sims Ltd* [1980] 1 QB 677. See further P Birks, *Restitution: The Future* (1992) pp 2-5.

11   On contracts void *ab initio* see p 244, n 18 below.

enjoyed long usage[12] in the courts, the thrust of which is that part performance by D bars recovery and confines C to a claim in contractual damages.

But it has long been recognised that this phrase can be quite misleading when what is at issue is the benefit conferred by C rather than D's performance.[13] In particular, the understanding of 'total' has led to some startling outcomes, most famously in *Rowland v Divall*,[14] where the fact that C, the buyer of a car, had resold it to a third party who enjoyed its use, did not preclude C from recovering the full price paid to the seller because the seller had failed to convey good title. Similar jarring decisions continue to be handed down.[15] The lack of the coherence of the law follows from attempts by the courts to evade the consequences which follow from the unsatisfactory nature of the concept of total failure of consideration.[16] In 1975 the Law Commission recommended that the partial performance bar to recovery should be abolished, so that if C has received part of the benefit of the promised performance he should be entitled to recover the amount he paid, subject to a deduction of the reasonable value of the benefit he actually received.[17] But the Commission itself later resiled from this recommendation,[18] and the law remains without any guiding principle. At a time when the relationship of restitution and contract is undergoing rapid shifts, it would not be useful to discuss this issue (which really is one of liability to make the restitutionary payment) here. We will merely note that a tendency to abandon the requirement of total failure (or to interpret it in such a way as amounts to its abandonment) may be detected in the decided cases, and alert readers to the likelihood that this issue may well be subject to argument.[19]

12  Birks has argued that the historical reasons for linking total failure to recovery but not to *quantum meruit* claims can no longer be justified: P Birks, 'In Defence of Free Acceptance', in A Burrows (ed), *Essays on the Law of Restitution* (1991) 105, p 112.

13  *Fibrosa Spolka Akayjna v Fairburn Lawson Combe Barbour Ltd*, above p 231, n 1 at 48. See further G Williams, 'The End of *Chandler v Webster*' (1942) 6 Modern Law Review 46, p 53.

14  [1923] 2 KB 500. See further MG Bridge, 'The Title Obligations of the Seller of Goods', in N Palmer and E McKendrick (eds), *Interests in Goods* (2nd edn 1998) 303, pp 318-327 and GH Treitel, *Law of Contract* (10th edn 1999) pp 980-984.

15  Eg *Rover International Ltd v Cannon Film Sales (No 3)* [1989] 1 WLR 912.

16  A Burrows, *The Law of Restitution* (1993) pp 259-261.

17  Law Commission, *Pecuniary Restitution on Breach of Contract*, Working Paper 65 (1975) ss 6, 48-56.

18  Law Commission, *Pecuniary Restitution on Breach of Contract*, Report No 121 (1983) pt 3.

19  For a recent comprehensive review see *Chitty on Contracts*, vol 1 (2000) ss 30.048-30.061.

The principal virtue which the action for recovery would appear to have for C is that, as with the action for debt,[20] the claim is simple to make since, as it is for a liquidated sum, it avoids problems of quantification.[1] However, it would also appear that recovery avoids an unfortunate consequence of the working out of the damages rules which can arise in certain circumstances. In *Dawood Ltd v Heath (Est 1927) Ltd*, C rejected a non-conforming delivery of steel and sued for recovery of the advance payment for that steel. 35.36 tons of steel, paid for at £73.10s per ton, were rejected, and £2598.19s. 2d was claimed. However, the market price of this steel had fallen and a substitute was available at £70 per ton. If C was confined to a claim for lost expectation, his claim would have been for 35.36 x £70 = £2475 4s, which D could have paid from the payment he had received from C and still be left with 35.36 x £3 10s = £123 15s 2d.[2] This *is* the right outcome if C is confined to his expectation interest, but it is manifestly unjust that D should keep the balance. This problem would arise whenever a falling market is the background to a similar breach. To avoid the unjust enrichment of D, C should be allowed to recover the entire payment, although this *does* give C a windfall profit which over-compensates him in terms of his expectation. This may well be of little practical significance, for the combination of payment in advance, seller's breach and a *falling* market must be rare.[3] The seller could have bought the steel at the lower market price and sold it to the buyer, keeping the difference by avoiding breach. Nevertheless, the availability of recovery in these circumstances is an excellent restitutionary solution to this particular problem thrown up by the normal operation of the contract damages rules, and is a salutary illustration of how it is impossible to devise any system of rules which works well in all circumstances.

### Services rendered by C to D

When under the contract C has conferred a valuable benefit by delivering goods or rendering services to D for which D does not make recompense by performing his obligations under the contract, C may be entitled to claim from D a reasonable sum, assessed by the court, for that benefit, so that D is not unjustly enriched. Though the distinction between delivery of goods and rendering of services continues to be observed in some

---

20   See pp 158-160 above.
1    Beale, *Remedies for Breach of Contract*, above p 232, n 6, pp 204-205.
2    [1961] 2 Lloyd's Rep 512 at 518.
3    This is the set of circumstances referred to as a 'double lightning bolt' in CJ Goetz and RE Scott, 'The Mitigation Principle' (1983) 69 Virginia Law Review 967, p 996.

discussions of restitution, we would say that the use of *quantum valebat* in relation to goods delivered as opposed to *quantum meruit* in relation to services rendered has largely given way to the use of the latter to cover both situations. We therefore will refer to an action for restitution of a valuable benefit (other than payment of money) as a *quantum meruit*.[4] A *quantum meruit* need not arise out of D's failure to perform his contractual obligation to pay for a service, but this is the only circumstance we will consider here.

If C has performed all or a substantial part of his obligations to render a service under the contract which D breaches, C seems to have an unconstrained choice[5] either to sue in contract (or debt) or seek a *quantum meruit* to recover a reasonable sum for the work he has done.[6] Should the actions yield different results, he obviously will choose that which will yield the greater, as is his right.[7] The reason the results may differ is that as a *quantum meruit* is independently assessed by the court, the contract rate of remuneration (which may be zero in an entire contract) need not directly govern quantification, though it is of course likely to be used as evidence about the size of the valuable benefit conferred and may in this way come to govern.[8] This latitude in the calculation of a *quantum meruit* is essential to the purpose of the restitutionary claim[9] but also, of course, it means that 'the identity and value of the ... benefit to the recipient may be debatable'.[10]

In the interpretation of what unfortunately has become the leading case, *Planche v Colburn*,[11] both aspects of this latitude have markedly emerged.

---

4   P Birks, *An Introduction to the Law of Restitution* (rev edn 1989) p 78. For this purpose, therefore, delivery of goods is a service.
5   No parallel to total failure of consideration as a limit on choice of action has been considered in the cases dealing with non-monetary benefits.
6   The actions may merge if the contract effectively leaves the assessment of payment for the service to the courts.
7   *De Bernardy v Harding* (1853) 8 Exch 822 at 824. With the greatest respect, this and other dicta to similar effect seem to contradict the claim in Goff and Jones, *The Law of Restitution*, above p 232, n 5, pp 530-531 that: '[t]here is no English authority to suggest that an innocent party, who has rendered services or supplied goods, may elect to sue in restitution if he has performed or substantially performed his contract ... We consider this conclusion to be historically sound and sound in principle'. Burrows, *The Law of Restitution*, above p 234, n 16, p 270 is right to point out that, even were Goff and Jones correct, there equally is no authority to the contrary. Of course, when there is no breach, a party who has rendered services or supplied goods cannot just move to a *quantum meruit*, and it may be to this case that Goff and Jones' statement principally refers.
8   *James T Burchell v Gowrie and Blockhouse Collieries Ltd* [1910] AC 614 at 626.
9   *Renard Construction (ME) Pty Ltd v Minister for Public Works* (1992) 26 NSWLR 234 at 276-278.
10  *BP Exploration (Libya) Ltd v Hunt (No 2)* [1979] 1 WLR 783 at 799, QBD.
11  (1831) 8 Bing 14, 5 C & P 58, 1 Moo & S 51.

D, a publisher, agreed to pay C £100 if he would write one volume of a series of children's books which D was to publish. After C began the work but before he tendered the script, D breached by cancelling the series and, on learning this, C accepted D's anticipatory repudiation of the contract. C was awarded £50 (or guineas) as a *quantum meruit* for his part performance. Though no report of this case gives any detail about the quantification of the *quantum meruit*, it would appear that it represented the court's acceptance of C's assessment of adequate recompense for 'the trouble he had taken in the business',[12] and one can see the impulse behind using a *quantum meruit* to give C something if one accepts Tindall CJ's observation that '[u]nder these circumstances [C] ought not to lose the fruit of his labour'.[13]

However, this case is attended by serious difficulty for this *quantum meruit* certainly cannot be regarded as having been quantified so as to correct an unjust enrichment, for it is hardly obvious that a valuable benefit was conferred at all.[14] D not only did not receive the script, which remained incomplete, but, of course, could not profitably have used it in the series, which he had cancelled 'upon the ill success of the early numbers'.[15] From consideration of all the reports of this case, it would appear, though those reports do not allow of a certain conclusion, that the point actually at issue was the reasonableness of C's acceptance of D's anticipatory repudiation, for D argued that he was ready to pay £100 should the script be delivered and C was obliged to argue that it was reasonable not to submit the script for publication outside the children's series for which it was written. This therefore would seem to be a case which should have been decided on normal contract principles.[16] If D agreed to pay £100 to publish the work in the children's series, upon

---

12   5 Car & P 59-60.
13   8 Bing 16. If C had conveyed a valuable benefit, then *a fortiori* he would consider the use of *quantum meruit* if, as is now usual, the author's remuneration was not fixed in advance but took the form of royalties upon sales, for the failure to publish the volume would make the contractual assessment of his loss uncertain: *Restatement (Contracts)* 2d, s 352, illus 1. These were not, however, the facts of the case.
14   A Burrows, 'Free Acceptance and the Law of Restitution' (1988) 104 Law Quarterly Review 576, p 588; Burrows, *The Law of Restitution*, above p 234, n 16, p 267 n 2; M Garner, 'The Role of Subjective Benefit in the Law of Unjust Enrichment' (1990) 10 Oxford Journal of Legal Studies 42; Goff and Jones, *The Law of Restitution*, above p 232, n 5, p 532 n 54; G Jones, 'Restitutionary Claims for Services Rendered' (1977) 93 Law Quarterly Review 273, p 281 and G Jones, 'Claims Arising Out of Anticipated Contracts Which Do Not Materialise' (1980) 18 University of Western Ontario Law Review 447, p 458.
15   8 Bing 14.
16   Some indication of this is given in J Beatson, *The Use and Abuse of Unjust Enrichment* (1991) pp 88-89.

repudiatory breach he should have been liable for £100.[17] If D agreed to pay £100 for the work but did not guarantee its publication in the children's series, D was not liable at all as it actually was C who was in breach by failing to deliver the script. One must conclude that the distinction between reliance and restitution was not well observed in this leading case. The award of a sum in this case dignified by the name of a *quantum meruit* would appear to have been something of a compromise which, whilst one might accept it in an out of court settlement, really is no basis for the construction of restitutionary or any other jurisprudence.[18]

In addition to the general problem of the court's latitude in quantifying a *quantum meruit*, a presently unsettled[19] question of 'the highest commercial importance'[20] may arise from the divergence of the quantification of contractual damages and a *quantum meruit*. If $C^1$ has made a bad bargain[2] and during his performance is fortunate enough to be met with a repudiatory breach by D, can he avoid the consequences of his bargain by suing for a reasonable sum for his uncompleted work, even where that would give him a better return than the pro rata contractual rate? In *Slowey v Lodder*,[3] C was allowed to claim a *quantum meruit* of £1,015 5s[4] for partially completed building works which D had unreasonably prevented him from completing. This sum would appear to include a margin of profit on the part of the works completed, although there was no evidence that C would have made any profit at all had he completed those works, and so the damages C would have received quantified according to the contract measure would have been only

17  Subject to the possibility of mitigation in terms of any saving of C's effort made possible by the early cancellation of the project.
18  More ordinary examples of the *quantum meruit* are particularly to be found in construction claims for incomplete works. See generally IN Duncan Wallace (ed), *Hudson's Building and Engineering Contracts* (11th edn 1995) ss 1.265-1.269.
19  The authorities up to 1978 are considered in *Morrison-Knudsen v British Columbia Hydro and Power Authority* (1978) 85 DLR (3d) 186 at 224-235, and the subsequent leading cases will be mentioned in the following text.
20  J Uff, *Construction Law* (7th edn 1999) p 130.
1   In *Hoenig v Isaacs* [1952] 2 All ER 176, D was of the belief that C had made an unreasonably good bargain, and, after C's substantial performance, D breached with the intention of paying a *quantum meruit*, that is to say, of having the court reassess the bargain. He failed, because the choice of action was C's, and C naturally chose the contract measure.
2   Other circumstances arising from the nature of specific types of performance can also raise this issue. For construction see Duncan Wallace (ed), *Hudson's Building and Engineering Contracts*, above n 18, s 4.230.
3   (1901) 20 NZLR 321, NZCA (affirmed on *quantum meruit* [1904] AC 442 at 453, PC).
4   The jury fixed the *quantum meruit* at £1,626 5s but C had already received £611. £1,626 5s was the exact mean between C's and D's estimates of the *quantum meruit*: *Slowey v Lodder*, loc cit at 356, NZCA.

nominal.[5] One can infer from the pleadings that the reason C's expectation was zero was that he had underpriced the contract,[6] and this was a attempt to take advantage of D's breach to avoid the consequences of this. This possibility is given support in US *Restatement (Contracts)* 2d, s 373(1)[7] and in a line of American authorities reviewed in a case which would appear to have taken its implications to extremes, *Boomer v Muir*, the facts of which arose in 1927. In that case, C was awarded a *quantum meruit* of US$257,965.06 for partly completed works (in addition to staged payments already made), although only US$20,000 remained to be paid on completion of all the works.[8] Though the reported facts of the case allow of no clear conclusion, those facts are perhaps a little less startling than they appear, for during the protracted disputes which led to D's breach, it may have been the case that D imposed extra costs on C which were captured in the *quantum meruit* (and, though not part of the original contract, could have been the basis of a claim for extra work). This then, unlike *Slowey v Lodder*, may not have been a case where C was using restitution *only* to evade the terms of a disadvantageous agreement, though, on the other hand, it is hard to put all of the tremendous disparity between the contract rate and the *quantum meruit* down to D's actions.

Accepting, then, that *Boomer v Muir* was at least in part a case of evading a bad bargain, it seems clear that a consistent application of restitutionary logic would allow this even when doing so had results of this magnitude,[9] which, in terms of contractual expectation, amount to a 'substantial injustice'.[10] Other than obtaining whatever value there is in asserting that restitution 'need not bow down to contract',[11] there is no reason completely to disregard the expectation interest when one shifts

5  Ibid at 350.
6  Ibid at 344-345.
7  Nb s 373 comment d.
8  *Boomer v Muir* 24 P 2d 570 at 578 (1933). A similar problem can arise in respect of cost to complete damages. In *Alfred McAlpine Construction Ltd v Panatown Ltd* [2000] 3 WLR 946, C paid £10 million for the construction of a multi-storey car park and office block. So serious were the defects in the construction that C alleged that their remedy, which might have required demolition of the car park, would have cost £40 million: B Coote, 'The Performance Interest, *Panatown* and the Problem of Loss' (2001) 117 Law Quarterly Review 81. In this context, this problem is subsumed under the general consideration of the strength of C's interest in obtaining cost to complete damages.
9  Birks, 'In Defence of Free Acceptance', above p 234, n 12, p 136. Cf the earlier Birks, *An Introduction to the Law of Restitution*, p 288, which seems to us to be right.
10  A May, ed, *Keating on Building Contracts* (6th edn 1995) p 227. See further Uff, *Construction Law*, above p 238, n 20, p 130.
11  Burrows, *Law of Restitution*, above p 234, n 16, p 269. Amazingly enough, Burrows goes on to accept the contract ceiling, but only after a tortuous attempt to make it appear part of restitutionary jurisprudence.

to the restitution interest in a case of this sort,[12] and it is submitted that the contractual rate of remuneration should be the ceiling for C's recovery in a *quantum meruit* claim.[13] This will reconcile C's interest (in not conveying an unjust enrichment) with D's interest (in the normal operation of contract principles) in the best way the rules allow. Unless one sees no value in that normal operation and sets D's interest at nought because he has breached, one should not allow C completely to avoid the contractual terms about the price merely because D has prevented him from completing performance.[14] To put the issue the other way around, the unlimited *quantum meruit* gives C an incentive to abandon the works in these circumstances, and we cannot agree that it is good policy that, by completing performance, C should put himself in a worse position than after part performance. In the often vexed circumstances of a construction (or similar) dispute, in which what becomes classified by litigation as the breach of one party is typically the result of the disputatious actions of both parties,[15] C should not be given a clear incentive not to complete.[16]

This notion of a ceiling has, however, not found favour with recent authority[17] on the ground that a 'mixture between a contract and an extra-contractual *quantum meruit*' would not be 'in accordance with principle'.[18] This is in its own terms correct, for if one holds that '[a]ll remedies necessarily must lie in the area of restitution'[19] and therefore has regard only to the restitutionary logic of the *quantum meruit*, then the result of *Boomer* is not 'anomalous'.[20] But, with respect, this is to give an unwise privilege to restitutionary logic over the parties' ability to calculate their liabilities when entering into contracts of the type *Boomer* is taken to represent, and it is not at all clear why this would be a good policy.

---

12   Duncan Wallace (ed), *Hudson's Building and Engineering Contracts*, ss 1.272, 4.230-4.231.

13   Following what appears to be a minority line of US cases traceable to *Wuchter v Fitzgerald* 163 P 819 (1917). See further Beale, *Remedies for Breach of Contract*, p 209; Goff and Jones, *The Law of Restitution*, above p 232, n 5, pp 533-534 and GE Palmer, 'The Contract Price as a Limit on Restitution for Defendant's Breach' (1959) 20 Ohio State Law Journal 264, p 281.

14   G McMeel, *The Modern Law of Restitution* (2000) pp 143-5.

15   NJ Canell, *Causation and Delay in Construction Disputes* (2000).

16   *Restatement (Contracts)* 2d, s 373, comment d. Cf Goff and Jones, *The Law of Restitution*, above p 232, n 5, p 532 nn 49-50 and Treitel, *The Law of Contract*, above p 234, n 14, p 989 n 71.

17   *Greenmast Shipping Co SA v Jean Lion et Cie SA* [1986] 2 Lloyd's Rep 277; *Rover International Ltd v Cannon Film Sales (No 3)*, above p 234, n 15 and *Renard Construction (ME) Pty Ltd v Minister for Public Works*, above p 236, n 9.

18   *Rover International Ltd v Cannon Film Sales (No 3)*, above p 234, n 15 at 927.

19   Ibid at 927-928.

20   *Renard Construction (ME) Pty Ltd v Minister for Public Works*, above p 236, n 9 at 277.

It is also submitted that the mitigation principle should be applied to a claim limited by a contractual ceiling. As soon as D has broken the contract, C's claim should be assessed on the basis that he should then have acted reasonably to minimise his loss. Thus, any salvage value of the work done by C which he retains should be taken into account in assessing the reasonable sum due to him from D.

## Rescission for common mistake and frustration

A discussion of restitutionary remedies must include the presently essentially restitutionary remedy for frustration. However, although the remedy for common mistake is not derived from restitutionary principles, any such discussion should now also make reference to common mistake.[1] Largely as a result of the relatively sympathetic recent reception of the economic analysis of risk allocation,[2] it is now generally recognised[3] that the jurisprudential basis for discharge on what previously had been taken to be the quite separate grounds of common mistake and frustration is that the performance of D's contractual obligation has, because of events not provided for in the contract, become 'impracticable in a commercial sense'.[4] As is recognised in UCC sec 2-615, commercial impracticability

1   From contemporary usage in eg *Chitty on Contracts*, above p 234, n 19, ch 5, it would appear that, despite GC Cheshire, 'Mistake as Affecting Contractual Consent' (1944) 60 Law Quarterly Review 175, terminological differences continue to beset the discussion of mistake, with a particular difficulty attending the uses of 'mutual' and 'common'. As the underlying issue is the unsatisfactoriness of the entire category of 'mistake" in English law (CJ Slade, 'The Myth of Mistake in the English Law of Contract' (1954) 70 Law Quarterly Review 385), there seems to be no other way to deal with this in this book other than to say that by common mistake we, following Cheshire, mean the type of mistake addressed in *Bell v Lever Bros Ltd* [1932] AC 161, where it is called a 'mutual mistake'.
2   J Swan, 'The Allocation of Risk in the Analysis of Mistake and Frustration', in BJ Reiter and J Swan (eds), *Studies in Contract Law* (1980) study 7, p 181. For a reinterpretation of the authorities in the light of awareness of risk allocation see J Beatson, 'Increased Expense and Frustration', in FD Rose (ed), *Consensus ad Idem* (1996) 121.
3   Treitel, *Law of Contract*, above p 234, n 14, p 862 rightly points out that frustration and (common) mistake are 'different juristic concepts' with different consequences. Indeed, but whether they should remain so is not decided by this commonplace observation, and that the extant law provides for different consequences for the same problem according to how it now has to be pleaded surely is a good reason to change that law: see E McKendrick, *Contract Law* (4th edn 2000) p 318. Of course, the changed law would have to respect any real differences there may be between common mistake and frustration, following from, say, the relative ease of verifying antecedent problems as opposed to predicting subsequent ones.
4   *Horlock v Beale* [1916] 1 AC 486 at 492, correctly defining 'impossibility' in this context, *pace* eg RG McElroy with G Williams, *Impossibility of Performance*

is the point of importance that lies behind all the particular circumstances that give rise to pleas of common mistake and frustration such as physical destruction of subject matter, delay, frustration of purpose, etc. 'Common mistake' is taken to cover factors existing prior to the agreement about which both parties were commonly mistaken and which become manifest during performance. 'Frustration' is taken to cover factors which the parties did not foresee and therefore did not provide for in the contract which arise during performance.[5] For the purposes of this book, the adequacy of our understanding of both common mistake and frustration and of the underlying concept of commercial impracticability and its relationship to breach need not be assessed as they speak to questions of liability. We will take common mistake and frustration to lawfully excuse D from performance.

In this circumstance, in which there is no breach[6] and *ex hypothesi* D is *not* liable for C's lost expectation,[7] the ideal remedy would be to discharge both parties from further performance and to return them both to their positions prior to the agreement; this is to say, to effect, so far as is possible,[8] *restitutio in integrum*. This is what in this book[9] will be meant by the term rescission (or rescission *ab initio*), though that term notoriously is one 'frequently used in alternative senses'.[10] Rescission must strongly be distinguished from termination,[11] which of course principally aims to put C in the position he would have been in after performance, both in its effect and in its means of operation. The parties may, of course, effect

---

(1941) pp 194-196, where, we can now say with a knowledge of risk allocation ultimately derived from economics, the issue simply is not properly understood.

5   *Bell v Lever Bros Ltd*, above p 241, n 1 at 225 and *Amalgamated Investment v John Walker* [1977] 1 WLR 164.

6   *Denny Mott and Dickson Ltd v James B Fraser & Co Ltd* [1944] AC 265 at 274.

7   The logical point is forcefully expressed in E McKendrick, 'Frustration, Restitution and Loss Apportionment', in Burrows (ed), *Essays on the Law of Restitution*, above p 234, n 12, 147, pp 168-169. The influential economic analysis in RA Posner and AM Rosenfield, 'Impossibility and Related Doctrines in Contract Law: An Economic Analysis' (1977) 6 Journal of Legal Studies 88 really turns on *not* accepting that there should be discharge on these grounds, and trying to thwart a law that does by refusing to design the remedies that should follow from this acceptance.

8   Though this will not be argued here, this use of rescission as a practical remedy requires the abandonment of the traditional view, which severely limits that practicality, that rescission is available only if it will effect *restitutio* perfectly, or, to put it the other way round, that a lack of such perfection bars rescission. *Contra Clarke v Dickson* (1858) EB & E 148 at 154.

9   In the following passages and in the treatment of misrepresentation in pp 553-563 below.

10  *Buckland v Farmer and Moody* [1979] 1 WLR 221 at 232.

11  *Heyman v Darwins* [1942] AC 356 at 399; *Horsler v Zorro* [1975] Ch 302 and *Johnson v Agnew* [1979] 1 All ER 883 at 889. See further W Alberry, 'Mr Cyprian Williams' Great Heresy' (1975) 91 Law Quarterly Review 337.

rescission by agreement,[12] adjusting their losses to their own satisfaction. If the common mistake becomes evident or the frustrating event takes place when there is no expectation loss and/or before substantial sums in reliance have been spent, one imagines that C will forebear to take action. If either of these is not the case, however, C obviously has an incentive to take action. It will here be considered to what extent the rules of common mistake and frustration manage to effect rescission when the parties' interests are potentially in conflict.

Whereas breach of condition gives rise to C's power to elect to terminate or to affirm, it would seem to be a necessary implication of D having a lawful excuse for non-performance that discharge from further performance should be automatic after a finding of common mistake or frustration, that is to say that discharge does not require the approval of C. The rather complicated rules relating to common mistake will be examined shortly but, in essence, discharge after frustration is automatic.[13] Two particular problems may, however, arise even in this case.

It has been argued that the automatic discharge rule gives rise to difficulties when the frustrating factor is delay, for D may fear a frustrating delay, and act as if the contract automatically is discharged when in fact the delay did not eventuate. In *Embiricos v Sydney Reid & Co*, D cancelled a charterparty because it reasonably feared its ship, under the Greek flag, would be seized by the Turkish government as it passed through Turkish waters, as it would have had to do had the contract been performed. As it happened, the Turkish government later unexpectedly extended permission to Greek vessels to sail through its waters, and had D attempted to perform, it would have been able to do so. Nevertheless, this contract was held to be frustrated because the belief that the frustrating delay would eventuate was a reasonable one at the time and 'commercial men ... must be entitled to act on reasonable commercial probabilities at the time when they are called upon to make up their minds'.[14] With respect, this is not a problem peculiar to this rule, or, indeed, to common mistake or frustration. A similar problem arises, for example, over anticipatory breach, when C acts in accordance with a reasonable but erroneous belief that he has a contractual right to terminate, or when a step taken in mitigation turns out not to be optimal.[15] This is a problem of respecting the beliefs on which parties take their decisions when these are reasonable at the time but later prove to be incorrect and requires no further discussion here.

---

12  *Davis v Street* (1823) 1 C & P 18.
13  *Denny Mott and Dickson Ltd v James B Fraser & Co Ltd*, above p 242, n 6 at 274.
14  [1914] 3 KB 45 at 54.
15  See pp 111-112 above.

The parties may have agreed a *force majeure* clause which provides that frustrating events be dealt with in a specific way, such as by requiring notice of intention to treat the contract as discharged, or by treating the frustration as merely suspending obligations, etc. Whether these provisions have themselves been discharged, along with the substance of D's primary obligation, by the frustrating event, is a matter of liability not within the purview of this book.[16] However, one general class of such clause must be mentioned here. The contract may contain a clause stipulating the compulsory reference of disputes to arbitration. It logically is the case that the discharge of the contract should discharge all the clauses which are in it, including arbitration clauses, but this would make arbitration clauses pointless as the quality of arbitration that distinguishes it from other forms of ADR is that there is an element of compulsion in it. It is submitted, then, that arbitration clauses must survive the frustration of the underlying contract, and that those clauses are 'separable' from the underlying contract, which is now the English position under the Arbitration Act 1996, s 7. The particular importance of this is that, as we shall now see, the shortcomings of the law following common mistake and frustration give the parties to complex commercial contracts a particular incentive to refer disputes arising from such events to arbitration.

In many circumstances, when either or both parties have made reliance expenditures and/or where C is faced with a substantial lost expectation, it may be a very difficult matter, or indeed impossible, to return the parties to the position they were in prior to the contract. Following *Bell v Lever Bros*,[17] the 'remedy' for a finding of common mistake at common law is to hold the apparent contract to be void *ab initio*. *Bell v Lever Bros Ltd* may be the most unsatisfactory contract decision handed down by the House of Lords in modern times. It is not merely its extraordinary restriction on the availability of common mistake that has created such an obstacle to the development of the common law of common mistake. It is also that holding a contract void *ab initio*, and therefore doing nothing to address the consequences of what may have been and may still remain to be done under the contract, or, as it is commonly said, letting the losses lie where they fall, is no remedy at all, and the parties will gain nothing from recourse to law of this quality.[18]

---

16    E McKendrick, 'Frustration and *Force Majeure*: Their Relationship and a Comparative Assessment', in E McKendrick (ed), *Frustration and Force Majeure* (2nd edn 1995) 33.

17    Above p 241, n 1.

18    Of course, a restitutionary claim may well arise as the ruling that contract was void *ab initio* creates the suspicion that benefits conveyed in the belief it was enforceable unjustly enrich the beneficiary. It was accepted by the House of Lords in *Bell v Lever Bros Ltd* that if money has been paid by C to D under a contract

An equitable alternative has been pursued to avoid the consequences of dealing with common mistake at common law. The use of equity to, in fact, contradict the common law in this way undoubtedly is unsatisfactory both as law[19] and policy,[20] but in this case it at least has held out the promise of the parties receiving a meaningful remedy.[1] The equitable remedy for common mistake is to hold the contract unenforceable at the election of the party who will suffer loss because of the mistake, and for the court to exercise its recognised equitable discretion[2] to apportion the losses of the parties in such a way as to approximate to rescission in the sense used here. In *Magee v Pennine Insurance*,[3] D compromised C's claim for the accidental destruction of his car under an insurance policy which D could have rescinded for C's innocent misstatements in his application for insurance. After the court held that this policy was agreed under an operative mistake at equity, D was able to recover the payment it had

---

which was void from the moment it was apparently made, C may in principle recover the amount by a restitutionary claim. So a payment made under a contract void for mistake may be recovered, such as the deposit paid by a hirer under a hire-purchase contract in *Branwhite v Worcester Works Finance Ltd* [1969] 1 AC 552. See Burrows, *The Law of Restitution*, above p 234, n 16, pp 304-312; *Chitty on Contracts*, above p 234, n 19, ss 30.062-30-063; Goff and Jones, *The Law of Restitution*, above p 232, n 5, ch 23; and Treitel, *The Law of Contract*, above p 234, n 14, pp 985-988, 990-991.

In addition, other categories of void contracts have their own rules about recovery of money paid by C, as with contracts void under statute, or for illegality, or for incapacity of a party. The special rules governing such claims are labyrinthine, contested and particularly subject to change in the current climate of restitutionary innovation and must be sought elsewhere: eg Treitel, *Law of Contract*, above p 234, n 14, chs 11-13. For one attempt to bring some coherence to this area see P Birks, 'Restitution After Ineffective Contracts: Issues for the 1990s' (1990) 2 Journal of Contract Law 227.

19  PS Atiyah and FAR Bennion, 'Mistake in the Construction of Contracts' (1961) 24 Modern Law Review 421, pp 439-440.

20  In a parallel to Posner and Rosenfeld's attitude to frustration, Atiyah's reservations (PS Atiyah, *The Law of Contract* (5th edn 1995) pp 219-229) about whether the parties should receive an equitable remedy in these cases in part turns on a suspicion that D is evading proper liability in some of them. Whilst this suspicion no doubt will be justified so long as risk allocation in contract remains inadequately understood (*William Sindall plc v Cambridgeshire County Council* [1994] 1 WLR 1016 at 1035), we will ignore this issue of liability and assume that a finding of common mistake or frustration rightly excuses non-performance.

1  *Solle v Butcher* [1950] 1 KB 671 at 692 per Denning LJ. In *Associated Japanese Bank International Ltd v Credit du Nord SA* [1989] 1 WLR 255, 270 Steyn J said that he would have set the contract aside even if he had not managed to find it void at common law. With respect, that finding paid *Bell v Lever Bros* even less respect than Denning LJ had in *Solle v Butcher*, which rather undermines Steyn J's criticisms in *Associated Japanese Bank* of Denning LJ.

2  *Cooper v Phibbs* (1867) 2 HL 149. See further P Matthews, 'A Note on *Cooper v Phibbs*' (1989) 105 Law Quarterly Review 599.

3  [1969] 2 QB 507.

made.[4] In a number of cases following *Solle v Butcher*, conveyances of interests in land at prices substantially affected by common mistakes as to the effect of housing or planning legislation were rescinded but, where appropriate, options to purchase at corrected prices were ordered by the court.[5] In *Solle v Butcher* itself, D rented a flat to C for seven years at £250 per annum. £250 was found to be 'the fair and economic rent', but it had been agreed in the common mistaken belief that the flat was free from rent control. When C found that the flat was subject to such control, he sought a declaration that the controlled rent was £140 per annum and claimed the excess rent he had paid. D counter-claimed for rescission of the lease, which would have left him free, after complying with certain formalities, to let to another tenant for £250. The court set the lease aside but gave C the power either to accept rescission of the lease or to enter into a new lease at £250. It does not seem possible, nor, it is submittted, would it be worthwhile, to attempt to give a detailed account of the terms on which the court should exercise its discretion to effect rescission in cases of this sort. As Lord Denning put it in *Solle v Butcher*, 'it is not beyond the wit of man to devise'[6] those terms, but they necessarily have been and should be contingent upon the facts.

Rescission in the sense used here following a finding of frustration has, however, been the subject of a more formal, restitutionary jurisprudence. Under the rule in *Chandler v Webster*, which essentially let losses lie where they fell, a finding of frustration was often as useless to the parties as a finding of initial voidness for common mistake.[7] The resources of restitution were drawn on to effect an improvement which was eventually[8] given statutory effect in the Law Reform (Frustrated

4    By failing also to order the repayment of the premiums following eg *Cornhill Assurance Co v Assenheim* (1937) 58 Ll L Rep 27 at 31, the court did not avail itself of all the possibilities of effecting rescission available to it, and therefore (accepting C's innocence) 'the decision seems to be unduly favourable to the insurance company'. Treitel, *Law of Contract*, above p 234, n 14, p 294. The premiums would be totally recoverable because, as the insurer was never really at risk, there was a total failure of consideration. This arguably is in itself another unsatisfactory consequence of the total failure of consideration rule, but some repayment (after, say, division of administrative expenses) would seem to have been required.

5    Eg *Grist v Bailey* [1967] Ch 532; *Laurence v Lexcourt Holdings Ltd* [1978] 1 WLR 1128 and *Redbridge London Borough v Robinson Rentals* (1969) 211 Estates Gazette 1125.

6    *Solle v Butcher*, above p 245, n 1, at 697.

7    As immediately emerges from a comparison of the outcomes for the parties of *Chandler v Webster* [1904] 1 KB 493 and *Krell v Henry* [1903] 2 KB 740.

8    Following extensive criticism of the rule in *Chandler v Webster* in the Law Revision Committee, *The Rule in Chandler v Webster*, Seventh Interim Report, Cmd 6009 (1939), the case was overruled in *Fibrosa Spolka Akayjna v Fairburn Lawson Combe Barbour Ltd*, above p 231, n 1. However, *Fibrosa* itself displays equally manifest if not equally drastic shortcomings, which the legislation was intended

Contracts) Act 1943.[9] When a contract[10] is found[11] to have been discharged by frustration, LR(FC)A 1943 adjusts the rights and liabilities of the parties in a way which, in the opinion of Robert Goff J (as he then was) in the leading case on the interpretation of LR(FC)A 1943, seeks to prevent unjust enrichment[12] and which certainly works through provisions derived from the restitutionary techniques of recovery of money paid and *quantum meruit*.[13]

Money payable or paid is dealt with in s 1(2). By this subsection, sums payable under the contract but not paid at the time of discharge are no longer payable and sums paid prior to the time of discharge are recoverable. This subsection avoids the unfortunate consequences of the former rule in *Chandler v Webster*, especially as they were exposed in *Krell v Henry*, and also avoids the problems in common law recovery caused by the requirement of total failure of consideration (which LR(FC)A 1943 does not mention and which, thankfully, has not been read into this subsection). Nevertheless, it is submitted that an unfortunate confusion is introduced at the outset, because, having decided to made something like the distinction between recovery and *quantum meruit* the basis of LR(FC)A 1943, that distinction is abandoned in s 1(2).

After making the basic discharge and recovery provisions, LR(FC)A 1943 adds the following proviso to s 1(2):

> if the party to whom the sums were so paid or payable incurred expenses before the time of discharge in, or for the purpose of, the performance of the contract, the court may, if it considers it just to do so having regard to all the circumstances of the case, allow him to retain or, as the case may be, recover the whole or any part of the

---

to avoid. The understanding of the present law is helped to an unusual degree by a study of the history of this episode of law reform. See A McNair, 'Law Reform (Frustrated Contracts) Act 1943' (1944) 60 Law Quarterly Review 160 and G Williams, *The Law Reform (Frustrated Contracts) Act 1943* (1944).

9   Hereinafter LR(FC)A 1943. The following criticisms of this Act will, so far as possible, be restricted to points of general theoretical interest. For an exhaustive technical analysis of LR(FC)A 1943 (which is not at all without theoretical interest) see *Chitty on Contracts*, above p 234, n 19, ss 24-072-24.096; McKendrick, 'Frustration, Restitution and Loss Apportionment', above p 242, n 7; E McKendrick, 'The Consequences of Frustration, The Law Reform (Frustrated Contracts) Act 1943', in McKendrick (ed), *Force Majeure and Frustration of Contract*, above p 244, n 16, 223; GH Treitel, *Frustration and Force Majeure* (1994) ss 15.044-15.075 and Treitel, *The Law of Contract*, above p 234, n 14, pp 851-854.

10  Or a frustrated severable part of a contract, the remainder being left in effect: LR(FC)A 1943, s 2(1).

11  LR(FC)A 1943 is silent about the grounds on which a contract may be discharged for frustration.

12  *BP Exploration (Libya) Ltd v Hunt (No 2)* QBD, above p 236, n 10 at 799.

13  Which were the basis of the reasoning in the *Fibrosa* case, above p 231, n 1.

sums so paid or payable, not being an amount in excess of the expenses so incurred.

This paragraph obviously allows a sort of counter-claim against payment of money payable or recovery of money paid, but of a curious sort. Fuller and Purdue wrote their seminal article in 1936: the clarification of the contractual interests in English contract scholarship and practice was by no means so clear in 1943 as now, and this paragraph seems to confuse the reliance and restitution interests.[14] '[E]xpenses ... for the purpose ... of the performance of the contract' would appear to set up a reliance claim, but the court 'may' recognise that claim only 'if it considers it just to do so', and it would appear that a sort of *quantum meruit* counter-claim is being allowed. But if this is so, this paragraph would appear on one view to be redundant, for not only, as we shall very shortly see, does s 1(3) provide for a sort of *quantum meruit*, but, as a s 1(2) counter-claim is limited to the amount of money paid or payable, a claim in excess of this must be pursued under s 1(3). The suspicion naturally arises that there must be something different about a s 1(2) counter-claim and a s 1(3) claim, otherwise they would always be combined as sometimes they must be,[15] but it is, in our opinion, impossible to be clear what it is.

To the extent that s 1(2) is used to resolve commercial problems, this is a point of practical significance. If before frustration C has run up substantial reliance expenses but has not actually conveyed a benefit to D, he will not be able to obtain a just sum covering all of those expenses under s 1(3), but he could set it against a s 1(2) claim as 'expenses' under s 1(2). However, he can do this only up to the extent of the *sums paid or payable before discharge*, and this of course need not be the time when, if ever, it is possible to desist from further reliance expenditure under a particular contract. This is a limit alien to the reliance interest with no clear justification.[16] A curious hybrid unknown to reliance or restitution as such appears to have been created. It is submitted that no sound foundation in either principle can be given to this hybrid, and that the claim by Garland J shortly to be considered that a court has a 'broad discretion' to interpret s 1(3) is, we submit, the wisest position that can be taken to s 1(2) as well.

Section 1(3) itself provides that:

Where any party to the contract has, by reason of anything done by any other party thereto in, or for the purpose of, the performance of

---

14    Williams, *The Law Reform (Frustrated Contracts) Act 1943*, p 9.
15    This would appear to have led Robert Goff J into error about a cash payment in *BP Exploration*: Treitel, *Law of Contract*, above p 234, n 14, p 852 n 56.
16    AM Haycroft and DM Waksman, 'Frustration and Restitution' [1984] Journal of Business Law 207, 217.

the contract, obtained a valuable benefit (other than a payment of money to which [s 1(2)] applies) before the time of discharge, there shall be recoverable from him by the said other party such sum (if any), not exceeding the value of the said benefit to the party obtaining it, as the court consider just.

Under s 1(3), a party who, in reliance on the contract before it is discharged by frustration, confers a valuable benefit (other than a payment of money) on the other party, can 'recover' a 'just sum' for the benefit from the other party. One might expect this sum to be a *quantum meruit*, but it cannot simply be so because it is stipulated that the value of the benefit is a ceiling upon the just sum, and, of course, were it a *quantum meruit*, these would be identical. In *BP Exploration* Robert Goff J appeared to approach the quantification of a s 1(3) award in essentially two separate stages,[17] but, we will argue, there actually was but one stage.

The first apparent stage was the valuation of the benefit, and here LR(FC)A 1943 puts many difficulties in the way of assessing a *quantum meruit* in the normal fashion. From his construction of LR(FC)A 1943, Robert Goff J reluctantly was constrained to conclude that the benefit is the 'end product' of the services rendered rather than the services themselves,[18] though the latter is the better approach. There are certain contracts where there will be no valuable end product, such as 'transporting goods'[19] or, a case which raises a somewhat different point, building work which, because of the client's specification, would have reduced the value of the client's property.[20] It cannot be right that C should obtain nothing under s 1(3) in these cases. Robert Goff J seems to contemplate departure from his construction in these cases which, with respect, would leave little of that construction intact. Furthermore, in the circumstances of a frustrated contract in which, if it had been performed, there might have been an identifiable end product, there may be no end product precisely because of the frustration, and *a fortiori* it cannot be right that C should obtain nothing in these circumstances,[1] though Robert Goff J is quite right to say that s 1(3)(b) would appear to provide exactly this. Were this not enough, it is perfectly possible that any end product could be the result of C's and D's joint efforts, and so some sort of direct

17 Treitel, *The Law of Contract*, above p 234, n 14, p 852. In *Chitty on Contracts*, above p 234, n 19, s 24-082 three steps are distinguished and in Goff and Jones, *The Law of Restitution*, above p 232, n 5, pp 563-571 (following Robert Goff J's judgment literally) four.
18 *BP Exploration (Libya) Ltd v Hunt (No 2)* (QBD), above p 236, n 10 at 801.
19 Ibid.
20 Ibid at 803.
1 Ibid. This would produce the result left by *Appleby v Myers* (1867) LR 2 CP 651, which it was intended that LR(FC)A would avoid.

valuation of C's services will in any case have to be undertaken in these cases to decide which part of the end product is attributable to C.[2]

In *BP Exploration*, C undertook to do all the work financing and exploiting an oil concession D had bought from the Libyan government in return for half the concession and 87.5% (ie 37.5% from D's 50%) of the first oil obtained until C had been 'reimbursed' 125% of its initial expenditure. Despite the great complexity of this contract, it was frustrated when, after only a short period of production, at which time C had received only a third of its reimbursement oil, the concession was compulsorily nationalised with inadequate compensation after the Libyan revolution. C sued for a just sum under s 1(3). Following his construction of s 1(3), Robert Goff J found the end product benefit received by D to be the *enhancement*[3] of the value of his concession represented by the net amount of oil and the value of the compensation he had received. Of this total, without much discussion, Robert Goff J accepted C's submission that half of the benefit was attributable to its actions and half to D's, so that eventually an overall benefit of US$169,902,000 was reduced to US$84,951,000.[4]

When turning to the just sum itself, accepting that the benefit was a ceiling on the just sum and not the just sum itself, Robert Goff J, it is respectfully submitted, remedied his reluctant acceptance of the end result measure of the benefit by assessing the just sum as the value, largely measured at contract rates,[5] of C's services to D in producing oil from the field. This is to say, he equated the just sum with a *quantum meruit* identifying benefit as services and thereby made the benefit as end result measure redundant. What LR(FC)A 1943 makes appear a two stage test was reduced to one stage. Subtracting from the services C had rendered the value of the oil C itself had received, Robert Goff J found the just sum to be US$35,403,146, which, being less than the benefit ceiling, was awarded in full.[6] At the cost of labouring a point, it is very convenient that Robert Goff J found the just sum to be less than the ceiling or it could not have been awarded in toto. If no oil had been produced (or compensation become payable), it would have defeated any ingenuity to have found a valuable benefit, but then, of course, one suspects that the case would not have come to trial. It remains the case, however, that LR(FC)A 1943 creates the possibility of what has been found to be a substantial just sum not being awarded in whole or in part.

2    This is referred to as 'apportioning the benefit' in *BP Exploration (Libya) Ltd v Hunt (No 2)* (QBD), above p 236, n 10 at 801.
3    Ibid at 817.
4    Ibid at 821.
5    Ibid at 823F-H, 826C-D.
6    Ibid at 827H.

We do not disagree with the substance of Robert Goff J's effective reduction of s 1(3) to a *quantum meruit* assessed as services rendered, or with the result he produced on this basis. But, having considered his thoroughly painstaking but, we feel obliged to say, undeniably unsatisfactory judgment, it is, with the greatest respect, submitted that in most circumstances in order to begin to reach a proper result under s 1(3), a court will have to ignore a number of irremediably unhelpful provisions in that subsection. It is because the present state of the law leads one to read 'discretion' in the rather regrettable sense of a departure from bad rules that one places a question mark against the essentially correct observations on dealing with the consequences of frustration of Garland J in *Gamerco SA v ICM/Fair Warning (Agency) Ltd*:

> It is self-evident that any rigid rule is liable to produce injustice. The words 'if it considers it just to do so having regard to all the circumstances of the case', clearly confer a very broad discretion. Obviously the court must not take into account anything which is not a 'circumstance of the case' or fail to take into account anything that is and then exercise its discretion rationally. I see no inclination in the Act, the authorities or the relevant literature that the court is obliged to incline towards total retention or equal division. Its task is to do justice in a situation which the parties had neither contemplated nor provided for, and to mitigate the possible harshness of allowing all loss to lie where it has fallen.[7]

Recognising this, an appeal cannot raise again what are likely to be one-off points of substance. Objection can be made only against manifest irrationality on the part of the trial judge, as Lawton LJ recognised when hearing *BP Exploration* on appeal:

> The responsibility lies with the judge: he has to fix a sum which he, not an appellate court, *considers* just. This word connotes the mental processes going to form an opinion. What is just is what the trial judge thinks is just. That being so, an appellate court is not entitled to interfere with his decision unless it is so plainly wrong that it cannot be just. [An appellate court] would not be justified in setting aside the judge's way of assessment merely because [it] thought that there were better ways.[8]

---

7   [1995] 1 WLR 1226 at 1237.
8   [1981] 1 WLR 232, CA. Lawton J seems to have been out of sympathy with Robert Goff J's restitutionary interpretation, declaring himself to have received 'no help from the use of words which are not in the statute': ibid at 243.

In the light of the difficulties of s 1(2) as well, this is the background attitude which one might expect to be taken to the interpretation of LR(FC)A 1943 whilst it remains in force. It is, we submit, not merely an understandable but a correct attitude if a more positive meaning is given to discretion.

As there are but a handful of Acts of Parliament which affect the basic structure of remedies for breach of contract, it is rather dismal to note that this one is so poorly drafted that it has given rise to problems of interpretation out of all proportion to its short length, and has brought very limited improvement to the common law.[9] If we acknowledge these shortcomings, the question arises what might be done to improve the law, and, with regard to frustration at least, a plea for extensive reform has been mounted, based on a sophisticated mixture of techniques for apportioning loss,[10] informed by authoritative comparative analysis of the Commonwealth parallels to LR(FC)A 1943.[11] It might be argued that the restitutionary character of some of these innovations rather departs from LR(FC)A 1943 in much the same way as Robert Goff J himself did in *BP Exploration*, but as it is our opinion that no amount of disciplined interpretation will ever make satisfactory law out of this Act, the force of this point is undercut in this instance. Rather, repeal of LR(FC)A 1943 must be thought highly attractive.[12]

Nevertheless, in our opinion, so far as it ultimately is based on abhorrence of discretion in awarding a remedy in these cases, this case for reform is misdirected.[13] Dispute resolution in this area is, *ex hypothesi*, highly contingent upon the unforeseen empirical circumstances of each case, and therefore it is pointless to regret that the law cannot develop detailed rules. The pursuit of such rules continues to hinder explicit recognition of the use of discretion which the nature of the case and not

9  An obvious parallel to the Misrepresentation Act 1967 presents itself, but in this case things were even worse in that the relationship between that Act and *Hedley Byrne & Co v Heller & Partners* [1964] AC 465 is even more difficult than that between LR(FC)A 1943 and the *Fibrosa* case. See pp 557-563 below.

10  McKendrick, 'Frustration, Restitution and Loss Apportionment', above p 242, n 7 and McKendrick, 'The Consequences of Frustration: The Law Reform (Frustrated Contracts) Act 1943', above p 244, n 16.

11  A Stewart and JW Carter, 'Frustrated Contracts and Statutory Adjustment: The Case for a Reappraisal' [1992] Cambridge Law Journal 66.

12  J Beatson, 'Should There Be Legislative Development of the Law of Restitution?', in Burrows (ed), *Essays on the Law of Restitution*, above p 234, n 12, pp 289-291 and Stewart and Carter, 'Frustrated Contracts and Statutory Adjustment: The Case for a Reappraisal', loc cit, p 112.

13  Beatson, 'Should There Be Legislative Development of the Law of Restitution?', loc cit, p 288; Goff and Jones, *The Law of Restitution*, above p 232, n 5, p 562 and McKendrick, *Contract Law*, above p 241, n 3, p 316.

the shortcomings of the statute make necessary.[14] Of course, this discretion should not be unbridled in the way that LR(FC)A 1943 now encourages. It should be discretion to effect rescission, and such discretion may be exercised in the way Garland J did, and reviewed in the way Lawton LJ set out. A limited jurisprudence on other than outright one-off points may then be developed.[15] To assess the plausibility of proceeding in this way, it is important to stress an aspect of the matter other than the formal rules.

The doctrines of common mistake and frustration are those parts of the classical law of contract remedies that should give most assistance in the modification of complex contractual obligations.[16] But they are signal failures as economic governance structures,[17] and, being the points at which the economic nature of incomplete, relational contracting has placed a strain on the classical law, are the points at which that law has fractured. One might wonder why a position as unsatisfactory as that left by LR(FC)A 1943 has been allowed to remain the law, and part at least of the answer has been that to a significant degree parties do not have recourse to the formal law to govern these aspects of economic action. Competent commercial parties, faced with the absurdity of the law of common mistake at common law or the weakness of the remedies for frustration, have included modification provisions in contracts of sufficient value and complexity to make this worthwhile. These clauses provide for non-binding alternative dispute resolution or arbitration (including arbitration *ex aequo et bono*),[18] which give the parties far more flexibility to apportion loss than any conceivable restitutionary recasting of the frustration rules might do.[19] Should provisions of this sort not prove

14  This is an acute example of the obsolete jurisprudence which continues to inform formal contract scholarship at a time when recognition of the value of reflexivity has become central to regulatory theory. Collins has recently taken a major step towards making the theoretical issues clear in relationship to contract in H Collins, *Regulating Contracts* (1999) ch 4.

15  Cf *Pioneer Shipping Ltd v BTP Tioxide Ltd* [1982] AC 724 at 743-744. To the extent that the rules as they are push parties towards arbitration *ex aequo et bono* or towards themselves resolving their disputes in defiance of the law, they hinder the development of any effective adjudication.

16  The corollary parts of the classical law of contract formation, displaying corollary weaknesses, are the doctrines of the insufficiency of existing obligations as consideration and economic duress: R Halson, 'Opportunism, Economic Duress and Contractual Modifications' (1991) 107 Law Quarterly Review 649.

17  D Campbell and S Clay, *Long-term Contracting: A Research Bibliography and Review of the Literature* (1995).

18  R David, *Arbitration in International Trade* (1985) ch 1.

19  IR Macneil, 'A Primer of Contract Planning' (1975) 48 Southern California Law Review 627, pp 676-702 and IR Macneil, 'Contracts: Adjustment of Long-term Economic Relations Under Classical, Neo-classical and Relational Contract Law' (1978) 72 Northwestern University Law Review 854, pp 965-899.

254 *Section I Remedies for unfulfilled contractual undertakings*

adequate, such empirical evidence as is available shows that the parties ignore the terms of their contracts to reach superior outcomes than those contracts provide.[20] The (extremely limited scope of and) the very inadequate remedies for common mistake and frustration provide a great incentive for parties to follow either or both of these courses, and the absolute paucity of cases on LR(FC)A 1943[1] would appear to be evidence that they are doing so.[2]

The weakness of the doctrines of common mistake and frustration[3] has been the principal reason for the non-use of contract in complex cases, for if this is the law, then it is good advice to tell parties not to incur the costs and delay of using it.[4] Furthermore, that the law adds little value to the governance of commercial relationships unfortunately does not mean that that law is irrelevant.[5] The poor remedies for common mistake and frustration give incentives to opportunistic behaviour even when the parties have been recognised to have a lawful excuse not to perform. It is submitted that a reform is needed which establishes the goal of rescission and extends discretion to the court to effect it. Appeal jurisprudence would be restricted to the correction of manifest failures to pursue this goal. This would make explicit what the law of common mistake in equity (and therefore the actually useful law of common mistake in toto) is. It would allow the law of frustration to develop along its best lines. It would bring the law into line with what, so far as we can tell, alternative dispute resolution practice is and what parties do when ignoring the law. It also would be what is economically and legally sensible if one accepts the assumption, on which common mistake and frustration rest, that there can be a lawful excuse for non-performance.[6]

20  D Campbell and D Harris, 'Flexibility in Long-term Contractual Relationships: The Role of Co-operation' (1993) 20 Journal of Law and Society 166.
1   *BP Exploration (Libya) Ltd v Hunt (No 2)* (QBD) above p 236, n 10 at 788E.
2   In the parallel case of the Misrepresentation Act 1967, statutory intervention provides consumers with far more protection against false representations than the law of misrepresentation. See ch 4 above.
3   And of insufficiency of existing obligations and economic duress.
4   Stewart and Carter, 'Frustrated Contracts and Statutory Adjustment: The Case for a Reappraisal', above p 252, n 12, p 112. The only point we would wish to add is that empirical studies of non-use emphatically showed that the otherwise good advice Stewart and Carter give was quite supererogatory.
5   See generally ch 2 above.
6   P Trimarchi, 'Commercial Impracticability in Contract Law: An Economic Analysis' (1991) 11 International Review of Law and Economics 63.

# 17 The expansion of restitution

## The problem of uncompensated loss

In *Wrotham Park Estate Co Ltd v Parkside Homes Ltd*,[1] a conveyance of land contained a restrictive covenant by which development of the land had to conform with a lay-out plan approved by the vendor or C, his successor in title. D, the purchaser's successor in title, breached the covenant by building houses which did not conform with the plan. It was found that '[n]o damage of a financial nature has been done to the plaintiff by the breach of the lay-out stipulation [and t]he plaintiff's use of the Wrotham Park Estate has not and will not be impeded.'[2] This would, of course, have meant that C's damages, calculated by the normal diminution in value measure, would be nominal.[3] The court was reluctant to grant a mandatory injunction which would have meant the houses had to be demolished, and an award of nominal damages effectively would have been a costless permission to D to breach. In this situation, the court gave C damages estimated at the price D would have had to pay to obtain a release from the covenant. Subsequently, however, in *Surrey County Council v Bredero Homes Ltd*,[4] on very similar facts, the Court of Appeal confined C to the nominal damages yielded by the diminution in value measure. *Wrotham Park* was, however, approved.[5]

The attempt to reconcile these cases has led to extensive consideration of the value of providing a remedy to C who would be left uncompensated by the normal operation of the contract damages rules in such situations.

1   [1974] 1 WLR 798.
2   Ibid at 811B.
3   Ibid at 812F.
4   [1993] 1 WLR 1361, CA.
5   Ibid at 1369-1370.

This recently has culminated in the identification, by a majority of the House of Lords in the recent, extraordinary case of *A-G v Blake*,[6] of *Wrotham Park* as one of the 'appropriate situations' in which a 'restitutionary claim for the profits made from a breach of contract' should be recognised. In what range of situations it would be appropriate to grant this remedy, and what the remedy actually is, remain extremely contentious issues, but it is indisputable that a real problem is being addressed. Throughout Part 3 of this book it has been noted that C may be left partially uncompensated when, denied literal enforcement because the cost to D of performance is disproportionately onerous, he is confined to compensatory damages. The problem is magnified when, as in *Wrotham Park*, the diminution measure yields only nominal damages, and D's obligations therefore are effectively unenforceable. In *Wrotham Park*, it was felt that 'justice [would] manifestly not have been done'[7] by an award of nominal damages. When it heard *Blake*, the Court of Appeal was of the opinion that:

> If the court is unable to award restitutionary damages for breach of contract, then the law of contract is seriously defective. It means that in many situations the plaintiff is deprived of any effective remedy for breach of contract, because of a failure to attach a value to the plaintiff's legitimate interest in having the contract duly performed.[8]

In the Lords, the importance of *Wrotham Park* was taken to be that it seemed to offer the possibility of correcting a situation in which contracts 'may be breached with impunity' which would be 'a sorry reflection on the law'.[9]

In *Blake*, the restitutionary remedy was used to attempt to correct an indisputably egregious wrong. Between 1944 and 1960, George Blake was employed by the security services. As a condition of his employment he signed a declaration of compliance with the Official Secrets Act and in the proceedings this was held to be a contractual undertaking not to divulge official information. In 1961 he was imprisoned in England for espionage. However, in 1966 he escaped from custody and has since lived in the foreign country for which he was a spy. In 1989 he agreed with a UK publisher to publish an autobiography for which he was to receive an advance of £150,000. Perhaps mindful of a previous Attorney General's humiliating failure to prevent publication of Peter Wright's *Spycatcher*

6   *A-G v Blake* [2001] 1 AC 268 at 283H, HL.
7   *Wrotham Park Estate Co Ltd v Parkside Homes Ltd*, above n 1 at 815B.
8   *A-G v Blake* [1998] Ch 439 at 457E, CA.
9   *A-G v Blake*, HL, above, n 6 at 238G.

disclosures,[10] the current Attorney General wisely did not seek to prevent publication, but he did seek to prevent Blake from receiving the £90,000 that remained to be paid of his advance. (£60,000 had been paid and obviously was practically irrecoverable.) The manifest injustice of allowing conduct like Blake's to yield a benefit to him has, it would appear, led their Lordships to generalise a restitutionary remedy which would cover Blake's breach of his undertaking not to divulge official information by enforcing recovery of his advance from his publisher.

In the course of a very powerful dissent, Lord Hobhouse emphasised, inter alia, that *Blake* was so extraordinary a case that its value as a precedent in commercial cases is highly questionable.[11] The availability of a restitutionary remedy as an alternative to expectation damages presently is so unclear that it would appear that the best way to describe the remedy is to trace the development of the argument for its expanded availability in the cases following *Wrotham Park*.

### D's hypothetical release from literal enforcement

An attempt has been made to distinguish *Wrotham Park* and *Bredero Homes* by regarding damages in the former as being awarded in equity under Lord Cairns' Act,[12] as a substitute for the mandatory injunction which would have required pulling down the houses which had been built, whereas in the latter the common law produced nominal damages as the diminution in value measure.[13] Brightman J certainly believed he was giving damages in lieu of an injunction in *Wrotham Park*,[14] and *Wrotham Park* has been followed on this point.[15] Even if one accepts this, it leaves the problem of determining the measure of damages in equity, which the judge calculated as the reasonable price D would have paid to be released from the covenant. In other words, this was compensation for C's opportunity to negotiate a release which was lost when D simply breached unilaterally. The argument is that if D's breach of contract has deprived C of the opportunity of negotiating the sale to D of permission to act in a

10  *A-G v Guardian Newspapers Ltd (No 2)* [1990] 1 AC 109.
11  Lord Hobhouse claimed outright that his brethren had been so anxious to punish Blake that they had departed from principle in order to do so: *A-G v Blake*, HL, above p 256, n 6 at 299F. This seems to be conceded at points in the other speeches, particularly in that of Lord Nicholls which searches for a 'just response', and in that of Lord Steyn which insists on the importance of 'the attainment of practical justice': ibid at 287G, 292C.
12  Chancery Amendment Act 1858, s 2 (now Supreme Court Act 1981, s 50), described at pp 488-490 below.
13  *Jaggard v Sawyer* [1995] 1 WLR 269 at 281H.
14  *Wrotham Park Estate Co Ltd v Parkside Homes Ltd*, above p 255, n 1 at 811D.
15  *Bracewell v Appleby* [1975] Ch 408 and *Jaggard v Sawyer*, above, n 13.

particular way, damages should be fixed at the reasonable price which should have been negotiated bilaterally.[16] If an order for specific performance or an injunction had been made, by negotiating a price for releasing D from the order, C would have been able to obtain some of the profits which D expected to make from his freedom to pursue the better opportunity which had arisen for him.

If one accepts that damages in *Wrotham Park* were a form of compensation, the law left by that case would appear to have been that there were three forms of compensatory remedy which might be available following breach of a contract in which literal enforcement might be sought. There was, first, literal enforcement by equitable remedy (specific performance or injunction which effects specific performance) or at common law (affirmation of the contract or award of cost to complete damages). Second, there were diminution in value damages when literal enforcement is refused both in equity and at common law. These may be nominal. Third, there were hypothetical release damages in lieu of an equitable remedy (but not, on the basis of *Wrotham Park*, in lieu of affirmation or of cost to complete damages at common law). One immediately notes that treating hypothetical release damages as compensatory in this way leaves one with the problem of choosing which form of compensatory damages one should apply in which situations, and this problem has dogged the subsequent cases. No overall answer to this problem has emerged, however, because subsequent attempts to deal with hypothetical release damages, both in terms of distinguishing the decided cases and of the general principle at issue, have encountered extreme difficulty with the idea that those damages are in lieu of an equitable remedy or compensatory at all.

### Can hypothetical release damages be regarded as compensatory?

It is possible to distinguish *Wrotham Park* and *Bredero Homes* by saying that C had more determinedly sought an injunction in the former than in the latter. In *Bredero Homes*, C had in fact no wish to bring D's actions into line with the agreed plan[17] and, having waited such a long time before bringing an action that a mandatory injunction certainly would have been refused,[18] sought damages only at common law. But distinguishing the cases on this basis is rather undermined not least because the determination

16   RJ Sharpe and SM Waddams, 'Damages for Lost Opportunity to Bargain' (1982) 2 Oxford Journal of Legal Studies 290.
17   *Surrey County Council v Bredero Homes Ltd* [1992] 3 All ER 302 at 309e, Ch D.
18   *Surrey County Council v Bredero Homes Ltd*, CA, above p 255, n 4 at 1368C.

of C to seek equitable relief is questionable even in the former case. In *Wrotham Park*, C had objected to the construction and issued proceedings, but had not sought interim relief to prevent the homes being built, though C's advisers should have been aware that after those houses were built it was most unlikely that a mandatory injunction would be granted. Once the homes were occupied, C did not even want 'to bulldoze the occupiers out of their homes'.[19] Furthermore, even ignoring the very poor support the facts of these cases give to this attempt to reconcile them, it is impossible to bring this view of compensatory damages into line with the very sensible position set out in *Johnson v Agnew*[20] that the principles of the quantification of damages should be the same at common law and equity. This impossibility is ignored in *Bredero Homes*,[1] for in that case Steyn LJ held that *Wrotham Park* damages for hypothetical release were 'a new development',[2] the nature of which we shall shortly describe, and not compensatory at all.

The rather transparent failings in holding hypothetical release damages to be compensatory arise because, with respect, such a holding is itself a transparent attempt to keep the response to the failure properly to compensate C in cases like *Wrotham Park* from disrupting the whole of the law of contract damages. This is the purpose of a number of cases following *Wrotham Park* such as *Jaggard v Sawyer*. We think all of these attempts at confinement were bound ultimately to fail, for if one is responding to the perceived injustice of breach without compensation, there is no consistent reason to restrict the argument for hypothetical release to cases where an equitable remedy might have been granted on the facts but was refused. For historical reasons, specific performance and injunction are, of course, recognised as a distinct category of equitable remedies relevant to contract. However, the other forms of literal enforcement of contract raise just the same issues. The loss caused by refusal of an injunction in *Wrotham Park* would also be caused not only by a refusal of direct specific performance,[3] but also by a refusal to allow a non-breaching party to affirm a contract,[4] and a refusal of cost to complete damages.[5]

---

19  *Wrotham Park Estate Co Ltd v Parkside Homes Ltd*, above p 255, n 1 at 809D.
20  [1980] AC 367 at 400.
1   *Surrey County Council v Bredero Homes Ltd*, above p 255, n 4 at 1366-1367, CA.
2   Ibid at 1369G.
3   *Co-operative Insurance Society Ltd v Argyll Stores Ltd* [1998] AC 1, discussed at pp 188-189, 224-226 above.
4   *Clea Shipping Corpn v Bulk Oil International Ltd, The Alaskan Trader* [1984] 1 All ER 129, discussed at p 164 above.
5   *Ruxley Electronics and Construction Ltd v Forsyth* [1996] AC 344, discussed at pp 213-214 above. For a general discussion of the grounds on which literal enforcement was refused in these cases see pp 154-157, 167-175, 221-226 above.

This was made perfectly plain in the very frank argument of Sir William Goodhart for C in *Bredero Homes*, for he tried to make what seems to be the weakness of C's position, that C did not actually want the injunction, *the reason* for awarding damages at common law: the accident of the potential availability of an equitable remedy should not affect the general response to the injustice of failure to pay for hypothetical release.[6] Dillon LJ found difficulty with this argument:

> because in theory every time there is a breach of contract the injured party is deprived of his 'bargaining power' to negotiate for a financial consideration a variation of the contract which would enable the party who wants to depart from its terms to do what he wants to do.[7]

However, it is precisely this sort of general revision that has followed from the attempt to give hypothetical release damages a sounder footing than they can enjoy if regarded as a form of compensation. Release damages have the essential nature of disgorgement (by reference to D's position) rather than of compensation (by reference to C's position), and the former has long been taken to be irrelevant to contract damages, the purpose of which is 'not one of making the defendant disgorge what he has saved by committing the wrong, but one of compensating the plaintiff'.[8] Hypothetical release damages can be justified only if their use as an *alternative* to expectation damages is justified, and in *Bredero Homes*, Steyn LJ, regarding the compensation argument as 'a fiction', gave hypothetical release a doctrinal foundation in restitution. Following the Fuller and Perdue three interests analysis, he regarded *Wrotham Park* as a restitutionary claim in a situation where expectation damages left an uncompensated loss but the restitutionary interest could be protected.[9] This was 'a useful development in our law' because 'a coherent law of obligations must inevitably extend its protection to certain restitutionary interests'.[10] For the reasons just given, Steyn LJ himself rejected the restriction of hypothetical release damages to cases in which specific performance had been refused.[11] But he went on to say that *Wrotham Park* was a case of 'invasion of property rights' which could be protected by restitution, as opposed to pure contract cases, of which he took *Bredero Homes* to be one. The fact that C in *Bredero Homes* did not really want

---

6   *Surrey County Council v Bredero Homes Ltd*, above p 258, n 17 at 309e, Ch D.
7   *Surrey County Council v Bredero Homes Ltd*, above p 255, n 4 at 1368B, CA.
8   *Tito v Waddell* [1977] Ch 106 at 332.
9   *Surrey County Council v Bredero Homes Ltd*, above p 255, n 4 at 1369, CA.
10  Ibid at 1369H, 1369F.
11  Ibid at 1370C.

the injunction meant that 'the case did not involve any invasion of the plaintiff's property interests'.[12]

It must be said that, for reasons given earlier, this is an unconvincing way of distinguishing these cases. However, it is not because of this that reference to property rights has in its turn failed to limit the scope of hypothetical release damages but because such a reference also is a transparent compromise.[13] The argument against special protection of equitable rights also works against special protection of property rights. All breaches can be regarded as releases from literal enforcement for which there should be a hypothetical release price, and the accident that some of these might be cases where what is presently identified as a property right is not involved should not stand in the way of extending the release price argument if that argument is sound. This was recognised in *Blake*, where Lord Nicholls, surely correctly, said:

> Property rights are superior to contractual rights in that, unlike contractual rights, property rights may survive against an indefinite class of persons. However, it is not easy to see why, as between the parties to a contract, a violation of a party's contractual rights should attract a lesser degree of remedy than a violation of his property rights ... it is not clear why it should be any more permissible to expropriate personal rights than it is permissible to expropriate property rights.[14]

Though it is important to state that the position is not clear, we submit that it has not proven possible to maintain that hypothetical release damages are compensatory and that, if they have a valid legal foundation, it has to be in restitution, which is the thrust of the majority decision in *Blake*.[15] In *Blake*, Lord Nicholls explicitly stated that, to the extent that *Wrotham Park* and *Bredero Homes* are inconsistent, the former is to be preferred.[16] Certainly, if it is rightly decided, *Blake* itself *must* stand for a *general* principle of restitution. The absence of any prospect of getting an injunction which barred the claim in *Bredero* was a blatant feature of

12  Ibid at 1369G, 1371A.
13  P Birks, 'Profits of Breach of Contract' (1993) 100 Law Quarterly Review 518.
14  *A-G v Blake*, above p 256, n 6 at 283D, HL. Cf *A-G v Blake*, above p 256, n 8 at 457D, CA.
15  M Chen-Wishart, 'Restitutionary Damages for Breach of Contract' (1998) 114 Law Quarterly Review 363. To the extent that it attempts to defend the analysis of hypothetical release damages as compensatory (*A-G v Blake*, above p 256, n 6 at 298G, HL), we believe that, with respect, Lord Hobhouse's dissent is unsustainable. However, this does not affect the strength of his criticism of the restitutionary position.
16  Ibid at 283H.

*Blake*,[17] in which C did not even pursue a private law restitutionary argument until, in the course of litigation, he was prompted to do so by their Lordships themselves,[18] after the public law arguments which he previously had used had met with such serious difficulty as to fail at first instance.[19] The private law interest which was found in *Blake* (based on Blake's undertaking), if it is a private interest at all, *has* to be contractual rather than proprietary. It therefore seems that there now may be a general restitutionary remedy of (partial) disgorgement of the profits of breach of contract in 'appropriate situations'. After *Blake*, the restitutionary remedy, whatever form it takes, need not be confined just to cases in which the refusal of literal enforcement was or could have been an issue, or just to cases in which there was a proprietary interest. One, but not the only, way of calculating the restitutionary payment effecting disgorgement may be the price of hypothetical release from literal enforcement, but total disgorgement (and perhaps apportionment on other bases) also is possible according to the majority of the House of Lords in *Blake*.

## The restitutionary disgorgement of the gains from breach

To the extent that *Blake* sets a precedent, it is a *general* denial that the normal remedies rules should leave C uncompensated in circumstances not only of extraordinary cases like *Blake* but of more usual cases like *The Alaskan Trader, Argyll Holdings, Ruxley* and *Wrotham Park*.[20] Those rules do, we think it should be clearly acknowledged, now leave C with an uncompensated loss. *Blake* makes it possible that a general restitutionary remedy might be employed to prevent D from ever being allowed to profit from his breach: 'there seems to be no reason, *in principle*, why the court must in all circumstances rule out an account of profits as a remedy for breach of contract'.[1] In an 'appropriate situation', the restitutionary remedy will apply, and it would only be in line with the course of development from *Wrotham Park* to *Blake* if many novel situations were now to be argued to be 'appropriate'. In Lord Nicholls' leading speech, 'a useful general guide, although not exhaustive' to the determination of appropriateness 'is whether the plaintiff had a legitimate

---

17  Ibid at 295G.
18  Ibid at 277H. The argument had been suggested by Birks in response to the *Spycatcher* failure. P Birks, 'A Lifelong Obligation of Confidence' (1989) 105 Law Quarterly Review 501. See also P Birks, 'Restitutionary Damages for Breach of Contract: *Snepp* and the Fusion of Law and Equity' [1987] Lloyd's Maritime and Commercial Law Quarterly 421.
19  *A-G v Blake* [1997] Ch 84.
20  Cited on p 225, n 1, p 259, nn 3-5 above.
1   *A-G v Blake*, above p 256, n 6 at 284H, HL.

interest in preventing the defendant's profit-making activity',[2] but, at its very best,[3] this merely rephrases the issue, which is left open for future development, though his Lordship clearly expected that 'an account of profits will be appropriate only in exceptional circumstances'.[4] Some classification of appropriate situations was attempted in the Court of Appeal hearing of *Blake*, and two situations – a performance had been 'skimped' or that 'D had obtained his profit by doing the very thing which he contracted not to do'[5] – were identified, but Lord Nicholls and Lord Steyn withdrew from both.[6] The matter is, then, to be 'hammered out on the anvil of concrete cases'.[7] Nevertheless, the suspicion one entertained from the outset, that the half-way house advocated most notably by *Jaggard v Sawyer* could not survive, has been realised by *AG v Blake*.[8]

In what has become the leading British authority for 'efficient breach', *Teacher v Calder*, it was stated that C cannot recover from D the profits D made from his breach of contract but can recover only for his own (C's) losses.[9] Though in the Court of Appeal, Lord Woolf expressly approved *Teacher v Calder*,[10] he gave no argument for doing so, and if one accepts the wider restitutionary argument developed in *Blake*, there is no consistent basis on which the principle of *Teacher v Calder* can be shielded from the logic of the *Blake* argument, which challenges the very notion of efficient breach for which *Teacher v Calder* is taken to stand.[11] *Blake*, we submit, now makes it possible to argue against the efficient breach view of contract remedies. The academic restitutionary

2  Ibid at 285H. Cf the 'legitimate interest' in affirmation in *White and Carter (Councils) Ltd v McGregor* [1962] AC 413 discussed at pp 163-165 above.
3  This observation is in one sense extremely misleading: see p 270 below.
4  *A-G v Blake*, above p 256, n 6 at 285G, HL.
5  *A-G v Blake*, above p 256, n 8 at 458, CA. See further pp 274-277 below.
6  *A-G v Blake*, above p 256, n 6 at 277G, 291D, HL. The account of the law in the latest reissue of *Halsbury's Laws* (4th edn reissue) vol 12(1), para 1000 is based on acceptance of these two cases.
7  *A-G v Blake*, HL, above p 256, n 6 at 291F.
8  C Mitchell, 'Remedial Inadequacy in Contract and the Role of Restitutionary Damages' (1999) 15 Journal of Contract Law 133, pp 143-150.
9  (1897) SC 661 at 672-673 (affirmed on this point [1899] AC 451 at 467-468 (HL(Sc))). The concept of efficient breach is discussed at pp 11-13 above. See also pp 7-11, 13-21 above.
10  *A-G v Blake*, above p 256, n 8 at 459A, CA. Cf *A-G v Blake*, above p 256, n 6 at 286E, HL where Lord Nicholls rejected the view that a 'deliberate ... breach [that] enabled the defendant to enter into a more profitable contract elsewhere... would be, by itself, a good reason for ordering an account of profits'.
11  LD Smith, 'Disgorgement of the Profits of Breach of Contract: Property, Contract and "Efficient Breach"' (1995) 24 Canadian Bar Journal 121. The whole tone of the restitutionary literature which now has led to *Blake* has been to disparage and question efficient breach in general and the principle in *Teacher v Calder* in particular: eg G Jones, 'The Recovery of Benefits Gained from a Breach of Contract' (1983) 99 Law Quarterly Review 443, pp 444, 453.

jurisprudence which so influenced the Court of Appeal and the House of Lords in *Blake* has recognised that there may be situations in which restitution for wrongdoing is impractical and has to be given up.[12] But it is clear that a breach remedied by what formerly were taken to be adequate compensatory damages is not such a situation, indeed it may well be an appropriate situation for restitution. The underlying concept in *Blake* is a recognition of a 'performance interest', for the assurance of actual performance given by a contractual obligation when remedies will be guided by the expectation interest is thought to be too weak:

> The essence of contract is performance. Contracts are made in order to be performed. This is usually the one and only ground for their formation ... This interest in getting the promised performance ... the performance interest ... is the only pure contractual interest [and] is protected by specific remedies, which aim at granting the innocent party the very performance promised to him, and by substitutional remedies.[13]

The perceived injustice addressed in the line of case from *Wrotham Park* is the insufficient ranking given to this performance interest, and the importance of *Blake* is that it goes some way to remedying this because a money payment on the basis set out in *Blake* obviously amounts to 'restitutionary damages to deter breach of contract.'[14] The entire law of damages based on compensation of lost expectation subject to mitigation, which as Farnsworth famously put it 'shows a marked solicitude for men who do not keep their promises,'[15] is thought defective, as is the law of literal enforcement, which not only comes into play only when damages are inadequate but also places limits on literal enforcement even when damages are found to be inadequate. Through recognition of the performance interest it is being sought more fully to make undertaking a contractual obligation *mean* performance.

One's opinion of this essentially depends on one's attitude to restitution of this sort as opposed to expectation damages, which in turn depends on one's attitude to the efficiency of breach. In this book,[16] it has been argued that not merely breach to maximise gain but also breach to minimise loss

---

12  P Birks, *An Introduction to the Law of Restitution* (rev edn 1989) p 24.

13  D Friedmann, 'The Performance Interest in Contract Damages' (1995) 111 Law Quarterly Review 628, p 629. Cf Friedmann's criticism of efficient breach: D Friedmann, 'The Efficient Breach Fallacy' (1989) 18 Journal of Legal Studies 1.

14  D Fox, 'Restitutionary Damages to Deter Breach of Contract' [2001] Cambridge Law Journal 33.

15  EA Farnsworth, 'Legal Remedies for Breach of Contract' (1970) 70 Columbia Law Review 1145, p 1216.

16  See ch 1 above.

are essential aspects of the efficiency of a market economy. The argument for the general restitutionary remedy threatens this efficiency. Or at least it does so in principle, for we do not for a moment imagine that this remedy could be given general application even after *Blake*. To say that '[t]he expectation interest is simply an inappropriate term describing the performance interest'[17] is utterly wrong. For it is in the gap between obligation and performance opened up by compensation of the expectation interest, in which mitigation does its work, that much of the efficiency of the legal structure of the market economy lies. We cannot but agree with Lord Hobhouse's dissent, which, it is submitted, is very wise and should guide further development:

> if some more extensive principle of awarding non-compensatory damages for breach of contract is to be introduced into our commercial law the consequences will be very far reaching and disruptive.[18]

The generalisation of a restitutionary principle to cover all appropriate situations is a *major* leap not properly dealt with in *Blake*, and that leap must be set out in a little detail here. As we have seen throughout the earlier Parts of this book, the court's main approach to contractual damages is to assess C's loss, not the profit made by D as a result of his breach. But it is, of course, entirely possible that if C is entitled to obtain restitution of a benefit conferred on D under a contract, he may obtain an amount exceeding his loss, and in this way the surplus over his loss could be viewed as partially depriving D of any profits arising from his breach. The expectation and the restitution interests *do* diverge; that is their point. But nevertheless, the restitutionary remedies of recovery of money paid and *quantum meruit* discussed in the previous chapter have a broadly quasi-contractual character in the sense that they can, it is submitted, be understood as supplementary to the basic principles of contractual damages. They come into play when situations arise which contractual principles do not adequately address, but they not only arise out of a contractual situation but share the contractual aim of correcting a defect in the claimant's position. Though *not* compensatory in the sense of contractual damages, they do restore to the claimant a benefit he has conveyed in the course of performance of a contract which otherwise would unjustly enrich the defendant. *Dawood Ltd v Heath (Est 1927) Ltd*[19] is a perfect example. Such cases address what Birks calls 'unjust enrichment

---

17  Friedmann, 'The Performance Interest in Contract Damages', above p 264, n 13, p 632.

18  *A-G v Blake*, HL, above p 256, n 6 at 299D.

19  [1961] 2 Lloyd's Rep 512, discussed in p 235 above.

by subtraction', in the sense that the benefit is 'subtracted' from the claimant who has paid money or rendered a service.[20]

It no doubt is theoretically unsatisfactory to have the two different principles of expectation and restitution simultaneously at work, for, of course, this means the problem always exists of deciding when each principle should be invoked, and a proper solution of this will logically require a third overarching principle which subsumes both of the original principles. It is highly arguable that Fuller and Perdue's analysis is ultimately unsatisfactory for just this reason. A subsidiary problem also will tend to arise that, until the overarching principle is understood, the scope of the original principles will be disputed, and this obviously is what has happened in the *Boomer v Muir*[1] situation. Nevertheless, we believe that these cases of unjust enrichment by subtraction, which it is helpful for this purpose to say are quasi-contractual, can be thought to stand in an analogous relationship to basic contractual principles as the literal enforcement remedies. That is to say, they remedy cases when compensatory damages are perceived to be inadequate to the claimant, and do so in a working relationship which has proven value and robustness but which nevertheless cannot really ultimately be theoretically defended (for the reason just given), and which invite the formulation of an overall better alternative basis for contractual remedies than the expectation analysis.

But in *Blake*, as part of the current development of the law of restitution as a foundation of the entire law of obligations, a restitutionary remedy has been recognised which, we submit, flatly conflicts with normal contractual principles. *Blake* allows the restitutionary redistribution of gains from breach in order to correct 'unjust enrichment by a wrong'[2] which, crucially, 'has not caused the [claimant] any harm' (except outraged feelings about the commission of the 'wrong').[3] The 'wrong' is against the principle of the abhorrence of unjust enrichment, and it is merely C's role to be the means of bringing about corrective justice through a restitutionary claim. It was noted in *Blake* that there was a 'dearth of judicial decision' on this whole issue, though 'no lack of academic writing'.[4] It clearly is the case that the development of the restitutionary remedy culminating in *Blake* has largely been driven by an abstract concern with an inconsistency in the law. This is manifest in *Blake* itself, which was not a contract case driven by commercial incentives.[5] It is impossible to believe a commercial party would have risked the hazards of litigation

20  Birks, *An Introduction to the Law of Restitution*, above p 264, n 12, pp 22-4.
1   24 P 2d 570 at 578 (1933). See pp 238-240 above.
2   Birks, *An Introduction to the Law of Restitution*, above p 264, n 12, pp 39-44.
3   M Jackman, 'Restitution for Wrongs' [1989] Cambridge Law Journal 302, p 302.
4   *A-G v Blake*, HL, above p 256, n 6 at 277H.
5   Ibid at 293F.

whose success depended on a major exercise of judicial legislation. It requires the lofty perspective given by command of public funds even to believe that it was a success to have obtained restitution of £90,000 at a cost of almost £1 million in legal fees[6] (leaving aside the costs run up by the Attorney General's office and the court administration costs).

But this curious quality which follows from lack of commercial interest has been present from the outset. There are cases of a refusal of an injunction where that refusal causes uncompensated commercial loss. The exposure of C to uncertain and irrecoverable loss which would have followed such a refusal in *Warner Bros Pictures Inc v Nelson*[7] is a clear example. But there was no such loss in *Wrotham Park*, in which, to repeat, '[n]o damage of a financial nature has been done to the plaintiffs by the breach of the lay-out stipulation [and t]he plaintiff's use of the Wrotham Park Estate has not and will not be impeded'.[8] We do not deny that there is a sort of loss in *Wrotham Park*, but it is distinct from the commercial loss which arises in cases when damages *really* are inadequate and an uncompensated loss follows from a refusal of literal enforcement.

In the light of this, the intention to leave the *Teacher v Calder* principle intact must immediately fail. Let us imagine that C in this case had his expectation fully protected by D's payment of compensatory damages. D still has not had to pay for the release as C's lost expectation did not include a release payment. Surely the restitutionary remedy would make D fully compensate lost expectation *and* pay for release. The only possible way in which the *Teacher v Calder* principle could be reconciled with *Blake* is to say that the release payment arises only when damages are otherwise nominal. But this is ridiculous in itself and, being unsustainable, would invite a repetition of the failed attempts to distinguish between equitable or proprietary cases and simple contractual cases. More importantly, it would not distinguish the absolutely typical case in which D, faced by unanticipatedly rising costs, breaches a contract to sell a generic good in the knowledge that C can take cover at no extra cost by purchasing the good from a third party. If D has to pay for release in this case, commercial law as we have it will collapse.

Though the instances of the use of the general restitutionary remedy which we are considering here arise out of a breach of contract, there is no real possibility of treating this remedy as quasi-contractual in the sense we have just used the term and thereby reconciling it with contract because, as there is no 'subtraction', the remedy conflicts outright with the contractual result. In the law of contract prior to *Blake* restitution has served a valuable function, and would continue to do so as long as it is not 'suggested that there is a universally applicable principle that in every

6   Anon, 'In the Courts' (8 September 2000) Private Eye 9.
7   [1937] 1 KB 209, discussed in pp 206-207 above.
8   *Wrotham Park Estate Co Ltd v Parkside Homes Ltd*, above p 255, n 1 at 811B.

case there will be restitution of benefit from a wrong.'[9] An understanding and assessment of this remedy requires one to form an opinion of the relative virtues of expectation and restitution as the foundations of the law of contract (or the contractual part of a general law of obligations). As we are in no doubt that the classical law of contract should be replaced, it is with regret that we will now submit that this restitutionary alternative is markedly inferior to the existing law of contract, and simply could not be widely adopted as a practical remedy in a market economy. Before setting out this argument, let us follow the implications of providing the remedy advocated in *Blake*.

## Would restitution correct the wrong?

If, for the sake of argument, one allows that there should be a general restitutionary remedy, then two further difficulties present themselves.

If one takes the restitutionary argument to what appears to be its logical conclusion,[9a] then D should have to restore all the benefit of the breach to C. However, in *Wrotham Park*, Brightman J did not do this. D made £50,000 from the development in breach of the lay-out plan, but Brightman J estimated the cost of the release to be 5% of that profit and awarded £2,500.[10] This is a rudimentary form of apportionment. No clear justification for such apportionment on restitutionary principles has emerged,[11] but one is driven to apportionment because the alternative of complete disgorgement by D, though clearly in line with those principles and wholly necessary if the performance interest is to mean anything, would have unattractive consequences.[12] The justification of hypothetical negotiation breaks down if disgorgement is total, because no rational D would have agreed to pay such a price for release. Indeed, as total disgorgement would utterly remove D's incentive to breach, and presumably would stop him breaching, he would make no extra profit to disgorge, but therefore neither would C. If C is allowed to get (nearly) all of the benefit, D may indeed decide to perform, but in that case, although C still gets the value of performance, the whole of the extra benefit is lost to both parties, and so lost to society. It seems clear that disgorgement

9    *Halifax Building Society v Thomas* [1996] Ch 217 at 227H.

9a   *Pace*. NJ McBride and P McGrath 'The Nature of Restitution' (1995) 15 Oxford Journal of Legal Studies 33.

10   *Wrotham Park Estate Co Ltd v Parkside Homes Ltd*, above p 255, n 1 at 815-816.

11   Such an apportionment was the result of what is to be taken to be the leading modern authority for the award of restitution, *Lipkin, Gorman v Karpnale Ltd* [1991] 2 AC 548. However, it has proven impossible to justify this result on any restitutionary principle.

12   *Halifax Building Society v Thomas*, above n 9 at 229.

must be partial, unless one puts such an overriding value on preventing the abstract wrong that D, C and society as a whole should be made to suffer in order that it be prevented.

Specific situations have long been recognised in which C can obtain, as part of his remedy, some of the gain made by D, and the 'light sprinkling of cases where courts have made orders having the same effect as an order for an account of profits'[13] was used as authority in *Blake* for the generalised restitutionary remedy. If D's breach of contract also amounts to a tort against C, the latter may have a claim in tort to deprive D of the gain.[14] C may have a proprietary remedy: if, after having sold land to C, D wrongfully sells it to a third person at a higher price, C is entitled to recover from D the proceeds of that sale.[15] If D makes any profits from the land after the date fixed for completion of the sale to C, D is treated as a trustee of the land for C, the equitable owner, so that C's 'loss' is not relevant. C may also have a restitutionary remedy for an account to deprive D as his agent of a secret profit,[16] or as his employee of profits arising from the misuse of a trade secret or confidential information.[17] C's equitable right to 'trace' his property into D's hands may entitle him to recover any increase in its value since the date of the wrong committed by D.[18] Another restitutionary remedy, the constructive trust, may achieve the same result: D, the 'trustee', will be compelled to account to C, the 'beneficiary', for any profit made from the trust property.[19]

But (though it will not be argued here) all of these cases are explicable without recourse to restitution of enrichment by mere abstract wrongdoing and, the significance of this, they all therefore have an element which leads to sensible quantification of damages based on legitimate prevention of D's breach. For example: in what seems to be the most influential of these authorities, *Penarth Dock*, D bought a pontoon which was moored at C's berth but did not move it as he was contracted to do. C sued both in contract and the tort of trespass and recovered a fair market rental for use of berth. C should not, in fact, have been awarded contractual damages, for C was discontinuing use of the dock and D's breach caused him no loss. But he should, as he appears to have been, awarded damages for trespass which amount to total disgorgement of the 'benefit' received

---

13  *A-G v Blake*, HL, above p 256, n 6 at 284C.
14  *Penarth Dock Engineering Co Ltd v Pounds* [1963] 1 Lloyd's Rep 359; cited in *A-G v Blake*, HL, above p 256, n 6 at 278G. See further ch 26 below.
15  *Lake v Bayliss* [1974] 1 WLR 1073; cited in *A-G v Blake*, HL, above p 256, n 6 at 284D.
16  *Regier v Campbell-Stuart* [1939] Ch 766.
17  *Printers and Finishers Ltd v Holloway* [1965] 1 WLR 1. The breach of fiduciary civil law duty is referred to in *A-G v Blake*, HL, above p 256, n 6 at 280G-H.
18  R Goff and G Jones, *The Law of Restitution* (5th edn 1999) pp 93-119.
19  *Reid Newfoundland Co v Anglo-American Telegraph Co* [1912] AC 555; cited in *A-G v Blake*, HL, above p 256, n 6 at 284D.

by D because we wish to prevent trespass per se. We also wish to prevent breaches of confidence, mismanagement of trusts, etc, and damages should be awarded on this basis, as they exceptionally are.[20]

These authorities support *Blake* so strongly because that case itself sets a markedly unfit *general* precedent because of its *outre* facts; C *did* want total disgorgement in *Blake* because the real goal of the proceedings was, precisely, the 'essentially punitive' one of depriving D of the benefit of this breach (and to prevent similar breaches in the future).[1] On the facts of *Blake*, this was at least arguably a legitimate goal, but it is important to realise that it is a goal which is very unlikely indeed to be appropriate in normal commercial cases, in which some form of apportionment will be needed. In sum, when Lord Nicholls said that 'a useful general guide, although not exhaustive' to the future determination of the appropriateness of the restitutionary remedy 'is whether the plaintiff had a legitimate interest in preventing the defendant's profit-making activity',[2] he was, with respect, in using the word 'preventing' interpreted naturally and in line with the result in *Blake*, giving a guide which will prove misleading in the extreme if used generally.

Because apportionment will be important even after *Blake*, the second difficulty arises: how is the hypothetical release payment as a form of apportionment to be calculated? One must ask what sum would a reasonable person in D's position have been willing to pay for C's consent, but only in quite artificial circumstances? It is obvious that a court would have to decide whether any revaluation of the bargain C made was a genuine attempt to price D's hypothetical release and not the 'ransom price'[3] which C may exact through opportunistic behaviour when general literal enforcement or a restitutionary substitute for this locks the two parties into a very strong bilateral monopoly. In *Wrotham Park*, although '[t]he lay-out covenant [was] not an asset which the estate owner ever contemplated he would have either the opportunity or the desire to turn to account', C initially asked for between £46,000 and £70,000 for a hypothetical release from which, as we have seen, D made £50,000.[4] So far as can be determined, the *only* reason C brought an action in *Bredero Homes* was to take advantage of the action established in *Wrotham Park*. Both Cs in *Bredero Homes* were local authorities which, in a strong sense, imposed the restriction through exercise of their planning powers rather than bargained for it. If a *Wrotham Park* claim had been recognised in this case, it would have extended a license to local authorities to impose planning restrictions of no commercial value on which they do not intend

---

20  Jackman, 'Restitution for Wrongs', above p 266, n 3.
1   *A-G v Blake*, HL, above p 256, n 6 at 295.
2   Ibid at 285H.
3   *Jaggard v Sawyer*, above p 257, n 13 at 282H-283A.
4   *Wrotham Park Estate Co Ltd v Parkside Homes Ltd*, above p 255, n 1 at 815.

to rely and then demand a payment for their relaxation. (The avoidance of this intolerable result (though no doubt it would have been corrected quickly) is the real key to understanding this case, and in particular why it was distinguished from *Wrotham Park*.)[5]

It was because Brightman J was anxious to avoid both total disgorgement, for he recognised C would never have agreed to this, and the possibility of strategic bargaining by C, that he assessed damages in *Wrotham Park* with 'great moderation' at £2,500. Though the learned judge identified the problems very acutely, as £2,500 would have worked out at £166 per house,[6] it is hard to see that this is very different from nominal damages, and, we submit, between the Scylla of total disgorgement and the Charybdis of nominal damages, there is no principled course to be followed. However, English courts have not hesitated to fix a reasonable price when the parties have failed to do so (but have agreed that there is to be a sale).[7] So where D leased equipment from C and retained it beyond the time when it should have been returned, C's damages for detinue were assessed at the reasonable cost of hiring which C might have fixed for the further use of the equipment.[8] Similarly, the ordinary letting value will be awarded as damages against a tenant who continues to occupy residential premises as a trespasser after his lease expires,[9] or a buyer who refuses to remove goods from the seller's premises.[10] In this type of situation, the court can give C damages at the amount which he could reasonably have charged D as rent or for storage facilities. But (accepting that there should be liability) these authorities all relate to enrichment by subtraction in which there is therefore in a sense a liquidated loss to which the court can refer. It is the absence of this that characterises enrichment by wrongdoing, and all the court can do is speculate. It is therefore impossible to agree with Lord Nicholls that the availability of the restitutionary remedy will not produce uncertainty in commercial cases.[11] With respect, his Lordship's apparent position that

---

5   In *A-G v Blake*, HL, above p 256, n 6 at 283C, Lord Nicholls sees this but, incredibly, approves of what the authority did, and consequently calls *Bredero Homes* into question. One can only imagine that, although he speaks of the local authorities 'imposing the covenant', Lord Nicholls imagines this imposition shares some of the legitimacy of a bargain.

6   *Wrotham Park Estate Co Ltd v Parkside Homes Ltd*, above p 255, n 1 at 815G-816.

7   Sale of Goods Act 1979, s 8(2).

8   *Strand Electric and Engineering Co Ltd v Brisford Entertainments Ltd* [1952] 2 QB 246.

9   *Swordheath Properties Ltd v Tabet* [1979] 1 WLR 285. See also *Inverugie Investments Ltd v Hackett* [1995] 3 All ER 841, in which the trespass continued for over 15 years.

10  *Penarth Dock Engineering Co Ltd v Pounds*, above p 269, n 14.

11  *A-G v Blake*, HL, above p 256, n 6 at 285F.

the unsettling effect will be restricted to exceptional cases not only seems to be an admission that it will be unsettling in those cases but, in light of the way the law has been developed, makes it no less unsettling for those situations which in future might well find themselves declared to be exceptional cases.

The court could approach this problem of quantification as a matter of elementary justice, and divide the benefit equally, in the absence of any special reason for a different division: 'equality is equity'. But, although this might well represent what would be the outcome of Alternative Dispute Resolution (ADR), it is neither compensatory nor restitutionary and, we shall now see, would actually be harmful. We have argued that the compromise payment approved by the House of Lords in *Ruxley* represented the sort of compromise which would be the outcome of ADR or an out of court settlement, and that such approval was unwise because it shifts the boundaries in which out of court settlements are made.[12] Similarly, leaving hypothetical release damages to be determined *ex post* by the court would make *ex ante* prices uncertain, for the parties would not know how much to factor in for release.[13] It is obvious that, faced with this uncertainty, competent parties would contract out of the problem by fixing the price themselves, and seeing this allows us to resolve the conundra of hypothetical release.

### Is there a 'wrong' in 'wrongful' breach?

The inevitable conundra which follow from an attempt to fix an *ex ante* price of hypothetical release arise because the criticism of efficient breach as a wrong per se is a lot of fuss about nothing at all. The reason there is no clear course to follow in determining hypothetical release damages is that there is no general wrong to be remedied. It is, in fact, the formalism and abstraction of the restitutionary approach, leading to the naïve assumption that contracts should and could absolutely assure performance expressed in the notion of the performance interest, which is itself the problem rather than a solution to any problem.

If all breaches are a wrong, little attention need be paid to establishing whether the reality of the 'wrong' done to C actually is of much commercial consequence. The whole point is, however, to distinguish efficient from inefficient, or, perhaps better, legitimate from illegitimate breaches. It is

---

12  See pp 214-216 above.
13  It has been argued at pp 246-254 above that the remedy for frustration amounts to elementary justice of this sort, but the harmful consequences do not arise because frustration must in general not be foreseen by the parties.

implicit in the concept of efficient breach that C is compensated,[14] and in critical writings on contract many unarguably bad cases have long been identified in which purportedly efficient breach arguably should not be allowed because it is not, in fact, efficient. If C suffers an idiosyncratic loss not compensated in damages, then a breach which on a mere calculation of the damages looks to be efficient may in fact not be so, for the damages rules are not working well. We have seen throughout Part 3 of this book that a fear of being under-compensated in this way has driven attempts to secure literal enforcement by actions for debt, specific performance, injunction and cost to complete damages. Two serious sets of problems have been identified.

First, the grounds on which damages are recognised to be inadequate and so give rise to a claim for literal enforcement may not be wide enough. It is this problem of idiosyncratic loss, or rather the profound inability of the formal remedies to deal with such loss, that gives rise to sophisticated contract planning of bespoke remedies (liquidated damages, arbitration clauses, etc) and the non-use of contract in complex commercial relationships.[15] Breaches that rode roughshod over this would actually be inefficient:

A model assuming away relations slips with the greatest of ease at any stage into favouring unco-operative and – ironically enough – highly inefficient human behaviour.[16]

The rules on mitigation[17] which are such a valuable aspect of compensatory damages obviously tend to reduce damages and so increase the disproportion between the costs and benefits of litigation which is such a barrier to a consumer's use of litigation for redress.[18] Breach that rode roughshod over this also would actually be inefficient:

Limiting remedies allows stronger parties to walk away from burdensome obligations at low or no cost. Courts frequently find that a stronger [party] has breached a contract, but so limit the remedy awarded the weaker that the victory is hollow.[19]

---

14 D Harris, 'Contract as Promise' (1983) 3 International Review of Law and Economics, 69, p 72.
15 See chs 2-3 above.
16 IR Macneil, 'Efficient Breach of Contract: Circles in the Sky' (1982) 68 Virginia Law Review 947, p 969.
17 See ch 7 above.
18 See ch 4 above.
19 S Macaulay, 'An Empirical View of Contract' [1985] Wisconsin Law Review 465, p 470. Cf IR Macneil, 'Essays on the Nature of Contract' (1980) 10 South Carolina Central Law Journal 159, pp 183-184.

For these reasons, the claim that breach is efficient has been widely disputed in many situations, and, indeed, questioned so often in consumer cases that the question has been posed whether the expectation rule is the best rule for those cases.[20] We suspect it is not. Nevertheless, the proper response to these issues is to look at the empirical detail of the way the civil legal system operates in these different situations, not merely at the substantive rules, for no sensible decision on which substantive rules are best can be made outside of that context, for it is the context that determines whether the rule enhances welfare or not.

Second, we have seen that even when literal enforcement has been pursued and a good case for it made out, it may be denied because the cost of it to D is held to be excessive. When properly understood, this is not so important an issue, and we shall defer its discussion for a moment. The point which should be made here is that the general restitutionary approach to breach is wholly misconceived. It does not attempt to do the necessary work of distinguishing when breach is and is not appropriate because it simply subsumes all these complex issues under the 'wrong' of breach, against which it would give a general remedy enhancing the performance interest. In its pure form, it takes it as axiomatic that any breach is a wrong which must be remedied, and it is the position taken in this book that there is no more sure way of misunderstanding the law of contract remedies. We do not believe it helpful to treat of breach *tout court* as a 'wrong' in this sense, and the ousting of normal contractual principles which accepting this would involve would be a very bad policy. However, it is the case that there is something specifically objectionable about the breach that occurred in *Wrotham Park Estate*, and the issue it is productive to consider is whether the application of restitutionary principles allows us to correct this specific defect in the law of contract.

Sadly, by proceeding purely formally, the restitutionary argument does none of the necessary work. In particular, neither of the specific grounds for the award of the restitutionary remedy which the Court of Appeal in *Blake* put forward – that a performance had been 'skimped' or that 'D had obtained his profit by doing the very thing which he contracted not to do'[1] – are actually at all compelling. In cases such as *Ruxley* performance is not skimped in the sense claimed and does not require a change in the law.[2] It is only if one thinks of a commitment to perform as absolute that

20  S Macaulay, 'The Reliance Interest and the World Outside the Law Schools' Doors' [1991] Wisconsin Law Review 247, pp 249-257. Atiyah suggests that it is a failure to recognise the extent of the effect of mitigation upon C's recovery that has allowed expectation to survive as the (inadequate) basis of damages in general: PS Atiyah, *Essays on Contract* (rev edn 1990) pp 124-5.

1  *A-G v Blake*, CA, above p 256, n 8 at 458.

2  *Pace* B Coote, 'Contract Damages, *Ruxley*, and the Performance Interest' [1997] Cambridge Law Journal 537.

this would be so.[3] Of course, the parties could in theory contract for, as it were, a stricter (if not absolute)[4] liability to perform, and contemplating restitution in the event of breach might be a technique for doing so. But such an obligation would be so onerous that D either would not undertake it, and so pools could not be built, or would be very expensive because D would have to take precautions such as extraordinarily careful ground surveys or taking out insurance against a potentially huge liability.[5]

As has been shown in chapter 6, the normal rules limiting damages are 'default rules' in that they will apply when the parties do not oust them by supplying their own, bespoke rules, which they are very largely legally free to do. It now is the case that, as a default rule, liability is limited by breach regulated by the expectation and mitigation rules, and prices such as the price of the pool in *Ruxley* reflect this. D did not skimp on performance but gave it to the extent the contract actually stipulated. It is quite wrong to hold that C should have a price which amortises liability based on compensatory damages principles and then be held to much stricter liability.[6] There is, of course, nothing (except bad advice about the degree of assurance of performance that a contract normally affords) to prevent the parties from ousting the default damages rules and undertaking a stricter liability to perform. C in *Ruxley* could have made it clear that the pool would have to be redug if not in perfect conformity because, say, it was to be used for competitive swimming over precisely measured distances rather than for ordinary, domestic use. It would be interesting to know what the effect of this would have been on the price of the pool or, indeed, on D's agreement to build it at all.

It is exactly the same defect of assuming that a contract leads to absolute commitment to perform that leads to the perceived injustice in respect of a performance which contradicts the obligation undertaken, as in *Wrotham Park* itself. The point at issue could be put in two ways: a floodgates argument[7] or a denial that there is anything to worry about. First, if we

3   On the current views of those in practice on this matter see IE Jacob, 'Is Near Enough Good Enough?' (1995) 139 Solicitors' Journal 676, p 677.

4   One can imagine circumstances which make the absoluteness of the obligation practically relevant, such as D encountering subsidence of such an extent that the pool either could not be built in that location or would require hundreds of tons of material to correct it. In these circumstances, the obligation would not, of course, be enforced, and D's liability would in any case be limited by voluntary liquidation. We are merely speculating about the consequences of absolute restitutionary liability.

5   R Cooter, 'Unity in Tort, Contract and Property: The Model of Precaution' (1985) 73 California Law Review 1, pp 11-19.

6   Cf the explanation of the second rule in *Hadley v Baxendale* in terms of C's disclosure of the risks D will bear under the contract, and of the remoteness rule as a default rule for the allocation of risk in general, in pp 91-93 above.

7   GH Treitel, *Law of Contract* (10th edn 1999) p 869.

restrict the category of doing the very thing one contracted not to do to obligations which would be protected by the award of an injunction, then we would just invite the repetition of the process by which the initial restriction of the hypothetical release payment to cases of refusal to grant an equitable remedy was undermined. Lord Nicholls quite rightly said that 'all express negative obligations' could come under this head, but one should add that *all* obligations can be regarded as of this sort, for when one breaches one is in a sense always doing what one contracted not to do.[8] A competent draftsman is all that would be needed to set up any obligation in a way that would attract the remedy.

The second point is that there is no general injustice. In respect of cases such as this, it is in effect argued that the goal of efficiency is not followed through in the argument for efficient breach because we cannot assess the efficiency of D's decision whether or not to breach by putting together two valuations of utility made at different times. If at the time of contracting the parties agree on an exchange of risk-taking, is not the effect of using information about post-contracting facts to reopen that agreed exchange? On this argument, it is not legitimate to take the revaluation of the use of his labour and resources made by D at the time of the breach, while holding C to his valuation made at the time of making the contract. Economic efficiency would require us to allow C also to revalue at the later time; and if he then increases his valuation of the utility to him of D's performance, the question should be whether the extra profit expected from D's alternative activity is more than sufficient to compensate C for the revised valuation of the loss which breach would cause him. The argument in terms of justice would be similar. Why should the law permit D to use later information to his advantage, while refusing C the opportunity to counter by doing the same?

These points have force but only on a mistaken understanding of the reasonable expectations of parties who enter into a contract. If the contract is made in the expectation that getting an agreement absolutely secures performance but the compensatory rules then defeat this expectation and allow only nominal damages, this seems unjust. But, of course, if C contracted with the benefit of good advice about the way the normal compensatory damages rules worked and the difficulties of obtaining literal enforcement, there would be no perceived injustice.[9] If C wanted

8   *Whitwood Chemical Co v Hardman* [1891] 2 Ch 416 at 426: 'If I agree with a man to be at a certain place at a certain time, I impliedly agree that I will not be anywhere else at the same time'. This issue is discussed in general at pp 200-208 above.

9   It is obvious that this is the obverse of the difficulties that the classical law of contract has had in recognising legitimate contract modifications, which that law rules out because of the existing obligations rule which is itself grounded in too absolute a view of the nature of a contractual obligation to perform.

a higher level of protection, he could contract for this stricter (though again not absolute) liability.[10] Between commercial parties it would be simply a matter of negotiation in which stipulating a price for renegotiation is one response to a stricter default rule. If C has, or is likely to obtain, an order of specific performance or an injunction in his favour, he may indeed be able to negotiate a price for releasing D from the (actual or potential) order, where the cost of D's complying with the order would exceed the loss which C would suffer from not getting the benefit of D's performance.[11]

But, of course, in any negotiation for a contract which contemplates renegotiation, D will adjust the price he is prepared to accept accordingly. With proper advice about the level of assurance of performance one actually gets by making a contract, the insuperable problems we have noted above in retrospectively fixing the price of a hypothetical release simply disappear because the problem is identified in advance and can be dealt with by negotiation. If competent parties agree to fix a release price, there can be no ground consistent with the values of the law of contract on which this agreement can or should be unpicked. If they do not agree to do this, this also should be accepted because it represents the parties' agreement to let the windfall lie where it accrues. If the court *ex post* in effect orders specific performance when the parties contracted in the expectation of compensatory damages, its order would substantially alter the agreed exchange of risk-taking which the parties contemplated at the time of contracting. The price demanded by D would have been substantially greater (or he would not have agreed at all) if he had expected his promise to be specifically enforced.

The extent of the error at work emerges in a passage of Lord Woolf's judgment in the Court of Appeal's hearing of *Blake*. In *City of New Orleans v Firemen's Charitable Association*,[12] D provided a perfectly satisfactory firefighting service to C but, after the expiry of the contract, C discovered that D had done so with less equipment than was stipulated in the contract. D made a considerable saving by doing this. It is possible to argue that D breached by failing to provide the extra security that, presumably, the contracted level of equipment might have furnished, but no such argument was mounted and C accepted that D had satisfactorily performed, or, to put it this way round, had not breached. It was held, and affirmed, that C

10 Subject to the present rules regulating, sometimes quite wrongly, the stipulation of damages. See ch 9 above.

11 C may similarly be able to negotiate an amount above his loss if there is a probability that the court will award him damages at the cost of getting substitute performance from a third person.

12 9 So 486 (1891).

had no cause of action when seeking to recover the money D had saved.[13] Lord Woolf[14] believes this decision is wrong:

> Justice surely demands an award of substantial damages in such a case, and the amount of expenditure which the defendant has saved by breach provides an appropriate measure of damages. This could be achieved by presuming that the plaintiff has suffered a loss of an amount corresponding to the amount by which he has been overcharged for the service actually provided [and] surely [the] preferable [way of doing this would be] to award restitutionary damages.[15]

Lord Woolf's belief that D breached this contract when he did not is highly significant.[16] From the point of view of 'justice' viewed not only after the event but when, surely unusually, all the facts have come to hand, one might think there is a problem here. But contracts are not made *sub specie aeternitatis*. They are made in situations in which the existence of positive transaction costs leads to bounded rationality and the negotiations by which one seeks what one wants from the contract never give perfect assurance that one will get it. If one does not get exactly what one wanted out of a freely negotiated contract, one has to put up with this unless one can show a breach. This not entirely obscure doctrine is called freedom of contract. One can barely imagine the haste with which Lord Woolf would himself have denied that C had a cause of action were C to have denied the existence of the contract at all because D had furnished inadequate consideration, or that the contract was unfair, or even (the ground that possibly but not necessarily might have substance in a reformed law of contract) that D had not bargained in good faith.[17]

13  The report does not allow one to say with absolute confidence what C sought to recover.

14  Making no reference to *White Arrow Express Ltd v Lamey's Distribution Ltd* (1996) 15 Tr LR 69.

15  *A-G v Blake*, CA, above p 256, n 8 at 458D-E. Lord Woolf's specific remedy would encounter the problems of total disgorgement.

16  Lord Woolf is led to this case by Jones, 'The Recovery of Benefits Gained from a Breach of Contract', p 455. Jones also seems wrongly to believe that D breached and C was prevented from recovering only because he had suffered no loss.

17  In *Blake*, that a breach is 'deliberate and cynical' is repeatedly stated not to be a sufficient ground for the award of the restitutionary remedy. *A-G v Blake*, CA, above p 256, n 8 at 457H; HL, above p 256, n 6 at 286E. We would suggest, however, that it is precisely in giving some greater force to an obligation to bargain and perform in good faith that an expanded notion of restitution may have place in supplementing the expectation interest. Cf Jackman, 'Restitution for Wrongs', above p 266, n 3, pp 322-323; R Nolan, 'Remedies for Breach of Contract: Specific Enforcement and Restitution', in FD Rose (ed), *Failure of Contracts* (1997), 35, pp 58-9 and, in general, SM Waddams, 'Restitution as Part of Contract Law', in

The mistake in the wrongful breach approach which so misleads Lord Woolf is to think that parties should be free to agree the terms of their contract but that the remedy for non-performance should be 'a matter of a normative theory external to the contract itself.'[18] Not only should choice of remedies be left to competent parties but, unless it is so left, agreement of terms is undermined, for part of the pricing of those terms is the costs of remedy for failure to perform the obligations those terms impose. The parties in *Ruxley* (were they properly advised) could have chosen a stricter liability rule but they did not. (The obverse could apply to a sale of a unique good to a consumer where specific performance would normally be awarded). There is no sensible ground on which the parties' choice, specific to the particular situation, should be altered in favour of a general, abstract rule:

> Damages rules should be understood solely as default provisions subject to variation by contract. The operative rules should be chosen by the parties for their own purposes, not by the law for its purposes ... On matters of both liability and remedy, the principle of freedom of contract should control so that all legal damages rules should be understood routinely as default provisions in lieu of express provisions, not as general rules of fairness or natural justice entitled to independent respect.[19]

When faced with a purported general rule that seeks to impose an inappropriate remedy, competent parties will contract out of that remedy. To some extent, then, bargaining around a new, restitutionary default rule by competent parties would tend to reduce that rule to insignificance. If the default rule is specific relief (or restitution to the same effect), then D can be released only if he negotiates with C and obtains his agreement (normally paying a price for the release). On the other hand, if the default rule is compensation for C's loss, D has a power unilaterally to discontinue performance, without negotiating his release or paying a price for it: the only condition imposed on this action by D is that he should be willing to pay damages (which will usually be assessed at C's net loss). In either case, the parties can contract out of the default rule.

But this is not to say that the rules are similarly efficient. For we suspect that the specific relief rule would often push the parties to fix a price about something they would rather ignore because it is too expensive to negotiate about it. This is very likely because making it necessary

---

A Burrows (ed), *Essays on the Law of Restitution* (1991) ch 8. On good faith generally see pp 604-606 below.

18  RA Epstein, 'Beyond Foreseeability: Consequential Damages in the Law of Contract' (1989) 18 Journal of Legal Studies 105, p 106.

19  Ibid, p 108.

expressly to deal with release gives too much scope for strategic bargaining, with each party holding out for too large a share of the benefit to D of his release, with the transaction costs mounting all the time they negotiate.[20] Having a default rule based on the present, somewhat confused, rules about the various forms of literal enforcement (now including restitution) would have an adverse effect on transaction costs. The less certain the judicial outcome, the less clear is the guidance to the parties, and the stronger the position of the party with greater resources to contest the matter. The discretion given to the court in granting specific relief means that (except with purchases of land) the parties face considerable uncertainty in predicting the decision. Only after an order has been made can negotiations be conducted against a background of certainty as to the strict legal position. Judicial discretion may lead to tailor-made decisions in court, but only at the expense of increasing the transaction costs of settling disputes before going to court: a trade-off must be made between these objectives. Transaction costs in settling disputes where the judicial outcome is predictable (eg a claim for a debt) must be lower than those over a claim to specific relief.

Once the breach of contract has been admitted, it is likely that the transaction costs involved in the parties settling a damages claim will also be lower, since, firstly, the range of possible outcomes is wider in a claim for specific relief, whereas it is usually certain that C will be awarded some damages, the dispute being over the amount; and, secondly, in a damages claim under existing rules the negotiations are about the assessment of C's loss, and not over a price for his releasing D from the prospect that specific relief might be granted to C. Even after a court order has been made, the subsequent transaction costs are likely to be higher with specific performance since D may wish to negotiate for a release for which C will demand a price, whereas with a damages award there is little scope for further negotiations. (C can only appeal to a higher court.) If the new default rule so increases transaction costs that it prevents agreement on the basic exchange or, as we suspect, typically has to be ousted, this would be evidence for the retention of the existing default rule which, we suggest, *is* the existing rule because it represents what competent commercial parties usually want, but must be a position from which they can contract away.

It is essential to appreciate that there is a very great difference between enforcing 'an agreement between the parties for a restitutionary damages remedy' and 'restitutionary damages perceived as a *general remedial response* to breach of contract'.[1] The former would be unobjectionable;

20  I Ayres and R Gertner, 'Filling Gaps in Incomplete Contracts: An Economic Theory of Default Rules' (1989) 94 Yale Law Journal 94.
1   Mitchell, 'Remedial Inadequacy in Contract and the Role of Restitutionary Damages', above p 263, n 8, p 134.

the latter entirely mistaken. Between commercial parties who wished to do this, the shift to the higher standard of liability should simply be a matter of agreement. Of course, the necessary negotiation might not be a practical matter in consumer contracts,[2] and it is highly arguable that consumer contracts for building works and similar services should contain an implied term giving a special degree of assurance of complete performance. Such a possibility has already been discussed in connection with the use of the entire obligation rule in such contracts in chapter 3,[3] and giving consumers a wider power to withhold payment in this way rather than adjust the payment they would receive in lieu of performance seems to us to be a far less complicated reform more addressed to the real problems of consumers. A generalised restitutionary remedy seems to us much more likely to increase unmet legal need than consumer satisfaction.

The effect of the proposed restitutionary reform would be to reverse the default rule for quantification from one broadly of compensation (subject to mitigation) to one of restitution (and stricter performance); the very purpose of the performance interest. The result of such a change would be to increase the present incentives on D actually to perform without resort to litigation. Whilst we have no objection in principle to this,[4] in this country no reason has been given for it other than the one thrown up by abstract restitutionary reasoning.[5] The question whether promisees in general are dissatisfied with the current rate of default by promisors is an empirical one on which virtually no evidence is available. Any, in effect, extension of literal enforcement or extension of a necessity to pay for release from it would need to be based on related issues of public policy which should be openly debated.[6] In the absence of the requisite

---

2    J O'Sullivan, 'Loss and Gain at Greater Depth: The Implications of the *Ruxley* Decision', in FD Rose (ed), *Failure of Contracts* (1997) 1, p 7.

3    See pp 46-48 above. Restitutionary arguments, it will be recalled, have been marshalled *against* trying to secure complete performance in this case.

4    Indeed, it has been argued in ch 9 above that this is a legitimate purpose of agreed damages clauses and that the present law on penalties that might render unenforceable some clauses to this purpose is wrong.

5    In the US literature, the case for general specific performance has not been argued on the grounds of securing more complete performances but on the grounds of reducing the transaction costs of (re)negotiating contracts when D contemplates breach or breaches: A Schwartz, 'The Case for Specific Performance' (1979) 89 Yale Law Journal 271.

6    Nolan, 'Remedies for Breach of Contract: Specific Enforcement and Restitution', above p 278, n 17, p 59. Crucial ancillary questions would have to be addressed if one really did wish to make performance strict. Eg should more promisees than at present be given access to the coercive powers of the state via contempt proceedings? Should more promisors be deprived of the potential protection of insolvency law (which is available in respect of debt or damages), and, in the event of their insolvency, should more promisees gain priority over the other creditors of promisors?

empirical evidence one can only speculate, but it seems to us likely that, in contracts between commercial parties, to adopt the restitutionary position would be to establish a default rule which such parties would normally have to oust through negotiation. If this is so it would, of course, be a bad policy mistake, for it would defeat the economisation of transaction costs which it is the purpose of default rules to effect.

At the cost of belabouring a point, we must add the following. All this reasoning assumes that C and the court have knowledge of D's profit even when it is not based on a subtraction from C. There is, of course, no necessity for C to have this knowledge and, if disgorgement were the default rule, there would be every reason for D to ensure that the profit was kept secret, which may well be easy in the absence of subtraction. It was just this that actually was at issue in the extensive litigation in *Teacher v Calder*. Are wrongs to be corrected only when chance leads to their discovery or would the general application of the restitutionary remedy lead to the imposition of disclosure requirements, and a means for monitoring compliance, with the attendant growth in transaction costs?[7]

## The proper limits of restitution following non-performance of a contractual obligation

Given the empirical investigations revealing that actually inefficient breaches may take place under the guise of efficiency and that the current rules do in some cases leave D uncompensated even when breach is efficient, we acknowledge that this is a matter which should be the subject of further (empirical) investigation. But not only is this a very different matter from attempting to correct an abstract wrong, but, paradoxically, such an investigation will make progress only if the naïve assumption is dropped that contractual obligations always should and could be performed (now formalised as the 'performance interest'). It must be recognised that a contract is but a legal institution guiding exchange and not an essential component of that exchange, and therefore the extent to which a contract should and could compel performance is always a live issue in any evaluation of potentially welfare enhancing reforms of the law of contract remedies.[8] It would appear that the main transaction cost preventing the requisite negotiation between the parties is the cost of

7   Cf the consequences of the growth of interest in tracing, which has not, to our knowledge, been the subject of any empirical study of the relative costs and benefits of the use of this device, although that those benefits have substantial costs is obvious.

8   D Harris, 'Incentives to Perform, or Break, Contracts' (1992) 45(2) Current Legal Problems 29.

obtaining correct advice[9] which points out that contractual obligations normally are not absolute and are priced in contemplation of the possibility of breach.[10] The typical advice they now receive unquestioningly assumes *pacta sunt servanda*,[11] and it is this misunderstanding that is driving the present restitutionary perception of a serious defect in the law of contract remedies by grossly exaggerating the extent of that defect as anything other than a formal inconsistency. What is utterly neglected in the restitutionary jurisprudence is an awareness that '[s]ocial efficiency ... requires [parties] to restrain [their] reliance in light of the ... probability of breach'.[12]

By seeking to make the law conform to their mistaken understanding of it, those presently advocating restitutionary reform are threatening to do a serious mischief to the law.[13] We therefore believe that the argument for the extension of a restitutionary remedy for efficient breach, and *a fortiori* the general replacement of compensatory by restitutionary quantification of damages for breach of contract, is very weak, indeed, it is almost entirely without merit. If the aim is not to correct abstract 'wrongs' but to provide workable remedies in support of commercial exchange, the extension of restitutionary remedies would be extremely ill-advised. Such an extension simply misunderstands the function of contract remedies and, leaving aside the problems the restitutionary remedies might themselves create, it could be done only at the cost of sacrificing those aspects of the existing law that make breach 'efficient' in the first place. It certainly should not be claimed that the results achieved by the present law are always perfectly efficient, for there are cases in which inefficient breach is not prevented, and, even when breach is efficient, the overall efficiency is sometimes secured at the cost of leaving C uncompensated for part of his loss. But because it largely proceeds in pursuit of an outcome deemed just on abstract rather than empirical grounds, the restitutionary

---

9   And, of course, adjudication which respects such advice.

10  This is so to the extent that the advice remains confined to the general principles of contract, but, of course, a sufficiently important client will be referred to the whole repertoire of techniques for getting greater security of performance as a separate matter of 'commercial law'. The extent of the error of treating commercial law separately from the general principles of contract is made evident in the notion of the performance interest. Some of these security techniques are discussed in ch 3 above. For a discussion of one technique which identifies the theoretical issue clearly see CR Knoeber, 'An Alternative Mechanism to Assure Contractual Reliability' (1983) 12 Journal of Legal Studies 333.

11  Or at least unquestioningly states it even if then to, quite rightly, depart from it, as was the case in Lord Mustill's speech at 360 in *Ruxley*'s case, above p 259, n 5.

12  Cooter, 'Unity in Tort, Contract and Property: The Model of Precaution', above p 275, n 5, p 13.

13  D Campbell, 'Classification and the Crisis of the Common Law' (1999) 26 Journal of Law and Society 369, p 377.

argument does not attempt to weigh the inevitable imperfections of the alternatives. If one does weigh these alternatives,[14] the shortcomings of compensatory damages are not nearly as great as those of general restitutionary damages would be.

14  R O'Dair, 'Restitutionary Damages for Breach of Contract and the Theory of Efficient Breach: Some Reflections' (1993) 46(2) Current Legal Problems 113 does weigh the alternatives to reach the opposite conclusion to the one advanced here.

# Section 2
# Tort: remedies for wrongdoing

# Part 5
# General issues in tort remedies

# 18 Objectives of the law

## Introduction

A brief review of the objectives of the law of torts is necessary for an understanding of the remedies. It will focus mainly on the tort of negligence, in view of its importance in practice, especially in cases of personal injury.

## Defining and protecting certain rights and freedoms

The first role of tort law is to define a number of legally-protected interests which the individual citizen may enjoy, and then to define and provide the degree of legal protection to which he is entitled if others interfere with the enjoyment of those interests. The obvious case is the protection given to proprietary and possessory interests in land and chattels.[1] The law specifies what these interests are and who is entitled to them. The defining role is clear where C seeks a declaratory judgment which sets out his rights against D but does not order the latter to do (or refrain from doing) anything. The declaration is an authoritative statement of the legal position between the parties, on which the parties can base their future actions.[2] If D acts in a way which contravenes the legal position laid down in the declaration he will usually become liable to an ordinary action leading to a coercive judgment. The defining role of the law of torts is illustrated by the use of injunctions in private nuisance. C claims an order

1  The extent of personal freedom is defined by the torts of false imprisonment, battery and assault (and by the writ of *habeas corpus*).
2  In the defining role of the law, the blameworthy nature of D's conduct should in principle be irrelevant.

prohibiting a specified level of interference with the use and enjoyment of his land. The order looks to the future, and tells D that if he thereafter allows certain activities to cause interference of a specified nature or beyond a specified level, eg of noise, C may return to court to ask that D should be coerced into compliance by the contempt jurisdiction of the court. Other tort actions may be used in a similar way. An action for trespass to land may be used simply to determine who is entitled to possession of a piece of land, eg in a boundary dispute. The trespass action is merely the vehicle by which C seeks a judicial ruling that he is entitled to possession, as where only nominal damages are sought.

Corrective justice is a concept built on the definition of rights. It is based on the belief that the autonomy of the individual depends on the protection of his rights. Corrective justice requires that the balance should be restored when the victim's previous position has been disturbed by wrongdoing: 'rendering to each person whatever redress is required because of the violation of his rights by another'.[3] This approach sees the law of tort as protecting the individual freedom of citizens; that freedom should be restricted only when harm is caused to another. Actually restoring the victim to his previous position is often not possible, so that the redress is the 'second-best' solution of giving money as a substitute for what has been lost. But money compensation is often a poor equivalent of what has been lost.

## Regulating behaviour: deterrence

In setting the standard of conduct which avoids the label of 'negligent' the law is regulating behaviour. Similarly, with other torts, the law decides the types of conduct which are not acceptable to society and should be deterred by legal sanctions. Deterrence of carelessness is based on the intuition that people will take more care to avoid causing harm if they must pay for any harm due to their negligence. The dominant approach of economists to tort law is that it should induce the 'efficient' (or socially desirable) level of precautions against avoidable harm to others.[4] D is free to choose whether he should engage in a particular activity, for example driving a car, and, if he does, he may choose which level of precautions to undertake – in the case of car driving, at which speed, with which level of built-in safety devices, with which level of regular maintenance, and so on. When deciding whether to drive at all, he will

3    RA Epstein, 'Nuisance Law: Corrective Justice and Its Utilitarian Constraints' (1979) 8 Journal of Legal Studies 49, pp 50, 99.
4    See eg S Shavell, *Economic Analysis of Accident Law* (1987); G Calabresi, *The Costs of Accidents* (1970); AM Polinsky, *An Introduction to Law and Economics* (2nd edn 1989).

automatically weigh the benefits against the costs of driving. In estimating costs he will naturally count those which fall directly on him (internal costs), not only the cost of the car itself and its running costs, but also the risk of injury to himself if he is involved in an accident. His overall expected benefit must exceed his overall expected cost before he will choose to drive at all. The risk of an accident will depend on the probability that it might occur, multiplied by the expected cost, if it did occur. If he can see that some precautionary steps will reduce the risk to himself (for example, driving a more expensive but safer car, or driving at a lower speed), he will balance the extra cost of those steps so that it does not exceed the extra benefit to him, that is, the amount by which the risk to himself is reduced.

The economist argues that the same approach should be used for an external cost, whenever D should see that his proposed activity will create the risk of loss or injury to others. Without some form of pressure, many might ignore these external costs. The law ensures that the expected harm to others (the probability of causing them harm, multiplied by the cost of that harm) is added to the internal costs which D will take into account. (The law compels him to 'internalise' what would otherwise be a cost to others.) The internalisation will occur whether the liability rule is based on the negligence standard or on strict liability. Under either regime, he should, as a rational decision-maker, determine the 'efficient' level of care in the same way. The economic approach is easiest to understand when we can think of care as a series of incremental units along an increasing scale of care, as in the example of reducing speed, or of increasing expenditure on safety. The theory is that D should choose the cost-minimising level of care against accidents: that efficiency is reached when the cost of the last additional unit of care exactly equals the value of the extra saving in expected accident costs. The extra unit of care might reduce the probability of an accident occurring, or it might reduce the severity of the expected harm (or both). In theory, there should always be a point at which it is no longer cost-effective to incur the cost of an additional unit of care, because it would produce only a smaller reduction in expected accident costs. At this point, it is cheaper for society as a whole to bear the remaining risk of incurring the expected accident costs than to spend more money on further reductions in the risk. (For the remaining accidents which occur despite the adoption of this 'efficient' level of care, the cost will be borne by victims under a negligence rule, but by actors under a strict liability rule: the cost-justified level of precautions remains the same, despite the different outcome in who bears the cost of any accident not avoided by that level of precautions.)[5]

---

5   See pp 412-427 below. The goal of deterrence could be achieved without any compensation being paid to the victims of negligence. So long as the cost of

*Appraisal of deterrence in personal injury accident cases*

Chapter 24 below reports that in practice damages are recovered by only a small proportion of victims in cases of personal injury caused by accidents. This fact reduces the deterrent effect of the law to a symbolic exercise. *Some* careless actors are held liable as an example to others. But the 'rational' actor will discount the deterrent effect by the small percentage of cases in which his possible carelessness will in fact lead to the payment of damages. No empirical study has been conducted in the UK to indicate what proportion of injuries caused by negligence lead to the recovery of damages. But the large Harvard study of medical malpractice in New York in 1990[6] showed that 3.7% of hospital patients suffered an 'adverse event', of which 27.6% were due to negligence: ie about 1% of all patients were injured by some negligent treatment. However, only one in sixteen of this group obtained any damages – tort liability was not imposed in 94% of the identified instances of negligence. It is unlikely that the situation in the UK is very different. Deterrence of medical negligence by the tort system operates in only about 6% of the instances of negligence identified by other doctors.

The deterrent effect of the law is blunted by the onus of proof being placed on C – no matter how careless D might have been, he can escape responsibility if C cannot prove it. Again, D may often escape responsibility for his carelessness because luckily he causes no harm; even where he does cause harm to C, the amount of damages is related to the degree of harm he in fact causes, not to the relative blameworthiness of his conduct. Serious negligence may cause little loss, but a trivial mistake may cause catastrophic loss. Deterrence, however, should operate *before* the accident occurs, when D is deciding how to act, and the degree of deterrence needed should depend on the potential risk.

The economic theory of the deterrence of reasonably avoidable accidents depends on the actor being held liable to pay *all* the costs of the accidents which he causes by failing to take a cost-justified measure of avoidance. If only some of the external costs are imposed on him, others in a similar position in the future will be tempted to ignore part of the expected costs which they should take into account, and so might take less care than is socially justified. The desirable level of deterrence will

---

negligently-caused accidents is imposed on the negligent injurers, the same deterrent effect would occur no matter who received the transfer – it could benefit the Exchequer, be paid to charity, or go to swell funds to which all accident victims have access on a no-fault basis. From the point of view of potential tortfeasors, negligent actions can have a 'price' attached to them no matter to whom the 'price' is to be paid.

6    *Patients, Doctors and Lawyers: Medical Injury, Malpractice Litigation and Patient Compensation in New York* (1990). The medical records of over 31,000 patients in New York hospitals were assessed by medically-qualified researchers.

not be achieved *either* if the negligent actor can avoid some of the costs he imposes, *or* if he can avoid paying any external costs because he escapes paying any damages at all. If an accident victim fails for any reason to recover the full cost from a person who was in fact negligent, the signal to other potential tortfeasors must be weakened. In Chapter 22 below it is shown that judicial awards often fall below 'full' compensation for personal injuries: eg the discount for future contingencies may be too high; future increases in the living standards of earners are ignored, as are any future changes in tax levels. Chapter 24 shows that settlements out of court usually lead to levels of damages below those of judicial awards.

### General or 'market' deterrence

The insulation of D from the full cost of his carelessness does not, however, prevent a form of general deterrence from operating through the market. If all those who engage in an activity have to pay an annual premium to cover the cost of fault-caused accidents arising in that activity, the premium-payers as a class are bearing the cost of those accidents, and that cost is therefore being internalised. This is a form of risk-relationship, under which those who benefit from a particular activity bear the cost of accidents arising in that activity, eg liability insurance for motorists, employers or manufacturers. For Calabresi,[7] minimising the total social cost of accidents should be the goal: this cost depends on various factors – the number of accidents, the severity of their consequences, the cost to society of compensating the victims (including the transaction costs) and the cost of avoiding accidents. Those engaging in a particular activity should be given an incentive to minimise the cost of accidents by taking steps to avoid them whenever that would be efficient, viz when the cost of avoidance is less than the expected cost of the accident. If the total cost of engaging in the activity went up as the result of internalising the cost of accidents, that might reduce the level of that activity in society. Even if various categories of activity and those who benefit from them could be identified,[8] the problem remains that under the present negligence rule the cost of only a small proportion of the accidents arising in that activity are internalised, viz those caused by fault, leaving the cost of non-tortious accidents to be borne by the actual victims or by the community as a whole. In virtually all categories of activity open to D, most of the cost of accidents is externalised under the present law.

---

7   *The Cost of Accidents,* above n 4.
8   P Cane, *Atiyah's Accidents, Compensation and the Law* (6th edn 1999) pp 378 et seq.

There are also many instances of externalities where part of C's losses is left on third parties who have no claim against D for reimbursement. Most medical, hospital and rehabilitation expenses fall on the NHS (and thus on the taxpayer);[9] the cost of sick pay falls on employers; the income tax, national insurance and pension contributions which C would have paid on his lost earnings are losses borne by taxpayers and the remaining contributors; the cost of payments under life, accident, and disability insurance policies falls on premium-payers; and the cost of charitable assistance falls on voluntary contributors. The existence of these many externalities prevents defendants or premium-payers from bearing the actual costs of accidents, and thus distorts the operation of general deterrence.

## Inquests into accidents

Tort law has a limited role as ombudsman to investigate what went wrong to cause an accident or mishap. Although public officials may decide whether an inquest should be held into fatal accidents, aeroplane crashes and other disasters, the private citizen may himself take the initiative in seeking a tort 'inquest'. But this role of tort is restricted: D can prevent a public inquiry by meeting C's claim in full, and the tort investigation does not focus on *future* accident prevention. The court investigates only those aspects of D's conduct which C selects for scrutiny, and the relevant standards are those current at the time of the accident. It is not a forward-looking enquiry directed at discovering on behalf of the public at large whether cost-effective steps could be taken to reduce the risk in future. Between the time of the accident and the 'tort liability' trial there could be technological advances which completely alter the situation, so that the costly investigation of D's responsibility at the time of the accident may contribute nothing to future safety: the whole of D's method of working or his type of production may have changed; indeed, it may even happen that no one is any longer producing the item in question, or engaging in the same activity.

## Compensation

Some legal writers claim that one of the main objectives of tort law is to compensate those injured in accidents. When account is taken of liability

9    However, under the Road Traffic (NHS Charges) Act 1999 the tortfeasor must pay the full cost (up to a ceiling of £10,000) of the NHS medical treatment of those injured in road traffic accidents.

insurance, the formulation of the compensation goal is revised to be the distribution of the cost of compensating accident victims among a wide group of premium-payers. But the law does not wish to discourage activities which in general benefit society. Hence the negligence standard was developed under which people were encouraged to engage in any type of activity by the knowledge that, even if they did cause injury to others, they would not be liable to compensate them in the absence of fault. Adoption of the negligence rule seriously restricted the role of tort as a compensation system, because it meant that C's loss is to be shifted to D (or to D's liability insurance) only where C can prove that D was at fault: in all other situations, the victim is left uncompensated.

Within the overall compensation goal, the House of Lords has recently used the concept of 'distributive justice' to justify their refusal to put some accident victims into a preferential group entitled to compensation, while other equally deserving victims are denied any compensation. So policemen 'rescuers' at the Hillsborough football stadium disaster, who were not themselves within the range of foreseeable physical injury, should not 'have the right to compensation for psychiatric injury out of public funds while the bereaved relatives are sent away with nothing'.[10] Nor should they be treated differently from first-aid workers or ambulance men attending the stadium who failed to obtain compensation.[11]

Apart from proof of D's fault, various rules restrict the achievement of providing compensation to accident victims. For instance, the rules on remoteness obviously divide C's losses into those for which D must pay and those which C must himself bear;[12] and the application of contributory negligence will also leave on C some of his loss, in respect of which he is unlikely to carry first-party insurance.[13]

The goal of compensation in personal injury claims is appraised in chapter 24 below.

---

10   *Frost v Chief Constable of South Yorkshire Police* [1999] 2 AC 455 at 510 per Lord Hoffmann. See also 502-504.
11   Ibid at 506, 510-511. See also *McFarlane v Tayside Health Board* [2000] 2 AC 59 at 82, per Lord Steyn: 'distributive justice ... requires a focus on the just distribution of burdens and losses among members of a society'.
12   See ch 20 below.
13   See pp 308-309 below.

# 19 Causation, mitigation and contributory negligence

## Limits on recovery of damages

As in claims for damages for breach of contract,[1] there are restrictions (or 'control mechanisms') on the extent of damages recoverable in tort. C must prove that the loss in question was *caused* by D's tort; even if the consequence in question does meet the legal tests for causation, it may be held to be *too remote* a consequence of the tort for damages to be awarded against D – if was a freak or unusual consequence; finally, D may show that C himself was *partly at fault* in causing the loss, which entitles the court to apportion the loss between the parties. The result of using these legal tests is to deny C entitlement to recover damages for part, or even all, of his loss. In theory, the question of causation is prior to that of remoteness. Only if D has caused a particular loss to C should the court proceed to consider whether that loss is nevertheless too remote for C to be entitled to recover damages from D. But since in regard to a particular category of loss both tests may produce the same result – a refusal to award damages – judges sometimes rule that the loss is 'too remote' without bothering to decide whether it was even a 'consequence'. If C suffers only one type of harm, his claim will fail whether the court says it was not caused by the tort or was too remote a consequence. But if there is more than one type of harm suffered by C, each type must be separately tested both by causation[2] and by remoteness. The result could be that D must pay for some, but not all the different types of harm in question. (Sometimes the duty of care in negligence is itself narrowly defined so as to refer only to

1   See pp 84-87 above.
2   House of Lords' authority supports the rule that causation must be tested separately in relation to the different types of damage: *Hotson v East Berkshire Area Health Authority* [1987] AC 750.

a specific type of causation and a specific category of consequence. This more recent development is discussed in the next chapter.)[3]

## Causation

Causation is rarely a problem in practice. The usual problem confronting C is to prove that the action by D which obviously caused the harm can be labelled 'negligent' (or satisfies the criteria for liability under some other tort). If he can prove that, it is usually obvious that the negligence caused the harm. As the leading authorities, Hart and Honoré, point out,[4] in practice causation is a disputed issue only when a number of separate actions by different people contributed to the harmful outcome, or where the harm occurred in an unusual set of circumstances. In a legal context, voluntary human conduct is more likely to be selected as a legal cause of harm because this enables responsibility to be attributed. But a court need not examine all possible causes of a given harm, since it is required to decide only whether the particular cause alleged by C was or was not a sufficient cause for the purpose of attributing responsibility to D. It need not be the sole cause: it need only be 'a material contributory cause'.[5] 'Where the wrong is a tort, it is clearly settled that the wrongdoer cannot excuse himself by pointing to another cause. It is enough that the tort should be a cause and it is unnecessary to evaluate competing causes and ascertain which of them is dominant.'[6]

Although the onus of proving causation is on C, he need prove only that it was 'more probable than not' (more than 50% likely) that D's tort caused the harm to him.[7] Occasionally the law comes to the aid of C when the causation is uncertain. Where a situation is under the exclusive control of D or his employees, and such an accident as C suffered would not be expected unless he or they were negligent, the court may infer negligence unless D can show that it happened without any negligence on his part or that of his employees (the *res ipsa loquitur* doctrine).[8] Occasionally, in

3   See pp 322-328 below.
4   HLA Hart and T Honoré, *Causation in the Law* (2nd edn) chs 6, 8.
5   *Hotson v East Berkshire Area Health Authority*, above n 2 at 237, but there may be 'causal apportionment' in assessing damages, eg deafness caused by excessive noise in C's working conditions may lead to liability on his employer D, but D is liable only for a tortious or blameworthy source of noise; the court must attempt to apportion responsibility between it and non-tortious sources: *Thompson v Smiths Shiprepairers Ltd* [1984] QB 405.
6   *Heskell v Continental Express* [1950] 1 All ER 1033 at 1047.
7   *Hotson v East Berkshire Area Health Authority*, above n 2; *Wilsher v Essex Area Health Authority* [1988] AC 1074.
8   *Scott v London and St Katherine Docks Co* (1865) 3 H & C 596, 601. The doctrine usually enables the *agent* of the causation to be identified.

other circumstances, the court may draw an inference to assist C in proving causation.[9]

A simple 'but for' test is useful in eliminating possible causes from further consideration, i.e. it eliminates non-causal factors. Would C have suffered the harm 'but for' D's action?[10] If the answer is 'no', this does not mean that D's action satisfies the legal test, but merely that it is a possible cause. For instance, the 'but for' test cannot solve the problem where each of two or more causes could on its own have produced the harmful result. Since more positive tests are needed, the courts search for a 'real', 'material', 'direct' or 'effective' cause (in the USA the search is for a 'proximate' cause). In deciding whether the cause alleged by C is a sufficient legal cause, the judge bears in mind the purpose of the enquiry: can responsibility to pay be pinned on D, an identified human agent? The judge's purpose is not future accident prevention nor the better design of equipment: it is to decide whether D should be compelled to pay for a given harm. His selection is made against the background of the law of torts, and his experience of the kinds of causes identified in previous tort cases as justifiable grounds for imposing liability to pay. He works by analogy from the decided cases. Although the judge will be guided by the ordinary attribution of responsibility made by the layman – which in turn will be subject to moral overtones – he will in marginal or difficult cases also pay attention to questions of justice and policy. Will it further the aims of the particular tort, such as deterrence of anti-social conduct, or compensation through risk-spreading or liability insurance, to attribute to D responsibility to pay? Social policy issues may arise in respect of both causation and remoteness. For some policy reason the courts may wish to say that in law $x$ cannot be treated as the cause of $y$; they might equally well say that in law $y$ is too remote a consequence of $x$ or that D owed C no duty of care in respect of $y$. These policy issues are discussed below.[11]

## Medical or scientific evidence

In some circumstances the layman cannot say how the harm came about, and prolonged medical or scientific evidence is needed to ascertain whether D was in any way responsible for the situation in which the harm arose. The causation of diseases is often particularly difficult to establish, because medical knowledge has not advanced sufficiently to enable the

---

9    See p 299 below.

10    An illustration is *Performance Cars v Abraham* [1962] 1 QB 33 (see p 532 below).

11    Pp 322-328. Special questions about causation arise in the so-called economic torts, which are discussed at pp 563-572 below.

cause or causes to be identified.[12] Frequently, a medical expert can say only that a factor for which D is responsible is a cause of a particular disease in a certain percentage of instances, but can say nothing definite about C's case. Apart from a few marginal situations discussed below, the law of torts has not developed any efficient mechanism to help C in this type of situation where any one of a number of different factors could have caused the harm.

If D's tort substantially increased the risk that C might suffer a disease or medical complication, the causal test is satisfied.[13] But the burden of proof is not reversed: even if D negligently created a risk and C's disease fell within that risk, D is not to be held liable merely because *he* cannot show that it had another cause.[14] D's substantially increasing the risk may, however, assist C where medical science cannot yet identify a precise cause of C's harm. So where D's action, in breach of his duty to C, materially enhanced the pre-existing risk of C's suffering a particular harm,[15] but the evidence could not show positively whether C would have suffered it even if D had fulfilled his duty, the House of Lords was willing to infer that D's action materially contributed to the harm.[16] On this basis, D was held liable for his employee C's dermatitis, on the ground that D had failed to provide showers for him after his exposure to brick dust, a known cause of dermatitis: D's fault had increased the risk that a single factor might have caused the harm to C. However medical research may indicate that there are several independent causes, each of which might have caused C's harm, some 'innocent' (or non-tortious) but one which is due to negligence. In this situation, C will fail unless he can prove *either* that in his particular case D's negligence was in fact the cause – this is often impossible to prove – *or* that the research statistics show that such negligence is the cause in more than half the cases observed in the research. In one case, the Court of Appeal held D liable for giving excess oxygen to C, since this added a further possibility to the list of risk factors which might have caused his blindness.[17] But the House of Lords reversed the decision and reverted to the traditional test that C must prove the causal

---

12   J Stapleton, *Disease and the Compensation Debate* (1986).

13   *McGhee v National Coal Board* [1973] 1 WLR 1.

14   *Wilsher v Essex Area Health Authority*, above n 7.

15   This principle in *McGhee v National Coal Board*, above n 13, does not apply where the medical evidence cannot establish that D's tortious action was capable of causing or aggravating C's harm: *Kay v Ayrshire and Arran Health Board* [1987] 2 All ER 417, HL.

16   '[A] failure to take steps which would bring about a material reduction of the risk involves ... a substantial contribution to the injury': *McGhee v National Coal Board*, above n 13 at 1014. See the discussion in Stapleton, above n 12, pp 46–9.

17   *Wilsher v Essex Area Health Authority*, above n 7.

link between D's negligence and C's harm.[18] If either D1 or D2 alone caused C's injury, but C cannot prove which was the cause, C will fail, unless both were employed by the same employer who will then be vicariously liable without C having to identify the responsible person.[19]

## Multiple tortfeasors

If each of several Ds materially contributed to causing C's harm, but the evidence cannot separate the relative causal effect of each fault, each D will be liable to C for the whole harm; but as between themselves, the responsibility of the Ds will usually be attributed equally.[20] Where D1's negligence created a continuing danger (eg blocking a road at night) but D2 was later negligent in the situation in another way (eg driving too fast) both are likely to be held causes of the accident.[1] Where successive employers wrongfully exposed C to asbestos dust, each will be liable to the extent that he contributed towards C's disability (where that can be quantified): normally a time exposure basis will be used to quantify the extent of each D's liability.[2]

## Successive causes of disability

In a leading case, *Jobling v Associated Dairies Ltd*,[3] the evidence showed that at the time of the accident in which C was injured by D's tort, he suffered a dormant medical condition which would at some future time cause total incapacity for work. Three years after the accident, the condition did cause a disease which was wholly unrelated to his injury from the accident. Thus, a tortious cause first led to C's partial incapacity, but a supervening natural or non-tortious cause later led to his total incapacity.[4] The House of Lords held D liable for C's loss of earnings only for the period up to the time when he suffered the disease. Thereafter, D's tort could no longer be treated as a continuing cause of C's inability to earn. Usually, the future vicissitudes of life are taken into account by the court

---

18  [1988] AC 1074.
19  *Cassidy* v *Minister of Health* [1951] 2 QB 66.
20  *Fitzgerald v Lane* [1989] AC 328. (Any reduction for C's contributory negligence must be made *before* the court proceeds to apportion responsibility between the Ds inter se: ibid.)
1   *Rouse v Squires* [1973] QB 889. (Apportionment between D1 and D2 reflected their relative degrees of fault: 25% to 75%.)
2   *Holtby v Brigham and Cowan (Hull) Ltd* [2000] 3 All ER 421, CA.
3   [1982] AC 794.
4   When the second cause is itself tortious, C has some chance of recovering some damages from the second tortfeasor: *Baker v Willoughby* [1970] AC 467.

making an allowance in assessing future loss of earnings,[5] but when an event actually occurs before the trial (such as C's death through an unrelated cause) the court uses its knowledge in lieu of speculation. The present common law is incapable of responding adequately to the consequences of successive accidents and illnesses. Such a response is possible only from a comprehensive scheme of compensation for all disabled people, irrespective of the cause of their disabilities.[6] In respect of illness, the problems of proving causation through medical evidence are so serious that the victim is very rarely able to take advantage of the law of tort.[7]

## Omissions

Causation may be a difficult issue when it is D's failure to act on which C relies. In a case of an alleged omission, D's conduct is seen as failing to prevent harm to C from the consequences of a third party's action or of a situation of danger arising from no one's fault, eg D's failure to abate flooding on C's land.[8] The problem is that the court must assess the hypothetical consequences of the hypothetical action which D should have taken. So where D failed to meet his obligation to supply C with safety equipment, D may claim that C would not have used it even if it had been supplied. The courts have held that C must prove, on a balance of probabilities, that he would have used it;[9] but C may argue that he would have done so if D had met his obligation to give him adequate instruction or advice.[10] However, it can be argued that the courts should be seeking to implement the policy of the legislation requiring an employer to take safety measures, and not using causation to give him an escape route to avoid tortious liability.

The alleged causation of C's harm from D's omission is often the basis of a claim for medical negligence. So where a doctor negligently failed to admit someone to hospital who died five hours later, his widow's claim failed on the ground that he would have died even if he had been admitted and treated properly.[11] Where C complains of delay in treatment he must show that, on a balance of probabilities, the delay materially contributed

5   See p 358 below.
6   D Harris et al, *Compensation and Support for Illness and Injury* (1984) ch 12.
7   Stapleton, above n 12.
8   Cf the different views expressed in *East Suffolk Rivers Catchment Board v Kent* [1941] AC 74.
9   *McWilliams v Sir William Arrol and Co Ltd* [1962] 1 WLR 295.
10  *Bux v Slough Metals Ltd* [1974] 1 All ER 262.
11  *Barnett v Chelsea and Kensington Hospital Management Committee* [1969] 1 QB 428.

to his disability. In *Hotson's* case,[12] through D's negligence C's injury was not correctly diagnosed for five days, but even with prompt treatment there would have been a 75% risk of his developing the disability. The House of Lords held that C failed on the issue of causation: he had failed to establish, on a balance of probabilities, that when he first came to the hospital his condition was such that he would not develop the disability. But, as an American judge has put it, this approach is in effect 'a blanket release from liability for doctors and hospitals any time there was less than a 50% chance of survival, regardless of how flagrant the negligence'.[13]

When the complaint is that D failed to advise C to do something, C must show (hypothetically) that he would have acted on the advice. So a patient who says that her doctor failed to advise her about the risks of an operation must prove that, had she been informed, she would have refused to consent to the operation.[14] D's negligent omission may raise the question what *he* would have done, as where a doctor failed to attend a patient. In *Bolitho's* case,[15] if the doctor had attended and adopted a particular procedure, the patient would not have suffered brain damage. But the doctor established that if she had attended, she would not have adopted it. The House of Lords held that her negligent failure to attend had not caused the brain damage because she was able to show that a responsible body of professional opinion supported her hypothetical decision not to adopt the procedure.[16]

## Loss of a chance

Damages for C's loss of a chance are recoverable for a breach of contract;[17] the Court of Appeal has recently awarded such damages in tort where the loss depended on the hypothetical action of a third party.[18] Where D, a solicitor, negligently failed to advise C to include a warranty in the draft of an agreement, C could prove (on the balance of probabilities) that, had

---

12  *Hotson v East Berkshire Area Health Authority*, above n 2. (The House overturned the judge's ruling that C was entitled to damages for loss of the 25% chance of avoiding the disability. Cf pp 81-82, 299 above.)

13  *Herskovits v Group Health Cooperative of Puget Sound* 664 P 2d 474, 477 (1983).

14  *Thompson v Blake-James* [1998] Lloyd's Rep Med 187, CA.

15  *Bolitho v City and Hackney Health Authority* [1998] AC 232.

16  This is the *Bolam* test by which the doctor is held not to be negligent even though the majority professional opinion was to the contrary: [1957] 1 WLR 582. The House of Lords has accepted this test.

17  See pp 81-82 above.

18  *Allied Maples Group Ltd v Simmons & Simmons* [1995] 1 WLR 1602 (the case was decided in negligence although there was a contract between the parties) and *Spring v Guardian Assurance plc* [1995] 2 AC 296 at 327.

he been so advised, he would have tried to negotiate the inclusion of the warranty:[19] provided he could show that there was a real or substantial chance (which could be less than 50%) that the other party might have agreed to this, he could recover damages from D which reflected the loss of that chance.[20]

### Voluntary intervention by a third party

Hart and Honoré place great emphasis on voluntary human action as a factor which may break the chain of causation between D's tort and the harm suffered by C. Where a third party[1] freely chooses to intervene in the situation created by D's tort the responsibility for the consequences will normally lie with the third party. The 'voluntary' aspect of the intervening conduct is clearly a matter of degree depending on factors such as the extent of the actor's knowledge of the situation, his freedom of choice, and his ability to control the situation without pressure from others.[2] An intervention by a child will therefore seldom break the causation. A person is not acting voluntarily if he is suffering from concussion, or acting in self-defence or self-preservation,[3] eg jumping from a vehicle imperilled by D's tort.[4] Similarly, reasonable action by a third party to protect his own or another's[5] interests will not break the causation.[6] An instinctive act, one done without reflection, is not treated as voluntary. Similarly, causation is not negatived if the actor does not properly appreciate the danger arising from D's action, as where D negligently delivered some combustible material in error to C's premises, where it was set alight by a woman with a lighted cigarette who approached it without realising how combustible it was.[7] But the chain of causation will be broken if the third party acted recklessly rather than

19  Once C can prove that he was more likely than not (more than 50%) to have acted, the court proceeds on the assumption that he *would* have acted.
20  The damages are discounted by reference to the percentage chance of the third party's accepting the warranty.
1   D cannot argue that his own intervening acts broke the causation between his tort and C's harm: *Ward v Cannock Chase District Council* [1986] Ch 546 at 571.
2   The so-called 'economic torts' illustrate pressure from D: see pp 563-572 below.
3   *Scott v Shepherd* (1773) 2 Wm Bl 892. (D threw a squib into a crowd, with the result that, in order to avert the risk of it exploding in their faces, several threw it away until it finally exploded and injured C. D was held liable.)
4   Cf *Jones v Boyce* (1816) 1 Stark 493 ('in the agony of the moment' C jumped off D's coach when the horses ran away).
5   As in the rescue cases: see *Haynes v Harwood* [1935] 1 KB 146.
6   *The Oropesa* [1943] P 32. D will be relieved from liability only if the third party's action was unreasonable, 'outside the exigencies of the emergency': ibid at 39.
7   *Philco Radio and Television Corpn of Great Britain Ltd v Spurling* [1949] 2 All ER 882.

simply negligently, or if in the circumstances his act was irresponsible.[8]
A gap in time between D's negligence and that of a third party may mean
that the latter was no longer 'in the grip of the casualty'[9] created by D.[10]
D may be held to be under a duty to guard against the third party's
subsequent negligence[11] or even, in rare circumstances, his deliberate
act.[12]

The deliberate exercise of an independent discretion will protect D
from liability, despite the fact that it was his wrongful act which created
the initial situation. So where D caused C to be wrongly detained in a
mental hospital, but other officials, acting independently of D, exercised
their discretion to continue C's detention, D was held not liable for the
consequences of their decisions.[13]

### Providing the opportunity for C to be harmed

In some situations, D is held responsible for harm to C where he has
failed to prevent that harm, or where he is responsible for creating the
situation in which a third party had the opportunity to harm C. The law
may say that D owed C a duty to prevent the third party's intervention
even where that intervention was a fully voluntary and deliberate act:
eg if D receives valuables for safe deposit, the whole purpose of the
deposit is that D should guard them against theft. The House of Lords
held that the Home Office owed a duty to owners of neighbouring
property to take care to prevent borstal boys from escaping, because
they were very likely to steal or damage nearby property.[14] Since the
duty was imposed for the explicit purpose of preventing the boys from
having the opportunity to commit crimes of the very sort which they
did commit in damaging C's property, the House found no legal problem
with the causation or remoteness of the harm.[15] But the police did not

---

8    *Ruoff v Long* [1916] 1 KB 148. Cf cases where repairs to a ship are delayed
     through a strike: see p 534, n 13 below.
9    *The Oropesa* [1943] 1 All ER 211 at 215.
10   *SS Singleton Abbey v Steamship Paludina* [1927] AC 16.
11   *Davies v Liverpool Corpn* [1949] 2 All ER 175 at 176 and *Northwestern Utilities
     v London Guarantee Co* [1936] AC 108.
12   See p 305 below.
13   *Harnett v Bond* [1924] 2 KB 517; affd [1925] AC 669. There are several cases on
     this type of problem, and some conflict among them: *McGregor on Damages*
     (16th edn) paras 163–164.
14   *Home Office v Dorset Yacht Co* [1970] AC 1004. Cf *Palmer v Tees NHS Trust*
     [1998] Lloyd's Rep Med 447 (mental hospital not liable for failing to take steps
     to supervise an out-patient who killed a child).
15   This use of a specific duty of care is considered at pp 322–328 below.

have sufficient control to owe a duty to the last victim of a serial murderer whom they negligently failed to catch.[16]

It is only in a few situations that the law has imposed the duty on D not to create an opportunity for a third party deliberately to harm C. The intervening act must be 'very likely to happen' if it is not to break the causation:[17] 'tortious or criminal action by a third party is often the "very kind of thing" which is likely to happen as a result of the wrongful or careless act of' D,[18] especially where D is responsible for the third party's actions, or is employed to prevent such actions.[19] In one case, D's tort led to foreseeable damage to C's house; the judge held that it was reasonably foreseeable, first, that the house would have to be vacated until repairs were carried out, and, secondly, that in the area where the house was located,[20] vandals and thieves were very likely to cause further damage to it.[1] But in most situations, D is protected from liability. Where D carelessly left a libellous letter (written by C) in a place where it was found by X, who showed it to the person libelled, D was held not liable for the consequence that C had to pay damages for the libel.[2] Similarly, where D negligently injured C, whose tools were stolen from his car while he was on the way to hospital, a Canadian court held that D was not liable for the loss of the tools – the risk of such a theft was too low.[3]

## Ulterior harm

A second injury to C, which he suffers in a subsequent incident which would not have occurred 'but for' the first injury, is sometimes called 'ulterior harm'; it may raise difficult problems which cannot be handled

---

16  *Hill v Chief Constable of West Yorkshire* [1989] AC 53. (The police are immune from negligence liability when investigating crime: ibid and *Osman v Ferguson* [1993] 4 All ER 344.)

17  *Home Office v Dorset Yacht Co*, above n 14 at 1030. See also *Hart and Honoré*, above n 4, p 198.

18  *Home Office v Dorset Yacht Co*, above n 14 at 1030.

19  *Lamb v Camden London Borough Council* [1981] QB 625 at 642. D may be merely under a duty to warn, as in an American case where a patient told his psychiatrist that he intended to kill a particular person: *Tarasoff v Regents of California* 551 P 2d 334 (1976).

20  The particular location is crucial: where D's tort led to C's house being unoccupied in Hampstead it was only a possibility that vandals or squatters might move in – hence the damage they caused was too remote: *Lamb v Camden London Borough Council* [1981] QB 625.

1  *Ward v Cannock Chase District Council* [1986] Ch 546 at 563–571. But vandal damage to C's chattels was too remote: ibid at 571–573.

2  *Weld-Blundell v Stephens* [1920] AC 956 (a contract case, but also relevant to tort – a tort case was approved).

3  *Duce v Rourke* [1951] 1 WWR 305, NS. Cf the contract case of *Stansbie v Troman* [1948] 2 KB 48 (discussed at p 85 above).

simply by using the foreseeability test as a layman would. D is not held responsible if the causation of the ulterior harm can be primarily attributed to some abnormal occurrence or to someone other than D. In a leading case, C's left leg had been injured by D's tort, so that C could not control it. Later, when he was descending steep stairs without a handrail, C did not use a stick nor call for assistance (which was available). As his left leg gave way, he jumped and broke his right ankle. The House of Lords ruled that D was not liable for this further injury, even though the reasonable layman might have foreseen this type of second accident. C's action in taking an unreasonable risk broke the causation: his own conduct was the sole cause of the second injury.[4] (The second injury might, on these facts, have been adequately met with reduced damages under the contributory negligence legislation.)[5] A contrast is offered by another case, where C had a collar fitted to her neck after being injured by D's negligence. She did recover from D for a further injury which she suffered two days later when she fell on some stairs. The collar made it more difficult for her to use her bi-focal glasses, and she was still shaken by the first injury.[6]

### Abnormal occurrences

The second feature which, according to Hart and Honoré, will regularly break the chain of causation from D's tort is an abnormal or highly unusual combination of events arising after the tort. An extraordinary combination of natural forces, such as an exceptional rainfall, which has this effect has for centuries been called an 'Act of God'. The term 'coincidence' may be used to refer to a most unlikely conjunction of events, such as the hypothetical case where D's negligence injures C, who on his way to hospital is killed by a falling tree.[7] Since, in ordinary experience, the conjunction of these two causes, the negligence and the falling tree, was highly unlikely to occur in such a short space of time, D would not be liable for the death: the fact that D had injured C could not be said to have increased the chances of C being struck by a falling tree.

One House of Lords decision deals with the unusual[8] coincidence of two separate causes, one tortious and the other not, but each of which

4    *McKew v Holland & Hannen & Cubitts* [1969] 3 All ER 1621. Cf the contract case of *Lambert v Lewis* [1982] AC 225 (discussed at p 111 above).
5    See pp 308-309 below.
6    *Wieland v Cyril Lord Carpets Ltd* [1969] 3 All ER 1006.
7    Cf *Hogan v Bentinck West Hartley Collieries* [1949] 1 All ER 588, 601.
8    Cf a reasonably foreseeable combination of events; the *Monarch Steamship Co Ltd v A/B Karlshamns Oljefabriker* [1949] AC 196 (discussed at p 86 above).

would have required repairs to be made to C's ship.[9] She was first rendered unseaworthy by D's negligence. After temporary repairs she sailed to a port for permanent repairs, but *en route* was again rendered unseaworthy, this time by heavy weather. Both sets of repairs were done at the same time. Since, however, the same period for repairs would have been necessary for the heavy weather damage alone, D was held not liable for C's loss of use of the ship during that period. D's negligence had not increased the likelihood of the later damage being suffered.

Where D intended to bring about a most unusual combination of events to harm C, he may be held to have caused the harm.[10] D cannot rely on the 'coincidence' defence if he knew of, and deliberately used, an unusual set of circumstances, eg if, by deceiving C, D hoped that C would do something unusual.[11]

## Mitigation

Although the rules of mitigation have been developed mainly in cases of breach of contract they also apply in principle to torts. The rules considered above[12] therefore apply to C in respect of his loss arising from D's tort. C cannot recover damages in respect of any part of his loss which he could have avoided by taking reasonable steps. This rule reduces social waste by giving C an incentive to take steps to minimise his loss, even though he is the innocent victim of a tort. C is usually better placed than D to reduce his loss and he is protected by the rule that D must pay damages to reimburse C for any extra expenses which he incurs in a reasonable attempt to mitigate, even when that attempt failed.

In the field of personal injuries there is obvious scope for mitigation. After his recovery, C must take reasonable opportunities to continue to earn.[13] If C unreasonably[14] refuses to undergo surgery[15] or to accept

---

9  *Carslogie Steamship Co v Royal Norwegian Government* [1952] AC 292. In the absence of the second damage, D would have been liable for loss of profits during reasonable repairs: see pp 533-534 below.

10  *Hart and Honoré*, above n 4, p 170.

11  In the same way, D cannot shelter behind the 'foreseeable consequence' test for remoteness when he intended to harm C: *Smith New Court Securities Ltd v Scrimgeour Vickers Asset Management Ltd* [1997] AC 254 (discussed at pp 330, 556-557 below).

12  Ch 7.

13  See pp 350-351

14  C must show that his refusal was reasonable: *Selvanayagam v University of the West Indies* [1983] 1 WLR 585, PC.

15  *Steele v Robert George and Co (1937) Ltd* [1942] AC 497 (workman's compensation claim) and *McAuley v London Transport Executive* [1957] 2 Lloyd's Rep 500.

hospital treatment,[16] his damages will be reduced on the ground that he failed to mitigate. A similar result would be justified if C delayed the recovery of an injured leg by an unreasonable attempt to walk too soon. Again, C may be suffering 'compensation' neurosis which will last until the outcome of his claim is known: in this situation, his unreasonable delay in pursuing his claim is a failure to mitigate.[17]

Damage to chattels and buildings will also create the need for C to act. When his chattel is damaged, he must act reasonably in deciding whether to get it repaired. If the cost of repairs would exceed its market value (viz the cost of a replacement) it is not reasonable to have it repaired; but when no reasonable substitute is available, this may be a reasonable decision.[18] Similar questions of reasonableness arise when C claims the cost of hiring a substitute car while his own is repaired,[19] or in his deciding what work to have done to restore his land after subsidence[20] or to repair his damaged building.[1]

## Contributory negligence

A brief mention must be made of contributory negligence, although it is properly a partial defence to liability rather than a remedy. But in some situations the court may use contributory negligence to deal with facts which might otherwise be dealt with under causation, remoteness or mitigation. The Act of 1945 empowers[2] the court to reduce C's damages 'to such extent as the court thinks just and equitable having regard to [C's] share in the responsibility for the damage ...' wherever C 'suffers damage as the result partly of his own fault[3] and partly of the fault[4] of any other person [D]'. The Act applies only where C's fault was a

---

16   *Marcroft v Scruttons Ltd* [1954] 1 Lloyd's Rep 395. The cost of medical treatment is recoverable as an expense incurred in C's attempt to mitigate: see pp 363-365 below.

17   *James v Woodall Duckham Construction Co Ltd* [1969] 1 WLR 903. (C received damages for loss of earnings for only three of the six years from his injury until the hearing.)

18   See p 531 below.

19   See p 533 below.

20   See p 525 below.

1   See pp 524-525 below.

2   Law Reform (Contributory Negligence) Act 1945, s 1(1).

3   C's 'fault' may be an intentional act: *Reeves v Metropolitan Police Comr* [2000] 1 AC 360 (suicide).

4   The definition in s 4 is wide enough to cover breach of statutory duty, nuisance, occupier's liability, etc. But contributory negligence cannot be pleaded in actions founded on conversion or on intentional trespass to goods: Torts (Interference with Goods) Act 1977, s 11(1); or on D's deceit: *Standard Chartered Bank v Pakistan National Shipping Corpn (No 4)* [2001] QB 167.

contributory *cause*[5] of the harm: the harm must be within the particular risk created by C's own fault.[6] D must show that C failed to take reasonable care for his own safety in respect of the harm which actually occurred. C's fault normally arises after D's fault, as where C fails to take avoiding action when D has created the situation of danger. C's intervening conduct can be viewed either as breaking the causation from D's conduct or as contributory negligence.[7] Once some loss or harm has been caused to C, his unreasonable failure to minimise the extent of his loss (eg by refusing medical treatment) can be viewed either as a failure to mitigate or as contributory negligence. But C's fault can sometimes lie in failing to take reasonable precautions in anticipation of someone else's fault, as with a passenger's failure to wear a seat-belt,[8] or a motor-cyclist's failure to wear a safety helmet,[9] both of which have been treated as contributory negligence.

In contributory negligence the apportionment of the loss between C and D must be 'just and equitable'. It must therefore take into account the relative effect of each side's fault as a factor causing the harm (its dangerous character or its 'causative potency') as well as the relative degree of 'blameworthiness'.[10] The second factor depends on how far each party's conduct fell below the standard of the reasonable man.

---

5   On causation, see p 297 et seq above.
6   *Jones v Livox Quarries Ltd* [1952] 2 QB 608.
7   *The Calliope* [1970] P 172.
8   *Froom v Butcher* [1976] QB 286. The House of Lords has accepted that the fault of C may precede that of D: *Platform Home Loans Ltd v Oyston Shipways Ltd* [2000] 2 AC 190 (an unreasonably incautious lending policy).
9   *O'Connell v Jackson* [1972] 1 QB 270.
10  *Davies v Swan Motor Co (Swansea) Ltd* [1949] 2 KB 291 at 326.

# 20 Remoteness

The test of remoteness is one of the control mechanisms used by the courts to restrict the extent of D's liability: it parallels the duty of care concept, which is an initial control used by the courts to restrict the imposition of any liability at all. The remoteness test enables the courts to discriminate between different types of harm suffered by C: eg where he was injured through D's negligence he may recover damages for loss of earnings caused by his physical incapacity, and even, where his injuries caused the breakdown of his marriage, for loss of the marriage; but he cannot recover damages to cover the amount of any orders made against him in matrimonial proceedings.[1] In broad terms, the remoteness rules hold D responsible for the usual, but not the unusual or freakish, consequences of his tort. Before the detailed legal rules are examined we should consider the social policies behind the rules.

## The justifications for restricting liability to usual consequences

Following the economic approach used in this book the question addressed in this section is whether insights into the legal rules may be derived from that approach. The economist would look at both incentives to take care and the allocation of risks.

### Incentives

One of the main reasons for imposing tort liability is to give an incentive to anyone planning an action or activity to take care not to cause harm to

1   See p 378 below.

others. The incentive arises from the actor's knowledge that, if he is careless, he will be liable to compensate anyone injured by his carelessness. But the implication in this statement of potential responsibility is that the actor will be liable for usual and normal consequences to the victim, and that this expectation will be sufficient to give the actor the appropriate incentive to take care. There is no need to add to this incentive any further liability for any rare and unusual consequence of his possible carelessness. Even if D were to be potentially liable for freak consequences, they are so rare that the rational actor would ignore the risk of causing them when he chooses which level of care he should adopt. Only a minimal additional incentive would therefore arise from imposing on him the risk of unusual consequences.

Another way of looking at incentives is to consider the position of the potential victim. He faces many risks in regard to injury to his own person or damage to his property, and (to the extent he knows the law) he should realise that the law of torts can give him protection against only a small fraction of the total: many risks do not directly arise from human activity, and of those which do, many do not involve tortious conduct by an identifiable person. Since in the vast majority of the risks he will not be protected by the law of torts,[2] it is only a marginal extension of the many non-tortious risks he faces for the law to say that they include the unforeseeable, freak consequences of another's tortious conduct. If the potential victim wants protection, he should use the first-party insurance market for comprehensive, 'all risks' insurance[3] which will give him compensation irrespective of the particular cause of his loss.[4] When the law of torts denies recovery of damages for freak consequences, it does so in the knowledge that an alternative mechanism – insurance – is available to potential victims, and that (at least in the case of property) it is frequently used. In the case of death and personal injuries, the denial of damages for freak types of consequences could also be justified by reference to the many non-tortious forms of support which are available to victims.[5]

Furthermore, the transaction costs involved in using tort law to transfer liability for freak consequences of tortious acts may not justify their inclusion in tort recovery. It might also be futile for the law to transfer the cost of freak consequences, except in those situations where potential tortfeasors are likely to be covered by liability insurance.

2   See, for instance, the statistics on disabilities at pp 410-412 below.
3   When the insurance is of the 'indemnity' type, eg fire insurance, the insurer, after meeting the claim under the policy, will be subrogated to any claim in tort which the policy-holder has against a person causing the harm.
4   The question whether tort should attempt to protect property against accidental loss is discussed in R Abel, 'Should Tort Law Protect Property against Accidental Loss?' in MP Furmston (ed) *The Law of Tort* (1986) 155.
5   See pp 412-427 below.

## Allocation of risks

The second way in which an economist might view the problem is as an allocation of risk-taking imposed by the law. In a voluntary exchange, the parties are free to agree upon any allocation of risk-taking which they wish. Only where their contract fails to deal with a category of risk is a legal rule required to fill out their agreement by reference to their implicit intention. In the typical tortious situation, however, the parties are strangers and had no opportunity to negotiate or to agree upon any reciprocal risk-taking. Hence the law must impose on them a standard allocation of risk applicable to all citizens who find themselves involuntarily involved in an accident which causes harm. The law must allocate risks between potential tortfeasors (those who are acting in some capacity, or who assume responsibility for some situation, eg occupation of land, manufacture of products, the keeping of animals, etc) and those who are the potential victims of their activities. The law allocates usual risks to negligent or tortious actors, and all other risks to accident victims. Potential victims must bear both the usual risks arising from the non-tortious action of others and also the unusual risks arising from their tortious action. C is expected to bear the risk of any freak consequences of D's negligence in the same way as he bears the risk of harm caused by D without negligence: both are treated as 'accidents' for which D is not liable. An element of reciprocity between citizens is involved, since all citizens are both potential actors and potential victims. If D is not liable to C for a freak consequence of his tort, neither will C be liable for any freak consequence any tortious action on his part may cause to D or others. A general argument supporting this rule is that the law should not discourage the activity of citizens since it normally benefits society: actors should not be deterred by any fear of being held liable for wholly unexpected consequences of their actions.

Although this philosophy may be justifiable when individual actors have to pay damages from their own resources, it should be reconsidered in the light of the widespread practice of potential Ds taking out liability insurance. If the burden of freak consequences of negligence can be spread over a large number of potential Ds the individualistic arguments used in *The Wagon Mound*, the leading case on remoteness, lose much of their force. The Privy Council said: 'It does not seem consonant with current ideas of justice or morality that for an act of negligence, however slight or venial, ... the actor should be liable for all consequences, however unforeseeable and however grave, so long as they can be said to be 'direct'. It is a principle of civil liability, subject to qualifications which have no present relevance, that a man must be considered to be responsible for the probable consequences of his act. To demand more of him is too harsh a rule; to demand less is to ignore that civilised order requires the observance of a minimum standard of behaviour.'[6] This passage wholly ignores the availability of insurance, although it is highly likely that *The Wagon Mound* itself was really a battle between two insurance companies. Unusual or abnormal risks are best handled by insurance; indeed, the practical message from the Privy Council (which denied C any recovery for losses suffered in a fire unexpectedly resulting from D's negligence) is that the owners of valuable property should insure it fully against all risks, because the law of torts offers only limited protection against damage to it.

## The legal rules on remoteness of damage[7]

Before considering the general rules on remoteness, we should note two recent developments. First, in some special situations the courts specify the duty of care in narrow terms so as to cover only a particular risk. This narrow categorisation of the duty may result in the issues of causation and remoteness being taken over by the detailed specification of the duty itself. Secondly, in some situations the courts have laid down narrow 'control mechanisms' which deal with issues which would otherwise have been decided under the general rules of causation and remoteness. Before examining these recent developments, we must consider the general rules on remoteness.

The first significant case in the modern law is *The Polemis*;[8] some knowledge of it is essential to understanding the present rules. D's stevedores carelessly allowed a plank to fall into the hold of C's ship; it hit something and caused a spark which ignited petrol vapour in the hold. The whole ship was destroyed in the resulting fire. Some (unspecified) damage could reasonably have been foreseen from the falling plank striking something in the hold, but the arbitrators found that the causing of the spark could not have been reasonably anticipated. But the Court of Appeal held that if D's employee was negligent in allowing the plank to fall, he was responsible to C for all the direct consequences, whether they were reasonably foreseeable or not. The concept of directness was not analysed in any depth, but Scrutton LJ considered that damage would be

6   [1961] AC 388 at 422–423 (the facts are given at p 314 below).
7   RMW Dias, 'Remoteness of Liability and Legal Policy' [1962] Cambridge Law Journal 178 and RMW Dias, 'Trouble on Oiled Waters: Problems of *The Wagon Mound (No 2)* [1967] Cambridge Law Journal 62 and Davies, 'The Road From Morocco: *Polemis* through *Donoghue* to No-fault' (1982) 45 Modern Law Review 534.
8   [1921] 3 KB 560 (the issue was whether D's negligence disentitled him from relying on an exemption clause. Although this dispute arose out of a contract between the parties, the Court of Appeal decided the question of remoteness by reference to the rules of tort).

314 Section 2   Tort: remedies for wrongdoing

indirect if it was 'due to the operation of independent causes having no
connection with the negligent act, except that they could not avoid its
results'.[9] The leading authority is now the decision of the Privy Council
in *The Wagon Mound*.[10] D had chartered a ship which was berthed at a
wharf in Sydney; while she was taking on furnace oil, some was carelessly
allowed to spill into the harbour. The oil floated to C's wharf 200 yards
away, where C was refitting another ship, using welding equipment. C
noticed the oil, but D assured C that there was no danger. But two days
later[11] some molten metal fell from C's wharf on to cotton waste floating
on the oil beneath the wharf; the waste ignited and the wharf was severely
damaged in the fire. The judge found that D could not reasonably have
been expected to know that the oil was capable of being set alight when
floating on water, but that it was reasonably foreseeable that some damage
would be caused to C's wharf by the oil congealing on the slipways (as in
fact happened). The judge applied the directness test in *Re Polemis* to
hold D liable for all the damage to the wharf, but the Privy Council held
that this was not the correct test. Remoteness of damage in the tort of
negligence now depended on whether the type of consequence and the
type of causation in question were reasonably foreseeable as a consequence
of D's negligent act or omission. The test of reasonableness would be
satisfied (according to the second *Wagon Mound* decision)[12] if, having
foreseen the particular risk, the reasonable man in D's position would have
taken steps to avoid it. The risk would not be reasonably foreseeable if it
was so unlikely to occur, or the foreseeable harm was so slight, that the
reasonable actor would have felt justified in ignoring it.

The first *Wagon Mound* decision depended on the evidence presented
by the particular C, the owner of the wharf. In a subsequent claim arising
from the same fire, which was brought by the owner of another ship lying
alongside the wharf, different evidence led to the finding that the risk of
fire was reasonably foreseeable by someone in D's position at the time
the oil was spilt into the harbour.[13]

As the result of *The Wagon Mound*, one verbal formula has been
substituted for another, but since both were necessarily expressed in
general terms, the courts still have a wide discretion in applying the current

---

9   Ibid at 577.
10  *Overseas Tankship (UK) Ltd v Morts Dock and Engineering Co Ltd, The Wagon*
*Mound* [1961] AC 388. In *Hughes v Lord Advocate* [1963] AC 837, the House
of Lords accepted that the Privy Council had correctly stated the law for the UK:
see also *Doughty v Turner Manufacturing Co Ltd* [1964] 1 QB 518, CA.
11  The Privy Council was clearly influenced by the delay in time between the escape
of the oil and the occurrence of the fire.
12  *Overseas Tankship (UK) Ltd v Miller Steamship Co Pty, The Wagon Mound (No
2)* [1967] 1 AC 617.
13  Ibid.

test to the facts of a particular accident.[14] If a judge considers it unfair to make D pay for a particular consequence suffered by C, he previously labelled it 'indirect' but must now label it 'unforeseeable'. The general impression gained from *The Wagon Mound*, however, is that the 'direct' test was regarded as too favourable to Cs, so that adoption of the 'foreseeable' test is a shift in favour of D.[15] In exercising his discretion the judge will evaluate the impact of the various factors which he considers should have weighed with D when deciding whether to act and, if so, what precautions he should take against causing harm to others. The existence of this discretion is supported by the view that the judge must adopt a 'robust and sensible approach' to the issue of remoteness.[16]

The tests for duty of care and for remoteness are not identical: both use the phrase 'reasonable foreseeability', but they are applied at different times in the sequence of events, and are therefore based on different sets of data. The purpose of using foreseeability of risk in the duty of care concept is to draw a conclusion as to whether D's action should be tested by the standard of care of the reasonable man. In the light of his foresight of possible risks, would the reasonable man in D's position (immediately before he acted) have considered that he should take care to avoid harming someone in C's position? It is more than the foresight of risk – would that foresight in the circumstances have led to precautions being taken? The reasonable man, in taking this decision, would weigh various factors, such as the chance of the risk occurring, the relative seriousness of the harmful consequences which might ensue, and the cost of taking precautions against the risk. In some special situations[17] the courts have imposed a specific duty of care on D in respect of a specific, particular risk to C. But generally it may be said that at the duty of care stage the risk need not be foreseen in any detail, nor need there be foresight of a particular way in which D might fall below the standard of reasonable care. There might be many ways in which he could be careless, but the duty test is phrased in general terms: 'If care is not taken by D in the action he is about to undertake, is there a risk of harm to someone in C's position?' The phrase 'if care is not taken' is applied in a general, unspecified way, without knowledge of the actual act or omission by D which will later be labelled negligent. But the causation and remoteness tests are applied after D has acted: the information given to the reasonable man has then expanded to include knowledge of the particular act or omission found to be negligent. The test of foreseeability is applied to D's specific action: what types of

14 Sir Robin Cooke, 'Remoteness of Damages and Judicial Discretion' [1978] Cambridge Law Journal 288.
15 The reasonable foreseeable test also makes it easier for the court to import policy considerations: see pp 324-328 below.
16 *Lamb v Camden London Borough Council* [1981] QB 625 at 647.
17 Discussed at pp 322-324 below.

consequence are foreseeable by the reasonable man in D's shoes, given the knowledge that, in the particular circumstances,[18] he has dropped this plank into this hold of the ship; or has spilled this oil into the harbour at this place; or has dropped this hardboard cover into this cauldron of chemicals;[19] or has given C this piece of inaccurate information?[20] The range of foreseeability will vary according to the nature of the negligent action in question: in most situations where D owes C a duty of care, the duty could be broken by many different acts or omissions on the part of D. The range of foreseeable risks will depend on the actual negligence in question. Some negligent acts will create only the risk of damage by physical impact, others the risk of damage by fire or explosion, others the risk that C will himself choose to take some step in reliance on D's statement, and so on. Knowledge of the particular action may widen foresight: if I drop a lighted cigarette, there may be a foreseeable risk of fire; but in other cases it may narrow the range of foresight: dropping this particular lid into this chemical mixture may create no foreseeable risk of a chemical explosion, but only risk of splashing from the liquid.[1]

### Categories of harm

Several limitations on the foreseeability test are found in *The Wagon Mound* itself, the main one being that 'the essential factor ... is whether the damage is of such a kind as the reasonable man should have foreseen'.[2] This use of a foreseeable category of consequence has its parallel in the test for remoteness in contract[3] and is a major restriction on the test in tort. Although not spelt out in *The Wagon Mound*, it is clear that the categorisation applies both to the type of consequence – the harm suffered by C – and to the type of causation. As will be illustrated by cases referred to later in this chapter, the categorisation between types of harm is at a broad level: for instance, personal injury or death; psychiatric injury suffered by C without his suffering physical injury; loss of a marriage caused by C's injuries;[4] physical injury to land or buildings; physical injury to chattels; loss of profits arising from damage to land or chattels; financial loss suffered without physical injury to C's person or property;

18   The circumstances known to D, and those of which he ought to have known.
19   *Doughty v Turner Manufacturing Co Ltd*, above n 10 at 528: 'Our inquiry must, therefore, be whether the result of this hard-board cover slipping into the cauldron, which we know now to be inevitably an explosion, was a thing reasonably foreseeable at the time when it happened'.
20   See p 323 below.
1    *Doughty v Turner Manufacturing Co Ltd*, above n 10.
2    [1961] AC 388 at 426.
3    See p 95 above.
4    See p 378 below.

or loss of reputation. The test of reasonable foreseeability must be applied to each category of harm in respect of which C claims damages. Thus, foreseeable harm to C's person will not support a claim for damages for unforeseeable harm to his property.

## Categories of causation

The courts also require reasonable foresight of the category of causation involved in causing the harm to C. In *The Wagon Mound* itself, damage to C's wharf was foreseeable, but only by the oil fouling it, not by the oil catching fire.[5] The Privy Council treated damage to the wharf by fire as a different category from damage to the wharf by the impact of the oil – this was the crucial point in their departure from *Polemis*. The 'type or kind of accident' must be foreseeable; the word 'accident' includes not only the type of consequence, but also the type of causation. But, provided the general type of accident was foreseeable, the details of how the particular accident occurred need not be foreseeable.[6] The decision of the House of Lords in *Hughes v Lord Advocate*[7] required the source of danger to be foreseeable, but not the actual details of how the accident did occur. Post Office workmen uncovered a manhole in the road, covered it with a temporary shelter, and left it while they went off for their tea-break. Four paraffin lamps were placed around the area to warn others. Two boys, aged eight and ten, carried one of the lamps into the shelter to explore it. One of them, C, the eight-year-old, tripped over the lamp and spilt the paraffin, which was vaporised by the heat of the lamp; it exploded and burnt him. The workmen were found negligent in leaving the open manhole unattended (it was an 'allurement' to children who might play with the lamp). Their Lordships held that a known source of danger, the lamp ('a potentially dangerous object'),[8] had led to burning by an unexpected explosion, but that this was not different in kind from burning by the paraffin coming into contact with the naked flame of the lamp. The distinction between burning and explosion was too fine to be accepted. The type of accident or occurrence – the burning of a child – was reasonably foreseeable although the means by which the source of danger led to the consequence was unforeseeable. This application of the *Wagon Mound* foreseeability test uses a broad categorisation of accidents, and amounts to a partial reinstatement of the *Polemis* test: provided the general

---

5   In *The Wagon Mound (No 2)*, above n 12 at 210-211, on different evidence, the judge held that there was a foreseeable possibility of fire arising from the spillage of oil: see p 314 above.

6   *Wieland v Cyril Lord Carpets Ltd* [1969] 3 All ER 1006 at 1009.

7   [1963] AC 837.

8   Ibid at 857.

categories of harm and of causation were foreseeable (eg personal injuries through burning from the lamp) the *Wagon Mound* test was satisfied. Similarly, where an abandoned boat with rotten planks was left alongside flats, it was a foreseeable danger to children tempted to play on it. But it was not a 'different type of accident' when the boat fell on a boy who jacked it up so he could work on it.[9] Within a foreseeable category of causation only the directness test need be satisfied.

The type of causation was crucial in another case.[10] D dropped an asbestos lid into a cauldron of liquid chemicals. The foreseeable risk was that C, who was nearby, might be splashed by the liquid, but in fact there was a chemical reaction between the lid and the liquid, leading to an explosion which splashed C. D was held not liable on the ground that splashing as the result of a chemical reaction expelling the liquid was a different type of accident from the foreseeable type, viz splashing by physical displacement of the liquid when an object fell into it. In the view of the Court of Appeal, the unusual nature of the causation, a chemical reaction, was the crucial feature of the accident, and since this was not reasonably foreseeable, the consequence was too remote. (Apart from causation, the type of consequence (personal injury) was a foreseeable risk.)

The category of causation which is usually foreseeable is where the harm is caused by the collision of one physical object or person with another object or person. The cases in this section show that burning by fire or explosion is a separate category, and that chemical reaction is a third. Special situations have been discussed under causation, eg the intervening act of a third person,[11] and others will be found below, such as harm to C's nervous system through his sight or hearing without any physical contact with his body;[12] financial loss caused by C acting in reliance on D's statement or advice;[13] or harm suffered by C in reasonably attempting to rescue a third person from danger created by D's negligence.[14]

### The unforeseeable extent of a foreseeable type of harm

The extent or gravity of a foreseeable type of loss need not be foreseen. Once the type or kind of harm meets the criterion of reasonable

---

9    *Jolley v London Borough of Sutton* [2000] 1 WLR 1082, HL. In *Jebson v Ministry of Defence* [2000] 1 WLR 2055, the CA also accepted a broadly defined risk.
10   *Doughty v Turner Manufacturing Co Ltd*, above n 10.
11   See pp 303-304 above.
12   See pp 324-326 below.
13   See pp 323-324 below.
14   *Haynes v Harwood* [1935] 1 KB 146.

foreseeability, D is liable for the full extent of that loss.[15] This is a major restriction of the *Wagon Mound* rule, because many consequences which the layman would consider to be 'unusual' are those where the actual extent of the harm was beyond anyone's expectation.[16] The *Polemis* test of direct consequences still applies within any particular category of harm which is reasonably foreseeable. The main illustration of this approach is the 'thin skull' rule. Provided some personal injury to C was reasonably foreseeable as a consequence of D's negligent act, D is liable to the full extent of all the personal injury directly caused by that act. So in C's personal injury claim, the fact that he was unusually susceptible to injury is ignored in assessing his damages once D's liability has been established. The 'wrongdoer must take the victim as he finds him';[17] 'it is no answer to the sufferer's claim for damages that he would have suffered less injury, or no injury at all, if he had not had an unusually thin skull or an unusually weak heart'.[18] This principle pre-dated *Polemis*, and has not been affected by *The Wagon Mound*.[19] It is reconciled with the latter by saying that the unforeseeable extent of a foreseeable type of harm is only a matter of degree.

In each of the following cases illustrating the 'thin skull' rule some personal injury was foreseeable, thus satisfying the *Wagon Mound* test. In one, C's husband was struck on the lip by a piece of molten metal: he suffered a small burn, which turned to cancer from which he died. D was held liable for the death.[20] In another, C's finger was pricked by frayed wire, and the injury affected his sight because his eye was already in an ulcerated condition. D was held liable for the aggravation of the eye complaint.[1] In a third, a minor graze led to C being seriously disabled after an anti-tetanus injection to which he reacted unforeseeably because he was peculiarly susceptible.[2] The same approach holds in psychiatric injury cases: provided there was a risk of some psychiatric injury to a person of average susceptibility in C's position, D is liable for the full extent of the shock actually suffered by C, despite his being hypersensitive.[3] The 'thin skull' rule is really a significant exception to

---

15 *The Wagon Mound*, above n 10 at 416; *Hughes v Lord Advocate*, above n 10 at 845 and *Doughty v Turner Manufacturing Co Ltd*, above n 10 at 532.
16 See the moralistic arguments used in *The Wagon Mound*, above n 10 at 422-423 quoted at pp 312-313 above.
17 *Bourhill v Young* [1943] AC 92 at 109–10.
18 *Dulieu v White* [1901] 2 KB 669 at 769.
19 *Smith v Leech Brain* [1962] 2 QB 405.
20 Ibid. But for the burn, the pre-malignant condition of the decreased's tissue might never have developed into cancer.
1 *Warren v Scruttons Ltd* [1962] 1 Lloyd's Rep 497.
2 *Robinson v Post Office* [1974] 1 WLR 1176.
3 An 'egg-shell personality' is to be treated in the same way as an egg-shell skull: *Malcolm v Broadhurst* [1970] 3 All ER 508.

the *Wagon Mound* rule. It is grounded in the judicial policy[4] of ignoring individual frailties when assessing compensation for injuries to human beings. The exception regularly allows some consequences of D's tort to escape from being labelled too remote, despite the fact that any layman would call them abnormal.

Once some personal injury to C is foreseeable, some resulting loss of his earning capacity is always within the range of reasonable foresight. From this it follows that the fact that C is an exceptionally high earner need not be foreseeable,[5] since that again goes only to the extent of a foreseeable type of harm, viz loss of earnings.

Whether the 'thin skull' rule applies to damage to property is not yet clear. Before *The Wagon Mound* it was assumed that D must pay damages for the full damage to or loss of C's property, even where that property was exceptionally valuable: 'you negligently and ignorantly injure the favourite for the Derby whereby he cannot run. You have to pay damages resulting from the circumstances of which you have no notice.'[6] Even after *The Wagon Mound* it can be argued that the exceptional value of C's property does not make it a different *type* of harm from that which was reasonably foreseeable, but only different in the extent of the financial consequences.[7] For instance, while damage to C's ship is being repaired, C may suffer a net loss of profits under the ship's current charterparty: before *The Wagon Mound*, this loss had been held not to be too remote a consequence of D's tort which caused the damage.[8] A similar situation arises when C's ship is totally destroyed: in assessing his damages the House of Lords (before *The Wagon Mound*) had taken into account her existing commitments under the contract under which she was operating at the time of the collision.[9] A similar problem arises with highly delicate property. If D jostles C, who is carrying a fragile chattel, must D take the victim chattel as he finds it? The courts have yet to give a definitive ruling, and it is obvious that the courts need not adopt an analogy based on the frailty of the human body. Even if they did, they might escape some of the effect of applying the 'thin skull' rule to hypersensitive chattels by

---

4    See pp 324-328 below for other policy considerations affecting causation and remoteness.

5    *The Arpad* [1934] P 189 at 202–203.

6    Ibid.

7    But C's impecuniosity is irrelevant if it prevents him from mitigating the loss of a valuable chattel by buying an available substitute in the market: see pp 326, 536 n 17, below.

8    See pp 533-534 below. Where, as the result of D's negligence, C's ship is in dock for repairs, the risk of delay through a trade-union strike is foreseeable: *Candlewood Navigation Corpn Ltd v Mitsui OSK Lines Ltd* [1986] AC 1, PC.

9    *Liesbosch Dredger v Steamship Edison* [1933] AC 449 (discussed at pp 536-540 below).

using contributory negligence whenever C should have taken precautions to protect his chattel.[10]

## Duty of care with an inbuilt limitation on liability

A novel use of the duty of care was made by the House of Lords in the *Banque Bruxelles* case[11] where the duty of care itself was defined so as to put a restriction on the extent of D's liability. C, the intending lender, instructed D, a valuer, to report on the current market value of a property which was offered to C as security for a proposed loan. D negligently over-valued the property and C, relying on the valuation, lent on the security an amount calculated by reference to the over-estimated value. Thus at the time of making the loan, C had less security than it believed it had, the initial 'deficiency in security' being measured by the extent of the over-valuation viz the difference between the negligent estimate and the amount of a proper (non-negligent) valuation. The borrower later defaulted and C realised the security, but it produced much less than the amount of the negligent over-estimate (the market had collapsed since the loan). As the net proceeds of sale were insufficient to meet the borrower's total indebtedness, C sued D for the 'basic' or 'ultimate loss', which was the lender's actual net loss, calculated as the amount of the original loan (and interest to date) less repayments from the borrower and the net proceeds of sale of the security. The decision of the House of Lords was that the lender could recover its ultimate loss, subject to any limitation imposed by the initial deficiency in the security. The whole of the ultimate loss was caused by, and was not too remote a consequence of D's negligence,[12] but D's duty of care was 'limited to the extent of the overvaluation'.[13] The fact that the duty of care imposed a limitation on D's liability was the novel feature: it is analogous to an express term in a contract which puts a limit on the damages payable by the contract-breaker.

The *Banque Bruxelles* type of duty of care subject to a limit on the extent of liability has been used in other lending situations eg where a solicitor's negligence led to the lender obtaining a valid title to only part of the intended security: the damages were restricted to the difference

---

10 Cf the cases in nuisance where C's property is abnormally susceptible to interference: eg *McKinnon Industries v Walker* [1951] 3 DLR 577, PC (C grew orchids, 'a particularly ... delicate operation').

11 Also known as the *South Australia* or the *BBL* case [1997] AC 191. The case has been interpreted by two subsequent decisions in the House of Lords: *Nykredit Mortgage Bank plc v Edward Erdman Group Ltd (No 2)* [1998] 1 All ER 305 and *Platform Home Loans Ltd v Oyston Shipways Ltd* [2000] 2 AC 190.

12 [1997] AC 191 at 205, 207, 210-216

13 *Nykredit Mortgage Bank plc v Edward Erdman Group Ltd (No 2)*, above n 11 at 1632.

between the value of the whole security and that of the part.[14] But it is unclear whether this technique will be developed elsewhere.

## Some duties of care which specify particular heads of loss

We now examine the recent developments affecting causation and remoteness, particularly the narrow definition of the duty of care and the introduction of detailed 'control mechanisms'. As put by one Law Lord: 'It is not a duty to take care in the abstract but a duty to avoid causing to the particular [C] damage of the particular kind which he has in fact sustained.'[15] In negligence cases this tendency is likely to be developed further. If C suffers different types of adverse consequence, D's duties may be specified separately in relation to each type, thus rendering it unnecessary to put the decision on remoteness. We now take first the latest House of Lords decision which uses these techniques.

### (A) UNWANTED PREGNANCIES

In *McFarlane v Tayside Health Board*[16] D, a doctor, negligently advised a man that a vasectomy had made him infertile so that it was not necessary to take contraceptive precautions. The result was that C, his wife, became pregnant and gave birth to a normal, healthy child. The House of Lords held that D owed C a duty of care in respect of the pain, distress and costs[17] associated with the pregnancy and birth, but not in respect of the costs of maintaining or educating the child until adulthood ('maintenance costs'). Both consequences were reasonably foreseeable consequences of D's negligence: it would have been in line with the approach of earlier authorities to say that damages were recoverable for the pain and distress since these were not too remote consequences of D's negligence, but that no damages were recoverable for the maintenance costs, because, for policy reasons, this type of loss was too remote a consequence.[18] However, the majority of the Law Lords put their conclusion in terms of the extent of D's duty of care – it was not fair, just or reasonable to impose liability on a doctor for such an economic loss. It was a question of the extent of

---

14   *Bristol and West Building Society v Cooke and Borsay* (one of the cases reported in [1997] 4 All ER 582).

15   Per Lord Oliver of Aylmerton in *Caparo Industries plc v Dickman* [1990] 2 AC 605 at 651.

16   [2000] 2 AC 59.

17   Such as medical expenses, clothing for C and equipment for the baby; and the loss of C's earnings due to the pregnancy and birth.

18   Lord Hope, dissenting, held in terms that the maintenance costs were not too remote: ibid at 95.

the duty of care[19] : although the doctor owed a duty in respect of the pain, distress and costs of the pregnancy and birth, he did not assume responsibility for economic losses like the maintenance costs and owed no duty of care in this respect.[20]

(B) FINANCIAL OR ECONOMIC LOSS CAUSED BY NEGLIGENT STATEMENTS

This is a topic where the duty of care is narrowly defined by reference to a specified type of causation and a specified type of loss, with the result that the general concepts of causation and remoteness are ousted. When C claims damages for a financial loss due to D's negligent statement, there must have been a 'special relationship'[1] between them: D must have voluntarily assumed responsibility towards C by making a statement (or giving advice) to C in circumstances in which it was reasonable for C, in reliance on the statement and without independently confirming its reliability, to enter into a particular transaction which put him at financial risk.[2] This statement of the scope of the duty of care specifies the causation (reasonable reliance[3] on D's statement) and the type of consequence (financial loss to C resulting from entry into the expected transaction). If C suffers any other type of loss, or suffers the foreseeable loss but not through the foreseeable type of causation, D will not be liable, despite his carelessness in making the statement. The loss to be compensated must be within the scope of the duty.

In *Smith v Bush*[4] a surveyor, D, on the instructions of the proposed lender, reported on the house which C intended to buy with a mortgage. Without getting his own survey report, C reasonably relied on D's report and bought the house. He recovered as damages from D the extra expense incurred by him in rectifying the defect which D had negligently failed to identify in his report. The duty was owed to the intending purchaser in respect of a particular type of loss caused by the particular causation.

But in *Caparo's* case[5] the purpose of D's statement did not extend to the use which C made of it. D as auditor reported on the annual accounts to the company and its shareholders. The House of Lords held that the purpose of the report was to enable C to exercise his powers as a shareholder but not to rely on it to buy more shares or to take over the company. The

---

19  Ibid at 75 per Lord Slynn.

20  Ibid at 76 per Lord Slynn.

1   *Hedley Byrne & Co Ltd v Heller & Partners Ltd* [1964] AC 465.

2   Ibid; *Henderson v Merrett Syndicates Ltd* [1995] 2 AC 145 and the cases cited below.

3   If it was not reasonable for C to rely on D's report, it may be held that causation is not satisfied, or that C was contributorily negligent.

4   [1990] 1 AC 831.

5   *Caparo Industries plc v Dickman*, above n 15.

decision was framed in terms that D owed no duty of care to C in respect of the financial loss arising from C's take-over at an over-value.

(C) ASSUMING RESPONSIBILITY FOR A TASK

The voluntary assumption of responsibility may be a task which D knows will benefit C. In *White v Jones*[6] D was a solicitor who negligently failed within a reasonable time to prepare a will under which C's father intended her to receive a legacy. After her father's death, it was held that D owed C a duty of care in respect of the intended legacy, and that the damages amounted to its full value.[7] The loss in question, and the relevant causation, were defined by the duty of care itself.

## Control mechanisms for psychiatric injury

Claims based on psychiatric, as distinct from physical injury, provide a fascinating illustration of the way in which the common law has used the tests of causation and of remoteness built into new 'control mechanisms' to restrict recovery of damages. ('Psychiatric injury' refers to cases recognised by current medical knowledge.) First, we consider fear for one's own safety, and then fear for that of others.

(A) PRIMARY VICTIMS

If D can reasonably foresee that his negligence might create the risk of physical injury to someone in C's position, he is liable to him if he suffers psychiatric injury from fear of himself suffering physical injury: it does not matter that C in fact escaped any physical injury, nor that psychiatric injury was not a foreseeable consequence of the negligence.[8] Such a C is a primary victim because he is physically imperilled by D's negligence, or reasonably believes that he is. Psychiatric injury to C is not too remote a consequence of negligence which puts C into physical danger.

(B) SECONDARY VICTIMS

The second category of psychiatric injury[9] is where D's negligence does not put C himself into physical danger, but C suffers through witnessing

---

6   [1995] 2 AC 207.
7   It should be noted that in some circumstances the intended third-party beneficiary may now have a contractual remedy under the provisions of the Contracts (Rights of Third Parties) Act 1999.
8   *Page v Smith* [1996] AC 155.
9   The term refers only to medically-recognised injury. No damages are awarded for shock, fear, anxiety or grief suffered as a result of witnessing a relative's death in distressing circumstances.

a traumatic event which puts someone else[10] into physical danger. In such cases, the test for the duty of care is, first, the orthodox one based on reasonable foreseeability: the bystander or spectator must show that psychiatric injury to him was a reasonably foreseeable consequence of exposing a person of reasonable fortitude to the trauma of seeing the accident or its immediate aftermath. But the Law Lords have not relied simply on the concepts of causation and remoteness to restrict liability after this initial test is satisfied: they introduced in *Alcock v Chief Constable of South Yorkshire Police*[11] several additional 'control mechanisms'[12] which partly overlap with the duty of care (No (1) below) and partly with causation and remoteness ((2) and (3)):

> (1) The plaintiff must have close ties of love and affection with the victim ... (2) The plaintiff must have been present at the accident or its immediate aftermath. (3) The psychiatric injury must have been caused by direct perception of the accident or its immediate aftermath and not upon hearing about it from someone else.[13]

Tests (2) and (3) set out the specific type of causation required in the bystander or spectator case: it is not enough merely to satisfy the test of the reasonable foreseeability of psychiatric injury.[14] The restrictive tests spring from policy considerations.[15]

In the *Alcock* case, the claimants were spectators at the Hillsborough Football Stadium where 95 people were crushed to death by over-crowding due to D's negligence. No damages were recovered by those relatives who saw the catastrophe only on television; nor by those who later identified bodies in the mortuary.

In the *Frost* case[16] the House of Lords also decided that the policemen on duty at the Hillsborough tragedy could not be given special treatment as 'rescuers' who had tended victims and handled the aftermath. A rescuer who had not himself been exposed to physical danger (or who did not reasonably believe that he had been so exposed) was a secondary victim in common with spectators and bystanders and so had to satisfy the control

---

10  The person who negligently or deliberately injures himself does not owe a duty of care to avoid psychiatric injury to another person: *Greatorex v Greatorex* [2000] 1 WLR 1970.

11  [1992] 1 AC 310.

12  The term used in *Page* v *Smith*, above n 8 at 189 and subsequent cases.

13  This is the summary of the *Alcock* decision given by Lord Hoffmann in *Frost v Chief Constable of South Yorks Police* [1999] 2 AC 455 at 502. None of the control mechanisms apply to primary victims (above).

14  Ibid at 491.

15  Ibid at 493.

16  Ibid.

mechanisms.[17] The strict application of the control mechanisms has denied damages to an employee whose psychiatric injury was induced by his feeling responsible for the death of a fellow-workman. C returned to the scene of the accident about 15 minutes later to be told of the fatality when a hydrant had exploded. His feeling of responsibility arose from his vehicle having struck the hydrant causing it to leak. But he was not himself at physical risk, did not witness the accident and could not meet the tests applicable to a secondary victim.[18]

### C's lack of financial resources[19]

At least in the case of a businessperson, C's impecuniosity is treated as an 'extraneous cause' if it prevents him from adopting a reasonable method of mitigating his loss arising from D's tort.[20] So where the tort causes the total loss of C's profit-earning chattel (such as the ship in the *Liesbosch* case)[1] but a substitute is reasonably available, C's damages will be assessed on the basis of the cost[2] of obtaining the substitute, whether or not C had the financial resources to buy it.[3] If his lack of resources forced him to take more expensive steps, such as hiring a substitute, he cannot recover the extra cost from D.[4] The implicit assumption in the decision to treat C's impecuniosity as irrelevant seems to be that, without waiting until D actually pays damages, the typical business owner of a profit-earning chattel should be able to raise the money to buy a replacement when it is destroyed – either he should be covered by insurance, or, if he chooses to 'self-insure', he should be sufficiently credit-worthy to borrow the necessary money. This is not spelt out in the leading speech of Lord Wright in the *Liesbosch* case, but it seems to be the only rational justification for the decision on this point.

A contrast with the *Liesbosch* case is found in a Privy Council[5] decision in which the roof of C's house was seriously damaged by corrosive dust

---

17 The House of Lords also held that the policemen's 'employment' relationship with D (the Chief Constable) did not entitle them to any special status when they suffered psychiatric injury by witnessing the accidents.

18 *Hunter v British Coal Corpn* [1999] QB 140, CA.

19 Cf the position in contract, where C may be able to show that his impecuniosity was within the parties' contemplation at time of contracting: see p 105 n 18.

20 *Liesbosch Dredger v Steamship Edison*, above n 9.

1 Ibid.

2 Ibid. (The facts of the case are considered in more detail at pp 536-540 below.)

3 For other consequential costs, see pp 536, 539 below.

4 Ibid.

5 *Alcoa Minerals of Jamaica Inc v Herbert Broderick* [2000] 3 WLR 23. In Coote's opinion, the Privy Council should have used this case as an opportunity to overrule the *Liesbosch*: B Coote, 'Damages, *The Liesbosch* and Impecuniosity' [2001] Cambridge Law Journal 511.

from D's smelting plant. The cost of repairs increased rapidly until the date when the court held D liable for the cost of repairs, but it was held to be reasonable (under the mitigation rules) for C to delay the repairs while D denied liability for the nuisance. It was foreseeable that the owner of an ordinary house might lack the funds to undertake the repairs; it was not like the *Liebosch* case, where C could be expected to go into the market to buy a substitute.

### Financial loss caused by negligent acts

In situations not involving C's acting in reliance on D's statements, D may act negligently and cause reasonably foreseeable financial loss to C. The main issue in these cases is whether D owes C a duty of care in various situations. But even where some duty is owed to C, the courts have restricted the types of causation which will be permitted to support recovery of damages for financial loss arising from D's negligent act. If D negligently causes reasonably foreseeable physical harm to C or his property, he will also be liable for any reasonably foreseeable financial loss to C which is consequent upon that physical harm. Damage to a profit-earning chattel, or to land or buildings used to generate rent or profits, is likely to cause loss of rent or profits. But if C's financial loss is not the consequence of physical harm to himself or his property, no recovery is allowed even where that loss was a reasonably foreseeable consequence of D's negligence. So where D's negligence cuts off C's supply of a utility, such as electricity, gas or water, then (if a duty of care is imposed on D) C may recover for foreseeable physical damage to his property, and for foreseeable loss of profits arising from that physical damage. But C cannot recover any loss of profits arising simply from his not receiving the supply of the utility.[6] In one case, D negligently damaged a cable carrying electricity to C's factory. The loss of power for 14 hours damaged molten metal in a furnace at the time of the cut-off, leading to a loss of profit on that melt (the first loss); a further loss of profit arose from the loss of further melts which C could have made during the period of the cut-off (the second loss). The Court of Appeal allowed damages for the first loss but not the second.[7] This restriction is an arbitrary one, designed simply to protect tortfeasors from a potentially crushing liability: it is in line with the refusal of the courts to impose a duty of care on D, even where reasonably foreseeable financial loss is likely to be

---

6   *Spartan Steel and Alloys Ltd v Martin & Co (Contractors) Ltd* [1973] QB 27. (D knew that under the road where he was excavating there was an electricity line to C's factory.)
7   Ibid (followed in *Muirhead v Industrial Tank Specialities Ltd* [1986] QB 507).

caused to C, if the causation is dependent on D's causing physical harm (or the risk of it) to a third person or his property.[8] The absence of physical harm to any property owned or possessed by C is the crucial factor in denying recovery to C.

## Consequences of defamation

Policy restrictions may lead to rulings that certain heads of loss fall outside the intended scope of the tort in question.[9] So where C's ill health was caused by being slandered, this type of harm was held to be too remote a consequence to be recovered in a claim for slander: this ruling amounts to a policy decision that good health is not an interest protected by that tort.[10] A similar decision was that in an action for slander not actionable per se, a woman could not recover damages for loss of her marriage when her husband turned her out because of the slander.[11] Although these decisions were based on the application of the then current test for remoteness, they were really attempts to limit the scope of the particular tort. The policy behind these old decisions should, of course, be reconsidered in the light of modern circumstances.

## Strict liability

In torts of strict liability, the risk of causing harm is placed on D because he chose to do something which created an unusual risk. So an occupier of land from which a dangerous substance escapes and causes damage to neighbouring land is liable under the rule in *Rylands v Fletcher*.[12] Escape from D's land is necessary, but liability is strict because the escape itself need not have been reasonably foreseeable. Nevertheless, in the *Cambridge Water* case[13] the House of Lords decided that the remoteness test was reasonable foreseeability in both *Rylands v Fletcher* and in private nuisance. D stored toxic chemicals on his land, a 'non-natural' use which

---

8    *Cattle v Stockton Waterworks Co* (1875) LR 10 QB 453; *Weller & Co v Foot and Mouth Disease Research Institute* [1966] 1 QB 569; *Candlewood Navigation Corpn Ltd v Mitsui OSK Lines Ltd*, above p 320 n 8. (The issues involved in this situation are discussed in D Harris and CJ Veljanovski, 'Liability for Economic Loss in Tort', in Furmston (ed) *The Law of Tort*, above n 4, 45).

9    HLA Hart and T Honoré, *Causation in the Law* (2nd edn) pp 304–307. This type of approach is adopted to decide whether a claim for damages may be based on breach of a statutory prohibition: *Gorris v Scott* (1874) LR 9 Exch 125.

10   *Allsop v Allsop* (1860) 5 H & N 534.

11   *Lynch v Knight* (1861) 9 HL Cas 577.

12   (1868) LR 3 HL 330.

13   *Cambridge Water Co v Eastern Counties Leather Co* [1994] 2 AC 264.

would lead to *Rylands v Fletcher* liability if it escaped from his land, despite the absence of any fault on his part in foreseeing or preventing the escape. Lord Goff said: 'it is plain that, at the time when the chemical was brought on to [D's] land, and indeed when it was used in the tanning process there, nobody at [D] could reasonably have foreseen the resulting damage which occurred at [C's] borehole'.[14] (The chemical seeped into D's land and was carried by percolating water to C's land 1.3 miles away.) The House of Lords made it clear in this sentence that they applied the test of reasonable foreseeability to the accumulation and use of the chemical, not to its escape from D's land. But it is the escape which is crucial for liability yet foreseeability was not tested by asking which types of harm could be foreseen, given the assumption[15] that (unforeseeably) the chemical had escaped outside D's land. By applying the test only to the accumulation and use, their Lordships seriously undermined the scope of this category of strict liability and brought it much closer to the ordinary tort of negligence. The *Cambridge Water* test applies to private nuisance but it is not clear how far it can apply to other torts of strict liability. Under the Consumer Protection Act 1987 the injured consumer need prove only that the product was defective, in that it failed to meet the expected standard of safety. Surely the test for remoteness should assume knowledge of the defect, since that defect might not have been foreseeable at the time it was manufactured.

By statute, there is strict liability for 'any damage ... caused by an animal which belongs to a dangerous species'.[16] The reference to 'any damage' would seem to import a directness test for remoteness. Similarly in wrongful interference with chattels, it would be artificial to use the *Wagon Mound* test, because D's liability need not depend on either fault or knowledge of the facts: strict liability is imposed in order to vindicate proprietary or possessory interests as such.

A more rational way of restricting the extent of liability for the consequences of a tort of strict liability would be to say that damages are recoverable only for the types of harm 'within the risk' which the legislature or judges had in mind when imposing strict liability.[17] (A causal test would still be needed,[18] especially to deal with ulterior harm.)[19] The US *Restatement of Torts*, s 519 makes the person who carries on an

---

14   Ibid at 306
15   Cf the application of the remoteness test of reasonable contemplation in contract which is applied on the *assumption* that the breach will occur.
16   Animals Act 1971, s 2(1).
17   This approach is illustrated by the Animals Act 1971, s 2(2) dealing with liability for damage caused by an animal which does not belong to a dangerous species.
18   Hart and Honoré, *Causation in the Law*, above n 9, pp 286–290.
19   See pp 305-306 above.

ultra-hazardous activity liable for 'resulting' harm if it was the risk of that kind of harm which rendered the activity 'abnormally dangerous'.

## Torts involving deliberate wrongdoing

The *Wagon Mound* test was obviously designed to place limits on liability for torts based on carelessness. Different justifications are needed for placing limits on D's liability for the consequences of deliberate or intentional wrongdoing, and the limits need not be drawn in the same way as for negligent acts: the justification given in *The Wagon Mound* for the reasonable foreseeability test clearly did not cover intentionally caused harm.

In one tort based on D's knowledge and intention we now have clear authority. In the *Smith New Court* case[20] the House of Lords held that the victim of fraud (deceit) was entitled to damages for all his actual loss (including consequential loss) directly flowing from the transaction which D induced him to enter. Their Lordships accepted that the test of directness is wider than reasonable foreseeability: of course, causation must be proved and C is always bound to take reasonable steps to mitigate his loss. If, however, on the particular facts, a type of harm resulting from D's deceit was 'reasonably foreseeable' but could not be labelled 'direct' – as where the voluntary act of a third party intervened – it is submitted that this consequence should also be held not to be too remote.[1] Finally, in deliberate torts, it should be accepted that, once causation is established, *intended* consequences are not too remote.[2] Thus, in deceit, D should be liable to pay damages in respect of any consequence suffered by C if it was an intended, or direct, or a reasonably foreseeable[3] type of consequence of D's deceit. The remoteness test should be widened in this way to increase the deterrent effect of any tort based on D's deliberate wrongdoing.

The remoteness tests in other intentional torts, such as intimidation, interference with contractual relations, assault, battery or

---

20  *Smith New Court Securities Ltd v Scrimgeour Vickers (Asset Management) Ltd* [1997] AC 254. At pp 560-561 below, we examine the method of assessing damages where C was induced by deceit to buy something.
1   Some authority for this extension may be found in the tort of intimidation: see pp 567-568 below.
2   *Quinn v Leathem* [1901] AC 495 at 537 (conspiracy: 'the intention to injure the plaintiff ... disposes of any question of remoteness of damage').
3   In *Wilkinson v Downton* [1897] 2 QB 57, D was liable for causing (foreseeable) nervous shock to C as the result of telling her a lie (that her husband had been injured) which D intended 'as a practical joke'.

malicious prosecution, should be the same as for deceit.[4] The special case of conspiracy is considered below:[5] the definition accepted by the House of Lords appears to have restricted Ds' liability, first by requiring that the harm to C must have been *caused* by their acts in pursuance of the agreement and, secondly, by requiring that their *purpose* in doing those acts must have been to injure C. If this excludes liability for direct or reasonably foreseeable consequences (though not intended) it is an unfortunate restriction to the scope of a tort which is explicitly based on an intention to harm C. If the type of harm suffered by C is different from that intended by D but is nevertheless a direct consequence of D's act, there can be no social justification for imposing liability on D in deceit but not in conspiracy.[6]

### Comparison with the rules on remoteness in contract

The superficial resemblance of the *Heron II*[7] test and the *Wagon Mound* test invites a comparison between the tort and contract rules for remoteness of damage. In the following comparison, the tort side examines the *Wagon Mound* test as applied to the tort of negligence. Different considerations apply to torts of strict liability and to intentional torts, and any comparison would be less useful in deepening understanding.

| **Contract** | **The tort of negligence** |
|---|---|
| *Purpose* | |
| The parties, having entered voluntarily into an exchange relationship, may convey information to each other, and are free to define precisely by the terms of their contract the extent of their responsibilities to each other. Their | In the typical[8] situation of tortious negligence the parties have not voluntarily entered into any relationship – they are strangers; there is no opportunity for them to exchange information about unusual risks or to agree upon any |

---

4   See pp 554-557 below.
5   See pp 565-567.
6   There might be a justification if all liability in conspiracy is considered anomalous, so that it should be restricted by any means available.
7   See pp 94-97 above.
8   Some tortious liabilities are imposed in contractual-type situations (eg the employment relationship, or in situations 'equivalent to contract', eg negligent mis-statement) but these marginal extensions of tort should not blind us to the typical type of situation where tortious liability is imposed.

obligations are self-imposed, and may be subject to any restrictions whether as to the primary obligations or as to the remedies for breach of those obligations. Breach of an undertaking depends on its actual wording, and is usually not dependent on any proof of fault. The promisee is entitled to the promised protection by D against the risks specified in the contract – the degree of protection which D expressly or impliedly promised and which C 'bought' by his own undertakings. (This is almost invariably greater protection than is given by the law to all citizens.)

reciprocal allocation of risks. the law itself imposes on all citizens the same community-wide minimum standard of conduct in the particular type of situation. The parties have no opportunity to restrict their potential liability, nor to specify the remedies they desire: the law imposes on them its own form of reciprocal risk-taking, which is usually based on concepts of fault, or on the responsibilities impliedly assumed when D engages in a particular activity.

### Formulation of the test

D is liable for the types of consequence which, on the assumption that D would break the particular undertaking, were within the reasonable contemplation of the parties.

D is liable for the types of consequence which were reasonably foreseeable as risks to be avoided by the reasonable man.

### The time for applying the test and for fixing the information to be used

At the time of contracting, and on the basis of the parties' actual or imputed knowledge at that time.

Immediately after the occurrence of the act or omission held to be negligent, and on the basis of D's actual or imputed knowledge at that time.

### Degree of probability of consequence occurring

Not unlikely

Usually, a lower degree of likelihood than 'not unlikely': the risk of the consequence occurring must be such that the reasonable man would have taken reasonable steps to avoid it

## *The nature of the typical type of loss*

Typically, the contract imposes a positive duty on D to produce a stated result for C's benefit; the breach is an omission – a failure to produce that result – and C's loss is his disappointed expectations, viz the fact that he has not received the anticipated benefit of D's performance.

The typical loss is physical harm to C himself or to his property, and consequential losses. (D is usually under a negative duty not to cause that harm.) Damages are not designed to put C into a better position than he would have been in had D not committed the tort against him.

Loss of expected profits (or consumer surplus) is recoverable even though it is not dependent on any physical harm to C or his property. Damages for physical harm are not excluded.

Normally, loss of earnings and of profits is recoverable only if it is consequential upon physical harm to C or his property, and only to the extent of restoring him to his position before the tort. (Even in the rare circumstances where purely financial loss is recoverable, the aim is to restore C to his former position, by compensating him for his reliance loss – not for his disappointed expectations.)

The cost of substitute performance is intended to give C the anticipated benefit of performance.

The cost of medical treatment or repairs is intended to restore C to his position before he suffered the harm.

# 21 Self-help

In tort, self-help has only a minor role in comparison with its role in contract, where the parties can agree in advance that C may unilaterally exercise various remedies.[1] Sometimes, however, self-help acts to prevent a tort being committed, rather than as a remedy after it has taken place. Self-defence is the obvious instance. A person may use a reasonable degree of force against another person to protect himself (or a third person) from an unlawful use of force by that other. But the force must be proportionate to the need for protection[2], and should normally be preceded by a warning.[3]

## Protection of the occupation of land

Action by C to protect his possession of land is another justification for self-help in tort. The occupier of land, or his agent, may use the minimum of force reasonably necessary to prevent a trespasser from entering his land, or to eject him from the land after he has had a reasonable opportunity to comply with a request to leave, but has failed to do so.[4] Self-help may also overlap with the defence of necessity, which may justify action which would otherwise be a tort. So a real and imminent danger to property justified D's trespass on C's land in order to prevent a heath fire from spreading.[5]

If D has actually taken possession of C's land, then provided C has the immediate right to possession he may enter peacefully to retake

1 See ch 3.
2 *Turner v Metro-Goldwyn-Mayer Pictures Ltd* [1950] 1 All ER 449 at 470–1; *Lane v Holloway* [1968] 1 QB 379 at 386–7; and *Revill v Newbery* [1996] QB 567 (CA discusses the limits on using force against a burglar to defend property).
3 Ibid.
4 *R v Chief Constable of Devon and Cornwall* [1982] QB 458 at 478. But the courts discourage the use of this remedy: ibid at 473.
5 *Cope v Sharpe (No 2)* [1912] 1 KB 496. See also *Rigby v Chief Constable of Northamptonshire* [1985] 1 WLR 1242 at 1254.

possession of it. But since 1381[6] it has been a criminal offence for C to use force to eject D. Under the Criminal Law Act 1977, s 6, it is an offence for C to use or to threaten to use violence to secure his entry into premises if he knows that the entry would be opposed by someone there. C must bring proceedings in court to recover possession where he cannot obtain it peacefully; a speedy procedure is available to enable C to recover possession of a house from which he has just been displaced.[7] But a landlord can recover possession of a dwelling-house from his tenant only by taking proceedings in court.[8]

The protection of occupation of land also justifies some self-help in cases of nuisance or encroachment. Without the sanction of the court, C, the occupier, or his agent, may himself abate a nuisance which is interfering with his enjoyment of the land in his occupation. It is an instance of mitigation in tort.[9] But, except for trees, there are in practice few nuisances where C can himself put an end to the interference.[10] The law does not favour self-help; it 'is justified only in clear and simple cases, or in an emergency'.[11] If C does himself abate, he must cause no more than the minimum harm to D's property[12], and the remedy must be exercised without delay.[13] C may cut off the branches of D's tree which overhang C's land,[14] or may sever the roots of D's tree which have spread into C's land.[15] But C must return to D the items he has severed.[16] Since C can cut them off at the boundary he need not enter D's land to do so, and hence he need not give any prior notice to D. But if C can abate a nuisance only by entering D's land, he must first request D himself to abate, and then give D prior notice of his intention to enter to abate.[17]

---

6    Forcible Entry Act 1381.
7    R Megarry and HWR Wade, *The Law of Real Property* (6th edn 2000) paras 22.128-22.301.
8    Protection from Eviction Act 1977, ss 2-3.
9    See pp 307-308 above.
10  However, in *Bradburn v Lindsay* [1983] 2 All ER 408, C was entitled to enter D's land to repair a party wall between them, after D's neglect to repair it had created a nuisance to C. See now the Party Wall etc Act 1996.
11  *Burton v Winter* [1993] 1 WLR 1077 at 1082, CA.
12  *Lagan Navigation Co v Lambeg Bleaching, Dyeing and Finishing Co Ltd* [1927] AC 226 at 244-245.
13  *Burton v Winter*, above n 11.
14  *Lemmon v Webb* [1894] 3 Ch 1, CA; affd [1895] AC 1, HL(E). No claim for damages arises until C suffers actual harm: *ibid* [1894] 3 Ch 1 at 11 and *Smith v Giddy* [1904] 2 KB 448.
15  *Butler v Standard Telephones and Cables Ltd* [1940] 1 KB 399 at 403. (Self-help is not C's only remedy: he may obtain an injunction: *McCombe v Read* [1955] 2 QB 429; or damages: *Davey v Harrow Corpn* [1958] 1 QB 60).
16  D could sue C in conversion if he wrongfully appropriated them: *Mills v Brooker* [1919] 1 KB 555.
17  *Lagan Navigation Co v Lambeg Bleaching, Dyeing and Finishing Co Ltd*, above n 12, at 245-246 and *Lemmon v Webb*, HL(E), above n 14 at 4-6, 8. See also the Access to Neighbouring Land Act 1992 (discussed at p 521 below).

(An emergency, where immediate harm is threatened, may justify C acting without prior notice.)[18]

## Retaking of chattels[19]

Where C is entitled to the immediate possession of a chattel but it is wrongfully held by D, C may retake it, provided he uses no more than reasonable force in doing so.[20] No case yet holds that C must previously have requested D to return it, but this would be a sensible analogy from the law on ejecting a trespasser (above). If the chattel is on land in D's occupation, C is entitled to enter the land in order to retake it, provided D himself is responsible for it being there; but in other situations, it is unsettled whether C may enter someone else's land to retake his chattel.[1]

## Detention of a 'trespassing' chattel

Distress damage feasant is the ancient, common law right of the occupier of land (C) to seize someone else's chattel[2] when it is still wrongfully on his land and is there causing harm to C, his land or chattels (or has caused harm while there on that occasion).[3] C's right is to detain the chattel as security until he receives adequate compensation for the harm it has caused, eg if a football breaks his window. In 1853, C was held to be entitled to seize D's railway engine wrongfully on C's line.[4] C's right is one of detention, similar to a lien[5] in that it confers no power on C to sell the chattel; but so long as it is exercised, it suspends C's right of action against D. In order to recover his chattel, its owner need not pay the amount demanded by C, but he must tender to C a sum which is adequate to compensate C for the harm suffered.[6] C is not entitled to distrain a vehicle parked without authority on his land but which causes no actual damage to the land.[7]

18  *Lemmon v Webb*, HL(E), above n 14 at 5.
19  CA Branston, 'The Forcible Recaption of Chattels' (1912) 28 Law Quarterly Review 262.
20  All the authorities, however, are old: eg *Blades v Higgs* (1865) 11 HL Cas 621.
1   *Salmond and Heuston on the Law of Torts* (21st edn 1996) p 574, n 20.
2   But the common law right does not extend to trespassing animals: the Animals Act 1971, s 7(1) abolished the right over animals, but s 7(2)-(7) substituted a new remedy to the occupier to detain (and ultimately to sell) straying livestock. Section 9 of the Act gives a person power to kill or injure a dog which is worrying livestock.
3   Reviews of the remedy are given in *Watkinson v Hollington* [1944] KB 16 (a cattle case: see preceding note) and in *Arthur v Anker* [1997] QB 564 (CA sought to limit the availability of the remedy).
4   *Ambergate, Nottingham and Boston Rly and Eastern Junction Rly Co v Midland Rly Co* (1853) 2 E & B 793.
5   See pp 48-49.
6   *Sorrell v Paget* [1950] 1 KB 252, 265–6 (an animal case, on which see n 2 above).
7   *Arthur v Anker*, above n 3 (the defence of *volenti* might apply).

# Part 6
# Compensation for personal injuries and death

# 22 Personal injury damages: the formal law

## Introduction

The aim of an award of damages for personal injury is stated to be to provide C with full compensation,[1] so far as an award of money can, for the loss he has suffered. The '100% principle', as it is sometimes described, is often referred to in terms which appear to admit of no alternative. In a recent decision of the House of Lords, it was described as 'common ground' and 'the premise of the debate'.[2] However there are alternative approaches[3] that are supported by other jurisdictions or systems of compensation.[4] Indeed these alternative approaches are sometimes supported indirectly by judicial decisions in this country.[5] Nonetheless the full compensation principle is now so entrenched in the case law that any retreat from it would have to be effected by legislation.[6] That the law

1 Eg see the following comments in the House of Lords *British Transport Commission v Gourley* [1956] AC 185 at 197; *Dews v National Coal Board* [1988] AC 1 at 12; *Hodgson v Trapp* [1989] AC 807 at 826 and *Wells v Wells* [1999] 1 AC 345 at 363, 382-383, 394, 398.
2 Ibid at 363, 382.
3 Patrick Atiyah has been a consistent and persuasive advocate of alternative approaches. See P Cane, *Atiyah's Accidents, Compensation and the Law* (6th edn 1999) pp 119-121, 126-134 and the highly readable PS Atiyah, *The Damages Lottery* (1997) (discussed at length at pp 453-461 below).
4 The New Zealand Accident Compensation Act 1972 provides for benefits of 80% of lost earnings and our domestic social security system generally provides benefits that fall well below full income replacement. See generally ch 24 below.
5 Eg the previous practices of imposing an upper limit for the 'multiplier' used in calculating damages for future pecuniary losses (see *McIlgrew v Devon County Council* [1995] PIQR Q66, Q77 and *Thomas v Brighton Health Authority* [1996] PIQR Q44 at Q57), 'discounting' the otherwise appropriate multiplier to reflect 'uncertainties' which have already been factored into the calculation. *Thomas* was one of the appeals consolidated in the House of Lords case of *Wells v Wells*, above n 1.

of personal injury compensation is committed to the 100% principle is sometimes obscured by the complexity of the detailed set of rules and sub-rules that seeks to effect it. It is easy to lose sight of the wood among the trees. When reading the account of the formal law that follows it is beneficial to bear in mind the overarching principle of full compensation that we will return to in the concluding part of this chapter. Although this chapter speaks of the court applying the formal rules we recognise that it is the parties who use the rules when negotiating an out of court settlement.

It should also be remembered that although damages for personal injury are most often sought in tort actions, eg an action in the tort of negligence arising from careless driving, such damages may also be a feature of contractual actions, eg arising from an employer's breach of the term implied by law into contracts of employment that the employer will take reasonable care not to endanger the health of employees.[7]

It is now the general practice of courts to itemise awards of damages for personal injury. The need to do so arose originally from the varying rates of interest[8] applicable to different 'heads of damage'.[9] Separate reasoning for each head is now usual, and appeals may be brought only in respect of the assessment for a particular head.[10] An appellate court, however, is reluctant to review a judge's award of damages: it will do so only if the judge made 'a wholly erroneous estimate' due to either a mistake of law or a misapprehension of the facts.[11]

The court must usually make a once-and-for-all assessment of all C's loss, both past and future; C's case cannot be reopened after the time for appealing has passed. Once-and-for-all assessment works satisfactorily where C's injuries are minor and C has recovered before trial. The situation is different where C's injuries are more serious and the court is necessarily called upon to assess future losses. In such a case the only inevitability about the award of damages is that it will be wrong. Despite the best efforts of the courts, given their imperfect ability to predict the future, the awards they make will, as events transpire either overcompensate or under-compensate C. For example C will be overcompensated if she returns to work earlier than anticipated and under-compensated if she returns to work later than expected. The best way to achieve full and accurate compensation for loss is to replace like for like. Lost future income is a loss of future periodic payments and so should be compensated for by an

---

6   *Wells v Wells* at 384.

7   *Johnstone v Bloomsbury Health Authority* [1992] QB 333 (junior doctors claimed that this term was breached when they were required to work long hours).

8   See generally pp 389-390 below.

9   The discussion that follows is structured around the distinct heads of damage.

10  *George v Pinnock* [1973] 1 WLR 118.

11  *Pickett v British Rail Engineering Ltd* [1980] AC 136 at 151, 172 and *Wells v Wells*, above n 1 at 376.

award of periodic payments.[12] The main advantage of periodic payments in place of a lump sum award is that the level of payment could, in the future, be adjusted to reflect changing circumstances. Periodic payments would also prevent C from 'squandering' a lump sum award (perhaps leaving the social security system, ie the taxpayer, to support C thereafter). They would also avoid C's estate receiving a 'windfall' in the event of C's premature death. However there are contrary arguments supporting the continuance of a system of lump sum awards. Accident victims prefer them because such awards empower them to make their own investment decisions[13] as well as avoiding a stressful[14] on-going relationship with the tortfeasor and his insurer. Insurers like them because they can 'close the book' once the claim is settled.

Some of the problems associated with the present system of lump sum awards may be avoided or ameliorated by a number of devices of varying breadth and efficacy. First in assessing damages, the court can take into account relevant facts which emerge between the injury (or death) and the time of trial. Where there is an appeal the appellate court may hear evidence of emerging facts.[15] The finality of a judgment or appellate decision may produce an incentive for one party to delay the trial or to appeal, in the hope that new facts will come to light which will assist his case. D may hope that C's medical recovery will be more rapid or greater than earlier prognoses predicted; while C may delay in the expectation that the cost of nursing care or other expenses will turn out to be higher than previously thought.[16] Inflation in the wage level relevant to C's occupation may also induce delay, because the court will take into account the level prevailing at the time of trial.[17] The timing of the trial or settlement may therefore be crucial. The court will not speculate about C's future on the basis of the facts immediately after the accident but will use all the subsequent facts that are known up to the trial.

Second there can be a 'split trial' where the issue of liability is settled with damages to be assessed later when better information is available concerning C's prognosis.[18] Where C has an immediate need for support

12   The general case for periodic payments is considered at pp 361-363 below.
13   See the Law Commission survey, *Personal Injury Compensation: How Much is Enough?* Law Com No 225 (1994) (hereinafter *How Much?*) p 181.
14   'Compensation neurosis' is a recognised psychological condition which has the effect of extending rehabilitation while levels of compensation are being worked out: see G Mendelson, '"Compensation Neurosis" Revisited: Outcome Studies of the Effects of Litigation' (1995) 39 Journal of Psychosomatic Research 695.
15   *Lim Poh Choo v Camden and Islington Area Health Authority* [1980] AC 174 at 183.
16   As happened in *Lim's case*, *ibid*.
17   *Cookson v Knowles* [1979] AC 556 at 575 (a fatal accident case; but the rule is the same for a surviving victim: see p 349 below).
18   Practice Direction 29, para 5.3(7).

this can be met by an order for an interim payment[19] so long as D is insured or a public authority.[20] Any application for an interim payment must now specify what it is to be used for.[1]

Third the court has the power to award periodic payments where both parties consent.[2] However such agreement 'is never, or virtually never, forthcoming', with the result that the present power to award periodic payments was described recently as 'a dead letter'.[3] Lord Steyn has argued that the courts should have the power to impose an award for periodic payment upon the parties.[4] The suggestion has not yet been acted upon, but the Lord Chancellor's Department has issued a consultation paper seeking views on the proposal.[5]

Fourth the court is able to award 'provisional' damages where 'there is proved... to be a chance that at some... time in the future the injured person will... develop some disease or suffer some deterioration in his physical or mental condition'.[6] Damages are awarded on the express assumption that C will not suffer any further deterioration, allowing further damages to be recovered if C does suffer that deterioration.[7] Further damages are not available where there has been a gradual deterioration in C's condition as opposed to a distinct and detrimental change.[8] Provisional damages have not proved popular in practice.[9]

Fifthly a new method of settling large[10] claims has emerged.[11] A so-called 'structured settlement'[12] may be agreed whereby C gives up his claim against D in exchange for a settlement which includes[13] periodic

19  Civil Procedure Rules, r.25.1(1)(k).
20  Civil Procedure Rules, r.25.7(2).
1   Practice Direction – Interim Payments, para 2.1.
2   Damages Act 1996, s 2.
3   *Wells v Wells*, above p 338 n 1.
4   Ibid at 502: 'Except perhaps for the distaste of personal injury lawyers for change to a familiar system, I can think of no substantial argument to the contrary'.
5   *Consultation Paper on Damages: The Discount Rate and Alternatives to Lump Sum Payments* (March 2000).
6   Supreme Court Act 1981, s 32A
7   Damages cannot be 'reduced' where C's condition improves.
8   *Wilson v Ministry of Defence* [1991] ICR 595.
9   See *How Much?* above p 340 n 13, pp 78-80.
10  It only seems to be used where the total claim is in excess of £0.5 m: R Lewis, 'The Damages Act 1996: The Future of Multipliers and Structured Settlements' [1996] Journal of Personal Injury Litigation 332, p 336.
11  The first use of a structured settlement was reported in 1981: see *Kelly v Dawes* (1990) Times, 27 September.
12  See generally R Lewis, *Structured Settlements* (1993) and IS Goldrein and MR de Haas (eds) *Structured Settlements* (2nd edn 1997).
13  Where the settlement consists of a lump sum as well as periodic payments this preserves C's ability to use his award to finance the purchase of a large capital asset such as a new house or to keep it as a contingency fund to meet his future needs which were not anticipated when the structured settlement was planned.

payments to be made to C. The periodic payments are financed by D's purchase of an inflation-proofed annuity.[14] The annuity will usually provide C with a regular income for the rest of his life. A structured settlement is attractive to C[15] because the risk of 'outliving' the judicial assessment of his life expectancy is effectively shifted to the insurer who provides the annuity. Further, C is relieved of the need to seek expensive investment advice.[16] Such settlements attract advantageous tax treatment[17] in so far as the income they produce is not taxable in the hands of the recipient. This enables D to provide a given level of income for C at less cost than would otherwise be possible. When this cost saving exceeds the set up costs such arrangements are popular with the insurers of defendants.

## Loss of earnings

Damages for loss of earnings or earning capacity are a major part of many claims for personal injury. In the majority of cases where the injury is minor C will have returned to work by the time damages fall to be assessed by the court. The more difficult scenario for a court is where the injury is more serious and the tribunal is required to make an assessment of its continuing effect on C's future income. The simple case is dealt with first.

### Loss of earnings up to the trial

C's loss of earnings between the accident and the trial is compensated by an award of so-called 'special' damages no matter how long the delay before the case comes to trial.[18] Such damages compensate C for his net loss of earnings, ie C's 'take home' pay after tax (including benefits in kind such as a 'season ticket loan')[19] and after the regular deductions from his pay have been made.[20]

The damages recovered by C reflect his full net loss. No reduction is made for contingencies between the date of the accident and the trial, eg unemployment, other incapacity which might have interrupted this stream of income; however the court will take into account the facts which have

14  An annuity is a periodic payment for the period of the annuitant's life.
15  *How Much?* above p 340 n 13, ch 12 recorded a high level of satisfaction among the beneficaries of structured settlements.
16  Investment advice 'costs' up to 1% p 9 of the sum invested according to *Wells v Wells*; above n 1 at 372-374.
17  Taxes Act 1988, ss 329AA and 329BB, as inserted by Finance Act 1996, Sch 26.
18  *Pritchard v JH Cobden* [1988] Fam 22.
19  *Liffen v Watson* [1940] 1 KB 556.
20  *Dews v National Coal Board*, above p 338 n 1.

occurred in this period. One consequence is that this produces an incentive for C to delay trial in the knowledge that this will increase his 'specials' to a greater extent than it diminishes his general damages for future income loss, where the multiplier applied reflects the uncertainties which are deliberately excluded from the calculation of pre-trial earnings. Nonetheless in a case where there was a delay of nine years between accident and trial the Court of Appeal has upheld the practice of making no reduction for contingencies.[1] It was said that 'the weapons' to be used to discourage delay were striking out the action for want of prosecution or depriving C of part of the interest which would otherwise be added to the special damages.[2]

A different approach to the assessment of loss of earnings up to trial would be for C to claim the cost of employing a substitute. This method of assessment may be used when such employment is a reasonable response to C's predicament. In one case[3] C, who was a working partner in a small garage business, recovered damages to cover the cost of employing a mechanic to do C's work. However C failed in his claim in respect of extra administrative duties formerly discharged by C but after the accident taken over by his wife. If C's wife had been employed under a contract to perform these duties a claim could have been made,[4] but she acted gratuitously.

## Income tax and other compulsory deductions from earnings

Damages for loss of earnings (past or future) must be assessed at the net amount which C would have received after deduction of income tax. The principle accepted by the House of Lords in *Gourley's* case[5] was that C should be compensated for his actual loss, which is the disposable amount[6] left in his hands after the deductions which his employer would be compelled[7] by law to make. Their Lordships claimed that 'to ignore the tax element at the present day would be to act in a manner which is out of touch of reality.'[8] The *Gourley* principle depends on two assumptions: (1) that C's earnings would have been subject to tax as

1   *Pritchard v JH Cobden*, above p 342 n 18.
2   Ibid. Of course the reform of civil procedure effected by Lord Woolf may in the future discourage delay on C's part.
3   *Hardwick v Hudson* [1999] 1 WLR 1770.
4   Such a claim may not have been to C's advantage because payment to C's wife would reduce the profits available to share between the partners: ibid at 1775.
5   *British Transport Commission v Gourley*, above n 1. (The principle applies to both employees and self-employed taxpayers).
6   In *Dews v National Coal Board*, above p 338 n 1 at 16 a similar phrase was used: 'income available for immediate expenditure ... for his immediate disposal'.
7   In *Dews* case, ibid, the principle was widened beyond compulsory deductions.
8   *British Transport Commission v Gourley*, above p 338 n 1 at 203.

income; and (2) that C's damages for the loss of these earnings will not be subject to tax.[9] Whenever C's earnings are high, the difference between gross and net income will be considerable, because the rate of tax to be used is that actually applicable to C's lost earnings.[10] Gourley was a consultant engineer whose earnings were reduced after the accident: the deduction for the then-current high levels of tax resulted in his damages for loss of earnings being reduced from £37,720 gross to £6,695 net. (The lost earnings must be treated as the top slice of C's notional total income, which slice would have been taxed at his highest rate.)[11]

The method of making the deduction is that the court should make a broad, 'rough-and-ready' estimate[12] of C's potential tax liability at the rates of tax and of allowances current at the time of judgment. This means that C will be undercompensated to the extent that income tax rates are reduced after the judgment (as, indeed, happened after *Gourley's* case itself). Some investigation is needed of C's total tax position – his investment income, his wife's income, his allowances and reliefs (eg covenants in favour of others) – as well as of the possibility that C could in future minimise his tax liability by various arrangements, such as by making covenants, gifts, and settlements.[13] D is entitled to reasonable particulars of C's taxable income from other sources, and of his tax assessments and allowances, but the courts discourage elaborate calculations that might increase costs.[14]

Taking account of tax may sometimes operate in another way. If through a period of unemployment C saves tax because he obtains a tax rebate[15] on his pre-tax earnings or on his earnings after his return to work (a 'tax holiday'), he must give credit for the saving in his claim for damages.[16]

The principle of *Gourley's* case has been applied to C's national insurance contributions to the Social Security Fund, which his employer

---

9    Damages for over £30,000 paid for removal from an office or employment are subject to tax Income and Corporation Taxes Act 1970 (as amended): On the tax payable on the income of the investments made by C with the damages see pp 359-360 below.

10    *British Transport Commission v Gourley*, above p 338 n 1 at 207.

11    *Lyndale Fashion Manufacturers v Rich* [1973] 1 WLR 73.

12    *British Transport Commission v Gourley*, above p 338 n 1 at 203, 207, 215. This is particularly true where C is engaged in a business or profession: his recent profits will normally be the base for future projections.

13    *Beach v Reed Corrugated Cases Ltd* [1956] 1 WLR 807.

14    *Phipps v Orthodox Unit Trusts Ltd* [1958] 1 QB 314.

15    This may arise from the way in which the PAYE Tables work: the allowances due to C are normally spread evenly over the whole tax year, but if there is a gap in his earnings during the year, the allowances for that period will later reduce the tax payable on his actual earnings for the balance of the year.

16    *Hartley v Sandholme Iron Co Ltd* [1975] QB 600.

is legally required to deduct from his wages.[17] Under his contract of employment, a deduction may also be made from C's wages in respect of his contributions to a pension scheme to which he is obliged to belong as one of the terms of his employment. The House of Lords recently held[18] that when C received no wages while he was away from work and so paid no contributions to the pension scheme, damages should be assessed only for his net loss, viz after deducting the amount of the unpaid contributions. If C has in fact lost some entitlement to an ultimate pension,[19] that diminution in his pension rights should be valued separately and general damages awarded for it.[20]

The *Gourley* principle has attracted much critical comment. Critics point to the difficult calculation the tribunal is called to make[1], the shortfall of revenue to the Treasury[2], the reduced deterrent of tort liability[3], the inconsistent treatment of damages,[4] the unjust advantage derived by D from his reduced liability and the potential under-compensation that might result because damages are 'reduced' when C would not otherwise have had a capital sum to invest and C will be taxed in any event upon the income produced from investing that sum.[5] As a result *Gourley* has not always been popular in other jurisdictions.[6]

17  *Cooper v Firth Brown Ltd* [1963] 1 WLR 418 (a wrongful dismissal case).
18  *Dews v National Coal Board*, above p 338 n 1. (D was C's employer at the time of the accident, but the same principle would apply even if D were a stranger). The deduction should be made even for voluntary contributions to a pension scheme, if C was likely to continue them.
19  In *Dews* case, ibid, C's ultimate entitlement was not affected.
20  Ibid and *Auty v National Coal Board* [1985] 1 WLR 784.
1  *North Island Wholesale Groceries Ltd v Hewin* [1982] 2 NZLR 176
2  AI Ogus, *The Law of Damages* (1973) p 114.
3  W Bishop and J Kay, 'Taxation and Damages: The Rule in *Gourley's* Case' (1987) 104 Law Quarterly Review 211. Since the burden of the loss of the tax which C would have paid is borne by taxpayers in general, D's tort imposes an external cost on the community.
4  JA Jolowicz, 'Damages and Income Tax' [1959] Cambridge Law Journal 86 points to the paradox of treating the receipt of lump sum damages as capital for Revenue purposes and as income when assessing the damages. Cf GH Treitel, *The Law of Contract* (10th edn 1999) p 863.
5  In exceptional circumstances the Court may take account of the greater tax liability imposed upon the recipient of a large damages award. See pp 359-360 below.
6  *Cunningham v Wheeler* (1994) 113 DLR (4th) 1 at 21-3 (Canada – not followed), *North Island Wholesale Groceries Ltd v Hewin* [1982] 2 NZLR 176 (New Zealand – not followed in a contractual claim for damages for loss of office – displaced for personal injury actions in tort by the statutory compensation scheme considered below in ch 24. In Australia *Gourley* has been followed after initial doubts, in *Cullen v Trappell* (1980) 146 CLR 1, overruling *Atlas Tiles Ltd v Briers* (1978) 144 CLR 202.

## Future loss of earnings

The more difficult (and interesting) aspect of assessment of loss of earnings comes when C is still unable to work at the time of the trial. This assessment requires the court to assess the expected period of incapacity from which to derive a 'multiplier' to be applied to the net annual loss (the multiplicand). At its simplest the award of damages for future loss of earnings is the product of these two variables.

## The expected period of incapacity

The period for which C will be unable to earn will depend on the medical evidence and the facts known up to the time of the trial. If C is permanently unable to earn, or his ability to earn will be permanently limited, the court must make a finding of his pre-accident expectation of his remaining years of working life up to his normal retirement age. This requires the court to estimate two things: the victim's pre-accident life expectancy and his pre-accident retirement age.[7] The Government Actuary's Department has for a considerable time produced life tables of various kinds.[8] These were based upon historic data derived from national censuses. Initially actuarial evidence was treated with considerable suspicion by the courts; in one case the predictions of actuaries were likened to those of astrologers.[9] This resistance was based partly upon the fear that such expert evidence would add to the length and so the cost of trials. Resistance to the use of actuarial evidence lessened following the production in 1984 by an inter-professional working party of actuaries and lawyers of a dedicated set of tables.[10] The *Ogden Tables*,[11] as they are known, were designed to indicate the appropriate figure (the 'multiplier') by which the net annual loss (the 'multiplicand'[12]) should be multiplied to produce a lump sum award. The House of Lords recently endorsed the *Ogden Tables* as the 'starting point' in the calculation of an appropriate multiplier rather than as a 'check' on the judge's calculation.[13] The latest version[14] includes tables based upon projected rather than historic mortality rates. This was a response to a fear

7    The 'normal' retirement age for men, and now also for women, is 65.
8    Some are helpfully reproduced in *Facts and Figures Tables for the Calculation of Damages* .
9    *Auty v National Coal Board*, above n 60.
10   Government Actuary's Department, *Actuarial Tables with Explanatory Notes For Use in Personal Injury and Fatal Accident Cases* (4th edn 2000) (hereinafter *Ogden Tables*).
11   After Sir Michael Ogden, the Chairman of the Working Party which produces the *Tables*.
12   See p 349 below
13   *Wells v Wells*, above p 338 n 1 at 376, 379, 388, 393 and 397.
14   4th edn 2000.

that the old tables would leave victims under-compensated because they failed to make allowance for future improvements in longevity. Judges now appear to be basing their calculations upon the tables incorporating projected mortality rates.[15] Different tables are available based upon retirement ages of 55, 60, 65 and 70 both for men and women together with guidance to permit interpolation for other retirement ages. The tables also permit a considerable degree of 'fine-tuning' to C's particular circumstances by means of further adjustments for contingencies other than mortality that might affect income earning such as possible unemployment or illness. These risks vary according to C's occupation and geographical location and the adjustments are made on that basis. Once an assessment of C's life expectancy has been arrived at, probably with the assistance of expert medical evidence, there is no justification for any further reduction in the corresponding multiplier. Such a practice, which might reflect judicial instinct that damages awards in serious cases are too high, is inconsistent with the stated aim of full compensation and has been expressly disapproved in the House of Lords.[16] The detailed rules concerning the calculation of the appropriate multiplier are examined below.[17]

### The 'lost years'

Where the injury has reduced C's expectation of life, so that she is not expected to survive until her normal retirement age, the pre-accident expectation of her working life is still the relevant period for the assessment of her future loss of earnings.[18] In the case of a young child the calculation of potential earnings in the lost years may be considered so speculative that no award at all is made. In one such case,[19] C was 7 at the date of the trial. His damages were based upon his post accident life expectancy of 40 years.[20]

15  Paragraph 9. See eg *Biesheuvel v Birrell* [1999] PIQR Q40.
16  *Wells v Wells* p 338 n 1 at 379.
17  See pp 354-360
18  *Pickett v British Rail Engineering Ltd* [1980] AC 136.
19  *Croke v Wiseman* [1982] 1 WLR 71. See also *Connolly v Camden and Islington Area Health Authority* [1981] 3 All ER 250 (C was 17 days old when accident occurred. Post accident life expectancy was $27^1/_2$ years. Due to the pre-trial delay the multiplier was derived from $22^3/_4$ years the balance of the post accident life expectancy with no allowance for the 'lost years'.
20  C was 21 months when the accident occurred. Where a claim is brought by a living claimant the multiplier is derived from the remainder of the post accident life expectancy at the time of trial (in this case 33 years because of the long delay in bringing the action to trial). The period from accident to trial is dealt with by an award of 'special damages' – see above p 342. Compare the approach to a Fatal Accidents Act claim considered in ch 23.

Where a lost year's claim is allowed a deduction must be made from C's potential earnings during those years to take account of the living expenses which C would have incurred. A deduction is made in respect of such sums as C would have spent exclusively on himself leaving out of account any sums C would have spent exclusively to benefit others.[1] The amount to be regarded as spent exclusively on C has become conventional. Where the family unit consists of a husband and wife the figure is 33%; where there are children the figure falls to 25%.[2] A single person is assumed, in the absence of pressing evidence to the contrary, to spend most of his income on his own maintenance and enjoyment.[3] Where the whole or part of C's net earnings is spent on living expenses for the joint benefit of himself and his dependants a proportion of those expenses is treated as part of C's deductible living expenses.[4] The exact proportion varies with the number of dependants. If C is married with no children ½ of the joint expenses are regarded as part of C's living expenses. If C is married with two children the proportion is ¼. An example will illustrate these deductions:

> C who is married with no children is involved in a non-fatal accident. C's life expectancy is reduced. C's claim for income in the 'lost years' is calculated by taking away from his net annual loss both the conventional percentage of expenditure exclusively attributable to C as well as a proportion of the shared expenses. If C's net income is £24000 pa then £8000 is regarded as spent solely on C and £8000 as spent for the joint benefit of C and his wife.

The lost year's calculation would be based upon:

$$£24000 - £8000 - (£8000/2) = £12000$$

Where the lost year's claim is speculative but not to the extent, as with very young claimants, to justify a nil award, the court may decline to do the elaborate calculation described above. Rather, compensation for the lost years may be effected by a small increase in the multiplier that would otherwise be applied. On this basis the multiplier of a 27-year-old was increased from 21.9 to 22.4 to take account of 11 lost years.[5]

1    *Harris v Empress Motors* [1984] 1 WLR 212.
2    Ibid.
3    *Adsett v West* [1983] QB 826.
4    A different approach is take to joint expenses in relation to claims by dependants under the Fatal Accidents Act 1976 where no reduction is made in respect of shared expenses such as car loan repayments. The law acts on the fact that you cannot drive half a car! See *Harris v Empress Motors*, above n 1 and see generally pp 339-340 below.
5    *Biesheuvel v Birrell*, above p 347 n 15.

The damages awarded for the lost years will enable C to make provision for dependants, but there is no obligation on him to use the damages in this way – he may have no dependants, and even if he does he could squander all the damages on himself during his shortened life, or give it away to non-dependants.

### The annual loss: the multiplicand

Once the future period is estimated, the next step is to establish the annual amount which, but for the accident, C would have been earning at the time of the trial.[6] To calculate this figure the court takes C's actual earnings at the time of the accident, and uprates them by reference to relevant pay awards since then. C therefore effectively gets the benefit of any wage-inflation up to the trial. If C's category of work was subject to routine unemployment (eg as a 'picker' of seasonal fruit or as an unskilled labourer working on construction sites), the expected annual loss of earnings should be adjusted downwards.[7] If C had good prospects ('a real possibility')[8] of promotion or career advancement this would justify an increase in the applicable multiplicand.[9] Where future promotion is contingent upon success in an exam or competition and such advancement was more likely than not, the extra earnings the promotion would have secured may be discounted by the likelihood that C would not pass the exam or succeed in the competition.[10]

Calculation of the appropriate multiplicand has proved problematic when C is self-employed or the major shareholder of a small company. The approach of the courts in such cases is to require C to produce full accounts but also to look beyond the formal arrangements where necessary. This is well illustrated by a case where for tax reasons the profits of a partnership were distributed evenly between the two working partners and their spouses. C recovered damages reflecting his real loss of 50% of the partnership profits rather than the quarter share to which he was formally entitled.[11]

---

6 *Cookson v Knowles*, above p 340 n 17. That C also had the benefit of substantial unearned income is irrelevant: *Phillips v London and South Western Rly Co* (1879) 5 CPD 280, 294.
7 *Rouse v Port of London Authority* [1953] 2 Lloyd's Rep 179 (dock labourer).
8 *Wynn v NSW Insurance Ministerial Corpn* (1995) 184 CLR 485.
9 *Roach v Yates* [1938] 1 KB 256, 269.
10 *Anderson v Davis* [1993] PIQR Q87 (multiplicand adjusted to reflect 2 in 3 chance that Polytechnic lecturer would be promoted to senior lecturer). Cf *Miles v Steele* (3 March 1989) (£3000 awarded as lump sum to reflect loss of 20% chance of passing an examination).
11 *Ward v Newalls Insulation Co Ltd* [1998] 2 All ER 690.

## Assessing the net loss

The objective in calculating C's earnings is to find his net loss. The figure should be his loss of 'take-home' pay, after deducting the income tax, and the national insurance and pension contributions which he would have paid on his gross earnings. The courts appear to take a robust approach to the calculation of the net loss that eschews overly elaborate calculation. On this basis the House of Lords have said that there should not be a routine deduction in respect of the travel expenses which C is 'saved'.[12]

The effect of deducting pension contributions from the multiplicand could without further adjustment leave C under-compensated to the extent that he is deprived of future pension entitlement. C is therefore entitled by way of addition to his general damages to the capitalised value of the difference between the pension (if any) he will in fact receive and the pension he would, but for D's wrong, have been entitled to. This exercise of representing as a present capital sum the loss of a future stream of pension income should reflect the court's approach to the same exercise in the context of loss of future income. Therefore it is to be expected that that reliance upon the *Ogden Tables*[13] will now displace more traditional methods of calculation.[14] The general principles of mitigation[15] 'require'[16] C to take reasonable steps to minimise the loss caused to him by the accident. Therefore if C either has obtained or could reasonably be expected to obtain alternative pensionable employment, the present value of that pension must be deducted from the element of general damages representing C's loss of pension rights.

More generally the principle of mitigation may 'require' C to seek alternative employment. The 'duty' to mitigate is a qualified rather than an absolute one. C must only take reasonable steps to make him eligible for and find alternative employment. C's damages will be assessed on the basis that he should have taken reasonable advantage of the medical and rehabilitation services available to him, and should have accepted

12  *Dews v National Coal Board*, above p 338 n 1 at 13.
13  See *Kemp and Kemp on the Quantum of Damages*, vol 1, paras 6.005-6.015.
14  As to which see *Auty v National Coal Board*, above n 60. Other methods might include costing the purchase of an annuity sufficient to provide the shortfall in future pension payments or not deducting C's pension contributions from his net annual loss and adding to his damages the capitalised value of C's employer's pension contributions. For a discussion of the competing methods see JJ Rowley, 'A Guide to Pension Loss Calculation' [1995] Journal of Personal Injury Litigation 107.
15  Which were developed mainly in contract cases but which also apply to those who are victims of torts. See ch 7
16  The so called 'duty' to mitigate only 'requires' C to act to minimise his losses in the sense that C's failure to do so will reduce the amount of damages he will receive. See above p 110.

reasonable opportunities to earn, even those involving a change in occupation. On this basis a general medical practitioner who could not continue in general practice might still be able to work as a radiologist.[17] The test of 'reasonableness' confers wide discretion on the court in assessing C's individual circumstances. A manual worker who used to do heavy work may still be able to do lighter work. But if he has no skills for non-manual work, and no chance of being trained for any more skilled work, his damages must be assessed on the basis of a total loss of earnings.[18] So long as C's decision to take up a new job was a reasonable one better conditions of service which are not readily converted into cash (such as shorter hours or longer holidays) will not reduce C's damages.[19] Where C changes his occupation C may be able to recover damages for the loss of congenial or satisfying employment irrespective of any loss of earnings. A modest award of such damages was made to a fireman who attended the Kings Cross disaster[20] and who as a result of his injuries later accepted employment as a fire prevention officer. The award of £5,000 was paid to compensate C for the lost sense of satisfaction as a member of emergency services responsible for rescuing those in danger.[1]

### Young victims

When called upon to assess the likely adult earnings of very young children the court is faced with a very difficult task. In one such case where C was injured shortly after his birth the judge described the assessment of damages as 'all very problematical, all very artificial, all very hypothetical, all very difficult'[2] and concluded that '[t]he only "yardstick", if it can even be dignified with that word, that could be taken was in the plastering trade, following in father's footsteps.'[3] An alternative method for deriving the appropriate multiplicand for very young children is to assume that C would earn the national average wage.[4] In other cases courts have

17 *Billingham v Hughes* [1949] 1 KB 643.
18 *Ransom v Sir Robert McAlpine and Sons Ltd* (1971) 11 KIR 141.
19 *Arafa v Potter* [1994] PIQR Q73.
20 Where several people died in a fire at an underground railway station.
1 *Hale v London Underground Ltd* [1993] PIQR Q30.
2 *Connolly v Camden and Islington Area Health Authority* [1981] 3 All ER 250, 255. To similar effect is the comment of *McGregor on Damages* (16th edn 1997) para 1582 that the assessment of a young C's damages in *Cassel v Hammersmith and Fulham Health Authority* [1992] PIQR Q168 was based upon no more than 'the propitious omens to be derived from ... the child's heredity and environment'.
3 Ibid. See also *Taylor v Bristol Omnibus Co Ltd* [1975] 1 WLR 1054 at 1061–2 , *Almond v Leeds Western Health Authority* [1990] 1 Med LR 370 (1.5 times national average wage) and *Cassel v Hammersmith and Fulham Health Authority* [1992] PIQR Q168 (2.5 times national average wage).
4 *Croke v Wiseman*, above p 347 n 19.

recognised the artificial nature of the calculation by rejecting a mathematical approach and awarding a broadly fair sum.[5]

### Disadvantage in the labour market

After his return to work C may suffer no immediate loss of earnings but nonetheless be at a disadvantage in the labour market if, for any reason including the disability caused by D, his present employment ended.[6] Compensation for this loss forms a recognised head of damages.[7] In such cases the court must attempt to assess the present value of the future risk that C's disability might reduce the employment opportunities open to him in the future. The risk must be real or substantial: if there is only a remote risk of an actual diminution in earnings, no award will be made.[8] Relevant factors include C's skills, his adaptability to new challenges, and the availability of suitable opportunities. A substantial award may be made under this head – £45,000 was awarded in a recent case where an electrician suffered a severe injury to his right wrist.[9]

### Unused earning capacity

When you read judgments (and textbooks) dealing with the assessment of damages for loss of earnings the impression is given that at the time of C's accident he or she was exercising their earning capacity to the full. Such accounts are often qualified by reference to a small number of poorly reported and contradictory cases and statements of principle involving male claimants who do not utilise their full earning capacity, such as an artist who prefers to paint pictures with little resale value rather than do lucrative restorations.[10] However two more common examples of unused

---

5   *Joyce v Yeomans* [1981] 1 WLR 549.
6   Under the Disability Discrimination Act 1995 it is unlawful for an employer (with a staff of more than 20) to discriminate against those suffering from long-term disability unless different treatment can be justified under the Act.
7   Sometimes called Smith *v* Manchester Corporation damages after *Smith v Manchester Corpn* (1974) 17 KIR 1.
8   *Moeliker v Reyrolle and Co* [1977] 1 WLR 132 and *Foster v Tyne and Wear County Council* [1986] 1 All ER 567, 572.
9   *Tait v Pearson* [1996] PIQR Q92. A similar approach is taken in Canada: *Reed v Steele* (1997) 148 DLR (4th) 695 where an award of Canadian $50,000 was made.
10  The usual opposition is *Keating v Elvan Reinforced Concrete Co Ltd* [1967] 3 All ER 611 at 613 discussing the example in the text ('the appropriate measure for damages is to take roughly the earning capacity which he would have had') and *Browning v War Office* [1963] 1 QB 750 at 767: 'A [claimant] is not entitled to damages for loss of capacity to earn money unless it is established that he would, but for his injuries, have exercised that capacity in order to earn money'.

earning capacity are where C is respectively a 'homemaker' or unemployed. In one case,[11] as a result of her injuries C became partially incapable of housework and so the home was run with her husband's assistance because before the award of damages they could not afford to employ paid help. The Court of Appeal held that C was entitled to recover the value of her future domestic services but not the cost of employing help in the period before trial when because of their impecuniosity no such help was retained. The Law Commission[12] has questioned this decision for the inconsistent treatment of past and future losses. The Court of Appeal criticised the artificiality of accepting as a pecuniary loss past housekeeping incapacity where no help is actually employed but went on to apply the same artificiality as regards the future by allowing recovery in respect of such services regardless of whether they will be used.[13] The Law Commission have proposed[14] that where C suffers a loss as a result of his or her inability to do work in the home this should be compensated as a past pecuniary loss where C has reasonably paid someone to do the work and as a future pecuniary loss where C establishes that he or she will reasonably pay someone to do it. In this way the inconsistency they identify is removed. Undercompensation is then avoided by proposing that if C 'battles on' and despite disability continues to do as much work as possible this could be reflected in the award of damages for non-pecuniary loss. Where the work has been or will be done gratuitously by a relative or friend (including D), consistently with the Law Commission's recommendations on gratuitously rendered nursing services,[15] C should be entitled to damages for the cost of the work and should be under a personal liability to account to the provider in respect of compensation awarded for past but not future services. The issue addressed by the Law Commission is a very important one when one considers that only a minority of the population including many women are wage-earners[16]

---

11  *Daly v General Steam Navigation Co* [1981] 1 WLR 120
12  Law Commission, *Damages for Personal Injury: Medical, Nursing and Other Expenses; Collateral Benefits*, Report No 262 (1999) (hereinafter *Medical Expenses*) para 3.88.
13  In the case itself C was not deprived of compensation because her award for non pecuniary loss was increased to 'compensate' for her pre-trial losses and the latter included something in respect of the income lost by the C's husband as a consequence of the domestic chores he performed.
14  Paragraph 3.91
15  See above pp 366-368.
16  The issue of damages in respect of C's inability to do work in the home will become even more important following *R v Gloucestershire County Council, ex p Barry* [1997] AC 584 which held that councils who provided care for disabled persons under the Chronically Sick and Disabled Persons Act 1970 did not act unlawfully when home care was withdrawn for economic reasons. As a result fewer claimants will receive such care in the future.

and that many others again including large numbers of women are in both categories as part time employees.

If C was unemployed but seeking work at the time of the accident, the court should estimate his pre-accident likelihood of obtaining suitable work and the wages that he would thereby earn. In doing so the Court may take into account C's past criminal tendencies which would probably result in his spending future periods in prison and reduce or eliminate his re-employment prospects.[17] In another case Cs made no claim for loss of earning capacity because they even if they were fit at the time when they in fact were suffering incapacity they would not have been able to find work.[18] If the court's approach to those whose settled pattern of living does not involve remunerative work is to limit or refuse damages for loss of earnings the same approach should be taken where C intends to live off unearned income and investments. However in either case the award should reflect the possibility, if it cannot be wholly ruled out, that C might at some point in the future respectively as a result of good luck or hard times gain paid employment.

### Discounting: the multiplier system

Full compensation requires C to receive complete replacement for lost income. In most cases this will be in the form of a lump sum award.[19] This lump sum is the replacement for a lost stream of future income. Account must therefore be taken of the accelerated receipt of the award. In other words C is entitled to only the present value of his future loss. When C receives his damages as a lump sum, he is able to invest it as capital to earn interest or other income, so that by the time he actually suffers the loss of a particular slice of his future earnings (or incurs a future expense) the amount available to meet that loss will have been augmented by the income which it has generated meanwhile. The 'present value' of a sum due at a future date is the reduced amount of capital which, together with the interest it will earn between now and that date, will produce the required sum. Hence, the courts conceive of an award of damages being invested and the income produced being augmented by gradual withdrawals of capital to make it up to the annual amount of the lost earnings. The fund should last for the required period of the loss[20], ie the

---

17  *Meah v McCreamer* [1985] 1 All ER 367.
18  *Halsall v Secretary of State for Social Security* [1995] 1 WLR 812.
19  For the exceptions see above, pp 340-342.
20  For this reason it is sometimes referred to as the 'cost of an annuity' approach. An annuity is an insurance product whereby a capital sum is paid in exchange for income for a period usually the rest of the annuitant's life. Underwriters responsible for pricing annuities address the same problem as the courts but 'from the other

capital should be exhausted by the end of the period.[1] The stream of future sums is *discounted* so as to produce the capital sum necessary to create such a fund. To take a simplified example suppose that C has been deprived of an income of £10,000 pa for a period of 20 years. A lump sum award of 20 times £10,000, ie £200,000, would overcompensate C because the accelerated receipt the outstanding income enables C to invest the lump sum and enjoy a return. The purpose of the discount is to eliminate this overcompensation. In this discounting, the crucial factor is the rate of interest or return to investment which is presumed. The higher the assumed return on capital, net of tax, the lower the lump sum. If a net return of 5% is applied the discounted sum would be £124, 600 but if a more modest 3% is assumed the figure would be £148,888 almost a 20% increase. In *Thomas v Brighton Health Authority*[2] the substitution of 4.5% for the discount rate of 2.5% used by the judge almost entirely accounted for the reduction of the award from over £1.6m to under £1.1m.

In the past the courts developed their own idiosyncratic response to this problem. Instead of relying on actuarial evidence their practice was to multiply C's net annual loss (the multiplicand) by a 'number of years purchase' called a multiplier. The starting point for deriving an appropriate multiplier was the number of years from the date of the trial until C's (pre-accident) expected retirement. This figure was then reduced to reflect the accelerated receipt of a capital sum and also the general vicissitudes of life, the many factors that might have disrupted the income stream such as unemployment, other injury etc. This somewhat impressionistic and unsophisticated technique has now been displaced by reliance upon semi-official actuarial tables – the *Ogden Tables* discussed above. These tables combine life expectation and annuity information based upon projected mortality rates. The tables are entered with C's age at the date of trial and the discount rate to be applied and will produce the multiplier to be applied to the traditionally derived multiplicand to produce the total award for loss of earnings. Different tables are available for males and females as well as for different retirement ages.[3] Other tables are available for pecuniary losses that either commence at retirement age such as pension rights or which will continue for the remainder of C's life such as medical and nursing expenses. In these cases

end'. The courts are called upon to reduce a future income stream to a present sum; the underwriters to reflect the value of a present sum in a guaranteed future income. However courts can follow the experience of underwriters by awarding a lump sum award sufficient to purchase an annuity which will replace the lost income.

1   *Taylor v O'Connor* [1971] AC 115; *Cookson v Knowles*, above p 340 n 17 at 568 and *Wells v Wells*, above p 338 n 1 at 383, 390, 395, 399.
2   One of the appeals heard together with *Wells v Wells*, ibid. The House of Lords increased to 3% the multiplier applied by the trial judge (2.5%).
3   Interpolation is necessary between the tabulated retirement ages.

the technique used is analogous to that for loss of earnings claims. The Civil Evidence Act 1995 which gives effect to the recommendations of the Law Commission provides that the *Ogden Tables* and the associated explanatory notes shall be admissible evidence. The Lord Chancellor's Department has announced their intention to bring this section into force '...to facilitate, but not to compel, the use of the Tables...'. The courts have anticipated the enactment of s 10 and the routine use of the tables as the starting point for the calculation of the correct multiplier has been endorsed by the House of Lords in *Wells v Wells*.

*Wells v Wells* further altered the computation of damages for loss of earnings when it substituted a discount rate of 3% for the 4.5% return upon which previous decisions had been premised. The 3% discount rate (net of tax) assumes a very low return to investment in low risk securities. The change was justified by reference to the availability of index-linked government securities[4] which have 'radically altered' the investment scene. These instruments provide a practicable and virtually risk-free way for investors to protect themselves against price inflation. The Law Commission had previously proposed that the award of damages for future pecuniary losses should be premised upon investment in such stock.[5] Lord Lloyd observed that '[i]n the end it comes back to the question of risk'. It was not unreasonable for C to invest his award in low risk investments and so awards should not be premised on more lucrative rates of return. This applies both to long- and short-term investments.[6] Although damages are assessed upon the assumption of such investment C is not in any way obliged to do so. How C *in fact* invests or intends to invest his money is irrelevant.

4    These were introduced in 1981 and became widely available from 1982.
5    The inter-professional working party which drew up the *Ogden Tables* recommended this policy in 1984 and 1994. See also the influential commentary of David Kemp, a member of the working party and author of the principal authority on damages: 'Discounting Compensation for Future Loss' (1985) 101 Law Quarterly Review 556 and 'Discounting Damages for Future Loss' (1987) 113 Law Quarterly Review 195.
6    It might have been expected that a greater element of risk should be assumed by long term investors who would be able to even out the highs and the lows of the equity (shares) market. This is reflected in the policy of the Court of Protection which administers awards on behalf of those unable through mental incapacity or immaturity to do so for themselves. Where sums are invested for over five years, up to 70% may be put into equities while for shorter term investments 'very little risk is acceptable'. In *Wells v Wells*, above p 338 n 1, the House of Lords chose not to follow this practice and considered risk aversion as prudent and acceptable for both categories of investor. Cf Lord Chancellor's Department, *Consultation Paper on Damages: The Discount Rate and Alternatives to Lump Sum Payments* (March 2000), which assumes that larger awards will be invested in a mixed portfolio of equities and gilts.

The social significance of the decision in *Wells v Wells* is immense. It has been estimated that the change in the discount rate increases by £115m pa the amount paid out by insurance company defendants. This will of course then be recouped from policy holders. Alone this would result in an increase of 1% for car insurance premiums, 2% for employer liability premiums and 7% for public liability policies. However the impact in the first year following the decision could have been up to four times higher because the new discount rate was applied to all pending cases and settlements whereas policy premiums could only be adjusted when the policy was renewed.[7] The decision in *Wells v Wells* alone caused an increase in 1999/2000 of £128m in awards of damages against state funded hospitals which funds would otherwise be available for the benefit of patients.[8] The House of Lords acknowledged that their decision would affect insurance premiums but were not addressed as to the extent. They said that the approach they adopted was not unjust because it was necessary to ensure full compensation for losses suffered.

The Damages Act 1996, s 1(1) empowers the Lord Chancellor to prescribe from time to time the discount rate to be used when calculating damages for future pecuniary loss in an action for personal injury. However whatever rate is prescribed 'shall not prevent the court from taking a different rate... if any party to the proceedings shows that it is more appropriate in the case in question'.[9] Since *Wells v Wells* the return on index-linked government stock has fallen, prompting the Ogden Working Party twice to urge the Lord Chancellor to use his statutory power to prescribe a new guide rate of 2%. After a period of consultation the Lord Chancellor responded and set the rate at 2.5% (clearly assuming a rate net of tax)[10] It was stated that the new rate should 'obtain for the foreseeable future' expressly disclaiming any intention 'to tinker with the rate frequently to take account of every transient shift in market conditions'. Following the approach of the House of Lords the Lord Chancellor decided to take a 'fairly broad brush' approach and to set the rate to the nearest 0.5%. The figure chosen was roughly in line with the gross redemption yield on index linked government stock for three years prior to 8 June 2001 which was said by the Lord Chancellor to be 2.61%.[11] The Lord Chancellor did not just take account of index-linked government stock partly because following *Wells v Wells* the market for

---

7   Ibid, para 13.
8   *Heil v Rankin* [2001] QB 272 at para 11.
9   Section 1(2).
10  Lord Chancellor's Department, *Setting the Discount Rate: Lord Chancellor's Reasons* (27 July 2001).
11  In *Wells v Wells*, above p 338 n 1, four Law Lords used the last three years average rate of return, the other referring to the previous year only.

such stock had become distorted.[12] Expert evidence suggested that the yields of such stock might temporarily be artificially low. Therefore he took a broader view and considered the yield from other minimal risk investments.[13]

## Contingencies other than death

The basic *Ogden Tables* reflect the projected statistical mortality of C. Depending on the table used further variables are incorporated to take account of the likely cessation of the income replaced before C's normal retirement age and any extra period of wait before the lost income would have been enjoyed as in the case of lost unaccrued pension rights.[14] However the tables permit even greater fine tuning to reflect C's individual circumstances and external factors that impact on him. The other contingencies that may be provided for are unemployment and illness. This is effected by adjustments based upon whether it is anticipated that national economic activity will in the future reflect the past 15 years. Three sets of figures are provided. The medium figures are to be used if the above assumption is correct. If it is not, the 'low' the figures provided should be used if lesser economic activity and so higher unemployment is expected; the 'high' figures should be used if higher economic activity and fuller employment is expected. Further adjustments reflect C's occupation and geographical region. The reductions are less for white collar and professional workers[15] for whom job security is greater and health risks less than they are for manual workers. The adjustment for geographical region proposes marginal increases for those resident in the South East and corresponding decreases for residents of the North or North West, reflecting the economic fortunes of these areas.

## Example of the use of Ogden Tables

Let us consider the following example:

C is male aged 50 resident in Manchester working in a factory. His retirement age was 65. His pre-retirement multiplicand has been

12  As a result of demand caused by changes in pensions legislation.
13  Further it was noted that even after the decision in *Wells v Wells* the Court of Protection continued to invest in multi-asset portfolios and not exclusively in the Index Linked Government Stock upon which awards were then premised.
14  Similar tables are available where C is a child and so would not, before the accident, have begun to earn for a number of years.
15  The adjustment reflects C's occupation not the industry he is employed in. See Explanatory Note 40.

assessed at £20000 pa. As a result of his injuries he has lost his job. His damages for future loss of earnings would be calculated as follows:

The steps one takes to determine future loss of earnings are:

1: enter C's age and current discount rate of 2.5% into Table 25 'Multipliers for loss of earnings to pension age 65 (males)' to derive multiplier of 12.06.

2: adjust for risks other than mortality.

2A: enter Table A 'Loss of Earnings to Pension Age 65 (males). Assume (say) medium economic activity to derive reduction by 0.93.

2B: adjust Table A factor for C's occupation. Permissible range of reduction for manual work is up to 0.05 at age 55 so reduce by say 0.03.[16]

2C: adjust Table A factor for geographical region. Permissible range of reduction for residents in North West is also up to 0.05 at age 55 so reduce by say 0.03.[17]

3: derive multiplier: 12.06 x 0.87 (ie 0.93 – 0.03 – 0.03) = 10.49

4: apply to multiplicand: 10.49 x 20000 = £209800 damages for future loss of earnings.

### Adjustment for higher tax on the income from the invested damages

Damages awarded as a lump sum are not subject to tax.[18] If the sum is invested in index-linked government stock the capital appreciation of the stock is not subject to capital gains tax[19] but the income produced is. This element of taxation is reflected in the choice of discount rate ie it justifies a lower rate (and so higher awards) than would otherwise be awarded. The incidence of tax on the income derived from the index-linked government stock could be reflected in the damages calculation

16  In more risky occupations adjustment can be reduced by up to 0.01 (up to age 25), 0.02 at age 40 and 0.05 at age 55. In less risky occupations adjustment can be increased by up to 0.01 (up to age 40) rising to 0.03 at age 55.
17  For residents in North, North West, Wales and Scotland adjustment can be reduced by up to 0.01 at age 25, 0.02 at age 40 and 0.05 at age 55. For residents in the South East, East Anglia, South West and East Midlands adjustment can be increased by up to 0.01 (up to age 40) and 0.03 at age 55.
18  Taxation of Chargeable Gains Act 1992, s 51(2).
19  *Wells v Wells*, above p 338 n 1 at 391.

in a more sophisticated way.[20] The House of Lords in *Wells v Wells* preferred the simple if crude expedient of adjusting the discount rate and so 'avoid the need for further calculations'.[1] It has been argued that this technique only makes allowance for tax at the standard rate and this disadvantages claimants who by virtue of the size of the award (perhaps because it includes a large award for future medical and nursing care) may become subject to higher rates of taxation which they would not have otherwise experienced. The House of Lords rejected the previous practice[2] of dealing with this problem by way of a small uplift in the multiplier to be applied subject to the caveat that in exceptional cases judges should be able to take account of the incidence of higher rate taxation.[3] However there has been a marked reluctance on the part of the courts to invoke this exception. The Court of Appeal have refused to apply it to an award of £3.1m even though higher rate tax would result in a gross return of 2.71% compared to the gross return of 3.53% which after allowance for basic rate tax produced the 3% discount rate approved in *Wells v Wells*.[4] In another case,[5] the same court dismissed the claim of a Dutch citizen to come within the exception on the basis of higher direct tax rates in Holland. Such a claim could not be accepted without a sustained examination whether such an imbalance in direct tax rates, if it existed, was balanced by a lesser incidence of indirect tax or more generous rates of return on Dutch government index-linked stock.[6]

## Inflation

Inflation is an ambiguous term. It may be used to refer to the rate of change in retail prices, eg as measured by increases in the Retail Price Index. Price-inflation is probably what the judges have in mind when they speak of inflation. Or it may be used to refer to the rate of increase in levels of earnings. This is 'wage-inflation' and is measured by changes in an index such as the average industrial wage. Over a long period, wage-inflation generally outstrips price-inflation, as improved productivity leads to an increase in the general standard of living enjoyed by earners. Judges have

---

20  The technique originated in family law and has becomes become known as a 'Duxbury calculation'. See *Duxbury v Duxbury* [1992] Fam 62n.
1   *Wells v Wells*, above p 338 n 1 at 393.
2   *Hodgson v Trapp*, above p 338 n 1.
3   *Wells v Wells*, above p 338 n 1 at 388, 393, 397, 405.
4   *Warren v Northern General Hospital NHS Trust (No 2)* `[2000] 1 WLR 1404.
5   *Van Oudenhoven v Griffin Inns Ltd* [2000] 1 WLR 1413.
6   It seems that such stocks may be issued on more generous terms by other national governments. See Lord Chancellor's Department Setting the Discount Rate; Lord Chancellor's Reasons 27 June 2001 available at www.lcd.gov.uk/civil/discount.htm

recognised that for loss of earnings the relevant question should be wage-inflation.[7] The choice of a discount rate that permits C to invest in index-linked government securities protects C against price inflation by linking the capital and income to movements in the Retail Prices Index.[8] This will not protect C against the extent to which wage inflation in the future exceeds price inflation. However it does show that the courts were prepared to insulate claimants from the future effects of inflation to the best extent they can based upon the financial instruments available at the time. With respect to lost earnings up to the date of trial C is completely protected against wage inflation because these special damages are based upon actual earnings in the same occupation up to that date.

### Lump sum or periodic payments?[9]

The damages system is almost unique in paying compensation for loss of future income in the form of a single, lump sum. Salaries and wages are paid periodically, and this is the method used for occupational sick pay, permanent health (or disability) insurance, and nearly all types of social security benefits – replacing like with like. But the lump sum is a central feature of the damages system and inevitably leads to some of its obvious deficiencies.[10] Although a few other compensation systems provide lump sums – criminal injuries compensation (which is explicitly based on the damages system); certain forms of accident insurance against specified types of injury; – the majority clearly favour regular payments to meet the regular expenses of the victim and his family. (The assurance of a regular income should also reduce some of C's anxieties about the future.) The lump sum approach requires a once-and-for-all assessment at a given point of time, so that all future contingencies must be crudely translated into a present value. A damages award intended to cover future loss of income or future expenses cannot be revised in the light of price- or wage-inflation or of changes in taxation, nor can it be altered when the victim's medical condition unexpectedly[11] deteriorates (only social security can now respond to this situation). It is a notable feature of the damages system that it turns future earnings into a present capital sum,

7   *Cookson v Knowles*, above p 340 n 17 at 569, 571, 574, 576.
8   Structured settlements offer a similar protection. They invariably involve periodic payments tied to the Retail Prices Index.
9   J Fleming, 'Damages: Capital or Rent?' (1969) 19 University of Toronto Law Journal 295.
10  *Lim Poh Choo v Camden and Islington Area Health Authority*, above p 340 n 15 at 182–3.
11  When the risk is anticipated, the court may reserve the assessment in some cases until it happens or award provisional damages. See above pp 340-342.

which is a procedure not offered by financial markets to able-bodied earners (no doubt because of the moral hazard problem – if I sell my future earnings in return for a lump sum price paid now, what assurance has the buyer that I shall continue to earn for his benefit?). This raises the question – Why should the damages system offer a facility which the market cannot offer? A system of periodic payments, such as social security, can handle future contingencies which are adverse to the beneficiary, such as price-inflation; it can sometimes lead to savings to the public purse, as where a new medical discovery enables a long-term disabled person to live a more normal life again.

Traditional defenders of the tort system point to some advantages of awarding lump sums.[12] It leads to finality in litigation, so that the insurer can close his file, and keep the transaction costs to a minimum. It also gives C the freedom of choice as to how to use the lump sum (but this is a freedom which is not available to uninjured people). Another advantage is that the lump sum award, after it has been made, does not distort C's decision to return to work and the need to encourage rehabilitation is being given increasing emphasis.[13]

The disadvantages, however, outweigh these advantages. A majority of the Pearson Commission favoured periodic payments for the pecuniary loss of a tort victim with a serious and lasting injury, or for the dependants of a deceased breadwinner.[14] They referred to the fact that the community as a whole would have to support him if his lump sum damages proved inadequate in the long run or were frittered away. Lord Steyn has recently emphasised the wasteful effect of awarding large sums which might turn out not to be needed.[15] The cost of such overpayments will also be borne by the community in the form of increased insurance premiums. The use of structured settlements and the court's statutory power to order periodic payments might be thought to go some way to meet these concerns. However the utility of the first is limited and that of the second non-existent. Structured settlements are only 'economic' in the view of defendant's insurers if the award is more than £0.5m.[16] The court's power under the Damages Act 1996, s 2 to order periodic payments is only available if both parties agree which in practice they never do. As a result Lord Steyn has made a powerful plea that the courts should be empowered

---

12  See the minority opinion in *Report of the Royal Commission on Civil Liability and Compensation for Personal Injury* (Chair: Lord Pearson) Cmnd 7054 (1978), vol 1, paras 615–630.

13  *Medical Expenses,* above p 353 n 12, para 1.17.

14  *Pearson Report,* above n 12, vol 1, paras 565–573. Periodic payments were envisaged only for losses likely to last for longer than 4-5 years after the award: *ibid,* para 574. Non-pecuniary loss should be met with a lump sum: ibid, paras 612–614.

15  *Wells v Wells,* above p 338 n 1 at 384.

16  See p 341 n 10 above.

of its own motion to make an award of periodic payments.[17] A possible objection to Lord Steyn's radical proposal is that it is not radical enough; that it would be an unnecessary duplication of administration to have a tort system of periodic payments operating alongside social security. The case for periodic payments should be subsumed under the larger question whether all long-term support for disabled people should be left to social security.[18]

## Expenses arising from C's disability

C's injury causes C to incur expenses such as medical and nursing costs which, but for the accident, C would not have had to meet. The '100% principle' requires that all expenses should be recoverable from D. The same principle actually prescribes a limit on compensation which must not exceed the full extent of C's losses. At several points in this section we will see this limit implemented by provisions designed to avoid over-compensation particularly as a result of overlaps between this and other heads of damage. The topic of medical nursing and other expenses in personal injury actions has been examined recently by the Law Commission.[19]

### Medical and hospital expenses

C is entitled to recover as part of his damages all the medical, hospital and rehabilitation expenses he has reasonably incurred, or will incur in the future. (These expenses may be considered as expenses incurred in C's attempting to mitigate the consequences of D's tort.)[20] Where C has not incurred any expenses, because he has been treated under the National Health Service (NHS) free of charge, he cannot claim any damages for the cost of his medical treatment.[1] However the NHS has a right to recoup the cost of treatment (based on a fixed tariff) from D's insurer where the insurer makes a payment to C following death or injury arising from the use of a motor vehicle.[2] Where C is not likely to incur any medical or hospital

---

17  Ibid.

18  D Harris *et al, Compensation and Support for Illness and Injury* (1984) ch 12.

19  *Medical Expenses*, above p 353 n 12.

20  With the result that such expenses may be claimed even where the attempt to mitigate fails eg where the diagnosis proves wrong: *Rubens v Walker* 1946 SC 215. Failed rehabilitation may be expected to generate such expenses.

1  *Harris v Bright's Asphalt Contractors Ltd* [1953] 1 QB 617.

2  Road Traffic (NHS Charges) Act 1999, s 1(3). The 1999 Act also introduced a new administrative machinery to exact recoupment. The old regime (Road Traffic

expenses in the future, because he will rely on the NHS, he cannot claim damages for those future expenses.[3] C is required to demonstrate on a 'balance of probabilities' that he would in the future make use of private care.[4] Where C has paid for private treatment in the past this will go some way to demonstrate his intention to do so in the future.[5] However C may have difficulty convincing the court of his genuine intention to 'go private' in the future where he has never done so in the past. This may work harshly against C when lack of funds alone has prevented him from utilising private services prior to the trial.

Medical expenses may only be claimed where treatment is reasonable. It would be hard to envisage how the services of a 'witch doctor' would qualify but the use of less extreme 'alternative' remedies may. Even if the type of treatment is reasonable the choice of provider may not be if equivalent services were provided by others at less cost. In these circumstances C bears the burden of demonstrating the reasonableness of his choice.[6] However where private medical expenses have or will be incurred statute provides that the availability of such services as part of the NHS is to be disregarded in assessing reasonableness.[7] So if C does pay as a private patient, he can recover the cost as if there was no alternative; and the fact that he is being reimbursed by private medical insurance, eg BUPA, is ignored when he claims these expenses. The Pearson Commission proposed that C should be permitted to recover private medical expenses only if it was reasonable on medical grounds that he should incur them.[8] There is much force in their proposal. It is difficult to see why liability insurance policy holders should as a group be asked to finance C 's private treatment when adequate provision for the need in question is already being paid for by another large group, ie taxpayers.[9] Nonetheless the Law Commission have recently endorsed the status quo[10] apparently on the ground that only a small number of

Act 1988, ss 157-158) will still apply to non-profit non NHS care providers. The Law Commission have recommended the extension of the 1999 Act to situations where D is not compulsorily insured and that, contrary to the 1999 Act, C's contributory negligence should limit the right of recoupment as it limits D's liability to pay damages to C: *Medical Expenses*, above p 353 n 12, para. 3.43.

3   *Cunningham v Harrison* [1973] QB 942 at 957. Cf *Lim Poh Choo v Camden and Islington Area Health Authority*, above p 340 n 15 at 188 where the House of Lords allowed a claim for private treatment despite doubts that the required treatment would be available outside the National Health System.

4   *Woodrup v Nicol* [1993] PIQR Q104.

5   *Thomas v Wignall* [1987] QB 1098.

6   *Rialas v Mitchell* (1984) 128 Sol Jo 704.

7   Law Reform (Personal Injuries) Act 1948, s 2(4).

8   *Pearson Report*, above p 362 n 12, vol 1, paras 340–342.

9   Such an argument of principle is unappealing to a government which is keen to reduce demand on the NHS.

10  *Medical Expenses*, above p 353 n 12, para. 2.7.

claimants use private care for all their needs.[11] However the same empirical study revealed that a large proportion of claimants use private services to meet some of their needs. A more convincing defence of the present regime might echo the fears of its originators that any other system would necessitate difficult qualitative comparisons between available private and public care.[12] The cases reveal a clear judicial instinct that the claim for private medical expenses may be abused and this finds expression in the closeness with which C's claimed intention is scrutinised unfortunately, as we have seen, sometimes to the detriment of the less well off.

An economist might seek to explain several features of the law we have just described on the basis that the costs of accidents should be 'internalised' ie borne by those who cause them or by the insurers of those who cause them.[13] Where costs are not so allocated (are 'externalised') classical economic theory predicts that there will be overproduction of the good in question, ie too many accidents will occur. The recovery of private medical expenses and the NHS recoupment provisions could be explained as attempts to internalise some of the costs of accidents.

### The 'domestic element' in the cost of care

Where C claims both his loss of earnings and the cost of his care in a hospital or similar institution, a problem of duplication arises. The cost-of-care damages must be reduced by deducting the 'domestic element' which he would have had to meet from his earnings if he had not been injured.[14] Even where C does not claim the cost (or the full cost) of his care, he will often make a saving because he is maintained (wholly or partly) at public expense in a hospital, nursing home or similar institution. By statute, this saving must be deducted from his claim for loss of earnings.[15] Such a saving of the 'domestic element' will arise if no charge, or only a reduced charge, is made upon C. But no deduction is made if after the accident C receives free board and lodging from relatives or friends

---

11 *How Much?* above p 340 n 13, pp 145-6.
12 See *Final Report of the Departmental Committee on Alternative Remedies* (Chairman: Sir Walter Monckton) Cmd 6860 (1946) paras 55-56; also referred to in *Medical Expenses*, above p 353 n 12, paras 2.15 and 3.12.
13 The first alternative describes so called 'specific' deterrence, the latter so called 'general' deterrence. See generally ch 24.
14 *Lim Poh Choo v Camden and Islington Area Health Authority*, above p 340 n 15 at 191–2. Similarly where C will 'earn' a modest wage in a dedicated workshop or rehabilitation unit this must be offset against C's claim for the future cost of care at that place: *Jenkins v Grocott* [2000] PIQR Q17.
15 Administration of Justice Act 1982, s 5.

## The cost of home nursing

Where C has a need for nursing services at home this may be met by a variety of persons[16] perhaps even the tortfeasor (if a member of the victim's family). Where it is reasonable for C to be nursed at home, he can recover, as part of his damages, the reasonable cost of the nursing care. The variety of providers and perhaps especially the possible presence among them of the tortfeasor have provoked a number of different approaches from the courts.[17] The justifications for these different analyses are rooted in the different answers given to two related questions: 'Who exactly has suffered a loss?' and 'Should the domestic or voluntary carer have an enforceable right to receive any monies?'. The courts seem agreed that for moral and practical reasons the work of such carers should be reflected in awards of damages. The moral argument for recognition in the damages award is more often assumed than expressed. The Law Commission state that the 'primary' argument in favour of such damages is that this will 'facilitate the adoption of the most appropriate care regime for a person who has been wrongfully injured'.[18] An indication of its force is that long-established principles appear to yield to it. For instance the present position established by the House of Lords in *Hunt v Severs* that the loss is regarded as that of the carer but that it can nonetheless be recovered by C is a stark derogation from the principle that damages should not be awarded to compensate a third party's loss.[19] The practical arguments are that the failure to recognise the valuable work performed by unpaid carers might discourage individuals from providing such care.[20] Other arguments emphasise the cost saving to defendants which results from the recognition of awards in respect of help given by friends and family (if commercial services were used they would be more costly) and the fact that the failure to recognise such help would encourage claimants to enter 'sham' contracts with their non-professional carers.[1]

In *Hunt v Severs* the House of Lords held that where care is provided for C by relatives or other private parties the 'loss' that is compensated is

---

16  *Lim Poh Choo v Camden and Islington Area Health Authority*, above p 340 n 15 (professional help), *Cunningham v Harrison*, above p 364 n 3 (spouse), *Housecroft v Burnett* [1986] 1 All ER 332 (parent) and *Hay v Hughes* [1975] QB 790 (grandparent). Care is also often provided by friends: *How Much?* above p 340 n 13, pp 48-50.

17  Prior to *Hunt v Severs* [1994] 2 AC 350 considered below the courts had held that the loss was C's who was obliged to pay the carer (see *Roach v Yates* [1938] 1 KB 256 and later that the loss was C's (see *Donnelly v Joyce* [1974] QB 454 overruled in *Hunt v Severs*).

18  *Medical Expenses*, above p 353 n 12, para. 3.48.

19  Compare in contrast pp 29-81.

20  *Hardwick v Hudson* [1999] 3 All ER 426, 435-6.

1   *Medical Expenses*, above p 353 n 12, para. 3.49.

that of the carer but that this is achieved by awarding damages to C which are held on trust for the carer. This is similar to the statutory regime in Scotland where the pursuer (C) is subject to a personal obligation to the carer to account for the damages awarded for past gratuitous care.[2] In *Hunt v Severs* no award was made in respect of the care provided by C's husband because he was also the nominal defendant and it was thought to be inappropriate for damages to be paid by and then held in trust for the same person.

The identification by the House of Lords of the carer as the party who suffers a loss is surely correct.[3] Where services are provided free of charge to C it is simply unrealistic to describe C as having suffered a loss. C may have a need but the way in which the need is being met prevents it from being a pecuniary loss. However the imposition of a trust to ensure that the damages awarded reach the carer[4] causes many difficulties especially when applied to future losses. The imposition of a trust would inconvenience C who could not use that part of the award as he wishes. A trust would be expensive to establish. What would happen to the trust fund if C died or recovered before it was exhausted? Would the fund revert to D (thereby derogating from the supposed finality of litigation)? Would it be given to the carer for care he is no longer going to provide? Or if C recovers would the monies be available to C as a 'windfall' gain?[5] A trust-based approach seems unsuitable in the light of the future uncertainties that confront C. If the carer is not to be given all the money following the trial what method will be prescribed for periodic payment? What happens if C's condition deteriorates or C's relationship with the carer breaks down? It is suggested that the Law Commission's recommendation that C should be subject to a personal obligation only to account to the non-professional carer in respect of damages awarded for past care and that C should not be subject to any obligation in respect of an award for future care should be acted on. The Law Commission also recommended the legislative reversal of the rule that damages should not be paid to C in respect of care provided by D.[6] This is an important recommendation because the percentage of serious accidents resulting in this arrangement may be greater than would at first be anticipated. This is because many

2    Administration of Justice Act 1982, s 8.
3    Cf *Kars v Kars* (1996) 141 ALR 37 the High Court of Australia preferred the principle of *Donnelly v Joyce* [1974] QB 454 where the loss was regarded as that of the victim.
4    A different solution to this problem would be to give the carer a direct right of action against D. This option is rejected by the Law Commission because of the difficulty of ensuring that after any such action the relevant care is delivered and the likely conflict between the interests of C and his carer: *Medical Expenses*, above p 353 n 12, paras 3.51-3.53.
5    Ibid, para 3.55.
6    Ibid, para 3.76.

cars contain several members of the same family who would feel a responsibility to care for each other if the need arose. The objection to the award of such damages in *Hunt v Severs* followed in part from the imposition of a trust in that case.[7] It also reflects an instinctive reaction to the idea that D should in any way 'profit' from his wrong. However it must be remembered that that wrong may consist of momentary inaction (perhaps a second's lapse of concentration while driving) to which it is difficult to attach moral blame. More important are the pragmatic considerations that the rule laid down in *Hunt v Severs* benefits no-one including the 'real defendant' – D's insurer. In his response to the Law Commission's Consultation paper Lord Bingham commented that the present rule creates 'an overwhelming incentive to employ outsiders at commercial rates with inevitable disadvantage to [C] and a greatly increased bill for the insurer'.[8]

## The quantum (amount) of damages

When damages are awarded in respect of non-professional care the courts must then place a value upon that care. In the leading case the Court of Appeal rejected the two 'extreme solutions' of valuing the care at the full commercial rate and that of valuing it at nil. Rather they took an intermediate position and assessed what would be reasonable compensation for the carer with the commercial rate as a ceiling.[9] In practice the courts have tended to award the commercial rate reduced by between a third and a quarter.[10] In some cases a different approach has been taken. Where the mother of an injured child gave up part-time work to look after him his damages were assessed on the basis of the lost earnings.[11] Such damages have also included a sum in respect of the carer's lost pension rights.[12] In some exceptional cases the courts have been prepared to make no discount or even exceed the commercial rate.[13] These cases were decided when the prevailing approach identified the loss as that of the carer. It might reasonably be expected that the shift in

---

7   See above, pp 366-367.
8   Quoted ibid, para 3.71. Other arguments are that *Hunt v Severs* impacts harshly on carers who are only partly responsible for C's injuries (ibid, para 3.72) and that the contrary rule encourages the carer to enter 'empty' contracts with C to provide care (ibid, para. 3.70).
9   *Housecroft v Burnett* [1986] 1 All ER 332, 343.
10  *Nash v Southmead Health Authority* [1994] 5 Med LR 79 (one third) and *Maylen v Morris* (21 June 1988, unreported) (one quarter).
11  *Donnelly v Joyce* [1974] QB 454
12  *Croke v Wiseman*, above n 79 (mother, a teacher, gave up work to look after disabled child).
13  Eg *Woodrup v Nicol* [1993] PIQR Q104.

*Hunt v Severs* to regarding the loss as that of the carer will cause a change to the calculation and level of these awards. In the future it will be more common for awards to be quantified by reference to the foregone earning opportunities of the carer (what an economist would describe as the 'opportunity cost' of providing the care)[14] with a resulting increase in the general level of awards. The Law Commission have rejected the suggestion that there should be any upper limit upon such awards beyond that of the general principle of mitigation of loss

### The calculation of damages

Where on the above principles C is entitled to damages for future medical expenses these are calculated in a similar way to damages in respect of future loss of earnings. After the multiplicand has been derived as described in the preceding paragraph for non-professional care the multiplier must be calculated. The *Ogden Tables* are again entered with the current discount rate and C's age. This will then produce the appropriate multiplier. Different tables[15] are used from those for the calculation of loss of earnings because retirement would terminate that head of loss whereas medical expenses may continue until C's death.

### Other expenses

C may recover the reasonable amount of any other expenses which he has reasonably incurred (or will do) as the result of his injuries. Where as a result of his accident C has special accommodation needs, these will need to be met. Where suitable new property is purchased C would be overcompensated if he received the net cost (ie cost of new accommodation – proceeds of sale, if any, of old house) 'since the larger house is a permanent addition to the family's assets'.[16] Such overcompensation is avoided by approximating the annual extra cost of the new accommodation in a conventional way and applying to it a multiplier appropriate to the period of C's need. The annual cost is calculated by applying the current discount rate[17] to the net capital cost

---

14   Where there is no loss of earnings the only practicable starting point will be the commercial rate.

15   Tables 19 (men) and 20 (women) 'Multipliers for pecuniary loss for life'.

16   *Wells v Wells*, above p 338 n 1 at 380 and *George v Pinnock*, above p 339 n 10 at 125: 'Obviously [C] is not entitled to the additional capital cost, since the larger house is a permanent addition to the family's assets'.

17   Previously the annual interest rate on C's mortgage had been used. See *Chapman v Lidstone* (1982) unreported. This method of calculation led to awards which

of the new purchase.[18] Eg C purchases suitable property for £200,000 having received £100,000 as the proceeds from the sale of his existing house. The annual loss would be $2^1/_2\%$ times $(200,000 - 100,000) = £2,500.$[19] Other expenses resulting from the new purchase are recoverable, eg legal costs, removal services and even higher utility bills.[20]

If it is more appropriate to adapt C's existing property to his new needs the cost of doing so may be claimed. Where the conversion works increase the value of C's property credit must be given for this.[1] Where the effect of the alterations is to reduce the value of C's home this could, in principle, justify a further award.

Where C reasonably requires the use of a motor vehicle and purchase is the most effective option this may also be claimed. A car however is a wasting asset and so its cost is calculated differently. The courts try to arrive at a capital sum which properly invested will finance the purchase of a suitable car and the net cost of its periodic replacement.[2] In addition the cost of any extra mileage may be claimed if such travel is reasonable.[3]

C may also claim any other miscellaneous expenses which will be reasonably incurred such as the provision of a wheelchair or other specialist equipment. Damages may even extend to cover the costs of specialist services to help devise an effective support strategy for C.[4] C may claim damages in respect of travel by relatives and friends to visit him in hospital.[5] By analogy with the approach of the House of Lords to the provision of non-professional care[6] such damages will now be regarded as an award to C in respect of a third party's loss and so will be held on trust for the visitors.[7]

---

almost equalled or exceeded the capital cost (in *Lidstone* £19,600 compared to £20,000 capital cost). In *Roberts v Johnstone* [1989] QB 878 the award so calculated would have exceeded the capital cost of purchase.

18   Ibid. (C was severely brain-damaged at birth which necessitated her adoptive parents moving to more appropriate accommodation).

19   This approach was approved by in *Medical Expenses*, above p 353 n 12, para 4.17.

20   Eg *Rahman v Arearose Ltd* [2001] QB 351 (£3000 removal expenses).

1   *Roberts v Johnstone*, above n 197.

2   *Woodrup v Nicol* [1993] PIQR Q104

3   This is usually calculated on the basis of the Motoring Associations' published figures. The Automobile Associations estimates are reproduced in *Facts and Figures Tables for the Calculation of Damages*.

4   *Goldfinch v Scannell* (26 March 1992, unreported).

5   *Walker v Mullen* (1984) Times, 19 January.

6   See the discussion *Hunt v Severs*, above n 177. Following that case, no such damages should be paid in respect of D's visits.

7   The Law Commission have made similar recommendations regarding such expenses ie that there should be a personal liability to account to the visitor for past expenses but none in respect of prospective ones. They have also proposed that such expenses may be claimed for visits by D. See *Medical Expenses*, above p 353 n 12, paras 8.6-8.6.

In respect of all expenses if the amount claimed is unreasonable, the damages will be reduced to a reasonable amount,[8] eg in one case, the cost of a specially constructed bungalow with a housekeeper and two nurses was held to be excessive.[9]

## Non-pecuniary loss

C may recover damages for losses other than the pecuniary ones – loss of earnings and expenses incurred or likely to be incurred. Such losses are here called simply non-pecuniary damages. They are also sometimes described as damages for intangible losses,[10] or psychic losses as they are often known in America. These damages are meant to compensate C for his pain and suffering (broadly understood to include embarrassment, humiliation and loss of dignity) as well as the consequent curtailment of his non-remunerative activities[11] (so-called loss of amenity damages).[12] One general sum is usually awarded in respect of both pain and suffering and loss of amenity. Sometimes, as presently is the case where C is unconscious, it is necessary to quantify these elements separately.

Most accounts of the law of damages for personal injury necessarily examine a lot of cases involving very serious injuries. Particularly in cases where C is young at the time of the injury there will be very large awards for loss of earnings and medical/ nursing care.[13] This should not give the impression that awards for non-pecuniary loss are globally insignificant. In fact the opposite is true. Approximately 95% of those injured in accidents have sufficiently recovered to return to work within three

---

8   *Shearman v Folland* [1950] 2 KB 43.

9   *Cunningham v Harrison*, above p 364 n 3.

10  Eg Cane, *Atiyah's Accidents Compensation and the Law*, above p 388 n 3, p 135.

11  To avoid overlap with damages for loss of earnings. A possible source of overlap was identified in *Fletcher v Autocar and Transporters Ltd* [1968] 2 QB 322 where C's hobby was a costly one. C would be overcompensated if the damages for loss of amenity reflected C's particular leisure activity and there was no credit for the earnings C would have to apply to produce that product. In practice this potential overlap is ignored and the Law Commission recommend no change to this policy. See Law Commission, *Damages for Personal Injury: Non-pecuniary Loss*, Report No 257 (1998) (hereinafter *Non-pecuniary Loss*) para 2.68.

12  And possibly also for physical or mental damage where there is no pain and suffering or loss of amenity. Examples of such damages for the injury itself are hard to identify. *Forster v Pugh* [1955] CLY 741 may be an example (compensation for abdominal injury necessitating removal of spleen – damages awarded for pain and suffering *and the injury itself*).

13  In *Thomas v Brighton Health Authority* (one of the appeals heard with *Wells v Wells*, above p 338 n 1), C who was born with cerebal palsy and is very severely handicapped was awarded only £110,000 for non-pecuniary loss by Collins J as compared with almost £1.2 m in respect of his pecuniary losses.

months.[14] In such cases the claim for pecuniary losses will be a fraction of that in the catastrophic cases. The award for non-pecuniary losses will of course also be less than in more severe cases but not to the same degree. This reflects the fact that pain and suffering is likely to be greatest in the immediate aftermath of the injury and that damages for loss of amenity do not seen to vary much according to C's age.[15] Work commissioned by the Pearson Commission[16] revealed that two thirds of the payments made by insurers were in respect of non-pecuniary losses.

The courts in this country are committed to the award of damages for non-pecuniary loss. In its recent report the Law Commission dismissed curtly the possibility that such damages should not be awarded.[17] In global terms the award of such damages are not inevitable. In particular such recovery is denied in some socialist and Islamic jurisdictions.[18] Several Australian states have imposed upper limits or thresholds upon the recovery of non-pecuniary losses arising from certain types of accident.[19] Compensation for non-pecuniary loss which had hitherto been part of the New Zealand no fault accident compensation scheme was abolished in 1992 following concern about the increasing size and so cost to the scheme of such awards.[20] It has been observed that 'The common law's willingness to compensate for non-pecuniary losses is usually not shared to the same extent by other compensation systems'.[1] In this country the unquestioning award of such damages is well established[2] and follows inexorably from the commitment to the 'principle of "full compensation" [which] applies to pecuniary and non-pecuniary damages alike'.[3]

14   *Pearson Report*, above p 362 n 12, vol 1, Table 2.
15   The *Guidelines* (below p 380) refer to 'age and life expectancy' as one of four factors considered in cases of paralysis; they also refer to life expectancy alone as one of three factors relevant to very severe (one of seven factors relevant to moderately severe) brain damage. It is only infrequently mentioned in relation to any other injury.
16   *Pearson Report*, above n 152, vol 2, Table 107.
17   *Non-Pecuniary Loss*, above p 371 n 11, paras 2.1-2.2 This conclusion was justified by reference to the view of the majority of respondents to their Consultation paper. The respondent's reasoning was not elaborated.
18   See H McGregor, 'Personal Injury and Death', *International Encyclopaedia of Comparative Law: Torts* (1986) ch 9 ss 35-38, 46-47 and SH Amin, 'Law of Personal Injuries in the Middle East' [1983] Lloyd's Maritime and Commercial Law Quarterly 446.
19   See N Mullany 'A New Approach to Compensation for Non-Pecuniary Loss in Australia' (1990) 17 Melbourne University Law Review 714, pp 721-727.
20   It was replaced by a modest disability pension. See G Palmer, 'New Zealand's Accident Compensation Scheme: Twenty Years On' (1994) 44 University of Toronto Law Journal 223.
1    Cane, *Atiyah's Accidents, Compensation and the Law*, above p 338 n 3, p 405.
2    For a history see J O'Connell and RJ Simon, 'Payment for Pain and Suffering: Who Wants What, When and Why?' [1972] University of Illinois Law Forum 1, appendix *v* especially pp 87-93, 98-99.
3    *Heil v Rankin*, above p 357 n 8.

However as Lord Steyn acknowledged in *Wells v Wells* 'It must not be assumed that the 100% principle is self evidently the only sensible compensation system'. It is suggested that the Law Commission gave insufficient weight to the arguments against and overstated the arguments for the award of damages for non-pecuniary loss when they recently proposed a substantial uplift in the level of these awards.[4] Indeed it could be argued that the Court of Appeal's[5] response to the Law Commission's proposal supports our criticism. In *Heil v Rankin* the general level of non-pecuniary awards was increased but not to the extent proposed and the court questioned the value of the evidence upon which the Law Commission based their views.[6]

The most powerful argument against the award of damages for non-pecuniary losses is that there is no convincing rationale for such awards. Where C's loss is financial there is no conceptual difficulty in converting this loss into a lump sum award of damages. Any difficulty the reader may have experienced in following our account of how damages for pecuniary loss are calculated arises from the ever more sophisticated calculations used by the courts to accurately quantify C's real life losses. But the conceptual aim of financial restitution is both simple to state and to comprehend. However 'There is no simple formula for converting the pain and suffering, the loss of function, the loss of amenity and disability which an injured person has sustained, into monetary terms.'[7]

English courts are said to adopt a 'diminution in value' approach.[8] Under this approach the purpose of the award is to put a value on what C has lost irrespective of the use to which the damages will be put. In contrast the 'functional' approach[9] holds that damages for non-pecuniary loss are awarded as a solace or comfort for C to enable him to purchase alternative sources of satisfaction. The 'diminution in value' approach itself has two variants depending upon whether C's loss is valued objectively or subjectively. The former has usefully been labelled a conceptual approach

4   See p 375 below.
5   The powerful Court of Appeal unusually consisted of five members: Lord Woolf MR, Beldam, Otton and May LJJ and Nelson J.
6   In particular the Court of Appeal questioned the scale, methodology and interpretation of an empirical survey commissioned by the Law Commission and conducted by the Office for National Statistics. See *Non-Pecuniary Loss*, above p 371 n 11, Appendix B.
7   *Heil v Rankin*, above p 357 n 8. See also *H West & Sons v Sheppard* [1964] AC 326 at 364 (The court has to perform the difficult and artificial task of converting into monetary damages the physical injury and deprivation and pain...'.)
8   *Non-Pecuniary Loss*, above p 371 n 11, para. 2.4.
9   The functional approach has been followed in Canada. See *Andrews v Grand & Toy Alberta Ltd* (1978) 83 DLR (3d) 452; *Arnold v Teno* (1978) 83 DLR (3d) 609; and *Thornton v Board of School Trustees of School District No 57* (1978) 83 DLR (3d) 480. It has also been canvassed in Australia: see Windeyer J in *Skelton v Collins* (1966) 115 CLR 94 at 131-133.

and the latter a personal one.[10] The difference between the conceptual and personal approaches is most marked when the case of an unconscious claimant is considered. A conceptual approach would allow full recovery. If a personal approach were followed C would recover nothing if he had no awareness of his condition.[11] Commitment to the diminution in value approach permits the development of a conventional tariff of damages for different injuries. This tariff is authoritatively recorded in the *Guidelines*. The functional approach is inimical to such development as the level of awards depends on what substitute pleasures are suitable for particular victims. The tariff based approach ensures consistency and so *relative* justice between awards. In relation to damages for pain and suffering it has been said that: 'All that can be said is that once you accept that £20 is the right award for one week of pain, the right award for two weeks of similar pain is in the region of £40 and not in the region of £400'.[12] The same point may be made with regard to damages for loss of amenity: if the loss of one finger can be monetised as £1k common sense tells us that the value of two digits will be greater. When the opinions of relevant experts are substituted for common sense a relative tariff can be constructed which gives a value to any bodily injury or mental impairment. The difficulty of this approach is justifying the starting point and so the absolute level of any individual award.

The Law Commission sought to answer this problem by considering the underlying basis of the law of tort. They assert that the law of tort is founded upon the principle of corrective justice rather than deterrence or compensation per se. This conception has been explained in these terms:

> The purpose of tort law [is to oblige] a person whose morally culpable behaviour has violated another's autonomy to restore the latter as nearly as possible to his or her pre-injury status... the purpose of tort law is to correct past injustices, not to deter future behaviour of other potential wrongdoers [n]or to compensate victims of misfortune whose misfortune is not directly caused by the morally culpable conduct of another.[13]

10  See generally the seminal article by AI Ogus, 'Damages for Lost Amenities: For a Foot, a Feeling or a Function' (1972) 35 Modern Law Review 1.
11  Law Commission, *Damages for Personal Injury: Non-Pecuniary Loss*, Consultation Paper No 140 (1995) para 4.15 preferred the personal approach. See para 4.15. Following consultation they favoured the conceptual approach.
12  *Wise v Kaye* [1962] 1 QB 638 at 664. Although the figures are 40 years out of date the principle they are used to illustrate is still valid.
13  D Dewees et al, *Exploring the Domain of Accident Law: Taking the Facts Seriously* (1996) p 8.

We have already observed that corrective justice in relation to pecuniary losses is simple to state but complex to effect. To apply a corrective justice approach to non-pecuniary losses requires a value judgment as to what particular injuries 'are worth'. A further logically prior problem is to identify who should make that value judgment. The Law Commission suggest that the appellate courts are the appropriate arbiters who should fix levels 'which to some extent conform with general perceptions of the sums of money that are commensurate with the different non-pecuniary losses suffered' and that 'the fairness and reasonableness of damages [should] be assessed in the context of the social, economic and industrial conditions prevailing at the time'.[14]

On this basis the Law Commission recommended a tapered increase in the previous level of damages for non-pecuniary loss.[15] The increases were justified because present levels of compensation were said to be out of step with public notions of appropriateness. The evidence said to support this conclusion was the responses of consultees following the Law Commission's initial report.[16] It is suggested that a 'head count' of respondents to the Law Commission's Consultation Paper is not a satisfactory way of discovering public perceptions of appropriate levels of award. Many respondents do not view the matter objectively; rather they speak for and represent a particular constituency (they are 'committed to a cause').[17] Also a simple counting exercise gives equal weight to all respondents whether individuals or representative bodies speaking on behalf of many individuals eg Victim Support or important commercial interests eg Association of British Insurers. The Law Commission were also 'influenced' by two empirical surveys.[18] These surveys involved asking victims of accidents in more or less sophisticated ways whether they were satisfied with their compensation. Surely we should not be surprised when a negative response was usually given. This reply might be prompted by many emotional factors – pity, justification for legal action – which are not necessarily relevant to the issue of compensation. It is interesting to compare these findings with those of an old American survey which revealed that most victims of road accidents in Illinois had no knowledge or expectation of receiving payment for non-pecuniary loss prior to the accident. The extent of the Law Commission's reliance

14  *Non-Pecuniary Loss*, above p 371 n 11, para 3.24.
15  Where the present award would be greater than £3k the increase should be 50-100%. Where the current award would between £2k and £3k the suggested uplift is not more than 50%.
16  75% of whom thought that damages for non-pecuniary loss for very serious injuries were too low and 50% thought the same for minor injuries.
17  *Heil v Rankin*, above p 357 n 8 at 310.
18  *How Much?* above p 340 n 13 and Office for National Statistics survey reproduced in *Non-Pecuniary Loss*, above p 371 n 11, Appendix B.

upon the second survey was criticised (it is suggested correctly) in *Heil v Rankin* on account of its limited scope[19] and its failure to adequately inform subjects about the cost of increasing damages for non-pecuniary loss.[20]

A further criticism of the Law Commission's approach is that their proposals are insufficiently sensitive to the context of victim compensation. In particular their proposals do not reflect the parallel provision made by the social security system. To the extent that accident victims now receive improved state benefits over those available in the past this might weaken the argument for an increase in damages for non-pecuniary loss.[1] The Law Commission also considered that they should not be dissuaded from their proposals on cost grounds. We have already seen that both the Pearson Commission and the New Zealand no-fault accident compensation scheme responded to the financial burden of non-pecuniary damages which the former said comprised two-thirds of all insurance payments;[2] the former by recommending that no action be available for the recovery of non-economic loss in respect of the first three months following the accident and the latter in 1992 by abolishing such claims altogether. In *Heil v Rankin* there was evidence before the court that the cost to the insurance industry of a 100% increase in non-pecuniary damages would be in excess of £2 b in the first year.[3] There would be also be a massive impact on the NHS which effectively funds many awards where hospitals are sued for negligence. The court, correctly it is suggested, responded that 'this [financial] impact should not be ignored' and the inevitable cost consequences of the 'very large increase proposed should not have been so extensively discounted.'[4]

Economists have tried to fill this conceptual lacuna and so provide a sound policy justification for the award of damages for non-pecuniary loss.[5] Economists usually value things by reference to a market. We have

---

19   Above p 357 n 8 at para 65.
20   Ibid at para 87. Apparently accepting (ibid at para 66) D's suggestion that: 'there can be a world of difference between answering a question, however skilfully crafted, and having to pay out the extra insurance premiums or tax which is necessary.'
1   See the evidence presented by Harris and Atiyah in *Non-pecuniary Loss*, above p 371 n 11, paras. 3.67-3.71.
2   See p 372 n 14 above. In 1978 in New Zealand compensation for non-pecuniary loss amounted to NZ$18.1 million out of NZ$89.1 m. In 1991 more was paid out in respect of non-pecuniary losses (NZ$259 m) than for medical and hospital treatment combined. See Cane *Atiyah's Accidents, Compensation and the Law*, above p 338 n 3, p 405 n 11.
3   Above p 357 n 8 at para. 15.
4   Ibid at para. 95
5   For an overview see MW Jones-Lee, *The Value of Life: An Economic Analysis* (1976).

already seen that many of the rules governing the damages payable for breach of a contract for the sale of goods are market based. However there is no developed market for the sale of body parts.[6] Therefore economists have tried to develop ways in which human behaviour can be analysed which will reveal information about how individuals value these things. This may be done by comparing salary rates in industries with different risks of physical injury.[7] This will reveal the amount that an individual will accept to assume a certain risk. A different approach derives indirect valuations from the amount that individuals would be prepared to spend to avoid injury.[8] These techniques tend to produce valuations that are higher than those used in the courts. A related technique examines the willingness of parties to insure against non-pecuniary loss. Several American studies suggest that damages for non-pecuniary loss are not justified because consumers would not in theory, and do not in practice take out their own insurance against such losses.[9] The economic literature is not decisive and so does not fill the conceptual need we identified.

### Pain and suffering

Damages for pain and suffering are awarded only to the extent that C is aware of it ie the pain and suffering are assessed subjectively. Pain refers to the physical hurt and discomfort caused by the injury and its reasonable treatment. The intensity and duration of the pain are the main factors. The claim will survive C's death for the benefit of his estate but it appears that a de minimis principle operates. In one case arising out of the Hillsborough football stadium disaster C had no claim for pre-death pain and suffering when he lost consciousness only a few seconds after the crushing began and died within five minutes.[10]

---

6   In some countries such as the United States blood may legally be sold by donors. Elsewhere there may be an unofficial market for duplicated body parts such as kidneys.

7   A Martin and G Psacharopolous, 'The Reward for Risk in the Labour Market' (1982) 90 Journal of Political Economy 827.

8   TC Sinclair, *A Cost-Effectiveness Approach to Industrial Safety* (HMSO 1972) Table 12.

9   G Priest, 'The Current Insurance Crisis and Modern Tort Law' (1987) 96 Yale Law Journal 1521, pp 1546-1547, 1553-1554, 1587-1588 and A Schwartz, 'Proposals for Products Liability Reform: A Theoretical Synthesis' (1988) 97 Yale Law Journal 353, pp 362-367. For a defence of the tort system see ES Pryor, 'The Tort Law Debate, Efficiency and the Kingdom of the Ill: A Critique of the Insurance Theory of Compensation' (1993) 79 Virginia Law Review 91 and SP Croley and JD Hanson, 'The Non-Pecuniary Costs of Accidents: Pain and Suffering Damages in Tort Law' (1995) 108 Harvard Law Review 1787.

10   *Hicks v Chief Constable of South Yorkshire Police* [1992] 2 All ER 65.

C's damages under this head will be increased by any mental suffering he experiences as a result of his injuries; embarrassment, feelings of dependence, distress at his inability to provide for his family, anxiety that his condition might deteriorate etc. Although damages are no longer awarded for C's loss of expectation of life[11], where C is aware of his reduced life expectancy this might increase his award for pain and suffering.[12]

### Loss of amenity

This refers to C's inability to do the things which before the accident he was able to do. In other words it is an award for his inability to fully participate in his pre-accident activities. Strictly the award is based upon C's post-accident life expectancy but the court's emphasis is usually upon the severity of the injury rather than C's age and life expectancy.[13] Damages under this head are assessed objectively; the award is not dependent upon C's awareness of his deprivations. However the award should reflect C's own personal circumstances. In this sense only the award may be said to have a subjective element. Where C's injuries affect his ability to engage in certain pre-accident hobbies, this can be reflected in the award.[14] Where C's sexual or reproductive abilities[15] are affected by the injury this may justify a substantial award. If C's injuries cause the breakdown of his marriage damages may be awarded for the loss of the marriage. However D will not be liable for the cost of any orders made against C in matrimonial proceedings.[16]

### The unconscious claimant

Even under the present law with its commitment to the award of damages for non-pecuniary loss it is a controversial question whether, and if so to what extent, a permanently unconscious claimant should be entitled to

---

11  A conventional sum of £1750 was awarded to C whenever the accident had the effect of reducing C's life expectancy. This claim was abolished by Administration of Justice Act 1982, s 1(1)(a).

12  Administration of Justice Act 1982, s 1(1)(b).

13  A rare example where the effect of age was mentioned is *Nutbrown v Sheffield Health Authority* [1993] 4 Med LR 187. (C, 72 with a life expectancy of 82, received £25,000 damages. The judge said C would have received twice as much if he was 30.)

14  *Moeliker v Reyrolle & Co Ltd* [1977] 1 All ER 9 (fishing) and *Miller v Tremberth*, (25 November 1982, unreported) (sketching, painting, reading and DIY – noted in *Kemp and Kemp on the Quantum of Damages*, vol 2, para D2-0.14.

15  *Cook v J L Kier & Co* [1970] 1 WLR 774 (loss of potency).

16  *Pritchard v Cobden* [1988] Fam 22.

such an award. It follows from what has been said above about the subjective nature of pain and suffering and the objective character of awards for loss of amenity that a permanently unconscious claimant is presently entitled to the latter only. Indeed the distinct characters of these two awards emerged in two cases dealing with such claimants.[17] In both cases the Court of Appeal and the House of Lords held by a majority[18] that a permanently unconscious claimant should receive damages for loss of amenity but not for pain and suffering. In 1980 the House of Lords were invited to reverse their earlier decision but declined to do so, at the same time acknowledging the forceful arguments on both sides.[19]

Those who support the present position argue that: it would be unjust to award lower damages for catastrophic injuries than for less serious ones; to fail to make an award would be to trivialise the victim's injuries and would reduce the deterrent effect of the law; such a failure would result in the position where it would be cheaper to kill a victim than to maim him; it is difficult to be sure about the victim's level of consciousness; and the damages would be valuable to C's dependants.

It is suggested that these arguments are not convincing. The aim of damages should be to meet C's needs. Unfortunately '[i]t is no more possible to compensate an unconscious man than it is to compensate a dead man'.[20] What is the point of awarding a sum of money that 'will in all probability be of no use to the victim'?[1] If the compensation is needed for C's dependants then they should be given a direct right of action.[2] The first argument for the status quo and perhaps others surely conceal a punitive motive when punishment (as opposed to corrective justice) is not a usual aim of the law of torts.[3] Further it must be doubted whether the law in this regard has a genuine deterrent effect particularly in view of the rarity of such cases. Also it can be pointed out that as a result of the prevailing approach to the assessment of damages following death it is presently cheaper to kill than to maim. Additionally the difficulty of proving C's sensory perception by effectively assuming it is tantamount to a reversal of the usual civil burden of proof.[4]

---

17  *Wise v Kaye* [1962] 1 QB 638 (C was brain damaged since the accident with no prospect of recovery) and *H West and Sons v Sheppard*, above p 373 n 7 (C may have had some limited insight into her condition but case was pleaded as if C was unconscious).

18  Diplock LJ dissented in *Wise* and Lords Devlin and Reid in *West*.

19  *Lim Poh Choo v Camden and Islington Area Health Authority*, above p 340 n 15.

20  *H West and Sons v Sheppard*, above p 373 n 7 at 341 per Lord Reid.

1   Ibid at 363 per Lord Devlin.

2   One respondent to the Law Commission pithily recommended the introduction of a Nearly Fatal Accidents Act.

3   *H West and Sons v Sheppard*, above p 373 n 7 at 362 per Lord Devlin.

4   Law Commission *Non-Pecuniary* Loss, above p 371 n 11, para. 4.15.

Therefore it is suggested that the practice of the Canadian courts where damages for non-pecuniary loss are not awarded to a permanently unconscious claimant is a better one.[5] This was the provisional view of the Law Commission.[6] However following consultation they were persuaded by the weight of opinion among consultees to recommend no change in the law.[7]

## The Guidelines

Despite (or maybe because of) the lack of a convincing justification for the level of any particular award of damages in respect of non-pecuniary losses the courts insist on comparability between awards for like injuries. It was the desire for comparability between awards that caused the Court of Appeal in 1966 effectively to abolish the use of juries in personal injury trials[8] and the Law Commission have recommended no change to this practice.[9] Comparability is further encouraged by the use of conventional sums. The idea of a tariff is not new.[10] Nonetheless the first edition of the *Guidelines* produced by the Judicial Studies Board only appeared in 1992. The latest version (5th edn 2000) is intended to summarise the cumulative effect of the cases decided up to May 2000, and incorporates the limited uplift in award levels made by the Court of Appeal in *Heil v Rankin*. The guidelines read like a morbid list of human defects and provide upper and lower limits for awards as well as guidance as to what factors should be used when locating any individual award within the proposed range. The figures in the *Guidelines* represent undifferentiated awards for total non-pecuniary losses ie pain and suffering and loss of amenity. The *Guidelines* are not in themselves law since their author the Judicial Studies Board has no legislative power.[11] However it is contemplated that judges

---

5   *Knutson v Farr* (1984) 12 DLR (4th) 658. In Canada this follows inexorably from the adoption of the 'functional' approach to the award of damages for non-pecuniary loss. In Australia the Courts apply a 'personal' approach which results in modest awards to permanently unconscious claimants. See *Skelton v Collins* (1966) 115 CLR 94 and *Densley v Nominal Defendant* [1993] ACL Reporter 500.

6   Law Commission *Non-Pecuniary Loss*, above p 371 n 11, para. 4.14.

7   *Non-Pecuniary Loss*, above p 371 n 11, para. 2.19.

8   *Ward v James* [1966] 1 QB 273. See now *H v Ministry of Defence* [1991] 2 QB 103.

9   *Non-Pecuniary Loss*, above p 371 n 11, para 4.4. It could be said that jury trial would be the best way to ensure that the level of awards reflected public perceptions of appropriateness.

10   The Laws of Ethelbert, c 600AD state that 'If there be exposure of the bone let *bot* be made with 111 shillings'.

11   *Arafa v Potter* [1994] PIQR Q73.

should routinely have recourse to them whenever damages for non-pecuniary loss are to be awarded. Indeed the Court of Appeal when reviewing the appropriateness of a particular award has developed the practice of referring both to the *Guidelines* and also to the case law from which they are derived.[12]

Some examples from the *Guidelines* are:

*Quadriplegia*: £160000-£200000. The level of the award within the bracket will be affected by the following considerations: the extent of any residual movement; the presence and extent of pain; depression; and age and life expectancy. The top of the bracket will only be appropriate where there is significant effect on the senses or ability to communicate.

*Loss of one arm amputated at the shoulder*: not less than £70,000.

*Severe post traumatic stress disorder*:[13] £30,000-£50,000. There must be a specific diagnosis of a reactive psychiatric disorder. Such cases will involve permanent effects which prevent the injured person from working at all or at least from functioning at anything approaching the pre-trauma level. All aspects of the life of the injured person will be badly affected.

*Loss of thumb*: £18,000-£28,000.

*Less serious leg fractures from which an incomplete recovery is made*: £9000-£14000. The injured person will be left with a metal implant and/or a defective gait, a limp, impaired mobility, sensory loss, discomfort or an exacerbation of a pre-existing injury.

*Minor neck injuries*: up to £3,750. Minor soft tissue and whiplash injuries and the like where symptoms are moderate and a recovery takes place within at most two years.

An economist would be surprised that C's own wealth is irrelevant to the calculation of non-pecuniary damages. Money is said to have a diminishing marginal utility. The first amount of money we receive is more valuable to us because it will be used to satisfy our most pressing needs; the next received to meet less urgent wants etc. If C is wealthy a tariff award might amount to little more than a symbolic gesture of public

---

12  *Reed v Sunderland Health Authority* (1998) Times, 16 October.
13  Post-traumatic stress disorder was first recognised amongst victims of disasters which because of their severity or scale are beyond common experience: eg the Marchioness, Hillsborough, Zeebrugge Ferry and Kings Cross station disasters. It manifests itself as nightmares, depression, temper, poor sleep, incontinence, racing pulse rate, breathlessness etc.

sympathy. If C was poor the same sum may transform his financial situation and so be very valuable to him.

## Collateral benefits: deductions from damages[14]

We have already discussed the general principle that C is entitled to the full net loss caused by the accident for which D is responsible. Two questions can arise:[15] first, what are the sums which C would have received but for the accident and which because of it he can no longer get? Second, what are the sums which C did in fact receive as a result of the accident but which he would not have received if there had been no accident? The first question was addressed when we considered C's damages for pecuniary losses, particularly his claim for loss of earnings. The second question is the one that we will address in this section.[16] The issue to be discussed is essentially whether the sums described in the second question should be deducted from those described in the first.

The law relating to the deduction of so called 'collateral' benefits is complex and displays no single unifying principle. Rather the mixture of common law and statute gives effect to a number of different and contradictory policy goals.[17] Some rules can only be explained in terms of history and expediency. Nonetheless it is a topic of huge practical importance. In the United States it has been estimated that two-thirds of the money paid to victims of road accidents comes otherwise than from D.[18] The approach of the common law has been influenced by two decisions of the House of Lords which we will briefly examine. In *Parry v Cleaver* it was decided by a majority that disablement pensions, whether contractual or voluntary, should be ignored when calculating damages for loss of earnings. In a much quoted statement of principle Lord Reid said that 'The common law has treated this matter as one depending on justice, reasonableness and public policy.'[19] In the later case of *Hussain v New Taplow Paper Mills*[20] it was held that long-term sick pay paid by an employer and funded under an insurance scheme should be deducted because it would be unjust for an employee who did not contribute to the

14  See generally Lewis, *Deducting Benefits from Damages for Personal Injury* (2000).
15  *Parry v Cleaver* [1970] AC 1.
16  To a limited extent we have already considered this issue when we discussed the provision of nursing services by a relative or friend of C. These services are a form of collateral benefit in kind. See above p.
17  See Lewis, 'Deducting Collateral Benefits from Damages: Principle and Policy' [1998] 18 LS 15.
18  Hensler, *Compensation for Accidental Injuries in the United States* (1991).
19  *Parry v Cleaver* n 15 at p 13. This approach was supported by Lord Pearce. Lord Wilberforce who made up the majority did not state such a broad principle.
20  [1988] AC 514.

insurance in effect to be compensated twice for the same loss. What is of general interest is that the presumption is now that collateral benefits will be deducted. Lord Bridge said that 'Financial gains accruing to [C] which he would not have received but for [the accident] are prima facie to be taken into account in mitigation of losses which that event occasions to him.'[1]

## Charitable payments

The courts have long acted[2] on the principle that charitable payments should be ignored when assessing damages and the rule has often been restated.[3] The policy behind the rule is that to hold otherwise would discourage such desirable acts of benevolence. Further it can be justified by reference to the donor's intention which was usually not to benefit the tortfeasor by reducing his liability to compensate C.[4] The same principle should apply whether the charity is a payment of money or a benefit in kind.[5] However the practice of the courts is to treat differently one kind of benefit, the provision of nursing care by a friend or relative. As we have seen the value of such care is formally part of C's award but is regarded as compensation for the carer's loss.[6]

Where C's employer makes an ex gratia payment the amounts are not deducted from C's damages against a third party.[7] Where the charitable or ex gratia payment is made by D[8] it has been suggested obiter dicta that such payments should be deducted from damages so as to encourage employers to make them and so perhaps save C the need to apply to the court for an interim payment.[9] This was apparently accepted in a case[10] where C received over £46,000 under a personal accident insurance policy taken out and paid for by the parent company of D, C's employer. However in that case no deduction was actually made because it could be inferred that the payment was not made on account of damages.

---

1   Ibid at p 527.
2   *Redpath v Belfast and County Down Rly* [1947] NI 167.
3   *Parry v Cleaver*, above p 382 n 15; *Hussain v New Taplow Paper Mills*, above p 382 n 20; *Hodgson v Trapp*, above n 1 at 819-820 and *Hunt v Severs*, above n 177 at 358.
4   See Lord Reid's judgment in *Parry v Cleaver*, above p 382 n 15.
5   *Liffen v Watson* [1940] 1 KB 556.
6   See the discussion of *Hunt v Severs*, above p 366 n 17.
7   *Cunningham v Harrison*, above n 163. Scottish law has a similar statutory provision: see Administration of Justice Act 1982, s 10(f)(iv).
8   Cf the approach to the gratuitous provision of nursing services by D. See the account of *Hunt v Severs*, above n 177.
9   *Hussain v New Taplow Paper Mills* in the Court of Appeal [1987] 1 All ER 417, 428.
10  *McCamley v Cammell Laird Shipbuilders Ltd* [1990] 1 WLR 963.

## The proceeds of insurance

The proceeds of insurance policies taken out by C or on his behalf are not taken into account in the assessment of damages. The old rule[11] was justified in two ways: first C should enjoy the benefits of his own foresight and secondly because it was not the accident but the policy of insurance which caused C to receive the benefit. It seems that the causal explanation has now been abandoned and so the rule now survives as an encouragement to persons to make provision for future misfortune.[12]

The courts have had difficulty applying the surviving rationale to many modern insurance products where the premium is not directly paid by C or in the case of 'self-insurance' where no premium is paid at all. Some cases have stated the rule broadly to apply irrespective of who in fact paid the premium.[13] However it is suggested that a better approach would be to retain the requirement that C has paid for the policy of insurance but to acknowledge that such payment may take different forms. It can be argued that an employee pays, by his labour, for all the benefits he receives from his employer or associated third parties. This approach is supported by a case where the House of Lords held C had paid for his entitlement to a disability pension which is 'the fruit, through insurance, of all the money which was set aside in the past in respect of his past work'.[14] On this basis the insurance-type pension was not deducted from C's award even though D was C's employer and the pension was paid for by self-insurance. This flexible approach[15] to the identification of the 'premium' paid by C combined with a broad conception of insurance (ie including self insurance) ensures that the widest possible encouragement is given to parties to make provision for downturns in their fortunes.

## Sick pay or wages

Where C has a contractual entitlement to sick pay C's damages will be assessed as his net loss ie the sick pay will be deducted from the award of damages for loss of earnings to which C would otherwise be entitled.[16]

---

11  *Bradburn v Great Western Rly Co* (1874) LR 10 Exch 1.
12  *Hussain v New Taplow Paper Mills*, above p 382 n 20 at 527 and *Hodgson v Trapp*, above p 338 n 1 at 819.
13  See the judgment of Lord Reid in *Parry v Cleaver*, above p 382 n 15. Cf *Cunningham v Harrison*, above n 163 at 950; *Hussain v New Taplow Paper Mills*, above p 382 n 20 at 527 and *Hodgson v Trapp*, above p 338 n 1 at 819.
14  *Smoker v London Fire Authority* [1991] 2 AC 502.
15  This might provide a better explanation of the result in *McCamley v Cammell Laird Shipbuilders Ltd* [1990] 1 WLR 963 discussed above.
16  *Parry v Cleaver*, above p 382 n 15 and *Hussain v New Taplow Paper Mills*, above p 382 n 20.

This will be the case even if the sick pay is long term and resembles disability insurance. In *Hussain*, C was entitled under the terms of his contract of employment to full sick pay for the first 13 weeks and thereafter to payments equivalent to half pay under D his employer's permanent health insurance scheme. In fact C received full pay for 15 months and thereafter half pay. The House of Lords held that all the payments under the scheme should be deducted from C's damages for loss of earnings. The payments should be treated as sick pay 'in the nature of wages' when C continued as an employee. The payments were distinguished from the proceeds of private insurance or a disability pension (which are not deducted).[17] It was said that C 'paid no premiums as such'[18] and the fact that the employer had insured his liability did not bring the payments within the insurance exception. A similar approach was endorsed by the House of Lords in one of the cases heard together with *Wells v Wells*.[19] If C is under a contractual obligation to repay sick pay in the event of C successfully recovering damages from D there will be no deduction.[20] The approach to voluntary sick pay is unclear.[1]

### Disablement pensions

In *Parry* the House of Lords established that disablement pensions, whether voluntary or not, were to be ignored when assessing C's damages.[2] This produces the wholly unsatisfactory distinction between sick pay paid by an employer which according to *Hussein* is deductible and a disability pension which according to *Parry* and *Smoker* is not. Yet the courts have not articulated any clear criteria to distinguish sick pay from disability pensions.[3]

17  See p 384 above and p 385 below.
18  *Hussain v New Taplow Paper Mills*, above p 382 n 20 at 532. Cf the approach suggested above, p 384.
19  *Page v Sheerness plc* [1966] PIQR Q26 (trial); revsd [1997] 1 WLR 652, CA; on appeal [1999] 1 AC 345, HL.
20  *Franklin v British Railways Board* [1994] PIQR P 1.
1   *Hussain v New Taplow Paper Mills*, above p 382 n 20 would implicitly seem to support deduction. See also *Williams v BOC Gases Ltd* [2000] PIQR Q 253 Cf *Cunningham v Harrison*, above p 364 n 3. Scottish Law has a statutory provision that would support deduction. See Administration of Justice Act 1982, s 10(f)(iv).
2   Confirmed in *Smoker v London Fire Authority* [1991] 2 AC 502.
3   See Law Commission, *Damages for Personal Injury: Collateral Benefits*, Consultation Paper No 147 (1997).

## Retirement pensions

A retirement pension will only fall to be considered as a collateral benefit where it would not have been received but for the accident such as where C's injuries cause him to retire early. In such circumstances a retirement pension, like a disablement pension, will not diminish C's award for loss of earnings up to the date of his normal retirement age.[4]

## Social security benefits

When following the *Beveridge Report*[5] the modern system of state support through social security benefits was introduced it was recommended that social security benefits should be deducted in full from awards of damages.[6] This proposal was not enacted until 1989[7] and then did not apply to cases where the compensation was less than £2,500.[8] The original proposal was that damages should be reduced to the extent that C was in receipt of state benefits. However the regime introduced in 1989 required D to deduct from the damages payable the benefits that would be received by C for five years following the injury and pay this sum over to the state. From C's perspective there is little difference between the two approaches but to the government there is. Under the original proposal D received the benefit of the deduction by paying less damages. Under the 1989 system the government benefits by recouping money it has paid to C. The new regime is simply a cost-saving scheme designed to reduce the extent to which the government has to fund the social security system out of general taxation. Taxpayers will gain little from the new scheme because they will have to pay increased insurance premiums levied by the insurance company defendants who make the payments over to the government.

---

4   See *Hopkins v Norcros* [1994] ICR 11 and *Longden v British Coal Corpn* [1998] AC 653.
5   *Social Insurance and Allied Services*, Cmnd 6404 (1942).
6   The recommendation was made by the Monckton Committee, above p 365 n 12, which was comprised mainly of lawyers.
7   Trade Unions objected to the proposal because state benefits were partly funded by a contribution levied on workers (national insurance) and to that extent should be treated like the proceeds of private insurance. Workers' contributions provided 5/12ths of the fund out of which industrial benefits were paid. The Law Reform (Personal Injuries) Act 1948 enacted a compromise whereby tortious damages would be reduced to reflect half the value of certain benefits which would likely be received in the five years following the accident. The 50% reduction presumably reflects lawyer's dislike of maths (5/12ths is almost ½) but the five-year limit had no apparent justification!
8   Social Security Act 1989 re-enacted as Social Security Administration Act 1992.

Two features of the 1989 scheme were heavily criticised. First it was said to be unjust to offset benefits against overall damage awards. This might result in C's entitlement to a social security benefit designed to provide income replacement reducing his damages for non-pecuniary loss. Further the £2500 limit was a source of problems as insurance companies put pressure on claimants to settle for less than that figure. In response to these criticisms a new scheme was introduced in 1997.[9] The lower limit was abolished (although there is power to enact one) and benefits received by C up to the date his damages are paid can be deducted by D only from heads of special damage that perform a similar function. No deduction can be made from damages for non-pecuniary loss.

The new system, like its predecessor, is administered by the Compensation Recovery Unit. Courts must assess damages without regard to C's entitlement to the benefits included in the scheme.[10] Before making any payment in satisfaction of any judgment or by way of out of court settlement D should obtain from the CRU a statement of the listed benefits payable to C up to date (but not exceeding the period of up to five years after the accident). When D makes payment to C, D is liable to pay the CRU C's full benefit entitlement up to that date, even though the amount may exceed the deductions which D is entitled to make from the amount payable to C as damages.

Where by virtue of his injury C becomes entitled to benefits outside the statutory recovery provisions those benefits can be set off against his losses.[11] In one case[12] this principle was applied to a sum payable to C under the Pneumoconiosis etc (Workers Compensation) Act 1979. (Benefits under the Act were not referred to in the 1997 legislation.)

### Appraisal of collateral benefits

In the law governing the deduction of collateral benefits we can see the courts trying to grapple with the realities of C's situation while the legislature has largely concerned itself with reducing government expenditure on the social security system. Unable to appeal to any single doctrine to solve the problems that confront them, the courts fall back upon intuitive and generalised notions of justice, reasonableness and public policy.[13] The specific policy considerations have not always been

---

9   Social Security (Recovery of Benefits) Act 1997 and the Social Security (Recovery of Benefits) Regulations 1997.
10  Social Security (Recovery of Benefits) Act 1997, s 17 and *Wadey v Surrey County Council* [2000] 1 WLR 820, HL.
11  *Hodgson v Trapp*, above p 338 n 1.
12  *Ballantine v Newalls Insulation Co Ltd* [2001] ICR 25.
13  See the discussion of *Parry v Cleaver*, above p 382 n 15.

spelt out, but the most convincing justification emphasises the source of the funds providing the collateral benefit. If the benefit is financed by a large section of the public in an institutionalised way (eg taxpayers and contributors to social security)[14] or by the defendant himself (eg an employer), it should be deducted from the damages.[15] On the other hand, if C has himself chosen to arrange the benefit and has himself contributed to its cost, directly or indirectly (eg private insurance), or if the benefit comes from voluntary donations to charity, no deduction should be made from his damages. The judges wish to encourage both first-party insurance and charitable giving. It can also be inferred from these cases that the intention of C or of the donors was not to relieve a potential tortfeasor, but rather to provide support for himself, or the victims, irrespective of any claim in tort which might be brought. These justifications have often been accepted as the guiding policies in the common law decisions. No single common law principle has emerged because no simple answer is possible to the diverse problems created by the present system.

Although deterrence of potential tortfeasors might be served by allowing no offsetting at all, the judges realise that the nominal defendant seldom pays the damages himself, and so have not adopted this approach. So far as social justice and economic efficiency are concerned, it is obvious that the present rules are an unsatisfactory compromise in modern conditions. The courts have expended much energy framing rules so as to avoid C receiving compensation for the same loss from more than one source unless there is a more powerful policy reason for allowing this. In this way the judges have tried to develop the system of tortious compensation so as to balance the need to encourage benevolence towards others and sensible provision for one's own future with a desire not to overload those who ultimately fund the awards. However the strains of trying to achieve these aims within the tort system by judge-made law are too apparent. The law on offsetting is complex, often contradictory and sometimes indeterminate. This was admitted by the Law Commission who surprisingly recommended no statutory changes to the law.[16] A better approach would look at the bigger picture and seek to integrate the various systems[17], so that C is entitled to receive compensation for one type (or one period) of his loss only from one source.[18] Double compensation from

---

14  '[W]hen the right to supplementary benefit was conferred, did Parliament intend that a plaintiff should enjoy it in addition to payment of his damages?': *Lincoln v Hayman* [1982] 1 WLR 488 at 492.

15  Both these factors are found in features of the codification of Scots law on deductions from damages: s 10 of the Administration of Justice Act 1982.

16  *Medical Expenses*, above p 353 n 12, para 13.1.

17  This was beyond the Law Commission's terms of reference.

18  Harris *et al*, *Compensation and Support for Illness and Injury*, above p 363 n 18, p 330 et seq.

public sources is inefficient, and, when resources are limited, is unfair to the many accident victims whose only support is state benefits. Once the law has fixed the single source to which C should look for support for a specified loss, loss-shifting should normally be avoided, because it simply increases transaction costs without achieving additional deterrence. This is most obvious when the loss-shifting would be from one large section of the public to another.

## Interest

By statute, courts must order payment of interest on damages for death or personal injury exceeding £200 'unless there are special reasons to the contrary'.[19] Guidelines have been laid down for the exercise of the court's discretion as to which parts of the damages should carry interest and for which periods. The courts have fixed different rates for different heads of damages, which has led to their regularly itemising their awards.

For special damages for financial loss up to the trial (the 'pre-trial loss' of earnings and expenses) interest is awarded on the full annual amount of the loss (averaged, if necessary) for the period from the accident to the judgment, but only at *half* the rate allowed on the investment of short-term funds in court.[20] Since loss of earnings and expenses would be incurred throughout the period, rough-and-ready justice is done by halving the rate over the whole period: since the court does not discount the amounts awarded to reach their present value at the time of the accident, interest is, in effect, already included in the amounts awarded for roughly half the period.[1]

General damages for future expenses or for loss of future earnings should carry no interest, since the loss has not yet been suffered.[2] Similarly, in a fatal accident, damages for the post-trial loss of dependency are compensation for a loss not yet suffered: hence, no interest should be awarded on that part of the damages.[2]

---

19 Supreme Court Act 1981, s 35A(2) (inserted by the Administration of Justice Act 1982, s 15). A similar power is in the County Courts Act 1984, s 69.
20 This rate is varied by statutory order from time to time to reflect market rates. If most of the pecuniary loss was incurred soon after the accident, the court may exceptionally award interest on damages for that loss at the full rate: *Ichard v Frangoulis* [1977] 2 All ER 461. Cf *Dexter v Courtaulds Ltd* [1984] 1 All ER 70.
1  *Cookson v Knowles*, above p 340 n 17 at 572–573.
2  Ibid at 572.

On other general damages for non-pecuniary loss (viz pain and suffering, and loss of amenity) interest at 2% should be awarded from the date the claim form was served on D until judgment or earlier payment.[3] (Since the award itself is adjusted for inflation up to the time of judgment, the rate of interest should not include any element to reflect inflation: it should reflect only compensation for the loss of the use of the money.)

3   *Wright v British Railways Board* [1983] 2 AC 773. In *L (Lawrence) v Chief Constable of Staffs* [2000] PIQR Q349 it was held that the rate should not be adjusted following the adoption of a 3% (now 2.5%) discount rate in *Wells v Wells* (for future loss of earnings and expenses).

# 23 Damages upon death

## Introduction

This chapter examines entitlements to damages following wrongful death. There are two types of action. The first is called the 'survival' claim. Any right of action[1] which the deceased had at the time of his death 'survives' for the benefit of his estate.[2] The second is known as the 'dependency' claim. This is a statutory action currently brought under Fatal Accidents Act 1976 which provides compensation for those who were financially dependent on the deceased at the time of his death. The 1976 legislation also provides for the recovery of two other heads of loss: funeral expenses and 'bereavement' damages. Claims under the Fatal Accidents Act have been examined by the Law Commission,[3] who have recommended a number of improvements designed to make the law more just, certain and to bring it in line with reforms proposed elsewhere.[4] The Law Commission[5] also invited the Working Party responsible for the compilation of the actuarial tables previously used in personal injury cases to consider their application to fatal accident cases. The latest edition of these tables responds to this invitation.[6] It therefore is now expected that, as with non-

1 Other than that for defamation, which is said to 'die' with the victim.
2 Rights of action against the deceased also survive his death but are not considered further here.
3 *Claims for Wrongful Death*, Report No 263 (1999) (hereinafter *Wrongful Death*).
4 Particularly those in relation to the provision of non-professional nursing care and the deduction of collateral benefits. See generally Law Commission, *Damages for Personal Injury: Medical, Nursing and other Expenses; Collateral Benefits*, Report No 262 (1999).
5 *Wrongful Death*, above n 3, para 7.14.
6 Government Actuary's Department, *Actuarial Tables with Explanatory Notes For Use in Personal Injury and Fatal Accident Cases* (4th edn 2000) (hereinafter *Ogden Tables*).

fatal injuries, the method of calculation outlined in the 'Explanatory Notes' accompanying the *Ogden Tables* describes the standard practice to be followed in such cases in the future.

Although the Pearson Commission found that tortious compensation is paid out more frequently following fatal, as opposed to non-fatal, accidents,[7] such accidents are far less common than their non-fatal counterparts.[8] The overall result is that only 2% of all payments are made in respect of wrongful death claims compared with 98% in respect of personal injury claims.[9] The figures suggest that the cost of implementing the Law Commission's proposals may be relatively low[10] which, in turn, may make them attractive to government.

## The survival claim

The Law Reform (Miscellaneous Provisions) Act 1934, s 1(1) provides that all causes of action (other than defamation)[11] vested in a person (or subsisting against him) at the time of his death survive for the benefit of (or against) his estate. The Act does not, like the Fatal Accidents Act 1976 considered below, create a cause of action; it merely provides that an already existing one will endure. Damages are recoverable by the estate under the same heads as for a living claimant.[12] The estate can recover for any loss of earnings up to the victim's death. A claim for damages for loss of income in respect of any period after death does not survive for the benefit of the deceased's estate.[13] In other words the claim for income lost in the 'lost years' dies with the victim. The purposes of establishing

---

7   Tort compensation is recovered following about one fifth of all fatal accidents whereas only 6-7% of those with non-fatal injuries receive payments through the tort system: *Report of the Royal Commission on Civil Liability and Compensation for Personal Injury* (Chair: Lord Pearson) Cmnd 7054 (1978) vol 2, paras 59, 73-4.

8   In the years analysed 4,500 payments were made following wrongful deaths compared to 210,500 in respect of personal injuries: ibid.

9   *Wrongful Death*, above n 3, para 1.22.

10  *Cf* their proposals for increases in the level of damages for non-pecuniary loss (pp 371-373 above) and the effect of the adoption of a lower 'discount' rate in *Wells v Wells* [1999] 1 AC 345 (see pp 356-358 above).

11  Defamation is excluded because the tort provides compensation for non-pecuniary loss suffered by the deceased and there is no reason why the deceased's estate should receive this. The rule that the living victim of defamation should have no action against the defamer's estate is hard to justify. In 1991, after consultation, the Lord Chancellor's Department recommended no change. See *Defamation: Death of a Party to Defamation Proceedings* (1990).

12  In addition the estate may claim a sum in respect of funeral expenses: s 1(2)(c) (if D's tort caused the death).

13  Section 1(2)(a) inserted by Administration of Justice Act 1982, s 4(2).

this limit were, first, to prevent non-dependants from benefiting from the damages under the deceased's will. When the main purpose of awarding 'lost years' damages was to support dependants, it is indefensible to require the tortfeasor to compensate the dependants in a Fatal Accident Act claim and also to pay damages for loss of earnings (out of which the dependency would, if the victim had lived, have been provided) which would benefit a non-dependant beneficiary of the estate.[14] A second justification for the limit is to prevent some dependants from obtaining higher damages through a surviving 'lost years' claim than they would have obtained through a 'loss of dependency' (fatal accidents) claim, eg as parents of a deceased child. Damages for pain and suffering and loss of amenity up to, but not beyond, death are available. Where death quickly follows the injury, this head of damages will be small. No award is made for pain and suffering for the few moments before death.[15]

## Claims under the Fatal Accidents Act 1976

### The bereavement claim

Damages for bereavement were introduced in 1982. These damages can be claimed by: the wife or husband of the deceased and the parents of a legitimate child under 18 or the mother of an illegitimate child of the same age.[16] The damages consist of a fixed sum which is awarded without reference to the recipient's financial dependency on the deceased. The original sum of £3,500 has been progressively raised to £7,500.[17]

Damages for bereavement have attracted considerable criticism. The list of claimants is very restricted and is narrower than those permitted to bring an action for lost dependency considered below. Any fixed list of qualifying applicants is bound to produce apparently arbitrary results. What justification is there for not extending the law to include cohabitants as well as spouses? Why should the mother but not the father of an illegitimate minor be able to claim? Why should parents be able to claim damages in respect of their child's death but children be denied such when

---

14  Other types of windfall gain for the beneficiaries of the deceased's estate eg pre-death pain and suffering and loss of amenity where there is a considerable period between injury and death are not prevented: see P Cane and D Harris, 'Administration of Justice Act 1982, s 4(2): A Lesson in How Not to Reform the Law' (1983) 46 Modern Law Review 478.

15  *Hicks v Chief Constable of the South Yorkshire Police* [1992] 2 All ER 65 (discussed at p 377 above).

16  Fatal Accidents Act 1976, s 1A(2), inserted by Administration of Justice Act 1982, s 3(1)

17  Damages for Bereavement (Variation of Sum) (England and Wales) Order 1990, SI 1990/2575.

their parent dies? Why restrict the parent's claim to children under 18? Are there not other relatives such as brothers and sisters of the deceased who have equal claims to compensation? Should the groom's entitlement differ when the bride is killed when driving to the church as opposed to the honeymoon (and vice versa)? Should the law not also reflect the feelings of those living in same-sex relationships as it does heterosexual ones? These problems were starkly illustrated by one case in which damages were refused in respect of the claimants' unmarried son who died as a result of D's negligence less than one month after his 18th birthday.[18]

A series of well-publicised national disasters, such as the Hillsborough stadium deaths, the Kings Cross tube fire and the Zeebrugge ferry sinking, drew public attention to the modest level of awards for bereavement. Unfavourable comparisons were made between the value placed upon human life by damages for bereavement and that placed upon a living individual's reputation by large awards of damages for defamation. Indeed, an unsuccessful private members bill, the Citizens' Compensation Bill, aimed at increasing the level of award to £10,000 and increasing the range of eligible claimants, was tabled.[19]

In order to assess these criticisms it is necessary to take a view on the underlying justification for awarding such damages. Damages for bereavement were introduced as compensation for the loss of the deceased's 'counsel' and 'guidance' as well as the consequent grief of the claimant.[20] The damages were also perceived as a symbolic recognition by the state of the effect of bereavement as well as a societal expression of the gravity with which it regards the loss of human life.[1] The introduction of damages for bereavement also served a strategic purpose of 'softening' the simultaneous removal of the conventional award of damages in respect of loss of expectation of life.[2] This head of damages evolved into a modest conventional sum which was justified as an indirect 'solatium' for the relatives of the deceased.[3] In effect, an uncertain[4] solatium was replaced by a directed one.

In its latest consultation paper to examine bereavement damages, the Law Commission correctly suggested that much of the controversy surrounding such awards follows from a misconception about their

---

18  *Doleman v Deakin* (1990) Times, 30 January. See A Unger, 'Pain and Anger' (1992) 142 New Law Journal 394.
19  *Hansard* (HC) 3 March 1989, vol 148, cols 519-521.
20  Law Commission, *Report on Personal Injury Litigation: Assessment of Damages*, Law Com No 56 (1973) para 172.
1   See respectively *Hansard* (HL) 30 March vol 428 col 1294 and 8 March 1982, vol 428 cols 41-2 and (HC) 3 March 1989, vol 148, col 544.
2   Law Commission, *Report on Personal Injury Litigation: Assessment of Damages*, Law Com No 56 (1973) paras 100, 107.
3   Ibid, para 100.
4   It might effectively be directed elsewhere by the deceased's will or intestacy.

function.[5] In their subsequent report they reiterated the view that 'bereavement damages are *compensatory,* in that they compensate *non-pecuniary* losses – specifically grief and sorrow, and the loss of care, guidance and society provided by the deceased'.[6] They specifically disclaimed the idea that they are intended to compensate for pecuniary losses, to punish the defendant, or to symbolise that the deceased's death was wrongful.[7] Viewed in this way, the modest level of the award is defensible. In order to compensate for the effect of inflation since the enactment of the current award and to add a small uplift to reflect that proposed for damages for non-pecuniary loss awarded to living claimants, a new figure of £10,000 was suggested.[8] In the interests of certainty and to avoid any temptation to a parade of false affection for the deceased, the Law Commission have proposed that the statutory list of persons entitled to damages for bereavement should be retained and that those include should continue to be entitled to damages without proof of mental distress or other actual loss.[9] However, consistency and justice required a radical expansion of those entitled to claim to include the following relatives of the deceased: spouse, parent, child, brother and sister (the last four categories to include those qualified by adoption) as well as fiancées[10] and cohabitees who have lived with the deceased as man and wife (or if the same sex in an equivalent relationship) for at least two years immediately prior to the accident.[11]

### The dependency claim

The Fatal Accidents Act 1976, s 1(1) creates a right of action for a defined class of dependants in respect of their actual and prospective pecuniary loss. The claim should be carefully distinguished from a claim made by a surviving victim of an accident, which is based on his own loss and on his extra needs arising from the accident. A fatal accident claim is restricted to the financial loss of the dependants, which will always be less than the deceased's loss of earnings. However, there is a sense in which the dependency claim is derivative. It is only available if D would have been

---

5   *Claims for Wrongful Death,* Consultation Paper No 148 (1997) paras 3.127 and 3.128.
6   *Wrongful Death,* above p 391 n 3, para 6.3.
7   Ibid.
8   Ibid, para 6.39. Up to three persons from the statutory list may claim this sum. Thereafter £30000 will be apportioned equally between all qualifying claimants: see para 6.51.
9   Ibid, para 6.34.
10  The status of a fiancé must be evidenced in a prescribed way: ibid, para 6.31.
11  Ibid.

liable to the deceased.[12] If the deceased had before his death obtained judgment[13] or compromised[14] his right of action against D, his dependants will have no claim. Statute now provides that an award of provisional damages[15] will not bar a claim under the Fatal Accidents Act 1976 but will be taken into account when calculating the damages payable to the dependants.[16] A complete defence such as *volenti non fit injuria* that would have been available against the deceased can be relied upon against the dependants. Contributory negligence on the part of the deceased will reduce the damages awarded to the dependants.[17]

The dependants may claim reasonable funeral expenses.[18] Reasonableness is determined by reference to the deceased's social position,[19] religious affiliation and racial origin.[20] On this basis the cost of a simple gravestone has been allowed[1] but that of a monument refused.[2]

Apart from funeral expenses, the Fatal Accidents Act 1976 allows damages to be awarded to 'dependants' of the deceased for loss of any benefit which the claimant could be reasonably expected to receive from the deceased had the deceased continued to live.[3] The aim of the award is to give the dependants the sum of money which will allow them material benefits of the same standard and for the same period of time as the deceased would have provided had he lived for his normal expectation of life.[4] Most obviously damages under the Act may represent compensation for the loss of money or other benefits such as a company car[5] brought into the household by the deceased's employment.[6] Less obviously such damages may extend to income obtained as a result of the deceased's unemployment. In one case, following the death in an

12  *Gray v Barr* [1971] 2 QB 554 at 569.
13  *Murray v Shuter* [1972] 1 Lloyd's Rep 6 (victim's claim adjourned so that his dependants could claim under the Act after his death).
14  *Read v Great Eastern Rly Co* (1868) LR 3 QB 555, also assumed in *Picket v British Rail Engineering Ltd* [1980] AC 136 at 146.
15  See generally p 341.
16  Damages Act 1996, s 3.
17  Fatal Accidents Act 1976, s 5.
18  Dependants can also recover funeral expenses under the Fatal Accidents Act 1976, s 3(5).
19  For an extreme application see *Quoinoo v Brent & Harrow Area Health Authority* (1982) 132 New Law Journal 1100 involving the death of a member of the Ghanaian royal family.
20  *Gammell v Wilson* [1982] AC 27 at 43.
1  *Hart v Griffith-Jones* [1948] 2 All ER 729 at 730-731.
2  *Stanton v Ewart F Youldon Ltd* [1960] 1 WLR 543 at 545.
3  Hence the 'reasonable expectation test'.
4  *Mallett v McMonagle* [1970] AC 166 at 174, 177
5  *Clay v Pooler* [1982] 3 All ER 570.
6  *Grzelak v Harefield and Northwood Hospital Management Committee* (1968) 112 Sol Jo 195.

accident caused by D of C's (already) severely disabled wife, C's damages under the Act included compensation for the loss of his dependency based on the state invalidity benefits which were previously paid to his wife.[7]

Though performed gratuitously, the services of a homemaker or primary care provider within a family amount to a financial benefit for this purpose.[8] Such a person does more than a housekeeper would do, since they give instruction to children and are available at all hours.[9] Where, after the death of the mother of young children, a nanny or housekeeper is engaged to look after them, the cost is recoverable as the measure of the loss of the mother's services.[10] Similarly, the damages may include the value of a relative's services in caring for dependent children.[11] Where after his wife's death a father gave up work to look after their five young children, the loss of her services was valued at the net loss of his own earnings.[12] It can be seen that the courts do not take a consistent approach to the valuation of such benefits, sometimes using a market based approach (ie the cost of hiring substitute services) and at other times an 'opportunity cost' approach (valuing the services by reference to the foregone opportunity – employment – of the substitute provider).[13] It is possible that following the decision of the House of Lords in *Hunt v Severs*[14] (with regard to damages awarded in respect of gratuitous care provided for the living victim), damages recovered by the dependant for the loss of the deceased's gratuitous services might also be held on trust for whoever actually provides those services after the death.[15]

The reasonable expectation test described above admits one established exception. Benefits expected to result from a business relationship between C and the deceased are not recoverable. In a colourful

---

7   *Cox v Hockenhull* [2000] 1 WLR 750 (severe disablement allowance and disability living allowance (both components) were allowed, but the invalid care allowance payable to carers did not form part of C's dependency).

8   *Berry v Humm & Co* [1915] 1 KB 627.

9   *Regan v Williamson* [1976] 1 WLR 305.

10  *Berry v Humm & Co*, above n 48 and *Jeffrey v Smith* [1970] RTR 279.

11  *Hay v Hughes* [1975] QB 790.

12  *Mehmet v Perry* [1977] 2 All ER 529.

13  KA Clarke and AI Ogus, 'What is a Wife Worth?' (1978) 5 British Journal of Law and Society 1 and FJ Pottick, 'Tort Damages for the Injured Homemaker: Opportunity Cost or Replacement Cost' (1978-9) 50 University of Colorado Law Review 59.

14  [1994] 2 AC 350 (discussed at pp 366-367 above).

15  *Wrongful Death*, above p 391 n 3, para 2.28. The Law Commission have proposed (ibid, para 5.53) reforms similar to those it recommended for personal injury cases (pp 367-368 above), ie that the dependant should be under a legal obligation to account for damages awarded for past but not future services to the provider of those services.

case, a husband was unable to recover damages for his loss of income as a dancer following the death of his wife who was also his dancing partner.[16]

The proof of the loss of future financial support from the deceased is usually[17] provided by showing actual dependence in the past. But if the claimant says that he would later have become financially dependent on the deceased, he must prove a reasonable expectation of enjoying a material benefit from the deceased:[18] eg by a parent showing that when his child began to earn he would have been supported[19] or that a house would have been purchased for him;[20] or by an estranged wife showing that there was a reasonable chance of a reconciliation with her husband.[1] If there are several dependants, such as a widow and children, a single action must be brought, but the court will apportion the damages between them according to their relative loss of dependency. As between children, the apportionment should take account of their different ages, since the dependency of an older child will end earlier than that of a younger child.[2]

### The category of dependants

The 1976 Act defines 'dependants':[3] the main categories are the wife or husband of the deceased; any cohabitant;[4] any parent or other ascendant; and any child or other descendant. The list also includes persons treated as a parent, or as a child of the family; illegitimate children; step-children; and certain relationships by affinity. Those included in the list of dependants are persons identified by the law as likely in fact to be

---

16  *Burgess v Florence Nightingale Hospital for Gentlewomen* [1955] 1 QB 349. Cf *Oldfield v Mahoney* (12 July 1968, unreported) (a school preferred to appoint married men to the position of housemaster; C, a teacher, recovered damages for his reduced chances of promotion following death of his wife – noted in *Kemp and Kemp on the Quantum of Damages*, vol 3, paras M3-055 and M3-122).

17  Strictly there is no need to show that a benefit has been previously enjoyed: *Betney v Rowlands and Mallard* [1992] CLY 1786.

18  *Taff Vale Rly Co v Jenkins* [1913] AC 1.

19  *Bishop v Cunard White Star Co Ltd* [1950] P 240 (the case of Appleby) and *Wathen v Vernon* [1970] RTR 471.

20  *Piggott v Fancy Wood Products Ltd* (31 January 1985, unreported) (noted in *Kemp and Kemp on the Quantum of Damages*, vol 3, para M5-012).

1  *Davies v Taylor* [1974] AC 207.

2  *Kassam v Kampala Aerated Water Co Ltd* [1965] 1 WLR 668. It might be appropriate to use different multipliers for different claimants: see *Cresswell v Eaton* [1991] 1 WLR 1113 at 1119 (mother died leaving children aged 7, 6 and 4 – multipliers of 8, 81/2 and 101/2 were used).

3  Fatal Accidents Act 1976, s 1(3) as amended by the Administration of Justice Act 1982, s 3.

4  To qualify the claimant must have lived with the deceased in the same household for at least two years immediately prior to the deceased's death.

dependent on the deceased. To qualify as dependants there is no need to prove actual dependency. Indeed loss of dependency is never directly in issue under the Act. We have already seen that the test[5] which governs the type of loss for which the claimant can recover is stated in wider terms than a loss of dependency.

Respondents to the Law Commission's Consultation Paper criticised this list as 'arbitrary' and 'discriminatory'. It is possible to envisage many individuals not recorded in the list who are likely to be as dependent on the deceased as those who are. Examples include cohabitants who fail to satisfy the 'two-year' rule; same-sex couples; children other than those of the deceased who were supported by him while living with, but not married to, the parent; other children supported by the deceased, eg friends' children; distant relatives supported by the deceased and non-relatives who live together but who do not enjoy a marriage-style relationship. The Law Commission have suggested that such lacunae are best addressed by supplementing the present list with a generally worded class of claimant. Their preferred formulation, borrowed from other legislation,[6] is any person who 'was being wholly or partly maintained' by the deceased immediately before the death or who would, but for the death, have been so maintained thereafter. A person should be treated as being wholly or partly maintained if the deceased 'otherwise than for a valuable consideration, was making a substantial contribution in money or money's worth towards his reasonable needs'.[7]

### The assessment of pecuniary loss: the multiplicand

The starting point for assessing the multiplicand is to calculate the annual value of the lost dependency. This may be done by simply cumulating all the benefits received by the dependants in a year. The court may alternatively deduct from the deceased's net annual income all sums spent exclusively on himself. The amount to be so deducted has become conventional for a married person.[8] In respect of any period when there are no dependent children it is 33%; for any period where there are dependent children it is only 25%.

---

5   Ie that there should be a reasonable expectation of a non-business benefit': see pp 396-398 above.
6   Inheritance (Provision for Family and Dependants) Act 1975. This Act allows those who were not provided for in the deceased's will to apply for support from his estate.
7   *Wrongful Death*, above p 391 n 3, para 3.46.
8   *Harris v Empress Motors* [1984] 1 WLR 212.

An example will illustrate this: V who is married with no children is involved in a fatal accident. V's wife W who has no paid employment[9] brings an action under the Fatal Accidents Act. If V's net income was £24,000 pa, then £8,000 is regarded as spent solely on V. The lost years calculation would be based upon: £24,000 − £8,000 = £16,000.

In contrast to the similar approach applied to the 'lost years' claim of a living victim,[10] no reduction is made in respect of shared expenses such as car loans. This is apparently because the law respects the fact that you cannot drive half a car. The value of the dependency at the date of the deceased's death is then reviewed to reflect likely changes to the deceased's income[11] between death and trial (to derive the pre-trial multiplicand) and in respect of changes in the deceased's income after trial (to calculate the post-trial multiplicand). The effects of pre-trial inflation are incorporated into the calculation. By using rates applicable at the time of trial, wage inflation from death to trial is reflected in the pre-trial multiplicand.[12] Where it is thought that the deceased's income would have risen in these periods, it could be suggested that the deceased would have reduced the percentage of his income applied to support his dependants. However the courts appear to ignore this complication.[13]

## The assessment of pecuniary loss: the multiplier

Where damages for personal injury are sought by the living victim of a tort, we have seen that post-trial damages for loss of income and medical expenses are calculated by applying a multiplier to a multiplicand. Such losses accruing before trial are simply totalled up. The practice with regard to the dependency claim is different because pre-trial losses are also assessed by a variant of the multiplier method. A single multiplier is calculated from the date of death rather than from the date of trial. Events occurring after death but before trial (eg the death of a dependant or an increase in the remuneration the deceased would have been paid) are taken

---

9   If V contributed income to the household the dependency would be calculated by applying the conventional deduction to the joint family purse less her net income. See *Coward v Comex Houlder Diving Ltd* (18 July 1988, unreported) (noted in *Kemp and Kemp on the Quantum of Damages*, vol 3, paras M2-042 and M2-232).

10  See p 348 above.

11  *Miller v British Road Services Ltd* [1967] 1 WLR 443.

12  *Cookson v Knowles* [1979] AC 556. The effects of post-trial inflation are now reflected by basing multipliers on discount rates applicable to investment in index-linked government stock, ie applying the logic of *Wells v Wells* (discussed at pp 356-358 above) to claims under the Fatal Accident Act.

13  *Cookson v Knowles* [1979] AC 556 at 568, 569, 575.

into account when assessing the damages to be awarded.[14] Nonetheless, it is still necessary to divide the single multiplier between damages to be paid for pre- and post-trial losses to apply the different rules as to interest applicable to each.[15]

The reason for deriving the multiplier from the date of death rather than that of trial is that the uncertainty which the multiplier is supposed to reflect begins at that date. From the date of the deceased's death, the court is required to speculate whether, if he had not died, he would have been able to continue to provide for his dependants.[16]

The method adopted by the courts in the past was to calculate the overall multiplier and then use as a pre-trial multiplier the actual number of years which have elapsed between death and trial. The balance of the calculated multiplier is then available to calculate future loss of dependency. Eg if the overall multiplier was 10 and the trial took place 4 years after the provider's death, the pre- and post-trial multipliers would be respectively 4 and 10-4 ie 6.[17] The overall multiplier was calculated in the same way as that for a living victim of a tort. After the recent period of revision involving the House of Lords, the Law Commission and the *Ogden Tables* Working Party,[18] it is expected that the use of the multiplier in fatal accident cases will follow the latest edition of the *Ogden Tables*.

First, the period of pre-trial dependency will usually be equal to the interval between accident and trial.[19] This figure should be further reduced to reflect the risk that the deceased would have died during this period. A table is provided for this purpose.[20] Where the period is small and the deceased was young at the time of the accident, the risk of his death in this period would be small and so no reduction is proposed. For instance, no reduction is proposed where a 30-year-old woman is killed and there is a 6 year delay between death and trial. However, where the deceased was a 70-year-old man and the delay was the same, the multiplier of 6 is reduced by a factor of 0.9.

---

14   *The Swynfleet* (1947) 81 Ll L Rep 116 at 121.
15   *Cookson v Knowles*, above n 12 at 572-573, 578-579.
16   Ibid at 576.
17   There is now a limited power to revise the multiplier applicable to the future loss of dependency where a long period of time between death and trial resolves some of the uncertainties informing the choice of overall multiplier: *Corbett v Barking Havering and Brentwood Health Authority* [1991] 2 QB 408 (multiplier of 12 used when trial took place 11 1/2 years after death – on appeal the multiplier applicable to future dependency was effectively raised from 0.5 (12-11 1/2) to 3 1/2).
18   See pp 346-347 above.
19   If it was likely that the provision would have ceased during this period perhaps because of the deceased's retirement or the dependant attaining his majority this shorter period of support should be used.
20   *Ogden Tables*, above p 391 n 6, Explanatory Notes 53-55 and Table D.

Second, the Working Group noted that the accurate calculation of post-trial dependency would not only require a set of tables similar to the one provided for living victims but for every combination of ages at the date of trial of the deceased and the dependant.[1] The view was taken that such a set of tables would be unwieldy and complicated to use when simplicity of application was sought. Therefore it was recommended that in complex cases or those involving very large claims, where small variations in the applicable multiplier produce exaggerated results in the global award, the advice of a professional actuary should be used. However, in the majority of cases the Working Group proposed a methodology which uses the tables and adjustments already described in relation to claims for future pecuniary loss brought by surviving victims of accidents. The multiplier so derived is then multiplied by a factor which reflects the further risk that the deceased would not in any event have survived to the date of trial in order to provide any post-trial dependency.[2] Again, this factor varies according to the age and sex of the deceased as well as the period from accident to trial. No reduction is proposed in respect of a 30-year-old man who dies three years before trial. In contrast, a factor of 0.45 should be applied where an 80-year-old woman is killed and it takes nine years for the case to come to trial. It is to be expected that in the future the tables based upon the current discount rate will routinely be used by the courts to calculate damages for lost dependency except where the calculations are complex or the award very large.

## Remarriage of the dependant

Until 1971 it was the practice of the courts to reduce damages claimed by a widow in respect of lost dependency to reflect her future prospects of remarriage and a fortiori to limit the claim when prior to the trial she had in fact re-married. This rule followed inevitably from the compensatory nature of the award. Where the claimant has, or will have, no loss of dependency because she has remarried, or intends to remarry, from the time of remarriage the dependency is extinguished or reduced. However, the courts attracted criticism along the lines that they were conducting a 'cattle market' when called upon to assess a widow's prospects of remarriage.[3] Much was made of the upsetting questions that might be asked in court and the intrusive activities of inquiry agents employed by

---

1    Ibid, para 52.
2    Ibid, Table E.
3    Several women's groups expressed strong disapproval: see *Hansard* (HC) 29 January 1971, vol 810, col 1122.

defendants.[4] As a result a provision was introduced to the effect that, in assessing the claim of a widow under the Fatal Accidents Act, the prospects of remarriage of a widow are to be ignored.[5]

Professor Atiyah has described this as 'one of the most irrational pieces of law 'reform' ever passed by Parliament'.[6] He illustrates the injustice to which this can give rise by a case in 1974 when a 25-year-old widow who had remarried an 'oil man with a five-figure salary' was awarded £65,000 damages in respect of the loss of her husband two years earlier.[7] The section can be further criticised for its untidy drafting because the widow's prospects of remarriage continue to be relevant to any dependency claim brought by her children. This provision starkly exposes the injustice of a tort-based compensation system which provides full compensation for the few (lucky) victims who are injured as a result of the fault of another as opposed to the many others who suffer the effects of injury or disease which is not so attributable and who have to rely on less generous schemes of compensation such as the social security system.

Comparison with the social security system may also suggest a better way to handle such problems. If compensation is paid in the form of periodic payments rather than a lump sum it is relatively easy to adjust the award to reflect the changing circumstances of the claimant. The Law Commission have rejected the award of revisable periodic payments mainly because they defeat the finality of litigation.[8] However, it is suggested that this is an advantage not a disadvantage. Rather, the Law Commission sought to balance the need to accurately assess a claimant's loss with that of avoiding an offensive investigation of the claimant's personal circumstances. In their opinion, this balance would be best struck by a new provision which instructs courts to ignore the prospects of future remarriage or supportive co-habitation when assessing damages for loss of dependency but to take account of any actual remarriage or supportive cohabitation. The new provision would apply equally to male and female dependants.[9]

## No deduction

The Fatal Accidents Act 1976, s 4 provides that 'in an action under this Act, benefits which have accrued or will or may accrue to any person from

4   Doubts were expressed that such concerns were exaggerated: see *Hansard* (HL) 20 April 1971, vol 317, col 541.
5   See now Fatal Accidents Act 1976, s 3(3).
6   P Cane, *Atiyah's Accidents, Compensation and the Law* (6th edn 1999) p 113.
7   *The Times,* 15 May 1974.
8   *Wrongful Death,* above p 391 n 3, paras 4.33-4.44.
9   Ibid, para 4.53.

his estate or otherwise as a result of his death shall be disregarded'. This section suggests that no deductions at all are to be made: this will therefore apply to any insurance moneys, pensions, benefits received from the estate of the deceased, or from any other source: social security benefits; the benefit of housing or domestic services provided free to the dependant; or payments from a fund raised for the victims of a disaster. Nor will any deduction be made if a dependant benefits from damages received by the deceased's estate in respect of his pain and suffering, or his loss of earnings for the period between the accident and his death.

However, the courts have drawn a distinction between the situation where the receipt of a benefit prevents the claimant from suffering a loss, and situations where the claimant can properly be said to have suffered a loss despite the receipt of the benefit. The courts have regarded the section as irrelevant to the former type of situation. In one case,[10] a child claimed damages under the Act following his mother's death. Although the child was receiving better care from his father's wife this was regarded as a benefit 'otherwise' accruing to the claimant and so did not in any way qualify the claim under the Act. In contrast, in a difficult case where a child's mother was killed in a car crash caused by the child's father the majority sought to exclude from the section the post-accident care provided by the father.[11] In order to avoid such fine distinctions, the Law Commission have recommended that the position in fatal accident cases should be made consistent with that in personal injury claims by a new provision that expressly provides that charity, insurance, survivors' pensions and inheritance are non-deductible.[12] A further proposal designed to clarify the law is that there should be a scheme for the recoupment of social security benefits paid to dependants similar to the one presently in force in relation to personal injuries.[13]

---

10  *Stanley v Saddique* [1992] QB 1.
11  *Hayden v Hayden* [1992] 1 WLR 986.
12  *Wrongful Death*, above p 391 n 3, para 5.39.
13  Ibid, para 5.69. See pp 386-387 above.

# 24 The damages system in practice

## Introduction

The first edition of this work published in 1988 was able to condense the results of a major empirical investigation into the actual operation of the damages system conducted by the Oxford Centre for Socio-legal Studies.[1] This was then the only major empirical investigation into the overall working of the damages system undertaken since the Pearson Commission.[2] It continues to enjoy that status.[3] Among the mass of relevant but uncoordinated (and for the purposes of assessing the damages system incomplete) data which has been accumulated subsequently,[4]

---

1   D Harris et al, *Compensation and Support for Illness and Injury* (1984) (hereinafter *Harris et al*) and H Genn, *Hard Bargaining* (1987) (hereinafter *Genn 1*). The data on which both of these works are based was largely collected between 1973-1977. The gist of *Genn 1* is given in H Genn, 'Negotiating the Settlement of Claims: Issues in Medical Negligence', in R Dingwall (ed) *Socio-legal Aspects of Medical Practice* (1989) 27.

2   *Report of the Royal Commission on Civil Liability and Compensation for Personal Injury* (Chair: Lord Pearson) Cmnd 7054 (1978) (hereinafter *Pearson*). Data was largely collected for 1973. Prior to *Harris et al* there also had been the *Report of the Personal Injuries Litigation Procedure Working Party* (Chair: Mr Justice Cantley), Cmnd 7476 (1979). This *Report* appears negligible to us but received an interesting defence in M Zander, 'Why Lord Woolf's Proposed Reforms of Civil Litigation Should Be Rejected', in AAS Zuckerman and R Cranston (eds) *Reform of Civil Procedure* (1995) 79, pp 83-84. A survey of taxed cases from 1986 carried out by members of the Faculty of Laws of University College London does not appear to have been fully published. Reference is made to papers by Swanson which draw on it at p 407 n 12, p 445 n 5, p 449 n 3 below.

3   The literature is surveyed in P Pleasence et al, *Profiling Civil Litigation: The Case for Research*, Legal Aid Board Research Unit Research Paper 1 (1996) ch 2.

4   Of eg the shortcomings of the litigation process before Woolf (Independent Working Party set up by the General Council of the Bar and the Law Society,

particular attention should be drawn to five pieces of work. The Law Commission has published a large-scale survey of the experience of successful personal injury claimants.[5] In the *Civil Justice Review*[6] and the *Woolf Report*,[7] two major evaluations of the working of the civil justice system overall, the Lord Chancellor's Department has provided some valuable additional information on the conduct of personal injury litigation. How well the civil justice system prior to the Woolf reforms was working has been described in an exhaustive independent survey: *Paths to Justice*.[8] Finally, the Legal Aid Board Research Unit[9] has examined in detail the conduct of legally aided personal injury litigation.[10] While there is an obvious need for a large scale project conducted with the goal of assessing the overall working of the damages system in a way which would replicate *Pearson* or *Harris et al*, the evidence available would seem to confirm that the very disturbing findings reported in the first edition of this work still broadly apply.

The typical undergraduate course on tort concentrates almost exclusively on questions of liability, the unstated assumption being that after a finding of liability C will receive an effective remedy for his injury. The remedy provided to those who suffer from illness and injury is a payment of damages for personal injury or death to C or his dependants. It is implicit in treating personal injury as a tort that the goal of damages for personal injury is 'full' compensation of C: 'compensation should as

---

*Civil Justice on Trial* (1993)); consumers' low level of satisfaction with that process (National Consumer Council, *Seeking Civil Justice* (1995)); the size of costs (see n 7 below) and the burden they place on ultimate payers (see pp 449-453 below), etc.

5    Law Commission, *Personal Injury Compensation: How Much Is Enough*, Report No 225 (1994) (hereinafter *How Much?*). Professor Genn was the author of this report.

6    *Report of the Review Body on Civil Justice* (Chair: Sir Maurice Hodgson) Cm 394 (1988) ch 7. The research on personal injuries was made available as a 'factual paper': Incubon International Consultants, *Civil Justice Review of the Study of Personal Injury Litigation* (1986). Though 1986 court statistics were used in the *Report*, the cases examined in detail were settled by 1984.

7    Lord Woolf, *Access to Justice (Final Report)* (hereinafter *Woolf*) (1996). This report commissioned some particularly valuable information on costs: ibid, annex 3 and H Genn, *Survey of Litigation Costs* (1996). On costs see further N Armstrong and J Peysner, *Costs in Personal Injury Litigation*, Report to the Association of Personal Injury Lawyers (1966) and S Fennell, *The Funding of Personal Injury Litigation*, Institute for the Study of the Legal Profession, University of Sheffield (1994).

8    H Genn, *Paths to Justice* (1999) (hereinafter *Genn 2*). There is a companion study of Scotland: H Genn and A Paterson, *Paths to Justice: Scotland* (2001).

9    Now Legal Services Commission Research Centre.

10   P Pleasence, *Personal Injury Litigation in Practice*, Legal Aid Board Research Unit Research Paper 3 (1998).

nearly as possible put the party who has suffered in the same position as he would have been in if he had not sustained the wrong'.[11] Tort is an individualised system which considers the particular circumstances of each C instead of using standardised rates of compensation. Damages are earnings-related, and are not subject to any ceiling; there is no direct political pressure on the courts to keep damages awards low. Damages may take account of a partial loss of earning capacity, and of earnings potential (such as promotion prospects). Unlike other systems of provision against personal injury, it attempts to compensate for non-pecuniary losses, such as pain and suffering or loss of amenities, and thus provides some compensation for non-earners, such as children, housewives and retired people. (There are no age criteria for entitlement.) As other systems do not aim at full compensation in this way, it is possible to claim that tort 'is the primary source of real compensation for accident victims in society'.[12]

However, it is the position taken in this book that this claim is so misleading as to be ridiculous.[13] The common assumption that the law of tort effectively remedies accidents, much less incapacity from all sources,[14] is almost entirely without foundation. As we will show in this chapter, the role the damages system plays in the compensation of incapacity overall is a failure judged by each and every one of the standards by which public investments are normally evaluated – economy, effectiveness, efficiency and equity. The first edition of this book and the empirical project whose findings were condensed in it carried into the 1990s the British form of 'the compensation debate' started by the creation of the post-Second World War welfare state as a response to the shortcomings of previous forms of provision, including tort;[15] or rather with the decision not to abolish tort at that time.[16] The resulting continuing comparison of tort and social security received enormous public attention

---

11   *Lim Poh Choo v Camden and Islington Area Health Authority* [1980] AC 174 at 187. See further chs 22 and 23 above.

12   TM Swanson, 'A Review of the Civil Justice Review: Economic Theories Behind the Delays in Tort Litigation' [1990] Current Legal Problems 185, p 211.

13   Cf *Pearson*, above p 405 n 2, vol 1, paras 174-175.

14   We shall use 'incapacity' to mean a substantial hindrance to the enjoyment of a normal standard of living caused by physical (including mental) sickness, injury, illness, disability, etc. The principal such hindrance is, of course, to work, leading to want through reduction of income.

15   *Social Insurance and Allied Services* (Chair: Sir William Beveridge) Cmd 6404 (1942) para 262: 'With the inevitable uncertainties of legal proceedings, suits for heavy damages on the grounds of negligence cannot escape having something of the character of a lottery'.

16   *Final Report of the Departmental Committee on Alternative Remedies* (Chair: Sir Walter Monckton) Cmd 6860 (1946) para 25. The decision to retain the damages system, though in a form that was perhaps intended to lead to its withering away, divided the Committee, and was taken despite the Committee as a whole finding

in the 1960s[17] from the exposure of the repugnant character of the thalidomide litigation.[18] In sum, it has been acknowledged at least since the war and it still is so that: 'there is a strong case for abolishing tort law and the tort system as a mechanism for compensating victims of personal injuries, illness and disability'.[19]

However, one can detect an increasingly desperate note in recent criticisms of the damages system, no doubt because that system, though occasionally shaken by distasteful episodes such as the personal injury litigation after the Hillsborough disaster,[20] continues to enjoy public legitimacy.[1] That this is the case poses an interesting sociological question, the answer to which really will have only two rational components: a lack of alternatives which appear clearly superior at a time of profound uncertainty about the appropriate role of welfare provision in general,[2] and the difficulty of undoing any reforms which prove worse. The scaling back of the New Zealand scheme for the provision of no-fault compensation by the state[3] has been thought to reduce the plausibility of the case which had

that: 'substantial advantages would be gained were it found possible to abolish the remedy by action and to substitute for it rights to benefits under national insurance'.

17   T Ison, *The Forensic Lottery* (1967) and PS Atiyah, *Accidents, Compensation and the Law* (1970).

18   The *Sunday Times* Insight Team, *Suffer the Children* (1979) chs 9-11. The legal points are emphasised in H Teff and C Munro, *Thalidomide* (1976) pp 57-61. The treatment of road accident victims was another particular source of concern: DW Elliot and H Street, *Road Accidents* (1968).

19   P Cane, *Atiyah's Accidents, Compensation and the Law* (6th edn 1999) p 423. See further, for the UK: PS Atiyah, 'Personal Injuries in the Twenty-first Century: Thinking the Unthinkable', in P Birks (ed) *Wrongs and Remedies in the Twenty-first Century* (1996) 1 and PS Atiyah, *The Damages Lottery* (1997) (discussed at pp 453-461 below); and internationally: D Dewees et al, *Exploring the Domain of Tort Law* (1996). For the US see p 430 n 15 below.

20   A Unger 'Pain and Anger' (1992) 142 New Law Journal 394. The latest shameful twist to the tale is described in A Chrisafis, '£330,000 for Hillsborough Officer's Late Stress Onset' (2 March 2001) *The Guardian*. In this particular case, a police officer claimed to have begun to suffer post-traumatic stress caused by his involvement in the disaster nine years after the event. On receipt of his award, he took early retirement (with a pension enhanced for medical reasons) at the age of 39. His claim was settled out of court by his negligent employer, the South Yorkshire Police Authority. This D was also liable to Mr Phil Hammond, Vice-chair of the Hillsborough Family Support Group, who was paid £3,500 for the death of his 14-year-old son after acrimonious litigation. Mr Hammond found the award to the officer 'offensive'.

1   Law Commission, *Damages for Personal Injury: Non-pecuniary Loss*, Report No 257 (1999) (hereinafter *Non-pecuniary Loss*) appendix B.

2   A Burrows, 'In Defence of Tort', in A Burrows, *Understanding the Law of Obligations* (1998) 120, pp 120-122, 130-134. Professor Burrows' work as Law Commissioner led to *Heil v Rankin*: see pp 440-442 below.

3   The history of the scaling back is authoritatively discussed in G Palmer, 'New Zealand's Accident Compensation Scheme: Twenty Years On' (1994) 44 University of Toronto Law Journal 223 and I Campbell, *Compensation for*

been made for adopting such a scheme in the UK.[4] What is worse for that case, however, is that under the New Zealand scheme existing common law rights were surrendered in return for the statutory rights which were given.[5] The scaling back arguably represented a breach of this unwritten 'social contract' under which the rights were surrendered,[6] but, of course, the common law rights have so far not been restored.[7]

Other, much more important, non-rational components of a full explanation of continuation of this system in the face of its shortcomings will include the development of a 'blame' or 'compensation culture' as an unfortunate side-effect of the growth of the welfare state; a continuing, stygian, popular ignorance of what the damages system actually accomplishes or can accomplish; the powerful advocacy of personal injury lawyers who believe in the system and, by happy coincidence, are the only clear beneficiaries of it; and a blatant want of capacity in the present political system to acknowledge openly that there are some hardships

---

*Personal Injury in New Zealand* (1996). Sir Geoffrey Palmer and Dr Campbell were, in their various capacities, extremely active and influential supporters of the scheme who believe that it continues to be overall extremely successful and that its shortcomings were exaggerated by a New Zealand government which very actively pursued the neo-classical economic policies of the 1980s: see further J Kelsey, *Economic Fundamentalism* (1996) pp 203-206. The best criticism of the philosophy of the New Zealand scheme is JA Henderson Jr, 'The New Zealand Accident Compensation Reform' (1981) 48 University of Chicago Law Review 781. Extensive references to criticisms of the working of the scheme are given by Palmer and Campbell.

4   Ison's views have, however, remained consistent: T Ison, *Accident Compensation* (1980) and T Ison, *Compensation Systems for Injury and Disease* (1994).

5   In this country, the replacement of quantification according to common law methods by a tariff for payments under the Criminal Injuries Compensation Scheme was substantially delayed by influential opposition on (a weak version of) this ground. The Scheme proposed in 1994 made no provision for loss of earnings or dependency, and in *R v Secretary of State for the Home Department, ex p Fire Brigades Union* [1995] 2 AC 513 this was held to be unlawful, although the proposal left it perfectly open for C to pursue a tort claim rather than a criminal injuries compensation claim. The tariff Scheme brought into force under the Criminal Injuries Compensation Act 1995 provides compensation for these heads of damage. See D Miers, *State Compensation for Criminal Injuries* (1997) sec 1.4.1.

6   For references see Campbell, above p 408 n 3, pp 74-76.

7   R Mahoney, 'Trouble in Paradise: New Zealand's Accident Compensation Scheme', in SAM McLean (ed) *Law Reform and Medical Injury Litigation* (1995) 31, p 77: 'The connection between the minimal cover provided by the [compensation scheme] and the continued bar on the right to sue remains a greater mystery than ever'. This argument is sound although Mahoney's criticisms of the scheme and comparisons with it are often suspect; eg he criticises the scheme for exempting disease (which its proponents did not wish to do but felt obliged to do) (ibid, pp 34-35, 39-43), with the breathtaking implication that the victims of disease would commonly be compensated if tort liability for personal injury had not been abolished! Another argument in this paper is discussed in n 19 below.

which government intervention is unable to remedy in a cost-effective fashion or, indeed, at all.

## The incidence of incapacity and of compensation by damages

The damages system cannot of its nature address all forms of incapacity. Usually C can obtain compensation through tort only if he is able to prove his loss was caused by D's negligent or intentional act (or omission). Incapacity which is not caused by an act, such as that caused by congenital sickness, or by injury such as the loss of a limb which was not caused by blameworthy conduct, will very rarely fall within tort's scope. These doctrinal limits are much further narrowed by evidential difficulties of proof to the standard required in civil proceedings, so that, for example, an illness caused by long (negligently caused) exposure to minute quantities of a toxin is likely to be extremely difficult to prove. The 'third party' nature of ultimate payment for tort liability gives D and his representatives a very strong incentive to dispute claims.[8] This all means that the damages system in practice responds almost exclusively to traumatic accidents.[9] *Harris et al*[10] found that damages were recovered in only 2 of the 952 cases of incapacity caused by sickness they surveyed. Contrary to the impressions of many lawyers, then, neither the seriousness of a cause of incapacity nor the length of time off work gives a strong indication of who is more likely to obtain damages; the tort system is effectively based on the cause of incapacity rather than on the relative severity of the consequences.

An assessment of that system's effectiveness in terms of compensating incapacity overall therefore requires one to appreciate the extent of incapacity arising from all forms of sickness, including both injury *and illness*.[11] There has been no attempt systematically to collect sickness data in a way which allows this assessment to be carried out since *Harris et al*, although it is possible to update certain data piecemeal.[12]

8    See pp 424-425, 430-434 below.
9    J Stapleton, *Disease and the Compensation Debate* (1986) p 3: 'although the law of torts does not formally sanction preferential treatment of accident victims, its conceptual machinery dramatically favours this class in practice'.
10   Above p 405 n 1, table 1.2 n 3 and table 1.3.
11   One quarter of all adults report that they have a longstanding, 'limiting' illness, and 37% of men and 48% of women are taking prescribed medication: Department of Health, *Health Survey for England 1996* (1998) tables 5.1, 5.3. On the incidence of (widely defined) disability see Office of Population, Censuses and Surveys, *The Prevalence of Disability Among Adults* (1988) and Department of Social Security, *Disability in Britain*, Research Report No 94 (1999).
12   When citing subsequent data, that data will be silently converted to correspond to *Harris et al's* categories as closely as possible.

According to *Harris et al*,[13] each year 10.3% of adults suffered an incapacity lasting a fortnight or longer;[14] 6.3% due to illness and 4% due to accidents.[15] 12% of the *accident* victims succeeded in recovering some damages for personal injury.[16] 3.5% of incapacity was caused by an accident at work,[17] 2.1% by a road accident, and 35% (86% of accidents) was caused by 'other' accidents (at home, on someone else's premises, at sport or leisure, etc).[18] However, not only are most illnesses outside the scope of tort, but fewer than one in three of road accident victims (29%), fewer than one in five of work accident victims (19%), and fewer than one in fifty of all other types of accident victim (2%) obtained any damages at all. It is obvious from these figures that the damages system provides compensation to only a minute proportion of all cases of incapacity. When illnesses are added to accidents, it is only in under 2% of the overall instances of incapacity that the victim will receive any damages. As 'adverse medical outcome' and liability for faulty drug products were part of *Harris et al's* 'other' category, it is likely that the recent dramatic growth in clinical negligence claims has made a marginal change to this picture.[19]

13  Above p 405 n 1, table 1.2.

14  In 1996, 6% of men and 7% of women reported having had within the preceding two weeks an acute sickness (ie illness or injury) leading to a disability which had lasted for 2 weeks or more: *Health Survey for England 1996*, above p 410 n 11, table 5.7.

15  The *Health Survey* reported that in 1996 8% of men and 7.5% of women suffered an accident which incapacitated them for more than a week: ibid, table 4.1. A claims management company recently gave evidence that there were 11.2 million accidents in the UK annually (in 2 million of which blame was attributed to someone else), and a 1994 Gallup poll conducted for the Law Society in connection with the establishment of its 'Accident Line' claims service found 6.8 million people sustained accidental injuries lasting over two weeks (and 2.5 million attributed the blame to someone else): *Report of the Lord Chancellor's Committee to Investigate the Activities of Non-legally Qualified Claims Assessors and Employment Advisers* (Chair: Mr Brian Blackwell) (April 2000) para 68 and Pleasence et al, *Profiling Civil Litigation: The Case for Research*, above p 405 n 3, para 2.2.2.

16  *Pearson*, above p 405 n 2, found that accidents account for 10% of incapacity (vol 2, para 35) and 6.5% of the victims of accidents receive damages (vol 2, para 74). *Pearson* defined accidents in such a way as to exclude minor injuries which were not severe enough to cause an absence from work of more than 3 days.

17  The Health and Safety Executive thoroughly analyses work-related injury and illness: Health and Safety Executive, *The Costs to the British Economy of Work Accidents and Work-related Ill-health* (1996). The Department of Trade and Industry has established its Home Accident Surveillance System which publishes annual reports: Department of Trade and Industry, *Working for a Safer World*, 23rd Annual Report of the Home and Leisure Accidents Surveillance System (2001). On road traffic accidents see Department of the Environment, Transport and Regions, *Road Accidents Great Britain 1999: The Casualty Report* (2000).

18  Cf *Pearson*, above p 405 n 2, vol 2, table 11.

19  Applying the Legal Services Commission's classification to all cases however funded, Fennell found that, of personal injury claims made in 1993, 52.5% were

Despite the protestations of lawyers, it is clear that, judged as a response to the problem of incapacity from all causes, the damages system is of extremely limited importance.

Moreover, *Harris et al*[20] found that the consequences of illness are on average much more serious than those of accidents, whether judged by length of stay in hospital, by use of medical or social services, by length of absence from work, by the degree of long-term incapacity, or by the effect on household income. On the basis of all these findings, a rational system of provision against incapacity should be much more concerned to plan to cope with the risk of suffering a serious illness than with the risk of a serious accident.

## Compensation outside the damages system

In order to appreciate the effectiveness of damages for personal injury in the social response to incapacity, we must take some stock of the general issues raised by the idea that some such response should be made. The extent to which the fact that the damages system does little to compensate incapacity overall is a criticism of that system depends on the answer to at least two questions: one, the extent to which incapacity should be compensated;[1] and two, the extent to which tort plays a useful role in compensating those whom it is thought desirable to compensate.

In his 1974 report on compensation in Australia, Woodhouse J, whose previous report led to the New Zealand accident compensation scheme, did recommend compensation for all forms of physical disability regardless of cause.[2] Largely for reasons of anticipated cost, it was not sought to implement this in Australia,[3] and it has not ever been sought to implement it anywhere else. The initial aspiration of the post-war British

---

road accidents, 26.4% were work accidents, 6.2% were medical negligence, 5.9% were tripping, and 5.7% were occupiers' liability: Fennell, *The Funding of Personal Injury Litigation*, above p 406 n 7, para 3.8. (These figures are corroborated by R Lewis, *Deducting Benefits from Damages for Personal Inujury* (1999) p 224 n 3 and Pleasence, *Personal Injury Litigation in Practice*, above p 406 n 10, p 48 n 28.)

20  Above p 405 n 1, pp 325-327. *Cf Pearson*, above p 405 n 2, vol 2, ch 17 and Department of Social Security, *Disability in Britain*, above p 410 n 11.

1   As Stapleton, *Disease and the Compensation Debate*, p 410 n 9 above, p 164 points out, the 'fundamental question is where to draw the boundaries of "disability" for the purposes of entitlement to benefits'. See further DA Stone, *The Disabled State* (1984) ch 6.

2   *Compensation and Rehabilitation in Australia: Report of the National Commission of Inquiry* (Chair: Woodhouse J) (1974) vol 1, pp 181-191.

3   *Report from the Senate Standing Committee on Constitutional and Legal Affairs: Clauses of the National Compensation Bill 1974*, Parliament of the Commonwealth of Australia Parliamentary Paper No 142 (1975) para 1.23. The history is discussed in G Palmer, *Compensation for Incapacity* (1979) chs 10-12, 20.

welfare state as set out in the Beveridge Report was more restricted. It was to provide 'freedom from want',[4] including want caused by all forms of incapacity. The welfare state was constructed against a background of a range of existing support schemes – through charity, poor relief, specific private and social insurance schemes particularly workmen's compensation, and tort.[5] These meritorious schemes lacked the coordination to avoid glaring anomalies in overall provision, and Beveridge recognised that a 'complete solution' to the problem of want caused by incapacity 'is to be found only in a completely unified scheme for disability without demarcation by the cause of disability'.[6] We shall return to these general issues at the end of this chapter.

As we are not approaching this question ab initio but attempting to assess the working of the existing damages system, the answer to the second question – the extent to which tort plays a useful role in compensating those whom it is thought desirable to compensate – can draw on empirical material about the alternative compensation mechanisms to tort and the performance of the damages system itself. Compensation outside the damages system is principally provided by social security.

## Social security benefits and sick pay

Britain no longer has a Department of Social Security. On 8 June 2001 its functions were taken over by the newly-created Department of Work and Pensions. Nevertheless, howsoever called, social security is by far the major source of financial support for the victims of accident or illness. In 1998-1999 social security spending on incapacity was £24 b, that is to say, 3% of gross domestic product (GDP), almost all of which went to those of working age whose incapacity prevented them from seeking work. (The overall social security budget was £97 b, 30% of all government expenditure and 11% of GDP. Spending on incapacity is the second largest

4   *Social Insurance and Allied Services*, above p 407 n 15, paras 11-16. The contemporary statement is 'to provide work for those who can and security for those who cannot': *A New Contract for Welfare: Principles into Practice*, Cm 4140 (1998) para 1 and *A New Contract for Welfare: Support for Disabled People*, Cm 4103 (1998) para 1. The notion of replacing Beveridge's 'negative welfare' with 'positive welfare' (eg 'in place of [protection from] want, autonomy') that (remotely) underpins this change in emphasis is set out in A Giddens, *The Third Way* (1998) ch 4 (quote at p 128). The criticism of Beveridge that underpins this change, that he did not place enough emphasis on work rather than receipt of benefit, is utterly spurious: *Social Insurance and Allied Services*, above p 407 n 15, para 440.
5   Ibid, appendix B.
6   Ibid, para 80. See further, on social security in general: TH Marshall, *Social Policy* (5th edn 1985) pt 1; and on incapacity in particular: JC Brown, *The Disability Income System* (1984).

414 Section 2 Tort: remedies for wrongdoing

head of social security expenditure after retirement pensions.)[7] About 55% of this enormous expenditure may be traced to contributions from employees and employers, the rest comes from general taxation (and local authority social services are in part paid from council taxes).

From the injured person's perspective, the crucial feature of social security is that in general it ignores the cause of a person's need. It therefore is not restricted to persons incapacitated by an accident, as tort effectively is. Unlike damages, social security does not aim to restore a person to his previous standard of living, nor to take account of his earning potential. A further contrast is that, apart from work-related cases, the social security system does not attempt to meet either partial loss of earnings or non-pecuniary loss. But benefits are paid weekly and are annually adjusted to take account of changes in the cost of living. In the past, the overall adjustment has actually run ahead of price inflation,[8] but since 1995 it has been brought into line with it and is expected to be held steady.[9] The benefits normally continue for so long as the need for support continues, and this future entitlement is often worth a substantial amount which must be taken into account in any comparison with damages.

It is not possible in a work of this nature to set out all the benefits to which a person suffering from incapacity may be entitled, much less the national insurance, tax and council tax credits, and other assistance to which such a person may also be entitled.[10] We shall merely mention some of the principal benefits.[11]

The great majority of employees are entitled to *statutory sick pay* from their employers for up to 28 weeks of sickness absence (excluding the first three days). It currently is £62.20 per week. (The average gross weekly income of all British households is £470 per week.)[12] The important feature of sick pay is that it is not dependent on any particular cause of the incapacity. Employers used to act merely as the government's agents in paying this benefit for they were able to deduct the whole cost from their national insurance contributions. However, except for very small employers, they no longer may do so. This burden was offset by

7   Department of Social Security, *The Changing Welfare State: Social Security Spending* (2000) ch 1.
8   On long-term sickness and permanent disability see M Evans, 'Social Security: Dismantling the Pyramids', in H Glennerster and J Hills (eds) *The State of Welfare* (2nd edn 1998) 257, pp 277-281.
9   *The Changing Welfare State: Social Security Spending*, above n 7, chs 2-3.
10  Child Poverty Action Group, *Welfare Benefits Handbook* (2001) pp 10-11 and Disability Rights Alliance, *Disability Rights Handbook* (26th edn 2001).
11  The heart of the social security system for those of working age now is the eponymous *jobseeker's allowance*. By its nature it is not for those suffering from incapacity, but if one is claiming jobseeker's allowance and one is sick for a short time, one need not sign off and claim a benefit related to incapacity.
12  Department of Social Security, *Family Resources Survey: Great Britain 1999-2000* (2001) table 3.1.

contemporaneous reductions in employers' national insurance contributions and it would appear that, despite many predictions to the contrary, the scheme is being administered overall properly.[13] The great majority of sick pay is therefore no longer really part of social security expenditure. It is better considered part of the minimum 'social wage' set by the government. Statutory sick pay, like ordinary pay, is subject to tax and national insurance contributions, and is paid through the employer's regular payroll arrangements.

In addition to this statutory minimum, the employer may be contractually bound to pay 'occupational' sick pay at a higher level – 'topping up' the statutory sick pay. Although membership of occupational sick pay schemes is high (over 90% of employees), the range of benefits (inevitably) differs considerably, and coverage is very uneven, especially amongst smaller employers. The protection against want caused by incapacity given by occupational sick pay has many obviously attractive features as a contractual rather than a social security mechanism,[14] and in particular it can embrace levels of coverage which social security *cannot*. But any extension of the already very important role which occupational sick pay now plays must seek to iron out present inadequacies of coverage,[15] and must recognise that, of its nature as part of the employment bargain, occupational sick pay *cannot* actually *replace* social security provision.[16]

One must earn £72 per week to be eligible for statutory sick pay. Earners[17] not entitled to statutory sick pay for this or another reason may be able to claim *incapacity benefit* at the short term lower rate of £52.60 (plus £32.55 for an adult dependant) for the first 28 weeks of their incapacity for work from any cause. A national insurance contribution record is needed (unless one became incapable of work in youth) and there is a waiting period of three days. For six months after the first 28 weeks, incapacity benefit is paid at the short term higher rate of £62.20 (plus

13   AI Ogus et al, *The Law of Social Security* (4th edn 1995) pp 160-161.
14   Department of Health and Social Security, *Report on a Survey of Occupational Sick Pay Schemes* (1977). This remains the most valuable official discussion of these schemes of which we are aware, and in itself it was not as well done as a previous, 1964, discussion which attempted to link these schemes to an enquiry into the incidence of incapacity for work. Research is urgently needed.
15   R Lewis, 'The Privatisation of Sickness Benefit' (1982) 11 Industrial Law Journal 245, pp 249-250.
16   See the discussion of the necessity of a social security floor and the great desirability of extra private provision at pp 453-461 below.
17   Plus some pensioners whose incapacity began during their working life for the first five years of their pensionable life. Though pensioners' incapacity obviously is long term, they are paid incapacity benefit at the short term rate. There is also some special conditions under which widows and widowers are entitled to incapacity benefit.

£32.55 for an adult dependant, plus £9.70 for one's eldest child, plus £11.35 for each other child); and after that at the long term rate of £69.75 per week (plus £41.75 for an adult dependant, plus £9.70 for one's eldest child, plus £11.35 for each other child). If one receives a pension (including an occupational pension but excluding statutory retirement pension), one's incapacity benefit after 28 weeks may be reduced or extinguished depending on the size of the pension payment.

Industrial injuries benefits are payable for work-related incapacity. *Disablement benefit* may be paid to an employed earner (ie not self-employed) whose incapacity was caused by an accident in the course of employment or from a disease specially prescribed in relation to the employment. For the first 28 weeks, statutory sick pay is payable. But after 15 weeks the long-term *disablement benefit* is also payable for a loss of physical or mental 'faculty' (capacity) resulting from a work accident or industrial disease. A statutory scale ranks various injuries: eg loss of both hands is a 100% disability (for which the rate is £112.90 per week); loss of four fingers of one hand is a 50% disability (£56.45 per week). The benefit is paid weekly, but no benefit is payable for an assessment under 14% (equivalent to the loss of an index finger). Entitlement to disablement benefit does not depend on any loss of earnings, and may be payable in addition to sick pay or incapacity benefit. Two other industrial injuries benefits, *constant attendance allowance* (paid at rates between £22.60 and £90.40 depending on degree of need) and *exceptionally severe disablement allowance* (£45.20), may be paid to those whose incapacity requires constant attendance upon them, in the latter case permanently.

*Income support* (for pensioners the *minimum income guarantee*) is paid from general taxation and is for those who are not in full-time employment and whose financial resources fall below a minimum based on the sum of a basic personal allowance, a premium for special needs most of which relate to incapacity, and housing costs such as mortgage interest payments. The minimum 'requirements' for families of different sizes and ages are calculated, and the benefit brings the actual resources of the beneficiary up to the 'applicable amount'. It is accordingly known as a 'means-tested' benefit. To take an example related to incapacity: let us consider an owner occupier paying a mortgage (of up to £100,000) who was the sole earner in a family and who is now in receipt of higher rate incapacity benefit. He will receive the difference between the benefit and the income support personal allowance for a couple with dependent children, plus the family premium, plus the disability premium, plus payment of mortgage interest.

*Disabled person's tax credit* tops up the wages of those in low-paid, full-time employment who are in receipt of an incapacity or disability benefit.

Several non-contributory benefits are designed to meet the extra needs of disabled people. *Disability living allowance* may be given to assist with mobility problems and care needs. The *mobility component* (£14.65 or £38.65) is for those who are unable (or virtually unable) to walk but are able to benefit from greater mobility. The *care component* (£14.65 or £37 or £55.30) is for a person in need of continual or repeated attention. (The *attendance allowance* is a benefit for those over 65 which corresponds to the disability living allowance care component.)

The *invalid care allowance* (£41.75 plus dependants' allowances) is paid to the carer (who is regularly and substantially engaged in caring and so not in gainful employment) of a person in receipt of disability living allowance care component at one of the higher rates, or attendance allowance, or constant attendance allowance.

### Other forms of 'social security'

Another form of financial 'social security' is the Criminal Injuries Compensation Scheme,[18] which is publicly funded and now administered by the Criminal Injuries Compensation Authority (formerly Board), a statutory body established by the Criminal Injuries Compensation Act 1995. Awards are made to those suffering personal injury directly attributable to a crime of violence, in assisting in an arrest or preventing a crime from being committed, or from an offence of trespass on a railway.[19] Eligibility is not dependent on a conviction against the offender, nor, in most cases, even on his identification; but the victim must have informed the police of the incident without delay. There would, of course, be a tort claim against the person causing the injury, but the Scheme was intended to stand in the place of the unidentified or impecunious offender. The overlapping of collateral benefits is for the most part prevented, but there are a number of complicated exceptions.

As originally established, the Scheme set upper and lower limits to the awards it would make, but assessed those awards in the same way as common law damages. This therefore included loss of earnings, earning capacity and non-pecuniary loss; and in fatal cases loss of dependency. As the Scheme was based on common law damages and, for the applicant, virtually cost-free, the Home Office's control over expenditure was tenuous; the annual amount of compensation paid grew by 4,000% between 1964 and 2000, which obviously was far beyond original anticipations. The annual value of compensation paid has increased 40

18  See further Miers, *State Compensation for Criminal Injuries*, above p 409 n 5 and D Miers, 'Criminal Injuries Compensation: The New Regime' *Journal of Personal Injury Law* [2001] Journal of Personal Injury Litigation 371.

19  The inclusion of this victimising event is both a tribute to the political influence of the railway unions in pressing for compensation for their members traumatised by people committing suicide on the tracks, and the vagaries of a compensation regime which privileges some forms of personal injury and death over others.

times in real terms, to around £205 million. Given the complexity of the assessment, applicants were, in many cases, unable to understand how the amount they were awarded was arrived at. And as the numbers of applications increased, their resolution became increasingly delayed.

The government's expectation was that the substitution of a tariff of injuries for the element of general damages would substantially meet these concerns: 'First, decisions in straightforward claims could be made speedily against publicly accessible injury descriptions with corresponding levels of award. Second, in the absence of any discretion under the tariff, decisions could be taken by relatively junior officials, rather than by the more experienced, and more expensive, Board members. Third, being no longer tied to increases in common law damages, the government could control exactly the tariff sums payable for each level of injury'.[20] After the abortive effort to reform the Scheme in 1994,[1] a statutory Scheme came into effect on 1 April 1996. This incorporated, first, a tariff specifying 310 injuries attracting any one of 25 levels of award between £1,000 (the minimum award) and £250,000 (the maximum award for any single injury). Second, it provided for compensation to be payable for loss of earnings and earning capacity and for long-term care, and, in the case of fatal injuries, bereavement, loss of dependency and loss of parental services. In 1999/2000 the Authority received 78,000 applications. Following a Home Office review, a revised Scheme came into effect on 1 April 2001. This maintains the existing structure, but there are now some 400 descriptions of injury.

Leaving aside the internal difficulties associated with the operation of the Scheme, the course of that operation has suffered from two defects obvious from the outset which, it is submitted, should have prevented its ever being implemented. The Scheme effectively adds another set to the class of those privileged by success in the damages system, and does nothing for those not so privileged other than make their relative position worse.[2] But, on the other hand, as monetary awards cannot actually

20   Miers, 'Criminal Injuries Compensation: The New Regime', above p 417 n 18, p 372.
1    See p 409 n 5 above.
2    This discrepancy would be accentuated were delinquent victims to be privileged by the operation of the Scheme. A claimant who was, at the time of his injury, himself engaged in some illicit behaviour may, in tort law, nevertheless succeed in damages against the defendant, probably reduced by virtue of his contributory negligence: *Revill v Newbery* [1996] QB 567 (claimant a burglar). The tax-payer funded Scheme permits the Authority to reduce or withhold an award because of the applicant's conduct or character (in the latter case, even where it is not causally connected to the victimisation). The implementation of this provision shows that it will be an exceptional case in which a burglar (or any other claimant committing an offence at the time) would receive any compensation at all. But needless to say, this is a highly contentious provision, and one which is difficult to apply: see Miers, *State Compensation for Criminal Injuries*, above p 409 n 5, sec 7.5.

compensate for the non-pecuniary losses of personal injury, there have been repeated distasteful episodes where, for example, the bereaved have criticised the awards they have received for being of a derisory amount.[3]

Proposals are being considered to set up a Board under the Ministry of Defence which will centralise the compensation for injury, illness or death suffered by those serving in the armed forces (and perhaps reservists) and will implement a system of tariffs somewhat similar to the Criminal Injuries Compensation Scheme.[4]

*Social services* are provided by the National Health Service (NHS) and local authorities (sometimes with central funding).[5] The NHS provides sick and injured people with hospital facilities, the services of general practitioners and specialists, rehabilitation services, and local community services (especially home nursing). The cost is supported by general taxation; no charge is made to the recipient of the services (except for prescriptions) and entitlement does not depend on the cause of the patient's need for the services. Similarly, local authorities offer welfare services to disabled people, irrespective of the cause of their need, and may provide, in addition to social work advice, home helps to assist with shopping and housework; the delivery of meals ('meals on wheels'); laundry services; telephones; adaptations to accommodation; special housing; transport assistance; day centres for light employment or recreation; and holidays or short-term care to give a break to members of the disabled person's family who are nursing him. The local office of Jobcentre Plus, part of the Department of Work and Pensions, will also help a disabled person to find employment, and there currently is a 'New Deal for Disabled People' which tries to address some of the problems specific to classes of the disabled. All these services are designed to meet needs with direct assistance rather than with money, although many local authorities have recently begun to make cash payments to disabled persons which they can spend on items which might formerly have been directly provided.

3   R Ford, 'Josie Russell to Contest Award for Mother's Loss' (2 April 1998) *The Times*. Ms Russell was a young girl who survived, but was seriously injured by, an appalling attack that left her mother and sister dead. She was initially awarded, *inter alia*, £18,500 for loss of parental services. In a statement entirely expressive of the typical overestimation of the possibilities of 'compensation' through law or the action of a public authority, Ms Russell's solicitor, one Ms Sara Harman, gave it as her opinion that: 'the authority ha[s] given paltry sums. It is a graphic illustration of the inadequacy of the Scheme. The authority had the possibility of exercising their discretion generously and compensating Josie for the terrible loss of her mother and her younger sister'.

4   Ministry of Defence, *Joint Compensation Review: A Consultation Document* (March 2001).

5   *Modernising Social Services*, Cm 4169 (1998). See further J Morris, *Independent Lives?* (1993).

Social services are also provided by the voluntary sector, sometimes in co-ordination with the state providers of social services.[6]

Another form of 'social security' is crucial to those who are sick or injured. This is the voluntary, informal care which victims receive mainly from members of their immediate families, but also from other relatives or neighbours. *Harris et al*[7] was in advance of its time in drawing attention to the contribution of such 'carers', who give regular assistance in nursing and self-care, in mobility and in housekeeping, in a way which does not depend upon the age or contribution record of the victim nor upon the cause of the incapacity. Britain has an estimated 5.7 million carers, with 17% of households containing a carer.[8] Following The Carers (Recognition and Services) Act 1995, a 'national strategy' for co-ordinating private caring and available public support has been developed.[9]

All these sources of support are often as important as or more important to disabled people than financial support. Some facilities, such as social or recreational centres, depend on community action; even a disabled millionaire could hardly buy the presence of others to make a success of such a centre. But the courts, in assessing damages for personal injuries, have paid little attention to non-medical services; they seem to assume that a sum of money will enable a person who is prevented by his injuries from continuing his previous activities to purchase some alternative satisfaction. However, the vast majority of incapacitated people cannot hope to obtain any damages, and for them the quality of their lives will depend largely on the support their families can give them, on social welfare services, and on the many voluntary agencies set up to help them.

### Evaluation of social security

There is no doubt that theoretically social security is a far superior mechanism for compensating disability than tort. It is not handicapped by the contradiction between the effective provision of compensation and the necessity of establishing tort liability which makes tort almost

6    Commission on the Future of the Voluntary Sector, *Meeting the Challenge of Change: Voluntary Action into the 21st Century* (1996).
7    Above p 405 n 1, pp 244-248. The Law Commission has recently taken notice of carers: *How Much?* above p 406 n 5, pp 48-50 and Law Commission, *Damages for Personal Injury: Medical, Nursing and Other Expenses; Collateral Benefits*, Report No 262 (1999).
8    *Family Resources Survey: Great Britain 1999-2000*, above p 414 n 12, ch 6.
9    Department of Health, *Caring About Carers: A National Strategy for Carers* (1999) ch 2, para 1.

irrelevant to the solution of the incapacity problem. But an unacceptable unevenness in social security provision identified by *Harris et al*[10] continues to characterise benefit provision. This unevenness arises in two ways. First, the level of service provided to claimants has been unacceptably low. Although the calculation of entitlement does not suffer from the inevitable arbitrariness of personal injury quantification, the system is in total complicated, with the combination of benefits being subject to difficult overlapping benefit rules. The claimant must be careful to frame his claim in such a way as to maximise his entitlement.[11] Proper submission of an at all complicated claim, such as one might expect in a case of prolonged incapacity, is very difficult unless the claimant receives good advice.[12] But while, unlike tort, social security does not have adversarial opposition to the incapacitated person's claim at its core, there is a long record of poor advice being given to claimants.[13] An atmosphere in the handling of claimants which may be daunting, and on occasion has a little of the quality of the thalidomide litigation,[14] and poor accuracy in decision-making (and appeals)[15] have led to substantial error in the payment of benefits.

Second, the social security system in general and incapacity related benefits in particular have not been ordered by any coherent commitment to a clear goal for the system. In part, of course, this stems from a tension created by the impossibility of eradicating significant 'moral hazard' from social security. Moral hazard has been particularly thoroughly identified in the economics of insurance. Having agreed an insurance contract, the insured may change his behaviour in a way prejudicial to the insurer, most acutely by fraudulently bringing about the event he is now insured against, but also, and more importantly, by not taking the precautions against the event's occurrence he did prior to having the policy. The point is that the 'policy might itself change incentives and therefore the probabilities upon which the insurance company has relied'.[16] Its relevance to health care (and to the provision of social security against incapacity) is manifest, for these are forms of 'insurance':

10  Above p 405 n 1, ch 5.
11  There are also complicated rules relating the payment of benefits to other sources of compensation: see pp 382-389 above.
12  Beveridge recognised this: *Social Insurance and Allied Services*, above p 407 n 15, para 397.
13  Lord Plowden, 'Foreword', in J Simkins and V Tickner, *Whose Benefit?* (1978) 11, p 11: 'nothing in my experience either as a civil servant or an industrialist prepared me for the Kafka-like world in which the disabled and handicapped [claiming benefit] have to exist'.
14  S Ward, *An Unfit Test: CAB Clients' Experience of the Medical Test for Incapacity Benefit* (1997).
15  J Baldwin et al, *Judging Social Security* (1992).
16  KJ Arrow, 'Information and Economic Behaviour', in KJ Arrow, *Collected Papers*, vol 4 (1984) 136, p 148.

'Health insurance' ... once taken out, is equivalent to a reduction in the price of medical care, and therefore the rational individual will increase his consumption, which increases the amount of medical insurance payments and ultimately causes an increase in the premiums. This is a social cost, since an increase in medical expenditures by any individual increases the premium for all.[17]

That the demand for health goods and social security is infinite and that demand will to some extent respond positively to greater access to provision are platitudes. But if not properly managed these platitudes may turn into strains on finite resources which undermine the legitimacy of social provision against incapacity.[18] In the light of this, a very cautious approach must be taken to the wider or more generous compensation of incapacity,[19] as Beveridge clearly recognised,[20] but successive governments including the present have taken the view that this has not been achieved in social security spending:

As worklessness is the main cause of poverty, the benefits system may have been more of a problem than a solution ... In many cases, such as Invalidity Benefit (whose more generous level of benefit encouraged people to define themselves as incapacitated rather than unemployed, and in which there was inadequate scrutiny of claims to benefit), it meant that the system itself may well have contributed to the problem it was designed to solve.[1]

17  Ibid. See further M Pauly, 'The Economics of Moral Hazard' (1968) 58 American Economic Review 531.

18  C Heimer, *Reactive Risk and Rational Action* (1985).

19  The Law Commission's recent recommendation that psychiatric illness be more readily recognised in tort was qualified because the Commission gave some force to the floodgates argument against it: Law Commission, *Liability for Psychiatric Illness*, Report No 249 (1998) para 6.8. The qualification was, however, gestural. Despite noting a case which should induce caution in any sensible person (*Vernon v Bosley (No 2)* [1999] QB 18) and receiving general evidence that the epidemiology of certain illnesses has been shown to vary with the compensation available for the illness, the Commission was able to make its recommendation because it thought that decisions about psychiatric injury would not be markedly worse than they now are in personal injury cases (Report, loc cit, para 6.7)! Leaving aside the extraordinary 'logic', the Commission's citation of back pain as an example of what is acceptable was singular. One of the main reasons public confidence in the New Zealand compensation scheme was damaged was the fact that in 1991, for example, 23% of the funds it paid out were for back pain: Accident Compensation Commission (New Zealand), *Annual Report 1992* (1993) p 24.

20  *Social Insurance and Allied Services*, above p 407 n 15, para 22: 'The insured persons should not feel that income for idleness, however caused, can come from a bottomless purse'. See further ibid, paras 22, 130, 131 (iii), 274 (ii), 443.

1   *The Changing Welfare State: Social Security Spending*, above p 414 n 7, p 34. See further Department of Social Security, *The Growth of Social Security* (1993) p 17.

The current evidence is that the problem of fraud in claiming incapacity benefits is very small,[2] but the steps now taken to prevent this are extensive.[3] So long as the majority experience work as a burden, ie so long as 'social security' as such is needed, there will be an irresolvable tension between the provision of benefits and the preservation of incentives to work.

This, however, cannot account for the continual adverse criticism of the incoherence of social security provision in respect of incapacity. The traditional goal of social security before Beveridge was to meet the needs of certain groups whose financial position was adversely affected by various contingencies such as old age, unemployment, death of a wage earner or congenital disability. With the creation of the general welfare state, these piecemeal provisions have been to some extent integrated into the overall goal of securing freedom from want. This underlies the modern form of support for those whose resources fall below minimum levels, whether or not they were affected by one of these particular contingencies. However, the fact that many incapacitated persons have to rely on income support shows that the benefits which are designed for incapacity are in themselves often not adequate to meet minimum needs. This failure to meet the 'adequacy of benefit' principle stipulated by Beveridge[4] is the great shortcoming of social security against want caused by incapacity as it has so far been developed,[5] and is an important reason why social security has not broken the strong link between incapacity and poverty.[6]

The most stark anomalies in social security provision overall are created by the Criminal Injuries Compensation Scheme: it is entirely possible that, for example, a person severely injured by a negligent, impecunious tortfeasor is confined to benefit when a person with identical injuries intentionally inflicted receives a huge award. But there are many other sources of incoherence in a social security system which started with a 'unified system' only as an aspiration and which has since been characterised by piecemeal tinkering in the course of interminable successive reforms which have created as many anomalies as they have

2  Department for Work and Pensions, *Fraud and Error in Claims to Incapacity Benefit* (2001).
3  Social Security Fraud Act 2001 and Department of Social Security, *A New Contract for Welfare: Safeguarding Social Security*, Cm 4276 (2000).
4  *Social Insurance and Allied Services*, above p 407 n 15, paras 17, 307.
5  Ibid, para 294: 'a permanent scale of benefit below subsistence, assuming supplementation on a means test as a normal feature, cannot be defended'.
6  H Barnes and S Baldwin, 'Social Security, Poverty and Disability', in J Ditch, *Introduction to Social Security* (1999) 156 and A Walker and L Walker, 'Disability and Financial Need: The Failure of the Social Security System', in G Dalley (ed) *Disability and Social Policy* (1998) 20.

removed.[7] The anomalies are less marked than in high value tort cases (because of the smaller sums involved)[8] but more extensive (because far more people are involved) within the benefit system. The welfare state has never unified provision so as to eliminate discrimination by cause of incapacity.

Short-term benefits for sickness and incapacity are now the same for work-related causes as for those which are not, but benefits for long-term industrial injuries are higher than those outside the scheme. A person who receives an injury at work may be entitled to greater benefit than a person who receives the same injury at home. Because entitlement to such benefits depends on previous work status, viz on satisfying certain contribution conditions, coverage must be uneven between those who have been able to build up a contribution record and those who have not (eg the long-term unemployed and women who have concentrated on raising their children). The relationship between incapacity to work (leading to earnings replacement benefits) and disability as such (leading to disability benefits) is not on a sure footing, so a disabled person of huge independent means can receive non-means tested benefits. One could go on.[9]

How far one believes this lack of coherence might be eliminated from the system depends on one's view of the administrative capacities of the welfare institutions. But even if one allows these telling criticisms of social security, it would appear to remain the case that comprehensive protection against want caused by incapacity must be provided by public social security. The live policy issues are how far one should seek to do more through social security provision than provide protection from want and, of particular relevance here, how far social security should coexist with third party insurance through the damages system and first person insurance.

## Private insurance

There are two different categories of insurance in this area.[10] Third-party or liability insurance is where an insurance company undertakes to

---

7    Despite Beveridge warning against this: *Social Insurance and Allied Services*, above p 407 n 15, para 454. See further N Timmins, *Five Giants* (1996).

8    The proliferation of special 'compensation' schemes to meet particular claims which have, for whatever reason, been politically effective – for blood products, CJD, vaccine damage, etc, etc – is a great step backwards in the attempt to give coherence to social security provision.

9    H Parker, *The Moral Hazard of Social Benefits* (1982) pp 103-104.

10   *Harris et al*, above p 405 n 1, ch 8. On the theoretical issues see further KS Abraham, *Distributing Risk* (1986) and SA Rea Jr, *Disability Insurance and Public Policy* (1981).

indemnify a policy-holder against any sum of damages which he is legally liable to pay a third person. For instance, where C claims that D, the insured person, is liable to him in tort for the losses he has suffered, the insurance company is contractually bound to pay D the damages and legal costs payable to C, and to indemnify D in respect of his own legal costs. The role of the courts and the government is essential in third party insurance, for it is they who, by taking the decisions about the extent of tort liability, create and set the size of the damages system, which is imposed on third parties. Liability insurance is compulsory for motorists and employers, but it is carried by many other categories of potential defendants, such as occupiers of premises, manufacturers, and suppliers of professional services. *Pearson*[11] found that 94% of the damages paid in awards or in out-of-court settlements are in fact paid by liability insurers; the great majority of the remainder are paid by defendants who are such large undertakings that it is cheaper for them to 'self-insure' by setting aside in their annual budgets a sum to meet their potential liabilities.[12]

A clear shortcoming of third party insurance against tort liability is that, because tort seeks to fully compensate C for lost earnings but the insurance burden is placed on a third party, there is little opportunity to make a wealthy C, who will receive a large amount in lost earnings if he makes a successful claim, pay a premium in proportion to his potential recovery. A regressive subsidy therefore is hidden in the operation of the damages system. Full compensation will mean that the high earner is compensated at a level much higher than that of a low earner with identical injuries. It is submitted that this can possibly be justified only if the high earner has made earnings-related contributions to the cost of the compensation. But liability motor insurance, for example, overall works in the opposite way: high-earning motorists pay into the insurance 'pool' according to the size and location of their car, but draw out (if they can prove another's liability) according to their income levels. As the increase (if any) in premium of the wealthy person's car insurance will bear little relationship to the differential in the award he will receive compared to a poor person, he is thus being subsidised by average and low earners who also pay liability insurance premiums.[13]

The second category of insurance is first-party insurance, where the potential beneficiary himself chooses to insure himself and pays for the level of insurance benefit he requires in a specified contingency. The paradigm case is life insurance, where the insured pays a premium calculated according to his expectation of life and the amount of cover.

---

11  Above p 405 n 2, vol 2, para 509.
12  Ibid.
13  D Harris, 'An Appraisal of the Pearson Strategy', in DK Allen et al, (eds), *Accident Compensation After Pearson* (1979) 85, pp 111-112.

The only parties involved are the insurance company and the insured person, whose representative claims against the company when his death occurs. Unlike the damages system, first-party insurance has the justification that the above-average earner pays a premium directly related to the level of his potential benefits.

In addition to life insurance, there are various types of first-party insurance against the risk of suffering incapacity. Private health care policies pay for medical treatment and hospital accommodation. A hospital cash policy pays a benefit for each day spent in hospital, irrespective of the actual cost, so that it is payable even when the insured is treated under the NHS. Personal accident insurance provides lump sums or periodic payments in the event of the policy-holder suffering personal injury by accident. Fixed sums are usually payable for specified impairments, such as the loss of a hand; regular income payments are made when the definition of incapacity in the policy is satisfied. Comprehensive motor insurance usually offers some personal accident cover for the policy-holder and his spouse.

Permanent health (or disability) insurance covers loss of income caused by the incapacity of the insured person. Once the insurer has accepted the proposal, he cannot refuse to renew the cover until the expiry date, which is usually the date of the policy-holder's expected retirement. If he suffers incapacity, the policy-holder usually expects to be supported by sick pay or social security for the initial period; so the periodic payments under the policy usually are payable only after a waiting period (sometimes of up to 12 months). The payments continue until the expiry date of the policy, and may be annually uprated by a fixed percentage. But the amount of the payments is limited to a fixed proportion of the insured person's pre-accident earnings, such as three-quarters or 80%, leaving the balance uninsured so as to reduce moral hazard.[14] In any case, a high earner would not wish to pay the premiums necessary to cover the whole of his current earnings. He would probably decide that, although some of his expenses would increase if he was disabled, he need not buy insurance to give him the same standard of living as previously enjoyed – he would choose to settle for a lower standard then, rather than to pay the increased premium now. It is an interesting comparison with the stated goal of the damages system that most first-party insurance is for less than 'full compensation' in the case of death or incapacity, and typically has nothing corresponding to non-pecuniary loss. The cost of permanent health insurance is relatively high if an individual policy is taken out, but the cost is greatly reduced if all members of a group are covered, eg all the employees in a particular employment.

14  See pp 421-422.

Though its wide use in Britain has recently been advocated by one of the leading contributors to the compensation debate,[15] first-party, private insurance plays only a small role at present in supporting people who are sick or injured.[16] Although at most ages the risk of suffering illness or injury is much greater than the risk of premature death, the latter is the only risk most commonly insured against. 17% of households now have some private medical insurance, but there has been no significant increase in the number of households insured against loss of income caused by sickness since *Harris et al* found[17] that 14% held a policy of this type. Only 16% now have a mortgage protection policy.[18] (Widespread occupational pension provision must, however, be added to these low figures to appreciate the overall extent of coverage.) First-party disability insurance should be regarded as an essential protection by all above-average earners for whom social security benefits may be insufficient. In the light of the meagre chances of recovering damages if incapacitated, the prudent person of sufficient means will see that he is covered against the risk of losing his earning capacity through long-term disability. In the face of the findings we have discussed, it would be irrational to rely on tort liability for protection.[19]

## Compensation for personal injury by accident

Even if the damages system plays an almost negligible role in the overall compensation of incapacity because so few causes of incapacity fall within its scope, the question remains of how well it treats the victims who do so fall. *Harris et al* found a high degree of 'unmet legal need', with nearly 75% of accident victims not even considering the possibility of claiming damages;[20] but *Genn 2*[1] appears to show some improvement. Although there was no resolution in 60% of the accident and work related ill-health

15  See PP 453-461 below.
16  T Burchardt and J Hills, *Private Welfare Insurance and Social Security* (1997) ch 2. See further Association of British Insurers, *Insurance: Facts, Figures and Trends* (2000).
17  Above P 405 n 1, table 8.1.
18  *Family Resources Survey: Great Britain 1999-2000*, above p 414 n 12, table 3.31.
19  The current incoherence of the overlapping benefits rules (see pp 382-389 above) handicaps the person wishing to take out an optimal insurance policy, and what in respect of retirement pensions is analysed as the problem of 'integrating' public and private provision (C Slusher, 'Pension Integration and Social Security Reform' (1998) 61 *Social Security Bulletin* 20) must be addressed.
20  Above p 405 n 1, p 65. This is consistent with the claims management company's evidence cited in p 411 n 15 above that annually there were over 2 million accidents in which the injured person blamed someone else, but only about 350,000 claims for personal injury damages were commenced.
1  Above p 406 n 8, pp 161-162.

cases she surveyed, it was found that 35% of those cases were settled by negotiation, presumably with some damages paid, and 5% were decided with the greater or lesser involvement of the court.

*Harris et al*[2] found that only one in seven accident victims reaches the stage of consulting a lawyer. A crucial role was played by advice from someone else (such as a relative, friend, workmate, trade union representative or employer) that the victim should consider making a claim; over two-thirds who saw a solicitor about claiming were prompted to do so by someone else's advice. This had the effect that trade union members and others who benefit from access to a network of advice and information were those most likely to get legal advice. Elderly victims and children were less likely to claim; victims in full- or part-time employment were much more likely to claim than those not in employment. *Genn 2*[3] found, however, that 69% of those suffering accidents or work related health problems obtained advice about the problem. Though the sources of initial advice were still predominantly non-legal, trades unions (18%), insurance companies (15%), the police (10%) friends and relatives (10%) and Citizens' Advice Bureaux (5%); solicitors (32%) were the largest single source of initial advice. Furthermore, 41% from the outset wanted advice about their legal rights, and around half contacted a solicitor at some time. It would appear that the expansion of legal expenses insurance and changes to the ways solicitors are able to seek business have markedly improved access to legal advice about personal injury.

*Harris et al's* finding that only one in seven of those receiving legal advice ultimately fails to get any damages have been broadly confirmed by later studies.[4] As these later studies now include clinical negligence cases which themselves have a less than 50% success rate, one would expect the overall success rate to have dropped a little, though the evidence we have does not allow one to be precise about this. There is, then, a high level of success in the sense of receiving some damages if, having begun the formal process of bringing a tort claim, C pursues the matter to the end. However, those who fail to obtain damages usually abandon the claim before trial.[5] This shows that the problems facing victims are more fundamental than mere access to legal services (we shall return to this).

2    Above p 405 n 1, pp 65-67.
3    Above p 406 n 8, pp 126-130.
4    Fennell, *The Funding of Personal Injury Litigation*, above p 406 n 7, paras 3.11-3.17; Pleasence *et al*, *Profiling Civil Litigation: The Case for Research* above p 405 n 3, pp 41-42 and Pleasence, *Personal Injury Litigation in Practice*, above p 404 n 10, p 10.
5    *Harris et al*, above p 405 n 1, table 3.12. See also Pleasence, *Personal Injury Litigation in Practice*, above p 406 n 10, p 13.

*Harris et al*[6] found that the main reasons for abandoning claims concern problems of obtaining sufficient evidence to establish D's liability (and the lack of finance to overcome these problems). The result is that of those who did recover some damages, *Harris et al* found that under 2% were awarded damages by a judge after a contested hearing in court (this amounts to 0.4% of all *accidents*, or 0.16% of all incapacity).[7]

Although initial advice was obtained very rapidly,[8] it would appear that the delays in obtaining compensation remain of great concern. *Harris et al*[9] found that the average time between the accident and the settlement was over 19 months, which meant that nearly all successful claimants were back at work before they received their damages. (This situation would clearly be intolerable but for the fact that health care is available through the NHS and that (statutory or occupational) sick pay, social security benefits and private self-insurance payments are available to many victims). This has been confirmed by later work.[10] The delay in the more extreme cases can be prima facie startling. The Civil Justice Review found that county court cases (where the amount in dispute was usually under £4,000 at today's prices) could take three or more years from incident to conclusion, and High Court cases frequently took four/five or six years.[11] This reflects general shortcomings in the civil law system which the Woolf reforms have addressed. But since damages are generally assessed on a once-and-for-all basis in a single lump sum to cover all C's loss, future as well as past, delay even beyond the normal delays of legal process is inherent in the system. *Harris et al*[12] found that in 40% of cases C's solicitor actually advised him to delay, in order to wait until his medical treatment had been completed, or at least until his condition had stabilised. It is clearly a risky venture to settle a case when the medical prognosis is still uncertain. In cerebral palsy cases, therefore, the average

---

6   Above p 405 n 1, pp 113-120. See also H Genn, *Meeting Legal Needs?* (1982) pp 33-35 and Pleasence, *Personal Injury Litigation in Practice*, above p 406 n 10, pp 18-19, 91-96.

7   Without heroic extrapolation from the available evidence, it is not possible to give later estimates. However, in 1998, 320 personal injury (including clinical negligence) cases were determined during or at the conclusion of a High Court trial; 1,830 personal injury cases were similarly determined in the county court; and 7,660 were determined by the arbitration (small claims) procedure: Lord Chancellor's Department, *Judicial Statistics 1998*, Cm 4371 (1999) tables 3.5, 4.12, 4.10.

8   *Genn 2*, p 406 above n 8, p 129.

9   Above n 1, p 105. *Cf Pearson*, above p 405 n 2, vol 2, table 17.

10  Pleasence et al, *Profiling Civil Litigation: The Case for Research* above p 405 n 3, pp 29-35 and Pleasence, *Personal Injury Litigation in Practice*, above p 406 n 10, pp 11, 14, 43-44, 64-68.

11  *Report of the Review Body on Civil Justice*, above p 406 n 6, para 432.

12  Above p 405 n 1, p 109.

time between incident and award is an absurd and shameful 12 years.[13] There are other difficulties peculiar to tort litigation which we shall now discuss.

### The settlement process

A central theme of the socio-legal criticism of the operation of the legal system has been that inequalities in access to justice undermine the rule of law's claim to be a system of equality before the law. Marked inequalities in the (potential) parties' access to justice will tend to make a mockery of equality before the law whatever the formal position of the parties. But access to justice (as opposed to the judicial system) is a matter both of being able to (threaten to) litigate appropriate matters, that is to say of access to legal services at all; *and* of being able competently to conduct one's case. In his seminal paper 'Why the "Haves" Come Out Ahead: Speculations on the Limits of Legal Change', Marc Galanter fleshed out this point with a detailed analysis of civil litigation in US in which 'Injury Victim *v* Insurance Company' was a paradigmatic illustration of inequalities of legal power.[14] A very large number of American journalistic accounts and scholarly analyses has since cast severe doubt on the justice of American personal injury litigation.[15]

*Harris* and *Genn 1* found that Galanter's basic thesis received strong confirmation from the conduct of personal injury litigation in England and Wales. Nearly all claims are settled out of court as the result of negotiations between the parties' representatives (usually between C's solicitor and a claims inspector from D's insurance company). In these negotiations there are many pressures on claimants to accept sums which heavily discount the amount which a judge would award if he found D 'fully' liable, viz if he decided every disputed question in C's favour.

---

13  *Handling Clinical Negligence Claims in England*, Report by the Comptroller and Auditor General, National Audit Office, HC 403 (3 May 2001) para 2.15. See further p 433 n 2 below.

14  (1974) 9 Law and Society Review 95, p 107. See also M Galanter and M Cahill, 'Most Cases Settle: Judicial Promotion and Regulation of Settlements' (1994) 46 *Stanford Law Review* 1139. See further HM Kritzer and SS Silbey (eds), 'Do the "Haves" Still Come Out Ahead?' (1999) 33 Law and Society Review 795 and HL Ross, *Settled Out of Court* (1970).

15  The parameters of the whole compensation debate were largely established by American tort scholars of the 40s: eg F James, 'Accident Liability Reconsidered: The Impact of Liability Insurance' (1948) 57 Yale Law Journal 549. The most dogged subsequent critic of the US damages system has been Jeffrey O'Connell: J O'Connell, *The Injury Industry* (1971); J O'Connell, *The Lawsuit Lottery* (1979); J O'Connell and CB Kelly, *The Blame Game* (1987) and PA Bell and J O'Connell, *Accidental Justice* (1997).

There will be a discount for every risk or uncertainty facing C: the risk that he does not have adequate evidence to prove D's fault (C can only guess the strength of the evidence available to D); that he might be found to have been partly at fault himself; that the medical reports on his side about his prognosis may not be accepted by the judge; that his evidence about his future employment prospects may not be accepted. Added to these are the uncertainties about how much further delay there would be in waiting for a court hearing; about how much the legal costs might amount to and whether part or all of them might fall on C himself; and about how much the judge might award for intangible losses, such as pain and suffering and loss of amenity. Every one of these risks or uncertainties is a negotiating weapon in the hands of D's insurance representative, and in most claims C is faced with the cumulative effect of several, and often many, of them. Because of this discounting for uncertainties affecting C's claim, it is often not worth the effort for the lawyers involved in negotiating to use the detailed legal rules on the assessment of damages to calculate the gross amount a judge would award for full liability. If there is to be a series of substantial deductions for the risk that a court may not accept all of the evidence given on C's behalf, and therefore may not resolve the uncertainties in his favour, it would be a waste of time to calculate the gross figure precisely. In out-of-court settlements, the law on damages is therefore used in a very rough-and-ready, indeed often arbitrary, way.

The impact of these risks and uncertainties on the parties differs greatly, because there is a structural imbalance between them which puts C into an unequal bargaining position.[16] First, insurance companies have the resources to collect all the available evidence as soon as possible, and to arrange for experts to report on the accident. Even while C is on his way to hospital, D will often be reporting the accident to his insurance company, which can then immediately arrange for assessors to take photographs of the scene and to seek out witnesses. (*Harris et al*[17] and *Genn 1*[18] showed that C's solicitor is often at a disadvantage in negotiating with the insurance claims inspector because the latter has much better information about the facts). Secondly, insurance companies are, in Galanter's terms, 'repeat players' to whom any particular case is merely one of many. They can afford to take a detached, neutral view of C's individual case, because they are concerned with the overall results of all the cases they handle. They can 'average' or spread their risks over them

---

16 The Woolf reforms recognised inequality between parties as a problem the alleviation of which will follow from the generally better working of the litigation system pursued by those reforms: Lord Woolf, *Access to Justice (Interim Report)* (1995) p 4 para 1; cf ch 3.

17 Above p 405 n 1, p 104.

18 Above p 405 n 1, ch 4.

all and so can be risk-neutral in their attitude to the individual case. But what is routine to the insurance man is unique to C. He is, again to use Galanter's term, a 'one-shotter' who is almost invariably risk-averse: if he is seriously injured, the case is of crucial importance to him and the risk of losing it is a powerful incentive on him to compromise for a smaller sum than he could hope to win in court on the basis of 'full' liability. He cannot spread his risk[19] and is also likely to be under financial and psychological pressure. If he is not back at work he may be in urgent need of money; he may also be fearful of facing the ordeal of a court hearing, including a public cross-examination.

An important feature of the relationship between the parties is that they are locked into it even though neither chose to deal with the other. C must negotiate with D's insurer and no one else, if he is to negotiate at all. He cannot seek a substitute insurer with whom he would prefer to deal – there is no 'market' choice open to him, and little market pressure on the insurer to control its conduct in the negotiations.[20] Economists describe this type of situation as a 'bilateral monopoly', in which there is a risk that one side could exploit the other by 'opportunistic' behaviour, behaviour that goes beyond legitimate self-interest by taking advantage of circumstances such as the lock-in created by bilateral monopoly. There is no supervision of the conduct of negotiations, and no publicity for the outcome: indeed, some out-of-court settlements have been made on the explicit undertaking of C not to give any information to anyone about the fact or the amount of the settlement. The only 'control' is C's ability to take his claim to court, but we have noted many pressures on him to avoid this. Insurance companies obviously try to settle claims as cheaply as possible; they operate within the existing fault-based system, and their principal responsibility is to their premium payers (and shareholders), not to protect the interests of accident victims.[1] They consider it legitimate to take advantage of any rule, whether of substance or procedure, which will assist them in minimising their expenditure. They search for and then expose any weakness in C's case; and they take advantage of the

19   The only spreading of risk available to C is to spread the risk of legal costs, and this is the purpose of the legal expenses insurance which usually accompanies the conditional fee under the new arrangements for funding personal injury litigation: see pp 450-451.
20   In first person insurance, unsatisfactory claims handling may be met by the insured changing his insurer, though this may, of course, be of little value in the case of a one-off claim as will almost inevitably be the case in major accidents. In these major cases, (regulatory) supervision, sanctions such as adverse publicity, and the decency of the insurer have an important part to play. They also, of course, have a part to play in third party insurance, but what economists call the structure of incentives is not so apt, for the (potential) consumers of that form of insurance want claims to be minimised.
1    In first person insurance, the victims are the premium payers.

inexperience of solicitors who handle claims only infrequently. But even where an experienced solicitor handles the claim, it is highly likely to end in an out-of-court settlement, though with a higher level of damages.

The evidence from *Harris et al* and *Genn 1* was that in a personal injury claim C is almost completely dependent on his solicitor's advice at all stages of the claim and particularly in regard to the amount he could expect to recover. The process of bringing a claim is so complicated, and the formal legal rules create such uncertainty, that C has no option except to give his solicitor effective control over all the crucial decisions – whether to go to court, to settle (and if to settle, for which amount), or to abandon the claim. The large number of uncertainties surrounding the claim has the effect of nearly always protecting the solicitor from criticism, no matter what advice he gives. Almost no case is so certain in regard to the amount of damages to be expected that his advice can be shown to be negligent; in practice, he can be held negligent only if he flagrantly fails to take a necessary step in the litigation procedure or fails to meet a specified time limit. (Except in rare circumstances, any court proceedings for personal injuries must be commenced within three years of the accident.)[2] The survey evidence shows that C will almost always be advised to settle, though sometimes not until the parties are just about to enter the court for the hearing. Most claimants who have not reached the door of the court are risk-averse, and would prefer the certainty of a smaller sum payable now to the chance of winning a larger sum at some uncertain time in the future.

That clients and their lawyers seek to advance the self-interest of those clients (and in a different way of the lawyers) in litigation is perfectly legitimate, and neither should nor could be prevented. But this self-interest equally should be confined within bounds which channel it towards the achievement of the publicly stated goals of the litigation.[3] *Harris et al* and *Genn 1* showed, in sum, that the rules of negligence and personal injury quantification and the practice of personal injury litigation

2   See generally ch 32 above. There is generally no limitation period in cases of catastrophic brain injury, and Cunningham John Solicitors recently was able to use the BBC radio programme *Law in Action* (broadcast 16 November 2001; factsheet available from the BBC) to advertise its eagerness to take cases decades after the accident. The firm has managed to obtain eg £2.5m in damages for a 28-year-old C who was injured at birth. One may question what the value of obtaining such an award is to C (if not his family and estate) and whether this is the best use of scarce health resources (C already being in receipt of as good a level of care as the NHS can provide to him and to others who have not won the damages lottery). One must question the cost achieving whatever it is that is achieved in cases of this sort, for it is very likely that the legal costs payable to Cunningham John will exceed the award C obtains.

3   AAS Zuckerman, 'Reform in the Shadow of Lawyers' Interests', in Zuckerman and Cranston (eds), *Reform of Civil Procedure*, above p 405 n 2, 61, pp 62-67.

underwritten by third party insurance presented so many opportunities and incentives to thwart these public goals by delay, vexatious argument and conduct, deliberate incurring of expense and increasing of uncertainty, etc that the actual conduct of litigation was best described by parody. Personal injury litigation, it was said:

> may be likened to a compulsory, long-distance obstacle race. The victims, without their consent, are placed at the starting line, and told that if they complete the whole course, the umpire at the finishing line will compel the race-promoters to give them a prize; the amount of the prize, however, must remain uncertain until the last moment because the umpire has discretion to fix it individually for each finisher. None of the runners is told the distance he must cover to complete the course, nor the time it is likely to take. Some of the obstacles in the race are fixed hurdles (rules of law), while others can, without warning, be thrown into the path of a runner by the race-promoters, who obviously have every incentive to restrict the number of runners who can complete the course. As the runners' physical fitness, and their psychological preparedness for the race, varies greatly, the relative difficulty of the obstacles also varies from runner to runner. In view of all the uncertainties, and particularly the difficulties which could be presented by unknown, future obstacles, many runners drop out of the race at each obstacle; others press on, but are progressively weakened by their exertions. At any stage of the race, the promoters alongside the race-track are permitted to induce a runner to retire from the race in return for an immediate payment, which they fix at a figure less than the prize they expect to be awarded by the umpire at the completion of the course. After waiting to see how many runners drop out at the early obstacles without any inducement, the promoters begin to tempt the remaining runners with offers of money to retire; the amounts of the offers tend to increase the longer the runner stays in the race. In view of the uncertainties about the remaining obstacles, their ability to finish the course, and the time it might take, most runners accept an offer and retire. The few hardy ones who actually finish may still be disappointed with the prize-money.[4]

## The settlement range

The first edition of this work was able to draw on *Harris et al* and *Genn 1* to put concrete detail on the perception of inequalities of legal power in

---

4   *Harris et al*, above p 405 n 1, pp 132-133.

the personal injury settlement process by identifying possible 'settlement ranges' – C's and D's differing views of the range of possible outcomes – and analysing the actual settlements reached in terms of a 'game' played within these parameters. Differing competences between repeat players and one-shotters to play the game obviously affect the outcome. The Woolf reforms make it impossible to apply these findings to current personal injury litigation. If it is effective, the general encouragement of a settlement mentality by Woolf[5] should have an impact.[6] More specifically, Woolf has radically revised the procedures by which offers to settle may be made.[7] What are now called 'Part 36 offers' or 'Part 36 payments'[8] may be made by C as well as D; may be made in respect of individual issues as well as the whole matter; and may be made at any stage before the commencement of proceedings[9] or at any stage of the proceedings. That a Part 36 offer or payment has been made is intended to have a substantial effect on the court's exercise of its discretion to determine the award of costs and interest,[10] which is intended to give both parties a clear incentive to settle, for if a rejected offer is matched or beaten by the eventual award, the party who refused the offer will normally suffer a heavy penalty in costs (and interest). The evidence of past practice was that the 'payment into court' system when only D could make such a payment placed a very powerful negotiating weapon in D's hands.[11] That C as well as D may make such an offer or payment will radically alter the way the settlement game is played.

5    JA Jolowicz, *On Civil Procedure* (2000) ch 19.
6    Initial reports are positive: Lord Chancellor's Department, *Emerging Findings: An Early Evaluation of the Civil Justice Reforms* (2001) and S Allen, 'Inconsistent Judges Plague Woolf Reforms' (29 March 2001) Law Society's Gazette 1 (an encouraging survey, with over 80% of solicitors interviewed finding the reforms an improvement, is reported under this headline). But see Zander, 'Why Lord Woolf's Proposed Reforms of Civil Litigation Should Be Rejected', above p 405 n 2.
7    CPR pt 36. See further *Woolf*, above p 406 n 7, ch 11 and Lord Woolf, *Access to Justice (Interim Report)*, above p 431 n 16, ch 24.
8    It is an obvious implication of C's being able to make an offer to settle under the new system that no actual payment is necessary, as it was under the previous system when only D could make a payment into court. An actual payment into court is now allowed but not required.
9    A specific 'Pre-action Protocol' for personal injury claims which seeks to guide settlement before proceedings are begun is issued as part of the CPR. See further *Woolf*, above p 406 n 7, ch 10 and T Goriely, 'The New Pre-action protocol for Personal Injury Claims' (1998) 148 New Law Journal 1547, p 1615.
10   Offers and payments can be made outside the Part 36 procedure, but, unless the court so orders in its discretion, such offers and payments will not have implications for costs and interest: CPR pt 36.1(2).
11   See the first edition of this work, pp 252-253, drawing on *Harris et al*, above p 405 n 1, pp 93-97 and referring to *Genn 1*, above p 405 n 1 pp 111-113. See also Pleasence et al, *Profiling Civil Litigation: The Case for Research*, above p 405 n 3, p 37.

It is obvious that any future proper understanding of the damages system will require the replication of *Harris* and *Genn 1* on settlement ranges when the Woolf reforms and the new arrangements for funding personal injury litigation have settled down.

### The amounts of damages actually awarded

Despite the theoretical generosity of the full compensation measure, the figures for the damages actually received by accident victims in out-of-court settlements are low. The figures in *Harris et al*[12] relate mainly to the years 1973–77 and so could not be given here without adjustment, but the picture they describe has been confirmed by subsequent but less comprehensive work.[13] In the Legal Aid Research Board's study of legally aided cases, the average (mean) damages were £8,631.55 but a better idea comes from the median, which was only £2,650; in other words, half the cases were under £2,650.[14] The damages system produces these relatively low amounts in large part as a result of the way that compensation is quantified.

As has been discussed in chapter 22 above, damages for personal injury include damages for consequential loss of earnings, medical costs, etc and non-pecuniary loss.[15] In court, the lump sum assessment requires a great deal of outright guesswork about C's future, and C will be undercompensated to the extent that the judge's prophecy about future contingencies overestimates the risks faced by C before the accident, or underestimates the long-term adverse effects of his injury. The actuarial difficulty of assessing long-term pecuniary loss, especially in the context of the risk of future price- or wage-inflation, makes the quantification of consequential loss so extremely uncertain as to amount to arbitrariness in many cases, and the necessity to discount the lump sum awarded compounds this arbitrariness. The judicial response to this arbitrariness has been to err on the side of caution. These factors all may mean that the long-term victim is left with less in real terms to meet his future losses or

---

12  Above p 405 n 1, p 260. The figures in *Pearson*, above p 405 n 2, vol 2, paras 72, 169, 180, 231 and table 43 were to the same effect.

13  Most work is on the outcomes of decided *cases*, but such cases are a tiny and one presumes unrepresentative sample of the damages recovered. The Compensation Recovery Unit of the Department of Work and Pensions must hold a full set of data, for all personal injury settlements have to be reported to it (Lewis, *Deducting Benefits from Damages for Personal Injury*, above p 412 n 19, ch 14), but it does not make public any analyses of this data.

14  Pleasence, *Personal Injury Litigation in Practice*, above p 406 n 10, p 16.

15  Damages for death have two analogous components: see in general ch 23 above and on damages for bereavement p 438 n 6 below.

expenses than was assessed in terms of the value of the currency at the time of the trial.

The improvement in accuracy of quantification which might be made even in the small number of appropriate cases of catastrophic injury[16] were the award of a lump sum to be replaced by periodic payments under structured settlements[17] is limited.[18] Nevertheless, in significant ways, especially when life expectancy is in serious dispute, these settlements can improve on the lump sum, which is particularly likely to create difficulties in these cases, and the very limited empirical research which has been done reports satisfaction with these settlements.[19] Since their first use in this country in 1981, over a thousand such settlements have been made, and that use has grown (in conjunction with the growth of clinical negligence cases) to the point where now over a hundred seriously injured persons each year are given part of their compensation in the form of a structured settlement pension.[20]

In sum, the practical achievement of full compensation will almost always be markedly deficient. It is therefore unsurprising that the Law Commission's survey of accident victims who obtained damages[1] found that only three in five considered that their damages had been adequate to cover even their *past* losses and expenses. Often extra future expense had not been fully anticipated at the time of the settlement. Over a third (especially those with higher damages) said that their standard of living had been reduced as a direct result of their accident, and many feared their future standard would suffer. Those who, at the time of their settlement, had been satisfied with their damages, were often later dissatisfied when they discovered the long-term impact of their injuries on their way of life.

Despite all these damning shortcomings, a coherent goal is at least theoretically being aimed at in consequential loss quantification. There is not even a coherent goal in the pursuit of non-pecuniary loss.

---

16  R Lewis, *Structured Settlements* (1993) ch 8. Structured settlements can possibly apply in only a fraction of cases; in the view of D's insurers they are 'economic' only if the award is more than £0.5 million: R Lewis, 'The Damages Act 1996: The Future of Multipliers and Structured Settlements' [1996] Journal of Personal Injury Litigation 322, p 336.

17  Law Commission, *Structured Settlements and Interim Provisional Damages*, Report No 224 (1994).

18  Lewis, *Structured Settlements*, above n 16, para 2.22. See further pp 361-363 above. Leaving aside the problems of making these arrangements as such, the basic attractiveness of a structured settlement is highly dependent on the prevalent annuity interest rates: ibid, paras 7.11-7.18 and P Andrews and T Lee, *Catastrophic Injuries* (1997) para 11.14.

19  *How Much?* above p 406 n 5, ch 12.

20  R Lewis, 'Structured Settlements and State Benefits' (2001) 151 New Law Journal 1066, p 1066.

1   *How Much?* above p 406 n 5, ch 11.

## Non-pecuniary loss

Damages for 'non-pecuniary' loss or damages for 'pain, suffering and loss of amenity' are not intended to compensate consequential loss of earnings, medical expenses, etc; they are intended to compensate for the injury itself. While the lack of clearly superior alternatives gives some justification to the continuation of the damages system in respect of consequential losses, it is submitted that the award of damages for non-pecuniary is wholly unjustifiable as 'compensation'.[2] Non-pecuniary loss awards are essentially fruitless and arbitrary.[3] The award of a sum of money to a person who loses a limb or a loved one does not compensate that loss. Of course, there are perfectly defensible instances of 'compensation', when 'compensation' slides into 'consolation', as when a child who has hurt itself is given a lollipop. But there are no such senses which leave intact the implication of proportionality in the concept of 'compensation' (and thus in the idea of non-pecuniary loss as a legal 'remedy'). This has the inevitable consequence that non-pecuniary awards given are fundamentally arbitrary.[4] Such awards may aspire to be internally consistent in the sense that each C in the same position will receive the same, and so may be governed by precedent,[5] but there is no reason why the loss of a limb or the death of a relative was ever worth whatever sum one may receive for it in personal injury litigation. Damages for non-pecuniary loss are inconsistent with the concept of compensation as a component of social security against want or as a right that justifies treating non-pecuniary loss as a matter for legal adjudication. There is *no* standard of 'full' compensation against which to measure the assessment of damages for non-pecuniary losses. The arbitrary sums awarded are an acknowledgement of these losses but can in no sense replace what has been lost.[6]

2   The use of 'compensation' in 'accident compensation' to cover charity, social security and tort is possible only because the link between compensation and remedy is broken. Cf *Pearson*, above p 405 n 2, vol 1, ch 2.

3   See pp 371-382 above. They may, in addition, represent a distasteful windfall payment in a significant number of cases: see p 433 n 17 below.

4   Cane, *Atiyah's Accidents, Compensation and the Law*, above p 408 n 19, p 135 and *Pearson*, above p 405 n 2, vol 1, paras 452-457.

5   Perhaps 'convention' is better than 'precedent': *West (H) & Son Ltd v Shephard* [1964] AC 326 at 346.

6   It could be decided to pay a fixed sum in consolation to a person who has suffered a personal injury from the social security budget, which would eliminate the extremely costly pretence of quantification of compensation. But not only is it unlikely that this extra compensation of accident victims would be found to be a just use of the social security budget, one suspects it would create a substantial and unmanageable moral hazard problem.
    The payment of a fixed sum (currently £7,500) of 'damages' to the bereaved under the Fatal Accidents Act 1976, s 1A replaced an award for the deceased's

This point is particularly worth making because of the overwhelming importance of non-pecuniary loss in the damages system. *Pearson* noted that over half of the total amount the damages system paid out was for non-pecuniary loss,[7] and such evidence as we have leads to the conclusion that this remains the case.[8] This is why median tort awards are so low. The conclusion that should be drawn from this is that:

> the main function of the tort system is not to provide for the future loss of income and care needs of those seriously disabled by accident or disease. Such especially needy claimants are relatively rare. Instead the damages system overwhelmingly deals with small claims, the great majority leading to damages of less than £5,000. In these cases claimants suffer very little, if any, financial loss. They make a full recovery from their bodily injury and have no continuing ill effects. They make no claim for any social security benefit as a result of their accident. In the minority of cases where benefit is claimed [non-pecuniary loss] is the only part of the award from which no social security can be deducted. This means that in a few cases the damages claim, in effect, is being made only for non-pecuniary loss. In settlements in general the largest component by far is the payment for pain and suffering. The stereotypical injury is the minor whiplash which follows a low-speed car 'shunt'. It is these type of cases which account for the extraordinarily high costs of the system compared to the damages it pays out. If it had been wholly in public hands, tort would have been radically revised and then privatised some years ago.[9]

That this position can obtain must to some extent reflect the way tort is represented in scholarship and teaching,[10] and certainly it is indeed the case that in general:

---

loss of expectation of life which had anyway settled in all but the most extraordinary cases into 'a moderate arbitrary sum'. These damages explicitly are meant to be a *solatium* (solace) (see pp 393-395 above), which is why they cannot be recovered by the deceased's estate. One trusts that the moral hazard problem arising from bereavement is confined to works of fiction, but the justice of this award may easily be called into question: Cane, *Atiyah's Accidents, Compensation and the Law*, above p 408 n 19, p 74, p 142 n 5. On the Law Commission's completely opposed recent views on this see above.

7   *Pearson*, above p 405 n 2, vol 1, paras 81, 382; vol 2, table 107.
8   R Lewis, 'Increasing the Price of Pain: Damages, the Law Commission and *Heil v Rankin*' (2001) 64 Modern Law Review 100, n 18.
9   Ibid, pp 103-104.
10  See J Conaghan and W Mansell, *The Wrongs of Tort* (2nd edn 1999).

much of the leading scholarship in tort law over the past 20 years has been dominated by abstract theorising and is characterised by sharp conflicts among proponents of competing normative goals for the tort system – disagreements that often reflect different empirical assumptions about the way the system works, without actually investigating the accuracy of these assumptions.[11]

One can, at least initially, find it amusing that a very great deal of intellectual effort currently is being put into the analysis of the philosophical bases of tort[12] when in practice the quantification of 'full compensation' and in particular non-pecuniary loss cannot possibly be put on a footing of minimal consistency with any of the bases being advanced. But the separation between doctrine and practice is of more concern when public policy is based on empirical error. In utter disregard of the facts, the Law Commission recently recommended an increase in the amounts awarded for non-pecuniary loss.[13] We have noted above that the Law Commissioner responsible, Professor Burrows, has mounted a telling argument against abolition of tort based on the absence of unambiguously superior alternatives. This 'negative' defence is, however, subordinate in Professor Burrows' thinking to a 'positive' claim that the tort system is 'a system of individual responsibility [which] pins responsibility for compensating another on an individual because of what the individual has, or has not, done'.[14] This claim, perhaps arguable in respect of abstract doctrine,[15] can be made only on the basis of an

11  Dewees et al, *Exploring the Domain of Tort Law*, above p 408 n 19, p v.
12  The notion of 'corrective justice' advocated in inter alia E Weinbrib, *The Idea of Private Law* (1995) has led this field, and (one extraordinary version of) the resultant statement of the English law of tort is given in N McBride and R Bagshaw, *Tort Law* (2001).
13  *Non-pecuniary Loss*, above p 408 n 1. See also Law Commission, *Damages for Personal Injury: Non-pecuniary Loss*, Consultation Paper No 140 (1995) paras 4.5-4.8.
14  Burrows, 'In Defence of Tort', above p 408 n 2, p 122.
15  However, Burrows runs into difficulty with the most elementary problem of the nature of tort, the conflict between compensation and deterrence. He (ibid, pp 124, 128) places heavy reliance on the following criticism of the New Zealand scheme by Mahoney, 'Trouble in Paradise: New Zealand's Accident Compensation Scheme', above p 409 n 7, p 33: 'the thug [who injures himself when he] headbutts a passer-by will ... receive compensation equal to that of the victim if the injuries and financial circumstances of the parties are the same.' It is unscrupulous to attempt to damn any proposal by exclusive concentration on an extreme case (the issue is how well does it handle cases overall?), but let us try to take this argument at its best and (ignoring the scheme's power to reduce or cancel payments to those imprisoned for an offence) agree that Mahoney has identified a worrying anomaly, as indeed he has. Tort would not compensate the thug. But Mahoney's argument works only if compensation is, in a sense, a luxury. Suppose the thug's injury reduced his income to zero. Would Mahoney let him (and his family) starve to punish him? Compensation in the sense of social security against want

absolutely thoroughgoing ignorance[16] or, what is worse, disregard[17] of the empirical evidence about the way the damages system actually works.[18] Burrows proceeds[19] as if the attributions of liability in abstract, formal scholarship applied in fact when the evidence is that this is not so. That evidence overwhelmingly confirms that 'the notion that the tort system adjusts the relationship between victim and harmdoer is a fiction ... The system cannot even be claimed to uphold the standards of behaviour embodied in the fault principle'.[20] In the light of this, the central point made yet again recently by Atiyah wholly escapes Burrows' criticism: 'the law must reflect the fact that in the great majority of cases damages are not paid by individual wrongdoers but by insurance companies or other large bodies. The consequences of this need to be faced'.[1]

Parliament did not respond to the Commission's invitation to implement the increase, and it surely is very unlikely that it would do so without first holding something like another Pearson Commission.[2] But

---

cannot be withdrawn when needed (but, of course, the type of compensation awarded in tort might well be able to be: see pp 442-445 above), and, absurdly, Mahoney's argument shows that the possibility of both compensating and punishing is needed, the very antinomy which undermines tort. The thug would receive compensation under the New Zealand scheme and (one hopes) be punished by the criminal law, but, of course, advocates of general compensation schemes have usually argued for other deterrence mechanisms outside the schemes because they make small claims for the deterrent power of such schemes (see n 1 below). The example is good evidence for this mix, for no one would argue that tort could both compensate and deter in this case. The only argument is to what extent it can do either in any given case.

16   Entirely predictably, Burrows has tried to elevate obscurantism about the social sciences to a principle of legal scholarship: A Burrows, 'Restitution: Where Do We Go from Here?', in Burrows, *Understanding the Law of Obligations*, above p 408 n 2, 99, pp 112-114.

17   Burrows, 'In Defence of Tort', above p 408 n 2, pp 120-121.

18   On the empirical evidence about deterrence see pp 290-294 above.

19   Burrows enters a quibble about the nature of individual responsibility which may be thought to give his whole argument away: ibid, p 123.

20   *Harris et al*, above p 405 n 1, p 160. Professor Burrows' remarks are yet a further disproof of Jolowicz's optimistic observation that: 'it cannot have escaped attention how inefficient and even inefficacious is the law of tort when seen as a deterrent': JA Jolowicz, 'Liability for Accidents' [1968] Cambridge Law Journal 50, p 54.

1   Atiyah, *The Damages Lottery*, above p 408 n 19, p 174. One consequence, of course, may be the encouragement of more effective punishment and deterrence of certain harms: ibid, pp 159-165. This argument again goes back at least to Beveridge: *Social Insurance and Allied Services*, above p 407 n 15, para 262.

2   Cf N Lyell, HC Deb, Standing Committee C, *Citizens' Compensation Bill* (3 May 1989) col 8. *How Much?* above p 406 n 5, was an attempt to deal with this problem, and as it has led to *Heil v Rankin*, in one sense it did so. But, as the author of the report was at pains to point out (ibid, pp 13, 262), by focusing on those in litigation, the Report said nothing about incapacity as a whole, and therefore did not address the central questions of the compensation debate; indeed it reproduced the

442    Section 2    Tort: remedies for wrongdoing

the damages system is so suspect that another commission of inquiry into it would be embarrassing in the extreme,[3] and might even lead to the recommendation of a reduction or abolition of damages for non-pecuniary loss or damages *tout court*. Avoiding the hazards of public accountability, the Court of Appeal, in an act of retrospective legislation which barely bothered to masquerade as a judgment, recently raised them in *Heil v Rankin*,[4] though to a lesser extent than the Commission had been so 'impertinent'[5] as to require.[6] If any empirical evidence of the effectiveness and equity of non-pecuniary loss as a remedy is taken into account, this increase is so ill-advised as to constitute a public scandal. As it will increase the burden of taxes and private insurance on almost all citizens in ways which the Court of Appeal could not and did not calculate, and for which adequate transitional provision could not be made, it is not merely an unconstitutional and unjust but an incompetent piece of judicial legislation. No good ethical answer has ever been given[7] to Calabresi's question: 'Why is compensation for illness even in highly welfaristic countries much less complete than compensation for accident victims'.[8] A good empirical answer which accurately describes the system of law reform that allows *Heil v Rankin* will have to stress the advantageous political influence enjoyed by the personal injury lobby. Certainly, no such answer can be based on the satisfaction of the needs of all who suffer from incapacity howsoever caused.

## The use of damages awarded

The House of Lords has held that the court should not be concerned with any question about the use of the damages awarded to C.[9] In this respect

---

concentration of those in litigation which that debate has shown to be a mistake: Atiyah, *The Damages Lottery*, above p 408 n 19 p 157 and Lewis, 'Increasing the Price of Pain: Damages, the Law Commission and *Heil v Rankin*' above p 439 n 8. In sum, the Report is by no means a justification of *Heil v Rankin*.

3    Assuming, as one can no longer assume, that the findings of such a commission would actually be made public.

4    *Heil v Rankin* [2001] QB 272 (discussed above at pp 375-376).

5    T Weir, *A Casebook on Tort* (9th edn 2000) p 636.

6    See further C Bennett, 'Personal Injuries: General Damages – Minor Increases Only' [2000] Journal of Personal Injury Law 129. Though hoping, with all personal injury lawyers, for a larger increase, Bennett very commendably is not sparing in his criticism of this method of making any increase: ibid, pp 133-136.

7    KS Abraham, 'Principle and Pragmatism in the Compensation Debate' (1987) 7 Oxford Journal of Legal Studies 302.

8    G Calabresi, *The Cost of Accidents* (1970) p 43.

9    *West (H) & Son Ltd v Shephard*, above p 438 n 5; *Lim Poh Choo v Camden and Islington Area Health Authority*, above p 407 n 11 at 188, 191 and *Wright v British Railways Board* [1983] 2 AC 773 at 781. On the unconscious victim see pp 378-380 above.

their Lordships have rejected the 'needs' approach: there should not 'be a paring down of the award because of some thought that a particular plaintiff will not be able to use the money'.[10] 'There is no condition that he should spend or use the damages. They are his to save or to spend or to dissipate in any useful or useless manner that he may choose.'[11] Judges accept that this approach creates a risk that the cost of supporting C may fall back on the taxpayer, or that his damages may in fact not be used for his benefit[12] but may benefit only the beneficiaries under his estate.[13] Occasionally, there is a hint of realism: eg a seriously injured child who because of his injuries is unlikely ever to have dependants, will not be given damages for loss of earnings during the 'lost years' to take account of the hypothetical support of dependants. On the other hand, even where a large award is made for future medical or nursing expenses the courts have not required any undertaking from C to use the damages for that purpose.[14] The courts' attitude seems to be in harmony with a popular belief that C should 'have complete freedom to choose' what to do with his award.[15]

Although few people have had any previous experience in handling a large sum, judges apparently believe that when C receives a large capital sum in damages, he will take advice as to its investment and use. In *Wells v Wells*,[16] this amounted to the House of Lords assuming that on receipt of very substantial damages C would adopt a sophisticated investment

---

10   *West (H) & Son Ltd v Shephard*, above p 438 n 5 at 349.

11   *Oliver v Ashman* [1962] 2 QB 210 at 224, CA.

12   *Taylor v Bristol Omnibus Co Ltd* [1975] 1 WLR 1054 at 1061.

13   *Murray v Shuter* [1976] QB 972 (eg damages for pain, suffering and loss of amenity suffered between the accident and the seriously injured victim's death). The size of the waste can be distastefully large. If C is catastrophically injured and receives a large award (including non-pecuniary loss), on his death such part of this award that has not been spent in his lifetime will pass to his heirs. Though awards are lowered to those whose life expectancy has been shortened, the guesses involved may very well be wrong. Anecdote amongst insurers and their representatives has it that one barrier to the use of structured settlements is the concern of potential beneficiaries taking decisions on C's behalf to benefit from this type of potential windfall.

14   See pp 363-371 above. The only restrictions on the use of damages relate to items where the expense has been incurred by, or a service given by, a third party, eg nursing of C by a family member or sick pay from an employer as a loan repayable out of damages.

15   *How Much?* above p 406 n 5, para 10.16.

16   [1999] 1 AC 345. The Lord Chancellor's subsequent attempt to recalculate the discount rate took a great deal of time and has been the subject of enormous controversy, for the calculation is extremely difficult, inexact and hazardous. *Kemp and Kemp on the Quantum of Damages*, Release Bulletin 79 (June 2001) criticised 'The Lord Chancellor's scandalous delay'. See further ibid, vol 1, ch 6 (appendix 1 reproduces Lord Chancellor's Department, *Setting the Discount Rate: Lord Chancellor's Reasons* (27 July 2001)). See in general pp 354-358 above.

strategy.[17] *Harris et al*[18] gave very little support to this assumption. It found that only one in twenty of those who obtained damages was given any advice on how to use them. The little empirical research that has subsequently been done on this vital issue shows an improvement. Although the great majority of those receiving damages received no investment advice, the picture changed depending on the size of the award. 72% of those obtaining under £20,000 received no advice, 67% of those receiving more than £20,000 did so, and 84% of those receiving £100,000 or more did so. Though this is encouraging, that there is room for further improvement is manifest,[19] for one can turn these figures around and say that almost a fifth of those awarded over £100,000, a third of those awarded £50,000-£100,000, and nearly half of those awarded £20,000-£50,000, still received no advice on how to use their money.

*Harris et al* found that many recipients bought tangible, durable items, such as furniture or household appliances; half saved some of the money for the future (but only one in twenty invested it in shares or something similar); while one in five put some money towards a house or house improvements. Because most victims were back at work before they received their damages, only a quarter of them used some of the money for living expenses, or to repay loans made to cover expenses while they were incapacitated. About one in five bought an enjoyable but passing experience, such as a holiday, or made a gift to relatives (often to those who had nursed them). The later research confirms this pattern of expenditure.[20]

The necessarily extremely limited use of structured settlements and otherwise basic disregard for what C does with his compensation stems from the contradiction between the abstract concept of compensating personal injury in tort and the efficient and effective use of 'compensation' funds, leading to an often quite surreal language in the cases[1] and an indefensibly wasteful attitude to the use of scarce resources. This is *not* a conflict between 'individual' freedom and 'social' efficiency, for the imposition by the state of tort liability (met by third party insurance) is a social decision (in the form of state imposition) about compensation

---

17  *How Much?* above p 406 n 5, ch 10 found that when awards were invested, this was in the conventional, 'safe' form of bank or building society accounts. Even for damages of over £100,000 only a third of recipients invested in company shares, two out of five in unit (or investment) trusts, and one in five in government stocks. This last is the form of investment on which the reasoning in *Wells v Wells* [1999] 1 AC 345 is based: see pp 357-358 above.

18  Above p 405 n 1, pp 120-123.

19  *How Much?* above p 406 n 5 secs 10.1-10.7.

20  Ibid, secs 10.8-10.14.

1   And in purported reform by statute: P Cane and D Harris, 'Administration of Justice Act 1982, s 4(2): A Lesson in How Not to Reform the Law' (1983) 46 Modern Law Review 478.

policy. However, it is a bad social decision, one that (taken with the other aspects of the damages system) would appear to be intended to foster inefficiency in the use of resources to meet incapacity except that, were this actually a goal, it might not be so thoroughly well accomplished. Although the judges may ignore the way in which damages are actually used, the policy-maker cannot avoid the comparison with alternative uses of the money now supporting the damages system, such as using it to improve the level of social security benefits for the long-term disabled.

## The costs of the damages system

The discussion of the damages system has been dogged by the suspicion or blatant accusation, maintained with varying degrees of sophistication, that this on its face indefensible system is maintained or, as we now see with *Heil v Rankin*, is expanded because it is in the interests of the lawyers who administer it,[2] for personal injury work must provide a considerable proportion of lawyers' income.[3] This argument rests on the fact that whatever the damages system accomplishes is accomplished at very high cost. The ratio of compensation obtained to costs of 1:0.85 given in *Pearson*[4] appears to be a reasonable mean of those given in other studies.[5] This is to say, every £1 of damages took 85p in costs to recover. In certain courts, for certain types of case, and at certain levels of damages, costs exceed damages. This prima facie enormously expensive system appeared even worse when *Pearson* contrasted it with an estimated 1:0.1 analogous ratio for the distribution of welfare benefits,[6] and this comparison has since repeatedly been drawn. Greater precision must, however, guide further use of this comparison.[7] *Pearson* calculated this ratio on the basis of all welfare provision, but retirement pensions and child benefit make

2   Eg M Joseph, *Lawyers Can Seriously Damage Your Health* (1984).
3   We are unaware of any direct evidence of this proportion. However, it has been found that, prior to the Access to Justice Act, solicitors in private practice devoted 13% of their overall fee earning time to personal injury work: B Cole, *Solicitors in Private Practice: Their Work and Expectations*, Law Society Research and Policy Planning Unit Research Study No 26 (1997) p 21. Almost one third of solicitors are 'regularly' engaged in personal injury work, but there was clear evidence of concentration of the work: *ibid* and G Chambers and S Harwood, *Solicitors in England and Wales: Practice, Organisation and Perceptions*, Law Society Research and Policy Planning Unit Research Study No 2 (1990) p 31.
4   P 405 n 2, vol 1, para 261.
5   Ison, *The Forensic Lottery*, above p 408 n 17, p 28; *Report of the Review Body on Civil Justice*, above p 406 n 6, paras 425-432; TM Swanson, 'The Importance of Contingency Fee Arrangements' (1991) 11 Oxford Journal of Legal Studies 193, p 196 and *Woolf*, above p 406 n 7, annex 3, table 4.
6   *Pearson*, above p 405 n 2, vol 1, para 121.
7   Cane, *Atiyah's Accidents, Compensation and the Law*, above p 408 n 19, p 338 n 6.

up the largest part of this and these are relatively easy to administer. We have not been able to calculate whether the particular set of benefits which address incapacity demonstrate this ratio,[8] but one suspects that, as they are much harder to administer than pensions or child benefit, they do not. Furthermore, some of the cheapness of the administration of welfare must be attributable to the unacceptably low level of service that has been given to recipients. Nevertheless, one surely is right to have confidence that the distribution even of incapacity related benefits does not remotely approach the costliness of the tort system.[9]

The less sophisticated criticisms of the self-interest of the profession in particular seem to be refuted by the sincere protestations by personal injury lawyers' professional associations that their members seek to do a great deal of good.[10] But the social scientific literature which demonstrates the crucial importance of groups of influential 'moral entrepreneurs' in identifying 'social problems' and framing the 'emergent' public response to these problems (or the 'capture' of existing regulations) does not seek to deny the public spiritedness of many or indeed most of those entrepreneurs.[11] It rather points to the fact that specific public policies, though they may seek the good of all, rest on the identification of that good by a particular, influential group, and that it is precisely the failure to recognise the inevitable contingency of any such identification must lead to an excess of confidence in the policy.

The confident profession of virtue by those advocating the increase of non-pecuniary loss in *Heil v Rankin* is, in fact, the surest sign of the unacceptability of what was done. One is tempted to say that only those dogmatically convinced of the virtue of abstract tort principles or of the 'right to compensation' could so blatantly disregard the empirical evidence of the likely consequences of their actions. It is submitted that the abstraction of much tort scholarship, teaching and even practice plays an important role in leading those whose decisions have important results in the real world to proceed in ignorance or virtuous contempt of those

8    It would in principle be possible to do so this from the accounts of the Benefit Agency and the Department of Work and Pensions, subject to the collection of the relevant data on sick pay from employers.

9    Cf R Lewis, *Compensation for Industrial Injury* (1987) pp 11-13.

10   The Association of Personal Injury Lawyers has a *Charter for Victims of Injury* which states: 'APIL recognises that people from all parts of society may suffer personal injury. Their accidents may have devastating effects on all aspects of their lives. Nothing can fully compensate people for their injuries. But where the accident is someone else's fault, society should ensure that those who cause injury are held accountable and take responsibility for their actions. Compensation should aim to rehabilitate the injured victim and assist them in buying the care needed to enable them to try to restore their quality of life'.

11   HS Becker, *Outsiders* (rev edn 1971) chs 7-8 and JR Gusfield, *Symbolic Crusade* (2nd edn 1986).

results. This abstracted attitude unfortunately is not always irrelevant, as one might think, but, when it has influence on policy, is actually harmful.

For this influence certainly is one of the principal obstructions to the construction of an alternative to tort. It has been noted above that the existence of moral hazard among the incapacitated makes it necessary to exercise caution in the extension of any compensation provision. However, the existence of moral hazard can lead to excess supply *only* if there is a propensity to supply to the consumer at less than cost, that is to say, the problem really is one of '*supplier* induced demand'.[12] The consumer's demands may be infinite; but supply will take place only if those demands are effective. Signalling effective demand is a role of money in the price system; in a non-price system something else must decide whether demand should be met by supply. The NHS, for example, purports to allocate health services according to 'need', but need is infinite and therefore useless as a rationing device;[13] and what this actually means is rationing according to the clinical choice of doctors who can thereby exercise very considerable choice over the expenditure of very large public funds.[14] Clinical choice is a matter of doctors' preferences, through which the good of the patient is mediated. That mediation will leave its mark, and the supply of health goods by the NHS is characterised by 'medical practice variations' which reflect the interests of the profession as well as the patient.[15] In particular, the fact that clinical choice has led to a concentration on medical procedures that convey professional status over relatively simple and cost effective procedures must be part of the reasons for the chronic existence of relatively long waiting lists for certain conditions in the NHS.[16] Moral hazard is, as we have said, a platitude; moral hazard which has an effect is, it may be said, a two or three way process: the (patient) demand must be made effective by supply side

12  RG Evans, 'Supplier-induced Demand', in M Perlman (ed), *The Economics of Health and Medical Care* (1974) 162.

13  M Cooper, 'Economics of Need: The Experience of the British Health Service', in Perlman (ed), loc cit, 89.

14  R Klein, et al, *Managing Scarcity* (1996) pt 2.

15  RG Evans, 'The Dog in the Night-time: Medical Practice Variations and Health Policy', in TF Anderson and G Mooney (eds), *The Challenges of Medical Practice Variations* (1990) 117.

16  S Frankel and R West (eds), *Rationing and Rationality in the National Health Service* (1993) p 12: '[t]he fact that the profession may find the management of certain conditions uninteresting is an important ingredient that may give rise to long waiting times, persisting from one decade to the next.' Waiting lists do not so much represent a lack of resources but are an inevitable concomitant of theoretically inexhaustible provision of this sort, for the inexhaustibility is always purely theoretical and such a list is the only rationing device available. The issue for the NHS is the relative length of waiting lists, and to what extent these relative lengths represent the 'underconsumption' or 'overconsumption' of various procedures.

(doctor) moral hazard, and there must be a third party (the public) which is obliged to pay.

The existence of a parallel to this situation, with all respect to the integrity of no doubt the vast majority of those concerned, would prima facie appear to be a plausible hypothesis for the retention of the damages system. A very influential body of legal opinion has been able to ensure that personal injury law has been maintained in such a way that public and private bodies *must* make (usually third party insurance) provision against it, and has further been able, in order to further access to legal services, argue for public provision such as legal aid in support of this. Conditional fees are an adjustment of the compulsory insurance intended to maintain the volume of use of legal services. The unwarranted stress on the value of the use of the law is, however, the problem, not the solution.[17]

Though we have seen that in many ways the damages system is a serious failure in terms of securing compensation even for those who fall within its ambit, the most telling criticism of it is, paradoxically, such success as it does enjoy in securing such compensation.[18] Though unevenness and inequity has hardly been eliminated from social security provision for incapacity, the dimensions of this failure are grotesquely magnified by maintenance of the damages system. Among those suffering incapacity, the minute proportion receiving damages are placed in a very privileged financial position by comparison with those suffering similar incapacity who do not. This is the case whether one speaks of a seriously injured person who receives a huge award for loss of earnings (for which, it will be recalled, he has not paid a proportionate 'insurance premium'); a catastrophically injured person who will receive superior care from a huge award for future nursing care; or the recipient of the small award for non-pecuniary loss only. The issue is: 'can one ethically defend a system that creates a "privileged" class of victims of one source of misfortune ... and treats victims of other sources of misfortune ... that generate similar income deficiencies much less generously?'[19]

---

17  Cf R Abel, 'The Paradoxes of Legal Aid', in J Cooper and R Dhavan (eds), *Public Interest Law* (1986) 379, p 386: 'legal aid is a social reform that begins with a solution – lawyers – and then looks for a problem it might solve.' See further P Alcock, 'Legal Aid: Whose Problem?' (1976) 3 British Journal of Law and Society 151 and M Cousins, 'The Politics of Legal Aid: A Solution in Search of a Problem' (1994) 13 Civil Justice Quarterly 111.

18  Stapleton, *Disease and the Compensation Debate*, above p 410 n 9, p 148.

19  MJ Trebilcock, 'The Social Insurance-Deterrence Dilemma of Modern North American Tort Law: A Canadian Perspective on the Liability Insurance Crisis' (1987) 24 San Diego Law Review 929, p 994.

*Evaluation of the damages system*

Work on the personal injury settlement process after *Harris et al* and *Genn 1* would appear to confirm the continuing applicability of Galanter's basic thesis to personal injury litigation prior to Woolf. However, the tone of the most theoretically advanced contribution is rather different from Galanter's and it takes its distance from *Genn 1's* emphasis on C's difficulties.[20] Though initially surprising, the reason for this is, it is submitted, entirely correct. Galanter's work was of a piece with the socio-legal work of its time in that it was very concerned to identify with C,[1] and had the obvious implication that one should seek to remedy C's unmet legal need. It was taken up in this way, with this implication, in *Genn 1*.[2] But once one appreciates that a personal injury claim is very rarely a claim on the resources of an individual but rather is a relationship between an individual C and a D who either is a merely legal person or a D whose liability will be met by a legal person, that is to say it is a relationship in which C seeks compensation ultimately from the public to an extent that the legal system specifies, then it is by no means clear that every C should always be compensated, or that steps towards this goal will be sensible.[3] And, paralysingly, this is so whether these steps are ineffective *or effective*. It is very hard to conclude that a system which cannot be made to run *better* without imposing a welfare loss[4] is other than indefensible.

The citizen's 'right to compensation' is based on a social relationship which establishes the right and the correlative duty to pay, and so is a call on finite social resources, and the effectiveness of such a right will be undermined if the right is established in a way which allows it to grow beyond the bounds of cost-effectiveness. The problem becomes acute when C's conduct appears less meritorious than D's or without merit at all, or when the personal injury lawyer benefits more than C, but this is not the fundamental issue, which is 'that sympathy for the victim comes with a price label attached if we want to do anything about it.'[5] The problems

20  R Dingwall et al, 'Firm Handling: The Litigation Strategies of Defence Lawyers in Personal Injury Cases' (2000) 20 *Legal Studies* 1.
1   The background 'methodological position' is concern with the 'underdog': HS Becker, 'Whose Side Are We On?', in HS Becker, *Sociological Work* (1970) 123.
2   See further Genn, *Meeting Legal Needs?*, above p 429 n 6. On Genn's more recent views see *Genn 2*, p 406 n 2 ch 8.
3   *Pace* Swanson, 'A Review of the Civil Justice Review: Economic Theories Behind the Delays in Tort Litigation', above p 407 n 12, p 211. This in many ways excellent paper is undermined by its exclusive focus on reform of the tort litigation process, not asking whether the goal of meeting all legal need is a sensible goal.
4   GL Priest, 'The Current Insurance Crisis and Modern Tort Law' (1987) 96 Yale Law Journal 1521.
5   Atiyah, *The Damages Lottery*, above p 408 n 19, p 113

are to ration scarce resources (eg to assess the relative needs of different groups, such as the needs of the elderly as against those of children), and to find the most efficient ways of using the resources to achieve particular goals, within a policy towards overall social provision for incapacity. Once the identification with an individual D is broken, as, in the light of the overwhelming importance of insurance, it has to be when forming a policy towards personal injury cases, then the direction of further reform of the damages system becomes uncertain, even in the light of continued findings of inequalities of legal power:

> Defendant insurers may be large corporations but the funds they administer come from the premiums paid by other citizens and there is no good reason to challenge the proposition that these funds should only be disbursed where a proper cause is established.[6]

It is in this light[7] that the very telling recent decision to withdraw legal aid from personal injury litigation[8] and institute costs rules which encourage the funding of litigation through conditional fee arrangements[9] must be assessed. Though personal injury took up only a small part of the legal aid budget,[10] prior to the Access to Justice Act 1999, half of personal injury litigation would appear to have been legally aided.[11] Though the Lord Chancellor's Department has argued that 'solicitors will take on the

---

6    Dingwall et al, 'Firm Handling: The Litigation Strategies of Defence Lawyers in Personal Injury Cases', above p 449 n 20, p 17.
7    In addition to the points we will make about tort as a compensation mechanism, it would seem that tort also is not merely an ineffective deterrent to clinical negligence but, because it encourages denial by using sanctions which are severe when (rarely) applied, it actually hinders the resolution of many NHS complaints and the scrutiny and improvement of clinical practices: L Mulcahy et al, *Mediating Medical Negligence Claims* (1999) paras 2.1-2.33. On the theory of determining the appropriate level of sanction to maximise compliance see B Fisse and J Braithwaite, *Corporations, Crime and Accountability* (1993) ch 5.
8    Access to Justice Act 1999, s 6(6) and Sch 2, para 1(a), brought into force on 1 April 2000 (SI 2000 No 774). In addition to the major exception of clinical negligence, there are some minor exceptions: Legal Services Commission, *Funding Code Guidance Section 3: Excluded Work*, paras 4-6.
9    Access to Justice Act 1999, s 27. A conditional fee is an 'uplift' or 'success fee' which legal advisers may charge above normal fees in winning cases. The system adopted has a scale of uplifts depending on the likelihood of winning.
10   Personal injury and clinical negligence were and are small parts of the entire budget (dominated by criminal legal aid) and overall spending on them marginally fell throughout the second half of the 1990s: *Legal Aid Board Annual Report 1999-2000* HC 664 (2000) p 5.
11   Fennell, *The Funding of Personal Injury Litigation*, above p 406 n 7, table 3.1. When kept, judicial statistics about the use of legal aid are broadly to this effect: eg *Judicial Statistics 1998*, above p 429 n 7, table 4.12.

cases' from which legal aid has been withdrawn,[12] this step has been 'one of the Government's greatest acts of manifest folly' in the opinion of the Association of Personal Injury Lawyers.[13] But legal aid was withdrawn from these cases because, *in nuce*, given that 'provision of scarce public resources cannot be without limit, nor can it be made without an assessment of the comparative benefits of expenditure',[14] the Lord Chancellor was both dissatisfied with the increasing expense of personal injury cases[15] and felt there were better ways to spend the legal aid budget:

> our plan is to focus legal aid on high priority social welfare issues. As a consequence, we believe legal aid should no longer be available for non-medical negligence personal injury cases. Instead, we believe that most personal injury cases should be financed using "no-win, no-fee" agreements.[16]

12 KPMG for the Lord Chancellor's Department, *Conditional Fees: A Business Case* (April 1998).
13 *Premature Abolition of Legal Aid Set to Cause Problems for Accident Victims*, Association of Personal Injury Lawyers Press Release No 93 (March 2000). See further Law Society, *Justice for All* (1999). To the extent that the Association's criticisms are of the way this measure was implemented as opposed to the measure *per se*, they appear to have substance, despite temporary transitional arrangements having been made. On this the Association is in apparent agreement with its traditional 'opponents', the Forum of Insurance Lawyers: A Parker, 'Conditional Fees: Kill or Cure' [2001] Journal of Personal Injury Litigation 68. There has been considerable argument leading to appeal litigation over who is to bear the costs of 'after the event insurance' premiums and uplifts: *Callery v Gray* [2001] EWCA Civ 1117 [2001] 3 All ER 833 and *(No 2)* [2001] EWCA Civ 1246 [2001] 4 All ER 1.
14 *Access to Justice with Conditional Fees*, Lord Chancellor's Department Consultation Paper (March 1998) para 5.1.
15 Since 1992, the costs of civil legal aid had risen by 35% per case: *Modernising Justice*, Lord Chancellor's Department White Paper, Cm 4155 (December 1988) para 38. It was highly suspicious that personal injury cases were 20% longer when legally aided, and the time between first instruction and issue of proceedings was 50% longer: *Woolf*, above p 406 n 7, pp 359, 360. In the Lord Chancellor's opinion the legal aid budget was 'rocketing' out of control prior to the Access to Justice Act 1999: The Lord Chancellor, *Civil Justice and Legal Aid Reforms: Keynote Address to the Solicitors' Annual Conference* (18 October 1997) and see further *Modernising Justice*, loc cit, ch 3. Personal injury and clinical negligence did not absolutely contribute to this (see n p 450 n 10 above), but the rising average cost of such cases and the stable overall budget together represent a considerable degradation of service, with the number of persons receiving civil legal aid falling by 35%: *Modernising Justice*, loc cit, para 38. Planned expenditure will hold the personal injury and clinical negligence budget steady: Legal Services Commission, *Corporate Plan 2001/02 –2003/04*, table D.
16 The Lord Chancellor, *Speech to the Association of Personal Injury Lawyers* (7 May 1998).

The position has been made stark in the UK because so much of the expense of clinical negligence is borne by the NHS.[17] The NHS in England has seen a 700% rise in the number of clinical negligence claims made against it since 1995-1996. In 1999-2000 it paid £400 m in settlement, but its position will have worsened because it received a new record of 10,000 new claims in that year. The NHS estimates that as of 31 March 2000 it faces 23,000 claims amounting to an outstanding potential liability of £3.9 bn. (The NHS's annual income is £40 bn). In 1999-2000, 28% of the expenditure on clinical negligence cases went to (claimants' and defendant's) legal costs, and if one deducts the extremely expensive brain damage and cerebral palsy cases this rises to 32%, with costs being larger than the damages awarded in 44% of all cases. The greater part of the clinical negligence claims brought against the NHS must have been legally-aided, for the Legal Aid Board as it then was issued 7,375 legal aid certificates to start such proceedings in 1999-2000 alone.[18] And in legally aided medical negligence cases, claimants' costs have exceeded the damages awarded![19]

The Lord Chancellor's Department has recognised that the bizarre spectacle of one government department (pursuing the good of 'justice') using public funds to ruin another (pursuing the good of 'health') so that those funds may in substantial part be transferred to the legal profession was indefensible:

> The presence of the Legal Aid Fund has not only allowed [clinical negligence] litigation to burgeon in recent years, but with its regular pay-outs from the taxpayer, has cushioned lawyers from the economic realities of operating in this field of law.[20]

17  *Handling Clinical Negligence Claims in England*, above p 430 n 13 and *Clinical Negligence: What Are the Issues and Options for Reform*, Department of Health Consultation Paper (August 2001). The volume of material on the emergent specialism of clinical negligence is large and is growing rapidly: see I Kennedy and A Grubb, *Medical Law* (3rd edn 2001) ch 4. However, the best overall appraisal of the issues of concern here as they arise in clinical negligence would appear to remain C Ham et al, *Medical Negligence: Compensation and Accountability* (1988) (another work produced at the Oxford Centre). The theoretical framework of this book and of *Harris et al* and *Genn 1* remains the foundation of the more penetrating recent accounts: P Hoyte, 'Unsound Practice: The Epidemiology of Medical Negligence' (1995) 3 Medical Law Review 53 and AF Phillips, *Medical Negligence* (1997) ch 3.

18  *Legal Aid Board Annual Report 1999-2000*, above p 450 n 10, table Civil 8. Similar numbers of certificates were issued in all years since 1995. Fennell, *The Funding of Personal Injury Litigation*, above p 406 n 7, table 3.1 found that 80.2% of medical negligence cases in 1993 were legally aided.

19  *Access to Justice with Conditional Fees*, above p 451 n 14, para 3.17. In only 17% of cases was £50 or more recovered!

20  Ibid, para 3.15.

Because the relatively new area of clinical negligence at the moment presents particular problems in the assessment of the likelihood of success in taking a case to practitioners and insurers, legal aid has for the present been retained for clinical negligence cases,[1] though the clear intention is that it will be removed in the medium term, with these cases also being in future funded through conditional fees.[2]


## Abandoning the goal of 'compensation': a new direction for reform?

In sum, there is no sensible positive defence of the damages system considered as part of the social response to the problem of incapacity.[3] Nevertheless, anyone who has great confidence that they know how to resolve the compensation debate is wrong. Personal injury advice is now largely[4] provided by a complicated market in which claims assessors, claims management companies, and the legal profession compete for market share.[5] This market is created by the present law of liability for

1   The Department of Health and the Lord Chancellor's Department have jointly sought to bring these cases under some control in the interim by concentrating the cases in, on the side of D, the newly formed NHS Litigation Authority, and, on the side of C, a limited number of solicitors' firms (currently 253) who have obtained a specialist quality mark from the Legal Services Commission to do this work on legal aid. The argument is that this concentration will lead to expertise, and consequently economy and efficiency (including expedition), in the handling of these cases: *Handling Clinical Negligence Claims in England*, above p 430 n 13, diagram 2.

2   *Access to Justice with Conditional Fees*, above p 451 n 14, paras 3.16, 3.27.

3   J Stapleton, 'Tort, Insurance and Ideology' (1995) 58 Modern Law Review 820 fairly concedes the point. Stapleton's, in our opinion wholly unconvincing, defence of tort nevertheless principally rests on her claim that the system (and aspects of liability insurance generally) cannot be reduced to their function as 'insurance'.

4   Citizens' Advice Bureaux, Law Centres and Trades Unions offer not-for-profit advice: cf p 428 above.

5   *Report of the Lord Chancellor's Committee to Investigate the Activities of Non-legally Qualified Claims Assessors and Employment Advisers* above p 411 n 15. Credit hire companies play a significant tangential role by carrying on a business which has been estimated to be worth at least £500 m pa: ibid, para 82. In a road accident in which C suffers personal injury and damage to his car, the personal injury and the property damage claim are usually handled together. Credit hire companies may repair C's car and/or hire him replacement, payment being deferred until an interim insurance payment is made or the claim is settled, the companies' costs ultimately being met by the liability insurer. Such companies obviously have an incentive to increase the cost of their services, which liability insurers have challenged, and there are regular reports in *Current Law* of many county court decisions on the reasonableness of the hiring charges for a replacement while C's car is being repaired. See also the House of Lords' decision in *Diamond*

personal injury, the expense very largely being met by the NHS (ie tax and national insurance payers), other public bodies (ie council tax and taxpayers), and private insurers (ie premium payers) as the third parties in third party insurance. It is too early to assess how well conditional fee arrangements for legal representation in particular or the regulation of these market participants in general will work, but, of course, current regulatory initiatives and proposals do not directly affect the size of the market,[6] that is to say of the amount of money spent on personal injury compensation, which is set by the extent of tort liability. They will not address the perennial questions of the economy, effectiveness, efficiency and equity of this spending within the overall context of dealing with incapacity.

The gigantic literature in which possible reforms of public provision for incapacity have been canvassed is authoritatively discussed elsewhere.[7] The goal of these reforms has been abolition of the damages system and its replacement by a scheme to provide comprehensive and equitable public compensation ultimately along the lines of the Woodhouse proposals for New Zealand or even Australia. We regard it as inconceivable that it should be sought to implement it in the UK now; not so much because the public funds will not be made available, but because 'the assumption of an easy transition from failed social insurance in the law of torts to successful public social insurance was too simple'.[8] We should like to argue that it is quite right that the funds for general (full) compensation of incapacity should not be made available, and that the assumption that 'compensation' is a good policy is questionable. We will do so in the course of making two points about Professor Atiyah's

---

*v Lovell* [2000] 2 All ER 897. *Cf* the discussion of the reasonableness of the replacement car selected at pp 531-532, 533 below.

6   A marked collapse in the volume of personal injury litigation following the withdrawal of legal aid would have this effect, but it shows no sign of happening, changes apparently being at the margin. Changes in the size of awards made and the success fees available can do a great deal to maintain or increase the volume of personal injury litigation whilst personal injury liability is imposed by the state. Without the imposition, the range of such changes would be limited by the elasticity of demand for first party insurance.

7   Cane, *Atiyah's Accidents, Compensation and the Law*, p 406 pt 6; Ison, *Compensation Systems for Injury and Disease*, above p 409 n 4 and Stapleton, *Disease and the Compensation Debate*, above p 410 n 9, ch 7 and SD Sugarman, *Doing Away with Personal Injury Law* (1989). An excellent British synopsis of the argument is M Maclean, 'Alternatives to Litigation: No Fault or Effective Social Security?', in Dingwall (ed), *Socio-legal Aspects of Medical Practice*, above p 405 n 1, 37. p 41: 'a more integrated social security system concerned with loss of income arising from disability'.

8   JF Keeler, 'Social Insurance, Disability and Personal Injury' (1994) 44 University of Toronto Law Journal 275, p 350.

recent reform suggestion, the basic thrust of which[9] is also to eliminate the damages system but not to make any public provision to replace it. Above a basic social security 'safety net',[10] those who wish and are able to take out first-party insurance against risks of any sort will be liberty to do so, the absence of the damages system giving an added incentive to them to do this.[11] Atiyah used to advocate something like Woodhouse, and though Conaghan and Mansell approach the criticism of these proposals from the opposite direction to Burrows, they join him in ridiculing the way Atiyah has changed his mind. In as powerful a criticism of the recent Atiyah proposals as those committed to general public compensation of incapacity will be able to mount,[12] they have said:

> Atiyah has not solved the problem of the damages lottery, but has simply substituted one system of arbitrary and fortuitous distribution for another. In what sense is it more justifiable for protection from injury and illness to depend on ability to pay premiums than on what causes the injury or illness in question? It is only if one accepts that the distribution of wealth is itself just ... that its outcomes appear defensible.[13]

With respect to Conaghan and Mansell, they miss the point why Atiyah has changed his mind. He is no longer *trying* to solve the problem of the damages lottery. Breaking the taken for granted connection between criticism of tort and Woodhouse-type proposals,[14] he is abandoning the idea of general compensation for all incapacity as a goal. This is, of course, exactly what Conaghan and Mansell do not like, but he was wise to do so for at least two reasons. First, social security spending just is not going the Woodhouse way, nor is there any foreseeable prospect that it will. Conaghan and Mansell concede the, as it were, negative point that tailoring one's proposal to this situation might indeed be practical politics.

9   Road accidents are treated differently: Atiyah, *The Damages Lottery*, above p 408 n 19, pp 185-188. It is in our opinion impossible to reconcile this exception to Atiyah's basic argument. Cf R Lewis, 'No-fault Compensation for Victims of Road Accidents: Can it be Justified' (1981) 10 Journal of Social Policy 161.

10  Ibid, p 193.

11  Ibid, pp 188-193. There is very substantial waste and duplication when first party and third party insurance coexist for the same risks which chills the use of the former.

12  Though see also the, as it were, first hand apprehensions about the extension of first-person insurance in M Howard and P Thompson, *There May be Trouble Ahead* (1995).

13  J Conaghan and W Mansell, 'From the Permissive to the Dismissive Society; Patrick Atiyah's Accidents, Compensation and the Market' (1998) 25 Journal of Law and Society 284.

14  Following Stapleton, *Disease and the Compensation Debate*, above p 410 n 9, p 178.

But there is a second, positive reason for accepting Atiyah's proposal, which is that we should now see that it was wrong to believe that something like Woodhouse should ever be set as a goal.

Atiyah calls his proposal '[leaving] the matter largely to the free market'.[15] With respect, he is mistaken to do so in two ways. First, it is impossible for the legal framework of a welfare enhancing incapacity insurance (or any other) market to be put in place without more or less extensive government involvement, and by putting his point the way he does Atiyah lays himself open to some very obvious criticisms of the shortcomings of an unregulated insurance market.[16] In particular, one would have thought it so deplorable as not to be countenanced that the government would fail to arrange that there be an insurer of last resort should the care of, say, a catastrophically injured person be jeopardised by the failure of his insurer.[17] But that which should not be countenanced has happened, and, for example, the recent failure of Chester Street Insurance Holdings Ltd has left certain terminally ill victims of asbestosis without payment of personal injury compensation.[18] Careful appraisal of the necessary 'reregulation' rather than 'deregulation' would be essential if Atiyah's proposal is to be implemented, for reasonable apprehension there could be a repetition of what happened (and still might happen) to deregulated pension provision would rightly prevent that implementation.[19] Identifying the necessary reregulation may answer some of the criticisms made by Conaghan and Mansell.

In particular, the second point we should like to make, despite the language in which he chose to express his point, Atiyah does not wish to eliminate direct welfare provision but, as we have mentioned, he takes it for granted that '[o]f course some state security safety net will still be needed for those who are not otherwise covered at all.'[20] Indeed, though he now sees limits to social security spending which were not acknowledged in his earlier work, he still seems to find it disappointing that the trend of such spending is not towards more generosity,[1] as indeed

15  Atiyah, *The Damages Lottery*, above p 408 n 19, p 190.
16  Eg R Ericson, et al, 'The Moral Hazards of Neo-liberalism: Lessons from the Private Insurance Industry' (2000) 29 Economy and Society 532.
17  Lewis, *Structured Settlements*, above p 437 n 16, ch 15, pp 261-262.
18  *Insurers Urged to Act After Company Collapse*, Association of Personal Injury Lawyers Press Release No 120 (April 2000).
19  Beveridge explored the ways in which the state might, 'by regulation, by financial assistance or by itself undertaking the organisation of voluntary insurance', set the framework for the provision of first party insurance, in part to ensure 'that in buying life assurance persons of limited means should be guided by advice from a seller which is wholly disinterested': *Social Insurance and Allied Services*, above p 407 n 15, paras 375, 188.
20  Atiyah, *The Damages Lottery*, above p 408 n 19, p 193.
1    Ibid, pp 180.

it is. It was a mistake for him to mention this so very briefly, for the plausibility of his (or indeed any) reform of the damages system turns on the relationship it establishes between the private and public compensation of incapacity. The necessity for social security stems from the way that market provision of all goods including insurance will, of its nature, not be uniform, and while this is simply the obverse of the flexibility of the market, it is intolerable if it means that significant numbers fall below minimum social security levels.[2] It is wrong to downplay the role of the state in providing general security against want.[3]

We are of the opinion that the continued existence of tort *prevents* general reform, and it is highly arguable that tort should be abolished just for that reason. Nevertheless, the case for abolition obviously gains strength if the freed resources are transferred to the replacement scheme for the more efficient and equable support of the incapacitated,[4] and we ourselves would hope that the floor should always be set at the highest level which is consistent with its being a floor. Unless there is some such transfer, one has to summon up enthusiasm for the abolition of tort largely from the rather barren satisfaction of achieving fairness by levelling down. It is important to note this because it would be reckless indeed to take it for granted that any savings would in fact be transferred to social security.[5] But an important barrier to raising the basic benefit level for incapacity is the legitimate fear that the scheme which replaced tort would have to treat all incapacity (something like) as generously as tort now treats the few who succeed in a tort claim. If tort continues and the general scheme is to be equitable, this obviously is so, and this is an insurmountable barrier to reform.

Atiyah plausibly argues that generalising the tort level of generosity would impose an unsustainable burden on public finances, for (leaving aside the fact that occupational sick pay and statutory sick pay (very largely) are not part of social security expenditure) it would mean spending *all* the current social security budget on incapacity, with the

---

2   Beveridge's principle of 'comprehensiveness' required that 'social insurance ... should not leave ... to ... voluntary insurance any risk so general and uniform that ... voluntary insurance can never be sure of covering the ground': *Social Insurance and Allied Services*, above p 407 n 15, para 308: .

3   In the much more thoroughly analysed issue of providing retirement pensions, even those to the (far) right of the British debate almost universally dismiss the idea that the state should not provide a 'tier 1' pension (corresponding to Atiyah's safety net) as 'a distraction': M Littlewood, *How to Create a Competitive Market in Pensions* (1998) p 117. The live issue in regard to such pensions (even amongst those who seek to lower the public pension budget) is 'integration': see p 427 n 19 above.

4   This was part of the New Zealand strategy: *Compensation for Personal Injury in New Zealand* (Chair: Woodhouse J) paras 462-466.

5   Lewis, *Deducting Benefits from Damages for Personal Injury*, above p 411 n 19, p 37.

implication that that budget would have to be increased.[6] We would add that presumably this budget would eventually have to be increased so that benefits paid to the non-incapacitated unemployed match the payments to the incapacitated, or one has merely reproduced the inequity of the damages system on a much larger scale. It is not a question of whether this is 'practical politics'. Such would be the size of the resultant welfare state that one is talking of state equalisation of all incomes, and this must be regarded as an insurmountable obstacle to reform unless one actually has it as one's ultimate goal (as Conaghan and Mansell may do). Furthermore, not only is the absolute incidence of the problem a bar to comprehensive compensation but we are now obliged to appreciate the problem of moral hazard in a way which was absent from the early contributions to the compensation debate.

Fortunately, security from want does not require the full compensation measure of tort and in particular it does not require compensation for non-pecuniary loss. Equitable treatment of all incapacity on the basis of 'full' compensation as in tort is almost certainly impossible and certainly is not cost-effective, for how can 'compensation' of incapacity above the level required to prevent want be given a higher priority than the alleviation of want for reasons other than incapacity?[7] *It is the virtue of social security protection against want that it does not require the 'compensation' of the victim of incapacity in the tort sense of compensation.* Social security makes it possible to seek to prevent want by a 'flat' rate of payments which avoid loss of earnings (and non-pecuniary loss). In sum, it is only by making it plain that the function of social security is to set a floor of protection from want, and (hopefully and plausibly) transferring resources only to raise the floor, that one can seek to replace tort with social security.

Of course, this will not meet everybody's requirements. And by envisaging that individuals be encouraged to pay for more protection than this if they wish and are able to do so, it would appear that Atiyah is setting out the *only* basis on which a flexible provision of security coverage might be achieved. We strongly suspect that no general scheme could be devised that has anything like the flexibility that might be achieved through the market, for the planning problems and the hindrances posed by treating benefits as rights (of all citizens) are simply

6    Atiyah, *The Damages Lottery*, above p 408 n 19, p 179.
7    The most damning criticism of the New Zealand scheme is that its benefits disproportionately go to improve the lot of the middle classes rather than the poor: Henderson Jr, 'The New Zealand Accident Compensation Reform', above p 408 n 3, pp 788-789. A generalised form of this criticism obtains to a greater or lesser degree for the British welfare state, most markedly in respect of higher education, but also in respect of health and social services: T Sefton, *The Changing Distribution of the Social Wage* (1997).

too huge. *Pearson* itself was a dreadful compromise which it was impossible to implement – 'the ultimate in the modern trend to "ad hockery"' as Conaghan and Mansell note Atiyah observed at the time.[8] Surely subsequent experience of the damages and the social security systems should lead us to have far less confidence than we had at the time of Pearson that a general scheme can be devised. There is, of course, no reason why a person should not buy insurance against incapacity just like any other good, but given inequality of income this will mean, of course, that above the floor of protection from want some will be better covered than others. But ours is a society which tolerates or places a positive value on at least a degree of inequality of income (not least because purportedly egalitarian societies have proven to be much worse), and it would be quite wrong to attempt to devise a compensation scheme on any other basis than creating a floor and allowing further coverage to be bought within the bounds of inequality of income found acceptable. It is possible that the 'mixed' scheme[9] proposed by Atiyah would have advantages over both the damages system, in that one's premium would at least vary in proportion to one's expected compensation, and over social security that it can establish a floor and above this be more closely tailored to an individual person's requirements.[10] If this is so, Atiyah was right to have changed his mind, for this is a condition of actually achieving reform.

It must be appreciated that it is Atiyah's proposal, rather than Conaghan and Mansells' criticism, that would mark a return to Beveridge's conception of the welfare state. We have noted that the *Beveridge Report* aspired to 'a completely unified scheme for disability without demarcation by the cause of disability'. The entire compensation debate continues because of the welfare state's failure to achieve this goal. But Beveridge himself thought this goal entirely compatible with a scheme like Atiyah's. The establishment of the 'unified Plan for Social Security' would leave 'those who felt the need for greater security, by voluntary insurance, to

---

8   Conaghan and Mansell above p 455 n 13, p 285. Atiyah made this observation in PS Atiyah, 'What Now?', in Allen *et al*, eds, *Accident Compensation After Pearson*, above p 425 n 13, 227, p 227. The papers in this book overall condemn *Pearson* most persuasively.

9   Cf Cane, *Atiyah's Accidents, Compensation and the Law*, above p 408 n 19, pp 6-11.

10  *Social Insurance and Allied Services*, above p 407 n 15, para 302. Concluding a valuable review of the issues, T Burchardt, *What Price Security?* (1997) p 77 says: 'If we believe that each individual should pay in proportion to the magnitude of the risk he or she faces, regardless of the determinant of that risk, then private insurance will meet our objective. But if we believe that society as a whole should bear the costs of those catastrophes which are not of an individual's own making, social security will provide a better alternative.' This way of putting the alternatives, with its implication that we should prefer social security, fails to conceive of a mixture of the two.

provide an addition to the flat subsistence guaranteed by the state'.[11] For Beveridge, 'unification' takes place at the level of security from want, and diversity is perfectly acceptable, indeed welcome[12] or even necessary,[13] above this level, and 'scope and encouragement for it must be provided'.[14] Beveridge's goal of 'abolition of want' clearly is somewhat different from the abolition of all inequalities sought by Conaghan and Mansell.[15]

Both goals have their attractions, some of which are mutually exclusive, but it would not be appropriate to fully discuss them here as they require an evaluation of a 'minimalist' as opposed to a 'maximalist' view of the welfare state.[16] However, the point we do feel able to make in connection with personal injury is that[17] experience since *Pearson* gives rise to the strong suspicion that aspiring to do more by direct government provision than Beveridge envisaged[18] is impossible within liberal democratic political and legal systems, which cannot equably draw the necessary line between that which is and is not to be 'compensated' on any other basis.[19]

---

11  *Social Insurance and Allied Services*, above p 407 n 15, para 80. See further ibid, paras 9, 66, 69, 73, 238-239, 302, 375-384, appendix F para 16(3).

12  Beveridge saw a major role for the voluntary sector after the creation of the unified scheme, both in providing services the state could not and preserving counterbalances to the dominating influence of the state: Lord Beveridge, *Voluntary Action* (1948) pt 3. This wheel is reinvented in currently fashionable theories of 'civil society'.

13  '[F]reedom in the management of a personal income' was one of the 'essential liberties' which Beveridge sought to preserve in his conception of the welfare state: WH Beveridge, *Full Employment in a Free Society* (1944) p 21; cf *Social Insurance and Allied Services*, above p 407 n 15, para 21.

14  Ibid, para 375.

15  Ibid, para 294: 'to give by compulsory insurance more than is needed for subsistence is an unnecessary interference with individual responsibilities. More can be given only by taking more in contributions or taxation. That means departing from a principle of a national minimum, above which citizens shall spend their money freely, and adopting instead the principle of regulating the lives of individuals by law'.

16  N Barry, *Welfare* (1990) pp 104-107.

17  *Pace* the abstract notion of positive welfare at p 413 n 4 above. That work on social security is informed by 'sociological theory' as opposed to 'blackletter law' is by no means a guarantee that it is any richer in appreciation of the institutional constraints of policy formulation and implementation.

18  *Social Insurance and Allied Services*, above p 407 n 15, para 294.

19  Cane, *Atiyah's Accidents, Compensation and the Law*, above p 408 n 19. See further Sir John Walley, *Social Security: Another British Failure?* (1972) pp 230-1: 'What troubles me most about the 'compensation' approach to state provision for the consequences of injury or disablement is [that] I have been unable to find a politically logical stopping place along this particular road ... In the foreseeable future, I believe that we will be wise, in trying to improve our public provision for the disabled, to stay with Beveridge in looking at the problem from the standpoint of meeting the essential requirements'.

Uniform compensation of incapacity is, we believe, impossible (unless 'compensation' is stripped of its connotations of being a legal remedy). Uniform prevention of want caused by incapacity is, on the other hand, an implicit, necessary goal of liberal democratic society. It may be that our persistent failure to appreciate the difference between the two has meant that the opportunity to effect some otherwise possible and necessary advances, including the abolition of the damages system and the setting of a fair and affordable (rising) floor, has so far been lost. The abstraction implicit in an exclusive concentration on the formal law of tort liability will mean that one simply cannot see the issues. But for acute critics of the workings of the tort system such as Conaghan and Mansell to criticise Atiyah's proposal for falling short of the bliss to be achieved in a utopia of equal incomes (including perfectly equitably distributed benefits) would be to make the best the enemy of the better, were it not that there is no consensus that such an equality is a utopia.

# Part 7
# Protecting property and financial interests

# 25 Interference with the enjoyment of land: private nuisance

## Introduction: the nature of liability for private nuisance

As questions of liability are avoided in this book so far as possible, this chapter attempts to confine itself to consideration of the remedies for private nuisance[1] and not to what amounts to a nuisance. However, an understanding of a remedy obviously presupposes some understanding of the nature of the harm it is to remedy, and the nature of the harm recognised in the law of nuisance appears to be so generally misunderstood that it is necessary to preface this discussion of nuisance remedies with a brief statement of the policy which guides findings of liability for private nuisance. It will also be necessary to give some assessment of the adequacy of that policy in order to evaluate the remedies for nuisance.[2] A private nuisance is an unreasonable interference with C's use and enjoyment of land in his occupation which either emanates from land in D's occupation or control, or results from a situation created by D. Typical nuisances arise from water, noise, smell, smoke, fumes, pollution, vibrations, heat, etc. Three crucial points about this definition must be noted.

1   This chapter does not consider public nuisance or statutory nuisance. On the relevant law of public and statutory nuisance see RA Buckley, *The Law of Nuisance* (2nd edn 1996) chs 4, 10-11 and, on the shortcomings of the distinctions between these forms of nuisance, see C Gearty, 'The Place of Nuisance in the Modern Law of Torts' [1989] Cambridge Law Journal 214 and JR Spencer, 'Public Nuisance: A Critical Examination' [1989] Cambridge Law Journal 55. However, to the now more or less complete extent that liability under *Rylands v Fletcher* (1868) LR 3 HL 330 is a matter of give and take rather than strict liability (JG Fleming, *The Law of Torts* (9th edn 1998) ch 16), these remarks on the remedies for nuisance would apply to *Rylands v Fletcher*.
2   See pp 496-510 below. This section may be omitted by those concerned only with the existing law of nuisance.

The tort protects C as an occupier of land, and in this sense the law on nuisance should be regarded as part of land law since it defines the level of enjoyment to which an occupier is entitled, in so far as it concerns the rights to be free from interferences emanating from outside his land which are some of the most important rights granted to an occupier as an incident of ownership.[3] Remedies for nuisance are among the legal rules which flesh out the concept of occupation of land by defining the level of enjoyment which will be protected against outside interference, in effect stating that the occupier may make any reasonable use of his right to occupy. From this 'land law' perspective, the courts' role in nuisance cases is to seek to ensure that the occupier may be deprived of his right to reasonable use only with his consent or under statutory powers. The first point that must be noted is, then, that nuisance remedies are remedies for loss of amenity caused by interference with the enjoyment of land.[4]

This has the consequences that only those with an interest in land have standing to take a nuisance action[5] and that, even if the nuisance causes them personal injury,[6] the remedy for nuisance must remedy the loss of amenity of the use of the land, not the loss of amenity in the sense of pain, suffering or loss of amenity caused by a personal injury.[7] The harm to the enjoyment of the land does not depend on the incident of how many persons, if any, sustain personal injury,[8] and a person without a proprietary interest has no standing to bring a nuisance action even if he suffers from a harm which otherwise would be regarded as a nuisance.[9]

---

3    AM Honoré, 'Ownership', in AG Guest (ed), *Oxford Essays in Jurisprudence* (1961) ch 5.

4    The case law has drawn a distinction between what has been called 'material damage to property' and 'interference with the use or enjoyment of land' proper, and it is unarguably the case that it has been easier for C to establish liability for 'physical harm' to his land: see BS Markesinis and SF Deakin, *Tort Law* (4th edn 1999) pp 422-435. A distinction between physical injury to land and physical encroachment, as by the roots or branches of a tree, has also been drawn: *Hunter v Canary Wharf Ltd* [1997] AC 655 at 695. However, we do not think such distinctions have merit and, without argument, we shall ignore such specific qualities, if any, that 'encroachment' and 'physical harm' have and treat them as species of interference with enjoyment of land. On trespass to land, which is a direct, physical invasion of C's land or of the airspace above it, see ch 26 below.

5    G Kodilinye, 'Standing to Sue in Private Nuisance' (1989) 9 Legal Studies 284.

6    As we shall shortly see, nuisance does not depend on D having been negligent, and thus when D has caused C a personal injury by an action which, though not negligent, has been found to be a nuisance, C will have an incentive to seek compensation for personal injury through an action for nuisance, though this should not be recoverable in this way: see pp 471-472 below. Of course, evidence of personal injury may be used to show the extent of the harm caused by an alleged nuisance.

7    *Hunter v Canary Wharf Ltd*, above n 4 at 702-708.

8    Ibid at 706.

9    Ibid at 687-699, 702-708, 711-719, 723-726. See futher J Wightman, 'Nuisance: The Environmental Tort' (1998) 61 Modern Law Review 870.

However, the second point to note is that the freedom to enjoy land protected by nuisance must still be regarded as part of a law of tort increasingly dominated by negligence[10] because nuisance is in a way analogous to negligence in that the protection it affords the occupier does not purport to be absolute or even strict[11] but is a protection from *unreasonable* interference. The typical nuisance dispute is a conflict of 'property rights'. D is usually the owner or occupier of neighbouring land, and the effect of his liability to C is to restrict what he may do on his own land, thus limiting his freedom to use and exploit his rights over his land, and therefore the value of the land at sale. If, say, D wishes to make a noise as an incident of carrying out his business and C obtains an injunction because the noise carries over to his premises,[12] C's property rights are declared to be enlarged and his amenity is improved, but D's are reduced. If C is unable to obtain the injunction, the obverse applies. Each extension of C's rights is at the expense of D's, and vice versa.

One possibility would be, of course, to make D liable for all interference, but the emergence of the modern law of nuisance has authoritatively been described[13] as a process by which distance was taken from the maxim *sic utere tuo ut alienum non laedas*,[14] under which D's liability approximated to this strict, if not absolute,[15] standard. Under the modern law, decisions about which harms constitute a nuisance try to maximise social welfare by refusing to regard reasonable interference as a nuisance.[16] Liability depends on 'what is reasonable [use of land] according to the ordinary

---

10  *British Road Services Ltd v Slater* [1964] 1 WLR 498 at 504.

11  *Sedleigh-Denfield v O'Callaghan* [1940] AC 880 at 904.

12  *Sturges v Bridgman* (1879) 11 Ch D 852.

13  JF Brenner, 'Nuisance Law and the Industrial Revolution' (1974) 3 Journal of Legal Studies 403. See also JPS McLaren, 'Nuisance Law and the Industrial Revolution: Some Lessons from Social History' (1983) 3 Oxford Journal of Legal Studies 155 and B Pontin, 'Tort Law and Victorian Government Growth: The Historiographical Significance of Tort in the Shadow of Pollution and Factory Safety Regulation' (1998) 18 Oxford Journal of Legal Studies 661.

14  *Broom's Legal Maxims* (10th edn 1939) p 238: 'enjoy your own property so as not to injure that of another person'. See further ibid pp 238-256. An illustrative leading case is *Tenant v Goldwin* (1704) 92 ER 222. On the departure from the rule see *Hole v Barlow* (1858) 140 ER 1113; *Bamford v Turnley* (1862) 122 ER 27 and their modern affirmation in *Sedleigh-Denfield v O'Callaghan*, above n 11 at 903. See further the discussion of *Bamford v Turnley* in RA Epstein, 'Nuisance Law: Corrective Justice and Its Utilitarian Constraints' (1979) 8 Journal of Legal Studies 49, pp 82-87.

15  Almost everything one does on one's own land can be shown (by the standards of the physical sciences) to 'interfere' with neighbouring land, but the *sic utere* rule did not, of course, turn on these standards. In particular, a right to light in the sense of a complete right to preserve the prospect from C's property was never part of the rule: *William Aldred's Case* (1611) 77 ER 816 at 821.

16  While it is hoped that this sentence captures the essence of the modern law, it is based on a non sequitur, as is that law: see pp 500-501 below.

usages of mankind living in ... a particular society';[17] 'it is a matter of balancing the conflicting interests of the two neighbours'.[18] Under 'the principle of give and take',[19] occupiers must accept as much interference with each other's enjoyment as is tolerable in the neighbourhood in question. Liability therefore often depends on the degree, extent or duration of the interference: a noise which is reasonable during daylight may be a nuisance after dark.[20] As regulated by nuisance, then, the enjoyment of private property is explicitly subject to reasonable 'reciprocal'[1] restrictions on the use of land: any occupier is both a potential C and a potential D. When he seeks a remedy in nuisance, C implicitly accepts that the same standard of liability would apply to him if D or any other neighbouring occupier complained of unreasonable interferences emanating from C's to D's land.

But although reasonableness is central to negligence and nuisance, and it would be wholly misleading to claim that the case law has established a clear distinction between the two,[2] a crucial difference must be noted as the third point we wish to make. If the harm caused by D's activity, such as the smell from a fish and chip shop, is held to be an unreasonable interference, it is irrelevant that he runs the shop non-negligently, or even to an unusually high standard, for instance by installing 'the most approved appliances'.[3] If the use is held to be unreasonable, the absence of negligence is simply not to the point, or, to put it this way, is no defence to an action for nuisance.[4]

## Damages for past interference

Having set out these three points about the nature of nuisance liability, we now turn to the legal rules which govern the award of nuisance

17  *Sedleigh-Denfield v O'Callaghan*, above p 467 n 11 at 903.
18  *Miller v Jackson* [1977] QB 966 at 981, discussed at pp 482-484 below.
19  *Bamford v Turnley*, above p 467 n 14 at 33; *Cambridge Water Co v Eastern Counties Leather plc* [1994] 2 AC 264 at 299 and *Hunter v Canary Wharf Ltd*, above p 466 n 4 at 711.
20  *Halsey v Esso Petroleum Co Ltd* [1961] 1 WLR 683, discussed at pp 471, 476 below.
1   *Bamford v Turnley*, above p 467 n 14 at 33.
2   *Goldman v Hargrave* [1967] 1 AC 645 at 656-657. See further FH Newark, 'The Boundaries of Nuisance' (1949) 65 Law Quarterly Review 480; JM Eekelaar, 'Nuisance and Strict Liability' (1973) 8 Irish Jurist 191; G Cross, 'Does Only the Careless Polluter Pay: A Fresh Examination of the Law of Private Nuisance' (1995) 111 Law Quarterly Review 453 and T Weir, 'The Staggering March of Negligence', in P Cane and J Stapleton (eds), *The Law of Obligations* (1998) 97, pp 102-107.
3   *Adams v Ursell* [1913] 1 Ch 269 at 272.
4   *Cambridge Water Co v Eastern Counties Leather plc*, above n 19 at 299. Cf US *Restatement (Torts)* 2d, sec 833(c).

remedies.[5] They are: damages for past interference; injunction; and damages in lieu of an injunction. The first of these remedies might well need to be combined with one of the other two to meet specific cases.

At common law, C is entitled to damages for any harm which has been caused by D's nuisance. Though these damages are for past harm, they will have some effect in deterring D and others from committing similar nuisances. If the court awards damages only in respect of past interference, it leaves it open to C to return to court in respect of any further harm or interference by D, and to seek either an injunction or further damages.[6] Where there is some uncertainty about the future, this may be the appropriate course for the court to take, since it postpones the decision until the situation develops.[7] Damages at common law would also be appropriate for harm caused on an isolated occasion, where a similar interference is unlikely to recur. All the normal rules on damages, such as causation, remoteness and mitigation, apply to the assessment. In particular, C may recover for consequential loss caused by the nuisance. Provided the test for remoteness of damage is satisfied, damages may be awarded for C's loss of profits or expenses incurred as a result of D's nuisance,[8] eg during the period of repairs to C's building, or for the loss of custom caused by excessive noise and dust from D's temporary building operations next door.[9] But when the nuisance is caused by D's interference beyond a permitted level (eg noise), the court must be careful to limit the damages only to the *excessive* interference. C is not entitled to be compensated for the harm suffered from the whole of the interference where part of it had to be accepted by him under the give and take rule.[10]

When D's nuisance has caused physical damage to C's land, and no other adverse consequence, the measure of damages is normally the diminution in the value of the land.[11] The reasonable cost incurred by C himself in abating the nuisance or in repairing the damage to his land or buildings will be allowed whenever that was a reasonable response to the nuisance: for example, where C was the current occupier of land affected

---

5   In the case of some nuisances (eg overhanging branches or protruding roots) C may have a self-help remedy, as by cutting the branches or roots at the boundary: see ch 21 above.

6   *Redland Bricks Ltd v Morris* [1970] AC 652 at 664, 668.

7   Uncertainty could also be met by an adjournment of the hearing, or the suspension of an injunction: see pp 475-476 below.

8   *Rust v Victoria Graving Dock Co* (1887) 36 Ch D 113 and *Dodd Properties (Kent) Ltd v Canterbury City Council* [1980] 1 WLR 433. When a public nuisance causes special damage to C, loss of profits has been awarded: *Campbell v Paddington Corpn* [1911] 1 KB 869 (C was prevented from using his house as a viewpoint from which to watch a royal funeral procession). Cf *Rose v Miles* (1815) 4 M & S 101 (extra expenses).

9   *Andreae v Selfridge & Co Ltd* [1938] Ch 1.

10   Ibid.

11   *Bunclark v Hertfordshire County Council* (1977) 243 Estates Gazette 381 at 455.

by subsidence from D's nuisance, C was entitled to recover the cost of remedying the damage to his building.[12] The time when the cost of repairs will be assessed will depend on when, in all the circumstances, it was reasonable for C to have the repairs done;[13] this will protect C against inflation up to that time.[14]

Assessing the extent to which repair is a reasonable response to the harm caused by a nuisance can lead to a problem where the extent of the cost of repair places such an onerous burden on D that it may appear unreasonable to impose it on him. This will especially be the case if there is a considerable disparity between the diminution in value of the land caused by the nuisance and the cost of repair, for then it is questionable whether imposing the burden of repair on D conveys a corresponding benefit on C. The cost of repair must be reasonable in order to comply with the goal of the rules of mitigation,[15] but this can lead to C who wishes to repair being confined to the smaller diminution in value measure and therefore believing himself not to have been fully compensated. C will believe the diminution in market value measure to be inadequate if he has a consumer surplus in his land beyond the value associated with its market price;[16] in nuisance cases this has been called 'the user principle'.[17] The issue of consumer surplus has already been explored in relationship to breaches of contract,[18] and it will be examined in more detail below in relationship to physical invasion of C's land, where it is more usual for C to seek the cost of repair.[19]

12  *Masters v Brent London Borough Council* [1978] QB 841 (damages were awarded despite the fact that the interference first arose during the occupation of his predecessor).
13  *Dodd Properties (Kent) Ltd v Canterbury City Council*, above p 469 n 8 (C's financial position was relevant to this decision).
14  See pp 104-106 above.
15  See ch 7 above.
16  The diminution measure will normally be legitimate when C uses his land for commercial purposes: *Tunnicliffe and Hampson Ltd v West Leigh Colliery Co Ltd* [1906] 2 Ch 22; or where C is a landlord of the premises affected by the nuisance: *Moss v Christchurch Rural District Council* [1925] 2 KB 750. There would appear to be no case in which a claim has been made for the cost of repair because of an idiosyncratic loss (which is irrecoverable in damages: see pp 171-175 above) caused to a commercial party by a nuisance, though the possibility of doing so presumably exists. Those nuisance cases which have considered the user principle in commercial cases have actually been concerned with disgorgement of D's profit: see n 159 and associated text below.
17  *Stoke-on-Trent City Council v W & J Wass Ltd* [1988] 1 WLR 1406 at 1416D: 'The law [has given] to the concept of loss or damage in such [cases] a wider meaning then merely financial loss calculated by comparing the property owner's financial position after the wrongdoing with what it would have been had the wrongdoing never occurred'. See further pp 490-491 below.
18  See pp 168-171 above.
19  See pp 524-526 below.

Often a nuisance causes the occupier C to suffer intangible loss, such as inconvenience, annoyance and discomfort, and it is difficult to calculate the damages which would compensate such a loss.[20] Despite nuisance being an interference with the enjoyment of land, it is, of course, tempting to refer to the relatively settled (if arbitrary) quanta which have been developed in personal injury litigation.[1] So in *Bone v Seale*,[2] where D's pig farm caused a most unpleasant smell on C's land for 12 years but, for reasons which do not fully appear,[3] C failed to show that that smell had diminished the value of the property. C recovered £1,000, a sum which had been determined by analogy to personal injury.[4] The only authority cited to the court in *Bone v Seale* was the case mentioned above in which what was called 'a sum in respect of the nuisances' but which appears to be personal injury compensation was awarded when an oil depot caused night-time noise.[5]

It has been held, it is submitted correctly, that it should not be possible to avoid the requirement of showing negligence in order to ground a claim for compensation for personal injury,[6] and it would appear that: 'there appears to be no English case in which a plaintiff has recovered damages for personal injury as such in [nuisance]'.[7] Of course, it is perfectly arguable that damages for 'nuisance' such as those given in *Bone v Seale* effectively allow C to avoid this requirement, and, with respect, Lord Hoffmann's attempt in *Hunter v Canary Wharf Ltd* to reconcile *Bone v Seale* with the requirement is unconvincing. His Lordship argued that the failure to prove diminution in value in *Bone v Seale* meant that:

> it had not been shown that the property would sell for less. But diminution in capital value is not the only measure of loss. It seems to me that the value of the right to occupy a house which smells of pigs must be less than the value of the occupation of a house which does not. In the case of a transitory nuisance, the capital value of

20 *Hunter v Canary Wharf Ltd*, above p 466 n 4 at 696.
1 See chs 22-23 above.
2 [1975] 1 WLR 797.
3 The nuisance was intermittent (ibid at 805G), but this does not seem to be nearly enough to explain this failure. An apparently absurd decision by the local authority that the smell was not a nuisance to public health because one who smelled it was not compelled to vomit was rejected: ibid at 800-801. See also p 472 n 9 below.
4 In the light of awards for loss of the sense of smell in personal injury cases, the Court of Appeal reduced the judge's award of £6,000: ibid at 802-804, 805, 806.
5 *Halsey v Esso Petroleum Co Ltd*, p 468 n 20 above at 702-703. 'Personal injury' compensation was also awarded in respect of a smell, and 'property damage' for linen damaged by smoke.
6 *Read v J Lyons & Co Ltd* [1947] AC 156 at 170-171 and *Cambridge Water Co v Eastern Counties Leather plc*, above p 468 n 19 at 300.
7 Buckley, *The Law of Nuisance*, above p 465 n 1, p 91.

the property will seldom be reduced. But the owner or the occupier is entitled for compensation for the diminution of the value of the amenity value of the property during the period for which the nuisance persisted. To some extent this involves placing a value upon intangibles. But estates agents do this all the time.[8]

Were his Lordship's argument that the value of a house that smelled of pigs 'should' be less than (an otherwise similar) one that does not, one would agree with him. But, presumably because of some vagary in the working of the property market, 'must' is wrong, and in point of fact in *Bone v Seale* it was not so, and there should have been no damages awarded in that case. This obviously is itself prima facie highly unsatisfactory,[9] but it is, with respect, difficult to see any alternative damages that the cases could throw up that do not further confuse an already confused position. It has plausibly been argued that anything like a satisfactory level of consistency in awards of damages for 'personal injury' caused by a nuisance cannot be expected without legislative intervention.[10]

It may also be the case that the diminution in value measure is unsatisfactory in a further sense. Cases may well arise in which the profit D made by carrying out the activity that caused the nuisance may be greater than the loss the nuisance causes to C, and in this case what would now be recognised as a restitutionary argument arises that D should have to disgorge this unjust enrichment. Were C confined to the diminution in value measure in these cases, D may be unjustly enriched because even after the payment of damages he would be left with a profit. Disgorgement on a restitutionary basis may be necessary to avoid this outcome. Analogies may be drawn from the cases on damage to land caused by other torts where other measures of damages have been used to effect (partial) disgorgement.[11] However, there do not appear to be any cases in which a restitutionary award in regard of the unjust enrichment obtained by inflicting only past harms has been pursued. Such awards have, however, been sought in regard of continuing nuisances, and they will be discussed in this connection below.[12]

8    *Hunter v Canary Wharf Ltd*, above p 466 n 4 at 706.
9    An injunction was C's obvious remedy in *Bone v Seale*, but the qualified injunction (see pp 474-475 below) granted in the first proceedings was a compromise under a consent order which permitted some smell, and whether D had contravened the permitted level was then difficult to prove: C 'won the war but lost the peace treaty': *Bone v Seale*, above p 471 n 2 at 800. Hypothetical release damages were not pursued in this case, in which the recently decided *Wrotham Park Estate Co Ltd v Parkside Homes Ltd* was not cited (see pp 488-491 below). In sum, the advice C received in this case was not outstanding.
10   *Salmond and Heuston on the Law of Torts* (21st edn 1996) p 64.
11   Eg restitutionary disgorgement of the profit D made by unauthorised use of C's land, such as a reasonable royalty for unauthorised mining: see pp 527- 529 below.
12   See pp 488-495

## Injunction

One would imagine that the injunction should play a particularly important role as a remedy for the type of harm caused by a nuisance. Damages for past harm can provide compensation for any loss of enjoyment which C has suffered up to the date of the trial, but the deterrent effect such damages may have in discouraging D from continuing to interfere in the future may well be very limited. An injunction, as a coercive order backed up by the threat of contempt proceedings and the ultimate sanction of imprisonment, is the most effective protection which can be given to C against his being deprived of some of the normal use of his land as the result of external conditions or activities for which D is responsible. An injunction may also reduce future costs. C will not have to begin a new claim for damages every time he suffers further harm and keep proving his loss.[13]

However, the fact that an activity has been identified as a nuisance does not mean that C will obtain an injunction, for this equitable remedy is, of course, granted at the discretion of the court,[14] and may be subject to conditions. The sanction for breach is contempt of court, punishable by either fine or imprisonment. The court will not itself take the initiative to enforce the injunction, but leaves it to C to monitor D's compliance and to return to the court to ask for it to be enforced if he can prove breach of the injunction.[15] The most important issue in litigation over nuisance remedies is the court's choice of injunction or damages, and a reasonably firm distinction has arisen between the treatment in this respect of prohibitory and mandatory injunctions. We shall, therefore, describe the specific forms of injunction before putting forward a general evaluation of the principles governing the granting of injunctions.

### Prohibitory injunctions

A final or perpetual injunction against D is designed to prohibit him from continuing the type and extent of interference which has been held to be

---

13  Of course, even with an injunction, C may have to return to court to seek its enforcement. For an example of what one fears is the typical relationship between parties involved in such proceedings see *Bone v Seale*, above p 471 n 2.
14  The grounds of appeal against a trial judge's decision are that 'the judge misdirected himself in law, took into account irrelevant matters or failed to take into account relevant matters': *Duport Steels Ltd v Sirs* [1980] 1 WLR 142 at 171.
15  This is an extremely important feature of the *private* nuisance injunction: see pp 500-501 below.

an actionable nuisance against C.[16] If, despite a prohibitory injunction against him, D continues a nuisance, C may recover damages for harm suffered after the injunction came into force.[17] These are not damages in contemplation of D's continuing the 'nuisance',[18] but damages for the harm caused by a nuisance which it is C's intention should be stopped. The injunction may be expressed in general terms: eg D is perpetually restrained from causing or permitting any effluent to flow or pass from his premises into a river so as sensibly to alter the quality of the waters.[19] However, the court should formulate the injunction so as to specify precisely the prohibited level of interference. D should know exactly what he must refrain from causing in order to avoid being in contempt.[20] Injunctions seldom prohibit all interference with C's land, but rather fix the maximum, tolerable level, so that D is prohibited from causing any interference beyond that level.[1] A prohibitory injunction usually focuses on the harm to C, not on D's activity causing that harm. Instead of forbidding D's activity, it in effect tells him that he is permitted to continue his activity only if he can avoid causing the harm to C.[2] It is left to D to decide what he must do to produce that result. He may, for example, continue making a noise if he effectively prevents C from hearing it.

A period of uncertainty over the court's attitude towards granting prohibitory injunctions in the wake of *Miller v Jackson* would now appear to be at an end,[3] and it can now be said that C will normally be granted such an injunction. The issue is, however, complex, and we shall examine the 'working rule' guiding the court's decision to grant an injunction at length below.[4]

### Qualified injunctions

Instead of defining the prohibited level of interference, the injunction may specify exactly what D is permitted to do on his land in regard to the activity which is causing the interference. Instead of having to decide upon the level of activity which will meet the level of C's freedom from

---

16 The injunction may be worded so as to protect C's successors in title: *Pride of Derby and Derbyshire Angling Association Ltd v British Celanese Ltd* [1953] Ch 149 at 155.
17 *Hole v Chard Union* [1894] 1 Ch 293.
18 See pp 488-495 below.
19 *Pride of Derby* case, above n 56.
20 Cf *Redland Bricks Ltd v Morris*, above n 26, a case of a mandatory injunction.
1 Cf *Kennaway v Thompson* [1981] QB 88, discussed at pp 482-484 below.
2 The effect of granting an injunction is that, to the extent covered by the injunction, C need not take steps to attempt to mitigate the harm.
3 See pp 482-484 below.
4 See pp 480-481.

interference specified in the injunction, D has the easier task of ensuring that he does not exceed the level of his own activity which is laid down in the injunction. A qualified injunction is particularly suitable when D's activity can be graduated according to time, extent, or numbers, eg as with an injunction permitting a playground to be used only by children under 12 and between 10 am and 6.30 pm;[5] or one restraining an oil depot from operating so as to cause noise between 10 pm and 6 am;[6] or one restricting the number and duration of motor-boat racing events on a lake, and fixing the noise level of boats using the lake at other times.[7]

### Modification of injunctions

One of the problems with a permanent or final injunction is that it could become out of date as circumstances change, and, of course, the more detailed the injunction, the more likely this is to happen. The parties themselves are free to negotiate an agreed change, but, where they cannot agree, there should be some judicial machinery to deal with obsolete injunctions. Injunctions will often, at the end of the order, grant the parties (and their successors in title)[8] 'liberty to apply'. This means that either party may return to court to ask for a modification of the injunction or its discharge in the light of new circumstances.[9] A detailed injunction ought always to give liberty to apply, since it could easily become out of date as the situation changed, but even less specific ones usually do so. In the absence of such leave, there should be a statutory method of review, as there is to deal with obsolete restrictive covenants.[10]

### Suspension of the injunction

When a nuisance was created in the course of the direct public provision of a service, such as repair of a sewerage system then under public ownership, it was a regular practice to suspend the injunction in order to allow D sufficient time to make arrangements to maintain essential

---

5  *Dunton v Dover District Council* (1978) 76 LGR 87.
6  *Halsey v Esso Petroleum Co Ltd*, p 468 n 20 above at 703.
7  *Kennaway v Thompson*, above p 474 n 1, discussed at pp 482-484 below.
8  *Pride of Derby* case, above p 474 n 16 at 187.
9  Ibid at 182.
10 Law of Property Act 1925, s 84. The Lands Tribunal is empowered to discharge or modify a restriction (eg when the neighbourhood has changed its character) and may award compensation to the person affected: R Megarry and HWR Wade, *The Law of Real Property* (6th edn 2000) paras 16.084-16.093.

services to the public.[11] The reduction in the number of directly publicly provided services has required the extension of this practice to now privatised service undertakers, but this would appear to have encountered no particular legal difficulty,[12] and there were precedents for it. The oil depot causing night-time noise mentioned above was privately owned but was given six weeks to abate the noise.[13] Even where the court fixes a definite period for the suspension, it usually grants D liberty to apply for a further suspension if he can 'satisfy the court that justice requires that a further suspension should be granted',[14] eg if D is unable reasonably to do more than he is doing,[15] or cannot get the licence he needs to do the work.[16]

The court is free to attach conditions to the suspension, which gives it flexibility in adjusting the conflicting interests of the parties. One condition regularly imposed is that D should undertake to pay C damages in respect of harm or loss suffered by C during the period of the suspension.[17] A suspension without this condition is a compromise splitting the cost of abatement between the two parties,[18] in that C is to bear his own loss meanwhile and D bears the cost of the adjustments necessary to comply with the injunction when it comes into operation: C gets the injunction at the 'price' of bearing the cost of the delay.[19]

11  In the *Pride of* Derby case, above p 474 n 16 at 155, 181, 192, 193-194, D was given two years to modify its sewerage works. In *Hole v Chard Union* above p 474 n 17, another sewerage works was allowed six months. In *Manchester Corpn v Farnworth* [1930] AC 171 an injunction affecting an electricity generating station was suspended for one year.

12  Of course, the operation of the utilities creates enormous problems of interference, but these are handled almost exclusively by public regulation, eg highway authorities have powers to charge utilities for unreasonable prolongation of road works causing annoyance to local residents (and road users) under the Street Works (Charges for Unreasonably Prolonged Occupation of the Highway) Regulations (SI 2000 No 1281).

13  *Halsey v Esso Petroleum Co Ltd*, above p 468 n 20 at 703, 704.

14  *Pride of Derby* case, above p 474 n 16 at 182, 194–195.

15  *Stollmeyer v Petroleum Development Co Ltd* [1918] AC 485. (For a further case on this situation see [1918] AC 498.) For a further illustration of a suspension (but with a fine of £1,000) see *Shoreham-By-Sea UDC v Dolphin Canadian Proteins Ltd* (1973) 71 LGR 261.

16  War-time difficulties have been recognised: *Haigh v Deudraeth RDC* [1945] 2 All ER 661 (liberty to apply to extend the suspension was given at 664).

17  *Stollmeyer v Trinidad Lake Petroleum Co Ltd*, above n 15 at 497; *Manchester Corpn v Farnsworth*, above n 11 and the *Pride of Derby* case, above p 474 n 16 (at first instance: the appeal does not deal with this point). The court will usually have ordered D to pay damages for harm suffered by C up to the time of the judgment.

18  Cf the injunction with compensation paid to D discussed at pp 515-516 below.

19  *Frost v King Edward VII Welsh National Memorial Association* [1918] 2 Ch 180 at 195 and *Reinhardt v Mentasti* (1889) 42 Ch D 685 at 690 (D given three months 'to consider and do what is best under the circumstances').

## Anticipated harm

The quia timet (because he fears) action is for an injunction to prevent an apprehended legal wrong, before any has been committed, and thus before C has any remedy at law for damages.[20] It is obvious that a quia timet injunction carries with it a great danger of being oppressive, and the courts have rightly been extremely reluctant to grant one.[1] Obviously, the magnitude[2] and imminence[3] of the interference play a part in guiding the court, but, it is submitted, attempts to circumscribe the courts' discretion in other than self-evident ways have proven unhelpful, and should not be further pursued.[4] The power under Lord Cairns' Act to award damages in lieu of an injunction has the effect of conferring on the courts a power to award damages for apprehended harm.[5]

## Mandatory injunctions

A mandatory injunction requires D to take positive[6] action to abate a nuisance, eg by restoring support for C's land or buildings. As a mandatory injunction may easily impose particularly serious costs upon D, the courts exercise a real discretion when C asks for such an injunction,[7] and never grant it 'as of course'. The courts will attempt a cost-benefit analysis of the potential burden on D in comparison with the potential benefit to C.

---

20  *Torquay Hotel Co Ltd v Cousins* [1969] 2 Ch 106. *In Redland Bricks Ltd v Morris*, above p 469 n 6, C had already suffered harm, and so a cause of action had accrued, but the court granted a *quia timet* injunction because further harm was possible (ibid at 664). Of course, it is very often the case that further harm is a possibility, and were the reasoning of *Redland Bricks* generally accepted, this would have the pointless effect of making almost all injunctions quia timet: JA Jolowicz, 'Damages in Equity: A Study of Lord Cairns' Act' [1975] Cambridge Law Journal 224, pp 242–245. (See also PH Pettit, 'Lord Cairns' Act in the County Court: A Supplementary Note' [1977] Cambridge Law Journal 369 although the position causing the problem Pettit described is no longer law: see p 488 n 5 below). This is a procedural matter which it would be very unfortunate to allow to have an effect on the substantive law, and this, with respect, mistaken reasoning 'is probably best disregarded': *Clerk and Lindsell on Torts* (18th edn 2000) para 30-16.
1  *Litchfield-Speer v Queen Anne's Gate Syndicate (No 2) Ltd* [1919] 1 Ch 407.
2  *Redland Bricks Ltd v Morris*, p 469 n 6 at 665.
3  *Lemos v Kennedy Leigh Development Co Ltd* (1961) 105 Sol Jo 178.
4  *Hooper v Rogers* [1975] Ch 43. The development of an unhelpful pleonasm of synonyms and antonyms of 'imminent' was wisely halted by this case.
5  See pp 488–495 below.
6  The court will look to the substance, not the formal wording: *Jackson v Normanby Brick Co* [1899] 1 Ch 438. But the fact that D must *in practice* do something in order to comply with a prohibitory injunction does not make it mandatory.
7  *Isenberg v East India House Estate Co* (1863) 46 ER 637 at 641: 'Every one of this class of cases must depend upon its own peculiar circumstances'.

478 *Section 2 Tort: remedies for wrongdoing*

In *Redland Bricks Ltd v Morris*[8] the House of Lords laid down principles to guide the exercise of the court's discretion to grant a mandatory injunction. This power must 'be exercised sparingly and with caution'. C must show 'a very strong probability' that without it he will suffer 'grave damage' for which damages would be an inadequate remedy. The court should compare the cost to D of complying with the injunction and the value to C of that compliance: if the cost to D is out of all proportion to the advantage to C, no order should be made. In 'fairness to' D, the injunction must tell him 'exactly in fact what he has to do ... so that in carrying out an order he can give his contractors the proper instructions'. But the work ordered to be done may be designed 'merely [to] lessen the likelihood' of the harm to C.[9]

In *Redland Bricks* itself, although D's clay-digging operations had undermined support for C's adjoining property, the House of Lords allowed the appeal from the grant of a mandatory injunction that D 'take all necessary steps to restore the support to [C's] land within a period of six months'. The injunction 'imposed an unlimited and unqualified obligation' on D and, whilst it was not clear how he could have attempted to comply with it,[10] compliance could have cost up to £35,000, whereas the whole of C's eight acres was worth only £12,000, and the acre needing support only £1,500. Their Lordships emphasised that a refusal to grant a mandatory injunction would still leave C free to claim damages and/or an injunction if he actually suffered further harm.

## The legal criteria for the choice between injunction and damages

The criteria which the courts claim to use when deciding whether to award damages instead of an injunction are extremely vague and unsatisfactory. The basic reason why this is so is that this decision, like the decision whether or not a harm is a nuisance at all, has required a balance to be struck between the goals of respect for property rights and maximisation of social welfare. The courts have found it very hard to strike this balance, but it is not going too far to say that the difficulty of reconciling these goals has been the main problem of all economic policy formulation in liberal democratic society.

---

8   Above p 469 n 6 at 665–667.
9   An example is *Kennard v Cory Bros & Co Ltd* [1922] 1 Ch 265; affd [1922] 2 Ch 1.
10  Above p 469 n 6 at 667.

*Preference for prohibitory injunction*

In a society which respects private property, it is obviously a just and fair
goal to make the enjoyment of ownership as free as possible from
interference by others, and we have seen that the grant of a prohibitory
injunction was traditionally considered to be C's primary remedy for
private nuisance even if this could be said to impose social costs.[11] In the
nineteenth century, the judges asserted that protection of C's property
rights must prevail over any argument based on the public interest: only
Parliament could prefer the latter.[12] 'Neither has the circumstance that
the wrongdoer is in some sense a public benefactor (eg a gas or water
company or a sewer authority) ever been considered a sufficient reason
for refusing to protect by injunction an individual whose rights are being
persistently infringed.'[13] This attitude has broadly been maintained.[14] In
1953, the grounds for granting an injunction were set out in *Pride of Derby
and Derbyshire Angling Association Ltd v British Celanese Ltd,*[15] a case
in which the public interest in maintaining a city's sewerage system did
not prevent, as has been mentioned, an injunction prohibiting this
pollution in general terms being granted (although it did justify its
suspension). In the *Pride of Derby* case, a local authority's sewerage works
were polluting a river by discharging insufficiently treated effluent. The
Court of Appeal held that when C proves that his proprietary rights are
being wrongfully interfered with by D, who intends to continue his wrong,
C is prima facie entitled to an injunction. He 'will be deprived of that
remedy only if special circumstance exist, including the circumstance
that damages are an adequate remedy for the wrong that he has suffered'.[16]
But the court will examine the feasibility of D's compliance with the
injunction: 'the court will not impose on a local authority, or on anyone
else, an obligation to do something which is impossible, or which cannot
be enforced, or which is unlawful'.[17] As we have seen, the operation of
the injunction may also be suspended, as it often has been when made
against those maintaining a public service.

In prohibitory injunction cases, the courts' concern to protect
individual property rights obviously has outweighed their concern to
maximise social welfare. C's rights as occupier are protected despite some

---

11  AI Ogus and G Richardson, 'Economics and the Environment: A Study of Private
    Nuisance' [1977] Cambridge Law Journal 284, pp 317–25. ('Social costs' are
    described at pp 482-483, 485-486 below.)
12  *A-G v Birmingham Borough Council* (1858) 4 K and J 528 at 539–40.
13  *Shelfer v City of London Electric Lighting Co* [1895] 1 Ch 287 at 316.
14  Though see the discussion of *Miller v Jackson* at pp 482-484 below.
15  Above p 474 n 16.
16  Ibid at 181.
17  Ibid. See also ibid at 194.

cost in inefficiency in the terms of welfare economics, viz the goal of maximising the 'social cake' or the resources available for distribution. If this is done deliberately and openly, with full acknowledgement of the cost to society in terms of the reduction in the social cake, we should at least be aware of the trade-off between 'respect for property' and 'social efficiency'. But normally English judges have ignored the social cost of their decisions in these cases.

This may, of course, be something of an own goal as, in a law of nuisance based on give and take, it may stack up the arguments for refusing to find a nuisance in the first place. Fear of the draconian effect of granting an injunction may sometimes tip the scales when the judge is deciding whether D's interference is sufficiently serious to be labelled a nuisance. In the very disquieting *Allen v Gulf Oil Refining Co Ltd*,[18] C's case could not have been stronger, but it failed because the court feared the likely 'remarkable consequences' of finding a nuisance which would make C 'entitled (subject only to a precarious appeal to Lord Cairns' Act)[19] to an injunction [which] may make it impossible for [D's business] to be operated.'[20] It is pointless to insist that prohibitory injunctions must be granted to protect the sanctity of property rights if fear of the consequences of granting an injunction will lead to a finding that D did not commit a nuisance which denies C any remedy at all.[1]

### Discretion to confine C to damages

The traditional tests for choosing damages as an alternative to a prohibitory injunction are laid down in *Shelfer v City of London Electric Lighting Co*:[2] '(1) If the injury to [C's] legal rights is small; (2) and is one which is capable of being estimated in money; (3) and is one which can be adequately compensated by a small money payment; (4) and the case is one in which it would be oppressive to [D] to grant an injunction.' The word 'small' in (1) and in (3) clearly gives some discretion to the court, but the tests in (2) and (4) are unclear. The test in (2) is meaningless, since the courts have (for good or ill) always taken the view that they can make some estimate in money for any wrong, however intangible. The fourth test (whether an injunction would be 'oppressive') will be examined in more detail in a moment. The court is not bound to grant an injunction if one of the four tests is not met, because the court always retains a

---

18    [1981] AC 1001.
19    See pp 488-495 below.
20    Ibid at 1013.
1     But see pp 496-510 below.
2     Above p 479 n 13 at 322.

discretion,[3] but the tests in *Shelfer's* case have often been quoted in later judgments and are taken to constitute a 'working rule' guiding the court's decision to grant a prohibitory injunction.[4] *In nuce*, the rule is almost invariably to grant the injunction.[5]

## The cost of the injunction

The fourth *Shelfer* test, whether the injunction will be oppressive, requires an estimate of the costs it imposes. Two sorts of costs have been recognised: the costs to D and the social costs to the public.

In breach of contract cases, in deciding whether to grant literal enforcement instead of damages, the courts have been willing to compare the potential benefit to C with the potential cost to D. If the latter is out of all reasonable proportion to the former, C is left to his remedy in damages.[6] But when a prohibitory injunction is sought in nuisance cases the courts have repeatedly said that they ignore both the cost to D of complying with the injunction[7] and any other loss (eg loss of profits) which D may suffer. For instance, in 1877 an injunction was granted to C, whose expected harm was only £100 pa, whereas D said it would close his undertaking at a cost of £190,000.[8] In order to preserve the private rights of a few individuals – sometimes for a benefit which a reasonable third party would think of little value – the heavy cost of compliance has sometimes fallen on (council) tax payers or on the consumers of a public utility or on consumers generally. The judicial policy of avoiding social waste is not carried over to prohibitory nuisance cases because in the cases the courts continue to consider it more important to protect proprietary rights than mere contractual rights.

3   *Fishenden v Higgs & Hill Ltd* [1935] All ER Rep 435 at 444–445, 448–449, 453–454.
4   12(1) *Halsbury's Laws of England* (4th edn reissue 1998) para 1123.
5   The courts have traditionally refused injunctions to protect C's right to light if the interference has been relatively small and there is a risk that C would use the injunction to obtain an 'extortionate' payment from D as the price for agreeing not to enforce it. Many commentators therefore continue to treat 'the right to ancient lights' as a distinct doctrine; eg *Clerk and Lindsell on Torts*, above p 477 n 20, paras 19.97-19.104, and the phrase certainly occurs in modern cases. We would submit, however, that the two points at issue, the smallness of D's injury (under the first *Shelfer* test) and the possibility of extortion (see pp 492-494 below) should be considered on their merits, and that 'ancient lights' are involved should not of itself determine the outcome. We hesitantly suggest that this would indeed happen in a difficult case.
6   See pt 3 above.
7   *Pride of Derby* case, above p 474 n 16 at 180, 192, 194 and *Redland Bricks Ltd v Morris*, above p 469 n 6 at 664.
8   *Pennington v Brinsop Hall Coal Co* (1877) 5 Ch D 769. C also argued that 500 jobs would be lost, a social cost.

## Social costs and the public interest

The choice of remedy may affect third parties or the public at large by imposing what in welfare economics is called a 'social cost' if D's activity is regarded as being in the public interest. If D's activity is not merely of benefit to him but, incidentally, to third parties, it conveys what welfare economics has called a 'positive externality', being, it is claimed, a benefit to those parties which is the incidental or external effect of the economic relationship of C and D. Modifying an example which used to be commonly given in economics textbooks,[9] if D pays X to operate a lighthouse so that D's ships may navigate safely, D enjoys the benefit of the light at a cost 'internal' to his relationship with X. However, as the light is incidentally available to all shipping in the area, the light may benefit third parties with no legal interest in the provision of the light, who enjoy it as a positive externality. If C, whose sleep is disturbed by the light, obtains an injunction closing the lighthouse, its value will be lost not only to D but to the third parties; that is to say, its prohibition has an internal cost to D and a social cost to the third parties.

Recognition of a positive externality (though not employing the economic jargon) was decisive in *Miller v Jackson* (1977),[10] in which the Court of Appeal weighed C's proprietary interest against the sum of the interests both of D and of the community in the continuation of D's activity, gave greater weight to the latter and, dramatically reversing what we have seen was the formerly almost axiomatic position, denied C a prohibitory injunction. Occasionally, cricket balls hit from D's cricket ground landed in C's adjoining garden. Lord Denning MR emphasised the public interest in the playing of 'village cricket [which] is a delight to all'[11] and held that there was no nuisance: 'the public interest should prevail over the private interest'.[12] Geoffrey Lane LJ would have granted an injunction (suspended for 12 months so D could find another ground).[13]

9    And in one of the most influential British discussions of these issues: G Richardson et al, *Policing Pollution* (1983) p 7.
10    Above p 468 n 18.
11    Ibid. Nothing could be further from economic jargon than Lord Denning's lyric prose in the paragraph which is begun with this sentence, which 'echoes Beethoven's pastoral symphony': BS Markesinis and AM Tettenborn, 'Cricket, Power Boat Racing and Nuisance' (1981) 131 New Law Journal 108, p 108. Nevertheless, this case gave a very powerful stimulus to the argument that the welfare calculation it carried out should be extended to other British cases: eg S Tromans, 'Nuisance: Prevention or Payment?' [1982] Cambridge Law Journal 87. *Miller v Jackson* came just too late for proper consideration in what seems to be the best of the British works to this effect: Ogus and Richardson, 'Economics and the Environment: A Study of Private Nuisance', above p 479 n 11.
12    *Miller v Jackson*, above p 468 n 18 at 982.
13    Ibid at 987.

Cumming-Bruce LJ in effect decided the matter. Finding there to be a nuisance, he applied the 'balancing of interests' approach to the decision whether to grant the injunction, and, taking account of 'the interests of the inhabitants of the village as a whole',[14] he denied it on discretionary grounds, confining C to £400 damages for both past and future losses.

*Miller v Jackson* is therefore some authority for the view that the court may take some account of the potential hardship which an injunction would cause to third persons or to the public at large. But the 'new ground of public policy'[15] which it therefore seemed to open up was criticised as law at the outset,[16] and the case has been followed so hesitantly that it is now of very limited, if any, authority. More influential now[17] appears to be *Kennaway v Thompson*,[18] in which the public interest in encouraging sporting activities was not allowed to prevent an injunction being given, the Court of Appeal reversing the trial judge's refusal to grant an injunction on *Miller v Jackson* grounds. (That injunction was, however, formulated in terms which amounted to a compromise which was obviously influenced by the public interest: motor-boat racing was permitted to continue on a lake, subject to restrictions as to the number and duration of the club, national and international events to be held there each season, and as to the noise level of boats using the lake at any other time.)[19]

In cases where the amount of interference can be graduated, the choice of the court is not a stark one between an injunction or damages, but between damages and a variety of injunctions prohibiting various levels of interference and with an infinite variety of conditions attached to them.[20] The assertion that the courts will not consider the public interest

14 Ibid at 989. In addition, C himself was taking advantage of the open space provided by the cricket ground. An economic argument (not considered by the court: cf ibid at 981G) is that the price which C paid for the house four years previously would have reflected any diminution in the market value of the house if the average potential buyer would have considered it a disadvantage to have the cricket ground next door.

15 (1977) 93 Law Quarterly Review 481, p 483.

16 Ibid and RA Buckley, 'Cricket and the Law of Nuisance' (1978) 41 Modern Law Review 334, p 337. It does not help that that *Miller v Jackson* is perhaps the most blatant example of 'political bias' in a nuisance case. There can be no doubt that Lord Denning's personal history played a large part in forming his decision in that case, not least because he says so himself: Lord Denning, *Landmarks in the Law* (1984) p 370.

17 Markesinis and Deakin, *Tort Law*, above p 466 n 4, pp 445-449, nb p 447: 'The importance of *Kennaway* is that it reiterated the *Shelfer* principle in the face of recent tendencies to undermine it in favour of greater discretion'.

18 Above p 474 n 1.

19 See also *Dunton v Dover District Council*, above p 475 n 5.

20 But in *Tetley v Chitty* [1986] 1 All ER 663 the court simply prohibited all go-karting on D's land without attempting to detail a level of acceptable activity. D was told to apply to the court to vary or discharge the injunction if he could later produce an acceptable scheme: ibid at 675.

is partly circumvented by the suspension of the injunction or by the way in which a detailed injunction is formulated. If the courts are to exercise their discretion over the remedy in ways which are consistent with the legislative policy revealed in statutes protecting the environment or regulating town and country planning, they will be obliged to exercise their discretion in such a flexible manner.[1] It is arguable that should they fail to take account of the public interest in this it way would lead to more and more statutory intervention and a resulting further diminution in the role of nuisance law. Of course, the shortcomings of remedies for past harm when the nuisance is, ex hypothesi, continuing, make this difficult, and in this situation have led to the development of a more sophisticated form of damages which is discussed below.[2]

## Suspension of the injunction

The courts do not, then, usually consider a cost-benefit analysis to be appropriate when C seeks a prohibitory injunction, but they are prepared to do so when a mandatory injunction is sought. Although a prohibitory injunction usually requires D to *cease* causing an interference with C's use of his land, the difference that is being driven at, between having negatively to refrain from an act and having to carry out a positive act, is often only formal, and compliance with a prohibition could easily cost more than compliance with a mandatory injunction. In some situations the effects of the two injunctions are indistinguishable,[3] and in many other situations the only way in practice in which D can comply with a prohibitory injunction is by taking positive steps, often at considerable cost, to abate the nuisance. Even if D can avoid actual expenditure, it is a cost to him in economic terms if he must abandon an activity which, in the absence of the injunction, he would choose to engage in. The whole operation of D's factory could be closed by a prohibitory injunction,[4] or very expensive modifications to his equipment could be required to avoid closing down. It is submitted that the courts cannot justify weighing the potential costs to D against the potential benefit to C in the one situation but not the other: the difference is not one which goes to the substance or merits of the situation.

---

1    But see pp 496-510 below.
2    See pp 488-495.
3    In *Bracewell v Appleby* [1975] Ch 408 a prohibitory injunction against D using a right of way would, if granted, have made D's home uninhabitable, and this was found to be tantamount to a mandatory injunction to pull the house down: ibid at 416.
4    *Pennington v Brinsop Hall Coal Co*, above p 481 n 8.

A balancing operation can in fact be undertaken with equally satisfactory (or unsatisfactory) results in all cases by the adoption of the technique of suspending the injunction for a period to enable D to adjust his activity in order to comply, and we have seen that this palliative may be used in many situations.[5] Thus in a nuisance by pollution of water, the Privy Council held that D could not 'excuse or defend their wrong by showing how disproportionate is the loss which they will suffer' (in comparison with the benefit to C). But the court proceeded to say that these 'considerations may be relevant to the form of the remedy, especially to the time and opportunities which should be given them for finding some way out of their difficulty'.[6] When the Privy Council delayed the injunction by two years, it was motivated by exactly the same cost-benefit analysis as is conducted openly in claims for mandatory injunctions, the difference being only that in the one case the outcome is the suspension of the order, whereas in the other the order is refused but a price paid by D in the form of damages. The suspension of an injunction for a fixed period imposes costs on C as the necessary consequence of the court's attempt to help D to minimise the costs imposed on him. Since the suspension (especially if it is not conditional on any compensation to C for the period in question) is clearly an interference with C's property rights (although temporary), it is submitted that the court's willingness to use its discretion to balance the respective interests of the parties should not be restricted to this single method. If they are willing to suspend an injunction on the ground that the 'loss [to D] ... would be out of all proportion of [C's] gain'[7] they should be willing in the same circumstances to consider awarding damages in lieu; both methods involve some invasion of C's sacred rights of property.

### Private nuisance and environmental protection

The *Miller v Jackson* argument for recognition of the public interest could, of course, work the other way around. Whilst village cricket which is 'a delight to everyone' conveys a positive externality on those watching for free, D's activity may impose a 'negative externality' on third parties if his activity is, say, running a factory which produces noxious smoke.[8]

5   *Stollmeyer v Trinidad Lake Petroleum Co Ltd*, above p 476 n 15. Cf the suspension of injunctions against trespass to land discussed at pp 521-522 below.

6   Ibid at 494.

7   Ibid at 500.

8   Ogus and Richardson, 'Economics and the Environment: A Study of Private Nuisance', above p 479 n 11 and Richardson et al, *Policing Pollution*, above p 482 n 9, pt 1. Subsequent British application of the welfare economics of environmental pollution to law do not seem to have improved on these works.

If C obtains an injunction, the prevention of the smoke will convey an external benefit on third parties who previously suffered from the smoke but were not involved in the action. However, the action for private nuisance is only one of many instruments used to regulate environmental pollution, and, in the light of the expansion of state intervention in this area, it is now 'something of a residuary category'[9] of relatively little importance.[10] Other methods are: regulatory control based on the work of an inspectorate with statutory powers; planning controls; licensing of specified activities; health controls; tax incentives and disincentives; or restrictive covenants attached to land.[11] However, in the recent climate of growing dissatisfaction with public regulation, the possibility has been recently canvassed that private nuisance may play a larger role in environmental protection.[12] C's pursuit of an injunction might be of particular value where there is a large number of occupiers affected by D's interference.[13] If each C is likely to suffer only a small loss, he will not have sufficient incentive either to negotiate with D or to bring costly proceedings for an injunction. An injunction given to an individual C who can finance his own claim would benefit the other potential victims of D's activity. Any further extension of the role of private nuisance in environmental protection will require substantial shifts in the law of nuisance liability,[14] but, in relationship to the choice of remedy, it can be said that the public interest might point positively towards the granting of an injunction if public health is at risk, eg by smoke, fumes, noise or water pollution. But even this remedy may not be an effective way of protecting public health, inter alia because C may choose not to enforce the injunction where he can use it to exact a high price from D.

However, there have been interesting developments in the application of welfare economics to the law of utility regulation generally: R Baldwin and M Cave, *Understanding Regulation* (1999) pt 1 and AI Ogus, *Regulation* (1994) pt 1.

9    *Winfield and Jolowicz on Tort* (15th edn 1998) p 491.

10   T Weir, *A Casebook on Tort* (9th edn 2000) p 423: 'Those barons of the modern age, the local authorities, are the vigilantes of the environment: only in the rare case where the noisome activity is agreeable to local politicians, or the problem is too hot to handle does the private lawsuit really answer'.

11   S Bell and D McGillivray, *Environmental Law* (5th edn 2000). See further K Hawkins, *Environment and Enforcement* (1984); JPS McLaren, 'The Common Law Nuisance Actions and the Environmental Battle: Well-tempered Swords or Broken Reeds' (1972) 10 Osgoode Hall Law Journal 505; Richardson et al, *Policing Pollution*, above p 482 n 9 and J Steele, 'Private Law and the Environment: Nuisance in Context' (1995) 15 Legal Studies 236.

12   D McGillivray and J Wightman, 'Private Rights, Public Interests and the Environment', in T Hayward and J O'Neill (eds), *Justice, Property and the Environment* (1997) 144.

13   Eg *Hunter v Canary Wharf Ltd*, above p 466 n 4, discussed in Wightman, 'Nuisance: The Environmental Tort', above p 466 n 9.

14   See pp 496-510 below.

## Conduct of the parties

As an equitable remedy, an injunction will also only be granted if C's conduct is such as to make it equitable to do so.[15] In a number of cases, C's conduct has disbarred him from taking advantage of equity. One judge in *Shelfer's* case referred generally to 'cases where the plaintiff has so conducted himself as to render it unjust to give him more than pecuniary relief'.[16] D's conduct can also be of relevance. In a number of cases, that D has behaved in a civilised fashion in the course of a vexed dispute has inclined the court to allow him to continue with his activity; that is to say, to deny C an injunction. In particular, in cases involving rights to light, if D 'has acted fairly and not in an unneighbourly spirit ... the Court ought to incline to damages rather than to an injunction'.[17] This attitude could apply more widely than merely to cases of rights to light. In *Redland Bricks Ltd v Morris*, the court said that the balancing operation it was prepared to carry out in deciding whether to grant a mandatory injunction would not be conducted where D has acted 'wantonly and quite unreasonably' or 'without regard to his neighbour's rights or has tried to steal a march on him'[18] by rushing ahead before C could get the court to intervene. The fact that D 'did not act either wantonly or in plain disregard of C's rights[19] entitled the Court to ask whether it would be 'unreasonable' to impose this cost on D in order to confer on C the benefit of avoiding the 'anticipated possible damage'.[20] Similarly, a negligent failure to consider C's rights should be relevant.

Delay in seeking an injunction may disentitle C to that remedy (in terms of equity, he is guilty of laches or acquiescence) but damages may still be appropriate as a second-best remedy. Of course, as the harm is ex hypothesi continuing, achieving even a reasonable second-best remedy is difficult, and to this we now turn.

---

15  In *Miller and Jackson*, above p 468 n 18, the court's positive evaluation of the conduct of D (who 'have done everything possible short of stopping playing cricket on the ground at all': ibid at 977) and negative evaluation of the conduct of C ('the female plaintiff has [disclosed] a hostility which goes beyond what is reasonable': ibid at 989) clearly played some role in the refusal of an injunction.

16  *Shelfer's* case, above p 479 n 13 at 317. An illustration is *Fishenden v Higgs and Hill Ltd*, above p 481 n 3 at 448–50. On rights to light see p 481 n 5 above.

17  *Colls v Home and Colonial Stores Ltd* [1904] AC 179 at 193.

18  *Redland Bricks Ltd v Morris*, above p 469 n 6 at 666. See also *Woodhouse v Newry Navigation Co* [1898] 1 IR 161.

19  *Redland Bricks Ltd v Morris*, above p 469 n 6 at 663. D had in fact employed engineers and a geologist to advise him.

20  Ibid at 666.

## Damages in lieu of an injunction

If D's activity is found to be a nuisance which D intends to continue but C is refused an injunction, giving C damages for harm he has suffered up to the time of the hearing may be a very poor remedy. If D obtains a profit from his activity which is greater than his liability in damages, then D obviously has an incentive to continue with the nuisance by paying for it, for even if C were repeatedly awarded damages, D would repeatedly make a profit. D therefore might think that damages for harm caused to C are a small price to pay if the interference is the result of a highly profitable activity on his land. But in *Shelfer's* case and in innumerable other cases, it has been urged that D should not be able to continue his nuisance 'because ... he is able and willing to pay for the injury he may inflict'.[1] It is not merely that in a series of actions for damages for the harm suffered up to date in each C would have to incur a vast expenditure of costs proving his case each time,[2] but that this expenditure would not even properly protect C's interest if he were confined to damages for past harm. Damages exclusively for past harm are appropriate when coupled to a resolve by C and the court to prevent future harm, but as the sole remedy for a nuisance likely to continue or be repeated, it is hard to imagine the circumstances in which they could be other than 'futile'.[3] Where the court is extremely reluctant to award an injunction despite the blatant inadequacy of common law damages for past harm, it is as well to consider whether a superior basis on which damages might be quantified could be devised.[4] As common law damages are unsatisfactory, one might consider the further possibility of equitable relief in lieu of an injunction, and the power to give this exists under what, in the context of nuisance cases, continues generally to be referred to as an award of damages under Lord Cairns' Act.

Damages could not be awarded by the Court of Chancery, in which equitable relief had to be sought, until 1858, when the power to do so was granted by s 2 of the Chancery Amendment Act 1858, known as Lord Cairns' Act. The power is now given by s 50 of the Supreme Court Act 1981: 'Where the ... High Court[5] has jurisdiction to entertain an application for an injunction or specific performance, it may award

---

1    Above p 479 n 13 at 315-316.
2    *Pride of Derby* case, above p 475 n 8 at 181–2 (see also 194). Of course, if his action is successful, C would recover a substantial part of his legal (but not other) costs. Nevertheless, D might well be able to take advantage of C's lack of stamina in regularly initiating litigation to claim for loss up to date.
3    *Leeds Industrial Co-operative Society Ltd v Slack* [1924] AC 851 at 859.
4    Jolowicz, 'Damages in Equity: A Study of Lord Cairns' Act', above p 477 n 20.
5    This power is extended to the County Court under the Courts and Legal Services Act 1990, s 3.

damages in addition to, or in substitution for, an injunction or specific performance.' This provision empowers the court to award equitable damages[6] in situations not covered by common law, and, of particular interest here, for a threatened injury, where no harm has yet been suffered, in lieu of a quia timet injunction;[7] or for future losses.[8] Section 50 is not confined to cases where C is prima facie entitled to an injunction or specific performance.[9] So long as the facts justify the court in exercising its general equitable discretion to choose the appropriate remedy, it may award damages under the section, despite a ruling that C is not, on the facts, entitled to an injunction.[10] (To read the Act so that the court can award damages in lieu only when it *should* award an injunction leads to absurdity: it makes the power to award damages redundant.) If the court 'could have ... however unwisely' made an order, it has jurisdiction to award damages.[11]

The section, by its wording, confers a wide discretion on the court, but in exercising this discretion, the court must take the following into account. The award of equitable damages in lieu of an injunction amounts to a compulsory grant by the court of permission to D to continue the interference of which C has complained. C (and his successors in title) have no future claim for any further harm, but must tolerate the interference so long as it does not exceed the type or extent established in the judgment. Since the judgment takes the place of a voluntary grant of permission in a contract or easement, it should, on the one hand, provide all the details necessary to clarify exactly what D is entitled to do, and, on the other hand, it must deal with C's claim (if any) on the 'future' benefit which D will enjoy through that entitlement.[12] This is to say, in fixing the damages in lieu of an injunction, the court is fixing the price for granting the

6   This term is used by the Court of Appeal in *Hooper v Rogers*, above p 477 n 4 at 47. See further PM McDermott, *Equitable Damages* (1994).

7   *Leeds Industrial Co-operative Society Ltd v Slack*, above p 488 n 3 at 857–8 and *Hooper v Rogers*, above p 477 n 4.

8   It has recently been held that awarding damages for future loss is compatible with the Human Rights Act 1998: *Marcic v Thames Water Utilities Ltd (No 2)* [2001] 4 All ER 326 at paras 15-16 (for the facts and earlier hearing of this case see p 439 n 18 and p 499 n 5 below).

9   *Elmore v Pirrie* (1887) 57 LT 333.

10  *City of London Brewery Co v Tennant* (1873) 9 Ch App 212 at 219; *Colls v Home and Colonial Stores Ltd* [1904] AC 179 at 193; *Bracewell v Appleby*, above p 484 n 3 at 419; *Jaggard v Sawyer* [1995] 1 WLR 269 at 285 and *Marcic v Thames Water Utilities Ltd (No 2)*, above n 8 at para 11.

11  *Hooper v Rogers*, above p 477 n 4 at 48. The parties need not plead the Act: *Betts v Neilson* (1868) 3 Ch App 429 at 441. Cf *Redland Bricks Ltd v Morris*, above p 469 n 6 at 665).

12  Once D has paid damages under Lord Cairns' Act, his future position can be safeguarded by an endorsement on the title deeds of both sides: *Crawford v Hornsea Steam Brick and Tile Co Ltd* (1876) 45 LJ Ch 432.

permission. Although in some earlier cases courts had spoken of damages being assessed to include both the past harm suffered by C and the harm to be expected in the future,[13] it is submitted that this must be the wrong approach since the court is imposing a 'sale' on C. If these damages are possibly to be a plausible remedy, the thinking has to be of a 'price' for 'hypothetical release' from the injunction which might have been granted, rather than of compensation for loss as usually understood. It has been argued that 'compensation' should include the lost opportunity to bargain for this price.[14] In awarding damages in lieu of an injunction, the court is, in effect, granting D the permission to continue the nuisance, but fixing a price to be paid to C for that permission.

That the price of hypothetical release is the proper form of equitable damages has been argued in a line of cases from *Wrotham Park Estate Co Ltd v Parkside Homes Ltd*.[15] The 'release' was from a restrictive covenant in *Wrotham Park* itself, and in the limited number of other cases, the 'releases' were from a range of obligations. In one of the very few nuisance cases, *Carr-Saunders v Dick McNeil Associates Ltd*,[16] damages for the loss of an hypothetical opportunity to bargain for release from an injunction which would have prevented construction which interfered with the right to light of C's residence were granted under Lord Cairns' Act as interpreted in *Wrotham Park*. The court estimated the sum which C might have accepted in a negotiated bargain as the price for his loss of amenity and for allowing D to make the profit which he (D) expected to make from developing his site. The *Carr-Saunders* case has, to our knowledge, been followed twice in the county court,[17] but on the only occasion where it has been considered by the Court of Appeal, that court refused to follow it. In *Stoke-on-Trent City Council v WJ Wass Ltd*,[18] D defied an injunction to hold a rival market to C's,[19] but as this caused C no loss, only nominal damages were awarded.[20] However, this case[1] is of

---

13   *Isenberg v East India House Estate Co*, above p 477 n 7; *Fishenden v Higgs and Hill Ltd*, above p 481 n 3 at 443–6, 448–50; *Hooper v Rogers* above n 84 and *Miller v Jackson*, above p 468 n 18.

14   See pp 257-258 above.

15   [1974] 1 WLR 798. See further ch 17 above.

16   [1986] 1 WLR 922.

17   *Marine and General Mutual Life Assurance Society v St James Real Estate Co* [1991] 2 EGLR 178 and *Deakins v Hookings* [1994] 1 EGLR 190.

18   Above p 470 n 17.

19   Which was held to be a (statutory) nuisance, though no great weight was placed on this point: ibid at 1410G.

20   At first instance C had been awarded the cost of the licence D would have had to obtain from C to make his (D's) market lawful. But, of course, this presumably amounted only to a fraction of D's profit (or else why would D hold the market?), and so was not complete or even substantial disgorgement.

1   And *Deakins v Hookings*, above n 17 at 195-196, which followed *Carr-Saunders v Dick McNeil Associates Ltd*.

unclear authority for it is, with respect, inextricably confused. Its argument for departing from the diminution in value measure was considered in terms of the 'user principle' (that C had a consumer surplus), when disgorgement of an unjust enrichment (an argument about D's position) was sought.[2]

The law is, it is submitted, most unsatisfactory. Any future influence that the *Carr-Saunders* case may have will depend on the way that *Wrotham Park* damages in general are developed after *A-G v Blake*,[3] which is an extremely vexed question turning principally on arguments for the expansion of restitution as the foundation of the entire law of obligations.[4] In terms of general restitutionary principle, there would appear to be no reason why, if hypothetical release damages are taken to be restitutionary, they could not be extended to nuisance cases, and in particular it would easily avoid the problems posed by *Surrey County Council v Bredero Homes Ltd*[5] as nuisance can be seen as a proprietary interest. If these damages are put on a restitutionary basis, they should in theory be available as of right, but the effect this would have on the court's formerly explicit discretion to grant these damages under Lord Cairns' Act is impossible to predict.

There are two good reasons which can be given for the courts' evident reluctance in nuisance cases to use the power under Lord Cairns' Act: the problem of quantification and the problem of expropriation, and to these we now turn.

### Quantification

It has proven impossible to calculate the price of a hypothetical bargain with any certainty. In his commendably frank remarks in *Carr-Saunders v Dick McNeil Associates Ltd*, Millett J conceded that when carrying out such a calculation he was merely speculating.[6] Total disgorgement of D's profit would be relatively certain, but would, presumably, prevent the nuisance, and this contradicts the point of awarding the damages in lieu rather than an injunction in the first place. From the perspective of D and of C who is prepared to countenance permitting the nuisance for a price, total disgorgement would actually be worse than even a prohibitory injunction, for D may be able to buy out an injunction at a price which

2   See p 470.
3   [2001] 1 AC 268.
4   See ch 17 above.
5   [1993] 1 WLR 1361. These problems may, as a matter of doctrine at least, have been eliminated by *A-G v Blake*: see pp 258-262 below.
6   Above p 490 n 16 at 930-932.

still leaves his nuisance-making activity profitable,[7] but total disgorgement would prevent this.[8] This makes apportionment essential, and no principled basis for apportionment has emerged in the nuisance cases or in restitution more widely; nor, it is submitted, is there a way in which it can.[9] Something of the quality of the quantifications that have been attempted is conveyed by the fact that in the *Carr-Saunders* case the 'disgorgement' was calculated without any evidence of the profit D expected to make![10] This would be amazing were such arbitrariness not perfectly typical of the hypothetical release cases.

One aspect of the way the courts have sought to control the influence of their decisions on actual out of court negotiations in nuisance cases has had an important impact on the grant of *Wrotham Park* damages in such cases. English judges clearly recognise that C's claim for an injunction often arises from a breakdown in negotiations, and that the award of an injunction will often lead to negotiations in which C will fix his own price for agreeing to release D from the injunction. Judicial statements openly acknowledge that an injunction may in this way put C into a strong bargaining position. When a mandatory injunction has been sought, the courts accordingly have been particularly concerned with the effect of the injunction on subsequent negotiations. The older cases use the word 'extortionate' when referring to the demand which C, armed with a mandatory injunction, could make of D in post-injunction negotiations. For example, in 1863, Westbury LC said that it is 'the duty of the Court in such a case as the present not, by granting a mandatory injunction, to deliver over the Defendants to the Plaintiff bound hand and foot, in order to be made subject to any extortionate demand that he may by possibility make [but rather to grant damages]'.[11] On the other hand, it appears to be no objection to the award of a prohibitory injunction (at least in a nuisance case) that C intends to use it as a bargaining chip,[12] and does not intend to enforce it unless D refuses to pay C's price. In the case of the prohibitory injunction, the ability of C to fix his own price usually is not seen as extortionate, but rather as a legitimate exercise of a major right deriving from ownership/occupation.

Yet, as has been argued, the difference between a mandatory and a prohibitory injunction can hardly be treated as hard and fast.[13] If one looks

---

7    See pp 500-501 below.
8    Unless the parties come to some far-fetched arrangement about what to do with the damages, in contradiction of the arguments needed to get the damages in the first place.
9    See pp 268-272 above.
10   Ibid at 931G.
11   *Isenberg v East India House Estate Co Ltd*, above p 477 n 7 at 641.
12   But in *Shelfer's* case, above p 479 n 13 at 317, one judge said equitable damages might be given in 'cases in which a plaintiff has shown that he only wants money'.
13   See pp 484-485 above.

at the substance rather than the form, one finds situations in which
prohibitory injunctions give a great deal of power to C, and the courts
have sometimes responded to this. As we have seen, some expropriation
is involved in their regular practice of suspending an injunction, even
where compensation is paid to C for the period of suspension; and that
period is sometimes a matter of many months, or even years. In cases in
which a prohibitory injunction has been sought to protect a right to light,
the courts traditionally have refused the injunctions because there is a
risk that C would use the injunction as a means of 'extorting money' from
D as the price for agreeing not to enforce a right which has 'never before
been considered of any great value'.[14]

Mandatory    injunctions    (or    prohibitory    injunctions    of
indistinguishable effect)[15] have been at issue in many of the *Wrotham
Park* cases, including *Wrotham Park* itself, and in them the court has both
refused the injunction and been anxious to avoid giving C damages which
would fully reflect the advantageous bargaining position into which the
injunction would have placed him.[16] In *Wrotham Park*, D made £50,000
from a development in breach of a restrictive covenant, but the court
estimated the cost of the release to be 5% of that profit and awarded
£2,500.[17] It no doubt is ill-advised to try to draw a conclusion from a
county court judgment which is one of (to our knowledge) but three[18]
nuisance cases in which *Wrotham Park* damages have been given in lieu
of a mandatory injunction, but *Deakins v Hookings*,[19] a right to light case
which followed *Carr-Saunders v Dick McNeil Associates Ltd*,[20] is at least
solidly argued. In that case, the county court was extremely anxious to

14  *Colls v Home and Colonial Stores Ltd* [1904] AC 179 at 193.
15  See p 484 n 3 above.
16  Above p 490 n 15 at 815 ('the court ought ... to act with great moderation'.) See
    also the easement case *Bracewell v Appleby*, above p 484 n 3 at 416 (an injunction
    'would put the plaintiffs into an unassailable bargaining position').
17  *Wrotham Park Estate Co Ltd v Parkside Homes Ltd*, above p 490 n 15 at 815-
    816.
18  In *Marcic v Thames Water Utilities Ltd (No 2)*, above p 489 n 8 damages were
    awarded in lieu of a mandatory injunction but were calculated on a variant of the
    *Wrotham Park* basis. D, a water undertaker under the Water Industry Act 1991,
    refused to effect repairs to a drain which caused flooding to C's home. Major
    works were required to which D gave very low priority on its list of required
    works, and this failure to repair was found to contravene the Human Rights Act
    1998 (see p 499 n 5 below). Damages were to be calculated as the difference
    between the value of D's property without the repairs and that value *at the date
    in the future* when the repairs should have been completed: ibid at para 18. This
    novel quantification was called a 'diminution in value' measure (ibid at para 8),
    but it is, of course, neither diminution in value as normally understood nor
    *Wrotham Park* damages as previously understood. *Marcic* is a decision of the
    Technology and Construction Court against which an appeal has been lodged,
    and a longer discussion of this case at this time would be premature.
19  Above p 490 n 17.
20  Above p 490 n 16.

avoid 'a ransom situation', and gave £4,500 when D had made £30,000 from the nuisance. It is impossible to tell how generous or otherwise the court was in the *Carr-Saunders* case itself,[1] but one suspects that (part of) an award of £8,000 which was to effect disgorgement of part of the profit to be made by adding two storeys to a commercial building in Covent Garden in the 1980s was a modest award.

The other nuisance case which has followed the *Carr-Saunders* case in the county court is *Marine and General Mutual Life Assurance Society v St James Real Estate Co.*[2] It would appear that, though another right to light case, this concerned a prohibitory injunction. However, it is not this that seems to have led to what in one sense was a most generous award of £18,000 in which the element of 'compensation' for hypothetical release must have played a major part.[3] Though D's expected profit is once again not reported in a purported disgorgement case, the court had evidence of an agreement by which D had paid £25,000 to a third party in a very similar situation to C, so that the third party would allow D to continue the nuisance. This influenced the court very heavily. It is submitted that nothing like this sum would have been awarded under *Wrotham Park* in the absence of this evidence, which again rather counts against the certainty of *Wrotham Park* damages. As by granting damages for hypothetical release the court militates against negotiations for actual release,[4] the wider use of *Wrotham Park* damages presumably will tend to make it less likely that this sort of solid evidence will be available in future.

### Expropriation

The second problem with having recourse to Lord Cairns' Act is that it is a judicially approved expropriation of part of the normal rights of the occupier, C. Where C is not willing to give any permission to D at all, it is arguable that C should be protected by an injunction, if he so wishes. Judges seem here to be influenced by the distributional effects of their nuisance decisions – who will get a larger slice of the social cake as a result of the particular decision? If a decision to award equitable damages would increase D's slice, but this is perceived to be at the expense of diminishing C's already small slice, the courts may prefer to protect C's

1    See pp 491-492 above.
2    Above p 490 n 17.
3    The servient property 'received only limited light: it was typical of many central London properties in not relying upon daylighting for beneficial use of the accommodation', and expert testimony placed C's loss at between zero and £6,375.
4    See pp 500-505 above.

existing slice by an injunction. But if the interference is of a type and extent which most occupiers would be willing to sell at a reasonable price,[5] the courts should, whilst nuisance liability is based on give and take, consider the wider use of equitable damages.

For the use of equitable damages in situations where simple damages for past harm are not adequate may have the effect of increasing the number of cases in which a nuisance remedy is used. We have noted that fear of the effect of granting an injunction may induce the court not to find a nuisance at all,[6] and the decision to award equitable damages makes it easier for the court to find that the interference did deserve some sort of remedy for future harm (as damages for past harm would not serve the purpose).[7] In *Miller v Jackson*, Cumming-Bruce LJ clearly was unsure whether his refusal of the (suspended) injunction proposed by Geoffrey Lane LJ was correct.[8] One suspects that D's being prepared to pay 'past and future damages' which were assessed at £400 although the trial judge, who had granted the injunction, assessed past damages at only £150,[9] will have inclined Cumming-Bruce LJ to grant the injunction.

However, the judicial discretion to award equitable damages is not able to deal *directly* with situations where D's activity benefits the community. The damages are paid only by D, whereas the appropriate response might be that they should be paid by the community which benefits from D's activity. It is accepted in the modern world that, subject to proper enquiry and to the payment of adequate compensation, expropriation of private property may be justified.[10] But there is no regular machinery to enable the public interest to be represented before the court in a case of private nuisance[11] and the courts would require statutory powers to make the (council) tax payer pay a 'price' as compensation to C when the refusal to grant an injunction was for the public benefit. *Explicit* expropriation at public expense is not a common law power vested in the judges.

---

5  And which D would wish to buy. Since the award of equitable damages assumes that D wishes to continue the activity causing the interference, no award should be made unless the court is confident that D does wish it to give him permission at a price fixed by it. (It may sometimes be cheaper for D simply to cease his activity on that site.)

6  See pp 479–480 above.

7  JA Jolowicz, 'Should Courts Answer Questions? Does Statutory Authority to Build Confer Immunity From Liability for Use? [1981] Cambridge Law Journal 226, pp 228–229 and Tromans, 'Nuisance: Prevention or Payment?' above p 482 n 11, p 108

8  *Miller v Jackson*, above p 468 n 18 at 969.

9  Ibid at 970-971, 982D. The reasoning behind the £400 figure is not given.

10  GM Erasmus, *Compensation for Expropriation* (1990).

11  The role of the Attorney-General in cases of public nuisance could be taken as a precedent.

## Interference and the problem of social cost

In the discussion of remedies for nuisance up to this point, the basis of
liability, and particularly the give and take approach, have been assumed
and such evaluations of the remedies as have been put forward have been
of them as remedies within this framework of liability. These evaluations
have tended to lead to the conclusion that the courts' discretion to weigh
up the appropriate remedy must be expanded because consistency with
the give and take test of liability demands this. However, an overall
evaluation of these remedies cannot be undertaken on this basis, for the
axiomatic assumption that nuisance liability must be decided on the give
and take basis has been called into the most serious question in the US
'law and economics' literature, and any competent contemporary
understanding of nuisance remedies must involve a grasp of the arguments
that have been made following the appearance of Ronald Coase's seminal
article on 'The Problem of Social Cost'.[12] A direct exposition of those
arguments, particularly as their British reception has been markedly weak,
is inappropriate in a work of this nature.[13] What follows is a discussion of
the English law of private nuisance which draws on those arguments.

### The position under the current liability rule

When a harm is held, on the give and take principle, not to be a nuisance,
this does not make the harm disappear; it is merely placed in a general,
imprecise category of the costs of social existence for which the law gives

12   (1960) 3 Journal of Law and Economics 1; reprinted in RH Coase, *The Firm, the
Market and the Law* (1988) 95. See the appendix to this chapter for a reading list
of the principal works. The best single commentary is SG Medema, *Ronald H
Coase* (1994) ch 4.
13   The basic mistake that has been made is to think that law and economics works
are committed to the dogma that a 'property rights' or 'market' based solution to
environmental harms will always produce optimal outcomes, and, as this is a
ridiculous belief, to dismiss the argument of 'The Problem of Social Cost', either
after proper consideration (eg P Burrows, 'Nuisance, Legal Rules and Decentralised
Decisions: A Different View of the Cathedral Crypt', in P Burrows and C
Veljanovski (eds), *The Economic Approach to Law* (1981) 151), or even out of
hand (eg Tromans, 'Nuisance: Prevention or Payment?' above p 482 n 11, p 104).
(See also p 504 n 17 below.) Though there are some law and economics works
which do subscribe to this dogma, it cannot be attributed to the law and economics
represented by Coase: D Campbell, 'On What is Valuable in Law and Economics'
(1996) 8 Otago Law Review 489, pp 496-505 and D Campbell, 'Of Coase and
Corn: A (Sort of) Defence of Private Nuisance' (2000) 63 Modern Law Review
197, pp 199-210. The confusion is confounded because the best known law and
economics scholar, RA Posner, subscribes to a view of the matter itself radically
opposed to Coase's: ibid, pp 206-210.

no remedy under the maxim '*damnum absque injuria*'.[14] There is a
tendency to think of these harms as de minimis, and one suspects that this
is one of the reasons why (of all the balances that have been struck) it is
rights of prospect that are so often cited as the example of *damnum absque
injuria* in nuisance cases.[15] But, of course, there is no need for these harms
to be de minimis, and, indeed, every reason to think that a harm which C
bothers to bring to court is not. The recent citation of *damnum absque
injuria* by Lord Lloyd in *Hunter v Canary Wharf Ltd* is a perfect example
of the thinking at work:

> The house owner who has a fine view of the South Downs may find
> that his neighbour has built so as to obscure his view. But there is
> no redress unless, perchance, the neighbour's land was subject to a
> restrictive covenant in the house owner's favour. It would be a good
> example of what in law is called '*damnum absque injuria*': a loss
> which the house owner undoubtedly has suffered, but which gives
> rise to no infringement of his legal rights.[16]

Because, inter alia, 'the analogy between a building with a view and a
building which interferes with television reception seems to me ... to be
very close', Lord Lloyd refused to find the construction of a building
which caused such extreme interference as to make it impossible for
hundreds of people living in the electromagnetic shadow of the building
to watch the BBC to be a nuisance.

It is submitted that the analogy between expropriation and a refusal to
find a nuisance in this case, and in the majority of nuisance cases, is at
least as close. Whilst in the final analysis one's views about the scope of
the tort of nuisance, and about the desirability of modifying the remedies
for it, will depend on one's own political and social philosophy, it is
submitted that it simply is a fact[17] that in cases of harm which are not
classified as a nuisance, C's amenity and the value of his occupation are
diminished by D but D does not have to pay for doing this. Despite
innumerable dicta traceable at least to Blackstone of which *Bamford v*

---

14  *Broom's Legal Maxims*, above p 467 n 14, p 120: 'a damage is sustained, but a
damage not occasioned by anything which the law esteems an injury'. See further
ibid, p 123.

15  Despite a right of prospect not being part of the *sic utere* rule: see p 467 n 15
above.

16  *Hunter v Canary Wharf Ltd*, above p 466 n 4 at 699. This drawing of this analogy
was commended in *Salmond and Heuston on the Law of Torts*, above p 472 n 10,
pp 58-59.

17  As a nuisance judgment defines the extent of C's right against interference, it is
logically possible to argue that there is no expropriation for there never was a
right against interference in excess of that defined in the judgment. Whilst this
would be correct were rights being defined on a *tabula rasa*, in cases involving
existing properties this is an unworthy argument.

*Turnley* (1862) is one example,[18] that the infliction of loss without compensation, albeit in the public interest, is unacceptable expropriation, it is arguable that this is the essence of private nuisance liability. The same argument applies, though typically with less force, when a nuisance is found but C is denied an injunction (or the injunction is qualified and/ or suspended), for even if C receives past harm and/or hypothetical release damages, these will compensate only partially, and leave a margin of expropriation.

The principal concrete reason given why nuisance liability is decided on a give and take basis rather than by adherence to the *sic utere* maxim[19] is that the latter would prevent economic growth. Taking this maxim to mean that D is under a strict if not absolute liability for any interference, then the spirit of the 'reasonable use' at the core of the English law of private nuisance is as it was expressed in *Hole v Barlow* (1858):

> It is not everybody whose enjoyment of life and property is rendered uncomfortable by the carrying on of an offensive or noxious trade in the neighbourhood that can bring an action. If that were so ... the ... great manufacturing towns of England would be full of persons bringing actions for nuisances arising from the carrying on of noxious or offensive trades in their vicinity, to the great injury of the manufacturing and social interests of the community.[20]

If this argument is accepted, then, in a very important sense, nuisance is *not* a system of expropriation because C, by sharing in the general benefits of economic development, receives indirect, general compensation for the harm he suffers in the particular case. The principal legitimation of government intervention is theoretical compensation under the various criteria devised in welfare economics.[1] Calculations of the social costs and the social benefits of an activity are made, the argument being that if the latter is greater than the former, then the activity should be undertaken[2] to maximise social welfare, for it is possible

18  Blackstone, *Commentaries*, i, 35 and *Bamford v Turnley*, above p 467 n 14 at 33. One of many modern affirmations was provided in *Shelfer's* case, above p 479 n 13 at 316: 'Expropriation, even for a money consideration, is only justifiable when Parliament has sanctioned it'.

19  Above p 467 n 14.

20  Above p 467 n 14 at 1114. See also *A-G v Doughty* (1752) 28 ER 290.

1   The most important is the 'Kaldor-Hicks' criterion derived from the work of Sir John Hicks and Sir Nicholas Kaldor: see FH Stephen, *The Economics of the Law* (1975) pp 57-62.

2   In 'undertaken' we mean to include both the direct provision of 'public goods' by public bodies and the clearing away by the state of obstacles to private investment. The role of the state in clearing away such obstacles to the private construction of the railway, and its environmental effects, is an extremely

theoretically to compensate those harmed by the activity out of the increase in overall welfare and still have a margin of increased welfare.[3] Though some compensation may well be paid to those harmed by these activities, it is *hypothetical* compensation that is the basis of the legitimacy of planned solutions in government policy in this area. No actual direct compensation need take place and it is important to see that any that is paid must be less than an agreed sale price. A 'compulsory' purchase at absolutely 'full' compensation, ie a price at which the owner wished to sell, is not compulsory at all, it is an agreement to sell. In nuisance cases, the sometimes terribly complicated mathematical techniques of welfare economics are replaced by recourse to the judge's assessment of what is, on balance, a reasonable use, but the effect of the two reasoning processes is much the same.[4] Nuisance law and planning are both systems by which permission may be given to those who wish to undertake an activity which will cause interference (including environmental harm), the permission typically eschewing or reducing the direct payment of those harmed. They do this because it is thought to be of overall social benefit that the activity takes place without its promoter having to bear the costs of securing actual agreement to his doing so.[5]

---

instructive study: see Campbell, 'Of Coase and Corn: A (Sort of) Defence of Private Nuisance', above p 469 n 13, pp 207-208 (and references therein) and AWB Simpson, *Victorian Law and the Industrial Spirit* (1994).

3 An example: let us assume a project has a social cost of 10 units, of which 5 units are actual costs and 5 units are the harm to some citizens. Let us further assume that the project yields a gross social benefit of 15 units. It should be undertaken as it leads to a net social improvement of 5 units, both items of social cost being amortised, including the 5 units of harm which are 'compensated' from the 15 units of gross benefit.

4 It is quite wrong of Simpson to argue that the courts do not do this because they do it so quickly as it hardly seems that they do it at all: AWB Simpson, *Leading Cases in the Common Law* (1995) pp 193-194. A decision is a decision however quickly it is made, though one suspects that a very quick decision may be a bad one.

5 In *Marcic v Thames Water Utilities Ltd* [2001] 3 All ER 698 (for the facts see p 493 n 18 above) D was not found liable in nuisance at common law or under statute but was held to have contravened The Human Rights Act 1998, s 6(1) in respect of Sch 1, art 8 (respect for private and family life and home) and Sch 1, pt 2, art 1 (protection of property). The Human Rights Act allows interference with these rights in the public interest, which in this case would have required D 'to strike a fair balance between the competing interests of [C] and ... other customers of [D], allowing [D] a margin of discretion': ibid at 732. In this case, it was held that D had not discharged the burden of justifying the low priority it gave to the works C wished to have carried out, which relegated those works to an indefinite future. However, it would appear certain that the give and take test (carried out by bodies carrying out public functions or by the courts) will be preserved under the Human Rights Act (albeit in a new terminology). Such change as there will be once the inevitable flurry of litigation in this area is over will be, it is submitted, to place a greater onus on bodies carrying out public functions to be able to show paper trail for their decisions.

## A defence of strict liability

Even from the perspective of those who welcome economic growth and who are prepared to countenance the possibility of expropriation in the public interest,[6] the legitimacy of these systems of permission is called into question when it is realised that the *sic utere*[7] rule would not necessarily prevent such growth, and the self-evident connection between the inevitability of reciprocal harms and the adoption of the give and take rule is realised to be a non-sequitur. Even if D was liable for all harm he caused[8] and C would of right be given an injunction against him, this does not mean, so long as the injunction is C's alienable private right as it is in private nuisance, that D would have to cease the harmful activity. The alienability of the private right gives a crucial potential flexibility to the working of the strict liability regime.[9] Leaving aside the possibility of abatement by D and the possibility of D buying the whole of C's interest in the land affected by the nuisance, both of which would terminate D's liability to C, D could pay C to release him from the injunction. If C values his freedom from interference more than he values the payment D will make for relaxation of the injunction, he will enforce the injunction. If D values the activity which causes the harm enough to be willing to pay C enough to relax the injunction, the activity will take place. (The parties could, of course, negotiate such detailed terms for and/or suspension of the injunction and its combination with damages as they wish.) The *sic utere* rule would not necessarily prevent the harm but would mean that D

6   It is, however, argued by staunch libertarians, whose views are a form of right-wing or conservative anarchism in this respect, that in the long run 'social welfare' will be enhanced by protecting certain private rights without conducting a cost-benefit analysis of the immediate situation of the parties. The occupier's freedom from indirect expropriation by a nuisance is a 'public good' contributing to social welfare generally, inter alia because of the high value which people place on the knowledge that their property rights are sacrosanct.

7   Above p 467 n 14.

8   The definition of harm, or the specification of recognised harms, would remain an essential and extremely difficult task for the law of nuisance, and in particular an analogue to the causation problems raised by the distinction between *The Polemis* and *The Wagon Mound* (see pp 310-318 above) would remain: see HLA Hart and T Honoré *Causation in the Law* (2nd edn 1985) pp lxvii-lxxvii. One cannot conceive that this definition could or should be attempted on anything other than a legislative basis: *Cambridge Water Co v Eastern Counties Leather Plc*, above n 19 at 305E; see further *Report of the Royal Commission on Civil Liability and Compensation for Personal Injury* (Chair: Lord Pearson) Cmnd 7054 (1978) paras 1643-1651. Two points may, however, briefly be mentioned. First, the definition of what constitutes a harm under this regime should be made with the aim of facilitating private negotiation about the harm, not deciding whether it should take place or not. Second, nothing that was defined as a harm for this purpose could then be denied to be a nuisance.

9   These remarks obviously do not apply to public or statutory nuisance, much less to a public law regulation.

would have to enter into negotiations with C to see if he could continue with his activity. The proper alternatives are not between standstill and growth but between growth on a *sic utere* basis, in which D has to negotiate in order to obtain permission to harm C, and growth on a give and take basis, in which D typically is given a permission to harm at zero direct cost. Of course, on the give and take basis when the tendency is to find economic growth a net social benefit, D has no need to negotiate, and the give and take basis of nuisance liability therefore will undermine any possible market in environmental harms based on private nuisance.

Once this is understood, then the issue is the choice of systems of liability. In a society based on dispersed private property[10] in which goods usually are allocated through a market, one might expect the *sic utere* alternative to be preferred, for under it more of the costs of economic growth will be goods allocated through a market, and one might expect more rational pricing of that growth because of this. When the harm C suffers from smoke is, for example, a 'cost' of operating D's smelter,[11] if D has to pay C for that harm, then the price D charges for the metal he produces will have to be able to bear the cost of C's harm. The greater the number of markets in the various harms D causes (a smoke market, a noise market, a water pollution market, etc), the more accurate the pricing of his metal. An economy satisfying the conditions of 'general competitive equilibrium' would be 'fully contingent' in that it would contain markets in all contingencies (including harms) related to the production of goods, and the pricing of goods would be perfectly efficient. Of course, this will mean that some goods are not produced which are produced when markets are imperfect, because they now do, though they did not then, have to amortise their full costs; but this merely tells us that the goods are less valuable than the goods such as enjoyment of land which have to be given up to their production, and it is optimal that such goods are not produced.[12]

10  The degree to which the initial distribution of property in land is just will determine the justice of an allocation of harms through private nuisance however efficient that allocation is carried out, and the injustice of the distribution of property played and plays a major part in reducing the attractiveness of private nuisance as a system of environmental regulation. Of course, the assumption implicit in this is that public systems of such regulation are based on a distribution of political power more just than the distribution of land, and will do so under plausible reforms of either or both. On the assessment of the distribution of resources when both wealth (positive income) and exposure to risk (negative income) are taken into account see U Beck, *Risk Society* (1992) ch 1.

11  *St Helen's Smelting Co v Tipping* (1865) 11 HL Cas 642.

12  At zero transaction costs, the argument works perfectly well the other way around. If D had a clear permission to cause a specific harm, then the negotiation could proceed around this, though, of course, C would have to start it rather than D start the negotiation if C had the injunction. This argument, what Coase himself seems to have meant by what came to be called 'the Coase theorem', has to some extent worked as a polemic against a position in welfare economics which need not be

We have seen that a perception that some (benefits and) harms of economic growth are 'externalities' lies behind the welfare economics' case for government intervention. But given that a fully contingent market would allocate the costs of harm completely efficiently, one must be precise about the ground on which this case lies. In a fully contingent market, there are no externalities, for there is a market in every harm and therefore every harm is internal to an economic relationship between those affected by it. The case for intervention is based on the concept of 'market failure', in that the existence of externalities represents a failure to provide all the necessary markets. If the market in smoke harm is missing, for example, then D can operate his smelter and impose the smoke harm on C at zero cost to himself; that is to say, smoke is an externality. The basis of much welfare economic criticism of the market as a system of environmental regulation has been to insist that the fully contingent market is a merely hypothetical construct and therefore externalities will in practice always exist. This is so, but we are now able to see that this actually is a banal criticism which has been influential only because it has been very misleading.

The generally competitive economy is an economy at zero transaction costs, which is to say it is a situation in which all the costs of establishing markets and making exchanges on them are zero,[13] and in this situation one can have markets in every conceivable good all of which will work perfectly. But, of course, in the empirical world, markets can exist only if one incurs the transaction costs of legal framework setting, negotiating, information seeking, enforcement, etc which are necessary to establish and trade on those markets. The core of the law and economics' position is to insist that a framework of legal rights is essential for any market to exist:

> If we move from a regime of zero transaction costs to one of positive transaction costs, what becomes immediately clear is the importance of the legal system in the new world...what are traded on the market are not, as is often supposed by economists, physical entities but the rights to perform certain actions, and the rights which individuals possess are established by the legal system...the legal

---

set out here but is of no relevance to the analysis of concrete legal rights and negotiations under positive transaction costs. The Coase theorem has been almost always misunderstood in the British literature.

13  The zero transaction costs world is a state of bliss about which nothing logically consistent can be said. One would not have markets at zero transaction cost because the existence of a market as an allocative structure is itself a cost; one would not have property rights at zero transaction cost for the same reason; indeed one would not have transactions at zero transaction costs. See further Campbell, 'On What is Valuable in Law and Economics', above p 496 n 13, pp 505-507.

system will have a profound effect on the working of the economic system and may in certain respects be said to control it.[14]

In the empirical world, then, all markets incur positive transaction costs, the price of goods traded on them has to include an aliquot part of the cost of the market just as much as raw materials, depreciation of plant, etc, and markets therefore will tend to operate only when the benefit of operating them outweighs (at least) this cost. The vast majority of conceivable markets (eg in devices to prevent being struck by a giant comet within the next 10,000 years, or being inundated by a tsunami within the next 300 hundred years, etc)[15] will be more costly to establish than will be rewarded by the benefits of operating them, and so they will not exist. To criticise market allocations by pointing to the existence of externalities is, then, formally right, but works rather too well to have much substance as a general criticism. Under positive transaction costs externalities are absolutely ubiquitous, and to seek to remove all externalities and approximate to the fully contingent market would be impossible as it would involve infinite transaction costs. To attempt to internalise *any* externality by creating a market in it need not be sensible, for on what ground is one disputing what the market's non-existence prima facie tells us, that the costs of operating that market exceed the benefits of doing so?

Though it has been very often thought that just to point to the existence of externalities is enough to ground a case for government intervention, this cannot be so, for, given the absolute legion of externalities, the further question has to be asked: why these particular ones, in this case some environmental harms?[16] Something in addition to market failure must be at work when a market economy is criticised for treating certain environmental harms as externalities, for it is not enough just to point to the existence of externalities to show why we focus on *these* harms as the objects of environmental protection policies. There are two possible arguments that can be made.

First, we could argue that the existing system of legal rights might be so revised so that some missing markets might be brought into existence under a different legal system. Now, the law of private nuisance would seem to be a perfect example of this case. The reason nuisance liability is

14  RH Coase, 'The Institutional Structure of Production', in RH Coase, *Essays on Economics and Economists* (1994) 3, p 11.

15  These examples are chosen from recent news stories calling for public investment into research in these hazards.

16  The same question should be asked of the current explosion in the trading of financial derivatives on markets heavily supported by national governments, and, as with environmental harms, it typically is not: D Campbell and S Picciotto, 'The Justification of Financial Futures Exchanges' in A Hudson (ed), *Modern Financial Techniques, Derivatives and Law* (2000) 121.

decided on the give and take basis of existing nuisance liability is to supplant the market which it is feared would exist given strict liability.[17] The courts clearly have been of the opinion that they can supply a hypothetical bargain which will improve welfare in a way which is better than the actual bargain (or absence of agreement) which would follow the granting of an injunction. In particular they seem to dislike the possibility that the parties may not reach an agreement which will allow the environmental harm to take place, either without direct cost if there is no nuisance, or at reduced cost if the injunction is detailed, modified, or supplemented or replaced by damages.

The sensible way to put the claims underlying the rejection of the *sic utere* rule is that industrialisation would have been prevented or slowed if developing industries had had to bear more of the costs of their harms, and that it therefore was wise that the give and take rule shifted those costs into the realm of externalities. The courts minimised the role of the market to remove the check it would place on harms for which it was thought (no doubt often rightly) that it would not be possible to obtain permission through private negotiation with many neighbouring occupiers. It is unarguable that there is a case for this way of handling the matter: it would seem to be almost universally agreed that the private and public works of industrialisation required this shielding from costs by reduction in the scope of the market.[18] Even if one broadly accepts this,[19] it does not alter the fact that it is because the give and take rule minimised interferers' costs that we are now in the position where it is thought necessary to undertake wide-ranging environmental interventions to make polluters pay. For the core of almost all discussion of environmental harm, including Coase's in 'The Problem of Social Cost',[20] is the

---

17 The most successful arguments ever mounted against Coase are those of AWB Simpson, the distinguished legal historian, who has shown that Coase plays very fast and loose with the facts of the cases he cites in order to imply that a negotiated solution was possible in them when, as a matter of fact, it was not: Simpson, *Leading Cases in the Common Law*, above p 499 n 4, ch 7 and AWB Simpson, 'Coase *v* Pigou Reexamined' (1996) 25 Journal of Legal Studies 53 (which is followed by Coase's reply and a rejoinder). Coase is guilty of this, and from this Simpson reaches pessimistic conclusions about negotiated 'economic' solutions in general. But amongst a number of reasons why Simpson's arguments ultimately are not, with respect, so devastating as he thinks, is that he takes it for granted that nuisance liability must be decided on the give and take basis (as, of course, it has been), when the logic of Coase's argument is that give and take will undercut negotiated solutions.
18 TH Teitenberg, *Environmental and Natural Resource Economics* (5th edn 2000).
19 Though individual case studies keep revealing counter-evidence: eg DN Dewees with M Halewood, 'The Efficiency of the Common Law: Sulphur Dioxide Emissions in Sudbury' (1992) 42 University of Toronto Law Journal 1.
20 Above p 496 n 12, p 133.

suspicion that the amount of harm which is produced when it is costless to produce it will exceed the optimum.

### Government failure

The second possible response to market failure has been, then, to move to government intervention, for the existing law of private nuisance has been regarded as 'the market' and 'the market' understood in this way is but little obstacle to activities which cause environmental harm. Here again, however, the case for intervention has not really been made out in the clearest possible way. The existence of market failure typically has led, without much further argument, to intervention, but if the argument is that an empirical market fails because it does not match the results produced by a fully contingent market, this is quite senseless.

Consider the following the following written in the early 1980s by Paul Burrows, one of the most distinguished British welfare economists who considered the plausibility of nuisance based solutions to environmental problems:

> [A] characteristic of a free market system which may induce interventionist policies is inefficiency in the allocation of resources between competing uses. We shall describe an inability of the market to allocate resources in a way which is efficient for society as 'market failure'. A socially efficient allocation of resources is one which yields the highest net benefits to society ... a perfectly operating competitive market system will automatically lead to a socially efficient allocation of resources. Perfection in this context means [inter alia] that no user of resources can ignore any of the costs of his inputs ... The consequence of the existence of external costs in a market system is ... to bring about an allocation of resources between competing uses which is less socially efficient than the allocation which would occur if producers (and consumers) were obliged to take account of *all* of the effects of their activities.[1]

The case for intervention is that the fully contingent market is a purely theoretical system which will, in empirical circumstances, fail. But what is the point of criticising an existing market for failing to live up to this utopian standard? No empirical market (nor any other method of allocating goods) could possibly live up to it, so there is no point in the criticism as such. What evidently has gone on in environmental regulation is that, under the rubric of market failure, the harms produced by activities

1   Richardson et al, *Policing Pollution*, above p 482 n 9, pp 4, 6.

disliked for ethical and political reasons (from water pollution to smoking in public) have been identified as 'externalities' and made subject to public regulation. These reasons may in some cases be perfectly good, but how particular harms come to be identified as 'externalities' is not a technical step taken towards the realisation of optimal social efficiency which, being an infinite distance away from the empirical world, remains just as far away after the intervention as before.

In this situation, which particular externalities are picked for action and the concrete notion of social efficiency which the action is to optimise is the product of the contingencies of the political process, which may indeed supply superior outcomes to the market, but also may not. The explanation of why a particular environmental harm has been singled out as the subject of intervention from among the legion of externalities does not always reveal either a rational reason for the choice or a clear perception that something very much actually can be done once the costs of the intervention are properly assessed. Of course, as Coase was himself at great pains to insist in 'The Problem of Social Cost',[2] in many cases, such as industrial smoke pollution, government intervention may produce the best available solution. However, overwhelming empirical evidence now exists to show that such intervention need not, and on many occasions has not, improved the situation.

An evaluation of public environmental regulation must be sought elsewhere.[3] What is apposite here is to say the process of public choice arguably is not helped by the language of externalities and the mathematics of welfare economic cost-benefit calculations, for these give a wholly misleading 'scientific' or 'economic' gloss to what is a political problem. Nor is it necessarily the case that the opinion of a judge that an activity is reasonable wholly settles the issue of whether the world will be a better place if the promoter of that activity is given a permission to harm others at no or reduced cost. The public interest is an abstract concept, and enthusiasm for intervention should be tempered by the recognition that in every contested case the finding by planning authorities or the courts that a use is reasonable represents the imposition of the public interest as defined by one group over the definition of that interest by another group. In political philosophy it has long been acknowledged that the public interest sometimes demands disregard of individual liberty, and this has been the central problem of liberal democratic political philosophy. The contribution of law and economics exemplified by

2   Above p 496 n 12, p 118: 'there is no reason why, on occasion ... such governmental regulation should not lead to an improvement in economic efficiency. This would seem particularly likely when, as is normally the case with the smoke nuisance, a large number of people is involved and when therefore the costs of handling the problem through the market or the firm may be high'.

3   See the appendix to this chapter.

Coase[4] has been to call into question more systematically then ever previously the process by which the public interest is identified. Nevertheless, many of those calling for state environmental intervention do so in the face of repeated evidence that what was once thought to be in the public interest has turned out not to be so, in the belief that they have correctly identified that interest *now*.[5]

Burrows continues the passage already quoted by saying:

> The failure of the market to provide socially efficient levels of production and consumption has been regarded as a prima facie case for attempting to regulate.[6]

Burrows puts '*prima facie*' in recognition of another difficulty. For even if one identifies a market failure which it is thought right to try to correct, it is not enough to ground intervention to point to that failure. One must show that the alternative of intervention would be superior to what the failed market has done. Simply to advocate intervention because one was dissatisfied with the market involves a further non sequitur. One's perception of 'market failure' must be complemented by a perception of 'government failure' when making choices between alternative governance structures for the allocation of economic goods. To do so, one must, of course, be aware of the costs of government intervention. What now seems amazing, but certainly was the case, is that it typically was not recognised that government intervention also involves transaction costs, and that this can lead government bodies to 'fail' as well. Given that the public bodies are themselves imperfect, there is no necessity for intervention to be superior to the market even when the market is shown to have failed. A theoretical solution may be shown on the blackboard which assumes perfectly functioning public bodies, but this is merely the opposite error to assuming that markets themselves will ever function perfectly. One must compare the costs of (a possible) market and (possible) government intervention under the empirical circumstances and choose the more effective and efficient in the full awareness that both will, to some extent, fail. Once this is done, the superiority of existing or

---

4   Coase has made little or no contribution to the analysis of the political processes which produce these outcomes, which has been carried by the 'public choice' school of law and economics centred on the University of Virginia. Strikingly, however, much of this work is based on the early contribution of Duncan Black, who was a colleague of Coase's in Dundee in the 1930s!

5   For a recent colloquium on what passes for thinking in this area see (2001) 35(5) Social Policy and Administration (special issue on environmental issues and social welfare).

6   Richardson et al, *Policing Pollution*, above p 482 n 9, p 7.

feasible environmental regulation by no means necessarily emerges as superior to the existing or feasible common law of nuisance.[7]

## Summary

The British response to arguments for greater use of nuisance in the regulation of environmental harms in particular and competing land uses in general has basically been one of incredulity. Consider again a passage from Burrows:

> Market and tort laws have existed for centuries. By comparison, a systematic statutory approach to pollution control is a recent innovation. If the markets, allied with private property rights and actions, were potentially so effective a method of controlling pollution, one may wonder why the pollution problems are now so serious. The answer is that markets do not handle the significant pollution problems, and it would be better if the legal analysts did not behave as if they do or can.[8]

Two points can, however, be made in response to this: about the nature of markets and the applicability of the lessons of the past.

First, the useless 'markets' are those produced by the give and take basis of nuisance liability, that is to say produced by a system of property rights which privileges judges' assessment of the public interest rather than seeks to create a market by which the parties will themselves reach such an assessment. It says little about markets and nothing about a system based on strict liability.

Second, these comments on the past say little about the possible role of nuisance *today*.[9] At the moment, private nuisance is little more than a system granting permission to harm at no or reduced direct cost. Even if one accepts that this may have been necessary to encourage industrialisation, does 'affluent', 'post-industrial', 'risk' society need this huge subsidy for industry now or does it need the deliberation and respect for individual choice which expanding the market in environmental harms would bring? And, of course, a nuisance system now would sit alongside a very highly developed system for compulsory acquisition. A strict

7   J Murphy, 'Noxious Emissions and Common Law Liability: Tort in the Shadow of Regulation', in J Lowry and R Edmunds (eds), *Environmental Protection and the Common Law* (2000) 52, p 74.
8   Burrows, 'Nuisance, Legal Rules and Decentralised Decisions: A Different View of the Cathedral Crypt', above p 496 n 13, p 164.
9   G Calabresi, 'Some Thoughts on Risk Distribution and the Law of Torts' (1961) 70 Yale Law Journal 499, p 517.

liability system of nuisance could be an individual's barrier to harms which, in the light of the development of the public intervention system, could subsequently be trumped by such intervention on grounds deliberated upon in public.[10] It surely is at least arguable that sacrifices of individual rights to the maximisation of the perceived social good should be achieved openly through public law and that judges should not attempt to redistribute resources indirectly through the occasional application of legal rules governing private relationships. A valuable mix of governance structures[11] might thereby replace the current heaping of permission on top of permission. The present relationship between the role of planning and licensing authorities and the role of the courts in nuisance cases overlaps to an extent that is unclear and unsatisfactory.[12]

One can be satisfied with the present system only if one has thorough confidence that the judge, in the court setting, will be able to carry out the more or less legislative task[13] of conducting a social welfare assessment under the rubric of deciding whether a use is reasonable, and that this will be a superior outcome to that which the parties themselves might reach were strict liability in force. Being obliged to reach this type of decision places a tremendous, unwelcome burden on the political beliefs of the judge, who *must* be very sympathetic to economic development.[14] It hopefully would be a further virtue of a strict liability regime that it should replace these explicitly political welfare decisions with adjudication over (statutorily allocated) purportedly bright-line rights, which is a task more fitting to a judge's competence and proper constitutional role under the common law.[15] It should at least challenge the characteristic muddle of current environmental debate, in which 'the

---

10  K Morrow, 'Nuisance and Environmental Protection', in Lowry and Edmunds (eds), *Environmental Protection and the Common Law*, above p 508 n 7, 139, p 159.

11  K Stanton and C Willmore, 'Tort and Environmental Pluralism', in Lowry and Edmunds (eds), op cit,  93.

12  J Rowan-Robertson, 'Compensation for "Regulation" in the UK Law in Relation to the Natural Environment', in Erasmus (ed), *Compensation for Expropriation*, above p 495 n 10, vol 2, 141.

13  J Bell, *Policy Arguments in Judicial Decisions* (1983) p 233.

14  J Conaghan and W Mansell, *The Wrongs of Tort* (2nd edn 1999) ch 6 and C Hilson, *Regulating Pollution* (2000) ch 9. The criticism of the Court of Appeal's finding D liable in *Cambridge Water Co v Eastern Counties Leather plc* as a decision acceptable only to 'the most verdant Green' shows what is at stake: T Weir, 'The Polluter Must Pay – Regardless' [1993] Cambridge Law Journal 17, p 19. Of course, a verdant green law would be as unsatisfactorily biased as the pro-corporations which allowed the development in *Allen v Gulf Oil Refining Co Ltd*, above p 480 n 18. The point is not to accelerate or hinder that growth through intervention but, so far as possible, create the system of legal rights that lets individual choice expressed through a market determine the rate of that growth.

15  Cf the discussion of *Bolton v Stone* in RA Epstein, 'A Theory of Strict Liability' (1973) 2 Journal of Legal Studies 151, 169-171.

market' is excoriated for causing pollution, which therefore must be reduced by state intervention, when the regulation of environmental harm by the law of private nuisance (and *a foriori* by public controls) has (for good or ill) had the exclusion of the market at its heart.

## Obstacles to negotiated solutions and the courts' response to these

In the light of the understanding that the issue is not merely to point to market failure but to compare market and government failure, it becomes absolutely essential to be able to compare in detail the comparative strengths and weaknesses of the alternative institutions. Until recently, the issue has been so completely misunderstood that the British literature comparing the give and take rule as it determines liability and the grant of an injunction with strict liability and injunctive relief as of right is vestigial. In a brilliant exception, Spencer very plausibly argued that strict liability would be the best available system for regulating motor accidents.[16] In the light of the absolutely abysmal record of the Ministry of Agriculture, Fisheries and Food to regulate the environmental impact of agriculture, it has been argued that a system of nuisance based on strict liability may have plausibility in this area.[17] In the British legal literature, detailed analysis of the obstacles to negotiation under the give and take rule is almost non-existent,[18] thought pointless because externalities called for government intervention (and intervention was taken to succeed), but some general comment may be made here on the obstacles to negotiations in the shadow of nuisance law.[19]

16  JR Spencer, 'Motor Cars and the Rule in *Rylands v Fletcher*: A Chapter of Accidents in the History of Law and Motoring' [1983] Cambridge Law Journal 65. To Spencer's argument we would add the possibility of reducing (eliminating?) the extent to which the criminal law relating to road traffic has perforce adopted strict (bureaucratically enforced) liability in flat contradiction of the legitimate bases of attribution of criminal responsibility.

17  Campbell, 'Of Coase and Corn: A (Sort of) Defence of Private Nuisance', above p 496 n 13. For the argument that common law tort should be given a wider role in the regulation of the introduction of new technologies generally see BR Furrow, 'Governing Science: Public Risks and Private Remedies' (1983) 131 University of Pennsylvania Law Review 1403; A Katz, 'The Function of Tort Liability in Technology Development' (1969) 38 University of Cincinnati Law Review 587 and ML Lyndon, 'Tort Law and Technology' (1995) 12 Yale Journal on Technology 137.

18  Ch 25 of the first edition of this work is the only substantial exception of which we are aware. On the US literature, see the appendix to this chapter.

19  Cf R Mnookin, 'Why Negotiations Fail: An Exploration of the Barriers to the Resolution of Conflict' (1993) 8 Ohio State Journal of Dispute Resolution 235.

In the empirical situation in which parties are confronted by substantial transaction costs, there is no certainty that the parties will come to any post-injunction agreement at all, even where that is in their joint interest and would be the optimal outcome and, in fact, clear reasons have been identified to lead us to fear that they will not. Take, for instance, the situation where D's cost in complying with the injunction would exceed C's benefit by a substantial amount. In other words, there is a 'surplus' to be gained by their reaching an agreement which they could share between them.[20] One party may be stubborn and may 'hold out' for the lion's share of the surplus. He may simply be greedy, or he may wish to establish a reputation as a hard bargainer who will not move from his initial demand, even though he risks losing the whole surplus if no agreement is made. Economists call this 'strategic behaviour'[1] which may prevent an optimal agreement or any agreement at all being reached.

A second obstacle to making a private bargain is the 'free-rider' problem. If there are many potential claimants (as with a factory polluting a residential suburb) there is the possibility that if only some claimants incur the cost of negotiating or litigating, the others will benefit from the outcome without contributing to that cost. This is a serious problem in abstract economic terms, for any sort of an external effect disturbs theoretical economic equilibrium, but its practical significance is typically overstated. It would be a peculiarly strong (but not unknown) misanthropy that would prevent a party from making a bargain which improves his own situation just because it would improve the situation of others.

A third problem is inequality of bargaining power based on asymmetries of information about the nuisance. (There obviously also is a general problem of access to justice.) In many nuisance situations it is likely that the parties will have unequal access to the relevant information. If D is an industrial concern or a large organisation, it will normally be better placed to assess the technological issues and the relative costs of different measures to abate the nuisance. An inefficient outcome may often arise from relative ignorance on one side.

It is to attempt to, in a sense, avoid these obstacles to negotiated solutions that we have seen the courts give detailed or suspended injunctions and combine these with or replace them by damages. The court has to decide whether the interference is sufficiently substantial to justify putting C into the strongest possible bargaining position by arming him with an injunction, or whether the court should itself adjust the relationship by granting permission to D at a judicially determined price. The courts

20  Cf the situation in regard of specific performance discussed at p 224 above.
1   Another phrase used by economists is 'opportunism in a situation of bilateral monopoly'; the only party with whom D can negotiate with is C, who knows that he can bargain from an impregnable position, since he can veto any bargain at all.

seem to have decided that (given that liability is established), the injunction will still be the appropriate remedy where C's benefit is likely to exceed D's cost, or where it may do so because C's benefit is difficult to evaluate objectively, eg if he has a special attachment to (consumer surplus in) a residential property. The larger C's benefit – in other words, the more serious the interference – the closer an award of equitable damages would approach a partial expropriation of C's property rights (and should therefore be avoided). Believing that D's cost clearly exceeds C's benefit and that a post-injunction agreement will not be reached, the courts have tried to fix damages at a reasonable price for C's foregoing the benefit. This 'hypothetical release' form of equitable damages which replace the actual release or failure to obtain a release which would be the outcome of the parties' negotiations in the light of an injunction perfectly encapsulates the welfare maximising impulse behind give and take reasoning.

### Incentives to compromise before trial

We are now also able to say something of the effect of judicial remedies as incentives to the parties to agree upon a compromise before going to court. In most respects, pre-trial negotiations will resemble post-injunction negotiations: there will be the same scope for strategic behaviour in a situation of bilateral monopoly. Most disputes will be settled at the pre-trial stage, because the transaction costs incurred in litigating are likely to exceed those incurred in negotiating a settlement. How far do the legal rules facilitate and encourage negotiations, so as to minimise total transaction costs? Settlements will be made in the light of the advice which the parties are given about the likely judicial decision: the more certain the judicial decision, the more likely a settlement. One justification for treating the injunction as the prima facie remedy is that the expectation of an injunction will be an incentive to a potential D, before he begins an activity which is likely to inconvenience C, to negotiate with C. Usually, it will be cheaper for D to pay a reasonable price now, instead of fighting until C wins an injunction, when D would have to pay the costs on both sides. After an injunction, C would be in an even stronger bargaining position than now, and so would probably demand a higher price.[2]

Although in theory C may fix his own price for agreeing to permit D's interference with his land, it is subject in practice to a ceiling, which is the expected cost[3] to D of complying with the type of injunction he

---

2   In some circumstances, however, the delay itself may be valuable to D.
3   This cost should include D's expected costs of the litigation in which an injunction would be made against him.

anticipates. The possibility of a pre-trial agreement depends on the relationship of D's expected cost to the value to C of the benefit he expects to receive from having the interference stopped. If C's benefit is expected to exceed D's cost, D is likely to agree to abate the nuisance. If C demands a price above D's cost, D will either voluntarily abate the nuisance or allow C to take him to court in the hope that the injunction might be qualified or suspended. If D's costs exceeds C's benefit, there is a 'settlement range' within which both parties would be better off with an agreement than with litigation. Since it will be cheaper for D to pay any price below his expected cost, C can hope to bargain for a price exceeding his expected benefit. He can exploit his bilateral monopoly up to the ceiling fixed by D's expected cost. This outcome will still satisfy the criterion of economic efficiency because the inefficient outcome would occur only if D actually abated the nuisance at a cost above C's benefit.

The incentive to compromise before trial is weakened by the discretion of the court to choose a remedy other than an immediate, final injunction. It may choose a qualified or suspended injunction, or award damages in lieu of an injunction, or simply damages for past harm. To the extent that there is uncertainty about the judicial decision, the party in the stronger bargaining position is favoured and his threat to fight the case is credible and powerful. Although it is an advantage to a judge to be able to choose a remedy at any point in a graduated scale of responses (eg a highly detailed injunction), this discretion has the effect of further weakening the negotiating position of the already weaker party.

## The possible outcomes

In the light of the above discussion, we can describe all the possible outcomes when C seeks a remedy for the harm caused by D's activity, and these are set out in Table 3 (see p 514). It is vital to note two points. First, though self-help remedies are ignored, Table 3 takes into account the negotiated (extra-judicial) outcomes as well as judicial remedies. Second, the law is the extant law: the give and take rule as it applies to nuisance liability and the decision whether to grant an injunction underlies these outcomes.

### Prohibition at D's expense

This is achieved by the court granting an injunction under which D is prohibited from interfering (usually, from continuing to interfere) with

| D is prohibited | | | | D buys permission to continue the interference (at least for a period) | | | D pays for harm suffered by C up to present date |
| --- | --- | --- | --- | --- | --- | --- | --- |
| *(a) At D's expense* | | *(b) At C's expense (D is not liable to C under the existing law)* | | | | | |
| 1 The court grants an *immediate injunction* prohibiting any interference of the specified type. | 2 The court grants a *limited injunction* prohibiting any interference beyond a specified level (eg when the harm to C is incremental, as with noise or smell). | 3 C may negotiate an *agreement* with D that D will refrain from causing the interference. D fixes the price which C must pay him. | 4 (Not yet in English law) The court grants C an *injunction* prohibiting D from continuing the interference, but *on condition* that C pays D a sum fixed by the court as (partial) compensation. | 5 Negotiated *agreement* — C fixes the price. *Before or after* an injunction, the parties agree that D is to be entitled to continue the interference indefinitely. | 6 *Compulsory permission* — the court fixes the price. Damages in equity awarded in lieu of an injunction. | 7 *A suspended injunction* — the court grants an injunction (as in 1 or 2) but suspends it for a stated period (eg to enable D to complete building operations, or to relocate his activity). The court may also award damages (as in Remedy 8) for past interference (and also for interference during the period of suspension). | 8 *Compensation* to C — common law damages assessed for *past* interference only. |
| *Consequences* Either: (1) C must monitor D's compliance with the injunction and return to court to enforce it if D defaults. Or (2) C may negotiate with D to release him from the injunction in return for a price (which is Remedy 5 in this outline). | | *Consequences* C must monitor D's compliance, and if D defaults, may seek an injunction (to enforce a negative covenant) and/or damages. | *Consequences* C must monitor D's compliance and return to court to enforce it if D defaults. | *Consequences* C has no future claim in respect of any interference within the terms of the agreement. | *Consequences* C has no further claim in the future, unless D exceeds the terms of the permission granted by the court. | *Consequences* At the end of the period D is subject to an injunction as in Remedy 1 or 2. | *Consequences* All remedies (1 to 7) remain available for any future interference. |

*Table 3*

C's enjoyment of land in his occupation. D must at his own expense take whatever steps are necessary to prevent the specified degree of interference being suffered on C's land. If D cannot abate the nuisance, or cannot afford to do so, he must cease his activity or move it to another location.

The injunction may be in general terms which leave it to D to decide for himself which steps are required to reduce the interference to the legally acceptable level (Remedy 1 in Table 3). The injunction may, however, be either limited (Remedy 2) or suspended (Remedy 7). A limited injunction spells out in considerable detail exactly what D is, or is not, permitted to do. The risk of D's interpreting the injunction is greatly reduced because the court specifies the level of his permitted activity, instead of leaving him to assess which level of his activity will avoid causing an unacceptable level of interference with C's occupation (as in Remedy 1).

### Prohibition at C's expense

The first instance of this is straightforward (Remedy 3). If D is held not liable to C for the interference (or if C fears that outcome in court), C may attempt to negotiate with D for a contract or restrictive covenant under which D binds himself to refrain from a particular activity (or at least from causing a specified level of interference with C's use of his land). D will obviously expect something in return for this, which in this chapter is called a 'price', although it obviously could be something else which D desires C to do or give. Under such an agreement, C must monitor D's compliance. If D defaults, C must sue him for breach of contract, and may seek an injunction (to enforce a negative covenant) or damages for his loss up to date. It is a question of land law whether D's agreement may bind his successors in title as with a restrictive covenant running with the land.[4]

### An injunction with compensation to D

Remedy 4 in Table 3 represents an interesting possibility canvassed in academic writing,[5] which was applied in the American case *Spur Industries Inc v Del E Webb Development Co*,[6] but which remains theoretical[7] in

---

4    Megarry and Wade, *The Law of Real Property*, above p 475 n 10, ch 16.
5    G Calabaresi and AD Melamed, 'Property Rules, Liability Rules and Inalienability: One View of the Cathedral' (1972) 85 Harvard Law Review 1089, pp 1115-1124.
6    (1972) 494 P 2d 700. See further E Rabin, 'Nuisance Law: Rethinking Fundamental Assumptions' (1977) 63 Virginia Law Review 1299.
7    But cf the supension of injunction without conditions discussed at p 485 above.

that, so far as we are aware, that case has never been followed in the US,[8] nor even considered by any court in this country.[9] This is that the court should grant an injunction on condition that C pays D a contribution towards the cost of complying with it. This sum could be the cost (or part of it) which D would incur in abatement, in moving his activity elsewhere, or simply a sum to compensate D for giving it up. It would be appropriate where the court might otherwise decide to refuse an injunction on the ground that the cost of compliance to D would be disproportionate to the benefit to C; or where C seeks a wider injunction than would otherwise be justified. *Spur Industries* illustrates this solution. D manufactured cattle food, which caused flies and smells affecting neighbouring occupiers. C, a property developer, bought some adjacent land and was in the process of building on it. The court granted C an injunction on condition that he paid D the cost of moving his factory to a new location. This was a compromise solution which called for the parties to share the cost of adjustment. The equitable jurisdiction of the English courts is sufficiently wide to permit the granting of an injunction on such a condition,[10] but it remains merely a theoretical possibility in English law. As with Remedies 1 and 2, C would have to monitor D's compliance, and, if necessary, return to the court to seek enforcement.

### D purchases permission to continue the interference in future

At any stage, D may negotiate with C for permission to continue his activity, despite the fact that it results in an actionable level of interference being suffered by C. D may seek an agreement before the court grants an injunction, or after one is granted. Judges anticipate that the parties may enter into post-injunction negotiations for its release, and often grant the injunction in order to vindicate C's right as occupier to fix his own price for permitting D to interfere with the use of his land.

8    W Farnsworth, 'Do Parties to Nuisance Cases Bargain After Judgment? A Glimpse Inside the Cathedral' (1999) 66 University of Chicago Law Review 373, n 22. According to one of those responsible for the original idea, a parallel to the compensated injunction is in common use in the public law governing takings in the US: AD Melamed, 'Remarks: A Public Law Perspective' (1997) 106 Yale Law Journal 2209.
9    The actual attitude taken by parties would appear to be expressed in *Leakey v National Trust* [1980] QB 485, in which, when an imminent landslip on D's land threatened harm to C's land, D initially refused C's offer to pay half of the cost of taking steps in abatement. In the light of the prevailing authorities at the time of these negotiations, it is submitted that D was entitled to take this (unreasonable) position, but those authorities were overruled and this harm was found to be a nuisance.
10   Cf the grant of specific performance subject to payment of compensation discussed at pp 193-194 above.

The agreement should specify exactly what it permits D to do in future, and for which period. If the agreement is simply to release D from a permanent injunction, the implication is that D is now permitted to do what the injunction prohibited.[11] If, contrary to the agreement, C seeks to enforce his previous entitlement to a remedy for D's nuisance, D will be able to defend the claim on the ground of C's permission. If, however, D's activity or the interference he causes exceeds the permitted level, C will still be able to sue in nuisance in respect of the 'excess' interference.

### Compulsory grant of permission to D

Remedy 6 is a compulsory sale to D of the entitlement to interfere in a specified way with the enjoyment of C's land. In this solution, the court refuses to grant an injunction to C, but in lieu awards him damages in equity as the 'price' for the granting of permission to continue the interference. The terms of the permission should be specified in detail in the judgment, since this replaces the specification which would be found in a contract or easement agreed by the parties (Remedy 5). The award of damages in lieu of an injunction looks to the future, but it may be coupled with damages for past interference (Remedy 8). As with Remedy 5, C retains his entitlement to sue in nuisance for any future interference which exceeds the level of D's activity or interference specified in the judgment.

### A suspended injunction

The permission granted by the court may be only temporary. It may grant C only a suspended injunction, which may be coupled with damages payable to C for harm suffered during the suspension. A period of suspension enables D to abate the nuisance, eg to complete the temporary building work which was interfering with C's use of his land, or to move his activity to another site. The court is in effect imposing a compromise on the parties, and may thereby impose on C some of the costs of the adjustments to be made by D. Although D is given a temporary licence to continue his activity, he is also given notice that he has only a limited time in which to make other arrangements.

---

11   As with Remedy 3, the rules of land law determine whether C's agreement binds his successor in title in favour of D and his successor in title.

*Damages for past interference*

In contrast to Remedy 6, an award of damages at common law for nuisance is designed only to compensate C for the harm or interference which he has suffered up to date. If it is unlikely that the particular interference will be repeated, damages assessed on this basis will be the only remedy which C needs. Even where he has sought an injunction, the court's refusal to grant one may be coupled with damages only in respect of the past. Such damages are not 'in lieu of' an injunction and the award does not affect the future legal position between the parties. If D commits a further nuisance, C is free to seek any remedy he chooses, as if this were the first occasion he was taking action against D. If after the award of damages for the past the nuisance has recurred, the court may be more willing to grant an injunction, but C may in any event recover further damages for the interference suffered since the previous assessment.

## Appendix: some law and economics works on nuisance

The works are listed in the order in which it is suggested they should be read.

### The critique of the externality

RH Coase, 'The Problem of Social Cost' (1960) 3 Journal of Law and Economics 1 (reprinted in RH Coase, *The Firm, the Market and the Law* (1988) 95, with commentary at pp 10-16, 20-30, 157-185); AA Alchian, 'Some Economics of Property Rights' (1965) Il Politico 816 (reprinted in AA Alchian, *Economic Forces at Work* (1977) 127); CJ Dahlman, 'The Problem of Externality' (1979) 22 Journal of Law and Economics 141

### Comparison of nuisance liability rules

G Calabresi and AD Melamed, 'Property Rules, Liability Rules and Inalienability: One View of the Cathedral' (1972) 85 Harvard Law Review 1089; FI Michelman, 'Pollution as a Tort: A Non-Accidental Perspective on Calabresi's Costs' (1971) 80 Yale Law Journal 647; BH Thompson Jr, 'Note: Injunction Negotiations: An Economic, Moral and Legal Analysis' (1975) 27 Stanford LR 1563; AM Polinsky, 'Resolving Nuisance Disputes: The Simple Economics of Injunctive and Damage Remedies' (1980) 32 Stanford Law Review

1075; I Ayres and E Talley, 'Solomonic Bargaining: Dividing a Legal Entitlement to Facilitate Coasean Trade' (1995) 104 Yale Law Journal 1027; JE Krier and SJ Schwab, 'Property Rules and Liability Rules: The Cathedral in Another Light' (1995) 70 NYU Law Review 440

## Empirical studies

L De Alessi, 'The Economics of Property Rights: A Review of the Evidence' (1980) 2 Research in Law and Economics 1; RC Ellickson, *Order Without Law* (1991); RC Ellickson, 'Property in Land' (1993) 102 Yale Law Journal 1314

## Government failure

F Michelman, 'Property, Utility and Fairness: Comments on the Ethical Foundations of "Just Compensation"' (1967) 80 Harvard Law Review 1165; RA Epstein, 'Nuisance Law, Corrective Justice and Its Utilitarian Constraints' (1979) 8 Journal of Legal Studies 49; RC Ellickson, 'Alternatives to Zoning: Covenants, Nuisance Rules and Fines As Land Use Controls' (1973) 40 University of Chicago Law Review 681; GJ Stigler, *The Citizen and the State* (1975); D Campbell, 'Of Coase and Corn: A (Sort of) Defence of Private Nuisance' (2000) 63 Modern Law Review 197

# 26 Protecting the right to occupy or use land

## Injunctions

Where D has prevented C from occupying land which C is entitled to occupy,[1] C's main remedy is based on the old action of ejectment; by the action for the recovery of land he will recover possession of the land itself.[2] When C is still in possession of the land, but D is responsible for a direct, physical invasion of it or the airspace above it, D is liable to C in trespass, for which the regular remedy is an injunction prohibiting further trespasses by D and the award of damages for any damage suffered by C from the past trespasses by D. An injunction is intended to vindicate C's right to possession against all the world, and is particularly appropriate when the past trespasses by D were committed deliberately and the likelihood is that he will continue his activity unless he is forbidden to do so. In these circumstances, the courts consider that the protection of C's property rights is even more justifiable than in the case of nuisance, where D's interference with the use of C's land is indirect.[3] The type of balancing operation – the cost of compliance compared with the value of the benefit to C, which is conducted in cases of mandatory injunctions in nuisance[4] – is not considered relevant. By granting an injunction, the courts are compelling D, if he wants to continue his activity, to negotiate with C to get his

---

1    Licensees granted a right to occupy land may bring a claim: *Manchester Airport plc v Dutton* [2000] 1 QB 133 (a contractual right to possession).
2    R Megarry and HWR Wade, *The Law of Real Property* (6th edn 2000) pp 1440-1447. C cannot be made to pay for any improvements to the land: R Goff and G Jones, *The Law of Restitution* (5th edn 1999) pp 241-245, 594-595.
3    See ch 25 above.
4    See pp 477-478 above.

agreement to grant a licence at whatever price C is willing to accept.[5] When the court gives C this remedy, it is refusing to impose on him a licence at a price fixed by the court.[6] The courts do not use the language of 'extortion' in relation to C's holding out for the highest price he can get,[7] and recognise that the grant of an injunction will put C into an 'extremely powerful bargaining position'.[8] C is not required to prove that D's trespass has caused him any harm.[9]

Building or repair work often requires some access to adjoining land which needs permission from its occupier. A limited degree of flexibility is given by the Access to Neighbouring Land Act 1992. This Act entitles the court to make an access order enabling C to carry out works which are reasonably necessary for the *preservation* of his land or buildings and which would be impossible or difficult without access to adjacent property.[10] A 'price' may be fixed by the court for granting an access order: 'the likely financial advantage of the order to the applicant'[11] is specifically mentioned as relevant in assessing the 'sum by way of consideration for the privilege of entering' the neighbour's land.

Some flexibility has been shown by the courts in suspending the operation of an injunction. If D trespasses in the course of temporary building work on his own land, eg where D erects scaffolding on C's land in order to repair his building, the courts are sympathetic to D. In one case,[12] C claimed an injunction to prohibit D from allowing the jib of a crane to swing over C's premises at a height which caused no harm to C. Because the construction work was in progress, an immediate injunction would have presented a major problem to D, who had not acted in 'flagrant disregard' of C's rights.[13] The court suspended the operation of the injunction to enable D to complete his work.[14] (But such a suspension should be coupled with an award of damages).[15] Although these building cases do involve technical trespasses, they seem to be analogous to the

5   *Goodson v Richardson* (1874) 9 Ch App 221 at 224 and *Eardley v Granville* (1876) 3 Ch D 826 at 832.
6   RJ Sharpe and SM Waddams, 'Damages for Lost Opportunity to Bargain' (1982) 2 Oxford Journal of Legal Studies 290.
7   Cf pp 492-493 above.
8   *Bracewell v Appleby* [1975] Ch 408 at 420.
9   See p 522 n 20 below.
10  See also the Party Wall, etc Act 1996.
11  Section 2(5) and (6). However the Act only covers 'preservation'; the construction of a new building is outside it.
12  *Woollerton & Wilson Ltd v Richard Costain Ltd* [1970] 1 WLR 411.
13  Ibid at 416. (D had in fact offered the substantial sum of £250 a week for the right to use C's airspace.)
14  Doubts as to this order were expressed in a later CA decision: *Charrington v Simons & Co Ltd* [1971] 2 All ER 588 at 592.
15  See pp 527-528 below. See *Jaggard v Sawyer* [1995] 1 WLR 269 at 278-279, 284, CA.

'give-and-take' approach of nuisance law.[16] the courts are using their discretion to suspend an injunction to moderate the unreasonable assertion of C's proprietary rights. Where an injunction is suspended, C still has a claim to common law damages for any loss which he can prove he has suffered; but this proof is often difficult. Damages would be more than nominal only if the courts thought in terms of a reasonable 'price' which C might have obtained from D for the temporary licence to invade C's land or airspace.[17] Through the trespass, C has been denied the opportunity to bargain.

Courts have occasionally been reluctant to use injunctions against trespassers who cause no injury. Where C, a large landowner, claimed an injunction to prevent local people from using coastal paths across his land, the court refused to make the order: 'The existing security of the tenure of land in this country is largely maintained by the fact that the owners of the land behave reasonably in the matter of its enjoyment.'[18] The public interest was also the ground for denying an injunction against a railway company whose genuine mistake led to its occupying C's land.[19] But the Court of Appeal has held that, in all but 'exceptional circumstances', C (whose title is not in issue) is entitled to an injunction to restrain a trespass, whether or not that trespass causes him any harm.[20]

Where D's invasion of C's land amounts to 'squatting', the courts always grant orders for possession or injunctions, even against homeless people.[1] Again, where D's trespass could cause serious harm to C's property, the court will not hesitate to grant an injunction. If D has acted deliberately, a mandatory injunction may be made ordering him to dismantle a structure,[2] but where D has inadvertently built on C's land, the courts are reluctant to make an order involving the waste of valuable resources.[3]

In the exceptional cases in which the court refuses to grant an injunction to prevent D from continuing to trespass on C's land, it may instead award damages under the special jurisdiction which began with Lord Cairns'

---

16  See pp 467-468 above.
17  See pp 527-528 below. Cf Access to Neighbouring Land Act 1992 discussed at p 521 above.
18  *Behrens v Richards* [1905] 2 Ch 614 at 622. See also *Llandudno Urban District Council v Woods* [1899] 2 Ch 705.
19  *Woods v Charing Cross Rly Co* (1863) 33 Beav 290.
20  *Patel v WH Smith (Eziot) Ltd* [1987] 1 WLR 853 at 858–9, 863 (in speaking of 'exceptional' or 'rare' cases, the court was referring to *Behrens v Richards*, above n 18).
1   *Southwark London Borough Council v Williams* [1971] Ch 734.
2   *Kelsen v Imperial Tobacco Co Ltd* [1957] 2 QB 334.
3   Eg where pipes for the local authority's water works had been inadvertently laid in C's land: *Rileys v Halifax Corpn* (1907) 97 LT 278.

Act in 1858,[4] and which is often used in less serious cases of nuisance.[5] This solution in the case of trespass would be, in effect, a compulsory licence granted to D to continue to use C's land in the same way as previously;[6] the proper measure of damages should be the reasonable 'price'[7] which the parties could have negotiated for the grant of such a licence.[8] Such a price might be a percentage of the profit derived by D from the transaction in question.[9]

## Damage to land

Various torts, such as trespass to land, negligence, *Rylands v Fletcher*,[10] or nuisance, may cause damage to C's land itself[11] or to buildings erected on it; or D may use or occupy part of C's land without his permission. These situations will be considered in turn.

If C is not an owner-occupier of the property but has only a limited interest in it, eg as a lessee, reversioner or mortgagee, his damages are restricted to the extent of the damage to his interest.[12] Where C's house, let out on lease, was almost completely destroyed by fire, his damages were measured by the diminution in the value of his reversion.[13]

### Physical damage

In practice, C will usually have insured his buildings against damage or destruction by fire and other contingencies, so that the real claimant will

---

4   See pp 488-495 above.

5   See p 480 above.

6   '[I]f the injunction is refused the result will be no more nor less than a licence to continue the tort of trespass in return for a nominal payment': *Woollerton and Wilson Ltd v Richard Costain Ltd*, above n 12 at 413.

7   But see the quotation ibid.

8   *Jaggard v Sawyer*, above n 15 (trespass as well as breach of a restrictive covenant). Cf damages in lieu of an injunction for breach of a restrictive covenant: *Wrotham Park Estate v Parkside Homes* [1974] 1 WLR 798 (discussed in ch 17 above).

9   *Bracewell v Appleby*, above p 521 n 8. The award of damages in lieu of an injunction in this case amounted to the grant to D of an extended right of way over a private road. See also p 268 above.

10   (1868) LR 3 HL 330.

11   This section does not deal with the special case of damage caused by trespassing livestock: see *McGregor on Damages* (16th edn 1997) paras 1491-1492.

12   Cf torts affecting goods: ch 27 below.

13   *Moss v Christchurch RDC* [1925] 2 KB 750. See also *Rust v Victoria Graving Dock Co* (1887) 36 Ch D 113 (flood damage would be repaired before reversioner entitled to possession).

be his insurance company, which is subrogated to his claim against D.[14] C, the owner of the damaged property, cannot recover twice over, once from his insurance company, and once from D. If C recovers from D, he cannot recover the same amount from his insurers; if the insurers pay C, they are subrogated to C's rights against D and can sue D in C's name.

Actual physical damage to land or buildings should be compensated by an award of damages for C's 'loss', but this leads to the problem of deciding what is this loss. As with the contract cases,[15] there are two possible views: first, the diminution in the market value of C's land[16] or, secondly, the cost of restoring C's land to the state it was in immediately before D's tort. The first view would be justified if C held the land purely as a speculation (eg he was not actually occupying it), but not if he intended to use the land in a way not measurable simply in terms of financial profit and loss. If C does not intend to restore his property he cannot recover the reinstatement measure of damages,[17] as, for instance, where he was keeping it for its potential value for redevelopment.[18] If C seeks the cost of reinstatement, the court must be satisfied that he does intend to incur the cost, if he receives the damages assessed on this basis.[19] In cases of doubt about his intention, C might sway the decision in his favour by offering an undertaking to reinstate, but in one case the judge held that such an undertaking was not 'appropriate'.[20] (He gave no reason for distinguishing the tortious case from the breach of contract case, where such an undertaking has been accepted.)[1] It will usually be reasonable for a business C, whose income-producing premises have been demolished as a result of D's tort, to rebuild and claim the cost.[2] But it may be cheaper and quicker to acquire other premises where the business can be carried

---

14  The position is the same as with chattels: D cannot use the fact that C has been compensated under first-party insurance: see p 530 above.
15  See pp 211-214 above.
16  In cases of unauthorised mining, in addition to damages for the coal extracted (p 545 below) and for use of the land (pp 527-528 below), C may recover damages for the damage to the land itself, eg 'for all injury done to soil by digging': *Morgan v Powell* (1842) 3 QB 278 at 284; or damage to C's houses on the surface of his land: *Livingstone v Rawyards Coal Co* (1880) 5 App Cas 25.
17  *Hole and Son (Sayers Common) v Harrisons of Thurnscoe* [1973] 1 Lloyd's Rep 345.
18  *CR Taylor (Wholesale) Ltd v Hepworths Ltd* [1977] 1 WLR 659. In this case, D's tort gutted C's building, thus saving C the cost of clearing the site; this saving was set off against C's claim.
19  *Ward v Cannock Chase Council* [1986] Ch 546 at 577. (But C can recover reinstatement damages only if he has, or will get, planning permission: ibid.)
20  Ibid at 580.
1   See pp 212-213 above.
2   *Dominion Mosaics and Tile Co Ltd v Trafalgar Trucking Co Ltd* [1990] 2 All ER 246, CA (C's claim for loss of profits was lower than it would have been if it had rebuilt).

on, and if C has acted reasonably the cost of acquisition will be the measure of damages.[3]

C is entitled only to the reasonable cost of doing reasonable work of restoration and repair. He is not 'entitled to insist on complete and meticulous restoration when a reasonable building owner would be content with less extensive work which produces a result which does not diminish to any, or any significant extent, the appearance, life or utility of the building, and when there is also a vast difference in the cost of such work and the cost of meticulous restoration'.[4] An illustration is the case where D mined under C's highway, letting down its surface; C restored it to its former level despite that fact that an equally good highway could have been built much more cheaply at a lower level. The House of Lords held that C could recover only the cost of the cheaper road.[5] In applying this test of reasonableness, the court is implementing its policy of giving C a strong incentive to avoid social waste; the same policy is found in decisions on the granting of an order of specific performance or an injunction,[6] or on the award of reinstatement damages for breach of contract.[7] Reasonableness must therefore be applied not only from C's point of view, but also from society's. The test of reasonableness confers a wide discretion on the court. It may refuse to award the cost of restoration if that would be seriously out of proportion to the diminution in the market value of C's land. As in the contract situation, a balance must be struck between the cost imposed on D and the advantage to C. Although the problem is not identical to the choice between specific performance (or injunction) and damages for breach of contract, or between an injunction and damages in nuisance, the situations are analogous and deserve comparison. Social waste would occur if scarce resources were used to produce a benefit to C which he values at considerably less than the cost to D.[8] C is allowed to give evidence of his subjective valuation of reinstatement, that the land and the house were 'of special and particular value' to him,[9] which accords with the economic concept of the consumer surplus.[10] Thus, when C's house had been damaged through a fire for which

3   Ibid.
4   *Dodd Properties Ltd v Canterbury City Council* [1980] 1 WLR 433 at 441 (appeal allowed on a different point: ibid). Where C will suffer loss of profits while repairs are made to the building where he carries on his business, he may also recover damages for that loss: see p 527 below).
5   *Lodge Holes Colliery Co Ltd v Wednesbury Corpn* [1908] AC 323.
6   See pp 180, 182-184, 208-209 above.
7   See pp 211-214 above.
8   The rule that C was always entitled to exact reinstatement 'cost what it might' and irrespective of alternatives open to him, was rejected by the House of Lords because it 'might lead to a ruinous and wholly unnecessary outlay': ibid at 326.
9   *Ward v Cannock Chase Council*, above n 19 at 574.
10  See pp 168-171 above.

D was responsible, C was given the cost of reinstatement because of its unique or special features – its size and location.[11] The arguments presented above (in the case of breach of contract) that the courts should avoid the two extremes, and be willing in appropriate cases to award damages between the full cost of reinstatement and the diminution in market value, could also apply to a tortious claim by C.[12]

### The time for assessing reinstatement damages

One aspect of the reasonableness test concerns the time for repairs or reinstatement. The general rule in tort is that damages should be assessed as at the date when the tort was committed (interest may be awarded to cover the delay from that time until D actually pays the money). But there are many exceptions: one is where the cost of repairs to C's land or buildings increases substantially between the time of the tort and the time when it was reasonable[13] for C to undertake the repairs. In this situation, the damages are assessed at the cost at the later date.[14] C's financial position may be relevant,[15] in that if D denies liability up to the trial, it may be reasonable for C not to incur the cost until then.[16]

When C is awarded reinstatement damages, no 'deduction' is made for 'betterment', viz the fact that the repaired or reinstated building has a higher market value than before.[17] If C was forced to accept a deduction for betterment, he would in effect be forced to invest money in modernising his property, which he might not have chosen to do had D not damaged it.[18] The same position holds with repairs to chattels.[19]

11  *Hollebone v Midhurst and Fernhurst Builders Ltd* [1968] 1 Lloyd's Rep 38.
12  See pp 214-216 above. These arguments were not considered in *Ward v Cannock Chase Council*, above n 19 at 578, 582, where the judge held that he had to choose between the two measures.
13  This is in line with the rules of mitigation.
14  *Dodd Properties (Kent) Ltd v Canterbury City Council*, above n 4. (It was not disputed that the cost of repairs was the appropriate measure.)
15  *Alcoa Minerals of Jamaica Inc v Herbert Broderick* [2000] 3 WLR 23, PC (treating it as a matter of mitigation). In this respect, there is a contrast with the situation where D's tort has destroyed C's chattel: C's impecuniosity which prevents him from buying a replacement in the market is ignored in assessing his damages: see pp 326-327 above, p 536 n 17 below.
16  Ibid and *London Congregational Union Inc v Harriss & Harriss* [1985] 1 All ER 335. (But C's delay in bringing the case to trial meant that the assessment was made at a date earlier than the trial.)
17  *Hollebone v Midhurst and Fernhurst Builders Ltd* [1968] 1 Lloyd's Rep 38.
18  *Harbutt's Plasticine v Wayne Tank and Pump Co* [1970] 1 QB 447 at 473 (a contract case discussed at p 113 above. This case has been overruled on another point: see p 113 n 9 above).
19  See p 532 below.

## Consequential loss

C may also recover damages for his loss of the net profits which he expected to arise from using his land or buildings, but which he was prevented from making by D's tort.[20] So where it was reasonable for C to repair the building damaged by D's nuisance, C was entitled to recover damages for the loss of profits caused by the dislocation to his business during the repairs.[1] Similarly, where C's building estate was flooded through D's negligence, he recovered damages for the cost of the repairs and loss of rents on his houses during the repairs.[2] The tort may also cause C to incur additional expense: in an old case, where D obstructed a canal, C sued in public nuisance and recovered the reasonable expense of unloading his goods from barges and transporting them by land.[3]

## Wrongful occupation or use of land

Where D's tort deprives C of the occupation of his land, C will first wish to recover possession. But he may also recover damages for the loss of his occupation and use of the land during the period he was wrongfully deprived of that occupation or use (the action for mesne profits).[4] In normal situations C's loss will be measured by the rental value of the land in the market for the period of his deprivation,[5] but this ignores the fact that C may value the occupation of his land more highly than this.[6] Even where C would not have used his land himself to produce a rent, he is entitled to recover its rental value from D.[7] In the cases on D's unauthorised use of C's mining passages, C has been awarded as damages a reasonable rent for the use of the passages. This is called a wayleave, and is awarded

---

20   *McArthur & Co v Cornwall* [1892] AC 75. (C can recover the expected gross profit less the expenses which he has saved.)
1   *Dodd Properties (Kent) Ltd v Canterbury City Council*, above n 4. (In this case, the dislocation would occur in the future, when C effected the repairs.)
2   *Rust v Victoria Graving Dock Co*, above p 523 n 13.
3   *Rose v Miles* (1815) 4 M & S 101.
4   The action for mesne profits may be joined with an action for recovery of land: CPR 7.3.
5   *Swordheath Properties Ltd v Tabet* [1979] 1 WLR 285, CA and *Inverugie Investments Ltd v Hackett* [1995] 1 WLR 713, PC (rent awarded as damages for the entire period of the trespass, despite the low level of occupancy of the apartments).
6   See pp 168-171 above.
7   Modern authorities on this are *Penarth Dock Engineering Co v Pounds* [1963] 1 Lloyd's Rep 359 at 362–363 (see p 269 above and p 528 below); *Swordheath Properties Ltd v Tabet*, above n 5 and *Inverugie Investments Ltd v Hackett*, above n 5.

despite the absence of any damage to the land or the passage.[8] The
principle has been extended to other situations, as where D trespassed on
C's land by tipping waste soil on to it. C's damages were the value to D of
the use of the land made by him,[9] and were not restricted to any diminution
in the value of the land itself.[10] So without having to prove any 'loss' the
Royal Air Force was entitled to restitutionary damages for trespass
assessed as a rent from a tenant who wrongfully ignored a notice to quit.[11]
Similarly, where D bought a floating pontoon from C but failed to remove
it from the dock leased by C, the damages awarded to C (both in trespass
as well as for breach of contract)[12] were fixed at the benefit to D from
using the dock premises after he should have removed the pontoon he
had bought.[13] The principle is similar to that applied to unauthorised use
of C's chattel.[14]

### Depriving D of his profit

Where D used C's land deliberately without C's permission, intending to
make a profit from the use, C will be able to claim exemplary damages
designed to deprive D of the profit he made.[15] For example, exemplary
damages may be justified where a landlord trespasses in order to evict his
protected tenant, hoping to take advantage of the great increase in value
of the property without a protected tenancy.[16]

Another type of potential attack on C's profits might have been
expected in restitution.[17] But, unfortunately, the majority of the Court of
Appeal in 1883[18] restricted the use of 'waiver of tort' in cases of trespass

---

8    *Phillips v Homfray* (1871) 6 Ch App 770.
9    This value was enhanced because it was the only land available to D for tipping.
10   *Whitwham v Westminster Brymbo Coal and Coke Co* [1896] 2 Ch 538. (The
     question whether D made a profit from the use was treated as irrelevant: ibid at
     543.)
11   *Ministry of Defence v Ashman* (1993) 66 P & CR 195, CA.
12   See p 269 above.
13   *Penarth Dock Engineering Co v Pounds*, above n 7. C had not lost any money
     because the dock premises were of no use to him and he had to pay no extra rent.
     (Similarly, in the *Swordheath* case, above n 5, the fair rental value of a house was
     awarded against trespassers without any proof by C that he would have let it to
     anyone else.)
14   See pp 547-550.
15   See pp 586-588 below.
16   *Drane v Evangelou* [1978] 1 WLR 455.
17   See chs 16, 17.
18   *Phillips v Homfray*, above n 8. D had used roads and passages under C's land to
     remove C's minerals. (The main problem facing the court was whether C's claim
     survived the death of the tortfeasor.) The case is criticised by Goff and Jones, *The
     Law of Restitution*, above p 520 n 2, pp 776-780.

to land, holding that where C suffered no loss from the trespass, he cannot recover under waiver of tort the value of the use made by D. Thus, the majority refused to award as damages the price which C could reasonably have demanded for giving D permission to use the land.[19] The view of the majority unnecessarily restricts recovery,[20] and is inconsistent with the approach used by the courts in awarding damages in lieu of an injunction,[1] or for unauthorised use of C's chattel.[2] It is a clear benefit to D to have saved himself expenditure, and if any corresponding 'loss' is needed it can be found in C's loss of the opportunity to exploit the potential of his land by charging D, which is one of the advantages of being an occupier of land.[3]

---

19  In the USA, C has regularly been permitted to recover from D the profits he made by wilfully trespassing on C's land; sometimes, C's claim has been in equity for an account of the profits made by D. See ibid, p 779.
20  Exemplary damages may now be used to extract the profit from D: see pp 586-588 above.
1   See pp 488-494 above.
2   See pp 547-549 below.
3   See pp 527-528 above.

# 27 Protecting the right to use chattels

## Introduction

When D interferes with a chattel in C's possession (or to whose immediate possession C is entitled), the nature of the remedy depends on the situation. If D *damages* the chattel while it remains in C's possession, C will seek damages for the cost of repairing it (and for any loss in its value despite the repairs); he may also seek damages for the loss of its use during the period of the repairs. If D *destroys* the chattel, C will seek its value (or the cost of obtaining a substitute). If D *misappropriates* the chattel, by taking it out of C's possession or by using it without C's permission, C will seek its recovery or its value, together with compensation for loss of its use during the period he was deprived of it.

A valuable chattel, such as a ship, a motor vehicle or a productive machine, is likely to be comprehensively insured by C, so that if it is damaged or destroyed, C will often have been reimbursed by his insurance company. If a claim is brought in C's name, the 'real' claimant will then be his insurer; after[1] meeting a claim by C, the insurer is subrogated to any claim which C has against a third person.[2] D, however, cannot take any advantage from the fact that it is C's insurer who will benefit from the success of C's claim.[3]

---

1  If C recovers damages from D, he cannot thereafter recover his loss a second time from his insurance company, because it is 'indemnity insurance'.
2  *Taylor (Wholesale) v Hepworths* [1977] 1 WLR 659 (damage to a building, but the principle applies also to chattels).
3  Ibid.

## Physical damage

Although many different torts may cause physical damage to or destruction of C's chattel, the rules on C's remedy will usually not differ with the type of tort. Many of the reported cases concern ships, but the principles laid down in them apply to all types of chattel.

### Cost of repairs or diminution in value

The prima facie measure of damages for damage caused to C's chattel by D's tort is the resulting diminution in its value.[4] In most cases, however, the reasonable cost of repairs is in practice taken as the measure of this reduction in value.[5] But C may also be entitled to damages for any reduction in value which remains despite the repairs.[6] To claim the cost of repairs, C must show that it was reasonable for him to have the repairs done instead of replacing the damaged chattel,[7] that the amount of work done was reasonable, and that the cost of the repairs was also reasonable.[8] If it was not reasonable to repair the chattel, C's claim will be as if the chattel had been totally destroyed, in other words a 'write-off'.[9] C cannot recover the cost of repairs if that substantially exceeds the cost of a reasonable and available substitute.[10] So where C repaired his vehicle at a cost of £192, but he could have purchased a similar vehicle for £80–100 in the second-hand market, the Court of Appeal assessed his damages at the lower figure.[11] (The rules on mitigation[12] are relevant.) However, C's chattel may not be a standard one, so that the question of a reasonable substitute does not arise:[13] in these circumstances, C may be entitled[14] to the cost of repairs despite the fact that others would not value the chattel as highly as he does.[15]

4   Interest may also be recovered for the period that C is deprived of use of the damages: see pp 107-108 above.
5   *Darbishire v Warren* [1963] 1 WLR 1067 at 1071, CA.
6   *Payton v Brooks* [1974] RTR 169 at 176. For instance, a repaired yacht may be less valuable than before: *The Georgiana v The Anglican* (1873) 21 WR 280.
7   *Darbishire v Warren*, above n 5.
8   Ibid.
9   See pp 535-541 below.
10  Ibid. (Cf in the case of nuisance, the cost of abatement to D in comparison with the benefit to C: see pp 477-478, 481-484 above.)
11  Ibid.
12  See pp 307-308 above.
13  Cf *O'Grady v Westminster Scaffolding* [1962] 2 Lloyd's Rep 238 (as interpreted in *Darbishire v Warren*, above n 5, at 1072, 1077. Cf *ibid* at 1079).
14  But in this situation, the court may seek some assurance that C will in fact have the repairs done: cf pp 212-213 above.
15  On the consumer surplus see pp 168-171 above. (There are indications of a consumer surplus in *O'Grady v Westminster Scaffolding*, above n 13.)

The need for the repairs in question must be due to D's tort.[16] If he damaged C's chattel when it was already in need of a particular repair (eg a respray of the paintwork of part of a car), D is not liable for the cost of this repair, even though his tort would otherwise have made it necessary.[17]

Since the cost of repairs is taken as the measure of the diminution in value of the damaged chattel, C is entitled to recover the cost without proof that he intends to spend the money in repairing it.[18]

The fact that the repaired chattel may be worth more than previously, because new parts have replaced old, or it has been modernised, does not reduce C's damages.[19] Any other rule, it is argued, would force C to spend his money on new parts before they were worn out, or on modernisation which he did not want. But this rule does mean that C can be better off as the result of D's tort.[20]

## Other expenses

In addition to the cost of repairs, C may recover any expenses reasonably incurred by him as a reasonably foreseeable consequence of D's tort, eg the cost of a tug to take a damaged ship to port, and the expenses of docking it there. Another head of recoverable expenses is for C's expenditure rendered futile[1] by the tort, eg the cost of the wages of the crew and other expenses which it was reasonable for C to continue to incur during the period of the repairs.[2] Where C's car was damaged, but C's own (first-party) insurance company met the cost of repairs without making a claim against D (or D's insurance company), C could recover

16  On causation generally see pp 297-307 above.
17  *Performance Cars v Abraham* [1962] 1 QB 33 (a third party had previously damaged C's car).
18  *The York* [1929] P 178 at 184–185 (ship lost through a different cause before claim for repairs was heard); *The London Corpn* [1935] P 70 at 78 (ship sold to be broken up). Cf the situation with reinstatement damages in contract (pp 212-213 above) and in tort (p 524 above), and with damages for personal injury (pp 442-443 above).
19  *The Gazelle* (1844) 2 Wm Rob 279 (replacing damaged timbers in a wooden ship), This rule has been followed in contract cases: *Harbutt's 'Plasticine' v Wayne Tank and Pump Co* [1970] 1 QB 447 (factory destroyed by fire and replaced by a new factory) and *Bacon v Cooper (Metals) Ltd* [1982] 1 All ER 397 (partly used working part of a machine).
20  Cf the contrary rule in the USA, where the value of any enhancement to C's chattel is deducted from the cost of repairs in assessing his damages: CT McCormick, *Handbook on the Law of Damages* (1935) p 471 and *Cato v Silling* 73 SE (2d) 731 (1952).
1   Cf the analogous situation in contract: pp 121-129 above.
2   *The City of Peking* (1890) 15 App Cas 438 and *Edmund Handcock v 'Ernesto' (Owners)* [1952] 1 Lloyd's Rep 467 (contract case).

from D the 'excess' (the first part of the loss which was not covered by the insurance) which he had to pay, and also damages for the loss of his 'no claims' bonus on his ensuing premiums.[3]

## Cost of hiring a substitute

C is usually acting reasonably if he hires a reasonable[4] substitute chattel during the period when the repairs are being made,[5] and the reasonable cost of hiring is recoverable as damages from D. This applies to a chattel not used for profit-making[6] as well as to one which is.[7] If C's prestigious company car was damaged, it may be reasonable to hire a less prestigious car for the period of repairs, so that C may not be able to recover the full cost of hiring an equally expensive car.[8] But it has been held to be reasonable for the private owner of a Rolls-Royce to incur the cost of hiring another Rolls-Royce.[9]

## Loss of profits[10]

Where C hires a substitute, he should be able to avoid any loss of profits arising from D's tortious damage to a profit-earning chattel. (There may be a loss of profits if a reasonable substitute is not immediately available.)[11] If C does not hire a substitute, he may claim his net[12] loss of profits during the period between the time when the damage occurred

---

3  *Ironfield v Eastern Gas Board* [1964] 1 WLR 1125 n.
4  The test of reasonableness applies to the question whether the substitute can perform the function previously performed by the damaged chattel.
5  It may be reasonable for C to delay the repairs until his insurers (and sometimes D's insurers) have approved the estimate: *Martindale v Duncan* [1973] 1 WLR 574 (taxi).
6  Eg the cost to a public authority of hiring a substitute lightship: *The Mediana* [1900] AC 113 at 122, 123.
7  Eg a ship: *The Yorkshireman* (1826) 2 Hag Adm 30n.
8  *Watson Norie v Shaw* [1967] 1 Lloyd's Rep 515. Cf the discussion of credit hire companies at p 435 n 5 above.
9  *HL Motorworks v Alwahbi* [1977] RTR. 276. Cf *Mattocks v Mann* [1993] RTR 13.
10  Cf the similar situation in contract, where D delays delivery of a profit-earning chattel: see pp 98-99 above.
11  Cf pp 536-540 below.
12  From gross expected earnings must be deducted the expenses normally incurred in producing them, and any wear and tear of the chattel which C avoided during the repair period.

and the time by which repairs should reasonably[13] have been completed.[14] General damages will be given for loss of the opportunity to earn profits,[15] eg for a ship, by taking her average daily profits from recent voyages.[16] But the test for remoteness of damage must be satisfied if C claims special damages for the loss of profits arising under a specific engagement. So where D is responsible for damage to C's ship, C may recover damages for his net loss of profits (caused by the delay for repairs) under a charterparty which he had already made for that ship.[17] But the rules of mitigation require C to take reasonable steps to minimise this loss, eg if he has lost a charterparty, by finding the next-best alternative use for his ship during the period she was free as the result of losing the charterparty;[18] or by his finding a substitute ship to perform the original charterparty.[19] When C's mitigating steps enabled him to begin a previously arranged charter earlier than would have been otherwise possible, an allowance was made in his damages to reflect the benefit of the earlier receipt of the high profits made under this charter.[20]

### Loss of use of a non-profit-earning chattel

In addition to the cost of repairs, C is entitled to general damages for loss of use of his chattel during its repair, even where he did not use it for a profitable activity at the time of D's tort, and where he did not hire a substitute during the period of the repairs.[1] So damages have been given for loss of the use of ships engaged in public services, such as a dredger or

---

13   The period for repairs to C's ship has been held to include delay due to a trade union strike while she was in dock; the risk of such delay was foreseeable as a possible consequence of D's negligence: *Candlewood Navigation Corpn Ltd v Mitsui OSK Lines Ltd* [1986] AC 1.

14   *The Argentino* (1889) 14 App Cas 519 at 523. The term 'demurrage' is sometimes used to refer to the earnings reasonably anticipated during that period but lost through the detention of a ship for repairs. On the problem when two separate causes create the need for repairs: see pp 306-307 above.

15   But if C was not operating his ship profitably at the time of the collision, he can recover nothing for loss of profits: *The Bodlewell* [1907] P 286.

16   *The Naxos* [1972] 1 Lloyd's Rep 149.

17   *The Argentino*, above n 14. (It is arguable whether this and similar cases should be reconsidered in the light of the *Wagon Mound* [1961] AC 388 (discussed at pp 314-317 above). Cf *The Soya* [1956] 1 WLR 714.

18   *The Star of India* (1876) 1 PD 466. (C recovered the difference between the net profits of the lost and of the substituted charterparties – he could not have fulfilled both).

19   *The World Beauty* [1970] P 144.

20   Ibid.

1   As he may do: see p 533 above.

a lightship,[2] or a cruiser or oil tanker belonging to the Admiralty;[3] or of buses run by a local authority[4] (which is a non-profit-making body). The first method of assessing the damages for loss of use of this type of chattel is to award interest at 5–7% on the current[5] capital value of the chattel.[6] This method assumes that C valued the use of the chattel at least at this figure: the rate of interest should meet the loss of the notional return on the capital locked up in the asset, as well as its current depreciation. The problem, however, is that this method values its use at a reducing level as the chattel's age increases (the total for depreciation increases), whereas C may actually value its use at a constant figure throughout its life. The second method for valuing the use of a non-profit-making chattel is to calculate the daily cost of maintaining it, including the daily rate of depreciation.[7] This cost is taken to be a fair measure of its value to C, and has been used for a bus operated by a local authority.[8] But the value of the chattel to C may often exceed this cost to him[9] so that this method may undercompensate him.

## Destruction

Where D's tort has caused the destruction[10] of C's chattel,[11] the basic measure of his damages is its market value at the time and place of the

---

2   *The Greta Holme* [1897] AC 596; *The Mediana* [1900] AC 113 and *The Marpessa* [1907] AC 241.

3   *Admiralty Comrs v SS Chekiang* [1926] AC 637 and *Admiralty Comrs v SS Susquehanna* [1926] AC 655.

4   *Birmingham Corpn v Sowsbery* [1970] RTR 84 (the damaged bus was replaced with one from the back-up fleet maintained for emergencies).

5   Viz its value when the damage occurred. In the earlier cases, this value was reached by taking the original cost to C and then deducting depreciation (*Admiralty Comrs v SS Chekiang*, above n 3) but this seems no longer appropriate in times of inflation. (The rate of interest should also be fixed to reflect current rates.)

6   Ibid and *The Hebridean Coast* [1961] AC 545. Where C actually replaced the damaged ship with a stand-by in its reserve fleet (eg a naval oil tanker) interest on the value of the stand-by has been awarded: *Admiralty Comrs v SS Susquehanna*, above n 3.

7   *The Marpessa*, above n 2 (dredger owned by a public authority).

8   *Birmingham Corpn v Sowsbery*, above n 4. (But this measure could put 'a premium on inefficiency' because higher costs would lead to higher damages: ibid at 86–7).

9   See pp 168-171 above.

10  Or where the chattel, although not totally destroyed, is not worth repairing, and is therefore treated as a 'constructive total loss'. The scrap value of the chattel must be deducted from C's damages.

11  If C has only a limited interest in the chattel his recovery may be restricted: see pp 546-547 below.

loss.[12] Whenever a replacement can be obtained in the market, this sum will enable C to buy one, if he wishes. (The situation is closely analogous to the seller's failure to deliver goods.)[13] The replacement cost is still the measure of damages where only a new chattel could be obtained to replace the used one, provided it would have been reasonable to replace it (eg it was not near the end of its life).[14] If C can immediately replace the lost chattel, he should be able to avoid any consequential losses arising from the tort. The main problems arise where C faces a delay in obtaining a suitable replacement.

### Loss of a profit-earning chattel

In the leading case, *Liesbosch Dredger v Steamship Edison*,[15] C's dredger was sunk by the negligence of D while it was working in Patras, a Greek harbour, under C's construction contract with the harbour authorities. C lacked the financial resources to buy a substitute dredger, although several were available in Holland.[16] Instead, C hired, at a high rate, a dredger from Italy which was more expensive to work. The House of Lords refused to give C, as part of his damages, the cost of hiring this replacement and the extra costs of working it, on the ground that his impecuniosity was an extraneous cause.[17] The House held that C's damages should be the value to C of the Liesbosch, capitalised as at the date of the loss. The value to C should, it was held, take account of various factors (their use is examined below): (1) the market price of a comparable dredger which was reasonably available as a substitute; (2) the cost of adapting the substitute to perform the function of the lost vessel, and of transporting it to Patras; and (3) compensation for disturbance and loss in carrying out the contract for the period between the loss and the time when the substitute could reasonably have been available in Patras. On the total sum, interest should run from the date of the loss.

12  *Liesbosch Dredger v SS Edison* [1933] AC 449 at 464. Interest on the amount has always been awarded in Admiralty cases: see now the statutory power to award interest (see pp 107-108 above).
13  See pp 100-101 above.
14  *Dominion Mosaics and Tile Co Ltd v Trafalgar Trucking Co Ltd* [1990] 2 All ER 246 at 254-255, CA (possibly some allowance should be made for depreciation: ibid at 255).
15  Above n 12.
16  On C's impecuniosity see pp 326-327 above.
17  C's impecuniosity may be relevant when the market value or price is not the measure of damages, eg where the question is when it would have been reasonable for C to incur the expense of repairing his building: *Alcoa Minerals of Jamaica Inc v Herbert Broderick* [2000] 3 WLR 23, PC (discussed at pp 326-327 above).

How should damages in tort for a lost ship or machine used in a business be assessed? Where a businessman, C, acquires a profit-earning chattel like a ship, he is really buying the right to the flow of its future net earnings over its expected life.[18] Let us take an example. Suppose C has bought a machine at a price of £1,000; that it has a working life of three years and is expected to earn £500 per annum, with operating and maintenance costs amounting to £100 per annum (thus providing net earnings of £400 per annum). The present value of this stream of earnings will be calculated as shown in Table 4 (a discount rate of 5% is used).[19]

When C was considering whether or not to buy the machine (the 'ex ante' position in economic jargon) he would have compared its cost (£1,000) with its present value to him as a profit-earning machine over three years, £1,090; this leaves a surplus of £90 (after allowing for the foregone interest over the three years). He bought the machine because he could not find any alternative use of his money which would produce a greater surplus than this over the three years. But once he has bought it, his position has changed. His initial outlay of £1,000 is a 'sunk cost' in the sense that once it has been made, it is beyond recall – what C now has is a machine. (Someone else may be prepared to buy it as a second-hand machine (almost certainly for less than £1,000) but C can no longer go back to his original position before the purchase, in which he had the free disposal of £1,000 in money.) The historic cost of the machine is not strictly relevant to his current position. Once C has the machine on his hands, he will value it from his point of view as the right to use it and thus to receive the stream of its earnings over its expected life. C's view of its value to him will obviously alter as the life of the machine shortens, and as other factors change; eg the demand for the product of the machine may fall, in which case its expected gross earnings must be revised downwards. C will calculate the sum of money which, at any given time, he would be willing to accept in return for giving up the machine at that time.[20] To take the above example: on the day after he bought the machine, C would value it at £1,090. At the end of the first year, and assuming that expected earnings continue to be £500 per annum, he would value it at £745 (the total of the last column of lines 1 and 2). At the end of year 2, he would value it at £381 (the last column of line 1). The value to C is the value of the opportunity cost of the machine to C at the given time, ie the potential return from alternative uses to which the resource could be put. According to the remaining life of the machine, at the different values in

---

18  This is partly recognised in the *Liesbosch* case, above n 12 at 464; in *The Llanover* [1947] P 80 and in *The Fortunity* [1961] 1 WLR 351 at 356 ('the price which reflected future earning capacity').

19  For discounting see pp 354-358 above.

20  In theory, C should be 'indifferent' between retaining the machine and giving it up in return for this sum.

the last column C is indifferent between retaining it and exchanging it for the relevant sum. To take the historic cost of the machine (£1,000) and then to deduct an arbitrary sum for its depreciation since its purchase is a fictional calculation: it is merely a book-keeping method of spreading the outlay on the machine over its expected life, so that an equivalent sum is notionally available at the end of its life to purchase a replacement (eg 'straight-line' depreciation of £1,000 over three years would produce £333 per annum but this calculation ignores the foregone interest). For the economist, the opportunity cost, the best potential return from an alternative use of the resource, as calculated at the given time, is the true value to C at that time.

Table 4

| | Years of working life | Outlay | Gross | Earnings Less operating costs | Net | Discount factor at 5% pa | Discounted value of net earnings |
|---|---|---|---|---|---|---|---|
| | 0 | 1000 | | | | | |
| Line 1 | 1 | | 500 | 100 | 400 | 1/1.05 | 381 |
| Line 2 | 2 | | 500 | 100 | 400 | 1/1.10 | 364 |
| Line 3 | 3 | | 500 | 100 | 400 | 1/1.16 | 345 |
| | | | | | | Present value | £1090 |

If, instead of using this concept of value (Table 4), the court uses the cost of buying a replacement machine in the market (as was done by the House of Lords in the *Liesbosch*: see item 1 in their list above) the method can be justified only as a second-best one, or as a 'proxy' for calculating C's valuation by the Table 4 method. (Although it is not spelt out in the cases, the relevant market value should be of an identical machine, with exactly the same expected working life as the original machine, and with the same degree of wear and tear: any alteration, particularly in the remaining period of its working life, will directly affect its market price, as Table 4 above shows.) The market price is the value placed on the replacement machine by the marginal buyer of similar machines at that time, which will be based on the marginal buyer's calculation of its present value to him of its expected future earnings (a calculation conducted in the same way as in Table 4 above). So instead of C's own calculation (which, after the loss of the machine through D's tort, might be artificially inflated by him through self-interest) the courts are taking the marginal buyer's calculation, which may not be the same. Lawyers should realise that the market price calculation is a second-best method of assessing the value to C (which is, however, more justifiable if a substitute is immediately available).

If C's chattel has been destroyed through D's tort, C's basic loss should ideally be calculated as the value to him in the Table 4 method. But there may be additional factors in determining that value when a suitable replacement is not immediately available at the same location as the lost chattel, as was the position in the *Liesbosch* case. The value of the lost chattel 'as a going concern'[1] to C may include the factors of its location at the time, the work on which it was currently engaged, and the availability of a suitable replacement. In the *Liesbosch*, the dredger (dredger I) was engaged in performing a contract in a particular location and no substitute was immediately available – it would take some months (the 'period of delay') to buy a substitute (dredger II) in the market in Holland and to transport it to Patras where it could take over the work of dredger I. Since dredger II would begin to earn only on its arrival in Patras, C would lose the *gross* earnings of dredger I from the contract during the period of delay. But if the value of dredger I is understood as in Table 4, that value already includes the net earnings for the period of delay. If, in addition to that value (usually taken by the courts as the market price at the time of the loss), C recovered his loss of earnings – whether gross or net – for the period of the delay, he would be compensated twice for the same net loss of earnings. However, during the period of the delay, C cannot avoid[2] continuing to incur some of the expenses of operating a dredger, such as the wages of its crew. These expenses will be wasted during that period, and there can be no objection to adding them to C's damages.[3] (Net earnings in Table 4 are calculated after deducting operating costs.) Thus, item 3 in the calculation of the House of Lords above, if understood in this sense, is correct.

C would also incur the extra cost of adapting dredger II to perform the function of dredger I at Patras (if necessary) and the extra cost[4] of transporting dredger II from Holland to Patras, which are other justifiable additions to the basic value (as in item 2 of their Lordships' list). Finally, a further item (item 4) would be the transaction costs incurred by C in coping with the aftermath of the loss of dredger I and the purchase and transport of dredger II, including the disruption to the performance of the contract (eg any extra costs involved in performing that contract and any compensation for the delay payable to the other contracting party).[5] If a hypothetical buyer were willing to pay C a price to cover all these items,

1   The *Liesbosch* case, above n 12 at 467–468. See also ibid at 465 ('the real value to the owner as part of his working plant'). This turns 'value' into a specific concept which is dependent on C's own (perhaps idiosyncratic) arrangements.
2   Under the rules of mitigation, C must take reasonable steps to minimise his loss, such as avoiding any further expenses which he can.
3   If C was calculating the price at which he would be willing to sell to a hypothetical buyer immediately before the collision, these expenses would be a factor in fixing that price.
4   Eg insurance, fuel, cost of crew, etc.
5   The word 'disturbance' in item (3) of the list given in the *Liesbosch* could be interpreted as covering transaction costs.

(1 to 4), immediately before the collision, it would be because he valued more highly than C the benefit of having dredger I immediately available, in comparison with the alternative of waiting for a substitute to be brought out from Holland in several months' time. (If the price were not paid immediately, C would also expect interest on the price, at the rate at which he could borrow in the market; the allowance of interest by their Lordships was therefore also correct.)

In a subsequent case,[6] C's vessel had been built for a specialised holiday trade on the Norfolk Broads, and could not be replaced until after the next holiday season. Since no reasonable substitute could be hired for that season, C was awarded the net loss of profits for that season, in addition to the market value of the lost vessel. If that value was assessed as at the date of the collision, it would include the present value of the earnings for the next season; to avoid compensating C twice over for loss of that season, the value should have been assessed at the time when the replacement was available, when the future working life of the lost vessel would have been reduced by one year.[7]

### Loss of a non-profit-earning chattel

There are few cases on the assessment of the value of C's chattel which he used for enjoyment or from which he derived a 'consumption benefit' not normally calculable in financial terms. By analogy with cases of profit-earning chattels, C's damages are prima facie assessed at the cost of buying a substitute in the market[8] as soon as reasonably possible after the loss (giving allowance for any scrap value of the destroyed chattel). It may be unreasonable for C to demand an exact replacement where that would cost an unreasonable amount, in which case he will have to accept damages sufficient to meet 'the reasonable cost of another [chattel] which reasonably meets his needs ... and which is reasonably in the same condition'.[9] C is also entitled to the reasonable cost of adapting the nearest equivalent chattel he can obtain so that it can fulfil the function of the

---

6    *The Fortunity*, above n 18.
7    As in the *Liesbosch*, C should have been awarded any unavoidable, but wasted expenditure for the missed season.
8    But the court must assume that normal conditions prevail: where C's yacht was destroyed shortly before the Second World War broke out, a time when the market for yachts was depressed, the court valued it on the basis of the peace-time market: *Piper v Darling* (1940) 67 Ll Rep 419.
9    *Uctkos v Mazzetta* [1956] 1 Lloyd's Rep 209 at 216 (a motor-boat of an unusual type). See also *Dominion Mosaics and Tile Co Ltd v Trafalgar Trucking Co Ltd* [1990] 2 All ER 246 at 255.

lost chattel and of transporting it to the place where his chattel had been destroyed.[10]

C should also be entitled to any reasonable expenses[11] arising from the tort, such as the cost of disposing of the wreck of his destroyed chattel, and the cost of hiring a substitute until he could reasonably have been expected to obtain a long-term substitute. In one case,[12] C's 18-month-old Rover car was written off after an accident caused by D's negligence. He hired a substitute Rover for the period before he could get a new Rover, which turned out to be much longer[13] than the fortnight in which he could have obtained another 18-month-old Rover. The Court of Appeal allowed the cost of hire for the longer period, on the ground that it was reasonable for C to wait for a new Rover, since he regularly changed his car every two years. But since C was not entitled to the cost of a new Rover, but only to the second-hand value of his old car, this seems to be an eccentric application of the reasonableness test.[14] If he did not hire a substitute for this period, he should be entitled to some compensation for loss of use, eg interest on the capital value of the lost chattel.[15]

## Misappropriation[16]

D may deprive C of his chattel without damaging or destroying it, or he may act in relation to it in such a way as to deny C's title to it. If D has it in his power to return the chattel to C, the remedy may be either an order for its specific delivery to C, or damages for its value.

The law on remedies for wrongful appropriation or use of C's chattels is complicated by the partial reforms brought in by the Torts (Interference with Goods) Act 1977.[17] This Act abolished the action for detinue but did not lead to a single tort of 'wrongful interference with goods'; although this generic term is used in the Act, it includes reference to both conversion and trespass, which are retained as separate torts. Detinue was a claim for specific return of the chattel, whereas the other two were claims to

---

10  By analogy with the costs of 'adaptation' of the dredger allowed in the *Liesbosch* case: see pp 536, 539 above.

11  Another type of expense would be one rendered futile by the tort: cf pp 121-129 above.

12  *Moore v DER Ltd* [1971] 1 WLR 1476.

13  Eighteen weeks: there was a strike at the Rover factory.

14  Cf the *Liesbosch* case, above p 536 n 12 (discussed at p 536 above) and the cases on damaged chattels discussed at p 531 above.

15  By analogy with the cases on damaged chattels: see pp 534-535 above.

16  This section does not consider the special rules on damages for wrongful distress of C's goods or in an action of replevin: see *McGregor on Damages* (16th edn 1997), paras 1455-1472. Cf the discussion of repossession at p 159 n 7 below.

17  Hereinafter the 1977 Act.

damages. In the present law, specific recovery may still be obtained, but the order can be made in a claim for conversion or in a general claim for wrongful interference with goods.

## Specific return of C's chattel

In proceedings for wrongful interference with goods C may ask the court to exercise its discretion to make an order that D should specifically deliver the chattel to C.[18] (C must show that he has the immediate right to possess it.) Normally, D is faced with an order for delivery of the chattel to C, which gives D the alternative of retaining the chattel on payment to C of its value as assessed by the court.[19] But the court has a discretion[20] not to make such an order,[1] and so to deprive D of the alternative of keeping the chattel and paying its value to C. The court requires a special reason for ordering specific delivery, which is unlikely to be the case with 'ordinary articles of commerce ... and of no special value or interest'.[2]

If C seeks an order for specific delivery of a chattel, the court may impose on him a condition requiring him to make an allowance to D for any increase in its value resulting from a repair or improvement made by D (provided D acted in the mistaken but honest belief that he had title to the chattel).[3]

## Damages for misappropriation[4]

Where C has lost possession of his chattel through D's misappropriation, and has not recovered possession,[5] the same rules apply to the assessment of his damages whether he sues in conversion or for trespass to goods. In this situation, the normal measure of damages for the loss of the chattel is

---

18   1977 Act, s 3. Cf the court's discretion to order specific performance of a contract for the sale of goods: see pp 171-173 above.

19   Ibid, s 3(2)(b).

20   Ibid, s 3(3)(b), (4) and (6). See *Howard E Perry and Co Ltd v British Railways Board* [1980] 1 WLR 1375 at 1382–1383.

1    This discretion is similar to that conferred on the court by the Sale of Goods Act 1979, s 52: *Cohen v Roche* [1927] 1 KB 169 at 180–181. See pp 172-173 above.

2    Ibid. CPR 40.14 deals with a claim by the part owner of the chattel.

3    1977 Act, s 3(7). *McGregor on Damages* (above n 16, para 1412) argues that the same result should be reached where D has incurred expenses in making the chattel saleable.

4    Special rules apply to some particular cases, such as negotiable instruments (eg a cheque).

5    See pp 545-546 below on D's voluntary redelivery of the chattel to C.

its market value. What would it cost C to buy a substitute in the market open to him (eg as a private customer, a retailer, a wholesaler, etc)?

The discussion in the preceding section (under 'Destruction' of C's chattel)[6] about the calculation of the value of a profit-earning chattel is also relevant here. Where an exact replacement is immediately available to C in the market, he should be able to avoid most consequential losses[7] and to continue earning profits as previously. But if no substitute is available,[8] the court must turn to another measure, such as the cost of commissioning the construction of a replacement.[9] In the absence of an exact substitute, the use of a notional market value to assess damages may not fully compensate C if he has a consumer surplus in the chattel; it is submitted that, in appropriate cases, where no substitute could give C equal satisfaction, the damages should take account of the loss of a consumer surplus.[10] This should be the court's approach whether its policy is compensation or deterrence of similar acts of misappropriation.

In assessing the value of the item converted, the court will look to the reality of the situation, as where D published material in which C held the copyright; although the technical conversion was the binding of the infringing sheets into the book, the value of the sheets was taken as a proportion of the value of the book as a whole.[11] If D has the chattel in his possession, but refuses to produce it to enable it to be valued, the court may infer that it is of the highest value of any chattel of that type, as where a chimney-sweep sued the jeweller to whom he had shown the jewel he had found in a chimney.[12]

## The time for assessing value

The law began with the uncompromising view that the value of C's chattel should always be assessed as at the time of D's conversion or misappropriation of it. But some statements prefer assessing the value at the date of judgment.[13] The date of conversion rule favours C if the market price of the chattel subsequently falls: in this situation, when D converted C's shares, the Privy Council allowed C to recover damages assessed at

6   See pp 536-540 above.
7   Cf pp 532-533, 539 above.
8   Cf the situation in the sale of goods where the buyer cannot buy an exact substitute: pp 100-101 above.
9   *JE Hall Ltd v Barclay* [1937] 3 All ER 620. (D had sold the chattels as scrap.)
10  See pp 168-171 above.
11  *Caxton Publishing Co Ltd v Sutherland Publishing Co* [1939] AC 178.
12  *Armory v Delamirie* (1721) 1 Stra 505. See also *Mortimer v Cradock* (1843) 12 LJ CP 166.
13  *Sachs v Miklos* [1948] 2 KB 23 and *Munro v Willmott* [1949] 1 KB 295.

their value of the time of conversion.[14] A later Privy Council case has upheld the date of conversion rule where the chattel (share certificate) had been 'irreversibly converted'[15] or disposed of; it was accepted that there is no universal rule as to the appropriate date for taking the value in conversion.[16] More recently the Court of Appeal ruled that the date for taking the value should be such as 'fairly' to 'compensate' C for his loss, taking account of what he would have done with the chattel eg would he have kept it, sold it or replaced it?[17] It could justifiably be argued by C that he could have chosen to sell at any time before the hearing,[18] which would support a rule allowing C to recover the highest value at any point between the conversion and the judgment, because C might have chosen to sell at that point.

The difficulty comes when the market price has risen after the date of conversion. If C knew, or ought to have known, of D's conversion, he cannot increase his damages by delay in bringing his action while the market rises.[19] But if C is not guilty of unreasonable delay, he may claim damages to give him the full value at the date of judgment, by treating the rise in value after the conversion as reasonably foreseeable consequential loss.[20]

## Improvements

Other problems in assessing the value of C's chattel arise when D has incurred expense or spent effort in repairing or improving it.[1] At common law, damages for conversion have been assessed at the value of the chattel in its unimproved state,[2] which indirectly allows D to retain the benefit

14　*Solloway v McLaughlin* [1938] AC 247.
15　*BBMB Finance (Hong Kong) Ltd v Eda Holdings Ltd* [1991] 2 All ER 129, PC, distinguishing cases where C has suffered only a 'temporary deprivation of his property', as in *Brandeis Goldschmidt and Co v Western Transport* [1981] QB 864, CA (C later received the copper which had been converted but failed to prove any loss caused by the delay).
16　The *BBMB* case, *loc cit* at 412.
17　*IBL Ltd v Coussens* [1991] 2 All ER 133 at 143.
18　Ibid.
19　*Sachs v Miklos*, above n 13. The rules on mitigation would lead to the same conclusion. (See now 1977 Act, s 12).
20　Ibid. In the (now abolished) action for detinue, in which C claimed actual delivery of the chattel, its value as at the date of judgment was the measure of damages in lieu of D's returning it: *Rosenthal v Alderton* [1946] KB 374. To the extent that conversion now fulfils the function of detinue, the same rule on damages should apply.
1　R Goff and G Jones, *The Law of Restitution* (5th edn 1999) pp 246-251.
2　*Munro v Willmott* [1949] 1 KB 295 (a claim in detinue, which has now been abolished: see p 541 above).

of his expenditure on improvements or in making it saleable.³ (This allowance at common law does not depend on D having acted in the honest belief that he had a good title to the chattel.) An analogy may be found in the many earlier common law cases concerning unauthorised mining by D, where C claimed damages for the value of the coal extracted. The courts allowed in all cases the cost of bringing the coal to the surface to be deducted from the value of the coal at the surface; in addition, where D had not been a wilful trespasser, the cost of severing the coal was also allowed.⁴ Where C could not himself have extracted the coal, his damages should be the reasonable royalty which adjacent owners would have paid for a licence to mine.⁵

Some statutory protection is now given to an improver by the 1977 Act. In proceedings for wrongful interference against D, who has improved the chattel in the honest but mistaken belief that he had a good title to it, the assessment of damages must allow D the benefit of the improvement to the extent that the value of the chattel is attributable to it.⁶

## Redelivery in mitigation of C's claim

If C accepts redelivery of the chattel before judgment in his claim against D, his damages will obviously be reduced,⁷ because his remaining claim will be only for loss of use during the period he was deprived of it or for any physical damage to it. If a virtually identical item is redelivered, such

---

3   However, D would not receive any allowance if C was able to recover possession of the improved chattel without bringing legal proceedings. (Similarly, no allowance against the proceeds of sale is given by 1977 Act, s 12, which gives a bailee the right to sell the chattel where he has taken reasonable steps to communicate with the bailor, but without success.) The question whether the improver has an *independent* claim against the owner is unsettled: *Greenwood v Bennett* [1973] QB 195 at 202, 203 (see Goff and Jones, *The Law of Restitution*, above n 1, pp 175-176); J Beatson, 'Discharge for Breach: The Position of Instalments, Deposits and other Payments Due Before Completion' (1981) 97 Law Quarterly Review 389, pp 410–11; P Birks, *An Introduction to the Law of Restitution* (rev edn 1989) pp 121-124 and P Matthews, 'Freedom, Unrequested Improvements, and Lord Denning' [1981] Cambridge Law Journal 340, p 366.
4   *McGregor on Damages*, above n 1, paras 1399-1410.
5   *Livingstone v Rawyards Coal Co* (1880) 5 App Cas 25.
6   1977 Act, s 6(1). (Section 6(2) provides that a similar allowance is to be made when C sues a bona fide transferee from the improver. S 6(3) deals with the consequential adjustment in any claim for a recovery of a price paid by the transferee.)
7   C will always be entitled to nominal damages, to signify that D had converted his chattel: *Hiort v London and North Western Rly Co* (1879) 4 Ex D 188 (a notional redelivery of the goods to C: ibid at 196).

as shares in the same company,[8] C's damages will similarly be reduced. Again, if D uses some of the proceeds of the conversion to pay off C's debts to a third party, C's damages for conversion may likewise be reduced.[9]

But C may refuse D's offer to redeliver the chattel to him, in which case the court may stay C's action and thus compel C to accept redelivery, provided the court is satisfied that the chattel remains in the same condition as before the tort, and provided C was claiming only its value, without any claim for consequential loss.[10]

### Where C has only a limited interest in the chattel

At common law, the fact that C, the possessor of the chattel, had only a limited interest in it (eg as a bailee) did not prevent him from recovering damages for its full value against a stranger, D, who converted it.[11] This held even where C, the bailee, was not liable to the bailor for loss of the chattel;[12] but if C in fact recovered its full value from D, he held for the bailor the excess beyond his own interest.[13] Where C sues for damages for wrongful interference, D is now entitled by statute[14] to show that a third party has a better right than C in respect of all or part of the interest claimed by C. D may bring the third party before the court,[15] which may then apportion the damages between the parties according to their respective interests.[16] If D does not avail himself of this procedure, the common law position set out above still applies.

---

8   *Solloway v McLaughlin* [1938] AC 247. (C was awarded the difference between the value of the shares at the time of the conversion (see pp 543-544 above) and their value on redelivery.)

9   *AL Underwood Ltd v Bank of Liverpool* [1924] 1 KB 775 at 794 (conversion of C's cheques). Cf *Lloyds Bank v Chartered Bank* [1929] 1 KB 40.

10  *Fisher v Prince* (1762) 3 Burr 1363. (D must pay C's costs up to the stay of proceedings.)

11  *The Winkfield* [1902] P 42. (The claim was for destruction of the chattels by D's negligence, but the assessment of damages was treated as it would have been in conversion.) The bailor has no further claim. If it is the bailor who recovers damages from D for damage to the chattel and loss of its use, the bailee has no further claim against D for loss of its use: *O' Sullivan v Williams* [1992] 3 All ER 385, CA.

12  *The Winkfield*, [1902] P 42. (The chattels in question were mails in charge of the Postmaster-General, who was not liable for their loss).

13  Ibid.

14  1977 Act, s 8.

15  CPR 19.5A.

16  1977 Act, s 7. If C has recovered more than his proper share of the value of the chattel, he may be required to account for the excess to another person entitled to claim (s 7(3)).

If D himself claims an interest in the chattel, C can recover damages in conversion only to the extent of his limited interest.[17] In the case of a pledge[18] where D, the pledgee, has converted C's chattel which he holds as security for a loan to C, C must tender the debt and interest due to D before he can sue D in conversion.[19] In the case of a sale of goods, where the buyer C was entitled to possession despite the fact that he had not yet paid the price (the sale being on credit terms) C could nevertheless sue the seller D in conversion for reselling the goods to a third person: but C's damages were the value of the goods less the price.[20] Similarly, in hire-purchase: C, a finance company, claimed the value of the car let to a hirer on hire-purchase terms, on the ground that the hirer had sold it to D, a dealer (which meant that both the hirer and D had converted it). C's damages were limited to the amount unpaid under the hire-purchase agreement at the time of the conversion, which was the extent of its loss.[1]

## Unauthorised use

When D, without C's authority, makes use of C's chattel (which has been returned to C's possession) a problem arises about the basis for assessing C's damages. The simplest situation is where C used the chattel in his business, and had to hire a substitute while D wrongfully deprived him of it: it is clear that C can recover the reasonable cost of the substitute.[2] The situation is less clear when C does not hire a substitute, but claims damages for loss of use. If the approach is to ask C to prove his actual 'loss', C may be unable to prove any. If, on the other hand, the approach is to charge D what it would have cost him to hire the chattel from C, a 'reasonable price' can be fixed by the court on the basis of the figure which reasonable parties, in the particular circumstances, would have been likely to negotiate for C's permission to D to use it. The second approach can be justified on

---

17 *Brierly v Kendall* (1852) 17 QB 937. But the unpaid seller of goods who has transferred both ownership and possession to the buyer, has no further interest in the goods themselves. If he retakes them, the buyer can recover in conversion their full value from the seller, whose sole remedy is to sue the buyer for the price: *Benjamin's Sale of Goods* (5th edn 1997) para 15-117.

18 See p 49 above.

19 *Donald v Suckling* (1866) LR 1 QB 585 and *Halliday v Holgate* (1868) LR 3 Exch 299.

20 *Chinery v Viall* (1860) 5 H & N 288.

1 *Wickham Holdings Ltd v Brooke House Motors Ltd* [1967] 1 WLR 295; *Belvoir Finance Co Ltd v Stapleton* [1971] 1 QB 210.

2 *Strand Electric and Engineering Co Ltd v Brisford Entertainments Ltd* [1952] 2 QB 246 at 254. To the same effect is *Davis v Oswell* (1837) 7 C & P 804 (C recovered the cost of hiring other horses when D converted and used his). Cf the situation where C hires a substitute while his damaged chattel is being repaired.

the argument that D has wrongfully deprived C of the opportunity to negotiate a hiring charge. This thinking reflects the economic concept of opportunity cost: D's tortious action has prevented C from being able to take advantage of any alternative use of the chattel, which should be valued at the most valued foregone use, such as hiring the chattel to a user like D.[3]

The courts have instinctively been feeling their way towards the concept of opportunity cost. In one case[4] C's business was to hire out electrical equipment. D had failed to return some equipment belonging to C, and continued to use it to earn profits during the period of detention. The Court of Appeal awarded as damages the full market rate of hire for the period of detention by D. It was held to be irrelevant that C usually had only 75% of its equipment let out on hire at any one time[5], and that it sometimes let it at no charge to the hirer. Two of the judgments felt constrained to search for C's 'loss', but Denning LJ (as he then was) treated it as restitution by D of the value to him of the benefit which he had taken without C's permission.[6] Although the judgment did not develop the point, because C sued in tort[7] not in restitution, 'waiver of tort' is a category of restitution in which C elects to sue to recover the benefit which D has obtained through his tort (instead of damages for the loss which C has suffered).[8] The ground for granting the remedy is that D has been unjustly enriched through his tort.[9] As an Australian judge has put it: if D 'be improperly enriched, on what legal principle can it claim to retain its ill-gotten gains merely because' C has not 'been correspondingly impoverished'?[10] This approach was first used in conversion in 1701, when C was able to recover from D, who had converted C's chattel, the price for which D had sold it to a third person.[11] Later, the approach was extended to recovery of benefits received by D from trespass to goods

---

3    Damages for conversion of coal extracted from under C's land have sometimes been fixed at the royalty which D could have been expected to pay for the privilege of mining there: see text at p 545 n 5 above.
4    *Strand Electric Co v Brisford Entertainments*, above n 2. Although the claim was made in detinue, which is now superseded by a statutory extension of the tort of conversion (pp 541-542 above), the principle about damages laid down in this case will apply to similar factual situations in conversion.
5    To the same effect see *Inverugie Investments Ltd v Hackett* [1995] 1 WLR 713, PC (damages for wrongful occupation of an apartment building not reduced on account of the probability that not all the apartments would have been let by C: see p 527 above).
6    *Strand Electric Co v Brisford Entertainments*, above n 2.
7    See n 4 above.
8    Goff and Jones, *The Law of Restitution*, above p 544 n 1, pp 773-798.
9    Ibid, p 11 et seq.
10   *Mason v The State of New South Wales* (1959) 102 CLR 108 at 146.
11   *Lamine v Dorrell* (1701) 2 Ld Raym 1216.

and to land.[12] C may, however, find it difficult to prove the extent of D's enrichment if, in addition to tortiously using C's chattel, D used his own skill and money in producing the profit.[13]

A different approach to depriving C of the profit he made is found in exemplary damages. If D used C's chattel with the intention of making a profit from it, the case would fall within one category where exemplary damages are permitted to deprive D of the profit he made.[14] This approach is aimed at deterring deliberate profit-making, whereas the restitutionary remedy will also cover profits made from torts committed without knowledge of their tortious character.

It is submitted that the same result could be reached by the courts assessing damages for unauthorised use of C's chattel at his opportunity cost, the best alternative use available to him. One advantage of assessing damages at the value of the benefit to D is that it avoids the question whether C could recover the market rate of hire as damages if he was not in the business of hiring out the chattel. Another advantage is that this method avoids the possible defence that D might seek to prove that C would not in fact have used the chattel to earn hiring charges or to make a profit.[15] It would be unfair to the private individual if he could not recover damages on this basis whereas the businessman could. Whether the law should aim at depriving D of the profits arising from his tortious activity depends on a policy question – do we wish to increase the deterrent effect of the law? So long as D can profit from his tortious conduct whenever C cannot show a corresponding loss, the deterrent effect is weakened. This effect is relevant only where D knew that he was misappropriating someone else's chattel; but the law, in order to protect proprietary and possessory interests in chattels, must also give protection to C when D acted innocently.[16]

A final issue is whether C can recover any loss of profits caused by D's misappropriation. If D deprives C of the use of a profit-earning chattel, can C claim loss of the profits which he would have made by using the chattel to fulfil a contract with a third party? The answer is 'yes' if it was reasonably foreseeable that D's tort could cause this type of loss,[17] as

---

12  A limitation has been imposed in cases of trespass to land: see *Phillips v Homfray* (1883) 24 Ch D 439 (discussed at pp 528-529 above).

13  *Re Simms* [1934] Ch 1 at 33.

14  See pp 586-588   below.

15  The two other Lords Justices in the *Strand Electric* case, above n 2, reserved their opinions on these points at 252, 257.

16  In cases of unauthorised mining, the courts have distinguished between a wilful and an innocent trespasser: see p 545 above.

17  *Re Simms*, above n 13 at 29. In *Saleslease Ltd v Davis* [1999] 1 WLR 1664, it was held that in order to claim consequential loss beyond the market value of the chattel, C must show that the type of loss was reasonably foreseeable by D at the time of the conversion.

where D converted C's tools of trade.[18] Whenever a substitute is available, however, C should be able to avoid any loss of profits as the result of D's depriving him of a chattel used to generate profits (this is another instance of mitigation). In *The Arpad*,[19] C sued for damages for conversion of part of a cargo of wheat, and claimed the loss of profit arising from a contract to sell it which he had previously made; the majority of the Court of Appeal rejected this claim, although the rules on remoteness might have allowed it.[20]

18  *Bodley v Reynolds* (1846) 8 QB 779 and *France v Gaudet* (1871) LR 6 QB 199
    at 205.
19  [1934] P 189 (applied in *Saleslease Ltd v Davis*, above n 17).
20  See p 534 above.

# 28 Protecting financial interests

## Introduction

This chapter considers the remedies available under those torts which are principally used to protect C against loss which lawyers call 'purely' financial or 'pure' economic loss: deceit, negligent misrepresentation, statutory misrepresentation under the Misrepresentation Act 1967, wrongful interference, conspiracy, intimidation, and injurious falsehood and passing off. Pure economic loss is loss of a type which, from C's point of view, can only be conceived of in financial terms, such as loss of profits, loss of earnings not arising from an injury to C, loss of the value of an investment, loss made in performing a contract, or loss of an expected legacy under a will. In terms of the present law, this category of loss normally[1] excludes C's financial loss which is consequential upon physical injury to himself or his property. Most of the torts giving a remedy for financial loss are based on D's intentional conduct in certain situations, where the objective of the law is to deter those in D's position from behaving in an unacceptable way.[2] The main situations found in the law reports arise out of commercial competition and industrial relations.

There are special problems of causation with these torts, because D's conduct is often the making of a statement, and C's loss is caused only when he or a third person acts in reliance on, or in response to, that statement. A further problem is the risk that many people could act on a

---

1   It should be noted that although the torts considered in this chapter are principally used in practice to recover damages for C's financial loss, he may exceptionally be able to recover damages for physical harm, as in deceit: see below.
2   H Carty, 'Intentional Violation of Economic Interests: The Limits of Common Law Liability' (1988) 104 Law Quarterly Review 250.

single statement, which could lead to crushing liability being imposed on a single defendant.[3] This latter reason has caused judges to hesitate before giving a remedy when D did not intentionally cause loss to C. Further protection, as by imposing liability on D for negligently causing financial loss to C, might inhibit healthy competition between businessmen, or other activities which generally benefit society. Thus, it is only in restricted situations that D can be liable for negligence in causing purely financial loss. Normally, C must look after his own financial interests, as by spreading them widely, or covering his risks by loss insurance.

The 'law of tort' other than negligence has a certain quality of being a residual category into which heads of civil liability not easily placed within contract, land law and to some extent restitution now are exiled, and have there been left without determined attempt to imbue them with overall coherence. This is particularly true of the torts used principally to protect financial interests. They have no real reason to be brought together here except that they are principally used to protect financial interests. Lack of doctrinal consistency need not be deplored if the law works tolerably well, and, even if it does not, it is not necessarily the case that the courts should attempt to do anything radical to remedy such a lack[4] because an improvement in consistency secured at the cost of the usefulness of the law is no improvement at all. Nevertheless, it should be pointed out that there is a *particular* lack of consistency about these torts which does impede their clear understanding.

These torts will be treated under two headings which, though they represent an obvious classification, themselves embody a great deal of confusion: *misrepresentation* (deceit, negligent misrepresentation and statutory misrepresentation) is a mixture of contract, tort and a statutory hybrid of the two;[5] and *the economic torts* (wrongful interference,

---

3    W Bishop, 'Economic Loss in Tort' (1982) 2 Oxford Journal of Legal Studies 1.
4    Lord Wedderburn has observed that the economic torts have 'lacked their Atkin' ('Rocking the Torts' (1983) 46 Modern Law Review 224, p 229, but he did so in the course of a criticism of attempts to look 'for a quick solution "in principle"': ibid, p 227 (cf Lord Wedderburn's discussion of these torts in *Clerk and Lindsell on Torts* (18th edn 2000) ch 24). This has, however, usually been read as a call for radical doctrinal tidying up: eg DF Partlett, 'From Victorian Opera to Rock and Rap: Inducement to Breach of Contract in the Music Industry' (1992) 66 Tulane Law Review 771, p 773: 'The economic torts *require* a Cardozo or Atkin to tell them where they belong' (our emphasis). The general liability in negligence for pure economic loss towards which this seems to drive is not reconcilable with the existence of a market economy.
5    DK Allen, *Misrepresentation* (1988) p 9: 'the law of contract is very frequently seen as protecting the expectation interest and the law of tort as protecting the

conspiracy, intimidation, and injurious falsehood and passing off) is merely a grouping by function.[6] So potentially vexed are the commercial, industrial and labour interests on which these torts impinge that, it is submitted, reform on other than a legislative basis would be quite wrong,[7] even if the best course for such legislation were to attempt to devise a general competition regime comprehensible and justiciable at common law.[8]

## Misrepresentation

The law of misrepresentation may provide C with a cause of action against D when C suffers loss as a result of an untrue statement made by D. The loss is usually (but not necessarily) economic rather than physical.[9] Misrepresentation is an amalgam of common law[10] and statute[11], contract[12]

---

reliance interest. The general law of misrepresentation may ... be regarded as occupying a kind of no-man's land between the two, and this autonomous status is a major source of difficulty in expounding and comprehending this area of the law, especially bearing in mind the significant role that equity still plays in cases of misrepresentation'.

6 The most determined attempt to give these torts consistency within a tort framework is the classification of 'contractual' and 'non-contractual expectancies' in P Cane, *Tort Law and Economic Interests* (2nd edn 1996) pt 2 (cf P Cane, *The Anatomy of Tort Law* (1997) ch 3). See also H Carty, *An Analysis of the Economic Torts* (2001) ch 10. Without entering into the discussion, we think the less formally rigorous attempts to gather these torts together in JD Heydon, *Economic Torts* (1978); T Weir, 'Chaos or Cosmos: *Rookes, Stratford* and the Economic Torts' (1964) Cambridge Law Journal 225 and T Weir, *Economic Torts* (1997) are more successful. Cf I Englhard, *The Philosophy of Tort Law* (1993) p 216: 'the theorists' various models of uniform theories of liability are unrealisable in practice and will remain an intellectual utopia'.

7 T Weir, *A Casebook on Tort* (9th edn 2000) pp 569-570.

8 Much of the relevant law must be sought amidst the often (for any practical purpose) incomprehensible complexity of combined (or at least overlapping) UK and EC legislation: R Whish, *Competition Law* (4th edn 2001). The character of a 'system' of law this distant from the implicit concerns with general comprehensibility and effectiveness which were taken for granted in jurisprudence after John Austin (LL Fuller, *The Morality of Law* (rev edn 1969) ch 2) is a most interesting sociological issue: N Luhmann, *The Sociology of Law* (1975).

9 See *Langridge v Levy* (1837) 2 M & W 519 (considering D's liability in deceit in respect of gun which exploded and injured C) and *The Nicholas H* [1996] AC 211 (advice of negligent ship surveyor resulted in loss of cargo – liability would have arisen but for the particular status of the surveyor – liability would upset established allocations of responsibility in the shipping industry).

10 Eg actions in deceit and under *Hedley Byrne & Co v Heller & Partners Ltd* [1964] AC 465 and elsewhere where rescission is sought in respect of a non-fraudulent and non-negligent misrepresentation.

11 Eg actions under Misrepresentation Act 1967, s 2(1) and 2(2).

12 Where a misrepresentation is incorporated into a contract (ie it is a term of that contract as opposed to a mere representation which induced it) any action for

and tort.[13] As a result the subject is rarely considered as a whole with parts examined in tort textbooks and others in standard contract works. In this discussion we will examine the remedies available in respect of a misrepresentation irrespective of the origin of the underlying cause of action. In this area it is difficult to understand the available remedies without some reference to the corresponding cause of action. For this reason a brief précis of the substantive law precedes the examination of available remedies.

The discussion that follows is divided into three sections to reflect the distinct contexts in which an action for misrepresentation may arise.

## Deceit

Deceit, also known as 'fraudulent misrepresentation' or simply 'fraud', is a tort. The tort is committed where D deceives C into believing that a certain fact is true with the intended consequence that C suffers loss.[14] The essence of the action is that D made the untrue statement deliberately ie he was aware of its untruth.[15] In other words an honest belief in the truth of the fact asserted will render D immune from an action in deceit.[16] If the belief was carelessly formed, D may be liable in an action for negligent misrepresentation. If D has the required mental state his motive is irrelevant.[17] If, besides D's deceit, there is another contributory cause of C's loss,[18] C's action for deceit is unaffected even if the contributory factor is a want of care on C's part.[19]

Despite the fact that all systems of civil liability enforce a protection against the deliberate propagation of misinformation there is a lack of unanimity about the underlying rationale. Some writers have stressed the moral wrong committed by those who are aware of the untruth of their assertion and the likelihood that others will suffer loss in reliance upon

---

misrepresentation is not formally affected by its status as a term: see Misrepresentation Act 1967, s 1(a). In practice C may prefer to pursue his remedy for *breach* rather than for *misrepresentation* in order to obtain damages assessed by reference to the position C would have been in if the representation had been true ie the expectation measure.

13   Deceit and negligent misrepresentation under *Hedley Byrne* are torts.
14   The loss may be suffered at a time and place other than where C acted on the misrepresentation: *Diamond v Bank of London and Montreal Ltd* [1979] QB 333 at 349.
15   *Derry v Peek* (1889) 14 App Cas 337 at 374.
16   Ibid at 373.
17   Ibid at 374 and *Foster v Charles* (1830) 7 Bing 105 at 107.
18   *Paul and Vincent Ltd v O'Reilly* (1913) 49 ILT 89.
19   *Pearson (S) and Son Ltd v Lord Mayor of Dublin* [1907] AC 351.

it.[20] Economists have proposed an instrumental argument which emphasises the wasteful effects to which the failure to control fraud would give rise. The 'investment' in making and unmasking untruthful statements 'is completely wasted from a social standpoint', for they consume resources for no beneficial product.[1] Where *ex hypothesi* D is aware of the untruth of the statement he does not need to carry out costly investigations to verify or refute it. This means that the costs of avoidance are comparatively low. A cost benefit analysis therefore supports the regulation of fraud.[2] To an economist the purpose of the legal prohibition on fraud is therefore to secure the benefits that flow from increasing the confidence that may be placed by actors in the veracity of statements made by others.[3] A distinction is sometimes drawn between so called procedural and substantive unconscionability.[4] The former refers to a concern with the procedures that precede the formation of a contract and the latter to the distributive effects (ie who gets what) of the completed bargain. The economic rationale for the control of fraud is in these terms concerned with procedural rather than substantive unconscionability and any distributive effect is purely incidental.[5]

Where C seeks rescission in respect of a fraudulent misrepresentation the courts dispense with a number of requirements that would otherwise have to be satisfied. First, whatever the position in respect of other misrepresentations,[6] there is no requirement that a fraudulent misrepresentation be a material one[7] ie one upon which a reasonable person in C's position would have relied. Second, rescission may be

20  See C Fried, *Contract as Promise* (1981) pp 9-12. For a judicial endorsement of this explanation see *Smith New Court Securities Ltd v Scrimgeour Vickers (Asset Management) Ltd* [1997] AC 254.
1   RA Posner, *Economic Analysis of Law* (5th edn 1998) p 122.
2   MJ Trebilcock, *The Limits of Freedom of Contract* (1993) p 104.
3   R Cooter and T Ulen, *Law and Economics* (3rd edn 2000) pp 276-277. For a critical account of the effectiveness of private law in this regard see H Collins, *Regulating Contracts* (1999) ch 4.
4   It originates in a well-known American article AA Leff, 'Unconscionability and the Code: the Emperor's New Clause' (1967) 115 University of Pennsylvania Law Review 485, p 487. Cf PS Atiyah *Essays on Contract* (rev edn 1990) p 333, which is critical of the distinction.
5   See Trebilcock, *The Limits of Freedom of Contract* (1993) 104.
6   *Museprime Properties Ltd v Adhill Properties* [1990] 2 EGLR 196 suggests that 'materiality' is relevant to the burden of proof in relation to inducement ie where the representation was not material (would not have induced a reasonable man to act as C did), C must prove that it did induce him so to act, and where the representation was material (would have induced a reasonable man to act as C did), D bears the burden of disproving inducement. See also *County Natwest v Barton* [1999] 33 LS Gaz R 31.
7   *Smith v Kay* (1859) 7 HL Cas 750 and *Rafsanjan Pistachio Producers Co-operative v Bank Leumi (UK) plc* [1992] 1 Lloyd's Rep 513 at 542. Cf *Downs v Chappell* [1997] 1 WLR 426.

'triggered' without the need for C to communicate this intention to D.[8] Third, lapse of time will not, of itself, prevent C from seeking rescission of a contract entered with D in reliance upon D's fraudulent representation (it would if the misrepresentation was non-fraudulent).[9] Further, the court has no power, as it does under Misrepresentation Act 1967, s 2(2) in respect of a non-fraudulent misrepresentation, to substitute for the claim to rescind an award of damages.

Deceit is a tort and so any damages awarded to C will seek, so far as an award of money can, to put C in the position he was in before the wrong occurred ie before the misrepresentation was made. In one case,[10] C was induced by fraudulent representations to exchange his yacht, sports car and a large sum of money for a villa and discotheque overseas. C recovered as damages the difference between the value of the property he received and that which he gave plus some incidental expenses such as delivering his yacht. In this way C was returned to his *status quo ante*. Damages for loss of profit are usually associated with the expectation or contractual measure of damages which seeks, so far as an award of money can, to put C in the position he would have been in if the promise had been kept.[11] In the context of misrepresentation such an award would put C in the position he would have been in if the representation had been true. However, damages for loss of profit were awarded in respect of a fraudulent misrepresentation made by the vendor of a hairdressing business that he would not compete in the locality of the business sold.[12] This award was justified by reference to the test of remoteness that governs awards of damages for deceit (all 'direct' losses) which is more generous than that used in the tort of negligence (all 'reasonably foreseeable losses').[13] The sum awarded still fell short of the full contractual measure of recovery. C received the profits she would have made from the business she would have bought if she had not contracted with D; C did not receive the profits she would have made from the business she in fact bought if D had not, in breach of covenant, worked at a nearby salon.[14] D's liability for unforeseeable losses has a further consequence that D effectively bears the risk of C's loss being increased by events subsequent to the fraud which lay beyond the control of either party, such as a general market decline

8   *Car and Universal Finance Co Ltd v Caldwell* [1965] 1 QB 525.
9   *Leaf v International Galleries* [1950] 2 KB 86. The other bars to rescission discussed below apply to a fraudulent misrepresentations as to any other.
10  *The Siben (No 2)* [1996] 1 Lloyd's Rep 35. C was also to receive an 'escort business' run from the villa. However, as this amounted to a business in prostitution it was left out of account by the court which acted on the maxim *ex turpi causa oritur non actio* (no action shall arise from a base cause).
11  See generally pp 74-75 above.
12  *East v Maurer* [1991] 1 WLR 461.
13  The so-called *Wagon Mound* test. See pp 313-316 above.
14  *East v Maurer* [1991] 1 WLR 461.

which further devalues the worth of the subject matter of the contract.[15] Again this contrasts sharply with the approach in the tort of negligence where the House of Lords have effectively decided that the risk of such events is borne by C.[16]

There is another way in which damages for deceit are quantified which is generous to C. Where C claims damages in the tort of deceit, contributory fault on the part of C does not operate, as it would if C brought his action in negligence, to reduce recovery. In one case, a fraud was perpetrated upon several lenders by a number of parties. The liability of the employer of a surveyor who was a party to the fraud was not reduced by the lender's failure to follow their own internal guidelines and properly scrutinise a loan application.[17]

Damages for deceit can extend to any form of consequential loss directly flowing from the fraudulent misrepresentation. This may consist of damage to property,[18] wasted expenses[19] or damages in respect of inconvenience and distress.[20] In one case a 'moderate' award of £500 aggravated damages was made to C when he had been induced to buy shares from D who did not own them.[1] This case left open the question whether exemplary damages could be awarded.[2]

### Non-fraudulent pre-contractual statements

Many things are said in contractual negotiations. Where a contract ensues, only some of the statements made in negotiations will be incorporated into that contract as terms.[3] When a statement so incorporated is revealed

---

15 *Smith New Court Securities Ltd v Scrimgeour Vickers (Asset Management) Ltd* [1997] AC 254.
16 *South Australia Asset Management Corpn v York Montague Ltd* [1997] AC 191.
17 *Alliance and Leicester Building Society v Edgestop Ltd* [1994] 2 All ER 38. See also *Corporacion Nacional del Cobre de Chile v Sogemin Metals Ltd* [1997] 1 WLR 1396 and *Standard Chartered Bank v Pakistan National Shipping Corpn (No 4)* [2001] QB 167.
18 *Mullett v Mason* (1866) LR 1 CP 559 (C lost other cows following purchase of cow which D fraudulently said was free of disease).
19 See *The Siben (No 2)* [1996] 1 Lloyd's Rep 35.
20 *Mafo v Adams* [1970] 1 QB 548 (D fraudulently tricked C into giving up protected tenancy – damages included compensation for inconvenience) and *Shelley v Paddock* [1979] QB 120 (C moved into Spanish house sold to her by D who fraudulently represented that he had good title to it).
1 *Archer v Brown* [1985] QB 401. On aggravated damages generally see pp 580-585 below.
2 Cf *Metall und Rohstoff AG v ACLI Metals (London) Ltd* [1984] 1 Lloyd's Rep 598, 612 suggesting obiter that they are not. On exemplary damages generally see pp 585-594 below.
3 See the standard contract texts for further discussion of express and implied terms: eg GH Treitel, *The Law of Contract* (10th edn 1999) ch 6.

to be false the representee (usually C)[4] will have a choice; he can either pursue his remedies for breach of contract or for misrepresentation.[5] Occasionally remedies for misrepresentation will be more attractive. This might be the case where C wants to 'escape' from the contract and rescission for misrepresentation is available but termination for breach is not (perhaps because the term breached was not a condition but a warranty).[6] Where C seeks financial compensation he will generally prefer to sue for breach of contract rather than for negligent misrepresentation in order to claim the contractual measure of damages. Where the untrue statement made in negotiations is not incorporated into any subsequent contract, the main remedies[7] available to C will be rescission (or damages in lieu) and damages for negligent misrepresentation either under Misrepresentation Act 1967 or under the common law tort deriving from *Hedley Byrne & Co Ltd v Heller & Partners Ltd*.[8] Indeed the latter route would be available to C if he suffers loss as a result of the untrue statement of D even though no contract is ever concluded between them.[9]

The law of misrepresentation is therefore an important part of the legal control of pre-contractual bargaining. It has been argued that liability should be assigned between parties to negotiations in a way which minimises the cost of transactions.[10] Such an approach requires responsibility to borne by the party which could at least cost have discovered the truth or at least have insured against the possible untruth of the statement. In this way the law will facilitate mutually beneficial exchanges between contractors.

## Rescission

When C enters a contract in reliance upon a misrepresentation of fact made by D, C is entitled to rescind (set aside) the contract. Untrue statements of

4    Exceptionally D may be the representee eg where misrepresentation is raised as a defence to an action for specific performance as in *Redgrave v Hurd* (1881) 20 Ch D 1.
5    See Misrepresentation Act 1967, s 1(a) and above p 553 n 12.
6    Or the term breached was an innominate one and the breach was not serious enough to justify termination: see pp 51-56 above.
7    C may also be assisted by the law of restitution as applied to 'failed contracts' (see 235-241 above) or proprietary estoppel. C may also be able to sue for breach of a collateral contract. See R Halson, *Contract Law* (2001) ch 2.
8    Above p 553 n 10.
9    This is also true of an action in deceit and is one of the few advantages in framing an action in tort. It is sometimes summarised by saying that a tort action is available in three as well as two party situations.
10   W Bishop, 'Negligent Misrepresentation: An Economic Reformulation', in P Burrows and CJ Veljanovski (eds), *The Economic Approach to Law* (1981) 167, p 178.

fact in respect of which rescission is available are often contrasted with untrue statements of opinion,[11] intention[12] and law[13] which do not (unless they contain concealed statements of fact), any more than 'meaningless puffery'[14], justify rescission. Rescission for misrepresentation seeks to put C (and D) in the position they were in before the wrong occurred. Typically it will involve the mutual re-exchange of goods and money. In this way the parties are literally restored to their status quo ante. Rescission for misrepresentation is effected by C giving notice to D before any so called 'bar' to rescission arises. The bars to rescission are the intervention of innocent third party rights,[15] affirmation by the representee,[16] lapse of time[17] and where restitution is impossible.[18] The latter bar does not limit the availability of rescission to circumstances where C is able to return the goods or property of D in exactly the state in which it was received. In many cases C will in some way alter the property or goods before he discovers the untruth of D's assertion eg Where a mine is 'worked' for a period before it becomes clear that the represented deposits are not present. Where restitution is ordered in such cases it should be accompanied by a financial order requiring C to account for any interim profit (eg on the sale of such deposits as are extracted) and also for any deterioration of the goods/property caused by C's negligence (eg if mine buildings were damaged by fire).[19]

Where goods and property are purchased for cash, rescission will effectively restore parties to the positions they were in before they entered the contract C now wishes to set aside. However, where part of the 'price' paid by C for the goods or property involves payments to third parties, the third parties will not be affected by the rescission of a contract to which

---

11 *Bisset v Wilkinson* [1927] AC 177 (a statement by vendor who had never farmed sheep that land 'would carry 2000 sheep' was held to be an opinion).

12 *Jorden v Money* (1854) 5 HL Cas 185 (creditor's statement that he would not enforce a debt was a statement of intention for purposes of estoppel).

13 This dichotomy may be affected by the recent decision of the House of Lords in *Kleinwort Benson Ltd v Lincoln County Council* [1999] 2 AC 349 (payment made under a mistake of law may give rise to restitutionary claim).

14 Ie vague and laudatory sales talk. For an application see *Fordy v Harwood* (30 March 1999, unreported), CA (car described as 'Absolutely mint. All the right bits ... and does it go?! Probably cost a fortune to build').

15 Such as sale to a third party with no notice of the misrepresentation. See *Ingram v Little* [1961] 1 QB 31.

16 Affirmation occurs where C indicates a desire to continue with the contract at a time when he is aware of both the circumstances giving rise to the right to rescind and the existence of that right. See *Peyman v Lanjarni* [1985] Ch 457 (Iranian with little English did not lose right to rescind lease of restaurant because he knew of circumstances giving rise to right but not the right to rescind itself.)

17 *Leaf v International Galleries* [1950] 2 KB 86.

18 *Erlanger v New Sombrero Phosphate Co* (1878) 3 App Cas 1218.

19 Ibid and *The Lucy* [1983] 1 Lloyd's Rep 188 at 202.

they are strangers. For this reason C may obtain from D, in addition to an order for rescission, an indemnity in respect of any expenditure he was obliged to incur under the terms of the contract now rescinded. An example would be where a tenant rescinds a lease which contained covenants requiring the tenant to keep the premises in good repair. Any sums so spent will be recoverable as an indemnity. An indemnity should be distinguished from an award of damages. In one case,[20] unsanitary premises represented to be in good condition were let to a poultry farmer under a lease which obliged the tenant to pay rent, rates and effect repairs. The tenant's successful action for rescission meant that he received back the rent paid and was indemnified in respect of the rates paid to the local authority and repairs effected. However the tenant received no further compensation for his loss of stock, loss of profit and medical expenses.

## Damages

Damages 'in lieu'[1] of rescission are available under the Misrepresentation Act 1967, s 2(2) when a party has entered into a contract in reliance upon a non-fraudulent misrepresentation. The court is empowered by this section to 'declare the contract subsisting' and to award damages 'where it is equitable to do so' taking account of the nature of the misrepresentation, the loss that C would suffer if the contract was upheld and the loss that D would suffer if it was not. The breadth of the discretion conferred on the court is illustrated by a case in which rescission was sought of a contract to purchase development land for over £5m.[2] The purchaser sought rescission on the basis that the vendor represented that there were no sewers running under the land to be developed. An undisclosed sewer was discovered which could be re-routed at a cost of £18,000. C wanted rescission of the contract because the value of the land had subsequently dropped by half. The Court of Appeal said that if the claim to rescission had been made out[3] it would have exercised its discretion to award £18,000 damages 'in lieu' of rescission. In this way the discretion conferred by the statute would be exercised to prevent C from escaping the consequences of his own bad bargain.

The Misrepresentation Act 1967, s 2(1) introduced a new liability where D negligently induced C to enter into a contract with D. If C suffers

20   *Whittington v Seale-Hayne* (1900) 82 LT 49.
1    This has been interpreted to require a continuing (ie at the time damages are sought) rather than an historic right to rescission: *Floods of Queensferry Ltd v Shand Construction Ltd (No 3)* [2000] BLR 81 and *Government of Zanzibar v British Aerospace* [2000] 1 WLR 2333.
2    *William Sindall plc v Cambridgeshire County Council* [1994] 3 All ER 932.
3    It was held that there had been no actionable misrepresentation.

'loss' as a result of D's misrepresentation, D is liable[4] 'unless he proves[5] that he had reasonable ground to believe and did believe up to the time the contract was made that the facts represented were true'. One effect of the way in which the statutory liability for negligent misrepresentation is created by reference to the tort of deceit[6] has been to make the measure of damages recoverable under the section the same as that recoverable in the tort of deceit. This conclusion was said to follow inexorably from the statutory wording which does not state that the representor shall be liable but that he shall be 'so liable' referring back to liability for deceit.[7] The measure of damages applicable is therefore the tortious one and the appropriate rule of remoteness is all 'direct', not all 'foreseeable', losses. This equivalence with the tort of deceit is not complete. The Court of Appeal have said, albeit obiter, that damages under s 2(1) may be reduced to reflect C's own want of care (contributory negligence).[8]

### The tort of negligent misrepresentation

The decision of the House of Lords in *Hedley Byrne*[9] created the possibility that there could be liability at common law in respect of negligent misrepresentation outside of a fiduciary relationship. Most of the cases address issues of liability rather than remedy but it is nonetheless difficult to state simply the requirements of the tort. Two different approaches can be discerned in recent cases. The first emphasises the need for a special relationship between the parties.[10] This relationship is usually stated restrictively in terms of D's knowledge as to whom the statement will be communicated and for what purpose. The adviser must know that the statement will be communicated to a particular person or restricted class of persons for a particular purpose. On this basis auditors of a company have been held to owe no duty of care to another company which acted

---

4   The subsection confusingly says 'if the person making the misrepresentation would be liable in damages in respect thereof had the misrepresentation been made fraudulently'.

5   Ie the usual burden of proof is reversed: see *Howard Marine and Dredging Co Ltd v Ogden & Sons (Excavations) Ltd* [1978] QB 574 (D unable to discharge burden cast upon him by showing that represented capacity of barges was taken from Lloyd's Register of Shipping when capacities were correctly recorded in ship's documents).

6   See above n 4.

7   *Royscot Trust Ltd v Rogerson* [1991] 2 QB 297. See also *Cemp Properties (UK) Ltd v Dentsply Research and Development Corpn* [1991] 2 EGLR 197.

8   *Gran Gelato Ltd v Richcliff Group Ltd* [1992] Ch 560. Cf the tort of deceit discussed at pp 553-554 above.

9   Above n 10.

10  *Smith v Eric S Bush* [1990] 1 AC 831 and *Caparo v Dickman* [1990] 2 AC 605.

on the accounts when launching a take-over bid.[11] In contrast a duty of care was owed by auditors who were commissioned to prepare accounts to be used to 'defend' a take-over bid which accounts would be inevitably relied upon by the predator company.[12] The second broader approach emphasises the necessity for an assumption of responsibility by the representor.[13] This approach may be criticised for stating a conclusion of law rather than providing a workable test for a duty of care.[14]

*Hedley Byrne* liability was held to be established when D induced C to take the tenancy of a petrol station by negligently overestimating the potential value of the leased site.[15] C recovered his loss of capital, the amount of the overdraft run up while trying to keep the business going as well as his loss of other foregone earnings. The exceptional nature of this liability has been emphasised by the Court of Appeal.[16] The imposition of liability in the case just considered is probably justified by the extreme informational asymmetry in the case.[17] The tenant would have no prior expertise (and no obvious means of commercial access to such expertise) in the assessment of potential estimated annual throughput of petrol for a particular geographical location.

### Other non-fraudulent misrepresentations

*Hedley Byrne* provides the only possible liability for non-fraudulent statements made in contexts other than pre-contractual negotiations. The lack of a clear test for the imposition of a duty of care has already been noted.[18] A recent decision of the House of Lords[19] creates further confusion about the proper computation of damages. Where there is a breach on the part of a valuer[20] or solicitor[1] of a duty to take reasonable care with regard to the provision of information, the valuer or solicitor may not be liable

---

11   Ibid.
12   *Morgan Crucible Co plc v Hill Samuel & Co Ltd* [1991] Ch 295. See also *Galoo v Bright Grahame Murray* [1994] 1 WLR 1360.
13   *Henderson v Merrett Syndicates Ltd* [1995] 2 AC 145.
14   See the judgment of Lord Griffiths in *Smith v Eric S Bush* [1990] 1 AC 831.
15   *Esso Petroleum Co v Mardon* [1976] QB 801.
16   *Glen-Mor Fashions v Jaeger Co Shops Ltd* (1991, unreported).
17   Bishop, 'Negligent Misrepresentation: An Economic Reformulation', above p 558 n 10.
18   Bishop argues that restriction of the duty of care is justified when the information is of a type that is valuable to many users but the producer is unable to reflect this benefit in the price charged for it and a wider imposition of liability would discourage the production of information: ibid, pp 180-183.
19   *South Australia Asset Management Corpn v York Montague Ltd* [1997] AC 191.
20   Ibid.
1    *Bristol and West Building Society v Mothew* [1998] Ch 1.

to the full extent of C's loss where this is in part caused by a fall in the market value of the property purchased. This is because the duty assumed was one to take reasonable care in the provision of information upon which their employer could choose to act; they did not undertake to advise whether and if so how to act on that information. On this basis a valuer has been held liable to a lender only to the extent of the 'initial security shortfall' ie the difference between the negligent valuation and the actual value of the property at the time of the valuation. This approach relieves the valuer of responsibility for the effect of general market movements going beyond this shortfall. However, it also fails to compensate C for a loss that was a reasonably foreseeable consequence of D's breach of duty.

A further difficulty with the computation of damages for negligent misrepresentation concerns the effect of contributory negligence on the part of C. Some statements of *Hedley Byrne* liability refer to a requirement of reasonable reliance,[2] thereby suggesting that unreasonable reliance by C will bar recovery altogether. In contrast, later cases[3] appear to suggest that contributory negligence operates in relation to careless advice as it does with regard to conduct to reduce rather than avoid recovery.

### The 'economic torts'

*Wrongful interference with contractual relations*

This tort is committed where loss is caused to C by D who, with knowledge of C's contract and without justification: (1) intentionally persuades, induces or procures the other party to the contract to commit a breach of it; or (2) intentionally does an act which directly interferes with, or prevents the performance of, the contract; or (3) by unlawful means, intentionally but in an indirect manner interferes with, or prevents the performance of, the contract.[4]

The most effective remedy for this tort may be a negative injunction to prevent the continuation of D's action.[5] An interim injunction may preserve the present position until trial, so that C can carry on his business

---

2   Eg see Lord Reid's judgment in *Hedley Byrne*, above p 533 n 10 at 486.
3   *Banque Bruxelles v Eagle Star* [1995] 2 All ER 769 at 819-820. The point was not discussed in the Court of Appeal or the House of Lords.
4   *Merkur Island Shipping Corpn v Laughton* [1983] 2 AC 570 at 606–609. A similar tort is committed where D uses unlawful means to interfere with C's trade (or possibly his business or economic interests generally, eg with his prospective contractual relations with third parties): ibid at 609.
5   *Lord Strathcona Steamship Co Ltd v Dominion Coal Co Ltd* [1926] AC 108; *Manchester Ship Canal Co v Manchester Racecourse Co* [1901] 2 Ch 37 and *Swiss Bank Corpn v Lloyds Bank Ltd* [1979] 2 All ER 853 at 869–874. (In trade disputes, however, legislation governs the use of injunctions: see p 566 n 6 below.)

as he did before D's action.[6] If D's interference is established, an injunction may restrain him from interfering with similar contracts which C may make in future.[7]

The authorities seem to have established no clear principle for the assessment of damages for this tort, beyond the vague statement that 'the damages are damages at large'.[8] Examination of the wrongful interference cases in particular and the exemplary damages cases in general leads one to conclude that holding damages to be at large has amounted to an invitation to C to try to claim for almost any loss. C often claims damages for his loss of profits or of business, such as loss made by C in not being able to sell confidential information to D;[9] or loss of profits on orders for business taken away from C when D induced a third party to break a covenant in restraint of trade made with C.[10] Subject to remoteness and mitigation, C may recover damages for the expenses he incurred as the result of D's wrongful interference, eg the expenses of investigating D's campaign against C's system of obtaining covenants from purchasers of new cars that they would not resell them for 12 months.[11] Subject to the general rules governing such combination, expectation and reliance claims may be combined.[12]

Courts in the past have been reluctant to award damages for injury to C's feelings or reputation arising from inducing breach of contract, for reasons similar to those which have meant that such awards have so far been isolated (but not unknown) in breach of contract cases *tout court*.[13] But analogies for doing this may be found in deceit,[14] and in *Pratt v British Medical Association*,[15] a conspiracy case, C obtained damages for his suffering 'humiliation and menace' in addition to his pecuniary loss. This issue of recovery for 'damages for distress' will be considered in connection with exemplary damages below,[16] but in so far as precedents from economic

---

6    *Torquay Hotel Co Ltd v Cousins* [1969] 2 Ch 106. On interim relief see ch 31 below.
7    Ibid. A declaration may be made in lieu of an injunction: *Bents Brewery Co Ltd v Hogan* [1945] 2 All ER 570 and *The Kalingrad* [1997] 2 Lloyd's Rep 35. On declarations see further pp 217-218 above.
8    *Exchange Telegraph Co Ltd v Gregory & Co* [1896] 1 QB 147 at 153. On damages at large see pp 582-583 below.
9    Ibid.
10   *Goldsoll v Goldman* [1914] 2 Ch 603 at 615–616.
11   *British Motor Trade Association v Salvadori* [1949] Ch 556 at 569.
12   *Falconer v ASLEF and NUR* [1986] IRLR 331. The highly controversial aspects of this case concern not the quantification of damages but the 'floodgates' implications of holding D liable at all: ibid at 334, para 49 and see further (3 June 1986) 306 Industrial Relations Legal Information Bulletin 13.
13   See pp 594-603 below.
14   See p 554-557 above.
15   [1919] 1 KB 244 at 281–282.
16   See pp 595-601 below.

tort cases are concerned, the Court of Appeal has strongly insisted that if C wishes to recover for injury to feelings or reputation, he must bring an action in defamation.[17] These particular losses are, it is hesitantly submitted, now unlikely to be recovered as an incident of an economic tort action, though it must be insisted that distinctions such as that drawn between 'aggravated general damages' and 'an additional claim for distress and injury to feelings' are most unsatisfactory, for it would appear that what amounts to the latter may, if it is pleaded in a different way, be allowed under the former head.[18] The law on this point may be so uncertain that one cannot say with confidence what would be decided in future cases, the outcome of which would appear to be very heavily dependent on the framing of the pleadings.[19]

## Conspiracy

The tort of conspiracy is committed where, without lawful justification, loss to C is caused by the implementation of an agreement between two or more persons whose main purpose is to injure C or to cause that loss. If the means employed by D are illegal, the agreement cannot be justified. But even where the acts agreed to be done by the defendants are criminal, C must still prove that their intention was to injure him, rather than to protect their own interests.[20]

17  *Lonrho plc v Fayed (No 5)* [1993] 1 WLR 1489 at 1496. This also was a conspiracy case, but see *Joyce v Sengupta* [1993] 1 WLR 337 at 351-352, a malicious falsehood case.
18  Sir Michael Kerr, ibid at 353 struck out an explicit claim for distress and injury to feeling but allowed 'that something of the same nature could still be awarded as an ingredient of a possible award of aggravated damages'. This seems to hold out a reward for obfuscation in statements of case. Sir Michael's frankness about the unsatisfactory character of this distinction is all that distinguishes his treatment of it from that in most other cases. For a perfectly representative example of the confusion at work see *Ketley v Gooden* (1997) 73 P & CR 305.

There were unjustifiable inconsistencies between the County Court and Supreme Court Rules of pleading aggravated damages: Law Commission, *Aggravated, Exemplary and Restitutionary Damages*, Report No 247 (1997) paras 2.37-2.38 which Lord Woolf has sought to address in the course of an attempt to improve the pleading of exemplary damages overall: CPR 16.4(1)(c).
19  In a postscript to his judgment in *Michaels v Taylor Woodrow Developments Ltd* [2001] Ch 493, in which a number of unreported decisions had been cited to him, Laddie J argued that steps must be taken 'if the increasing ease with which prior decisions can be accessed is not going to choke the system' (ibid at 522G). Without wishing to derogate from Laddie J's wise point, which stands on its own, we would add that when the law is so incoherent that its outlines cannot be reduced to a statement of agreed principle, it invites this type of attempt to win by weight of citation.
20  *Lonrho Ltd v Shell Petroleum Co Ltd (No 2)* [1982] AC 173.

The cases state that damage is an ingredient in the tort, but give little guidance on the causation involved. Some implementation of the agreement by the defendants is obviously necessary in order that the harm should result: 'the tort of conspiracy is constituted only if the agreed combination is carried into effect in a greater or less degree and damage to the plaintiff is thereby produced';[1] 'the tort ... consists not of agreement but of concerted action taken pursuant to agreement'.[2] The formulation of the tort in the leading case requires the 'predominant purpose' to 'injure the plaintiff's commercial interests' to be applied not only to the agreement between the defendants but also to 'the acts done in execution of it which caused damage to' C.[3] So if the defendants, by implementing their agreement to injure C, caused him loss in some unintended way, that loss would not be recoverable in this tort. This is a restriction on the scope of the tort, and precludes use of the analogy from the tort of deceit, where D is liable for an unintended consequence, provided it satisfies the test of directness.[4] If in the tort of conspiracy the acts of the defendants which actually cause C's loss must be acts intended by them to injure C, this is an even narrower test of remoteness of damage than the *Wagon Mound* test of reasonable foreseeability.[5]

Few cases deal with the assessment of damages in conspiracy. The loss of which C complains usually concerns his commercial interests or contractual relations, such as C's loss of business suffered through the withdrawal of his chief customer.[6] In regard to other losses, it is submitted

---

1   *Crofter Hand Woven Harris Tweed Co Ltd v Veitch* [1942] AC 435 at 439.
2   *Lonrho Ltd v Shell Petroleum Co Ltd (No 2)* [1982] AC 173 at 188.
3   Ibid at 189. See further the extensive recent discussion of *Lonrho v Shell (No 2)* in *Michaels v Taylor Woodrow Developments Ltd* [2001] Ch 493, *passim*.
4   See pp 556-557 above.
5   See pp 313-322 above.
6   *Quinn v Leathem* [1901] AC 495. At 498 it is reported that the trial judge permitted the jury, in assessing damages, to take account of the defendants' conduct.

   Lord Lindley's speech in this case has been subjected to one of the most searching examinations ever made of a judgment, exposing his depiction of Leatham's position as resting on 'the ordinary rights of a British subject' as mere façade: WN Hohfeld, *Fundamental Legal Conceptions* (2001) pp 16-17 (cf introduction by NS Simmonds, ibid, pp xix-xx). The political controversy Hohfeld shows is inherent in the legal conceptions at work in *Quinn v Leatham* (and *Rookes v Barnard* etc) has made this area ripe for legislative intervention. The necessary balancing of interests (Heydon, *Economic Torts* (1978) pp 25-26) has repeatedly been remade in line with the then prevailing political views (Lord Wedderburn, *Labour Law and Freedom* (1995) ch 1) until, broadly, the current New Labour governments continued the policies of the previous Conservative ones: IT Smith and G Thomas, *Industrial Law* (7th edn 2000) pp 628-633. The crucial point is that the broad political consensus on which trying to develop a defensible common law position of any sort depends has largely been absent from the economic torts. On the current influence of labour law legislation on these torts see *Clerk and Lindsell on Torts* (18th edn 2000), paras 24.138-24.205.

that the courts should follow the decisions in other torts involving D's intention,[7] eg recovery of expenses.[8] It is undecided whether exemplary damages could be awarded where the defendants intended to make a profit from their conspiracy.[9]

## Intimidation of a third person[10]

The tort of intimidation is established where: (1) D makes a threat to a third person to do an unlawful act affecting him, unless he acts in a certain way, which D intended should cause loss to C (or ought reasonably to have foreseen was likely to cause loss to C); and (2) the third person complies with the threat, by acting in the required way, with the consequence that C does suffer loss. In the leading case, *Rookes v Barnard*,[11] the defendants threatened their employer that they would strike in breach of their contracts of employment unless their employer dismissed C, another employee.

The causation is of a specific type, which involves a third party's action in acceding to D's threat to him. If the third party was actually coerced into his action, it need not be tested by the standard of reasonableness – the fact that a reasonable person would not have succumbed to the threat is irrelevant. (Of course, whether the action will be found to have amounted to coercion will, as a matter of fact, depend on how threatening the action was.) The intention of D that the third party should comply with the threat is sufficient to meet the causal test. Although the essence of the tort is the unlawfulness of what D threatens to do to the third party, it is not clear whether the coercive effect of the threat must come from its unlawful aspect. Would it be a defence for D to show that the threat would have been just as coercive if the unlawful aspect had not been present?[12]

A further issue concerns remoteness of damage. In intimidation, the loss to C is usually the loss which D intended to cause to him, eg threats 'directed at' C, 'being designed to cause an end of his employment' with his employer.[13] If an analogy is taken from the tort of conspiracy,[14]

---

7   See pp 330-331.
8   *British Motor Trade Association v Salvadori* [1949] Ch 556 at 569.
9   See pp 588-590 below.
10  Intimidation of C himself should, in respect of remedies, be treated in the same way as deceit: see pp 555-557 above.
11  [1964] AC 1129.
12  Eg if in the leading case of *Rookes v Barnard*, ibid, there had not been a 'no strike' clause, and if the union had given a week's notice of striking (thus avoiding the illegality) the threat would have been just as powerful in its impact upon the employer: see *Morgan v Fry* [1968] 2 QB 710 at 738 at 739, CA.
13  *Rookes v Barnard* [1964] AC 1129 at 1182.
14  See pp 566-567 above. But another analogy from deceit would support the test of directness: see p 557 above.

intended consequences might also be covered. But one judge has said that D's threat is actionable 'if it is likely to harm' C, and causes 'reasonably foreseeable' damage to him.[15]

Decisions on assessing damages for intimidation concern industrial disputes where C has been dismissed from his employment. His damages are for his loss of earnings, less the amount he is earning, or ought reasonably to be earning, in substitute employment.[16] But the period for assessing the loss is not the same as in contract, because C can rely on his reasonable expectation that his contract will continue in force.[17] In *Rookes v Barnard*, C recovered damages for his loss of employment even though the strict legal position was that his employer could terminate his employment on a week's notice.[18]

## Injurious falsehood and passing off

Injurious falsehood consists in D's publishing to a third person a false statement about C, his property or his business, which D intends to, and does, cause the third person to act to C's detriment. C must prove that D had some dishonest or improper motive. The standard case is where D falsely says to others that C has ceased to carry on his business.[19] The common law required proof by C of 'special damage', which was often difficult to establish.[20] But by statute,[1] this is no longer necessary – (1) if D's words were published in writing or other permanent form and were calculated to cause pecuniary damage to C; or (2) if D's words were calculated to cause C pecuniary damage in respect of any office, profession, calling, trade or business held or carried on by C at the time of publication. Before the statute, it was held that C could establish his claim by proving a general loss of business, without showing the loss of particular customers.[2] It has been held after the statute that C can recover

---

15  Ibid at 1202.
16  *Morgan v Fry* [1968] 1 QB 521 at 548–549 (appeal allowed on a different point: CA, above p 567 n 12).
17  *Morgan v Fry* [1968] 1 QB 521, QB at 548-549.
18  See the discussion of wrongful dismissal at pp 601-603 above.
19  *Ratcliffe v Evans* [1892] 2 QB 524.
20  Ie the falsehood caused a specific loss which may be particularised, not merely the 'damage' the promulgation of a falsehood causes by definition. For discussion see CT McCormick, *Law of Damages* (1935) paras 113-115 and for examples see 28 *Halsbury's Laws of England* (4th edn 2000) paras 258-259 and *McGregor on Damages* (16th edn 1997) paras 24, 1871-1878.
1   Defamation Act 1952, s 3(1) (as recommended by *Report of the Committee on Defamation* (Chairman Lord Porter) Cmd 7536 (1948) para 54).
2   *Ratcliffe v Evans* [1892] 2 QB 524.

substantial damages only if he can prove pecuniary loss; otherwise he will receive nominal damages.[3] Once he has shown pecuniary loss, however, other damages may be claimed, except for injury to reputation and feelings.[4] As we shall see, with passing off C's remedies are not limited to damages. He may also seek an injunction to prevent repetition of the false statement, or a declaration as to C's title to the goods (slander of title or of goods).[5]

In one type of injurious falsehood, the tort of passing off, D deceives third parties into acting to C's detriment. This tort is established where one trader, D, makes a false statement to members of the public, which induces them to believe that his goods or services are those of another trader, C (or are associated with, or sponsored by C).[6] By using a misleading name, description, mark,[7] label, appearance or packaging, D 'passes off' his goods or services as those of C, taking advantage of C's trade or business reputation. It is unfair competition arising from the confusion of customers, and is often considered to be an injury to C's right of 'property' in the goodwill of his business.[8] C need not prove that D had an intention to deceive the public; it is enough that D's practice is likely to deceive the typical customer.

An injunction is a regular remedy for passing off. C may obtain an injunction preventing D from carrying on his business under a name which confuses the public.[9] The House of Lords has upheld the award of an injunction restraining D from using the words 'Yorkshire Relish' in connection with his sauce 'without clearly distinguishing it from' C's sauce.[10] In another leading case,[11] the injunction restrained D from selling or distributing any product bearing the name 'advocaat' unless it consisted of spirit and eggs (the distinctive ingredients of the product to which the reputation attached) and did not include wine (as C's product did).

---

3  *Fielding v Variety Inc* [1967] 2 QB 841. (C can recover damages for his 'probable money loss, and not for [his] injured feelings': ibid at 850.)
4  *Joyce v Sengupta* [1993] 1 WLR 337 at 351-352.
5  *Reuter (RJ) Co Ltd v Mulhens* [1954] Ch 50 at 75.
6  *Erven Warnink v J Townend & Sons (Hull) Ltd* [1979] AC 731 at 742.
7  More extensive protection is given to registered trademarks by domestic legislation, principally the Trade Marks Act 1994, and by other EU and international trade legislation: see 48 *Halsbury's Laws of England* (4th edn reissue 2000), paras 1-14 for a summary statement and, at greater length, *Kerly's Law of Trade Marks and Trade Names* (13th edn 2001) chs 17-18.
8  *AG Spalding and Bros v AW Gamage Ltd* (1915) 84 LJ Ch 449 at 450.
9  *Henricks v Montagu* (1881) 17 Ch D 638.
10  *Birmingham Vinegar Brewery Co Ltd v Powell* [1897] AC 710. The same qualification to the injunction was made by the House of Lords in *Parker Knoll v Knoll International* [1962] RPC 265.
11  *Erven Warnink v J Townend & Sons (Hull) Ltd* [1979] AC 731.

Damages for passing off are recoverable for the loss suffered by C as the result of his potential business being diverted to D.[12] Such damages for lost future business are, in the nature of the case, difficult to assess because of the uncertainty of C's loss.[13] C is, of course, entitled to nominal damages even without proof of actual loss; but such damages are little deterrent.[14] It is for this reason that C may well seek injunctive relief with regard to a product which D intends to continue to produce, but this will leave him with the burden of monitoring D's compliance with the injunction.

An alternative to compensatory damages for loss of his own profits which C is at liberty to elect in these cases[15] is an account of profits, the purpose of which is to give C the actual profits improperly made by D.[16] Cases of passing off may well now be argued to be one of the 'appropriate situations' in which the wider use of this essentially restitutionary remedy[17] would appear to have been sanctioned by *A-G v Blake*.[18] However, there are two major problems with the use of this remedy which *Blake* does not affect, or, indeed, adequately address.

First, if the account of profits is limited (as it logically must be) to the gains D has made, the worst that can happen to D[19] is that he must disgorge all those gains. It must be questionable whether this is a sufficient deterrent. A 'punishment' of merely depriving a person of any gain he may make through wrongdoing is punishment at zero risk, that is to say, it is not punishment at all.[20] D may just repeatedly pass off, and disgorge

---

12  Ibid. The Defamation Act 1952, s 3(1) applies to passing off: see DI Bainbridge, *Intellectual Property* (4th edn 1999) pp 635-637.

13  *United Horse-shoe and Nail Co Ltd v John Stewart and Co* (1888) 13 App Cas 401 at 413. Cf the problems of proof of consequential loss in contract discussed at pp 88-97 above.

14  Other non-legal sanctions (see pp 13, 44-45 above) will tend to be of little relevance because the parties in a passing-off action are likely to have no positive relationship.

15  *Lever v Goodwin* (1887) 36 Ch D 1 at 7. One would have thought it unarguable that 'double recovery' by framing overlapping claims in both ways should be prevented, but questions about this have been raised by A Burrows, *Remedies for Torts and Breach of Contract* (2nd edn 1994) p 305 and Law Commission, *Aggravated, Exemplary and Restitutionary Damages*, Report No 247 (1997), paras 3.64-3.72. The damages for breach of copyright now available under the Copyright Designs and Patents Act 1988, s 97(2) have been interpreted in such a way as to make them consistent with avoidance of double recovery: D Allen, *Damages in Tort* (2000) paras 7.014-7.016.

16  *Draper v Trist* [1939] 3 All ER 513 at 522 and *My Kinda Town v Soll* [1983] RPC 15 (reversed on another point [1983] RPC 407, CA).

17  Ibid at 55: 'The purpose of ordering an account of profits ... in a passing-off case is not to inflict punishment on the defendant. It is to prevent an unjust enrichment of the defendant by compelling him to surrender those profits'.

18  [2001] 1 AC 268. See in general ch 17 above.

19  Leaving aside the question of costs, which D can limit by early settlement.

20  P Jaffey, 'Restitutionary Damages and Disgorgement' (1995) Restitution Law Review 30, pp 37-38.

when caught. If one's goal is to prevent passing off, one actually is pushed away from restitution to outright punitive damages not calculated with reference to unjust enrichment,[1] or, indeed, to seeking an injunction.

Second, and more importantly, in these cases an account of profits in practice suffers from defects similar to, but one imagines sometimes far worse, than those encountered in quantifying damages to compensate for loss of future business. Logically, the plausibility of this remedy rests on C being able to provide evidence of the gains D has made by his wrongful conduct, and this must encounter the proof problems analogous to those C's own expectation damages claim will encounter,[2] with the added very serious complication that the evidence must be sought from D, who obviously will not wish to provide it. The civil legal system does in theory have the mechanisms for searching for and compelling disclosure of evidence in these circumstances,[3] but the litigation this involves can be extremely fraught and expensive.[4] In practice, however, C's difficulties have been reduced because, to be frank, the courts often have adopted a very rough and ready approach to the quantification of awards given on broadly restitutionary bases,[5] and C may be able to obtain something through an account of profits even if it is impossible to justify the precise sum awarded.[6] It is likely that this sum will be 'fair and temperate',[7] for the courts have typically adopted a 'moderate' attitude when making these difficult-to-justify awards.[8] Even were the facts available, C is not entitled to recover all of D's profits but only those 'which are properly attributable to'[9] the passing off, and distinguishing the two may be very difficult.

1 *Pace My Kinda Town v Soll* [1983] RPC 15 at 55 (quote at n 17 above). This issue was inadequately considered as it arose in *Blake*: see p 608 below.
2 *Price's Patent Candle Co Ltd v Bauwen's Patent Candle Co Ltd* (1858) 70 ER 302 at 303.
3 See the 'inquiry into [expectation] damages at their own risk' ordered in the protracted litigation over the 'Orb football': *AG Spalding & Bros v AW Gamage Ltd* (1918) 35 RPC 101 (the order was made in the House of Lords, above p 569 n 8).
4 Passing off is one of the principal areas of law in which search (formerly Anton Piller) orders are used (Lord Chancellor's Department, *Anton Piller Orders: A Consultation Paper* (1992) para 1.9) and Sir John Donaldson MR (as he then was) has called such orders (together with freezing orders (Mareva injunctions)) 'the nuclear weapons' of commercial litigation: *Bank Mellat v Nikpour* [1985] FSR 87 at 92. Such orders may be needed to establish liability irrespective of the way damages are quantified.
5 See pp 235-238 above.
6 This imprecision evidently is what Slade J meant by 'fair apportionment' on the basis of a 'reasonable approximation' in *My Kinda Town v Soll* [1983] RPC 15 at 58.
7 *Draper v Trist* [1939] 3 All ER 513 at 527.
8 See pp 492-494 above.
9 *My Kinda Town v Soll* [1983] RPC 15 at 56. In particular, if at first D's practice was innocent, the account of profits will relate only to those profits arising after D had notice of C's rights: *AG Spalding & Bros v AW Gamage Ltd* (1918) 35 RPC 101 at 149.

In sum, while there would appear to be no objection to C having the account of profits available as a potential remedy, it remains to be seen even after *Blake* whether this will prove to be a superior alternative to compensatory damages if C does not seek or is denied an injunction in passing off cases.

## An Australian remedy

In his discussion of injurious falsehood, Fleming[10] mentions that the Australian[11] Trade Practices Act 1974 (Cth), s 52[12] offers a superior alternative remedy to the English law. Section 52 provides that 'a corporation shall not, in trade or commerce, engage in conduct that is misleading or deceptive or is likely to mislead or deceive'. The Australian experience would appear to be that this has had a very positive effect on the regulation of misleading trade practices,[13] not merely in relationship to injurious falsehood and passing off[14] but in relationship to many misleading statements,[15] and in particular it has more or less replaced the common law of misrepresentation in disputes to which it applies.[16] The principal virtue of s 52 is that it is that *rara avis* in contract, a clear statutory improvement upon the common law position as to liability, something beyond the UK Parliament in regard of misrepresentation.[17] Certain aspects of the remedies which follow from a successful claim under s 52 are,

---

10  JG Fleming, *The Law of Torts* (9th edn 1998) p 781.

11  See also the New Zealand Fair Trading Act 1986, s 9 and the US *Restatement of Unfair Competition* 3d (1995) § 3 (and ch 2 *passim*).

12  This is an Act of the Australian Commonwealth, and for constitutional reasons which need not be discussed here there is parallel state legislation throughout Australia, with only the position in Queensland being materially different in respect of remedies.

13  F Hanks and PL Williams (ed), *The Trade Practices Act: A 25 Year Stocktake* (2001).

14  RS French, 'The Law of Torts and Part V of the Trade Practices Act', in P Finn (ed), *Essays on Torts* (1989) 183, 201-202.

15  The extent to which s 52 applies to contractual terms (not covered by other consumer protection legislation) is a disputed issue: see JW Carter and DJ Harland, *Contract Law in Australia* (3rd edn 1996) para 1109.

16  Ibid; JA Connors, 'Intellectual Property and Consumer Protection: The Australian Overlap' (1980) 2 European Intellectual Property Review 211 and DJ Harland, 'The Statutory Prohibition of Misleading or Deceptive Conduct in Australia and Its Impact on the Law of Contract' (1995) 111 Law Quarterly Review 100. Harland's article is the basis of the chapter on the statutory prohibition of misleading or deceptive conduct in perhaps the leading Australian contract textbook: Carter and Harland, *Contract Law in Australia* (3rd edn 1996) ch 11.

17  Of the Australian states, only the Australian Capital Territory and South Australia enacted something like the Misrepresentation Act 1967.

however, worthy of note in themselves. These remedies are contained in the general section on remedies in Pt 6 of the Trade Practices Act 1974.

First, damages for contravention of s 52 are available under s 82,[18] and although this section does not guide quantification, it has been settled in the case law[19] that the tort or reliance measure should normally[20] be used; obviously a major clarification of the English position. Damages are not limited to economic losses,[1] but nominal[2] and exemplary[3] damages are not recoverable, which has the positive effect of concentrating the litigation on substantial and certain losses.

Section 87 gives the court a general discretion to make a wide range of orders which, again, constitute a major clarification of the broad rescission remedy available in the English law of misrepresentation.[4] Section 80 allows C to obtain an injunction against D's misleading and deceptive conduct, and this has been the principal remedy sought in passing off cases.

The most interesting aspect of the remedies for misleading and deceptive conduct is, however, the way they expand the number of possible Cs and Ds. Section 82 provides that: 'a person who suffers loss or damage by conduct of another person that was done in contravention of [s 52] may recover the amount of the loss or damage by action against that other person or against any person involved in the contravention'. The definition of 'a person who suffers loss or damage' is not confined to a consumer,[5] not only in that a business may bring an action if it has been induced to buy unsatisfactory goods by D's misleading and deceptive conduct, but businesses may bring an action even if it is not they who have bought the goods. The losses they suffer are those following from an unfairly diminished market share: loss of profits on diminished volume, loss of reputation amongst retailers, etc.[6] In English terms, the remedy of damages that may be sought in passing off cases (and the like) may also be sought

18 And, in special circumstances, under s 87: *Leazam Pty Ltd v Seabridge Australia Pty Ltd* (1992) ATPR 41.171.
19 *Gates v City Mutual Life Assurance Society Ltd* (1986) 160 CLR 1.
20 In cases similar to deceit cases at common law, a different measure may be adopted at the court's discretion: *Mister Figgins Pty Ltd v Centrepoint Freeholds Pty Ltd* (1981) ATPR 40.226 at 43.067. Contracts found to be unconscionable (understood widely) are treated separately under s 52A.
1 *Brabazon v Western Mail Ltd* [1985] ATPR 40.549 at 46.454 (injury to reputation). Whether damages for mental distress are recoverable is uncertain: *Flamingo Park Pty Ltd v Dolly Dolly Creation Pty Ltd* (1986) 65 ALR 500 at 523-525.
2 *JLW (Vic) Pty Ltd v Tsiloglou* [1993] ATPR 41.257.
3 *Musca v Astle Corpn Pty Ltd* (1988) 80 ALR 251.
4 *Henjo Investments Pty Ltd v Collins Marrickville Pty Ltd* (1988) 79 ALR 83.
5 Though s 52 appears in Pt V of the Trade Practices Act, headed 'Consumer Protection': see Carter and Harland, *Contract Law in Australia* (3rd edn 1996) para 1106.
6 *Prince Manufacturing Inc v ABAC Corpn Aust Pty Ltd* (1985) ATPR 40.506.

in misrepresentation cases. An injunction under s 80 is available in a similar way, and as seeking this remedy avoids the proof problems of quantifying loss, and indeed may be brought to avoid anticipated loss, s 80 has become an extremely widely used remedy. In sum, manufacturers who engage in all forms of misleading or deceptive conduct 'are susceptible to suit by competitors, non-competitors, consumer groups, officious bystanders and action groups, product purchasers, as well as the Trade Practices Commission'.[7] This expansion of the number of C's has, it would appear, done a great deal to avoid the enforcement problems which have beset either relying on directly affected consumers or a public authority[8] to carry out the enforcement,[9] for this burden has largely been shifted to private businesses.[10] One's concern that there may, indeed, be too much of a burden on business is alleviated by the facts that private litigation will be undertaken only when D's conduct is (feared to be) sufficiently serious to justify the cost, and that D can always reduce this burden by desisting from the misleading or deceptive conduct.[11]

The extension of liability beyond the person contravening s 52 to include 'any person involved in the contravention' has greatly widened the number of possible Ds. Under s 75B, in essence all those who knowingly were involved in the misleading and deceptive conduct may find that their businesses and themselves personally are held liable for that conduct. This has made it very difficult for D to avoid liability by erecting a legal structure for his business which effectively isolates him (and culpable others) from liability.[12]

The possible clarification of the remedies for misrepresentation, injurious falsehood and passing off, and the innovative approach to enforcement strategy set out in s 52 are, it is submitted, worthy of consideration in this country.

7   E Beerworth, 'A Manufacturer's Guide to Section 52 of the Trade Practices Act' (1991) 19 ABLJ 325, p 326.
8   The Trade Practices Act 1974 does have certain criminal provisions, though contravention of s 52 is not, per se, a criminal offence: Trade Practices Act 1974, s 79(1).
9   Beerworth, 'A Manufacturer's Guide to Section 52 of the Trade Practices Act', (1991) 19 ABLJ 325 at 364: 'a protective effect has been achieved even in the absence of substantial consumer or government intervention'.
10  B Kercher and M Noone, *Remedies* (2nd edn 1990) pp 310-311. Kercher and Noone are, with respect, wrong to regret the fact that business interest rather than cause lawyering (and legal aid) carries the bulk of the regulatory burden.
11  Of course, this argument depends on the definition of 'misleading and deceptive' being kept within reasonable bounds, and this is a point of dispute: Carter and Harland, *Contract Law in Australia* (3rd edn 1996), paras 1105, 1107 and Kercher and Noone, *Remedies, loc cit*, pp 299-300.
12  Carter and Harland, *Contract Law in Australia* (3rd edn 1996), paras 1114, 1121.

# Section 3
# Common issues

# 29 Concurrent liability in contract and tort

## Introduction

Before 1994 concurrent liability in both contract and tort had been accepted in cases of physical injury eg employees suing their employers for personal injury, patients suing doctors or dentists and building owners suing architects or engineers. In *Henderson v Merrett* in 1994,[1] in respect of a claim for purely financial loss, the House of Lords permitted one party to a contract to sue the other for the tort of negligence committed in the course of performing the contract, even though on the same facts the defendant would also have been liable for breach of contract in respect of the same loss. The implied contractual duty of a Lloyd's insurance agent to take reasonable care of his principal's business was co-extensive with the tortious duty of care founded on the agent's 'voluntary assumption of responsibility'.[2] This ruling enabled the principal, a Lloyd's Name, to take advantage of limitation rules in tort which were more favourable to him, because in contract time runs from the breach, whereas in the tort of negligence, time runs from when actual damage was suffered (damage is an essential element in the cause of action in tort). A further advantage is that in tort (but not in contract) the latent damage rules may give the claimant a secondary period of time within which to sue – three years from the time he did discover, or ought reasonably to have discovered, that he had a cause of action against the defendant.[3] The *Henderson v*

1   *Henderson v Merrett Syndicates Ltd* [1995] 2 AC 145.
2   The 'voluntary assumption of responsibility' is, in effect, parasitic upon the contract. However, it may be limited to cases where D possesses a special skill and agrees to perform a service for C requiring that skill. The tortious duty of care may also require some 'reliance' by C on D's statement or undertaking.
3   There is a final 'cut-off' point in that the latent damages rules cannot benefit the claimant for more than 15 years from the time of the defendant's act (or omission).

*Merrett* principle now applies generally, whenever one party to a contract, C, can build a tortious claim on either the other's undertaking founded on the contract itself or on the other's negligence in performing the contract in such a way as to cause harm to C, his property or his financial interests.

Beside limitation, there are other rules in tort[4] which may give an advantage to C over the corresponding contract rules eg in remoteness of damage: instead of asking what types of risk were within the reasonable contemplation of the parties at the time of contracting, the tort test is what types of risk were reasonably foreseeable at the time of the negligent act.[5] In regard to damages, however, there remains a contrast between the concept of 'expectation loss'[6] for which damages may be awarded only in contract (where D has contractually undertaken to produce a profit or other benefit for C) and the concept of 'loss' in tort, where the damages are usually designed to restore C (so far as money can do so) to the position he was in before D committed the tort. Remedies in tort attempt to restore the pre-accident situation, whereas those in contract also attempt to achieve the post-performance situation. In contract, where D promises to do something for C, the damages are designed to put C into the better position he would have been in if the contract was performed. Although 'loss' in contract is often C's failure to obtain an expected benefit, it may also cover 'loss' in the tortious sense of C's being worse off than before as a result of the breach. If C suffers an 'expectation loss' his claim lies only in contract – concurrent liability in tort will not give him damages for such a loss.

## The relationship between the contract and the extent of the tortious duty

The terms of the contract are crucial in determining the extent of the concurrent tortious duty of care – in these cases, without the contract there would be no 'assumption of responsibility' to found the duty of care in tort. The contract creates the tortious relationship. The contract will set the scene for the tortious duty of care; it will 'indicate the nature of the relationship which gives rise to the common law duty of care, but the nature and scope of the duty of care [in tort] ... must not depend on specific obligations or duties created by the express terms of the contract'.[7] But

4   Further examples may be found in the rules on the capacity of the parties; in the conflict of laws; or in the rules governing service of a claim form on D outside the jurisdiction.
5   See p 313 et seq below.
6   See pp 74-75 above.
7   *Central Trust Co v Rafuse* (1986) 31 DLR (4th) 481 at 521.

the contractual obligation of D may go beyond a duty of care in tort[8] eg D may undertake to produce a stated result, whether or not his failure to produce it is due to his fault. The contract may be construed to impose a wider liability than in tort. So although a travel agency was not itself negligent, it was held liable for the negligence of its agent, on the basis that the travel agent had contracted that the services which it undertook to perform would be carried out with reasonable care.[9] On the other hand, the terms of the contract cannot be used to *extend* the tortious duty beyond one to take reasonable care.[10] But the court may rely on a factual context wider than the contract itself. D may voluntarily assume a responsibility which goes beyond his contractual obligation to C; his negligence in this responsibility will lead to liability so that he will be liable in tort but not in contract.[11]

The contract may often expressly restrict D's duty by a qualifying or exclusion clause or a limitation of liability clause. It may also give a complete exemption from tortious liability or a defence to a possible claim in tort eg consent to medical treatment or a licence to enter land. If contract law provides a limited remedy (rescission) for a breach of a contractual duty, the courts are unlikely to impose a duty of care in negligence to give an additional remedy in damages.[12] The duty of care in tort imposed on a party to the contract must not be inconsistent with the terms of the contract[13] eg if the contractual duty was lower than a duty of care, as where the Privy Council held that a bank customer owed his bank only a duty to act honestly in the running of his own account: he was not under a duty to take reasonable care.[14]

A strict contractual obligation owed to A may be the basis of a (lower) tortious duty to take reasonable care owed to C. So where a solicitor undertook to prepare a new will for his client (the provisions of the new will were clearly defined, being the same as in a former will) but the solicitor failed to do so 'with due expedition', he was held liable to the intended beneficiaries when the client died before making the new will

8   *Aiken v Stewart Wrightson Members Agency Ltd* [1995] 1 WLR 1281. (The contract permitted D to be held liable for the negligence of an agent to whom work had been delegated; whereas in tort the delegate alone is liable in negligence if he is properly employed by D and is apparently competent to do the work.)

9   *Wong Mee Wan v Kwan Kin Travel Services Ltd* [1996] 1 WLR 38, PC.

10  *Aiken v Stewart Wrightson Members Agency Ltd* [1995] 1 WLR 1281.

11  *Holt v Payne Skillington* [1996] PNLR 179.

12  *Bank of Nova Scotia v Hellenic Mutual War Risks Association (Bermuda) Ltd* [1990] 1 QB 818 (reversed on other grounds [1992] 1 AC 233).

13  *Henderson v Merritt* [1995] 2 AC 145 at194.

14  *Tai Hing Cotton Mill Ltd v Lin Chong Hing Bank Ltd* [1986] AC 80. Similarly, no tortious duty can be imposed on D if the relevant equitable principles place no duty on him: *Parker-Tweedale v Dunbar Bank plc* [1991] Ch 12 and *China and South Seas Bank v Tan* [1990] 1 AC 536 at 543-544.

in their favour.[15] The duty to the client to prepare the will was probably a strict contractual duty not dependent on fault,[16] but the tortious duty to the intended beneficiaries was only to take reasonable care. The complete failure to fulfil the contractual obligation in this case amounted to the negligent failure in tort to fulfil a responsibility which he had voluntarily undertaken.

## Contributory negligence

The availability of concurrent liability may benefit the contract-breaker: he may not plead contributory negligence against a claim brought in contract, except in the situation where, on the same facts, he could have been sued in tort.[17] For example, this will be helpful to a professional person, D, who is sued in contract for a failure to exercise professional skill and care: if, on the same facts, D could have been sued by C in the tort of negligence, he may claim that the damages should be reduced where the client's loss was caused partly by his own fault. In one case[18] a firm of solicitors was sued in contract for its failure to ensure that a transaction was completed in accordance with the terms of certain letters. Their liability in contract arose from breach of the implied term that they would carry out their contract of retainer with the skill and care reasonably to be expected of a reasonably competent solicitor, which was the same as their liability would be (on the same facts) for the tort of negligence. Hence, damages could be reduced for C's contributory fault. Thus, to the great benefit of contract-breakers, concurrent liability is being used to circumvent the rule that contributory negligence is no defence to a claim in contract.[19]

---

15  *White v Jones* [1995] 2 AC 207.
16  Lord Goff said that the solicitor's 'assumption of responsibility ... towards his client should be held in law to extend to the intended beneficiary' (which statement clearly implies that he had assumed a *tortious* responsibility to his client): ibid at 268. Lord Goff also said that the terms of the contract were significant in setting the contents of the duty of care in tort: ibid.
17  *Barclays Bank plc v Fairclough Building Ltd (No 2)* [1995] IRLR 605, CA (following *Vesta v Butcher* [1989] AC 852, CA; which, however, has not been followed by the High Court of Australia: *Astley v Austrust Ltd* [1999] Lloyd's Rep PN 753).
18  *UCB Bank plc v Hepferd Winstanley & Pugh (a firm)* [1999] Lloyd's Rep PN 963, CA.
19  In *Barclays Bank plc v Fairclough Building Ltd (No 2)*, above n 17, cleaning contractors used their potential concurrent liability in tort to reduce by half the damages paid for their breach of contract: C was held to be at fault in failing to inform itself of the problems arising from the intended method of cleaning.

# 30 Exemplary damages

## Introduction

It is not possible to give a definition of 'exemplary' (or 'aggravated', 'punitive', etc)[1] damages that is both internally coherent and accurately describes what passes for the law in this area. It may preliminarily be said that such damages are an award that goes beyond the amount necessary to compensate C for his loss in the normal way and therefore effectively punishes D for serious misconduct. An 'example' is made of that misconduct. Of course, C obtains an award greater than he would receive on normal compensatory principles, whether the intention is to punish D, to give C a greater than normal award, or a mixture of both. Though an extremely wide range of problems have on occasion been addressed through the use of these damages,[2] their use is wholly anomalous in terms of the normal principles of damages in contract and tort,[3] and the effects

1  For reasons which will become apparent, these are the three most important of the many terms which have been used to refer to these damages. A list of all terms which has been so used is given in Law Commission, *Aggravated, Exemplary and Restitutionary Damages*, Consultation Paper No 132 (1993) (hereinafter *Consultation Paper*) para 1.12.
2  The Law Commission gives a useful list of examples of the cases in which exemplary damages have or might be used in *Aggravated, Exemplary and Restitutionary Damages*, Report No 247 (1997) (hereinafter *Report*), para 1.24. Despite the length of this list, it is one of the Law Commission's principal criticisms that exemplary damages are sometimes unavailable when they may be needed: ibid, para 1.2.
3  Lord Devlin's characterisation of these damages as 'an anomaly [in] the law of England' in *Rookes v Barnard* [1964] AC 1129 at 1221 which, however, could not be judicially abolished (ibid at 1225-1226) was affirmed by the House of Lords in *Broome v Cassell & Co Ltd* [1972] AC 1027 at 1087 and has since been cited innumerable times: for a recent example see *Kuddus v Chief Constable of Leicestershire* [2001] 2 WLR 1789 at 1808-1809.

of this anomaly pervade the decided cases. The result yielded by those cases is a body of law which is, in the words of the Law Commission, 'unprincipled and illogical',[4] and is almost universally held to be in grave need of reform.[5] It can be said that, in essence, it is possible to award exemplary damages in tort in restricted circumstances; but they normally are not available in contract. The issues which need to be considered when deciding whether exemplary damages should be awarded are different in tort and contract and the positions will be considered separately; but in a concluding section an issue that in the US has been analysed as one of concurrent liability will be examined.

## Tort

### Aggravated damages

Damages in tort seldom go beyond the amount deemed sufficient to make up for C's loss. Any deterrent effect which tort law may have must, therefore, lie almost exclusively in the fear of potential liability for actual loss (and associated legal costs) caused by tortious behaviour.[6] Exceptionally, however, exemplary damages may be awarded to C which exceed the amount necessary to meet his loss. Traditionally, the common law permitted these damages whenever D's conduct was so outrageous as to demand punishment. But concern about the overlap of the function of these damages with that of the criminal law, without the safeguards for D built into the criminal law, led the House of Lords in *Rookes v Barnard*[7] in 1964 drastically to reduce their permissible use. The House did, however, support the continued use of a more limited category called 'aggravated' damages. Following Lord Devlin's analysis in *Rookes v Barnard*,[8] the Law Commission has recently defined aggravated damages as:

> damages awarded for a tort as compensation for [C's] mental distress, where the manner in which [D] has committed the tort, or his motives in so doing, or his conduct subsequent to the tort, has upset or outraged [C]. Such conduct or motive 'aggravates' the injury

4    *Consultation Paper*, above n 1, para 1.8.
5    *Report*, above n 2, para 5.3.
6    On deterrence by tort see pp 290-294 above.
7    Above n 3.
8    Ibid at 1221-1231.

done to [C], and therefore warrants a greater or additional compensatory sum.[9]

The definition of aggravated damages in the glossary to the new Civil Procedure Rules is: 'additional damages which the court may award as compensation for [D's] objectionable behaviour'.

Aggravated damages are intended to compensate for insult and injury to C's feelings and dignity. They are not in theory designed to punish but rather to compensate C for his hurt feelings arising from the way in which the tort was committed.[10] The award must be supported by evidence that C suffered unusual hurt from the tort, but in situations like rape or sexual assault this will nearly always be satisfied.[11] Nevertheless, no matter how much injury to C's feelings and dignity has taken place, aggravated damages are available only when the injury has been caused by D's outrageous conduct: a non-compensatory 'trigger' of outrageous conduct which 'aggravate[s] the injury'[12] done to C is still required in these claims. In *Kralj v McGrath*,[13] C experienced difficulties during the delivery of her twins and D's 'horrific' negligent obstetric treatment killed one of her children and caused her excruciating pain. D admitted liability but aggravated damages were not awarded because D's negligence was held not to amount to outrageous conduct. Woolf J held that such an award would be 'wholly inappropriate' where a doctor is held liable for negligence (ie not intentional harm) when treating a patient. The Law Commission has called this the 'exceptional conduct' requirement of an award of aggravated damages, and the Commission's analysis has received authoritative endorsement at tribunal[14] and in a court at first instance.[15]

---

9  *Report*, above n 2, para 2.1. The Law Commission has recommended that aggravated damages should be replaced by the label 'damages for mental distress': *Report*, above n 2, para 2.42.

10  *Archer v Brown* [1985] QB 401 at 424–426.

11  *W v Meah* [1986] 1 All ER 935 (aggravated damages for rape or sexual assault upheld; but the judge said that the aim of the award should be compensatory, and be related to awards in ordinary personal injury cases).

12  *Rookes v Barnard* [1964] AC 1129 at 1221, 1232 and *Thompson v Metropolitan Police Comr* [1998] QB 498 at 502: 'aggravating features'.

13  [1986] 1 All ER 54 (see further p 584 n 13, p 588, n 4 below). This was a contract case, C being treated privately. However, its principle would govern tort cases brought after negligent treatment on the National Health Service (NHS). The Law Commission is right to regard *Kralj* (and the cases in which it has been followed) 'as modern authorities to the effect that aggravated damages are unavailable for the tort of negligence and for breach of contract': *Report*, above n 2, para 2.36. See also p 597 n 20 below.

14  *Ministry of Defence v Meredith* [1995] IRLR 539 at 542 para 29. The statement of the law has been applied to similar issues in *Ministry of Defence v Mutton* [1996] ICR 590 and *Ministry of Defence v O'Hare (No 2)* [1997] ICR 306.

15  *Appleton v Garrett* [1996] PIQR P1 at P4.

Neither Lord Devlin[16] nor the Law Commission[17] have purported to maintain that a consistent distinction between aggravated and other exemplary damages is supported by the cases; and it must be said outright that indeed it cannot. The point of making the distinction is to say that in some cases 'extra compensation' (but nevertheless compensation) of C by aggravated damages is appropriate, and in other cases exemplary damages are appropriate in order to punish D. Damages of this latter sort are, perhaps, better called punitive, and the Law Commission has recommended this usage.[18] This usage would be an improvement were the confusion merely terminological, but it is not. The decided cases inextricably tangle the 'compensatory' and the 'punitive' aspects of exemplary damages and, it will be submitted, the concept of aggravated (as opposed to punitive) damages is itself unsustainable. If this is so, it is pointless to adopt the Commission's revised terminology and we will continue to use 'aggravated' and 'exemplary' damages here. The latter does *sometimes* but not always embrace the former; this is an obviously unsatisfactory position, but nevertheless a position which accurately captures the confusion that characterises the law.

Little can be said about how aggravated damages are 'calculated'. Even if one recognises that this word cannot in the context of exemplary damages refer to a nicely balanced mathematical procedure,[19] this can hardly excuse the arbitrariness of what has passed for 'calculation'. In *Rookes v Barnard*,[20] Lord Devlin said these were damages 'at large', that is to say, 'not limited to the pecuniary loss that can be specifically proved', so that they can embrace insult and injury to C's feelings and dignity. This is, in essence, to seek to award damages for intangible losses,[1] and therefore displays the same shortcomings as the award of damages for non-pecuniary loss for personal injury:[2] in essence, these damages are fruitless and arbitrary. There is also the major added complication that in many instances, in defamation cases in particular, the quantification of exemplary damages is determined by a jury (whereas jury trial has been all but eliminated from personal injury cases),[3] so that the settling of awards into at least internally consistent patterns which has taken place in personal injury has not taken place with exemplary damages. Even the moderation exercised by judges to try to keep some sort of control in the face of these

16   *Rookes v Barnard* [1964] AC 1129 at 1221, 1229.
17   *Report*, above p 579 n 2, para 2.1.
18   Ibid, para 5.39.
19   *Broome v Cassell & Co Ltd* [1972] AC 1027 at 1078–1079, 1094, 1101, 1130.
20   [1972] AC 1027 at at 1221.
1    *Broome v Cassell & Co Ltd* [1972] AC 1027 at 1070D-1072H and *Consultation Paper*, above p 579 n 1, paras 2.11-2.29.
2    See pp 438-442 above.
3    *Consultation Paper*, above p 579 n 1, para 1.16.

difficulties need not apply in these cases, and hence the simply ridiculous (if the offensive can be ridiculous) sums awarded in some libel cases.[4] The result has been that aggravated damages claims have been made and obtained for almost anything relating to C's widely defined distress caused by the outrageous conduct of D (and the connection between the two has been *very* loose).[5]

There is simply no hope whatsoever of the law being reduced to reasonably consistent principles in these circumstances, and writers of a book of this nature can do little more than advise readers wishing to know the law which would apply to a particular situation to turn to the cases themselves, with the caution that those cases may yield only very limited instruction. This is an area where the courtroom experience and skill of the advocate will have an extremely large influence on the outcome;[6] indeed, it is submitted, an unacceptably large influence. Though this area of the civil law has an obvious grip on the popular[7] and, to a lesser extent, professional[8] imaginations, if by 'law' one means a system in which outcomes are determined in accord with a reasonably consistent and comprehensible set of rules rather than by a battle between legal champions,[9] it is not really law at all. This makes litigation a particularly

4    See the cases listed at ibid, para 3.59 (there is an outright punitive element in some of these damages) of which *John v MGN Ltd* [1997] QB 586 (discussed at p 587 n 15 below) is a good example. Some attempt to control these awards by increasing the guidance the judge gives to the jury has been made following *Rantzen v Mirror Newspapers* [1994] QB 670 and *John v MGN Ltd*, the latter case allowing reference to be made to non-pecuniary loss in personal injury cases. The practice of giving similar guidance in other than defamation cases had previously been only intermittently canvassed (eg *Broome v Cassell & Co Ltd* [1972] AC 1027) but now appears to be more firmly established after *Thompson v Metropolitan Police Comr* [1998] QB 498.

5    *Rookes v Barnard* [1964] AC 1129 at 1221: 'when one examines the cases in which large damages have been awarded for conduct of this sort, it is not at all easy to say whether the idea of compensation or the idea of punishment has prevailed'.

6    D Price, *Defamation: Law, Procedure and Practice* (2nd edn 2001). In order to serve as the successful guide to courtroom practice which it is, this book has to be frank about the 'tricks of the trade' it describes.

7    For an example of the numerous popular treatments of defamation cases see H Montgomery Hyde, *Their Good Names* (1970).

8    See eg PF Carter-Ruck, *Memoirs of a Libel Lawyer* (1990). It is instructive to read this book while making cross-reference to *Carter-Ruck on Libel and Slander* (5th edn 1997).

9    Engaging the late George Carman QC was thought by libel solicitors to be so likely to lead to success (ie irrespective of the merits) that '[h]is very name became a tactical tool for resolving a dispute'. Whatever the truth of the apocryphal story that solicitors often would settle on disappointing terms for their client rather than face Carman in court, Carman was able to command a very substantial retainer on the basis of belief in it: M Berlins, 'Last of the Great Advocates' *Guardian*, 23 January 2002, G2 section, 16, p 17.

powerful weapon in the hands of the relatively wealthy, who can afford to gamble. An explanation of why defamation law in particular continues in its utterly anomalous and extremely unsatisfactory form would have to emphasise the political influence of those who are able to wield that law.[10]

In the laudable belief that 'reasoned, consistent and proportionate awards are vital',[11] the Law Commission has made certain proposals to rectify this situation, all of which depend on the core proposal of eliminating the jury's role in quantification.[12] The plausibility of this depends on thinking that non-pecuniary loss quantification represents an acceptable standard of adjudication to which the award of aggravated damages usefully may aspire, and we do not. If it is maintained that aggravated damages are compensatory in the sense that they purport to be based on a one-off assessment of C's loss, then they must be recognised to be even worse than damages for non-pecuniary loss for personal injury; that is, to repeat, they are also fruitless and arbitrary, but even more so.

As aggravated damages can only be awarded on the 'triggering event' of D's conduct being outrageous, aggravated damages can never be separated from their punitive aspect,[13] and it is as well to concentrate exclusively on the punitive value of exemplary damages, for aggravated damages will never have an economic, effective, efficient and equitable compensatory function.[14] It is our opinion that aggravated damages

10  The most thoroughly analysed example of the way the law in this area can be used *in terrorem* by those enjoying greater resources is the 'SLAPP' suit (strategic lawsuit against public participation) brought by corporations to stifle criticism of their products and business practices: see P Canan and G Pring, *SLAPPs: Getting Sued for Speaking Out* (1996) and, for Commonwealth jurisdictions, F Donson, *Legal Intimidation* (2000). The most famous SLAPP suit in this country was the 'McLibel trial', an anomalous example in which the intimidation did not work, indeed had disastrous results for C, the McDonalds 'fast food' corporation, because the Ds were impecunious political activists who disregarded the threat of ruination and welcomed their involvement in a 313-day trial: see J Vidal, *McLibel* (1997). For a very thought provoking investigation of the (lack of any) basic value of the law of defamation see T Gibbons, 'Defamation Reconsidered' (1996) 16 Oxford Journal of Legal Studies 587.
11  *Report*, above p 579 n 2, para 1.3.
12  Ibid, para 1.21, 5.81-5.98.
13  The Law Commission was quite right to conclude in its *Consultation Paper*, above p 579 n 1, para 2.29 that, because of the exceptional conduct requirement for an award of aggravated damages, such an award inevitably 'looks like punishment'. See also *Report*, above p 579 n 2, paras 2.18-2.20. The Law Commission was also quite right to observe that *Kralj v McGrath* (and the cases in which it has been followed) are impossible to understand unless 'aggravated damages are in reality, and contrary to Lord Devlin's views [in *Rookes v Barnard*], a form of punitive damages': ibid, para 2.36.
14  Exactly the opposite is authoritatively argued in J Stone, 'Double Count and Double Talk: The End of Exemplary Damages' (1972) 46 Australian Law Journal 311.

should be abolished, and, if it is thought appropriate, their function be taken over by exemplary (in the sense of punitive) damages, quantified without any pretence of reference to C's loss.[15] We now turn to the case for exemplary damages.

## Exemplary damages

Without wishing to convey the misleading impression that the law relating to the award of exemplary damages is coherent, it may be said[16] that the decision to make such an award depends on three issues: the 'categories' test; the 'cause of action test'; and 'other discretionary factors'. In *Rookes v Barnard*,[17] their Lordships held that exemplary damages may be awarded in tort in only three categories. The first was where statute expressly authorised the award. The other two were common law categories: where government officials had acted oppressively, or where D's conduct was calculated to make a profit for himself. Statutory authority is rare (arguably non-existent if by 'exemplary' is meant 'punitive' damages),[18] and so of little importance, but the common law categories can be used more widely.

The first common law category where exemplary damages may still be awarded is where there has been 'oppressive, arbitrary or unconstitutional action by the servants of the government',[19] which will include the police and local government officials.[20] Exemplary damages were first awarded in eighteenth-century cases of this type, as where D searched C's premises under illegal general warrants.[1] The law can check the use of power by

---

15  On the *separate* issue of contract damages for distress, disappointment and loss of enjoyment see pp 595-601 below. One of the classes of contractual cases is loss of enjoyment of a holiday. Very moderate damages for this would be appear to be recoverable in negligence, not as aggravated damages but simply as part of the specification of the harm C suffered as a result of personal injury: eg *Bush v Phillip (No 2)* [1986] CLY 1065 (at the start of a cycling holiday C, a boy of 15, was taken to hospital after a road traffic accident. He was not detained but missed the first week of the holiday. Awarded £200 (£300 at current rates) for loss of enjoyment of the holiday. His father's claim is also reported).

16  Following *Report*, above p 579 n 2, pt 4.

17  Above p 579 n 3 at 1226-1227.

18  Lord Devlin, ibid at 1225, cited The Reserve and Auxiliary Forces (Protection of Civil Interests) Act 1951, s 13(2) (damages for conversion of the goods of servicemen), in which the words 'exemplary damages' are used; but Lord Kilbrandon has interpreted 'exemplary' in this sub-section to mean 'aggravated': *Broome v Cassell & Co Ltd* [1972] AC 1027 at 1133-1134. The question whether the Copyright, Designs and Patents Act 1988, s 97(2) (and formerly the Copyright Act 1956, s 17(3)) authorises the award of exemplary damages is much disputed: ibid at 1080, 1134 and *Report*, above p 579 n 2, paras 4.21-4.22.

19  *Rookes v Barnard* [1964] AC 1129 at 1226.

20  *Broome v Cassell & Co Ltd* [1972] AC 1027 at 1077–8, 1087–8, 1130.

1  *Wilkes v Wood* (1763) Lofft 1 in which C sued a public officer in trespass.

officials, who should be 'servants of the people' as well as of the government.[2] C's wrongful arrest by a police officer, D, falls within this category, and even when D acted under a mistake it should be left to the jury to decide whether to award exemplary damages.[3] 'Unconstitutional action' does not require evidence of 'oppressive behaviour'[4] but newspapers have reported large awards against the police where there is such evidence. However, the use of exemplary damages to check the obvious power of large corporations or of trade unions,[5] which arguably poses a similar threat of oppression to that posed by governmental bodies, has not been developed.[6]

The main common law category is where D's 'conduct has been calculated by him to make a profit for himself which may well exceed the compensation payable to' C.[7] Here, the award is intended to deter others like D from 'a cynical disregard' for C's rights where he 'has calculated that the money to be made out of his wrongdoing will probably exceed the damages at risk'.[8] The category covers D's 'seeking to gain at the expense of [C] some object – perhaps some property which he covets – which either he could not obtain at all or not obtain except at a price greater than he wants to put down'.[9] The House of Lords in *Broome v Cassell & Co Ltd* used this category to uphold exemplary damages of £25,000 (in addition to compensatory damages of £15,000) for a serious libel which D published in order to make a profit for himself.[10] If D weighs

2    *Rookes v Barnard* [1964] AC 1129 at 1226.
3    *Holden v Chief Constable of Lancashire* [1987] QB 380, CA. The case decides implicitly that exemplary damages may be awarded where D himself is liable only vicariously. The recent consideration of this matter in *Kuddus v Chief Constable of Leicestershire*, above p 579 n 3 questions whether vicarious liability for exemplary damages should continue to be  recognised but reaches no definite conclusion on the matter. By far and away the strongest substantive argument in *Kuddus* is, however, that of Lord Scott, who points out that the outrageous conduct can hardly be attributed to a party whose liability is *purely* vicarious (ie is not even the result of a culpable failure to supervise): ibid at 1824B-D.
4    *Holden v Chief Constable of Lancashire* [1987] QB 380 at 388.
5    Though *Rookes v Barnard* [1964] AC 1129 itself concerned a trade union: see p 567 n 11 above.
6    *Broome v Cassell & Co Ltd* [1972] AC 1027 at 1108E-G. The most forceful criticism of this position stated in a Commonwealth case would appear to be that of Taylor J in *Uren v John Fairfax & Sons Pty* (1966) 117 CLR 118 at 132-133, 137.
7    *Rookes v Barnard* [1964] AC 1129 at 1226. The criminal standard of proof beyond a reasonable doubt should be satisfied: *Mafo v Adams* [1970] 1 QB 548 at 556, 559 (approved in *John v MGN* [1997] QB 586 at 592).
8    *Rookes v Barnard* [1964] AC 1129 at 1227. Another formulation given in *Broome v Cassell & Co Ltd* [1972] AC 1027 at 1079 was that D's 'prospects of material advantage outweigh the prospects of material loss'.
9    *Rookes v Barnard* [1964] AC 1129 at 1227.
10   The amount of damages was upheld only by a majority of 4 to 3.

the risk of loss against the chance of getting away with it, exemplary damages may be awarded against him even if he did not in fact make a gain.[11] 'It is only if there is a prospect that the damages may exceed [D's] gain that the social purpose of this category is achieved – to teach a wrongdoer that tort does not pay.'[12]

Awards on this profit-calculation basis have been made against newspapers for libel,[13] but there must be evidence to show the knowledge of a reporter or editor that the item was defamatory and his intention to boost sales of the paper by a 'cynical calculation' that the risk of paying damages was worth taking.[14] However, the mere fact that a newspaper business is run for profit does not mean that every libel published in the newspaper falls within the category.[15] Landlords also run the risk of exemplary damages.[16] If a tenant enjoys a protected tenancy, a landlord who unlawfully evicts that tenant stands to make a profit by selling the house with vacant possession or by reletting it at an unrestricted rent.[17] In

---

11  *Broome v Cassell & Co Ltd* [1972] AC 1027 at 1130.
12  Ibid. But it is doubtful whether the facts justified an award under this category against a trade union in *Messenger Newspaper Group Ltd v National Graphical Association* [1984] IRLR 397.
13  *Riches v News Group Newspapers Ltd* [1986] QB 256.
14  Ibid.
15  *Broadway Approvals v Odhams Press* [1965] 1 WLR 805; *Manson v Associated Newspapers* [1965] 1 WLR 1038 at 1040–1041 and *Broome v Cassell & Co Ltd* [1972] AC 1027 at 1079. It may, of course, even be held as a matter of fact that because he was acting in accordance with a reasonable and honest belief D was not acting outrageously: *Eliot v Allen* (1845) 135 ER 441. In defamation cases it is very likely that D knows that the statement is defamatory, for this may be the very point of making it, but if he reasonably and honestly (but wrongly) believes he has a defence, exemplary damages should not be awarded. In *John v MGN* [1997] QB 586, this principle was firmly stated (ibid at 618), but nevertheless C was awarded very substantial exemplary damages when a national newspaper wrongly claimed he was bulimic. The jury concluded that when D proceeded inter alia in the belief that C's undisputed past history of 'dietary abuse' (and drug abuse for which he was 'extremely fortunate not ever to have been prosecuted') meant that he was unlikely to sue (ibid at 624), this was a cynical calculation as to profit. It awarded D £275,000 exemplary damages (and £75,000 aggravated damages), about three times the then maximum conventional award for non-pecuniary loss following quadriplegia! Noting this (ibid at 614), the Court of Appeal reduced these sums to £50,000 and £25,000. Though this case has had a strong influence toward the reduction of libel damages (see p 583 n 4 above) which is most welcome, the outcome of this case was hardly satisfactory as the total of the sums awarded by the Court of Appeal was itself was only little less than the then maximum non-pecuniary loss award for complete loss of sight.
16  The measure of the exemplary damages used to counter 'unlawful eviction' under the Housing Act 1988, ss 27-28 is restitutionary: *Jones v Miah* (1992) 24 HLR 578 at 587. Of course, as the restitutionary damages are in excess of the (perhaps slight) compensatory award, these damages are in a sense exemplary.

588 Section 2   Tort: remedies for wrongdoing

*Broome v Cassell & Co Ltd*[18] unlawful eviction by harassment was given as an obvious example of the profit-seeking category, and the Court of Appeal subsequently upheld an award of £1,000 against a landlord who used force to break into his tenant's house in his absence and put his belongings outside.[19]

A formidable criticism of this 'categories test' restriction on the use of exemplary damages is that it does not permit their use where D did not act for profit but rather 'had been high-handed, insolent, vindictive or malicious or had in some other way exhibited a contumelious disregard for'[20] C's rights. To the extent that *Rookes v Barnard* turns on an acceptance that deterrence of flagrant wrongdoing is an important aim of civil law, the House of Lords should have authorised the use of exemplary damages for such conduct by D. The decision not to do this is a further sign of the irrelevance of deterrence to policy making in tort law.[1]

Prior to *Rookes v Barnard*, as a matter of historical chance, exemplary damages had been awarded only in connection with a limited number of torts: assault and battery, defamation, false imprisonment, intimidation, malicious prosecution, private nuisance, trespass to goods and land and wrongful interference with business.[2] *Rookes v Barnard* left it unsettled whether the profit-calculation category allowed the scope of exemplary damages to be extended beyond the situations covered by previous case law, eg to deceit,[3] injurious falsehood, negligence[4] and public nuisance.

17  *Drane v Evangelous* [1978] 1 WLR 455 at 459. See in general *Arden and Partington on Quiet Enjoyment* (3rd edn 1990) pp 31-34. The circumstances usually involve harassment, but if the landlord's tort is deceit, the position is uncertain because the status of deceit under the cause of action test is uncertain: see n 3 below. Some exemplary damages for nuisance by a landlord against his tenant were awarded in *Guppys (Bridport) Ltd v Brookling and James* [1984] 1 EGLR 29.

18  Above p 579 n 3 at 1079E-F.

19  *Drane v Evangelous* [1978] 1 WLR 455.

20  *Uren v John Fairfax & Sons Pty* (1966) 117 CLR 118 at 129. In *Broome v Cassell & Co Ltd* [1972] AC 1027 at 1088, Lord Reid said that the distinction between greed and malice could be justified only by reference to authority.

1   The most crucial such sign is the fact that it has not been settled that it is impossible to get insurance against exemplary damages, whereas it is, of course, impossible to insure against the consequences of committing a crime: *Lancashire County Council v Municipal Mutual Insurance Ltd* [1997] QB 897 and *Report*, above p 579 n 2, paras 4.108-4.112, 5.234-5.273. Serious misconduct by D may, however, in itself be a factor influencing the court to grant a discretionary remedy such as an injunction which will do more to prevent that conduct.

2   *Consultation Paper*, above p 579 n 1, paras 3.55-3.64. Many arguments could be raised about this (or any) list, and in particular intimidation and private nuisance are extremely difficult cases to classify: ibid, paras 3.63-3.64.

3   In *Mafo v Adams* [1970] 1 QB 548 at 548, 555, 558-559 the Lords Justices divided on this issue. See also *Archer v Brown* [1985] QB 401 at 420-423 and *Metall und Rohstoff AG v ACLI Metals (London) Ltd* [1984] 1 Lloyd's Rep 598 at 612.

4   Negligence fails the cause of action test for exemplary damages, but there are sound substantial reasons for exemplary damages not being available for this

D's conduct could, of course, be as outrageous in connection with many of these torts as with those recognised prior to *Rookes v Barnard*. On the other hand, equally obviously there is a floodgates argument and a parallel can be drawn to the way negligence liability decided according to the overarching neighbour principle has, for good or ill, wildly expanded beyond traditional categories after *Donoghue v Stevenson*.[5] In *Broome v Cassell and Co Ltd*, two Law Lords thought that the formulation in *Rookes v Barnard* was not intended to widen the use of exemplary damages;[6] the purpose of that decision 'was to restrict, not to expand, the anomaly of exemplary damages'.[7] These remarks were not central to the case, but, on the face of it, the question appeared to have been settled by the decision of the Court of Appeal in *AB v South West Water Services*,[8] which, striking out claims for exemplary damages based on a number of torts, held that such damages can be claimed only for causes of action that were recognised as ones in which exemplary damages could be awarded before *Rookes v Barnard*.

However, it is very difficult to view the obvious compromise represented by this 'cause of action test' as sustainable, and it has repeatedly been attacked, most recently by the House of Lords in *Kuddus v Chief Constable of Leicestershire*.[9] If one is in favour of exemplary damages, the cause of action test is an absurd restriction: if D's conduct is outrageous, it should be punished.[10] Even if one is not in favour of exemplary damages, one cannot be satisfied with the obvious inequity that exemplary damages are available for some torts and not for others because of historical chance.[11] In sum, the present position is indefensible (unless any change will be worse or insufficiently better to justify the expense involved, which is very hard to conceive in this case). Furthermore, this position is bound to invite the argument that a tort not explicitly in the pre-*Rookes* category actually was implicitly in;[12] an argument which will have to be conducted by reference to antique cases (which very rarely can now be understood properly from the typically inadequate reports) in a way which will be an expensive parody of proper

---

    tort, mere negligence being, of its nature, not outrageous conduct: *AB v South West Water Services* [1993] QB 507, 523C-D, 528E-F, 530H. See *Kralj v McGrath* [1986] 1 All ER 54.

5    [1932] AC 562.

6    Above p 579 n 3 at 1076, 1080 1130–1131.

7    Ibid at 1131.

8    Above p 588 n 4.

9    Above p 579 n 3.

10   Ibid at 1795H–1796B.

11   Ibid at 1978G, citing *Winfield and Jolowicz on Tort* (15th edn 1998) p 746.

12   The Law Commission ominously opines that confirmation of its (controversial) inclusion of the economic torts within the pre-*Rookes* category 'ultimately depends upon the proper interpretation of the pre-*Rookes* authority': *Consultation Paper*, above p 579 n 1, para 3.64.9 (despite para 3.60 n 262).

legal argument. In *Kuddus*, understandable impatience with this type of ratiocination[13] led the House of Lords (overturning the decision at first instance and on appeal) flatly to state that the fact that the only recently emergent tort of malfeasance in public office[14] was not, of course, recognised prior to *Rookes v Barnard* would not prevent it from grounding exemplary damages. However, this very aggressive course creates no clear precedent for not only is it wholly unreconcilable with *AB v South West Water Services* but it creates whole new vistas of liability the wisdom of which it was impossible for the court to assess and therefore the longevity of which it is impossible to estimate. As this is written, it is too early to assess the full impact of this case, but it is obvious that its tendency is to completely undermine the cause of action test. However, highly critical things are said about exemplary damages as such throughout *Kuddus*, and the aggressive course taken in that case may, perhaps, have been as much intended to provoke abolition of exemplary damages *tout court* as of the cause of action test in particular (two actions with very different outcomes). Their Lordships clearly indicated their disappointment that the parties failed to invite them to consider whether exemplary damages should ever be awarded.[15] In order to forestall the inevitable further confusion of an already indefensible existing situation, the law of exemplary damages must be legislatively reformed.[16] The Law Commission has recommended that, in essence, exemplary damages should be awarded for any tort or equitable wrong which shows 'a deliberate and outrageous disregard of [C's] rights'.[17]

Even if D's conduct falls within a *Rookes v Barnard* category and is a pre-*Rookes v Barnard* cause of action, the judge or jury retain a complete discretion not to award exemplary damages in the light of their evaluation of that conduct, and in *Broome v Cassell & Co Ltd*[18] Lord Hailsham was of the opinion that this must inevitably be the case. This obviously will be so as long as a jury is involved in the decision,[19] but it also turns on the inevitable subjectivity of any evaluation of the general outrageousness of conduct (ie *not* identified by the breach of the specific rule which has grounded normal liability). Whether or not our opinion that arbitrariness is inevitable is correct, it certainly is the case that the existing law again

13  *Kuddus v Chief Constable of Leicestershire*, above p 579 n 3 at 1796C, 1821A.
14  See *Clerk and Lidsell on Torts* (18th edn 2000) paras 17.133-17.146 and 45(2) *Halsbury's Laws of England* (4th edn reissue 1999), para 495.
15  *Kuddus v Chief Constable of Leicestershire*, above p 579 n 3 at 1798D-E, 1807G, 1808F, 1818A-E; but see contra 1796G-1797A.
16  The government recently declined to do so: HC Deb (9 November 1999) col 502.
17  *Report*, above p 579 n 2, para 1.20. The immense difficulties are reviewed at ibid, pt 5.
18  Above p 579 n 3 at 1060B.
19  Ibid at 1087C-F per Lord Reid and *Report*, above p 579 n 2, para 4.57.

does not display the consistency which really allows one to divine any principle which can be said to have guided the award of exemplary damages. The Law Commission has made a sustained attempt to develop an analysis of the 'additional factors which limit the availability of exemplary damages' to which the reader is referred;[20] but it must be read in the full understanding that it cannot explain the weight given to any particular factor in any particular case, for this *cannot* be explained. This law has rightly been characterised as 'unpredictable' and 'uncontrollable',[1] and we are again obliged to observe that such law is no law at all. The Law Commission's decision to recommend the expansion of exemplary damages obviously requires the abolition of the role of the jury if these damages are to be placed on a principled footing.[2] It also requires that a judge be able to determine unspecified outrageous conduct in a principled way, and while the Commission recognises the problem,[3] we are obliged to say that it does not give sufficient weight to the complete contradiction involved in what it asks of the judge.

One's attitude to this issue will to a large extent depend on one's view of the 'law'. If one has a sort of 'social policy' view, in which it is right for the power of the state to be wielded in pursuit of worthy ends even if one

20 Ibid, paras 4.29-4.55. We would draw particular attention to the policy question raised by the case in which D has already been punished by a criminal sanction. In *Archer v Brown* [1985] QB 401 at 423, 426, Peter Pain J held that no exemplary damages could be awarded where D had already been punished by a criminal court for the conduct in respect of which C sued in tort because a 'man should not be punished twice for the same offence'. The Law Commission (*Report*, above p 579 n 2, paras 4.36-4.43) has objected that by this sweeping injunction Peter Pain J rules out any inquiry into the adequacy of the criminal sanction. But, of course, even if one accepts that this sort of question is justiciable (does it make any sense to say that one year's imprisonment plus £1,000 exemplary damages equals a sufficient punishment?), why would one think that the civil law can handle it in a way superior to the criminal law? The exhaustive consideration of the doctrinal issues in NJ McBride, 'Punitive Damages', in P Birks (ed), *Wrongs and Remedies in the Twenty-first Century* (1996) 175, pp 188-194 bases part of its case for the use of exemplary damages on their being used 'to remedy the inevitable failures of the criminal justice system' (ibid, p 193). Absurdly but not surprisingly, this is done without any comparison with the inevitable failures of the civil system (cf ibid p 199). What, one wonders, would Mr McBride have said of the enormous damages awarded against those who deliberately and with a view to profit said that Lord Archer was a compulsive liar and crook before it became incontrovertible that he was, and had indeed obtained those damages by a most calculated perjury? See generally M Crick, *Jeffrey Archer: Stranger than Fiction* (rev edn 2000).
1 *Broome v Cassell & Co Ltd* [1972] AC 1027 at 1087D-F.
2 *Report*, above p 579 n 2, para 5.44.
3 Ibid, paras 5.16-5.39. The personal views of the Law Commissioner at the time of the *Report*, Professor Burrows, tend towards abolition of exemplary damages: A Burrows, *Remedies for Torts and Breach of Contract* (2nd edn 1994) pp 282-285 and A Burrows, 'Reforming Exemplary Damages: Expansion or Abolition', in Birks (ed), *Wrongs and Remedies in the Twenty-first Century* (1996) 153.

cannot give much of a principled statement about the way that this will be done, then one will tend to sympathise with the Law Commission's expansionist view. If one has a 'classical liberal' view of the law,[4] in which the state's power should be wielded only when it can be done in a sufficiently principled way as to respect the demands of legality, one will tend to find the Law Commission's expansionist view worthy[5] but wrong, and its claim that expansion can take place along 'reasoned, consistent and proportionate' lines an attempt to avoid the basic choice.[6] The Law Commission is, however, drawing on a long tradition in tort of awarding really quite arbitrary sums in the belief that it is better that something (anything) be done rather than the law, from respect of legality, be reluctant to become entangled in non-justiciable matters. This certainly is the case with exemplary damages.

In *Rookes v Barnard* the House of Lords suggested guidelines for the assessment of exemplary damages.[7] But these would appear to be largely irrelevant if the purpose is to deprive D of the profit he actually made. They are relevant if D intended to make a profit but failed to do so, or if the award is against a government official. The award should be moderate in amount;[8] should take account of D's means (as with a fine) and of C's own conduct (as where he provoked an assault by D).[9] It should also take account of the amount awarded as compensatory damages: if D has to pay a substantial sum as compensation, that in itself may be a sufficient

---

4    N Barry, 'The Classical Theory of Law' (1988) 73 Cornell Law Review 283, p 291: 'lawyers have become ... less concerned with the *adjudication* of cases and more with the implementation of what they believe to be socially acceptable values'.

5    There is, of course, a perfectly good case that privacy is not adequately protected in this country, but wishing to do something effective about this will require the use of means other than the law of tort or the law of tort's very substantial reform: BS Markesinis, 'Our Patchy Law of Privacy: Time To Do Something About It' (1990) 53 Modern Law Review 802 and B Niell, 'Privacy: A Challenge for the Next Century', in BS Markesinis (ed), *Protecting Privacy* (1999) 1. See also Gibbons, 'Defamation Reconsidered' p 584 n 10 above.

6    The necessity of the choice is not obvious to all. The Law Commission received evidence that it was a good thing that exemplary damages are unpredictable, for unpredictable awards are a better deterrent. The Commission had no objection in principle to this argument that the state should use its power *in terrorem* for worthy ends, but (unconvincingly) argued that the principled awards to which it imagines its reform proposals will lead will not be a less efficient deterrent: *Report*, above p 579 n 2, para 5.36.

7    Above p 579 n 3 at 1227–1228.

8    *Rookes v Barnard* [1964] AC 1129 at 1227–1228 and *Broome v Cassell & Co Ltd* [1972] AC 1027 at 1081. (But an award of £25,000 was upheld: see p 586 above.

9    *Lane v Holloway* [1968] 1 QB 379 at 391 and *O'Connor v Hewitson* [1979] Crim LR 46.

deterrent to others.[10] But the fact that the judge has publicly castigated D for his conduct should not reduce the amount of either aggravated or exemplary damages.[11]

Problems may also arise with multiple Cs or Ds. Where there are several Cs, the *total* amount for exemplary damages should be fixed by the jury, and then divided equally between the Cs.[12] Where several Ds are sued jointly, the misconduct of only one does not entitle the award of exemplary damages in a single judgment against them all.[13]

The Law Reform (Miscellaneous Provisions) Act 1934, s 1(2)(*a*)(i) does not permit a tort claim to exemplary damages to survive for the benefit of the estate of a person who died before his claim was settled or adjudicated.

Without defending this opinion against many powerful objections here,[14] it is submitted that it is a necessary (but not sufficient) condition of any retention (though not in their present form) of exemplary damages that their quantification be legislatively placed on a schedular basis. This will be easier if the idea that these damages are compensatory (the idea behind distinguishing aggravated and punitive damages) is completely dropped[15] for this idea is unsustainable. This does not mean, however, that the punitive aspect of exemplary damages is sustainable, which very arguably it is not.[16] Very little of the literature will help one to come to a conclusion about this. As Street put it as long ago as 1962:

It is believed that in the present state of knowledge, one cannot say whether exemplary damages are desirable. That study of law in action which would show how efficiently they contribute to the attainment of [desirable] purposes ... remains to be done. And the practical usefulness of exemplary damages is the basic question, one to which no amount of theorising can provide an answer.[17]

10  *Broome v Cassell & Co Ltd* [1972] AC 1027 at 1082 and *Riches v News Group Newspapers Ltd* [1986] QB 256. D will also have to pay C's legal costs.
11  *Dingle v Associated Newspapers Ltd* [1964] AC 371 at 402–404.
12  *Riches v News Group Newspapers Ltd* [1986] QB 256.
13  *Broome v Cassell & Co Ltd* [1972] AC 1027.
14  The most powerful objections turn on the undeniable fact that schedular punitive damages look very like a fine, to put it mildly, and so acutely raise the problems of the relationship of exemplary damages and the criminal law: Ontario Law Reform Commission, *Exemplary Damages* (1991) pp 43-46.
15  In the light of the pronounced difficulties in formulating the statutory reform which it believes is the necessary condition of retaining a form of exemplary damages, the Law Commission has welcomed the growth of extra-compensatory restitutionary remedies, but holds that further development should be left to the courts: *Report*, above p 579 n 2, pt 3. Though the Law Commission envisages this development in connection with contract, tort and equitable wrongs, we shall consider it only in relationship to contract at pp 606-608 below.
16  *Kuddus v Chief Constable of Leicestershire*, above p 579 n 3 at 1817H.
17  H Street, *Principles of the Law of Damages* (1962) p 36.

That this has recently been approvingly cited in *Kuddus v Chief Constable of Leicestershire*[18] gives one a little, no doubt naïve, hope that the necessary work might now be undertaken.

## Contract

If one holds to a view of the law of contract based on *pacta sunt servanda*, the view which lies behind the recent promotion of what has been called the performance interest, the fact that exemplary damages are so exceptional as to be basically unknown in the law of contract is a tremendous puzzle. Few, however, have carried the logic of holding such a view through to its extreme where the law of contract damages *tout court* are thought to be defective for this reason.[19] It has already been argued that to reform the law of contract to enhance the so-called performance interest would be mistaken because it is too sweeping a reform.[20] On the view of contract taken in this book,[1] which gives legitimate breach a positive role, the irrelevance of exemplary damages is easy to understand. General extra-compensatory damages would be utterly disruptive as they are incompatible with a market economy.

Two issues will be pursued in the rest of this chapter. First, it is in a sense wrong to say that aggravated damages have not been awarded in contract, but this is because of a widespread confusion of aggravated damages in tort and damages for distress, disappointment and loss of enjoyment in contract. Second, as the view of contract taken in this book does not seek to prevent all breaches, it allows the possibility of distinguishing those legitimate breaches which should not be prevented from those illegitimate ones that, in fact, should be (if a good way of doing this can be devised). We will discuss this in the context of the US doctrine of 'bad faith breach' and the English position towards breach of employment contracts and restitutionary damages.

---

18  Above p 579 n 3 at 1800C per Lord Mackay. Lord Mackay generously implies that this passage was cited by Lord Devlin in *Rookes v Barnard* [1964] AC 1129 at 1221. It was not.
19  But see NJ McBride, 'A Case for Awarding Punitive Damages in Response to Deliberate Breaches of Contract' (1995) 24 Anglo-American Law Review 369. See also p 599 n 12 below.
20  See ch 17 above.
1   See ch 1 above.

## Distress, disappointment and loss of enjoyment

It is obvious that in many[2] cases a breach of contract will cause distress and disappointment to C, and in some cases when a good which was to be enjoyed by a consumer is lost or spoilt, that enjoyment will be lost or impaired. Damages which compensate for any of these as such are exceptional in contract. The stoical attitude of the law of contract has been heavily influenced by the denial of exemplary damages in *Addis v Gramophone Co Ltd*,[3] where an employee was wrongfully dismissed in a 'harsh and humiliating'[4] manner before an assembly of employees. This case has not been confined to an authority on wrongful dismissal,[5] but has been generalised to stand for a general refusal to award damages for distress and disappointment in contract.[6]

In general it can be said that if this stoical approach were applied in every contract case it would sometimes deny compensation to C for genuine losses which were within the parties' contemplation, and the courts have in fact made a number of exceptions to their general disinclination to award damages in contract in respect of non-pecuniary losses, which will here be called damages for distress and disappointment and loss of enjoyment.[7] This rather long phrase embraces two[8] situations

---

2   Or indeed all: GH Treitel, *Law of Contract* (10th edn 1999) p 923: 'anxiety is almost an inevitable concomitant'.

3   [1909] AC 488, discussed at pp 601-603 below.

4   Ibid at 493.

5   The employment contract issues are briefly discussed below.

6   Treitel, *Law of Contract* (10th edn 1999), p 920.

7   They are exhaustively listed in *McGregor on Damages* (16th edn 1997) paras 98-106.

8   With some hesitation, it may be stated that damages may usually be recovered in what has been regarded as the distinct situation of physical inconvenience caused by D's breach: the principal modern authority is *Bailey v Bullock* [1950] 2 All ER 1167. This was an unusual and unpleasant case in which the employee of D, a firm of solicitors, fraudulently hid the fact that he had failed to pursue C's attempt to repossess his house from a tenant. C's consequent prolonged failure to obtain possession caused him, his wife and child considerable distress as they had to live in one bedroom of his in-laws' small house until they did regain possession. It being conceded that this was a contract case, *Addis v Gramophone Co Ltd* should have meant that non-pecuniary loss could not be recovered. However, it was recovered because this was distress caused by 'physical inconvenience', which was distinguished from distress and disappointment as such.

   It is by no means unknown for the law of tort and even contract to show particular solicitude for 'physical' harms, and it may well be best to regard *Bailey v Bullock* as confined to its facts, the product of clever pleading to an understandably receptive court. The case certainly cannot yield a robust ratio, for the fact that it involved physical inconvenience does not address the real issue at all, which was the distress caused by the inconvenience. However, quite predictably, the argument that distress caused by physical inconvenience cannot be distinguished from distress caused in other ways has intermittently been drawn

that have been treated somewhat differently in the cases,[9] and are indeed factually distinct,[10] though they raise the same contractual issue: (1) protection from distress and disappointment and (2) provision of enjoyment.

Where the purpose of the contract may be to protect C from annoyance and mental distress, it is obviously contemplated that D's breach may be a 'cause' of C's continued suffering. In such a case a woman employed solicitors to protect her from being molested by a former friend, who was causing her mental distress; the damages for the solicitors' culpable failure to obtain protection for her included a sum for the foreseeable annoyance and mental distress which she continued to suffer as a result of their breach of contract.[11] Damages have also been awarded for nervous shock (psychiatric injury) or an anxiety state (an actual breakdown in health) suffered by C, if that was, at the time the contract was made, within the contemplation of the parties as a not unlikely consequence of the breach of contract.[12] Certainly at appeal level, these cases are very isolated.

Much more widely discussed are cases arising when the purpose of the contract extends beyond the avoidance of distress, unhappiness or displeasure to the actual provision of enjoyment. Damages for non-pecuniary loss repeatedly have been recovered in actions for breach of contract in this situation. The awards in such cases tend to be modest and so attract little attention from the appellate courts. This causes many writers to overstate the court's disinclination to award such damages at first instance, as a visit to the county court (or a perusal of *Current Law* where

---

upon in those cases which have sought to chip away at Addis as an argument not that distress damages should not have been awarded in *Bailey v Bullock* but that they should be awarded more widely, including *Jarvis v Swan Tours* [1973] QB 233 at 237-238 and *Archer v Brown* [1985] QB 401 at 424. The physical inconvenience basis of recovery in *Bailey v Bullock* has recently gained the support of being cited with this expansionist intention in two House of Lords cases: *Johnson v Gore Wood & Co* [2001] 2 WLR 72 at 108H and *Farley v Skinner* [2001] 3 WLR 899 at 923B (see also 907H). Whatever the position in the authorities, physical inconvenience as a specific ground of recovery cannot be given a coherent basis.

9   *Watts v Morrow* [1991] 1 WLR 1421 at 1445G-H.
10  R Halson, *Contract Law* (2001) p 485.
11  *Heywood v Wellers* [1976] QB 446.
12  *Cook v Swinfen* [1967] 1 WLR 457 (a solicitor's failure to defend divorce proceedings).
13  But in *Farley v Skinner* [2001] 3 WLR 899 at 907 Lord Steyn, after considering a description of litigation in the County Courts, has recently said: 'I am satisfied that in the real life of our lower courts non-pecuniary damages are regularly awarded on the basis that [D's] breach of contract deprived [C] of the very object of the contract, viz pleasure, relaxation, and peace of mind'.
14  Interestingly, non-pecuniary damages have been recovered for the breach of contracts for the sale of a car: see *Jackson v Chrysler Acceptances* [1978] RTR 474 and *Bernstein v Pamson Motors (Golders Green) Ltd* [1987] 2 All ER 220. Both were consumer cases, and indeed the former can be interpreted as a holiday

many such decisions are noted) would confirm.[13] The paradigm examples[14] of contracts for the provision of pleasure involve holidays[15] and weddings.[16] These cases can be viewed as an attempt to compensate a disappointed promisee's consumer surplus which could not be measured by the price he had paid for the service.[17] In the holiday contract cases, if D had broken the contract before C had travelled to the place it might have been possible for him to find a substitute holiday. But the timing of D's breach may rule out this possibility, as where D, who had been employed to take photographs at C's wedding, failed to appear. Damages were awarded for C's being 'permanently denied' the 'pleasure in the years ahead' from the 'recollection of a happy occasion'.[18]

Discussion of this matter is handicapped because the working of the law of contract as a system of default rules simply is not properly understood in much of that discussion.[19] It should be and is perfectly possible for the parties to provide that D will be liable for distress, disappointment and loss of enjoyment caused by D's breach of their contract. If the prevention of distress, disappointment and loss of enjoyment are identified in the contract in this way,[20] then D should be

---

case, and it is, of course, possible to argue that a contract for the purchase of a car by a consumer can be said to be one where the essence of the contract is the provision of pleasure. But this argument surely must mean that these cases hold out the possibility that the provision of pleasure may be identified in all or at least a great many sales of goods to consumers: see PS Atiyah *et al*, *The Sale of Goods* (10th edn 2001) pp 551-552. (*Jackson* has recently been approvingly cited by Lord Steyn in a speech which clearly intends to expand the use of exemplary damages in contract: *Farley v Skinner* [2001] 3 WLR 899 at 907F-G). This is a possibility that must be handled with *extreme* caution. If this sort of liability (and the legal costs of establishing it) was ever found to be a normal part of sales of goods, it might prove that the consequences of this could not be minimised by the seller explicitly excluding this liability because of the regulation of exemption clauses. For these reasons, the pricing of consumer goods might therefore be radically shifted in ways courts acting on their own initiative cannot possibly understand or evaluate.

15   *Jarvis v Swan Tours* [1973] QB 233 and *Jackson v Horizon Holidays* [1975] 1 WLR 1468.

16   *Cole v Rana* [1993] CLY 1364 (transport to); *Diesen v Samson* 1971 SLT 49 (photographs of); *Dunn v Disc Jockey Unlimited Co Ltd* (1978) 87 DLR (3d) 408 (entertainment at); *Hardy v Losner Formals* [1997] CLY 1749 (clothing for) and *Morris v Britannia Hotels Ltd* [1997] CLY 1748 (suggesting that the level of damages in wedding cases should be higher than that in the holiday cases).

17   H Beale, 'Exceptional Measures of Damages in Contract', in Birks (ed), *Wrongs and Remedies in the Twenty-first Century* (1996) 217, p 224. For the concept of the consumer surplus see pp 168-171 above.

18   *Diesen v Samson* 1971 SLT 49 at 50.

19   See the discussion of default rules at pp 88-94 above and its application to restitution at pp 272-282 above.

20   *Bliss v South Eastern Thames Regional Health Authority* [1987] ICR 700 at 718 and *Watts v Morrow* [1991] 1 WLR 1421. When in the latter case it was held that it was 'impossible' to interpret 'the ordinary surveyor's contract' as warranting

liable for damages to compensate this loss. Of course, it may be expected that D will charge more for, say, providing a package holiday if he is to be liable in this way than if he is not, or, given the difficulty of quantification of these losses and the legal costs to which this may give rise, in the face of this liability he may withdraw from the market. It would appear that, as a default rule, package holidays are sold with either no or limited liability for these losses,[1] and we would hazard that this reflects the preference of package holidaymakers for cheapness rather than paying for insurance against this sort of loss. What would be utterly wrong would be to change the law to say that damages of this sort should *or* should not be made available in these (or similar) cases from the point of view of an abstract consideration of the wrongfulness of breach. Policy must be determined in full awareness of the costs of the alternative forms of liability, and the views of the parties to specific contracts (and their trade and consumer associations), including the propensity of consumers to pay, must be decisive in the choice of form of liability.[2]

In *Watts v Morrow* it was said that the provision of 'pleasure, relaxation, peace of mind or freedom from molestation' should be the 'very object' of the contract if liability was to follow when 'the fruit of the contract was not provided';[3] but the relative clarity of this formulation, which at least

---

the provision of 'peace of mind and freedom from distress' (ibid at 1442), this was not to state an 'absolute rule' that a contract between house purchasers and their surveyor could not include such a term, but that such a contract would be 'exceptional' (ibid at 1445). This is a welcome correct analysis in terms of default and bespoke rules.

The disquieting aspects of *Kralj v McGrath* [1986] 1 All ER 54 might be addressed along these lines: a private patient could seek to contract for a level of liability that, one imagines, will be always unacceptable as a general position even for (grossly) negligent NHS treatment. Of course, the private medical practitioner may well be unwilling to absorb this risk, and so this possibility may be purely theoretical.

1   Clause 26 of the *Code of Conduct of the Association of British Travel Agents* contemplates that its members will be able to seek to limit (including exclude) this sort of liability. In an explanatory leaflet distributed to holidaymakers, *Providing Help and Protection for Consumers*, it is explained that: 'For a claim to succeed it's not enough that you didn't enjoy your holiday. There may be many reasons for this, eg bad weather or simply a wrong choice of holiday for you, and things beyond the tour operator's control'. The *Code of Conduct* does, however, appear fully to acknowledge (though it allows the limiting of) liability for a wide range of pecuniary losses. (The Association's documents are available on the Association's website http://www.abtanet.com). Cf The Package Travel, Package Holidays and Package Tours Regulations 1992/3288 inter alia in respect of reliance upon 'misleading information'.

2   Citing *Wong Mee Wan v Kwan Kin Services Ltd* [1995] 4 All ER 745, Professor Atiyah draws our attention to what appears to be an absurd result of proceeding in just the wrong way: PS Atiyah, 'Personal Injuries in the Twenty-first Century: Thinking the Unthinkable', in Birks (ed), *Wrongs and Remedies in the Twenty-first Century* (1996), p 3 n 3.

3   Above [1991] 1 WLR 1421 at 1445.

has the benefit of stressing that the fulfilment of the purpose *must* be
identified in the contract, has been dissipated by the House of Lords in
*Farley v Skinner*.[4] Regarding the 'very object' formulation as too narrow,
Lord Steyn said that '[i]t is sufficient if a major or important object of the
contract is to give pleasure, relaxation or peace of mind'.[5] Unfortunately,
this is not merely an attempt at semantic clarification; this was explicitly
done to reconcile these developments in the law with the loss of amenity
award given in *Ruxley Electronics and Construction Ltd v Forsyth*.[6] But[7]
as *Ruxley* was *not* a case where the purpose of enjoyment was identified
in the contract,[8] *Farley v Skinner* (though arguably right on its facts)[9] is
a most regrettable muddying of a pool which had begun to clear.[10] *Farley
v Skinner* undoubtedly tends to a position where the default rule will be
one of liability, which (so far as one can judge from the cases)[11] is a
complete reversal of the present position as it is understood by commercial
parties.[12] This may possibly be the right thing to do (though we do not
think so);[13] but as it is not being done after any sort of consultation with
potentially affected parties we cannot know, and surely things should be
left alone unless a very strong case is made for changing them. In any
case, the way this change is being broached in *Farley v Skinner* will ensure
confusion and litigation while commercial parties who have failed to keep

4   [2001] 3 WLR 899.
5   Ibid at 910B.
6   [1996] AC 344 (facts set out at pp 213-214 above).
7   Leaving aside that D's conduct in *Ruxley* was not outrageous (see pp 274-274
    above) and that the quantification of the amenity award was entirely arbitrary in
    that case (see pp 214-215 above).
8   See p 214 n 7 and pp 274-275 above.
9   The matter is not luminously clear: the House of Lords restored the trial judge's
    award after the Court of Appeal denied liability.
10  The overruling of *Knott v Bolton* (1995) 11 Const LJ 375, which on its reported
    facts seems to be an absolutely correct following of *Watts v Morrow*, is extremely
    regrettable but certainly necessary to reconcile the law with *Ruxley*. Nothing is
    said of the many other cases which have followed *Watts v Morrow* in a way
    indistinguishable from *Knott v Bolton*: *Farley v Skinner* [2001] 3 WLR 899 at
    909-910.
11  Eg the interpretation of 'the ordinary surveyor's contract' in *Watts v Morrow*
    discussed in p 597 n 20 above.
12  In *Farley v Skinner* [2001] 3 WLR 899 at 909G, Lord Steyn is strongly influenced
    by D Capper, 'Damages for Distress and Disappointment: The Limits of *Watts v
    Morrow*' (2000) 116 Law Quarterly Review 553, p 556, which allows that 'if [D]
    is unwilling to accept this responsibility he or she can say so and either no contract
    will be made or one will be made but including a disclaimer'. This at least shows
    some understanding of the working of default rules, if none of the illegitimacy of
    changing the law without any attempt to determine whether affected parties want
    it changed or telling them in advance what is to happen. Capper gives no
    consideration to the implications of the possibility that this liability might not be
    able to be excluded in consumer cases (see p 596 n 14 above).
13  See pp 279–282 above.

up with the latest academic literature learn that they must exclude a liability they had no idea they were undertaking.[14]

What, so far at least,[15] is clear is that the courts are not sympathetic to claims for non-pecuniary losses in commercial disputes. The point was forcefully made by Staughton LJ who said he 'would not view with enthusiasm' the prospect that a shipowner would be able to add to an action for unpaid carriage or liquidated damages 'a claim for mental distress suffered while he was waiting for his money'.[16] It is suggested that this antipathy should be viewed as a default rule against recognising these losses which simply reflects the empirical fact that in commercial disputes it will not usually be reasonably contemplated as a consequence of breach that C will suffer non-pecuniary loss. Breach is endemic to commercial life, and to normally give damages for mental distress would increase the transaction costs of contracting, perhaps by a considerable amount if one looks at the difficulties of proving the analogues to mental distress in tort. The present default rule of not considering damages for mental distress in commercial cases presumably reflects the fact that a commercial party who wished to recoup them would be at a considerable competitive disadvantage to one who did not (and may also suffer very considerable injury to his reputation). It is likely then, that losses of this sort are not in the reasonable contemplation of commercial parties. This fact should not be elevated to an absolute refusal to compensate such losses should they exceptionally be perfectly clearly identified in a contract made in a commercial context.

In sum, all these cases should be understood as having nothing to do with exemplary (ie including aggravated) damages as such.[17] They are cases in which the issue is whether the loss for which compensation was sought was identified in the contract, and, as a general default rule, it has not been and should not be regarded as being so identified. It would be quite wrong to suggest, however, that the cases turn on a clear appreciation

---

14  Or, far more likely, until *Farley v Skinner* becomes interpreted in ways reconcilable with *Watts v Morrow* (or just ignored).

15  The most recent House of Lords case remains firm on this point: *Johnson v Gore Wood & Co*, above [2001] 2 WLR 72 at 96B-97D, 101B-C, 107G-109G, 114H-115B, 127C, though Lord Cooke's position clearly invites criticism of *Addis* and approval of *Ruxley* in non-commercial cases, and questions whether cases like *Johnson* are commercial cases: ibid at 109B-G. This case was heard only a month after *Farley v Skinner* by an entirely differently constituted House and in his leading speech Lord Bingham (ibid at 96B-97D) placed a much more restrictive interpretation on *Ruxley* than did Lord Steyn in *Farley v Skinner*. This is an issue currently in flux.

16  *Hayes v James & Charles Dodd* [1990] 2 All ER 815 at 824. See also the discussion of the case of the surety in *Addis v Gramophone Co Ltd* [1909] AC 488 at 496.

17  But see p 585 n 15 above.

of this or that, especially after *Farley v Skinner*, a sort of aggravated damages claim in contract might not succeed in future.

## Outrageous breach of an employment contract

Despite C's undoubted humiliation, it was held that no damages in contract could be awarded for his injured feelings, distress, annoyance or social discredit[18] in *Addis v Gramophone Co Ltd*,[19] and this narrow principle has recently been confirmed by the House of Lords in *Johnson v Unisys*.[20] While the respect shown to *Addis v Gramophone Co Ltd* is explicable (and eminently correct) in terms of a reluctance to award exemplary damages in contract *tout court*,[1] it is very arguable that this case produces an unsatisfactory outcome in the employment cases it specifically covers. D's conduct in *Addis* was outrageous and is as strong a case of an iniquitous wrong it is sensible to try to prevent as one is likely to find in the common law.[2] To the extent that *Addis v Gramophone Co Ltd*[3] would limit the awards which would be made in wrongful dismissal cases at common law to less than is provided by legislation against 'unfair' dismissal,[4] it arguably is inconsistent with the purpose of that legislation. This may produce anomalous outcomes in the relatively small number of employment cases where the common law remedies are available but the statutory remedies are not, or where the outcomes would be different depending on how the case was pleaded.[5] This clearly is giving rise to employment litigation of which *Johnson v Unisys* and *Malik v Bank of Credit and Commerce International* (which is about to be discussed for

---

18 Loss of reputation should be protected by the tort of defamation. It has been held, however, that if the contract gave an opportunity to C to enhance his reputation as an author or an actor, damages may be awarded for the loss of that opportunity when D breaks the contract: *Clayton and Jack Waller Ltd v Oliver* [1930] AC 209 and *Joseph v National Magazine Co Ltd* [1959] Ch 14. But damages in contract cannot be awarded for injury to an existing reputation per se: *Withers v General Theatre Corpn Ltd* [1933] 2 KB 536.

19 [1909] AC 488.

20 [2001] 2 WLR 1076.

1 The arguments to this general effect in *Addis* itself are highly cogent and persuasive. In particular, an appreciation of the likely costs of proceedings in cases of this nature, a point to which Lord Hoffmann has wisely drawn attention in a recent case (see p 603 below) was clearly heavily influential in *Addis*.

2 Beale, 'Exceptional Measures of Damages in Contract', in Birks (ed), *Wrongs and Remedies in the Twenty-first Century* (1996) 217, pp 229-230.

3 And the other common law authorities which tend to place even greater restrictions on the remedies for employer's breach at common law as opposed to statute: IT Smith and G Wood, *Industrial Law* (7th edn 2000) pp 376-397.

4 Employment Rights Act 1996, pt X.

5 Smith and Wood, *Industrial Law* (7th edn 2000), pp 398-399.

its general implications) are examples; but it is the width of the authority that has been accorded to *Addis* as covering exemplary damages in general that raises the basic problem we shall address here.

Impetus has recently appeared to be given to the wider recovery of damages for non-pecuniary loss (subject only to the usual constraint of remoteness) by the House of Lord's decision in *Malik v BCCI SA (in liquidation)*.[6] Senior employees of a bank which went into liquidation following a massive fraud (of which they were not aware) sued their former employer when they were unable to obtain other employment because, they believe, of their past association with the bank. The House of Lords held that such 'stigma compensation' could in principle[7] be awarded where the disadvantage in the market was a reasonably foreseeable consequence of the employer's breach of contract,[8] ie applying the usual test of remoteness. Although the case involved a claim for pecuniary loss of future earnings[9] rather than non-pecuniary loss, it is important here because it was framed in terms of a claim for financial loss based on damage to reputation.

Once this sort of damage to reputation '[a]t the borderline between pecuniary and non-pecuniary loss'[10] was allowed, it might be thought that *Addis v Gramophone Co Ltd* would become subject to criticism for in that case compensation of lost future earnings caused by damage to reputation was simply ruled out (ie even if the loss was allowed to have occurred, it was irrecoverable). However, leaving aside its novelty, *Malik* (as it stands) sets a very uncertain precedent. Stigma claims must raise serious proof problems.[11] General contractual principles stipulate that for stigma compensation, disadvantage in the labour market must be actual

6   [1998] AC 20. This case is also known as *Mahmud v Bank of Credit and Commerce International (in liquidation)*.
7   These claims have so far been dealt with on an assumed set of facts and are still being litigated. After being dismissed, the employees compromised their claims against the bank in return for what they, with the hindsight of knowing how fraudulent the bank's conduct was and how difficult it has been for them to resume banking careers, believe were extremely small sums. It has recently been held that these agreements do not cover the stigma claims, which therefore proceed: *Bank of Credit and Commerce International v Ali* [2001] 2 WLR 735.
8   The term allegedly breached was the employer's implied contractual obligation not, without reasonable cause, to conduct his business in a way likely to damage the reciprocal relationship of 'trust and confidence' (or 'trust and respect') between employer and employee which has been recognised in modern labour law: Smith and Wood, *Industrial Law* (7th edn 2000), pp 124-125.
9   See also *Dunk v George Waller & Sons Ltd* [1970] 2 QB 163 (apprentice who was wrongfully dismissed received damages for the reduction in his future prospects, which was the purpose of his training as an apprentice) and *Edwards v Society of Graphical and Allied Trades* [1971] Ch 354 (member of a trade union wrongfully expelled from the union can receive damages for the loss of his employment prospects).
10  H Collins, *Law of Contract* (3rd edn 1997) p 390.
11  *Malik v Bank of Credit and Commerce International* [1998] AC 20 at 53.

and proven, not merely conjectural, and furnishing this proof will, of its nature, be extremely difficult. In the 'vastly expensive' BCCI litigation, which so far 'has produced benefits for no one except the lawyers involved',[12] this certainly has proven to be the case. Though their claims now proceed, no C has so far proven that his unemployment was prolonged by stigma. It is inconceivable that contract litigation on such claims will ever be anything other than immensely difficult and expensive.[13] Drawing attention to all this, Lord Hoffmann has questioned whether such claims should be allowed and, if one accepts his argument that: 'there comes a point at which the object of achieving perfect justice for everyone has to be tempered by some consideration of the resources required to investigate every possible claim',[14] it is very arguable they should not.[15] Furthermore, as BCCI is in liquidation (as D may well be in such cases), any damages awarded will have to be taken from the assets available to other creditors at least as innocent as the Cs and with typically much more certain, or indeed liquidated, claims.[16]

In recognition of basically these arguments, *Addis v Gramophone Co Ltd* has, as we have mentioned, recently been approved by the House of Lords in *Johnson v Unisys*,[17] which has sought to limit the scope of *Malik* (as it then stood). Much will depend on what now happens in *Malik*, and particularly what is made of *Johnson v Unisys*; but, it is submitted, nothing can nor should be done to really unsettle *Addis v Gramophone Co Ltd* as a general contractual principle at common law unless it is recognised that there are breaches which it is right to try to prevent (to which *Addis* should not apply) and breaches which it is not right to try to prevent (to which *Addis* should apply). Paradoxically, in terms of the outrageousness of D's conduct at least, wrongful dismissal is as strong a case as can be given of the *former*. (This is not necessarily a compelling case.) It is to a possible way of 'fine tuning' the notion of breach so that 'wrongful' breach can be distinguished from 'legitimate' breach that we now turn.[18]

---

12  *Bank of Credit and Commerce International v Ali* [2001] 2 WLR 735 at 760.
13  Smith and Wood, *Industrial Law* (7th edn 2000) raise the, it is submitted, entirely unwelcome possibility that quantification of these losses should be carried out in something like the way it is in personal injury cases. (It is not possible to be entirely clear what they have in mind.) It is, we submit, inconceivable that competent contractual parties would not generally contract out of liability which involves such legal costs (unless, as in most personal injury, the state prevents this).
14  *Bank of Credit and Commerce International v Ali* [2001] 2 WLR 735 at 761.
15  See p 601 n 1 above.
16  Ibid at 760-761.
17  [2001] 2 WLR 1076.
18  CA Remington, 'Intentional Interference with Contract and the Doctrine of Efficient Breach: Fine Tuning the Notion of Contract Breacher as Wrongdoer' (1999) 47 Buffalo Law Review 646.

## Concurrent liability and bad faith breach

A peculiar situation now exists in the law of contract as it is classically
understood. By generally assuming *pacta sunt servanda* and, what is the
other side of the same coin, refusing to recognise a general obligation to
perform in good faith (for all contracts must be strictly performed), the
classical law is unable to rationally distinguish between legitimate and
illegitimate breaches of contract. (It also reduces other purported
modifications to breaches and so is unable to distinguish between
legitimate and illegitimate modifications more generally.) Much of this
is a matter of the determination of liability outside of the scope of this
book. But it is this failing that presently is driving three arguments about
remedies: that literal enforcement should be more readily (or even usually)
granted; that a general restitutionary remedy should be available when
appropriate; and that exemplary damages should be more widely used.
On the positive view of breach as taken in this book, these arguments for
the so-called performance interest must all be rejected and the conclusion
be reached that reform of the law can make no progress until a choice is
made between the two sensible alternative courses now open to it.
Preferably, legislative encouragement should be given to the law of
contract to attempt to distinguish between modification and breach in
good faith and bad faith breach,[19] and impose remedies which are intended
to prevent the latter but not the former. Or, if it is decided that this
distinction is too difficult to draw,[20] the law should be left alone to develop
by growth of case law. General use of exemplary damages cannot be a
sensible policy.

Not recognising the necessity to make the distinction between breach
in good and bad faith, the Law Commission has adopted the second of
these alternatives,[1] and this is much better than arguing for exemplary
damages as a way of trying to realise *pacta sunt servanda* as a general
policy. However, though it will not be argued here, we are of the opinion
that the law of contract in effect does have a doctrine of good faith presently
composed of many disparate and indeed inconsistent doctrines,[2] and that
general good faith *will* be consciously recognised as a result of further

---

19  We go so far as to say this only because we believe EU led developments about
    to be discussed make it necessary.
20  The issues are reviewed and exemplified by PH Marshall, 'Wilfulness: A Crucial
    Factor in Choosing Remedies for Breach of Contract' (1982) 24 Arizona Law
    Review 733.
1   *Report*, above p 579 n 2, para 5.44.
2   D Campbell, 'The Relational Constitution of the Discrete Contract', in D Campbell
    and P Vincent-Jones (eds), *Contract and Economic Organisation* (1996) 40, pp
    62-63.

integration of English law into EU law.[3] If this is so, remedies appropriate to breach in bad faith will be necessary, and the argument for exemplary damages for 'bad faith breach' has been recognised in a number of US jurisdictions.[4] The employment case is, it is submitted, an obvious example which could be extended to other appropriate cases.[5]

As a matter of establishing liability, US bad faith damages work by establishing concurrent liability.[6] When the conduct which amounts to a breach of contract is wrongful and so also amounts to tort,[7] bad faith damages may be imposed.[8] To follow this line will very likely lead to the

---

3    O Lando and H Beale (eds), *Principles of European Contract Law* (2000) arts 1.201 and 1.202. On the whole issue of good faith see the review by R Brownsword, *Contract Law* (2000) ch 5.

4    L Curtis, 'Damage Measurements for Bad Faith Breach of Contract: An Economic Analysis' (1986) 39 Stanford Law Review 161 and B Perlstein, 'Crossing the Contract Tort Boundary: An Economic Argument for the Imposition of Extra-compensatory Damages for Opportunistic Breach of Contract' (1992) 58 Brooklyn Law Review 877.

5    In the US the most developed law seems to be the criticism of the bad faith practices of insurers (not insureds, to whom *uberrimae fidei* seems to be applied with a lack of mutuality) which deny what have come to be called the 'reasonable expectations' of insureds: for a review of the literature see PN Swisher, 'A Realistic Consensus Approach to the Insurance Law Doctrine of Reasonable Expectations' (2000) 35 Tort and Insurance Law Journal 729 and for recent contributions see 'Symposium on the Doctrine of Reasonable Expectations' (1999) 5 Connecticut Insurance Law Journal 1. There is a highly developed network of claimants' organisations: eg Fight Bad-faith Insurance Companies at <http://www.badfaithinsurance.org>. For an English example of the type of practice by an insurer at which the bad faith and reasonable expectations doctrines are aimed see *Sprung v Royal Insurance (UK) Ltd* [1999] Lloyd's Rep IR 111 (the Court of Appeal felt obliged to give judgment for the insurer, D, although Evans LJ did 'not find [D's] submissions attractive either from a commercial or a moral point of view': ibid at 118. Dismissing C's appeal 'with reluctance' Beldam LJ said that 'early consideration should be given to the reform of the law in similar cases': ibid at 119).

6    See ch 29 above.

7    The extent to which 'bad faith breach' has become a tort in itself or is a collective noun for specific torts which still retain particular features is a matter of dispute.

8    S Choturian. 'Note: Tort Remedies for Breach of Contract' (1986) 86 Columbia Law Review 377 and J Monaghan, 'Note: Extending the Bad Faith Tort Doctrine to General Commercial Contracts' (1985) 65 Boston University Law Review 355, p 355: 'The bad faith tort doctrine is a judicially created tort theory of recovery available only to parties to a contract. This tort has been applied with so little explanation of its necessary elements that it is not possible to derive a broadly applicable definition from the case law. The bad faith tort doctrine is significant, however, in that it pursues its underlying policy of providing for the recovery of damages suffered from a breach which are not recoverable under a contract theory by recognising a tort action where traditionally only a contract action would have been allowed. Thus, where the bad faith tort is applicable, a plaintiff is not limited in his recovery by common law restrictions on contract damages but is able to recover the generally more liberal measure of tort damages'.

idea that bad faith damages are compensatory, and we would not advise this for reasons we trust are clear from our criticism of aggravated damages.[9] In the US it has led to a tortured reinterpretation of the cases in order to yield useful results. The issue should be directly examined in terms of its value, or otherwise, in promoting welfare enhancing exchanges through contract. If the recognition of general good faith in contract is imminent, consideration of the specific levels or forms of good faith appropriate to particular breaches is essential, for it undoubtedly is the case that impositions of inappropriate levels of good faith 'could well work practical mischief if ruthlessly implemented in our law'.[10]

As a matter of determining quantum, apart from our general observation about the necessity of a schedule,[11] we submit that no conclusions should be derived from an abstract discussion from the perspective of exemplary damages in general. The appropriate schedular level of bad faith damages for each specific type of exchange must be determined in the light of an empirical examination of the exchange and a consultation with the affected parties.

### Restitution as exemplary damages

Many of the established instances of concurrent liability were cited in *A-G v Blake* as examples of 'appropriate occasions' on which the restitutionary remedy of partial or total disgorgement of the profits D makes from breach of contract should be used,[12] and *Blake* makes it more likely that they will be used in this way. These damages are exemplary in the sense that they may, of their nature, be in excess of the damages that would be awarded on normal compensatory damages principles (obviously this is when C will claim them), and, following much academic argument,[13] the Law Commission recently welcomed the greater use of these damages

---

9    Above pp 580-585.

10   MG Bridge, 'Does Anglo-Canadian Contract Law Need a Doctrine of Good Faith' (1984) 9 *Canadian Journal of Business Law* 385, p 426. The first commercial case which has relied on *Blake*, *Esso Petroleum Co Ltd v NIAD Ltd* (22 November 2001, unreported), Ch D, effectively extends the scope of good faith in a franchise contract by changing the rules on remedy rather than the rules on liability, without any consideration of the issues raised by Bridge and discussed in the context of franchises by JM Paterson, 'Good Faith in Commercial Contracts? A Franchising Case Study' (2001) 29 *Australian Business Law Review* 270.

11   Above p 593.

12   *A-G v Blake* [2001] 1 AC 268 at 284C. A relatively uncomplicated example is *Penarth Dock Engineering Co Ltd v Pounds* [1963] 1 Lloyd's Rep 359; cited in *Blake* at 278G and discussed at pp 269-270, 528 above.

13   Eg the first edition of this book: D Harris, *Remedies in Contract and Tort* (1988) pp 232-233.

in this exemplary way by the courts.[14] We have argued that the generalisation of the restitutionary remedy to cover an ever wider range of contractual situations is mistaken.[15] But, of course, if the breaches *are* so offensive that one *does* wish to prevent them (which is not the case with the great majority of breaches), the argument we have made against the general restitutionary remedy does not apply, and restitutionary remedies may play a role in preventing bad faith breach.[16] However, a rather different point should be made.

If the goal is to prevent breaches found offensive, then very arguably restitution may not be enough. Exemplary damages have two functions which could not be taken over by the law of restitution if that law is not to become hopelessly convoluted:[17] namely, the deterrence of oppressive conduct by government officials, especially where other officials may not choose to prosecute or discipline them;[18] and, secondly, the deterrence of tortious conduct which, although intended to be profitable, failed to be so. Consideration of this second point leads to a more general concern about the use of restitution as exemplary damages. Even if the restitutionary remedy is total (as opposed to partial) disgorgement, a 'punishment' of merely depriving a person of any gain he may make through wrongdoing is punishment at zero risk, that is to say, it is not punishment at all.[19] D may just 'offend' and disgorge what he has made when he is challenged. His only extra expense will be legal costs, which he can minimise by early settlement, and as he may expect not to be challenged on every (or even many) occasions, this type of deterrent is weak. Extra punishment is needed to prevent rational calculation leading D to conclude that, in his own interest, he *should* 'offend'.[20] If it is legitimate to prevent a particular sort of breach, one actually is pushed

14  *Report*, above p 579 n 2, pt 3.
15  Ch 17 above.
16  See R Nolan, 'Remedies for Breach of Contract: Specific Enforcement and Restitution', in FD Rose (ed), *Failure of Contracts* (1997) 35, pp 58-59 and, in general, SM Waddams, 'Restitution as Part of Contract Law', in A Burrows (ed), *Essays on the Law of Restitution* (1991) 197. But see p 606 n 10 above.
17  Seeing this point, the Law Commission has seemed to allow that 'an unexpectedly larger award' might sometimes be made in what it nevertheless analyses as restitutionary cases (*Report*, above, p 579 n 2, para 5.36), entirely giving away its insistence that 'reasoned, consistent and proportionate awards are vital' (ibid, para 1.3).
18  Some oppressive conduct by officials will fall outside the scope of the criminal law.
19  P Jaffey, 'Restitutionary Damages and Disgorgement' (1995) Restitution Law Review 30, pp 37-38. Cf the justification of the damages awarded in *Broome v Cassell & Co* above p 579 n 3 quoted at p 587 n 12 above.
20  Cf the role of (the lack of) certainty of punishment in determining the level of criminal sanctions in JH Bentham, *An Introduction to the Principles of Morals and Legislation* (1970) ch 14 § 16.

away from restitution to outright punitive damages not calculated with reference to unjust enrichment. There is no way of settling this point by ratiocination; empirical studies of the comparative effectiveness of restitutionary and outright punitive exemplary damages in specific situations are the only guide to sensible policy.

This issue was very inadequately considered as it arose in *Blake*, which really must be seen as an opportunistic attempt to extend restitution as a good in itself rather than to punish Blake himself (much less to assist the development of the law of contract). The House of Lords in *Blake* placed a great deal of reliance on *Snepp v United States*,[1] a very similar espionage case. The US Supreme Court divided over the issue of the appropriate remedy in *Snepp*, with the dissent turning inter alia on the argument that 'to the extent that the Government seeks to punish Snepp for the generalised harm he has caused ... and to deter others from following in his footsteps, punitive damages [rather than restitution are] clearly the preferable remedy'.[2] With respect, Lord Nicholls' citation of *Snepp* in *Blake*[3] is very tendentious, for *Snepp* is like *Blake* not least because the dissent in it is an unusually strongly worded and powerful criticism of the majority decision.

In sum, though the argument that it is wrong to seek to prevent all breaches by the use of restitution obviously cannot apply to those breaches it is thought right to try to prevent, it will not necessarily be the case that those breaches themselves are right occasions for the use of restitution, for restitution may not be such an effective deterrent as outright punitive damages. However, the matter cannot be decided generally but must be considered in relationship to specific empirical exchanges.

1    444 US 507 (1980). This course had been advocated by Birks: P Birks, 'Restitutionary Damages for Breach of Contract: *Snepp* and the Fusion of Law and Equity' [1987] Lloyd's Maritime and Commercial Law Quarterly 421.
2    *Snepp v United States, loc cit* at 523 per Brennan, Marshall and Stevens JJ.
3    [2001] 1 AC 268 at 287-288

# 31 Interim protection

## Interim injunctions

An interim[1] injunction is an order restraining D until trial of the action begun by C (or its other disposition). It usually protects C's alleged rights by preventing D from changing the situation to C's detriment during the delay until the trial. For many years these orders were used flexibly by the courts. They were regularly sought by the parties to a dispute in order to get a quick and cheap decision on the merits of the claim as the judge perceived them from reading the affidavit evidence. The judge looked to see whether C could show a good prima facie case and was likely to be given a final injunction at the trial. Unless C had shown a very strong case, the judge proceeded to consider the 'balance of convenience' between the parties, viz which of them would suffer greater hardship if the interim decision went against him. If the injunction were granted, C had to give an undertaking that, if he lost at the trial, he would pay damages to D for any loss suffered from his complying with the injunction. The decision in this preliminary trial usually led the parties to settle out of court, and so finally disposed of nearly all disputes in which court proceedings were seriously contemplated.[2]

However, in the *American Cyanamid* case in 1975[3] the House of Lords disapproved of this practice of treating the application for an interim injunction as a preliminary but 'real' trial of the merits. One reason was

1 'Interim' replaces the former word 'interlocutory'.
2 P Prescott (1975) 91 Law Quarterly Review 168, p 169.
3 *American Cyanamid Co v Ethicon Ltd* [1975] AC 396. C wanted to prevent D from marketing a product which C claimed infringed his patent. The 'guidelines' laid down in this case were examined further in *R v Secretary of State for Transport, ex p Factortame Ltd (No 2)* [1991] 1 AC 603 at 671-674.

that the evidence on affidavits was not tested by cross-examination, and so it was unsatisfactory for the judge to attempt at this stage to resolve difficult questions of fact or of law. In the leading speech, Lord Diplock held that at the interim hearing, the first test is whether C has shown 'that there is a serious question to be tried'; the 'court ... must be satisfied that the claim is not frivolous or vexatious'.[4] This formulation rejected the previous practice under which C had to show a strong prima facie case, and substituted one which is much easier for C to meet. If C does meet it, the court must then consider whether a remedy in damages for each side would be adequate, and whether each could pay any damages awarded against him. So the second test or 'guideline' is whether damages awarded at the trial would be an adequate remedy for C's loss up to the trial, and whether D could in fact pay them. If so, no injunction should be granted. But if damages to C would be inadequate,[5] the third test is whether, if D should win at the full trial, C's undertaking in damages would in fact give D adequate compensation for the loss suffered by him in complying with the injunction. If the answer to this is 'yes', C has a strong claim to an injunction. Fourthly, if the court is in doubt about the adequacy of the respective remedies in damages, it may use a 'balance of convenience' or relative hardship test and compare 'the extent of the uncompensatable disadvantage to each party'.[6] If this does not point clearly in favour of one party, the court may then (and only then) consider whether it is desirable to maintain the status quo,[7] and may weight the relative strength of the two cases on their merits, and favour one side if its case is much stronger. Thus, the prediction of ultimate success is to be used only if the other factors do not point to a decision. This relegation of the merits to the last stage of the enquiry, to be used only as a last resort, is the crucial change made by the *Cyanamid* decision. However, the rejection of the practice of using the interim hearing as a preliminary trial of the merits led to much dissatisfaction among practitioners and judges in the lower courts, so that later cases have a tendency to restrict the effect of the decision by creating exceptions and by interpreting it to allow some flexibility.[8]

---

4    The *American Cyanamid* case [1975] AC 396 at 407.
5    This led to the House upholding C's interim injunction in the *American Cyanamid* case itself because without it C's virtual monopoly arising from its patent would have been destroyed forever.
6    Ibid at 409.
7    Ibid at 408. But there is no simple test for what constitutes the *status quo*: *Garden Cottage Foods Ltd v Milk Marketing Board* [1984] AC 130 at 140.
8    *Fellowes & Son v Fisher* [1976] QB 122, 141. The Civil Procedure Rules 1998 do not seem to affect the application of the *Cyanamid* approach, but see the overriding objective in CPR 1.1.

The major exception to the *Cyanamid* approach is where, on the particular facts, it is clear that the interim decision will in practice settle the final outcome of the dispute;[9] where, in other words, an injunction would go beyond being 'a holding operation pending the trial'.[10] In this type of situation requiring urgent decisions the courts are entitled to look to the merits of the parties' cases, and to decide accordingly. So courts have seldom followed the *Cyanamid* approach in industrial disputes,[11] where Parliament itself has intervened;[12] nor in some commercial disputes, where immediate action by one or other side is essential in business terms.[13] Similarly, the *Cyanamid* decision has not been applied to an interim hearing where the facts and the law are clear eg an injunction to enforce an obviously valid restrictive covenant.[14]

Other departures from *Cyanamid* have occurred when the courts have taken account of the public interest, as where D is a local authority;[15] where an injunction would prevent the public from benefiting from a drug;[16] or where strike action by D would harm the public.[17] The public interest in freedom of speech nearly always leads to the refusal of an interim injunction, where D raises a defence to C's defamation claim;[18] or in a claim based on D's breach of confidence, where D puts forward a serious defence of public interest in publicly disclosing the information.[19] Writers

---

9   *NWL Ltd v Woods* [1979] 1 WLR 1294, 1305–7, HL. On the application of this principle to an employer's claim to enforce a covenant in restraint of trade, see *Lawrence David Ltd v Ashton* [1991] 1 All ER 385, CA and *Lansing Linde Ltd v Kerr* [1991] 1 WLR 251, CA.

10  *Cayne v Global Natural Resources plc* [1984] 1 All ER 225 at 234, 237.

11  Eg where the injunction would stop picketing: *Thomas v National Union of Mineworkers* [1986] Ch 20.

12  Trade Union and Labour Relations (Consolidation) Act 1992, s 221(2) (re-enacting a 1974 provision. Where D acted in furtherance of a trade dispute, the court must have regard to C's likelihood of success at the trial.) Damage to the public interest has been taken into account in *Associated British Ports v Transport and General Workers' Union* [1989] 3 All ER 796, CA. See further S Deakin and GS Morris *Labour Law* (2nd edn 1998) pp 916-920.

13  *Cayne v Global Natural Resources plc* [1984] 1 All ER 225. As the result of an interim injunction the claimants would have been able to become the new directors of the defendant company.

14  *Office Overload Ltd v Gunn* [1977] FSR 39, CA.

15  *Smith v Inner London Education Authority* [1978] 1 All ER 411 and *R v Secretary of State for Transport, ex p Factortame Ltd (No 2)* [1991] 1 AC 603 (no interim injunction granted to restrain the enforcement of a statute on the grounds of incompatibility with European law).

16  *Roussel-Uclaf v GD Searle & Co* [1977] FSR 125 (affirmed [1978] 1 Lloyd's Rep 225).

17  *NWL Ltd v Woods* [1979] 1 WLR 1294, 1305.

18  *Holley v Smyth* [1998] 1 All ER 853, CA.

19  *Lion Laboratories Ltd v Evans* [1985] QB 526 and *Francome v Mirror Group Newspapers Ltd* [1984] 1 WLR 892.

have argued that strict compliance with the *Cyanamid* ruling can also make it too easy for C to interfere with D's civil liberties by obtaining an interim injunction.[20]

An appeal from the judge's interim decision should be allowed only where the judge misunderstood the law or the facts, or there has been a significant change in circumstances. The appellate court may not interfere simply because its members would have exercised their discretion in a different way.[1]

## Interim mandatory injunctions

The courts are willing to grant an interim mandatory injunction but they are far more reluctant to do so than in the case of a comparable prohibitory injunction.[2] But such an injunction would be appropriate if D is trying to steal a march on C by acting quickly to make a permanent change to the situation before C can get a full hearing.[3] The courts are very cautious in granting an interim mandatory injunction to enforce a contract, since this drastic remedy is a form of 'specific performance' granted before a full hearing: it should be granted 'only in a clear case'.[4] But where speed is essential and the case is clear, it may be granted. So the House of Lords has approved the use of such an injunction when a letter of credit was shortly to expire; D, the buyer, was ordered to fulfil his contractual obligation by signing the notice which C needed to present to the bank to obtain the release of the credit.[5] In a similar type of situation, an interlocutory prohibitory injunction was granted to restrain D, an oil company, from withholding petrol supplies from C's garage until the trial of C's case.[6] If D stopped supplying him, C would be forced out of business because he had no alternative source of supply. By preserving the position under the contract, the order in practice amounted to specific performance until the full hearing.

---

20  P Wallington, 'Injunctions and the "Right to Demonstrate"' (1976) 35 Cambridge Law Journal 82 and D Newell, 'Trade Unions and Non-striking Members' (1981) 97 Law Quarterly Review 214.
1   *Hadmor Productions Ltd v Hamilton* [1983] 1 AC 191 at 220–1.
2   *Shepherd Homes Ltd v Sandham* [1971] Ch 340 at 351.
3   Ibid at 352 and *Luganda v Service Hotels Ltd* [1969] 2 Ch 209.
4   *Locabail International Finance Ltd v Agroexport* [1986] 1 WLR 657. (The *Cyanamid* approach does not apply: ibid at 664.)
5   *Astro Exito Navegacion SA v Chase Manhattan Bank NA* [1983] 2 AC 787 (if D failed to sign, the order authorised a court officer to sign on D's behalf).
6   *Sky Petroleum Ltd v VIP Petroleum Ltd* [1974] 1 WLR 576 (discussed at pp 174-175 above).

## Interim injunctions without notice

Several types of injunction are available to assist C to obtain evidence or to preserve the *status quo* until the trial of his claim against D. In cases of urgency, C may obtain an interim injunction (without notice to D) to restrain D from committing an act alleged to contravene C's rights. C must show that the delay to give notice to D would risk serious injury to him, and his counsel must make full and frank disclosure of all the material facts. The injunction is usually granted for a short time to enable notice to be given to D, so that he can seek a contested hearing.

A search order (which used to be called an *Anton Piller* order) is an interim order permitting C to enter D's premises to search for, inspect and seize documents relevant to C's claim or items which infringe C's rights (as with a breach of copyright or patent). The secrecy is justified in order to forestall any attempt by D to destroy these items before they can be used against him. Since the order is obtained without notice to D, safeguards for him are built into the order.

A freezing injunction (which used to be called a *Mareva* order) is an interim order designed to ensure that D will not be able to frustrate a money judgment which C may later obtain against him. It is an interim injunction obtained (without notice by C) to prohibit D from removing his assets from the jurisdiction. (It may also prohibit him from disposing of his assets wherever they are located eg by freezing his bank accounts.) Both freezing injunctions and search orders have spawned their own extensive case law, which is beyond the scope of this book.

# 32  Time limits for claims

## Introduction

The traditional view is that it is against the public interest to enforce stale demands. Claims should be tested before the evidence is lost, and potential defendants should be able to know when they can safely plan their affairs without taking account of the risk of claims arising out of a particular event. The general rule is laid down in the Limitation Act 1980. No action in contract[1] or tort[2] may be brought after the expiration of six years from the date[3] when the cause of action accrued. Some special periods are fixed for particular types of claim,[4] the most important of which is the three-year limit for personal injury claims.[5]

D must actually plead the defence of limitation, because the court itself will not take the point against C. Time runs from the earliest date when an action could have been brought, but various provisions allow for some postponement when C neither knew, nor ought to have known, crucial

1  Limitation Act 1980 (hereinafter 1980 Act), s 5. But the period for an action upon a 'speciality' (a deed under seal) is twelve years: ibid, s 8(1); cf ss 19 and 20(5). The same periods apply to C's claim to a debt, and (probably) to restitutionary claims. For concurrent causes of action in both contract and tort see ch 29 above.
2  1980 Act, s 2.
3  The claim form must be issued within the period but may be served anytime within four months after issue: CPR 7.5.
4  Eg for accidents at sea (Merchant Shipping Act 1995, Sch 6) or in the air (Carriage by Air Act 1961, 5(1): two years); for libel and slander (Administration of Justice Act 1985, s 57: three years); for claims under the Consumer Protection Act 1987 (s 11A: three years with a ten year long-stop); and for contribution between tortfeasors (1980 Act, s 10: two years from the date when the right to contribution accrued).
5  See pp 616-617 below. For claims following death see p 618 below.

facts,[6] or was under a disability (under age or suffering mental disorder),[7] or in cases of mistake, fraud or concealment.[8] Since most torts, like negligence, require proof of damage caused to C, the cause of action arises only when C suffers damage.[9] But where the tort is actionable without proof of actual damage (as with wrongful interference with goods), time runs from when D committed his wrongful act, even where the damage does not occur until later.[10] In contract, time runs from when the breach occurs, not from when C suffers any loss.[11] So in an action against a seller for delivering defective goods, the cause of action arises upon delivery, not when the buyer discovers the defect. During a current period of limitation, a written acknowledgement or a part-payment of a debt by D allows time to begin to run afresh.[12]

The expiration of the limitation period under the 1980 Act bars C's remedy through the courts, but does not extinguish his right.[13] Thus, in contract, a debt is still due to C, so that if D voluntarily pays it, or C can enforce it in some other way, C is entitled to retain the amount. For instance, if D pays money to C without specifying any particular debt, C may appropriate it to a statute-barred debt. C may also exercise a lien in respect of such a debt.

## Personal injuries

If C claims damages for personal injury (whether in contract or in tort), the limitation period is three years from either the date on which the cause of action accrued, or, if later, 'the date of knowledge' of the injured person[14] (who is assumed in the following account to be C). Detailed rules define 'the date of knowledge',[15] which refers to the date when C first had

---

6    See pp 616-618 below.
7    Where, at the time the cause of action arose, C was under 18, or suffering a mental disorder (see 1980 Act, s 38(3)), the six-year limitation period (or, in the case of personal injuries, the three-year period) runs from either his death or from the date when he ceased to be under the disability: ibid, s 28(1). So if C was injured while a child, he can sue D at any time until three years after he turns 18: *Tolley v Morris* [1979] 1 WLR 592, HL.
8    See pp 616-618 below.
9    *Cartledge v E Jopling & Sons Ltd* [1963] AC 758.
10   Where C's chattel has been converted successively, time runs from the original conversion: 1980 Act, s 3(1).
11   But there may be concurrent liability in tort, under which time runs from the occurrence of the damage. See ch 29 above.
12   Sections 29(5) and 30.
13   But title to land or to goods is extinguished: 1980 Act, ss 3(2) and 17.
14   1980 Act, s 11.
15   1980 Act, s 14(1). It is irrelevant that C did not know that, as a matter of law, D's liability could be based on the acts or omissions in question: ibid.

knowledge of four factors: (1) that 'the injury was significant';[16] (2) that it was 'attributable in whole or in part to the act or omission' alleged to create D's liability; (3) the identity of D; and (4) if it is alleged that the act or omission was of a person other than D (as in vicarious liability), the identity of that person and the additional facts supporting the claim against D. C's knowledge is extended to cover some categories of imputed knowledge. It covers 'knowledge which he might reasonably have been expected to acquire – (a) from facts observable or ascertainable by him, or (b) from facts ascertainable by him with the help of medical or other appropriate expert advice which it is reasonable for him to seek'.[17] But C is not fixed with knowledge of facts in category (b) so long as he 'has taken all reasonable steps to obtain (and, where appropriate, to act on) that advice'. But although the 1980 Act contains very detailed rules on the date of C's knowledge, the court has a wide discretion[18] to 'disapply' them (a) if 'it appears to the court that it would be equitable to allow an action to proceed'; and (b) if application of the detailed rules would 'prejudice' C.[19]

## Latent damage

Apart from personal injuries, damage not discoverable by C can arise in other situations, as with the construction of buildings, or where D's advice causes financial loss.[20] At common law the House of Lords gave the unsatisfactory ruling[1] that in the case of defective building work the cause of action is complete when some damage occurs, whether or not it could reasonably have been discovered at that time. This meant that if it later appeared that the physical damage must have occurred six years or more before it was discovered, the claim was statute-barred before C knew of the defect. However, a later Privy Council decision[2] held that where there

---

16 Defined by 1980 Act, s 14(2) as one where C would 'reasonably have considered it sufficiently serious to justify' proceedings against D.

17 1980 Act, s 14(3).

18 By 1980 Act, s 33 (which covers claims arising out of death as well as personal injury claims). The discretion is unfettered: *Thompson v Brown* [1981] 1 WLR 744, HL. 1980 Act, s 33(3) lists factors which the court should consider in exercising its discretion.

19 The prejudice to C must be compared with that to D if the action is allowed to continue: *Brookes v J and Coates (UK) Ltd* [1984] 1 All ER 702 at 714 and *Thompson v Brown* [1981] 1 WLR 744.

20 The date when C suffers 'damage' in these cases may precede the time when he suffers 'financial loss': *Forster v Outred & Co* [1982] 1 WLR 86.

1 *Pirelli General Cable Works Ltd v Faber & Partners* [1983] 2 AC 1. This was followed by the 24th Report of the Law Reform Committee, Cmnd 9390 (1984).

2 *Invercargill City Council v Hamlin* [1996] AC 624.

is a latent defect in a building (eg defects in the foundations) the claim is for *economic* (not physical) loss, which occurs only when the market value of the house is depreciated because the defective foundations have been discovered. Hence, the cause of action accrues (and time begins to run) only when the defects would have become apparent to any reasonable homeowner. But English courts are reluctant to follow the Privy Council on the common law position.[3] Legislation now gives C a secondary period within which to sue. For negligently caused damage (not including personal injury) the new limitation period[4] is the later of *either* the normal one (six years from when the cause of action first arose) *or* (if later) three years from the date when C knew or ought to have known facts[5] about the damage and his cause of action.[6] But there is an overriding limit of 15 years from the date of D's negligent act or omission.[7] This is a 'long stop' protection for potential defendants which will facilitate their taking out liability insurance.

## Death

When C dies within the limitation period, any claim surviving for the benefit of his estate[8] must be brought within three years of his death or of the date of his personal representative's 'knowledge'.[9] A fatal accident claim by dependants must be brought within three years of the death, or of the date of the dependant's 'knowledge'.[10] Where it is D who dies, the normal periods apply to claims brought by C against his estate.

## Mistake, fraud or concealment

Where C's claim is for relief from the consequences of a mistake, or is based on D's fraud, or where D has deliberately concealed from C any fact

3    *Havenlodge Ltd v Graeme John and Partners* [2001] Lloyd's Rep PN 223, CA.
4    On the date when a new owner acquires an interest in property subject to latent damage, he acquires a new cause of action: Latent Damage Act 1986, s 3.
5    The facts in question are similar to those needed for an extension of time under 1980 Act, s 14: see pp 616-617 above (personal injuries).
6    1980 Act, s 14A (inserted by Latent Damage Act 1986, s 1). The court has no discretion to extend this period. Section 14A does not apply to claims in contract.
7    1980 Act, s 14B (also inserted by the Latent Damage Act 1986, s 1). D's fraud or deliberate concealment of relevant facts will prevent the limit from applying: section 32(5).
8    Eg see pp 392-393 above.
9    1980 Act, s 11(5). 'Knowledge' is defined in s 14(1): see pp 616-617 above.
10   1980 Act, s 12 (which may be overridden by s 33: see p 617 above). For these claims see p 395 et seq above. If the deceased's own limitation period had expired before he died, no claim may be brought by a dependant: 1980 Act, s 12(1).

relevant to his cause of action, time runs from when C discovered the mistake, fraud or concealment, or could with reasonable diligence have discovered it.[11]

## Equitable remedies

Claims for equitable relief, such as specific performance or injunctions, are not subject to any statutory time limits.[12] They are left to the equitable doctrines of laches and acquiescence, which focus on C's conduct. Relief is denied if C has not been reasonably diligent in pursuing his claim or has waived it.[13] It must, in view of the prejudice caused to D, be unconscionable for C to enforce his claim after he has stood by and done little or nothing, despite his awareness of the relevant facts.[14] The question of time limits for claiming equitable damages[15] should be subject to the same rules.

---

11  1980 Act, s 32(1). By s 32(3) and (4), the *bona fide* purchaser for value of property (and his successors in title) are exempted from this provision.
12  But 1980 Act, s 36(1) says that courts may apply the statutory limits by analogy. Even a relatively short delay in seeking specific performance will lead to its being denied.
13  1980 Act, s 36(2) preserves these rules
14  *Shaw v Applegate* [1978] 1 All ER 123.
15  See p 488 et seq above.

# Index